Predictions in the Brain

Predictions in the Brain

USING OUR PAST TO GENERATE A FUTURE

Edited by

MOSHE BAR

Originating from a Theme Issue
published in *Philosophical Transactions
of the Royal Society B: Biological Sciences*.

OXFORD
UNIVERSITY PRESS

Oxford University Press, Inc., publishes works that further
Oxford University's objective of excellence
in research, scholarship, and education.

Oxford   New York
Auckland   Cape Town   Dar es Salaam   Hong Kong   Karachi
Kuala Lumpur   Madrid   Melbourne   Mexico City   Nairobi
New Delhi   Shanghai   Taipei   Toronto

With offices in
Argentina   Austria   Brazil   Chile   Czech Republic   France   Greece
Guatemala   Hungary   Italy   Japan   Poland   Portugal   Singapore
South Korea   Switzerland   Thailand   Turkey   Ukraine   Vietnam

Published by Oxford University Press, Inc.
198 Madison Avenue, New York, New York 10016
www.oup.com

Oxford is a registered trademark of Oxford University Press

Library of Congress Cataloging-in-Publication Data

Predictions in the brain : using our past to generate a future / edited by Moshe Bar.
p. cm.
Includes bibliographical references and index.
ISBN 978-0-19-539551-8
1. Consciousness–Research. 2. Self-consciousness (Awareness) 3. Brain–Evolution. I. Bar, Moshe. II. Title.

BF311.P734 2011
153--dc22
2010036273

9 8 7 6 5 4 3 2 1
Printed in China

PREFACE

Predictions: A Universal Principle in the Operation of the Human Brain

Moshe Bar

It is possible to explain complicated facets of nature in simple terms: Darwin's natural selection in evolution, Einstein's E = mc², Maxwell's equations in electromagnetics, the Big Five personality traits in psychology (and Murphy's "laws" for most other aspects of everyday life). Similarly, it might be possible for the multidisciplinary study of the brain to produce a short list of universal principles that can explain the majority of its operation. Given exciting developments in theory, empirical findings, and computational studies, it seems that the generation of predictions might be one strong candidate for such a universal principle. Predictions in the brain is the focus of the collection of chapters in this book. The contributions here range from addressing cellular underpinnings to computational principles, and from systems neuroscience to cognition, emotion, and happiness. They cover predictions that range from the next turn for a rat navigating a maze and food-caching in scrub jays to predictions required in decision making and social interactions, from the retina to the prefrontal cortex, and from early development to foresight, or its lack thereof, in nonhumans.

There is an intriguing analogy when thinking about the brain in action. The F-16 fighter plane is the first airplane intentionally designed to have an aerodynamically unstable platform. This design was chosen to enhance the aircraft's maneuverability. Most airplanes are designed to be stable such that they strive to return to their original attitude following an interruption. While such stability is a desired property for a passenger airplane, it opposes a pilot's effort to change headings rapidly and thus can degrade maneuvering performance required for a fighter jet. As can be evident from the collection of ideas presented here, the brain might be similarly flexible and "restless" by default. This restlessness does not reflect random activity that is there merely for the sake of remaining active, but instead it reflects the ongoing generation of predictions, which relies on memory and enhances our interaction with and adjustment to the demanding environment.

The topics that one might expect to learn about and hopefully be stimulated from by reading this book are naturally diverse. For example:

- The association and overlap between future-related thinking and memory. An intriguing idea in this context is that recollection relies on reconstruction, a mechanism that could also provide a valuable tool for generating future-related thoughts. What are the neural mechanisms mediating such constructive processes?
- The connections between imagery, simulation, mental reconstruction, pattern completion, action plans, spatial navigation, and more.
- The cellular mechanisms that balance the need to store stable memories and the need to be able to update them with novel experiences.
- Reasoning for past and future: "what if" questions and mental scenarios in the context of

preparation, "what if" questions that seem more like fantasizing, and "what if" questions that relate to self versus to others. Are they all different? Perhaps not as much as it may seem, with all promoting simulations and imagery, and possibly creating "memories" for future situations.

- Is prediction-related processing primarily cortical or subcortical?
- What are the computational elements involved in the ability to predict?
- How do neural oscillations help in information organization for predictions?
- How do we learn what we need for subsequent generation of accurate predictions, and how does error in predictions promote such learning?
- What is the role of language in learning and sharing future-related information?
- Does the ability for future simulations exist exclusively in humans, or are we simply unique in the magnitude and level of complexity of our foresight?
- What is the role of predictions in emotion, and vice versa? How does the association of past experiences with affective values influence how we predict and perceive related information? Are we as good as we think in predicting emotional consequences? If there is a discrepancy between our ability to foresee affective states and rewards and our ability to predict nonaffective outcome, what is the source of this discrepancy? How does the ability to plan and simulate futures affect our happiness, and what might be the implications to well-being and mental disorder?

We learn, encode, recollect, attend, recognize, evaluate, feel, and act. The chapters in this book put forth ideas describing the possible interactions between these rich processes and the mechanisms that mediate them by showing how they all rely on predictions in their core.

Some of the contributions here may appear to be describing similar ideas, which is an encouraging sign of potential validity. For example, consider the idea that predictions rely on memory. While it may be hard to think of what other source if not memory can mediate predictions,

these proposals are in striking agreement on many of the details, including the cortical structures involved (e.g., medial temporal lobe and medial prefrontal cortex), the complexity of the underlying memory structures, the way they are encoded, and the reconstructive way by which they are recalled and used in predictions.

On the other hand, some chapters might seem to contradict each other. For example, consider the issue of whether foresight is exclusive to humans. There seems to be evidence either way, and the question is whether the fact that rats, for example, show future planning-like operations, such as transitive inference and prediction of upcoming positions, implies that they are able to predict like humans, or similarly but to a lower capacity, or not at all; these demonstrations in nonhumans can instead be interpreted as something different than foresight. Other interesting debates include whether the underlying computational principles are Bayesian in nature. Such orthogonal proposals are particularly interesting because they show how the same solutions can be reached via different mechanisms and pathways.

As much as this collection offers answers to important questions, it raises and emphasizes outstanding ones. How are experiences coded optimally to afford using them for predictions? What is the mechanism underlying reconstruction, and how do we construct a new simulation from separate memories? How specific in detail are future-related mental simulations, and when do they rely on imagery, concepts, or language? What is the difference in the mechanism and cortical underpinnings of predictions that stem from sequence memory (i.e., replaying existing memories) and predictions that stem from construction? What is the role of hierarchies in representations and in predictions?

Finally, this collection developed from an earlier and shorter collection we had published as a special theme issue with the *Philosophical Transactions of the Royal Society B* in 2009. The idea to concentrate on the same topic in a book now was meant to achieve two goals: to add important and exciting new contributions, and to reach a wider audience that may be interested and stimulated. Therefore, in the resulting collection presented here, some are older papers with either minimal or significant modifications, and some are new and complementary in thought-provoking and expanding ways. It is hoped that the ideas and questions that emerge from this volume would inspire and steer future research on predictions in the brain.

This book was originally published as an issue of the *Philosophical Transactions of the Royal Society B: Biological Sciences* (Volume **364**; Issue **1521**) but has been materially changed and updated.

Moshe Bar
Charlestown, Massachusetts

CONTENTS

CONTRIBUTORS

Donna Rose Addis
Department of Psychology
University of Auckland
Private Bag 92019
Auckland 1142, New Zealand
d.addis@auckland.ac.nz

Kathleen M. Arnold
Psychology Department, CB 1125
Washington University
One Brookings Drive
St Louis, MO 63130
kathleen.arnold@wustl.edu

Cristina M. Atance
School of Psychology
University of Ottawa
200 Lees Avenue, Room E228
Ottawa, Ontario, Canada, K1N 6N5
atance@uottawa.ca

Moshe Bar
Martinos Center at Massachusetts
   General Hospital
Harvard Medical School
149 Thirteenth Street
Charlestown, MA 02129
bar@nmr.mgh.harvard.edu

Aron K. Barbey
Cognitive Neuroscience Section
National Institute of Neurological
   Disorders & Stroke
National Institutes of Health
Building 10; Room 7D49;
   MSC 1440
Bethesda, MD 20892
BarbeyA@ninds.nih.gov

Lisa Feldman Barrett
Department of Psychology
253 Nightingale Hall,
Northeastern University,
Boston MA 02115-5000
l.barrett@neu.edu

Lawrence W. Barsalou
Department of Psychology
Emory University
Atlanta, GA 30322
barsalou@emory.edu
http://userwww.service.emory.edu/~barsalou/

Antoine Bechara
Department of Psychiatry, Faculty of Medicine,
   and Desautels Faculty of Management
McGill University
Montreal, Canada
Department of Psychology, and Brain and
   Creativity Institute
University of Southern California, Los Angeles
bechara@usc.edu

Michael J. Berry II
Department of Molecular Biology and Princeton
   Neuroscience Institute
Princeton University
Washington Road
Princeton, NJ 08544
berry@princeton.edu

Lucy G. Cheke
Department of Experimental Psychology
University of Cambridge
Downing Street
Cambridge, CB2 3EB
United Kingdom

Nicola S. Clayton
Department of Experimental Psychology
University of Cambridge
Downing Street
Cambridge, CB2 3EB
United Kingdom
n.clayton@psychol.cam.ac.uk

Michael C. Corballis
Department of Psychology
University of Auckland
Private Bag 92019
Auckland 1142, New Zealand
m.corballis@auckland.ac.nz

Katherine A. DeLong
University of California, San Diego
Cognitive Science Department
9500 Gilman Drive #0515
La Jolla, CA 92093-0515
kadelong@cogsci.ucsd.edu

Yadin Dudai
Department of Neurobiology
The Weizmann Institute of Science
Rehovot 76100, Israel
yadin.dudai@weizmann.ac.il

Shimon Edelman
Department of Psychology
Cornell University
Ithaca, NY 14853
se37@cornell.edu

Howard Eichenbaum
Center for Memory and Brain
Boston University
2 Cummington Street
Boston, MA 02215
hbe@bu.edu

Norbert J. Fortin
Department of Neurobiology and Behavior
University of California at Irvine
1203 McGaugh Hall
Irvine, CA 92697
norbert.fortin@uci.edu

Karl J. Friston
The Wellcome Trust Centre for Neuroimaging
Institute of Neurology
Queen Square
London WC1N 3BG, United Kingdom
k.friston@fil.ion.ucl.ac.uk

Dileep George
Numenta, Inc.
811 Hamilton St.
Redwood City, CA 94063
dgeorge@numenta.com

Daniel T. Gilbert
Department of Psychology
Harvard University
Cambridge, MA 02138
gilbert@wjh.harvard.edu

Jordan Grafman
Chief, Cognitive Neuroscience Section
NINDS, NIH
Building 10; Room 7D43
10 Center Drive; MSC 1440
Bethesda, MD 20892-1440
grafmanj@ninds.nih.gov

Stephen Grossberg
Center for Adaptive Systems
Department of Cognitive and Neural Systems
Center of Excellence for Learning in
    Education, Science, and Technology
Boston University
677 Beacon Street
Boston, MA 02215
steve@bu.edu
http://www.cns.bu.edu/~steve

Laura K. Hanson
School of Psychology
University of Ottawa
200 Lees Avenue, Room E271A
Ottawa, Ontario, Canada, K1N 6N5
ljack033@uottawa.

Demis Hassabis
Wellcome Trust Centre for Neuroimaging,
    Institute of Neurology
University College London
12 Queen Square
London WC1N 3BG, United Kingdom
d.hassabis@fil.ion.ucl.ac.uk

Jeff Hawkins
Numenta, Inc.
811 Hamilton Street
Redwood City, CA 94063
jhawkins@numenta.com

Stefan Kiebel
Max Planck Institute for Human Cognitive
    and Brain Sciences
Stephanstraße 1A
04103 Leipzig, Germany
kiebel@cbs.mpg.de

Stephen M. Kosslyn
844 William James Hall
33 Kirkland Street
Cambridge, MA 02138
stephen_kosslyn@harvard.edu

Frank Krueger
Center for the Study of Neuroeconomics
Krasnow Institute for Advanced Study
George Mason University
Fairfax, VA 22030
FKrueger@gmu.edu

Marta Kutas
University of California, San Diego
Cognitive Science Department
9500 Gilman Drive # 0515
La Jolla, CA 92093-0515
kutas@cogsci.ucsd.edu

Nira Liberman
Department of Psychology
Tel Aviv University
P.O. Box 39040
Tel Aviv 69978, Israel
niralib@post.tau.ac.il

John Lisman
Brandeis University
Department of Biology and Volen Center
    for Complex Systems
415 South Street, MS 008
Waltham, MA 02454
lisman@brandeis.edu

Eleanor A. Maguire
Wellcome Trust Centre for Neuroimaging,
    Institute of Neurology
University College London
12 Queen Square, London WC1N 3BG,
United Kingdom
e.maguire@fil.ion.ucl.ac.uk

Kathleen B. McDermott
Department of Psychology, CB 1125
One Brookings Drive
Washington University
St. Louis, MO 63130-4899
kathleen.mcdermott@wustl.edu

Samuel T. Moulton
844 William James Hall
33 Kirkland Street
Cambridge, MA 02138
moulton@wjh.harvard.edu

Jamie Niemasik
Numenta, Inc.
811 Hamilton Street
Redwood City, CA 94063
jniemasik@numenta.com

A. David Redish
University of Minnesota
Department of Neuroscience
6-145 Jackson Hall
321 Church Street SE
Minneapolis, MN 55455
redish@umn.edu

SoYon Rim
Department of Psychology
New York University
6 Washington Place
New York, NY 10003
sr635@nyu.edu

Daniel L. Schacter
Department of Psychology
Harvard University
33 Kirkland Street
Cambridge, MA 02138
dls@wjh.harvard.edu

Gregory Schwartz
Department of Physiology and
Biophysics
University of Washington
Seattle, WA 98195
gregws@u.washington.edu

Nathaniel J. Smith
University of California, San Diego
Cognitive Science Department
9500 Gilman Drive # 0515
La Jolla, CA 92093-0515
njsmith@cogsci.ucsd.edu

Thomas Suddendorf
Department of Psychology
University of Queensland
St Lucia, Qld 4072, Australia
t.suddendorf@psy.uq.edu.au

Karl K. Szpunar
Department of Psychology
Harvard University
33 Kirkland Street
Cambridge, MA 02138
szpunar@wjh.harvard.edu

Shelley E. Taylor
Department of Psychology
University of California, Los Angeles
1285 Franz Hall
Los Angeles, CA 90095-1563
taylors@psych.ucla.edu

James M. Thom
Department of Experimental Psychology
University of Cambridge
Downing Street
Cambridge, CB2 3EB, United Kingdom

Yaacov Trope
New York University
Department of Psychology
6 Washington Place, Room 768
New York, NY 10003
yaacov.trope@nyu.edu

Endel Tulving
Rotman Research Institute of Baycrest Centre
3560 Bathurst Street
Toronto, Ontario, Canada, M6A 2E1
tulving@psych.utoronto.ca

Timothy D. Wilson
Department of Psychology
University of Virginia
P.O. Box 400400
Charlottesville, VA 22904
tdw@virginia.edu

Predictions in the Brain

CHAPTER 1
Varieties of Future Experience

Karl K. Szpunar and Endel Tulving

In this volume, the concept of "prediction" is proposed to be an overarching principle of brain function that encompasses the general capacity to anticipate a broad range of external events in the service of promoting adaptive interactions with one's environment (Bar, 2009). Nonetheless, the various "predicitive" capacities that are discussed here may be distinguished from one another and it will be important for psychologists and neuroscientists to specify how any one "predictive" capacity is different from, or similar to, other related capacities. This practice would serve the purpose of reinforcing the important observation that is central to Bar's (2009) characterization of "prediction"—that it is a heterogeneous concept and that all "predictive" capacities that have thus far been identified, and that will undoubtedly be identified in the future, are not necessarily equal.

As a modest starting point, we propose a straightforward distinction between "predictions" that are either: (i) inherent to actions and behaviours tied to the present moment (e.g., as is typically observed when humans or other animals produce intelligible and adaptive behaviours) or (ii) inherent to mental operations predicated on the conscious awareness on the part of the individual that his or her self extends temporally into the "non-immediate" future (i.e., a time that does not follow a presently ongoing sequence of events; e.g., as occurs when human beings contemplate scenarios that have yet to take place).

For instance, over an extended period of training, a rat is capable of learning to infer that one stimulus is more preferable (i.e., leads to a reward) than another, even though the rat has never experienced those two stimuli in conjunction in the past (see Eichenbaum & Fortin, 2009). In terms that will be used in the current volume, the rat is said to correctly "predict" the most beneficial manner in which to interact with its environment. This kind of "prediction" has to do with an ongoing sequence of events (in the present moment).

Of course, the same characterization can be made about various kinds of human behaviours. For instance, consider your ability to "predict" how much force will be required to lift a carton of milk (see Linas & Roy, 2009). The fact that you are consistently able to lift a carton of milk without dropping it or hurling it up towards the ceiling is a testament to the fact that you are able to anticipate the approximate weight of the carton (again, in the present moment).

The capacity to "predict" one's interactions with the immediate environment will be considered in much greater detail in various chapters that follow. In the remainder of this chapter, we focus on the other type of "prediction" outlined above, the kind that has to do with thinking about events that may not take place for some time to come (see Hassabis & Maguire, 2009; Schacter & Addis, 2009).

Specifically, this chapter is organized into two main sections. First, we provide an overview of the concept of "autonoetic consciousness," which is defined as the capacity to be consciously aware of one's continued temporal existence (Wheeler, Stuss, & Tulving, 1997). Second, we outline various "predictive" mental activities that deal with the extended, or "non-immediate," future of the individual. These include, future orientation, episodic future thought, planning, and prospective memory. Furthermore, we consider the nature in which these "predictive" mental activities relate to one another and how, ultimately, each depends on the capacity of autonoetic consciousness.

Autonoetic consciousness

To take full advantage of the "predictive" capacities of the brain that extend out beyond the present moment, one must first be aware that one's self will continue to exist in the future. It has been proposed that the capacity to appreciate the connection of one's current self with the future (and past) reflects the functioning of a special form of conscious awareness called "autonoetic consciousness" (Tulving, 1985, 2005; Wheeler et al., 1997). Further, it is has been argued that autonoetic (or self-knowing) consciousness is fundamentally different from a more general type of conscious awareness that underlies the capacity to simply know that the past and future exist, in a way that we know a myriad of other facts about the world. This latter, and more general, form of conscious awareness has been called noetic (or knowing) consciousness (see Tulving, 1995). Accordingly, only "autonoetic consciousness" is thought to bear a personally meaningful relation to time (see also Suddendorf & Corballis, 1997, 2007).

Evidence in support of this distinction was first presented in relation to the now well-known case of patient K. C. (Tulving, 1985; see also Rosenbaum et al., 2005). K. C. has global amnesia induced by diffuse brain damage sustained in a motorcycle accident. He possesses many intact cognitive capacities but can neither remember any single episode from his life nor project himself mentally into the future. When asked to do either, he states that his mind is "blank;" when asked to compare the kinds of blankness in the two situations, he says it is the "same kind of

blankness" (Tulving, 1985, p. 4) (see Rosenbaum, Gilboa, Levin, Winocur, & Moscovitch, 2009 for a more recent example of K. C.'s inability to apprehend his personal future and past). A similar profile is exhibited by patient D. B., studied by Stanley Klein and his colleagues (Klein, Loftus, & Kihlstrom, 2002); D. B. experienced an anoxic episode following cardiac arrest and can no longer project himself into the future or recollect his past.

It is critical to note that both K. C. and D. B. possess an intact understanding of the concept of time; they know that there is a future and a past and they can tell time on a clock. What they lack is the awareness that their current self extends into their personal future and past.

Relatively little attention has been devoted to the concept of "autonoetic consciousness" as a brain-based capacity that enables various mental acts (e.g., mental time travel into the personal future and past). In the remainder of this chapter, various mental activities that require the individual to appreciate that a particular personal experience may occur in the future, without necessarily being required to think about the experience itself, are identified and it is argued that each depends on the capacity of "autonoetic consciousness."

Varieties of future experience

In this section, we focus on various future-directed, or "predictive," mental activities that extend out beyond the present moment and that have each received a considerable amount of empirical attention. These include the following: *(1)* future orientation—the tendency for a particular individual to devote a considerable amount of his or her mental life to thinking about the future; *(2)* episodic future thinking—a particular mode of future thinking that involves imagining specific personal scenarios; *(3)* planning—a multicomponent process aimed at achieving some goal; and *(4)* prospective memory—a multicomponent process that underlies memory for intentions. As will become apparent, these various approaches to understanding the temporally extended future have been largely studied in isolation from one another, although close relations exist between them. As the neurocognitive study of the future (i.e., various "predictive" capacities of the brain) continues to evolve, it will be important to actively negotiate relations between the various concepts that have emerged and those that will doubtless emerge in the future. We attempt to draw a preliminary sketch here.

Future Orientation and Modes of Future Thought

Historically, the most common approach to studying the future, in the realm of psychological science, has been to ask people how often they actually think about it and whether the propensity to do so is associated with positive consequences. Next, are mentioned two influential contributions.

First, Jerome Singer and his colleagues developed the Imaginal Processes Inventory (IPI), a questionnaire aimed at characterizing the flavor of a person's mental life (Giambra, 1980; Huba, Singer, Aneshensel, & Antrobus, 1982; Singer, 1966, 1975; Singer & Antrobus, 1963, 1970, 1972). Among its various scales, the IPI includes questions regarding the frequency with which people report daydreaming about various aspects of their past, present, and future. A number of studies implementing the IPI have reported that people spend most of their time daydreaming about the future (although, not surprisingly, this tendency declines with increasing age; Giambra, 2000). Although largely descriptive in nature, this line of work underscores the relevance of future-directed thought in healthy human cognition (see also Klinger & Cox, 1987).

Second, the concept of "time perspective," which reflects the propensity of people to approach life's experiences with their past, present, or future in mind (Lewin, 1951; Zimbardo & Boyd, 1999) is briefly considered. Research in this area has convincingly demonstrated that adopting a future orientation is associated with many positive consequences, including higher socioeconomic status, superior academic achievement, and fewer health risk behaviors (e.g., Nuttin, 1985; Zaleski, 1994). Hence, not only do people spend a considerable amount of time thinking about their personal future, but the more they apply such thoughts to their daily

experiences the more likely they are to draw positive consequences from those experiences.

One limitation of the information gleaned from studies on future orientation, although those studies were not specifically designed for this purpose, is the absence of any insight regarding the manner in which people think about their future. For instance, one's thoughts about one's future may be general or specific (Atance & O'Neill, 2001; Klein et al., 2002; Okuda et al., 2003; Suddendorf & Corballis, 2007). A recent study by D'Argembeau, Renaud, and Van der Linden (2009) demonstrated that people (college-age students) spend a considerable amount of time thinking about upcoming life experiences from both general and specific perspectives (e.g., a general, self-imposed, reminder that a particular event is fast approaching as opposed to imagining a specific scenario related to the upcoming event). Hence, two people who devote a considerable, and equal, amount of their mental lives to thinking about their futures may, nonetheless, exhibit strikingly different profiles when it comes to the mode in which they frame these thoughts. It will be interesting for future research to examine the utility of approaching one's future from either perspective (i.e., general or specific).

Next, we shift focus to the considerable amount of empirical attention that has been devoted to understanding the capacity to think about one's future in terms of specific episodes. In particular, we discuss the benefits and potential shortcomings of orienting one's self to the future in a specific manner, allude to some provocative data regarding the manner in which specific thoughts about the future are implemented by the human brain/mind, and highlight the terminological variability associated with this particular "predictive" mental activity.

Episodic Future Thinking

Episodic future thought is defined as the ability to imagine specific personal episodes that may potentially occur in the future (Atance & O'Neill, 2001; Szpunar, 2010). Indeed, it has long been known that such specific thoughts about one's future can be beneficial, albeit somewhat inaccurate. In terms of positive consequences,

Shelley Taylor and her colleagues have demonstrated the utility of episodic future thought in the context of dealing with personal problems (e.g., resolving relationship issues) and achieving task goals (e.g., planning where and how one will study for a test) (Pham & Taylor, 1999; Taylor, Pham, Rivkin, & Armor, 1998; Taylor & Schneider, 1989). Consider the social psychological phenomenon known as the planning fallacy. According to research on this phenomenon, people typically underestimate the resources they will need to complete a task (e.g., time and money) and overestimate the ease with which they will complete a task (Kahneman & Tversky, 1979). For example, Buehler, Griffin, and Ross (1994) asked students to predict how long it would take them to complete various class projects (e.g., term paper). Only one-third of the students surveyed met their self-imposed deadline. However, Taylor et al. (1998) discuss a study showing how goal completion in this context could be improved if students were trained to imagine how they would specifically go about accomplishing this goal in the future. In fact, students were almost twice as likely (41% versus 21%) to meet a self-imposed deadline after they had been induced to imagine how they would complete the task.

On the other hand, Daniel Gilbert and his colleagues have identified some potential shortcomings of episodic future thinking (Gilbert and others also variably refer to this capacity as "preplay" and "prospection"; Buckner & Carroll, 2007; Gilbert & Wilson, 2007, 2009). According to Gilbert, people typically draw upon episodic future thinking to inform their decisions about the future. Some of these decisions (e.g., Should I have dessert after dinner?) reflect short-term consequences, whereas other decisions (e.g., Should I accept that new job halfway across the world?) reflect more long-term consequences. That is, although people are not able to presently experience what it would feel like to eat a mouthwatering piece of chocolate cake or how happy they will be in the second or third year of their prestigious job that is located in a new city, they are able to imagine what it would feel like. However, the ability to accurately predict the future does not come easily. One common source

of error associated with imagining one's future is the influence of current affective/physiological states. For instance, although people are able to imagine what it might feel like to consume a delectable piece of chocolate cake, the ability to do so is largely influenced by currently accessible physiological states. In one study, one group of participants was asked to imagine how much they would enjoy eating potato chips the following day. A second, satiated group of participants was also asked to imagine this future scenario. A day later, the group of participants who had made their prediction on a full stomach was found to have underestimated the extent to which they enjoyed their snack (see Gilbert, 2006). The imagination of the future event (i.e., eating the potato chips) was colored by their currently accessible physiological state (i.e., being full).

More recently, researchers have become interested in identifying how the human brain/mind implements episodic future thinking. The general idea that has emerged is that to generate a plausible future scenario, one must draw upon usable information from semantic and episodic (declarative) memory (e.g., appropriate context, emotional reactions, etc.) and recombine that information into a coherent mental representation of a novel event (Schacter & Addis, 2007). This claim is supported by converging evidence from neuroimaging (e.g., Addis, Wong, & Schacter, 2007; Botzung, Denkova, & Manning, 2008; Okuda et al., 2003; Szpunar, Watson, & McDermott, 2007), neuropsychology (e.g., Hassabis, Kumaran, Vann, & Maguire, 2007; Klein et al., 2002; Rosenbaum et al., 2009), clinical psychology (e.g., D'Argembeau, Raffard, & Van der Linden, 2008; Williams et al., 1996), and developmental psychology (e.g., Addis, Wong, & Schacter, 2008; Atance & O'Neill, 2005; Busby & Suddendorf, 2005).

For instance, research from the neuroimaging literature has revealed a striking similarity in the neural activity that characterizes episodic future thinking and the capacity to call to mind specific experiences from one's personal past (i.e., episodic memory) (e.g., Addis et al., 2007; Szpunar et al., 2007). Of particular interest are posterior cortical and subcortical regions (e.g., posterior cingulate cortex, posterior parietal cortex, parahippocampal cortex, hippocampus) that are known to play a particularly important role in remembering (Cabeza & St. Jacques, 2007; Maguire, 2001; Svoboda, McKinnon, & Levine, 2006). That episodic future thinking engages these regions in a similar manner as remembering suggests that a similar set of processes are involved as participants think about their past and future (Buckner & Carroll, 2007; Hassabis & Maguire, 2007; Schacter & Addis, 2007, 2009; Spreng, Mar, & Kim, 2009; Szpunar, Chan, & McDermott, 2009).

Importantly, patient populations who lack or have impoverished episodic memory exhibit an accompanying deficit in episodic future thinking. This pattern of impairment has been identified in brain-damaged amnesic patients (e.g., Hassabis et al., 2007; Klein et al., 2002; Tulving, 1985), suicidally depressed individuals (Williams et al. 1996), patients with schizophrenia (e.g., D'Argembeau et al., 2008), children under the age of 5 years (e.g., Busby & Suddendorf, 2005), and older adults (Addis et al., 2008). Taken together, the evidence suggests a close relation between future thought and memory.

Incidentally, the identification of a close relation between episodic future thinking, episodic memory, and other mental activities that involve imagining hypothetical scenarios (see Spreng et al., 2009) has led to a proliferation of terms that essentially refer to the same general capacity. These include *mental simulation* (Taylor & Pham, 1996; Taylor et al., 1998; Taylor & Schneider, 1989), *episodic simulation* (Schacter & Addis, 2007, 2009; Schacter, Addis, & Buckner, 2008), and *self-projection* (Buckner & Carroll, 2007; see also Barbey, Kruger, & Grafman, 2009; Barsalou, 2009 who provide more intricate conceptualizations and also present their own idiosyncratic terms). Such a state of affairs has the potential for negative side effects (see Gardiner & Java, 1993; Tulving, 2000). Hence, we stress the importance of terminological clarity as interest in the general imaginative capacity of the human brain/mind continues to grow (see also Szpunar, 2010).

Multifaceted Modes of Future Thought

As evidenced by the intriguing data that have emerged in relation to episodic future thinking,

it will be important to study the various modes by which healthy human adults are capable of contemplating their future. Perhaps even more important will be the task of examining how these various modes of future thinking interact with one another to produce more complex future thinking capacities. Next, we discuss two such capacities: planning and prospective memory. In so doing, we pay special attention to the manner in which each is capable of incorporating episodic future thinking as a subcomponent to the overall process of enacting a complex future-directed behavior.

Planning

Planning is considered a multicomponent process that operates at various levels of abstraction (e.g., general versus specific) and which serves as a predetermined course of action aimed at achieving some goal (Alexander & Stuss, 2000; Burgess, Veitch, de Lacy Costello, & Shallice, 2000; Fuster, 1995, 1999, 2001; e.g., Haith, 1997; Hayes-Roth & Hayes-Roth, 1979). For instance, a task as simple as planning one's daily activities involves defining a variety of goals and subgoals (e.g., attending a meeting, having lunch with a friend, dropping off the car at the shop, writing a lecture), prioritizing those goals (e.g., "I definitely have to attend this meeting" "I can always take the car to the mechanic tomorrow if there is no time today"), monitoring one's progress, reevaluating the original plan, and so on. In terms of levels of abstraction, one may have both general thoughts (e.g., "I have to remember to prepare my lecture for tomorrow") and specific thoughts (e.g., "I will prepare my lecture in my office after the meeting and will make sure to lock my door to avoid any distractions") about various goals that one wishes to accomplish (Hayes-Roth & Hayes-Roth, 1979). In relation to episodic future thinking, the ability to think about specific future events and to adjust plans according to the results of those thoughts (e.g., "Seems like I may not have enough time to prepare my lecture after the meeting, and before lunch, so I should set aside some time when I get home this evening") represents one important aspect of the planning process. However, it is important to keep in mind that evoking episodic future thinking in the course of planning represents only one component of the process.[1]

Prospective Memory

Prospective memory is defined as the ability to remember to carry out intended activities in the future (Brandimonte, Einstein, & McDaniel, 1996; Burgess, Quayle, & Frith, 2001; Einstein, McDaniel, Marsh, & West, 2008; McDaniel & Einstein, 2007; Simons, Scholvinck, Gilbert, Frith, & Burgess, 2006). Researchers have identified three varieties of prospective memory situations that people encounter in their daily lives: *(1)* those that are event based (e.g., remembering to relay a message to a coworker at a future meeting), *(2)* those that are time based (e.g., remembering to attend a meeting at a particular time), and *(3)* those that are activity based (e.g., remembering to write an e-mail after a meeting). In each case, intentions refer to a specific event that will plausibly occur in the future. However, forming an intention does not necessarily require one to think about that event in a specific manner. That is, one can form or be reminded of the intention in a more general sense (e.g., I have to do X). Nonetheless, imagining how that future event will transpire may greatly facilitate successfully carrying out one's intentions. Specifically, Peter Gollwitzer and his colleagues have demonstrated that imagining when, where, and how one plans on executing one's intentions provides a considerable benefit for carrying out those goals (Gollwitzer, 1993, 1996, 1999). In one study, women who set themselves the goal of performing a breast self-examination in the next month benefited considerably from specifying when and where they would perform the procedure (Orbell, Hodgkins, & Sheeran, 1997). Although future work will need to determine more clearly the extent to which implementation intentions are characterized by full-blown imaginations of personal future scenarios (i.e., episodic future thinking), there exists some indication that this

may be the case (see McDaniel, Howard, & Butler, 2008).

Relation to Autonoetic Consciousness

Finally, we note the manner in which the four future-directed, or "predictive," mental activities discussed earlier (i.e., future orientation, episodic future thinking, planning, and prospective memory) depend on the capacity of "autonoetic consciousness." Importantly, each noted mental activity requires the individual to be aware that his or her current self will one day encounter novel experiences. In the absence of this awareness, which reflects "autonoetic consciousness," we argue that it would be difficult, if not impossible, for an individual to do the following: *(1)* devote a considerable amount of one's mental life to thinking about the future (future orientation), *(2)* conjure detailed future scenarios that revolve around personal circumstances (episodic future thought), *(3)* conceive that there exist future goals to plan for (planning), or *(4)* conceive that there exist actions that one will need to carry out in the future (prospective memory). Next, we consider a few relevant observations and data that are pertinent to this conjecture.

Perhaps the most relevant observation, and one on which the concept of "autonoetic consciousness" was founded, is that of patient K. C., who spends little, if any, time thinking about his future (no future orientation) and who is incapable in engaging in episodic future thinking (Tulving, 1985; see also Klein et al., 2002 and Hassabis et al., 2007 for similar reports with other amnesic patients). Other relevant data have been reported in the context of frontal lobe patients who exhibit a profound indifference for their temporally extended existence (future or past) (e.g., Freeman & Watts, 1941; Luria, 1969; Luria & Homskaya, 1964; Robinson & Freeman, 1954; Stuss & Benson, 1986). Along the lines of this chapter, various authors have reported that frontal lobe patients have extensive difficulties with planning (e.g., Shallice & Burgess, 1991) and prospective memory tasks (e.g., Burgess et al., 2000; Cockburn, 1995).

A particularly fruitful avenue for future research will no doubt involve assessing the extent

---

[1] Of course, the concept of "planning" involves many executive functions aside from general and specific thoughts about the future.

to which various future-directed, or "predictive", capacities become impaired together following various instances of brain dysfunction.

Conclusion

In closing, as the concept of "prediction" continues to attract attention, it will be important to keep in mind the heterogeneous nature of the concept and how various "predictive" capacities are related to and differ from one another. Here, we have taken an initial step by suggesting that only those "predictive" capacities that extend out beyond the present moment require one to be consciously aware that one's self will continue to exist in the future.

REFERENCES

Addis, D. R., Wong, A. T., & Schacter, D. L. (2007). Remembering the past, imagining the future: Common and distinct neural substrates during event construction and elaboration. *Neuropsychologia, 45,* 1363–1377.

Addis, D. R., Wong, A. T., & Schacter, D. L. (2008). Age-related changes in the episodic simulation of future events. *Psychological Science, 19,* 33–41.

Alexander, M. P., & Stuss, D. T. (2000). Disorders of frontal lobe functioning. *Seminars in Neurology, 20,* 427–437.

Atance, C. M., & O'Neill, D. K. (2001). Episodic future thinking. *Trends in Cognitive Sciences, 5,* 533–539.

Atance, C. M., & O'Neill, D. K. (2005). The emergence of episodic future thinking in humans. *Learning and Motivation, 36,* 126–144.

Bar, M. (2009). Predictions: A universal principle in the operation of the human brain. *Philosophical Transactions of the Royal Society of London: B, 364,* 1181–1182.

Barbey, A. K., Kruger, F., & Grafman, J. (2009). Structured event complexes in the medial prefrontal cortex support counterfactual representations for future planning. *Philosophical Transactions of the Royal Society of London: B, 364,* 1291–1300.

Barsalou, L. W. (2009). Simulation, situated conceptualization, and prediction. *Philosophical Transactions of the Royal Society of London: B, 364,* 1281–1289.

Botzung, A., Denkova, E., & Manning, L. (2008). Experiencing past and future events: Functional neuroimaging evidence on the neural bases of mental time travel. *Brain and Cognition, 66,* 202–212.

Brandimonte, M., Einstein, G. O., & McDaniel, M. A. (Eds.). (1996). *Prospective memory: Theory and applications.* Mahwah, NJ: Erlbaum.

Buckner, R. L., & Carroll, D. C. (2007). Self-projection and the brain. *Trends in Cognitive Sciences, 11,* 49–57.

Buehler, R., Griffin, D., & Ross, M. (1994). Exploring the "planning fallacy": Why people underestimate their task completion times. *Journal of Personality and Social Psychology, 67,* 366–381.

Burgess, P. W., Quayle, A., & Frith, C. D. (2001). Brain regions involved in prospective memory as determined by positron emission tomography. *Neuropsychologia, 39,* 545–555.

Burgess, P. W., Veitch, E., de Lacy Costello, A., & Shallice, T. (2000). The cognitive and neuroanatomical correlates of multitasking. *Neuropsychologia, 38,* 848–863.

Busby, J., & Suddendorf, T. (2005). Recalling yesterday and predicting tomorrow. *Cognitive Development, 20,* 362–372.

Cabeza, R., & St. Jacques, P. (2007). Functional neuroimaging of autobiographical memory. *Trends in Cognitive Sciences, 11,* 219–227.

Cockburn, J. (1995). Task interruption in prospective memory: A frontal lobe function. *Cortex, 31,* 87–97.

D'Argembeau, A., Raffard, S., & Van der Linden, M. (2008). Remembering the past and imagining the future in schizophrenia. *Journal of Abnormal Psychology, 117,* 247–251.

D'Argembeau, A., Renaud, O., & Van der Linden, M. (2009). Frequency, characteristics, and functions of future-oriented thoughts in daily life. *Applied Cognitive Psychology,*

Eichenbaum, H., & Fortin, N. J. (2009). The neurobiology of memory based predictions. *Philosophical Transactions of the Royal Society of London: B, 364,* 1183–1191.

Einstein, G. O., McDaniel, M. A., Marsh, R. L., & West, R. (2008). Prospective memory: Processes, lifespan changes, and neuroscience. In J. Byrne (Series Ed.), *Learning and memory: A comprehensive reference: Vol. 2. Cognitive psychology of memory* (pp. 867–892). Oxford, England: Elsevier.

Freeman, W., & Watts, J. W. (1941). The frontal lobes in their relationship to the ego and the future. *North Carolina Medical Journal, 2,* 288–290.

Fuster, J. M. (1995). Memory and planning: Two temporal perspectives of frontal lobe function. In H. H. Jasper, S. Riggiom & P. S. Goldman-Rakic (Eds.), *Epilepsy and the functional anatomy of the frontal lobe* (pp. 9–20). New York: Raven Press.

Fuster, J. M. (1999). Cognitive functions of the frontal lobes. In B. L. Miller & J. L. Cummings (Eds.), *The human frontal lobes: Functions and disorders* (pp. 187–195). New York: Guilford Press.

Fuster, J. M. (2001). The prefrontal cortex—An update: Time is of the essence. *Neuron, 30,* 319–333.

Gardiner, J. M., & Java, R. I. (1993). Recognising and remembering. In A. Collins, S. Gathercole, M. Conway, & P. Morris (Eds.), *Theories of memory* (pp. xx–xx). Hillsdale, NJ: Erlbaum.

Giambra, L. M. (1980). A factor analysis of the items of the Imaginal Processes Inventory. *Journal of Clinical Psychology, 36,* 383–409.

Giambra, L. M. (2000). Daydreaming characteristics across the life-span: Age differences and seven to twenty year longitudinal changes. In R. G. Kunzendorf & B. Wallace (Eds.), *Individual differences in conscious experience* (pp. 147–206). Amsterdam, Netherlands: John Benjamins Publishing Company.

Gilbert, D. T. (2006). *Stumbling on happiness.* New York: Vintage Books.

Gilbert, D. T., & Wilson, T. D. (2007). Prospection: Experiencing the future. *Science, 317,* 1351–1354.

Gilbert, D. T., & Wilson, T. D. (2009). Why the brain talks to itself: Sources of error in emotional prediction. *Philosophical Transactions of the Royal Society of London: B, 364,* 1335–1341.

Gollwitzer, P. M. (1993). Goal achievement: The role of intentions. In W. Stroebe & M. Hewstone (Eds.), *European review of social psychology* (pp. 141–185). Chichester, England: Wiley.

Gollwitzer, P. M. (1996). The volitional benefits of planning. In P. M. Gollwitzer & J. A. Bargh (Eds.), *The psychology of action: Linking cognition and motivation to behavior* (pp. 287–312). New York: Guilford Press.

Gollwitzer, P. M. (1999). Implementation intentions. *American Psychologist, 54,* 493–503.

Haith, M. M. (1997). The development of future thinking as essential for the emergence of skill in planning. In S. L. Friedman & E. K. Scholnick (Eds.), *The developmental psychology of planning: Why, how, and when do we plan?* (pp. 25–42). Mahwah, NJ: Lawrence Erlbaum.

Hassabis, D., Kumaran, D., Vann, D. S., & Maguire, E. A. (2007). Patients with hippocampal amnesia cannot imagine new experiences. *Proceedings of the National Academy of Sciences USA, 104,* 1726–1731.

Hassabis, D., & Maguire, E. A. (2007). Deconstructing episodic memory with construction. *Trends in Cognitive Sciences, 11,* 299–306.

Hassabis, D., & Maguire, E. A. (2009). The construction system of the brain. *Philosophical Transactions of the Royal Society of London: B, 364,* 1263–1271.

Hayes-Roth, B., & Hayes-Roth, F. (1979). A cognitive model of planning. *Cognitive Science, 3,* 275–310.

Huba, G. L., Singer, J. L., Aneshensel, C. S., & Antrobus, J. S. (1982). *The short imaginal processes inventory.* Port Hurson, MI: Research Psychologists' Press.

Kahneman, D., & Tversky, A. (1979). Intuitive prediction: Biases and corrective procedures. *TIMS Studies in Management Science, 12,* 313–327.

Klein, S. B., Loftus, J., & Kihlstrom, J. F. (2002). Memory and temporal experience: The effects of episodic memory loss on an amnesic patient's ability to remember the past and imagine the future. *Social Cognition, 20,* 353–379.

Klinger, E., & Cox, W. M. (1987). Dimensions of thought flow in everyday life. *Imagination, Cognition, and Personality, 7,* 105–128.

Lewin, K. (1951). *Field theory in the social sciences: Selected theoretical papers.* New York: Harper.

Llinas, R. D., & Roy, S. (2009). The 'prediction imperative' as the basis for self-awareness. *Philosophical Transactions of the Royal Society of London: B. 364,* 1301–1307.

Luria, A. R. (1969). Frontal lobe syndromes. In P. J. Vinken & G. W. Bruyn (Eds.), *Handbook of clinical neurology* (Vol. 2, pp. 725–757). Amsterdam, Netherlands: North Holland.

Luria, A. R., & Homskaya, E. D. (1964). Disturbance in the regulative role of speech with frontal lobe lesions. In J. M. Warren & K. Akert (Eds.), *The frontal granular cortex and behavior* (pp. 353–371). New York: McGraw-Hill.

Maguire, E. A. (2001). Neuroimaging studies of autobiographical memory. *Philosophical Transactions of the Royal Society of London: B, 356,* 1441–1451.

McDaniel, M. A., & Einstein, G. O. (2007). *Prospective memory: An overview and synthesis of an emerging field.* Thousand Oaks, CA: Sage.

McDaniel, M. A., Howard, D. C., & Butler, K. M. (2008). Implementation intentions facilitate prospective memory under high attention demands. *Memory and Cognition, 36*, 716–724.

Nuttin, J. R. (1985). *Future time perspective and motivation: Theory and research method.* Hillsdale, NJ: Erlbaum.

Okuda, J., Fujii, T., Ohtake, H., Tsukiura, T., Tanji, K., Suzuki, K., et al. (2003). Thinking of the future and past: The roles of the frontal pole and the medial temporal lobes. *NeuroImage, 19*, 1369–1380.

Orbell, S., Hodgkins, S., & Sheeran, P. (1997). Implementation intentions and the theory of planned behavior. *Personality and Social Psychology Bulletin, 23*, 945–954.

Pham, L. B., & Taylor, S. E. (1999). From thought to action: Effects of process- versus outcome-based mental simulations on performance. *Personality and Social Psychology Bulletin, 25*, 250–260.

Robinson, M. F., & Freeman, W. (1954). *Psychosurgery and the self.* New York: Grune & Stratton.

Rosenbaum, S. R., Gilboa, A., Levin, B., Winocur, G., & Moscovitch, M. (2009). Amnesia as an impairment of detail generation and binding: Evidence from personal, fictional, and semantic narratives in K.C. *Neuropsychologia, 47*, 2181–2187.

Rosenbaum, S. R., Kohler, S., Schacter, D. L., Moscovitch, M., Westmacott, R., Black, S. E., et al. (2005). The case of K.C.: Contributions of a memory-impaired person to memory theory. *Neuropsychologia, 43*, 989–1021.

Schacter, D. L., & Addis, D. R. (2007). The cognitive neuroscience of constructive memory: Remembering the past and imagining the future. *Philosophical Transactions of the Royal Society of London: B, 362*, 773–786.

Schacter, D. L., & Addis, D. R. (2009). On the nature of medial temporal lobe contributions to the constructive simulation of future events. *Philosophical Transactions of the Royal Society of London: B, 364*, 1245–1253.

Schacter, D. L., Addis, D. R., & Buckner, R. L. (2008). Episodic simulation of future events: Concepts, data, and applications. *Annals of the New York Academy of Sciences, 1124*, 39–60.

Shallice, T., & Burgess, P. W. (1991). Deficits in strategy application following frontal lobe damage in man. *Brain, 114*, 727–741.

Simons, J. S., Scholvinck, M. L., Gilbert, S. J., Frith, C. D., & Burgess, P. W. (2006). Differential components of prospective memory? Evidence from fMRI. *Neuropsychologia, 44*, 1388–1397.

Singer, J. L. (1966). *Daydreaming.* New York: Random House.

Singer, J. L. (1975). Navigating the stream of consciousness: Research in daydreaming and related inner experience. *American Psychologist, 30*, 727–738.

Singer, J. L., & Antrobus, J. S. (1963). A factor-analytic study of daydreaming and conceptually-related cognitive and personality variables. *Perceptual and Motor Skills*, Monograph Supplement, *3-V-17*, pp. xx–xx.

Singer, J. L., & Antrobus, J. S. (1970). *Manual for the Imaginal Processes Inventory.* Princeton, NJ: Educational Testing Service.

Singer, J. L., & Antrobus, J. S. (1972). Daydreaming, imaginal processes, and personality: A normative study. In P. Sheehan (Ed.), *The function and nature of imagery.* New York: Academic Press.

Spreng, R. N., Mar, R. A., & Kim, A. S. (2009). The common neural basis of autobiographical memory, prospection, navigation, theory of mind and the default mode: A quantitative meta-analysis. *Journal of Cognitive Neuroscience, 21*, 489–510.

Stuss, D. T., & Benson, D. F. (1986). *The frontal lobes.* New York: Raven Press.

Suddendorf, T., & Corballis, M. C. (1997). Mental time travel and the evolution of the human mind. *Genetic, Social, and General Psychology Monographs, 123*, 133–167.

Suddendorf, T., & Corballis, M. C. (2007). The evolution of foresight: What is mental time travel, and is it unique to humans? *Behavioral and Brain Sciences, 30*, 299–313.

Svoboda, E., McKinnon, M. C., & Levine, B. (2006). The functional neuroanatomy of autobiographical memory: A meta-analysis. *Neuropsychologia, 44*, 2189–2208.

Szpunar, K. K. (2010). Episodic future thought: An emerging concept. *Perspectives on Psychological Science, 5*(2), 142–162.

Szpunar, K. K., Chan, J. C. K., & McDermott, K. B. (2009). Contextual processing in episodic future thought. *Cerebral Cortex, 19*, 1539–1548.

Szpunar, K. K., Watson, J. M., & McDermott, K. B. (2007). Neural substrates of envisioning the future. *Proceedings of the National Academy of Sciences USA, 104*, 642–647.

Taylor, S. E., & Pham, L. B. (1996). Mental simulation, motivation, and action. In P. M. Gollwitzer & J. A. Bargh (Eds.), *The psychology of action: Linking cognition and motivation to behavior* (pp. 219–235). New York: Guilford Press.

Taylor, S. E., Pham, L. B., Rivkin, I. D., & Armor, D. A. (1998). Harnessing the imagination: Mental simulation, self-regulation, and coping. *American Psychologist*, *53*, 429–439.

Taylor, S. E., & Schneider, S. K. (1989). Coping and the simulation of events. *Social Cognition*, *7*, 174–194.

Tulving, E. (1985). Memory and consciousness. *Canadian Psychology*, *26*, 1–12.

Tulving, E. (1989). Memory: Performance, knowledge, and experience. *European Journal of Cognitive Psychology*, *1*, 3–26.

Tulving, E. (1995). Organization of memory: Quo vadis? In M. S. Gazzaniga (Ed.), *The cognitive neurosciences* (pp. 839–847). Cambridge, MA: MIT Press.

Tulving, E. (2000). Concepts of memory. In E. Tulving & F. I. M. Craik (Eds.), *The Oxford handbook of memory* (pp. 33–43). New York, NY: Oxford University Press.

Tulving, E. (2005). Episodic memory and autonoesis: Uniquely human? In H. S. Terrace & J. Metcalfe (Eds.), *The missing link in cognition: Origins of self-reflective consciousness* (pp. 3–56). New York: Oxford University Press.

Wheeler, M. A., Stuss, D. T., & Tulving, E. (1997). Toward a theory of episodic memory: The frontal lobes and autonoetic consciousness. *Psychological Bulletin*, *121*, 331–354.

Williams, J. M. G., Ellis, N. C., Tyers, C., Healy, H., Rose, G., & MacLeod, A. K. (1996). The specificity of autobiographical memory and imaginability of the future. *Memory and Cognition*, *24*, 116–125.

Zaleski, Z. (1994). *Psychology of future orientation.* Lublin, Poland: Towarzystwo Naukowe KUL.

Zimbardo, P., & Boyd, J. N. (1999). Putting time in perspective: A valid, reliable individual-differences metric. *Journal of Personality and Social Psychology*, *77*, 1271–1288.

CHAPTER 2
The Proactive Brain

Moshe Bar

ABSTRACT

It is proposed that the human brain is *proactive* in that it continuously generates predictions that anticipate the relevant future. In this proposal, analogies are derived from elementary information that is extracted rapidly from the input to link that input with representations that exist in memory. Finding an analogical link results in the generation of focused predictions via associative activation of representations that are relevant to this analogy, a process that is proposed to be aided by context-based inhibition. Predictions in complex circumstances, such as social interactions, combine multiple analogies. Such predictions need not be created "from scratch" in new situations, but rather rely on existing *scripts* in memory, which are the result of real as well as previously imagined experiences. This cognitive neuroscience framework can help explain a variety of phenomena, ranging from recognition to first impressions, and from the brain's "default mode" to a host of mental disorders.

INTRODUCTION: THE GENERAL FRAMEWORK

A common belief that might be implicit but not entirely accurate is that there is a clear boundary between perception and cognition, whereby "perception" pertains to the analysis of information about the physical world around us, conveyed by the senses and analyzed by the sensory cortex, while "cognition" refers to the analysis and operations that take place beyond what is required for perceiving the input—faculties such as attention, memory, and categorization. But our perception of the environment relies on memory and expectations as much as it does on incoming information, which blurs the artificial border between perception and cognition. For example,[1] the assumption is that when we encounter an object in our environment, its recognition requires an exhaustive analysis of its properties (e.g., contour, color, texture), and this relies exclusively on a bottom-up, sensory-triggered propagation of information. However, rather than seeing the challenge of vision (or of any of the senses) as answering the bottom-up question "What is this?" we should look at the goal more as linking the input with an analogous representation in memory, and simultaneously with the information associated with it, by asking instead "What is this like?" Such recognition by analogy, and the concomitant associative activation of predictions, puts an emphasis on how we use experience by affording immediate access to analogies and associated representations. Support for this notion that sensory information interacts with existing representations for the purpose of perception proper is related to the concept of embodied cognition (Barsalou, 2003; Noe, 2005) and was recently supported by functional

---

[1] The examples here will tend to focus on the world of visual object recognition, because it is a field in which intense ';esearch activity has been invested for several decades now, and because recognition is unique in how it straddles the definitions of perception and cognition by relying on both to be accomplished.

magnetic resonance imaging (fMRI) studies (Wang et al., 2008).

At the heart of the proposed framework lies the idea that we do not interpret our world merely by analyzing incoming information, but rather we try to understand it using a proactive link of incoming features to existing, familiar information (e.g., objects, people, situations). More specifically, when encountering a novel input (and all inputs are novel to some degree because we never encounter anything twice under exactly the same conditions), our brains "ask" what is this input like that we are already familiar with? Critically, this question is being asked actively using top-down guesses that are based on rudimentary input information (Bar et al., 2006). Once an analogy is found (e.g., "this is the driver's seat of a car"), associated representations are activated rapidly, a process that provides the platform for predictions that presensitize the representations of what is most likely to occur and be encountered next (e.g., "this must be the stick-shift, that must be the headlight switch, and I am sure there is a cup-holder here somewhere").

This process of analogy→associations→ predictions can be seen as providing the basis for a universal principle. Naturally, our environment and needs involve circumstances that are considerably more complex than the basic process described here, but this process can be expanded to any level of complexity. Specifically, multiple analogies can be found in parallel, relating to multiple aspects of the input, and they can be integrated to generate compound predictions that go beyond simple perception and cognition and are as complex as those required, for example, in social interactions. In other words, predictions do not merely rely on reactivation of previously experienced environments and situations, but rather can be derived from a combination of representations in memory to generate a novel mental scenario.

Analogies, associations, and predictions are all issues that have been studied extensively in the past, individually. The present proposal brings them together by synthesizing previous findings and building upon them to provide an integrative framework for how the brain generates proactive predictions that facilitate our interactions with the environment, where analogies provide the trigger and associations serve as the building blocks. The next sections elaborate on these individual components and on their integration.

ANALOGIES: THE TRIGGER

Analogy is typically seen as a sophisticated cognitive tool used in specific types of problem solving (Gentner, 1983; Holyoak & Thagard, 1997; Muter, Snowling, & Taylor, 1994). Here the term is used instead simply to refer to the link of a novel input to a similar representation existing in memory: What is this like? (A *metaphor* could have been another choice.) Analogical mapping facilitates interpretation, but more importantly it connects with a set of associated representations that provide a platform for predictions. Analogies can be based on similarity in various levels: perceptual, conceptual, semantic, functional, and so on. Indeed, analogies as considered here can facilitate anything from the recognition of a cat never seen before to helping us decide what to pack when going on vacation in a new destination.

To demonstrate how analogy can help interpret the input rapidly, using only rudimentary information, consider a proposed model of how a visual object can be recognized rapidly using only global information about its general appearance and about the context in which it is embedded (Fig. 2.1). The top part is derived from an earlier proposal (Bar, 2003) and supporting evidence (Bar et al., 2006; Kveraga, Boshyan, & Bar, 2007), whereby in addition to the systematic analysis of detail along the ventral visual pathway, global appearance properties, conveyed by low spatial frequencies (LSFs), are projected directly from early visual areas to the orbital frontal cortex (OFC). The OFC then triggers the activation of the most probable object identities that share the same global appearance as the input target object with which an analogy in memory is sought.

In parallel (bottom part of Fig. 2.1), an LSF image of the input scene is typically sufficient for extracting the context in which the target object appears (Bar, 2004; Oliva & Torralba , 2001; Torralba & Oliva, 2003), thereby activating the

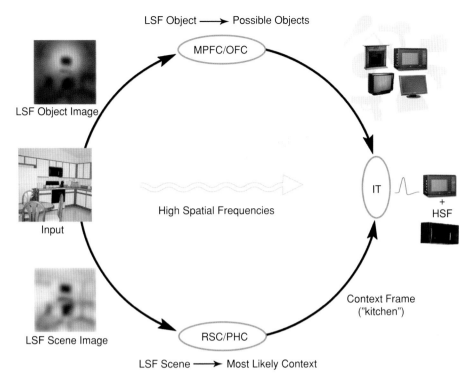

Figure 2.1 Combining object and context information to find a quick and reliable analogy. In parallel to the bottom-up systematic progression of the image details along the visual pathways, there are quick projections of low spatial frequency (LSF) information, possibly via the magnocellular pathway. This coarse but rapid information is sufficient for generating an "initial guess" about the context and about objects in it. These context-based predictions are validated and refined with the gradual arrival of higher spatial frequencies (Bar, 2004). HSF, high spatial frequency; IT, inferior temporal cortex; MPFC, medial prefrontal cortex; OFC, orbital frontal cortex; PHC, parahippocampal cortex; RSC, retrosplenial complex. The arrows are unidirectional in the figure to emphasize the flow during the proposed analysis, but all these connections are bidirectional in nature. (Adapted from Bar, 2004.)

representations of objects and relations that are common to that specific context (*context frames*; Bar & Ullman 1996; Bar, 2004), using a cortical network involving the parahippocampal cortex (PHC), the retrosplenial complex (RSC), and to some extent also the medial prefrontal cortex (MPFC) (Bar, 2003, 2004). Together, a simple intersection of the candidate object interpretations (top) with the objects that typically appear in such context (bottom) yields a quick recognition of the target object on a basic level. This basic-level recognition provides the analogy (i.e., input-memory link) that triggers the associative generation of predictions. The question of how the OFC and MPFC trigger these predictions in

the temporal cortex, and what kind of information they convey to do so, is important and still under investigation. As elaborated later, one alternative is that the OFC/MPFC exert their predictive influence on inferior temporal cortex (IT) by way of inhibition that focuses the associative activations in the temporal cortex and limits them to only the contextually relevant coactivations.

Such analogy matching requires generic representations in memory, which in addition to being typical of the exemplar that they represent, should be invariant to variations that are not meaningful to the analogy. (In the research of analogy, as defined traditionally, there have been numerous arguments and demonstrations that individual exemplars can actually be more appropriate for category representations than prototypes [e.g., Allen & Brooks, 1991], but this is beyond the scope of the current discussion and the different manner by which the term analogy is defined here.) How might such generic representations be accomplished? This has proven to be an extremely difficult question to answer. One proposal could be based on the observation that various instances of the same exemplar (e.g., object or context) can vary dramatically in their specific details, but they nevertheless share global properties. In the realm of visual cognition, we can consider LSF scene images as prototypical representations of contexts, because they only contain such instance-invariant visual features and do not represent details that vary from one instance to another. An LSF image of an input scene typically will match and activate one such global/prototypical context frame in memory (i.e., the analogy; such as the ones activated in the bottom part of the network depicted in Fig. 2.1). This is sufficient in most cases to generate rapid predictions that guide our pressing goals, such as navigation and avoidance. The arrival of the specific detail, with the high spatial frequencies (HSFs), gradually makes the initially activated prototypical representation more episodic, in that it "fills" the LSF blobs with image-specific details (e.g., the microwave in

Fig. 2.1 changes from a prototypical one to the specific instance).

One possibility for the development of prototypical representations in memory (e.g., the context frame) with experience is by averaging accumulated instances of the same context, which could be seen as analogous to LSF filtering. Indeed, the street prototype (Fig. 2.2, left) is a result of averaging over 100 street images (Torralba & Oliva, 2003). In addition to providing the trigger for the generation of predictions, analogies that are based on such "averaged" representations can be used as a powerful tool for accommodating the infinite variations in appearance of the physical world around us, where properties tend to be familiar but not identical, as has been demonstrated impressively in computer vision (Jenkins & Burton, 2008). In other words, a global, coarse representation of a certain concept can be activated by different exemplars of that concept in spite of changing details, and it therefore affords both analogy and a more invariant recognition.

Everyday situations tend to carry additional regularities and diagnostic properties beyond their "average" physical appearance. Consider, for example, your actions when you pick up the phone to discover (i.e., by analogy with your previous experience) that it is a telemarketing call. The appearance of the phone and the room you are in, as well as the voice and even the content of

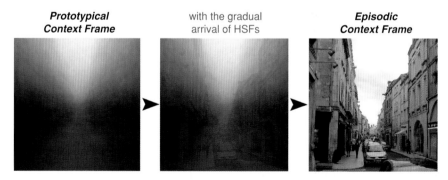

Prototypical Context Frame   with the gradual arrival of HSFs   **Episodic Context Frame**

Figure 2.2 When seeing a novel image of a scene, its low spatial frequency version rapidly activates a prototypical context frame (*left*) in memory (i.e., an analogy). The relatively slower and gradual arrival of detail in the high spatial frequencies (HSFs, *middle*) results in a more episodic context frame (*right*), with scene-specific information. (Image on left courtesy of A. Torralba.)

the conversation do not influence your reaction; you largely execute a familiar response, with only minor variations, based on knowledge that is considerably higher level than simple perceptual properties.

In sum, when entities in our environment occur frequently enough with repeating diagnostic properties, these regularities can be used to link, via analogy, to similar representations in memory, which then allows the use of associated information as predictions that facilitate our interaction with the environment.

ASSOCIATIONS: THE BUILDING BLOCKS

The importance of associations to our mental lives has been widely recognized and has been discussed already by early philosophers, dating back to Plato, Aristotle, and Vives. Associations provide the vehicle for memory encoding and retrieval, but here they are also proposed to serve as the building blocks of predictions: by activating a certain analogy, information that is associated with this analogy in memory is triggered, generating an "expectation" by becoming presensitized.

Seeing the brain as proactive implies that, by "default," when we are not engaged in some demanding and all-consuming task, the brain generates predictions. Therefore, if generating predictions is a continuous operation of the brain, and predictions rely on associative activation, one needs to show that associative activation is an ongoing process in human thought. We recently provided such demonstration (Bar, Aminoff, Mason, & Fenske, 2007) by showing a striking overlap between the cortical network that mediates contextual associative processing and the cortical network that has been termed the brain's "default network" (Raichle et al., 2001).

The default network is believed to subserve the mental processes that take place in the brain when subjects are not engaged in a specific goal-oriented task (Binder et al., 1999; Mason et al., 2007; Mazoyer et al., 2001; Raichle et al., 2001). The major components of this "default" network overlap remarkably with the same regions that we have found as directly related to contextual

associative activation (Aminoff, Gronau, & Bar, 2007; Bar, 2003; Bar et al., 2007) (Fig. 2.3). This overlap between the default network and the network subserving associative processing of contextually related information is taken as the cortical manifestation that associative predictions are crucial elements of natural thought. This account allows a more specific ascription of a cognitive function to the brain's "default" activity (Bar et al., 2007).

Interestingly, the regions of the contextual associations network and of the default network that exhibit the greatest overlap—MPC (medial parietal cortex; also termed RSC earlier), structures in the medial temporal lobe (MTL) and the MPFC—have been reported to be activated in an exceptionally wide variety of studies: navigation and spatial processing (Maguire, 2001; O'Craven & Kanwisher, 2000), execution errors and planning of saccadic eye movements (Polli et al., 2005), episodic memory (Ranganath et al., 2004; Wagner, Shannon, Kahn, & Buckner, 2005), decision making (Fleck, Daselaar, Dobbins, & Cabeza, 2006), emotional processing (Maddock, 1999),

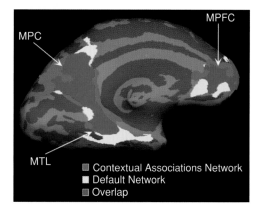

Figure 2.3 Medial view of the left hemisphere, demonstrating the overlap between the default network (defined, for example, using the contrast between activation at "rest" baseline vs. activation in an n-back working memory task) and the associative predictions network (defined, for example, using the contrast between recognition of highly associative objects vs. recognition of only weakly associative objects). MPC, medial parietal cortex; MPFC, medial prefrontal cortex; MTL, medial temporal lobe.

self-referential processing (Kelley et al., 2002; Macrae, Moran, Heatherton, Banfield, & Kelley, 2004), social interactions (Iacoboni et al., 2004), and mental state attribution (i.e., theory of mind; Frith & Frith, 2006; Mitchell et al., 2005; Saxe & Kanwisher, 2003). How could the same cortical regions apparently mediate so many different functions? Our proposal has been that the basic operation that is shared by all these diverse processes is the reliance on associations and the generation of predictions (Bar et al., 2007). In fact, it is hard to imagine another role that could be assigned to this network that can bridge such a wide variety of mental processes.

Our first approximation of the division of labor between the primary three components of this central cortical network is that the MTL represents episodic, physically specific representation of an immediate context, MPC/RSC contains prototypical representations for typical contexts (e.g., kitchen, theater, beach), including general but diagnostic information on each, and the MPFC uses this associative information to generate predictions (Aminoff, Schacter, & Bar, 2008; Bar, 2007; Bar et al., 2007). Indeed, the MPFC, the MPC, and the MTL have all been reported to show selective activation in recent studies of thinking about the past and the future (Addis, Wong, & Schacter, 2007; Buckner & Carroll, 2007; Burgess, Maguire, Spiers, & O'Keefe, 2001; Okuda et al., 2003; Szpunar, Watson, & McDermott, 2007), consistent with the roles we have assigned to this network.

It is important to note that the term *associations* is fairly broad in that it is certain to involve more than one type of mechanism and representations, and therefore more regions are expected to be involved in the processing of other types of associations. For example, the striatum, the caudate nucleus, and the cerebellum have all been shown to be involved in various paradigms related to associative processing (Pasupathy & Miller, 2005).

In the framework proposed here, associations can vary in the automaticity of their activation. On one extreme, associations are automatic, simple, and unique, like a basic Hebbian association where associated concepts are coactivated when the representation of one of them is activated. Basic associations have been the primary

focus of research on associations, and they have largely been shown to be mediated by a region within the MTL (Aminoff, Gronau, & Bar, 2007; Eichenbaum & Bunsey, 1995; Miyashita, 1993; Petrides, 1985; Ranganath et al., 2004; Schacter, 1987; Shallice et al., 1994; Sperling et al., 2003; Stark & Squire, 2001; Suzuki & Eichenbaum, 2000). Other associations are more deliberative, and their selective coactivation depends on the specific context in which they are embedded (Bar, 2004). Yet more complex types of associations might combine the output of different modules performing mental simulations and other relatively higher level operations. It is proposed here that even complex mental experiences are derived from associations with simpler elements. These associations are formed through experience based on similarity and frequent co-occurrence in space and time.

The concept of associative activation is powerful beyond the generation of predictions about what other objects, people, and events to expect in a given context. With the broad activations afforded by associative structuring of memory, associative activations can be seen as guiding our behavior more globally by determining a "mindset." This proposed concept of mindset might be seen as composed of a broad set of predictions—a repertoire of what is expected and what is not—which constitutes a *state* for guiding behavior and for tuning our perceptions and cognitions. It is elicited and shaped by a prime such as the given context, and it can be modified based on ongoing circumstances. This idea is still in its infancy, but it is interesting to consider here at least one (extreme) example of how such associative activations affect somewhat unexpected aspects of behavior. Specifically, Bargh and his collaborators (Bargh, Chen, & Burrows, 1996; Dijksterhuisa, Aarstb, Bargh, & van Kippenburg, 2000) have shown that associative activations, which their stereotype priming techniques can be seen as, can have surprisingly powerful effects on behavior. For example, priming rudeness in participants made these participants later interrupt the experimenter more frequently, and priming subjects with elderly traits (simply by exposing them to a trait-related collection of words) made them subsequently walk slower in the hallway when leaving the laboratory. While these links might seem far-fetched at first, they suggest that priming even a very high-level concept can activate associative predictions and action patterns that together constitute a mindset that is congruent with the prime.

One idea that stems from the concept of mindset is that our response to a certain stimulus or situation is not absolute, but instead determined by the mindset. This has been demonstrated repeatedly in the realm of emotion and affect, but it is valid in other settings as well. For example, certain behaviors might be acceptable in a "dance club" context and the corresponding mindset but the exact same behaviors will be rude in a "formal dinner" context (e.g., pushing on your way to get a drink). A second hypothesis is that a great deal of the ubiquitous activations seen in the "default" network can be explained as reflecting a mindset, and such default activity would change dramatically when subjects are in different mindsets. We tend to think that cortical representations are activated either by perception or internally retrieved with recall, imagery, and simulations. But mindsets imply that we have a sustained (and updateable) list of needs, goals, desires, predictions, and context-sensitive conventions and attitudes. This list constitutes our ongoing mindset, which is maintained continuously and imposed by activity in the contextual/default network. Mindsets can be suspended temporarily for performing an immediate task or achieving a short-term goal. It is possible that mindsets can also be suspended for longer durations by methods such as meditation for example.

Finally, the central role of associations in our mental lives has far-reaching implications to clinical mental disorders. Particularly interesting to note is that the pattern of activity typically observed at "rest" (i.e., "default mode") in healthy individuals differs in patients with major depression. For example, the MPFC exhibits hypoactivity during periods of rest in depressed individuals (Drevets et al., 1992; Soares & Mann, 1997). Furthermore, the structure, function, and connectivity of the same default/associative network are compromised in depression (Anand et al., 2005; Drevets, 2000; Mayberg et al., 1999), and its integrity is improved with antidepressant-related clinical improvement (Anand et al., 2005; Mayberg et al., 1999). And foresight is severely impaired in depressed individuals (Williams et al., 1996). These findings provide critical support to the recent hypothesis that mood can be modulated by associative and predictive processing (Bar, 2009).

PREDICTIONS AND SOME IMPLICATIONS

The proposal that memories are encoded in an associative manner (e.g., context frames) and that their holistic activation generates predictions gives rise to several interesting issues. First, one might wonder why would the brain invest energy in mind wandering, fantasizing, and revisiting existing memories. After all, if these operations are not geared directly toward a specific goal (such as in concrete planning), why not just rest? I propose that a central role of what seems like random thoughts and aimless mental simulations is to create "memories" (Bar, 2007), which are like actual experience-based memories, but are the outcome of imagined rather than experiences. Information encoded in our memory guides and sometimes dictates our future behavior. One can look at our experience as stored in memory like scripts. The notion of such scripts is similar to proposals in language and artificial intelligence (Schank, 1975), and similar to the idea of stored motor plans (Mushiake, et al. 2006; Schubotz & von Cramon, 2002), which contain information on what was the proper response and expectation under similar conditions in the past (see also Barbey, Krueger, & Grafman, 2009; Barsalou, 2009). The idea of behavior scripts existing in the cortex is supported to some extent by findings of behavior "segments" in Broca's area (Koechlin & Jubault, 2006). But why should these scripts only be derived from real experiences, given that our mind is powerful enough to generate simulated experiences that did not happen but could happen in the future? Unlike real memories, these simulation-based "memories" have not really taken place, but we benefit from them just like we do from memories that did occur previously. Therefore, one primary, if not the cardinal, role of memory is to guide our behavior in the future based on similarities (i.e., analogies), and this memory can be a result of real as well as imagined experience. This idea is related to Ingvar's visionary, concept of "memory of the future" (Ingvar, 1985).

An example might help make this point more vivid. You are waiting for your turn for a haircut, and with nothing good to read but an old shampoo catalogue, you let your mind wander. You imagine a scenario of an earthquake: "What if a powerful earthquake erupts?" Your thoughts can become very specific about your actions in this hypothetical case: how you will locate your family, how you will be ready to help other patrons in that hairdresser's place, and so on. Now it is a "memory." A future "memory" of an event that has never happened, but has some chance, even if slim, of happening; it can help facilitate your actions if it ever happens in reality, just like a real memory that is based on actual experience. Interestingly, not only can such "memories" be helpful in guiding our actions in various situations, they can suffer the same types of memory distortion to which real memories are prone. For example, you could swear you had actually written an e-mail that in reality you had only planned to, in detail, while stuck in traffic. Overall, this perspective promotes considering imagined scenarios, and what might appear like random mind wandering, as beneficial to our learning and future behavior as much as real experiences.

A second interesting issue is that while memory is clearly used for generating predictions, we do not know what influence predictions have on memory. A proposal that stems from the framework described here is that aspects of new experiences that meet our expectations are less likely to be encoded compared with novel ones. We primarily encode what differed from our memory and predictions: surprises as well as details if they are sufficiently important. Some have argued that such deviations from predictions provide the basis for learning (e.g., Schultz & Dickinson, 2000). The issue of what remains in memory from a given experience is interesting and is not fully understood, but it is worth noting how many of the known criteria for memory encoding, such as saliency, emotional value, surprise, and novelty, relate to predictions.

A third topic pertains to the intriguing interplay between the generation of predictions and the allocation of attention. Of course, when the predictions relate to upcoming items and events that are relevant for accomplishing a specific task at hand (e.g., looking for a friend in a restaurant), predictions directly guide our attention (e.g., spatial locations as well as identity features). Indeed, performance errors can be predicted by failures of preparatory attentional allocation (e.g., Weissman, Roberts, Visscher, & Woldorff, 2006), and studies demonstrated the role of predictive associations and memory in the allocation of attention (e.g., Moores, Laiti, & Chelazzi, 2003; Summerfield, Lepsien, Gitelman, Mesulam, & Nobre, 2006). But, otherwise, one of the foremost benefits afforded by accurate predictions is that they rid us of the need to exert mental effort and allocate attention toward predictable aspects of the environment. In other words, the power of predictions is that we can anticipate some context-specific aspects, to which we do not have to allocate as much attention, and therefore remain with the resources to explore our environment for novelties from which we can learn, and surprises we should avoid.

To summarize these last two points, generating predictability (and thus reducing uncertainties) based on our experience is therefore a powerful tool for detecting the unexpected. One way to look at this issue is to consider predictions as top-down influences that bias the presensitization of certain representations based on what is most likely to be relevant in that specific situation. In most typical environments, these predictions are met with corresponding incoming (bottom-up) information, which helps us "not worry" about those aspects of the environment. But in some cases, the bottom-up information ascending from the senses does not meet our expectations (e.g., a shoe hanging from a tree branch, a technology gadget we have never seen before, or an unexpected sound of an explosion). Those unpredictable incoming aspects that do not meet the possibilities offered by the top-down predictions (i.e., mindset) can provide a signal both for attentional allocation as well as for subsequent memory encoding. An issue that will not be covered here but is nevertheless related and interesting pertains to the constant act of balancing our need to learn by exploring new information and our need for certainty afforded by seeking the familiar (Cohen & Aston-Jones, 2005; Daw et al., 2006).

Inhibition is another concept that bears direct relation to predictions. Similarly to the implication of the prefrontal cortex (PFC) in predictions, the PFC has been implicated in many other high-level functions, including executive control, attentional guidance, response to uncertainty and reward value, understanding consequences, self-reference, and inhibition. With the exception of inhibition, all these functions can be directly seen as involving association-based predictions. It is interesting then to consider what could be the role that inhibition possibly plays in the generation of predictions. One might see the generation of predictions that activate specific

representations as limiting the alternatives by inhibiting those representations that are less relevant in the given context. Of course, this does not mean that all representations we have in memory are actively inhibited with each predictive signal. Instead, certain aspects of the environment can give rise to associations that result in somewhat irrelevant or even misleading predictions. For example, an image of a towel might be associated in memory (e.g., MTL or visual cortex) with many other objects; some are relevant in a bath context (a toothbrush), some in a beach context (a beach umbrella), and so on. Activating the representation of a towel might cause all these associates to be activated as well. But only some of them are relevant in the given context; automatically activating the representation of a soap bar when seeing a towel on the beach, rather than in a bath context, will be wasteful and misleading (Bar, 2004). Similarly, representations in our memory are all connected to each other with some direct or indirect association (Fig. 2.4a). But a given situation calls for only a partial set of these representations to be

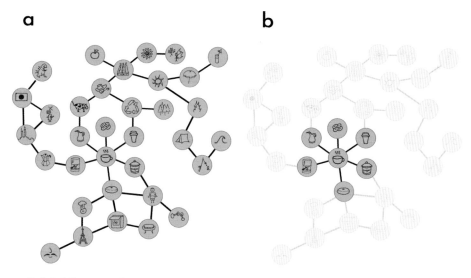

Figure 2.4 Inhibition as the source for making predictions focused and relevant. (*a*) Representations are connected to each other in an immense web of associations. (*b*) When we encounter a certain object, such as a cup of coffee, it is useful for us to activate objects associated with it that are relevant in that context (e.g., a coffee-maker) but not other things that might be less directly relevant (e.g., a tent). It is proposed that inhibition is the primary source of making such associative coactivation limited so that this process results in relevant predictions.

coactivated for the ensuing predictions to be focused and relevant (Bar, 2009). The irrelevant associations will be distracting if automatically coactivated, and inhibiting their activation might be accomplished via top-down processes (Fig. 2.4b). The inhibition proper does not need to take place in the PFC. Once predictions are conveyed to the relevant lower cortex, these predictions can start local processes that inhibit contextually incongruent associative activations as necessary. Taken together, inhibition can play a powerful role in helping the selective activation of only the most relevant representations as predictions, therefore maximizing their usefulness. A lack of inhibition might cause overly broad associative activations and therefore unhelpful, nonspecific predictions. Abnormally increased level of inhibition, on the other hand, might prevent associative activations, which could result in disorders such as clinical depression (Bar, 2009).

One everyday manifestation of the proposed framework of finding a rapid analogy that then serves the generation of predictions is that of first impressions and stereotypes. Consider first impression about someone's personality traits. It has been shown that such judgments can be formed with extremely brief exposures (Bar et al., 2006; Willis & Todorov, 2006), and that they rely on the rapidly arriving global details conveyed by the LSF (Bar et al., 2006). By extracting those rudimentary properties and forming an opinion, our brains find an analogy ("this guy looks *like* Zach") that then serves as a platform for predictions ("so he is probably frugal and a music expert"), which will directly influence our interactions with that newly introduced person. Similarly, whatever we might be judging based on body language (e.g., someone standing too close), typically even without the awareness of either the perceiver or of the "transmitter," could be seen as a cue that connects with analogy and predictions (e.g., "She seems to really like me."). Such predictive first impressions might be useful and possibly somewhat accurate when the judged traits directly pertain to our survival (e.g., potential threat) and less so for other traits (e.g., intelligence; Bar et al., 2006). A related example is people's response when listening to an exceptionally gifted speaker with oratorical talents that

make the listeners automatically assign credibility and authority to that speaker, with less emphasis on the content compared with their reaction to the message carried by more ordinary speakers. Such examples might all be seen as types of prejudiced prediction that are based on global, rudimentary information.

In summary, the generality of information within an activated associative context frame permits it to be applied to new instances of the relevant context such that previous experience can help guide new experiences (Bar, 2007; Bartlett, 1932; Brewer & Nakamura, 1984).

CONCLUSIONS

Predictions, and their constructions from associations, span a wide range of complexity and function: from basic Hebbian-like associative activation, to complex scenarios involving simulations and integration of multiple elements. Their application is correspondingly highly versatile, from simple and procedural automatic learning to language and social interactions.

There is clearly a need for developing models of how this framework of analogies→associations→ predictions is realized, a task that will undoubtedly prove to be complex. The framework proposed here includes various facets. First, the brain is proactive in generating predictions. Second, interpretation via analogies is meant to answer the question "What is this *like*?" Third, associations play a central role in foresight. Fourth, the information stored in our memory exerts its contribution to behavior by way of predictions. This information in memory may be represented as scripts for guiding behavior, some of which were acquired from actual experience and some of which are a result of mental simulations. Fifth, inhibition shapes and fine-tunes the selectivity and thus the relevance of the predictions activated in a given context. Finally, the web of activations that is elicited in a certain situation provides a set of predictions that determines a mindset that dictates our responses and actions.

At a given moment, we integrate information from multiple points in time. We are rarely in the "now," but rather combine past and present in anticipation of the future. How the brain integrates representations from different points in time, while still distinguishing among them, is an important question for future research. It is also important to understand the largely understudied issue of the computational operations, and the underlying cortical mechanisms, mediating the transformation of a past memory into a future thought. Furthermore, it is possible to imagine how the principle properties of an image could be represented in memory (e.g., by way of low spatial frequencies that exclude details but preserve diagnostic, global properties), but it is unclear how our experience with more complex situations (e.g., traveling) can be encoded at a gist level in a way that can easily be applied in novel, analogous circumstances. Revealing the cognitive and neural mechanisms underlying these important issues will fundamentally promote our understanding of how our brains rely on predictions as a universal principle for its operation.

ACKNOWLEDGMENTS

I thank L. Barrett, L. Barsalou, J. Boshyan, K. Devaney, K. Kveraga, K. Shepherd, M. Tousian, and C. Thomas for constructive comments and help with the manuscript. This chapter is an updated version of the following article: Bar, M. (2009) The proactive brain: Memory for predictions. *Philosophical Transactions of the Royal Society B*, 364, 1235–1243. Supported by NIH grant NS050615 and NSF grant 0842947.

REFERENCES

Addis, D. R., Wong, A. T., & Schacter, D. L. (2007). Remembering the past and imagining the future: Common and distinct neural substrates during event construction and elaboration. *Neuropsychologia*, 45(7), 1363–1377.

Allen, S. W., & Brooks, L. R. (1991). Specializing the operation of an explicit rule. *Journal of Experimental Psychology: General*, 120, 3–19.

Aminoff, E., Gronau, N., & Bar, M. (2007). The parahippocampal cortex mediates spatial and nonspatial associations. *Cerebral Cortex*, 27, 1493–1503.

Aminoff, E., Schacter, D. L., & Bar, M. (2008). The cortical underpinnings of context-based memory distortion. *Journal of Cognitive Neuroscience*, 20(12), 2226–2237.

Anand, A., Li, Y., Wang, Y., Wu, J., Gao, S., Bukhari, L., et al. (2005a). Activity and connectivity of brain mood regulating circuit in depression: a functional magnetic resonance study. *Biological Psychiatry*, 57(10), 1079–1088.

Anand, A., Li, Y., Wang, Y., Wu, J., Gao, S., Bukhari, L., et al. (2005b). Antidepressant effect on connectivity of the mood-regulating circuit: An FMRI study. *Neuropsychopharmacology*, 30(7), 1334–1344.

Bar, M. (2003). A cortical mechanism for triggering top-down facilitation in visual object recognition. *Journal of Cognitive Neuroscience*, 15, 600–609.

Bar, M. (2004). Visual objects in context. *Nature Reviews Neuroscience*, 5(8), 617–629.

Bar, M. (2007). The proactive brain: using analogies and associations to generate predictions. *Trends in Cognitive Sciences*, 11(7), 280–289.

Bar, M. (2009). A cognitive neuroscience hypothesis of mood and depression. *Trends in Cognitive Sciences*, 13(11), 456–463.

Bar, M., & Aminoff, E. (2003). Cortical analysis of visual context. *Neuron*, 38(2), 347–358.

Bar, M., & Ullman, S. (1996). Spatial context in recognition. *Perception*, 25(3), 343–352.

Bar, M., Aminoff, E., Mason, M., & Fenske, M. (2007). The units of thought. *Hippocampus*, 17(6), 420–428.

Bar, M., Kassam, K. S., Ghuman, A. S., Boshyan, J., Schmid, A. M., Dale, A. M., et al. (2006). Top-down facilitation of visual recognition. *Proceedings of the National Academy of Sciences USA*, 103(2), 449–454.

Bar, M., & Neta, M. (2006). Very first impressions. *Emotion*, 6(2), 269–278.

Barbey, A. K., Krueger, F., & Grafman, J. (2009). Structured event complexes in the medial prefrontal cortex support counterfactual representations for future planning [Special Theme Issue]. *Philosophical Transactions of the Royal Society B: Biological Sciences*, 364, 1291–1300.

Bargh, J. A., Chen, M., & Burrows, L. (1996). Automaticity of social behavior: Direct effects of trait construct and stereotype activation on action. *Journal of Personality and Social Psychology*, 71(2), 230–244.

Barsalou, L. W. (2003). Abstraction in perceptual symbol systems. *Philosophical Transactions of the Royal Society of London Part B: Biological Sciences*, 358(1435), 1177–1187.

Barsalou, L. W. (2009). Simulation, situated conceptualization, and prediction [Special Theme Issue]. *Philosophical Transactions of the Royal Society B: Biological Sciences, 364*, 1281–1289.

Bartlett, F. C. (1932). *Remembering: A study in experimental and social psychology.* Cambridge, England: Cambridge University Press.

Biederman, I., Rabinowitz, J. C., Glass, A. L., & Stacy, E. W. (1974). On the information extracted from a glance at a scene. *Journal of Experimental Psychology, 103*, 597–600.

Binder, J. R., Frost, J. A., Hammeke, T. A., Bellgowan, P. S., Rao, S. M., & Cox, R. W. (1999). Conceptual processing during the conscious resting state: A functional MRI study. *Journal of Cognitive Neuroscience, 11*(1), 80–95.

Brewer, W. F., & Nakamura, G. V. (1984). The nature and functions of schemas. In R. S. Wyer & T. K. Srull (Eds.), *Handbook of social cognition* (pp. 119–160). Hillsdale, NJ: Erlbaum.

Buckner, R. L., & Carroll, D. C. (2007). Self-projection and the brain. *Trends in Cognitive Sciences, 11*(2), 49–57.

Burgess, N., Maguire, E. A., Spiers, H. J., & O'Keefe, J. (2001). A temporoparietal and prefrontal network for retrieving the spatial context of lifelike events. *Neuroimage, 14*(2), 439–453.

Cohen, J. D., & Aston-Jones, G. (2005). Cognitive neuroscience: Decision amid uncertainty. *Nature, 436*(7050), 471–472.

Daw, N. D., O'Doherty, J. P., Dayan, P., Seymour, B., & Dolan, R. J. (2006). Cortical substrates for exploratory decisions in humans. *Nature, 441*(7095), 876–879.

DeLong, K. A., Urbach, T. P., & Kutas, M. (2005). Probabilistic word pre-activation during language comprehension inferred from electrical brain activity. *Nature Neuroscience, 8*(8), 1117–1121.

Dijksterhuisa, A., Aartsb, H., Bargh, J. A., & van Kippenburg, A. (2000). On the relation between associative strength and automatic behavior. *Journal of Experimental Social Psychology, 36*(5), 531–544.

Drevets, W. C. (2000). Functional anatomical abnormalities in limbic and prefrontal cortical structures in major depression. *Progress in Brain Research, 126*, 413–431.

Drevets, W. C., Videen, T. O., Price, J. L., Preskorn, S. H., Carmichael, S. T., & Raichle, M. E. (1992). A functional anatomical study of unipolar depression. *Journal of Neuroscience, 12*(9), 3628–3641.

Eichenbaum, H., & Bunsey, M. (1995). On the binding of associations in memory—clues from studies on the role of the hippocampal region in paired-associate learning. *Current Directions in Psychological Science, 4*, 19–23.

Fleck, M. S., Daselaar, S. M., Dobbins, I. G., & Cabeza, R. (2006). Role of prefrontal and anterior cingulate regions in decision-making processes shared by memory and nonmemory tasks. *Cerebral Cortex, 16*(11), 1623–1630.

Frith, C. D., & Frith, U. (2006). The neural basis of mentalizing. *Neuron, 50*(4), 531–534.

Gentner, D. (1983). Structure-mapping: A theoretical framework for analogy. *Cognitive Science, 7*(2), 155–170.

Hassabis, D., & Maguire, E. A. (2009). The construction system of the brain [Special Theme Issue]. *Philosophical Transactions of the Royal Society B: Biological Sciences, 364*, 1263–1271.

Holyoak, K. J., & Thagard, P. (1997). The analogical mind. *American Psychologist, 52*(1), 35–44.

Iacoboni, M., Lieberman, M. D., Knowlton, B. J., Molnar-Szackas, I., Moritz, M., Throop, C. J., & Fiske, A. P. (2004). Watching social interactions produces dorsomedial prefrontal and medial parietal BOLD fMRI signal increases compared to a resting baseline. *Neuroimage, 21*(3), 1167–1173.

Ingvar, D. H. (1985). Memory of the future: An essay on the temporal organization of conscious awareness. *Human Neurobiology, 4*(3), 127–136.

Jenkins, R., & Burton, A. M. (2008). 100% accuracy in automatic face recognition. *Science, 319*(5862), 435.

Kelley, W. M., Macrae, C. N., Wyland, C. L., Caglar, S., Inati, S., & Heatherton, T. F. (2002). Finding the self? An event-related fMRI study. *Journal of Cognitive Neuroscience, 14*, 785–794.

Koechlin, E., & Jubault, T. (2006). Broca's area and the hierarchical organization of human behavior. *Neuron, 50*, 963–974.

Kveraga, K., Boshyan, J., & Bar, M. (2007). Magnocellular projections as the trigger of top-down facilitation in recognition. *Journal of Neuroscience, 27*(48), 13232–13240.

Macrae, C. N., Moran, J. M., Heatherton, T. F., Banfield, J. F., & Kelley, W. M. (2004). Medial prefrontal activity predicts memory for self. *Cerebral Cortex, 14*, 647–654.

Maddock, R. J. (1999). The retrosplenial cortex and emotion: new insights from functional neuroimaging of the human brain. *Trends in Neurosciences, 22*(7), 310–316.

Maguire, E. A. (2001). The retrosplenial contribution to human navigation: a review of lesion and neuroimaging findings. *Scandinavian Journal of Psychology*, *42*(3), 225–238.

Mason MF, Norton MI, Van Horn JD, Wegner DM, Grafton ST, Macrae CN. 2007. Wandering minds: The default network and stimulus-independent thought. *Science* 315, 393–395.

Mayberg, H. S., Liotti, M., Brannan, S. K., McGinnis, S., Mahurin, R. K., Jerabek, P. A., et al. (1999). Reciprocal limbic-cortical function and negative mood: Converging PET findings in depression and normal sadness. *American Journal of Psychiatry*, *156*(5), 675–682.

Mazoyer, B., Zago, L., Mellet, E., Bricogne, S., Etard, O., Houdé, O., et al. (2001). Cortical networks for working memory and executive functions sustain the conscious resting state in man. *Brain Research Bulletin*, *54*(3), 287–298.

Mitchell, J. P., Banaji, M. R., & Macrae, C. N. (2005). General and specific contributions of the medial prefrontal cortex to knowledge about mental states. *Neuroimage*, *28*, 757–762.

Miyashita, Y. (1993). Inferior temporal cortex: Where visual perception meets memory. *Annual Review of Neuroscience*, *16*, 245–269.

Moores, E., Laiti, L., & Chelazzi, L. (2003). Associative knowledge controls deployment of visual selective attention. *Nature Neuroscience*, *6*(2), 182–189.

Moulton, S. T., & Kosslyn, S. M. (2009). Imagining predictions: Mental imagery as mental simulation [Special Theme Issue]. *Philosophical Transactions of the Royal Society B: Biological Sciences*, *364*, 1273–1280.

Mushiake, H., Saito, N., Sakamoto, K., Itoyama, Y., & Tanji, J. (2006). Activity in the lateral prefrontal cortex reflects multiple steps of future events in action plans. *Neuron*, *50*(4), 631–641.

Muter, V., Snowling, M., & Taylor, S. (1994). Orthographic analogies and phonological awareness: their role and significance in early reading development. *Journal of Child Psychology and Psychiatry*, *35*(2), 293–310.

Noe, A. (2005). *Action in perception (representation and mind)*. Cambridge, MA: The MIT Press.

O'Craven, K. M., & Kanwisher, N. (2000). Mental imagery of faces and places activates corresponding stimulus-specific brain regions. *Journal of Cognitive Neuroscience*, *12*(6), 1013–1023.

Okuda, J., Fujii, T., Ohtake, H., Tsukiura, T., Tanji, K., Suzuki, K., et al. (2003). Thinking of the future and past: the roles of the frontal pole and the medial temporal lobes. *Neuroimage*, *19*(4), 1369–1380.

Oliva, A., & Torralba, A. (2001). Modeling the shape of a scene: A holistic representation of the spatial envelope. *International Journal of Computer Vision*, *42*(3), 145–175.

Pasupathy, A., & Miller, E. K. (2005). Different time courses of learning-related activity in the prefrontal cortex and striatum. *Nature*, *433*(7028), 873–876.

Petrides, M. (1985). Deficits on conditional associative-learning tasks after frontal- and temporal-lobe lesions in man. *Human Neurobiology*, *4*, 137–142.

Polli, F. E., Barton, J. J., Cain, M. S., Thakkar, K. N., Rauch, S. L., & Manoach, D. S. (2005). Rostral and dorsal anterior cingulate cortex make dissociable contributions during antisaccade error commission. *Proceedings of the National Academy of Sciences USA*, *102*(43), 15700–15705.

Raichle, M. E., MacLeod, A. M., Snyder, A. Z., Powers, W. J., Gusnard, D. A., & Shulman, G. L. (2001). A default mode of brain function. *Proceedings of the National Academy of Sciences USA*, *98*(2), 676–682.

Ranganath, C., Cohen, M. X., Dam, C., & D'Esposito, M. (2004). Inferior temporal, prefrontal, and hippocampal contributions to visual working memory maintenance and associative memory retrieval. *Journal of Neuroscience*, *24*(16), 3917–3925.

Sanocki, T. (1993). Time course of object identification: Evidence for a global-to-local contingency. *Journal of Experimental Psychology: Human Perception and Performance*, *19*(4), 878–898.

Saxe, R., & Kanwisher, N. (2003). People thinking about thinking people. The role of the temporo-parietal junction in theory of mind. *Neuroimage*, *19*(4), 1835–1842.

Schacter, D. L. (1987). Memory, amnesia, and frontal lobe dysfunction. *Psychobiology*, *15*, 21–36.

Schank, R. C. (1975). Using knowledge to understand. In R. C. Schank & B. Nash-Weber (Eds.), *Theoretical issues in natural language processing* Arlington, VA: Tinlap Press.

Schubotz, R. I., & von Cramon, D. Y. (2002). Predicting perceptual events activates corresponding motor schemes in lateral premotor cortex: an fMRI study. *Neuroimage*, *15*(4), 787–796.

Schultz, W., & Dickinson, A. (2000). Neuronal coding of prediction errors. *Annual Review of Neuroscience*, *23*, 473–500.

Schyns, P. G., & Oliva, A. (1994). From blobs to boundary edges: Evidence for time- and spatial-dependent scene recognition. *Psychological Science, 5*(4), 195–200.

Shallice, T., Fletcher, P., Frith, C. D., Graby, P., Frackowiak, R. S., & Dolan, R. J. (1994). Brain regions associated with acquisition and retrieval of verbal episodic memory. *Nature, 368*(6472), 633–635.

Soares, J. C., & Mann, J. J. (1997). The anatomy of mood disorders—review of structural neuroimaging studies. *Biological Psychiatry, 41*(1), 86.

Sperling, R., Chua, E., Cocchiarella, A., Rand-Giovanetti, E., Poldrack, R., Schacter, D. L., & Albert, M. (2003). Putting names to faces: Successful encoding of associative memories activates the anterior hippocampal formation. *Neuroimage, 20*(2), 1400–1410.

Stark, C. E., & Squire, L. R. (2001). Simple and associative recognition memory in the hippocampal region. *Learning and Memory, 8*(4), 190–197.

Summerfield, J. J., Lepsien, J., Gitelman, D. R., Mesulam, M. M., & Nobre, A. C. (2006). Orienting attention based on long-term memory experience. *Neuron, 49*(6), 905–916.

Suzuki, W. A., & Eichenbaum, H. (2000). The neurophysiology of memory. *Annals of the New York Academy of Sciences, 911*, 175–191.

Szpunar, K. K., Watson, J. M., & McDermott, K. B. (2007). Neural substrates of envisioning the future. *Proceedings of the National Academy of Sciences USA, 104*(2), 642–647.

Torralba, A. (2003). Contextual priming for object detection. *International Journal of Computer Vision, 53*(2), 153–167.

Torralba, A., & Oliva, A. (2003). Statistics of natural image categories. *Network, 14*(3), 391–412.

Wagner, A. D., Shannon, B. J., Kahn, I., & Buckner, R. L. (2005). Parietal lobe contributions to episodic memory retrieval. *Trends in Cognitive Science, 9*(9), 445–453.

Wang, K., Jiang, T., Yu, C., Tian, L., Li, J., Liu, Y., et al. (2008). Spontaneous activity associated with primary visual cortex: A resting-state fMRI study. *Cerebral Cortex, 18*(3), 697–704.

Weissman, D. H., Roberts, K. C., Visscher, K. M., & Woldorff, M. G. (2006). The neural bases of momentary lapses in attention. *Nature Neuroscience, 9*(7), 971–978.

Williams, J. M., Ellis, N. C., Tyers, C., Healy, H., Rose, G., & MacLeod, A. K. (1996). The specificity of autobiographical memory and imageability of the future. *Memory and Cognition, 24*(1), 116–125.

Willis, J., & Todorov, A. (2006). First impressions: Making up your mind after a 100-ms exposure to a face. *Psychological Science, 17*(7), 592–598.

CHAPTER 3
Simulation, Situated Conceptualization, and Prediction

Lawrence W. Barsalou

Accumulating evidence suggests that simulation constitutes a central form of computation throughout diverse forms of cognition, where simulation is the reenactment of perceptual, motor, and introspective states acquired during experience with the world, body, and mind (Barsalou, 2008). As described next, the reenactment process has two phases: *(1)* storage in long-term memory of multimodal states that arise across the brain's systems for perception, action, and introspection (where "introspection" refers to internal states that include affect, motivation, intentions, meta-cognition, etc.), and *(2)* partial reenactment of these multimodal states for later representational use, including prediction. Each phase is addressed in turn.

Storage of Modal States

When an entity or event is experienced, it activates feature detectors in the relevant neural systems. During visual processing of a bicycle, for example, neurons fire for edges and surfaces, whereas others fire for color, configural properties, and motion. The overall pattern of activation across this hierarchically organized distributed system represents the entity in vision. Analogous patterns of activation in other sensory modalities represent how the bicycle might sound and feel. Activations in the motor system represent actions on the bicycle. Activations in the amygdale and orbitofrontal areas represent affective reactions.

As a feature system becomes active to represent an entity or event, conjunctive neurons in association areas capture the activation pattern for later representational use. Populations of conjunctive neurons code the pattern, with each individual neuron participating in the coding of many different patterns (e.g., Damasio, 1989; Simmons & Barsalou, 2003). Locally, association areas near a modality capture activation patterns within it (e.g., visual association areas capture patterns of visual features). In turn, higher association areas in the temporal, parietal, and frontal lobes integrate activations across modalities.

Reenactments of Modal States

The architecture just described has the functional ability to produce modal reenactments (simulations). Once associative neurons capture a feature pattern, they can later activate it in the absence of bottom-up stimulation. When retrieving a memory of a bicycle, associative neurons partially reactivate the visual state active during its earlier perception. Similarly, when retrieving an action performed on the bicycle, associative neurons partially reactivate the motor state that produced it. A reenactment never constitutes a complete reinstatement of an original modal state, and various sources of bias may often distort it. Thus, reenactments are always partial and potentially inaccurate. Regardless, some semblance of the original modal state is reenacted for representational use during cognitive activity.

Reenactment is not necessarily conscious but may also be unconscious, probably being unconscious even more often than conscious. Unconscious reenactments may occur frequently during perception, memory, conceptualization, comprehension, and reasoning, along with conscious reenactments. When reenactments reach awareness, they can be viewed as constituting mental imagery, given that imagery is typically assumed to be conscious.

SIMULATORS AND SIMULATIONS

Barsalou (1999, 2003a) developed a theory of cognition based on the neural reenactment of modal states. *Simulators* and *simulations* constitute the theory's two central constructs. Simulators integrate information across a category's instances, whereas simulations are specific conceptualizations of the category. Each is addressed in turn.

Simulators

Because the instances of a category typically have statistically correlated properties, encountering these instances should tend to activate similar neural patterns in feature systems (e.g., Cree & McRae, 2003; Farah & McClelland, 1991). Additionally, similar populations of conjunctive neurons in association areas—tuned to these feature conjunctions—should typically capture these patterns (Damasio, 1989; Simmons & Barsalou, 2003). After experiencing a category's instances over time, a distributed multimodal system develops to represent the category as a whole. Barsalou (1999) referred to these distributed systems as *simulators*. Theoretically, a simulator functions as a concept or type in more traditional theories by integrating the multimodal content of a category across instances and by providing the ability to interpret individuals as tokens of the type (Barsalou, 2003a).

Consider a simulator that represents the concept of *bicycle*. Across encounters with different instances, visual information about how bicycles look becomes integrated in the simulator, along with auditory information about how they sound, somatosensory information about how they feel, motor sequences for interacting with them, affective responses to experiencing them, and so forth. The result is a distributed system throughout the brain's feature and association areas that accumulates and integrates modal content processed for the category. As Barsalou (2003a) describes, many additional simulators develop to represent properties, relations, events, and mental states relevant to *bicycles* (e.g., *spokes, mesh, pedal, effort*).

Simulations

Once a simulator exists to represent a category, it can reenact small subsets of its content as specific *simulations*. As mentioned earlier, these simulations may never reach consciousness, although some aspects may become conscious, as in mental imagery. All content in a simulator never becomes active simultaneously—only small subsets become active to represent the category on particular occasions. Diverse factors such as frequency, recency, and context determine the simulations that become active during a specific simulation of the category (Barsalou, 1987, 1989, 1993). The *bicycle* simulator, for example, might simulate a touring bike on one occasion and mountain bike or a cross bike on others. Because all the experienced content for bicycles resides implicitly in the *bicycle* simulator, diverse subsets can be reenacted on different occasions, tailored to specific contexts. Often, simulations may represent specific instances of a category (e.g., individual bicycles), but they may also represent groups of individuals in a more generic manner (Medin & Ross, 1989).

Simulations are almost certainly never exact reenactments of previously experienced category instances. Instead simulations may typically only reenact instances partially, with various factors producing distortion (see examples later for simulations in perception and action). Furthermore, the level of detail in a simulation may vary widely, from being relatively vague and skeletal to being vivid and detailed, depending on the amount of information available or required. Finally, when simulations of events occur over time, they may often only include a small subset of the originally perceived points within the temporal sequence, rather than being a complete reenactment of all points.

Barsalou (1999, 2003a) proposed that simulations, combined with simulators, perform a wide variety of functions. Simulations represent a category's instances in their absence during memory, language, and thought. Simulations produce inferences and predictions about a category's perceived instances using the pattern completion inference mechanism described later. Simulations combine productively to produce infinite conceptual combinations. Simulations represent the propositions that underlie type-token predication and complex propositional structures. Simulations represent abstract concepts. In general, simulations implement the functionality of classic symbolic systems, with this functionality emerging implicitly in modal and association systems rather than being represented explicitly in symbolic structures, as in predicate calculus and frames.

Sources of Simulators

An infinite number of simulators can develop in long-term memory for objects, settings, events, actions, introspections, properties, relations, and so forth. Specifically, a simulator develops for any component of experience that attention selects repeatedly (Barsalou, 1999, 2003a). When attention focuses repeatedly on a type of object in experience, such as *bicycle*, a simulator develops for it. Analogously, if attention focuses repeatedly on an action (*pedaling*), introspection (*happiness*), or relation (*mesh*), simulators develop to represent them as well. Such flexibility is consistent with Schyns, Goldstone, and Thibaut's (1998) proposal that the cognitive system acquires new concepts as they become relevant. Because selective attention is flexible and open ended, a simulator develops for any component of experience selected repeatedly.

An important issue concerns how simulators for abstract concepts develop. Barsalou (1999) proposed that simulators for abstract concepts generally capture complex multimodal simulations of temporally extended events, with simulation of introspections being central. According to this account, simulators develop to represent categories of internal experience just as they develop to represent categories of external experience. In support of this account,

Barsalou and Wiemer-Hastings (2005) found that concrete and abstract concepts both contain extensive amounts of situation information, but that abstract concepts tend to contain more information about introspections and events (also see Wiemer-Hasting, Krug, & Xu, 2001).

Empirical Evidence

Accumulating evidence implicates simulation as a basic computational mechanism in the brain. Reviews of relevant evidence can be found in Barsalou (2003b, 2008), de Vega, Glenberg, and Graesser (2008), Gibbs (2006), Martin (2001, 2007), Pecher and Zwaan (2005), Pulvermüller, (1999, 2005), Semin and Smith (2008), Smith (2005), Smith and Gasser (2005), and Thompson-Schill (2003).

SITUATED CONCEPTUALIZATIONS

Barsalou (2003b) proposed that concepts are not typically processed in isolation but are typically situated in background settings, events, and introspections. When representing *bicycle*, for example, people do not represent a bicycle in isolation but represent it in relevant situations. According to Yeh and Barsalou (2006), people situate concepts for the following reason: If the brain attempts to simulate a perceptual experience when representing a concept, it should typically simulate a situation, because situations are intrinsic in perception. At any given moment in perception, people perceive the immediate space around them, including agents, objects, and events present. Even when people focus attention on a particular entity or event in perception, they continue to perceive the background situation—the situation does not disappear. If perceptual experience takes the form of a situation, and if a conceptual representation simulates perceptual experience, then the form of a conceptual representation should take the form of a perceived situation. When people construct a simulation to represent a category, they should simulate the category in a relevant perceptual situation, not in isolation.

Barsalou (2003b) referred to situated representations of categories as *situated conceptualizations*. Across different occasions, diverse situated conceptualizations represent a category. Because a single general conceptualization would be too vague to support relevant inferences in specific situations, more specialized representations are constructed instead.

Consider the representation of *bicycle*. According to traditional views, *bicycle* is represented as a generic set of amodal propositions that becomes active as a whole every time the category is processed. According to the view proposed here, however, the cognitive system produces many different situated conceptualizations of *bicycle*, each tailored to helping an agent interact with bicycles in different situations. For example, one situated conceptualization for *bicycle* might support riding a bicycle, whereas others might support locking a bicycle, repairing a bicycle, and so forth. On this view, the concept for *bicycle* is not a single generic representation of the category. Instead the concept is the skill or ability to produce a wide variety of situated conceptualizations that support goal achievement in specific contexts.

Multimodal Simulations Implement Situated Conceptualizations

Barsalou (2003b) proposed that a complex multimodal simulation becomes active to represent a situated conceptualization. Consider a situated conceptualization for riding a bicycle. Such a conceptualization might simulate how riding a bicycle appears perceptually from the perspective of riding one. When riding a bicycle, one views the bicycle from above, sees wheels rolling below, hears the sprockets and chain meshing, feels the wind blowing by, and so forth. All these perceptual aspects of the situation can be represented as modal simulations in a situated conceptualization that represents the experience in its absence. Rather than amodal propositions representing these perceptions, simulations represent them in the relevant modal systems.

A situated conceptualization of riding a bicycle is likely to simulate actions that the agent takes, such as peddling, changing gears, and watching for traffic. Modal simulations could also represent these aspects of a situated conceptualization via simulations of the actions.

A situated conceptualization of riding a bicycle is likely to include simulations of introspections, such as effort, happiness, the goal to reach a destination, planning a route, and motivation to push ahead at maximum speed. Again simulations of these internal states could represent them in the situated conceptualization. Just as external experience can be simulated, so can internal experience.

Finally, a situated conceptualization for riding a bicycle simulates a setting where the event could occur—the event is not simulated in a vacuum. Riding a bicycle, for example, might be simulated on a route to work or on a mountain trail. Again such knowledge can be represented as simulations of particular settings.

In summary, a situated conceptualization typically simulates four basic types of information from a particular perspective: *(1)* perceptions of relevant people and objects, *(2)* actions, *(3)* introspections, and *(4)* settings. Putting all these together, a situated conceptualization is a multimodal simulation of a multicomponent situation, with each modal component simulated in the respective neural system.

A further assumption is that a situated conceptualization consists of simulations from many different simulators (Yeh & Barsalou, 2006). A situated conceptualization for riding a bicycle is likely to include simulations from simulators for people, objects, actions, introspections, and settings. Thus, a single simulator alone does not produce a situated conceptualization. Instead many simulators produce the components that a situated conceptualization contains.

Finally, a situated conceptualization places the conceptualizer *in* the respective situation, creating the experience of "being there" (Barsalou, 2002, 2003b). By reenacting actions and introspections from a particular perspective, a situated conceptualization creates the experience of the conceptualizer being in the situation—the situation is not represented as detached and separate from the conceptualizer.

Entrenched Situated Conceptualizations

Across the life span, people experience many situations repeatedly while interacting with people, artifacts, social institutions, and so forth. As a consequence, knowledge about these familiar situations becomes entrenched in memory, supporting skilled performance in them. Situated conceptualizations represent this entrenched knowledge. When a situation is experienced repeatedly, multimodal knowledge accrues in the respective simulators for the people, objects, actions, introspections, and settings. Components of the conceptualization become entrenched as simulations in the respective simulators, as do associations between simulations and simulators. Over time, the situated conceptualization becomes so well established that it becomes active automatically and immediately when the situation arises. After riding a bicycle on many occasions, a situated conceptualization becomes entrenched in memory such that minimal cuing activates it when relevant. Different but similar situations may also activate entrenched conceptualizations by analogy on later occasion. Indeed, most experienced situations, regardless of how novel they are, may typically activate whatever situated conceptualization happens to be most similar. As described next, activating situated conceptualizations plays central roles in processing a current situation.

Inference via Pattern Completion

Once situated conceptualizations become entrenched in memory, they support a pattern completion inference process (Barsalou, 2003b; Barsalou, Niedenthal, Barbey, & Ruppert, 2003). On encountering a familiar situation, an entrenched situated conceptualization for the situation becomes active. Typically, though, only part of the situation is perceived initially. A relevant person, setting, event, or introspection may be perceived, which then predicts that a particular situation—represented by a situated conceptualization—is about to unfold. By running the situated conceptualization as a simulation, the perceiver anticipates what will happen next, thereby performing effectively in the situation. The agent draws inferences from the simulation that go beyond the information given (e.g., Bruner, 1957).

When a situated conceptualization becomes active, it constitutes a rich source of prediction

via a pattern completion inference mechanism. A situated conceptualization is essentially a pattern, namely, a complex configuration of multimodal components that represent a familiar situation. When a component of this pattern matches something experienced in the environment, the larger pattern becomes active in memory. The remaining pattern components—not yet experienced—constitute inferences, namely, educated guesses about what might occur next. Because the remaining components co-occurred frequently with the perceived components in previous situations, inferring the remaining components is plausible. When a partially viewed situation activates a situated conceptualization, the conceptualization completes the pattern that the situation suggests.

Imagine seeing a bicycle with a flat tire in someone's garage. Further imagine that the perceived bicycle matches components of one or more situated conceptualizations entrenched in memory for *bicycles*. Once one conceptualization wins the activation process—perhaps one containing bicycles with flat tires—it provides inferences via pattern completion, such as introspections likely to be present (being unhappy about a flat tire), actions likely to result (taking the wheel off the bicycle), tools that might be useful (a wrench), and so forth. The unfolding of such inferences—realized as simulations—provides a powerful source of prediction.

Empirical Evidence

Accumulating evidence implicates situated conceptualization and pattern completion inference on situated conceptualizations as basic computational mechanisms in the brain. Reviews of relevant evidence can be found in Barsalou (2003b, 2005), Barsalou et al. (2003), Yeh and Barsalou (2006), and Robbins and Aydede (2008).

SIMULATIONS AND SITUATED CONCEPTUALIZATIONS AS SOURCES OF PREDICTION

Simulations and situated conceptualizations—coupled with pattern completion inference—produce continual predictions across the spectrum of cognitive activities. The perception of something familiar in the environment, body, or introspection activates a simulation or situated conceptualization that contains it. Components of the simulation or situated conceptualization not yet experienced constitute predictions about events likely to occur, actions likely to be effective, and introspections likely to result. Because simulations represent predictions, predictions are simulated in the same modalities in which they would be experienced. As a consequence, predictions can be readily matched to corresponding components, should they actually occur.

Imagine seeing a coffee bean container that activates a situated conceptualization for making espresso. Although only this component of the situated conceptualization is perceived, it activates simulations of the other components as predictions about what could happen next: The container could be opened to reveal coffee beans inside; further actions could be taken to grind the beans and make espresso; psychological states such as pleasure, feeling stimulated, and being more awake could result. As this situated conceptualization becomes active, its simulated components can be used to monitor perceptions, actions, and introspections as they actually occur, assessing whether the situated conceptualization's predictions are satisfied. Because simulated predictions reside in the same systems that perceive the environment, carry out actions, and introspect on internal states, they can be matched to actual experience as it occurs, thereby assessing whether events have unfolded as predicted. Assessing the accuracy of predictions determines whether the situational conceptualization currently active is likely to provide effective guidance for interacting with the current situation. If initial predictions match, then the active conceptualization can be trusted to provide further predictions. If not, a new conceptualization must be retrieved or constructed.

The remaining sections illustrate how simulations and situated conceptualizations generate predictions in this manner across cognitive processes from perception to social cognition.

Perception

Goldstone (1995) illustrated how simulations produce perceptual predictions in a simple perceptual learning paradigm. Participants learned associations between a visual stimulus (e.g., the letter E) and a color (e.g., dark red). Later, when a colored stimulus was flashed as a standard (e.g., a red E), participants used a slider to reproduce its color on an adjustable token of the same stimulus simultaneously present in black (e.g., a black E). Interestingly, participants distorted the reproduced color of the second stimulus toward the *prototypical* color of the perceived standard across trials (i.e., the actual color of the standard was distorted). Perceiving the standard's shape activated a simulation of its prototypical color across trials, which then distorted the standard's perceived color, perhaps fusing with it. Although these simulations of the prototypical color distorted perception of the standard's color, they produced predictions about color likely to be true, statistically speaking, across instances of the stimulus. If the perceiver were searching for the stimulus in the environment, these color predictions would be maximally informative in finding it (for a similar finding, see Hansen, Olkkonen, Walter, & Gegenfurtner, 2006).

Simulations that originate in situated conceptualizations for objects produce predictions about motion. During motion continuation, viewers view the visual trajectory of a moving object. As they view the actual trajectory, they simultaneously simulate the object's future trajectory, predicting where it is likely to move next (e.g., Freyd, 1987). Knowledge about whether an object moves quickly or slowly affects these simulated trajectories accordingly (e.g., Reed & Vinson, 1996). Similarly, during apparent motion, simulations of possible human actions predict interpolated motion likely to be present between two alternating pictures of a human body in different positions (e.g., Shiffrar & Freyd, 1990, 1993). Stevens, Fonlupt, Shiffrar, and Decety (2000) showed that simulations in the motor system underlie these predictions.

During auditory perception, lexical knowledge produces predictions via simulation that contribute to speech perception. In the phoneme restoration effect, listeners use auditory knowledge about a word's phonemes to simulate and predict a missing phoneme (e.g., Warren, 1970). When a phoneme is missing, information present for surrounding phonemes is sufficient to activate a simulation of the word that includes the missing phoneme. Simulations appear present because participants hear speech sounds that are not present physically. Samuel (1997) showed that these simulations originate in early auditory processing. In the McGurk effect (McGurk & McDonald, 1976), perceiving a mouth producing a particular phoneme (e.g., ba) produces a corresponding auditory simulation that conflicts with hearing a different phoneme actually uttered (e.g., ga). Once the simulated phoneme is fused with the perceived phoneme, the result is the auditory perception of a phoneme that is the average of the simulated and perceived phonemes (e.g., da). Thus, an auditory simulation fuses with a perceived auditory phoneme to create the perception of a phoneme neither spoken visually nor heard auditorally. Because multiple modalities underlie the McGurk effect—visual information triggering auditory simulations—multimodal simulations like those in situated conceptualizations generate predictions about the phonemes spoken.

Action

As people perceive visual objects, situated conceptualizations produce predictions about actions likely to be effective while interacting with them. When people perceive a cup, for example, a situated conceptualization for interacting with cups produces a simulation of grasping it. Tucker and Ellis (2001) showed that when a cup handle is on the left, people simulate grasping it with the left hand, but that when the cup handle is on the right, people simulate grasping it with the right hand. In each case, a simulation predicts which hand is likely to be most effective in grasping the cup. Bub, Masson, and Cree (2008) further showed that a perceived object (or its name) automatically triggers simulations of both grasping and functional actions

predicted to be effective during interactions with the object.

Using functional magnetic resonance imaging (fMRI), Chao and Martin (2000) showed that perceived objects activate situated conceptualizations for interacting with the objects. On perceiving a hammer, for example, the grasping circuit in the brain becomes active, predicting—via a motor simulation—appropriate actions to take on the object. As in Tucker and Ellis (2001), these predictions are hand specific, with the grasping circuit for the right hand becoming active in right-handed participants. Lewis (2006) reviews similar and related findings.

Researchers report a wide variety of other findings also consistent with the conclusion that situated conceptualizations produce ubiquitous predictions about action via simulation. In Bosbach, Cole, Prinz, and Knoblich (2005), accurately predicting the weight of an object lifted by another agent required simulating the lifting action in one's own motor and somatosensory systems. In Repp and Knoblich (2004), a pianist's ability to identify auditory recordings of his or her own playing depended on simulating the motor actions underlying it. In Proffitt (2006), simulations of perceived effort appeared to affect the perceived steepness of a hill and the perceived length of a path.

Motor simulations of predicted limb position are central for motor control. As an action is performed, the motor system constructs a feedforward simulation of the action that monitors and guides it (e.g., Grush, 2004; Wolpert, Ghahramani, & Jordan, 1999). These motor simulations also play roles in predicting the anticipated actions of agents perceived visually (Wilson & Knoblich, 2005) and in speeding visual object recognition (e.g., Helbig, Graf, & Kiefer, 2006).

Implicit Memory

Implicit long-term memory is closely related to perceptual prediction. In both cases, perceptual memories—implemented as simulations and situated conceptualizations—become active and affect perception. As we just saw for perception, simulations and situated conceptualizations create perceptions and actions that go beyond stimulus information. In implicit memory, simulations increase perceptual fluency by facilitating the processing of perceptual information and speeding the formation of perceptions (repetition priming). According to the account proposed here, when a perceptual stimulus activates a similar perceptual memory, the perceptual memory runs as a simulation of the stimulus and speeds its processing by activating relevant processing areas, with the simulation perhaps fusing with the stimulus information. To the extent that the perceptual memory matches the stimulus, the memory predicts that the stimulus is another instance of itself, thereby increasing the fluency of perceiving it via top-down activation. When, for example, a perceived face activates an implicit memory, the face memory predicts that the perceived face is another instance of itself and speeds its processing.

Numerous findings support the proposal that the prediction underlying implicit memory results from the simulation of perceptual memories (Roediger & McDermott, 1993; Schacter, Dobbins, & Schnyer, 2004). First, perceptual processing is important for establishing robust repetition priming effects, consistent with the proposal that perceptual memories play central roles in priming (e.g., Jacoby, 1983). Second, repetition priming is strongest when the modalities of the memory and the perceived stimulus match (e.g., when an auditory memory exists to help process an auditory stimulus; Kirsner, Dunn, Standen, 1989). Third, repetition priming is strongest when the perceptual details of a memory and a perceived stimulus match, such as orientation, size, font, and so on (e.g., Jacoby & Hayman, 1987; Jolicoeur, 1985). Fourth, imagining a stimulus produces repetition priming similar to actually perceiving it, suggesting that perceptual representations underlie both (e.g., Roediger & Blaxton, 1987; Schacter & Graf, 1989). For these reasons, simulations of perceptual states appear central to the predictions that implicit memories generate about corresponding perceptions.

Working Memory

Mental imagery can be viewed as the conscious and explicit manipulation of simulations in working memory to predict future events. When imagining a rotating object, for example, a person attempts to predict the object's future orientation, analogous to the less intentional and less conscious inferences in simulating perceptual trajectories discussed earlier. Considerable evidence indicates that simulations in working memory underlie visual imagery (e.g., Finke, 1989; Kosslyn, 1980, 1994; Shepard & Cooper, 1982), motor imagery (e.g., Grèzes & Decety, 2001; Jeannerod, 1995), and auditory imagery (e.g., Halpern, Zatorre, Bouffard, & Johnson 2004). In all cases, imagery attempts to predict what is likely to occur next if an imagined event on the respective modality actually occurred.

When action is relevant to visual imagery, the motor system becomes engaged, implying the presence of a situated conceptualization. When visual rotation of a body part is imagined, for example, bodily constraints shape the rotational trajectory (e.g., Parsons, 1987a, 1987b). Similarly, mental rotation of visual objects is often accompanied by motor simulations of making them turn (e.g., Richter et al., 2000). In both cases, predictions on multiple modalities are conveyed via multimodal simulations.

Conceptual Processing

When entities and events are categorized, conceptual knowledge about the respective categories becomes active to predict what is likely to happen next. As we saw earlier, when people categorize visual objects, such as hammers, conceptual knowledge associated with the respective categories becomes active to predict relevant actions (e.g., Chao & Martin, 2000; Lewis, 2006). Because multimodal simulations represent these predictions, situated conceptualizations appear responsible. Similarly, when people categorize instances of food categories, situated conceptualizations—again implemented via multimodal simulations—produce predictions about how foods will taste and how rewarding they will be to consume (Simmons, Martin, & Barsalou, 2005). Additionally, perceiving an object predicts settings in which it is likely to occur. Bar (2004), for example, found that perceiving isolated objects activates neural systems that represent their environmental contexts. Indeed, recognizing the presence of certain objects is a powerful means of predicting the scene or situation likely to be present.

Much behavioral research supports these conclusions (for a review, see Yeh & Barsalou, 2006). In object perception, for example, perceiving an object activates a background scene that can speed object categorization (e.g., Bar & Ullman, 1996; Biederman, 1972, 1981; Palmer, 1975). Perceiving an object activates a situated conceptualization associated with its category, which—via interactive activation—speeds processing of the object, along with related objects and events in the situation.

Situated conceptualizations also play central roles when people attempt to predict information associated with categories in the absence of category exemplars being present. When people are asked to describe the properties of an absent object category (e.g., *watermelons*), they do not simply generate properties of the object itself. Instead they also generate properties for likely settings (*porch*), events (*eating*), and introspections (*pleasure*). Rather than simply describing the object per se as instructed, people further predict other aspects of situations likely to be present (Barsalou & Wiemer-Hastings, 2005; Chaigneau, Barsalou, & Zamani, 2009; Santos, Chaigneau, Simmons, & Barsalou, 2008; Wu & Barsalou, 2008). As people describe an object, they situate it from their own perspective, simulating themselves in the situation as well. In other words, people construct the experience of "being there" with the object to generate its properties (Barsalou, 2002, 2003b; Yeh & Barsalou, 2006).

Language

Prediction lies at the heart of language comprehension. When processing language, a comprehender's task is to predict what the language means. Accumulating evidence indicates that simulations and situated conceptualizations convey these predictions. Consider research reviewed by Zwaan and Madden (2005) on the role of visual simulation in comprehension. In these experiments, participants read sentences that implied something perceptual not stated

literally. For example, participants read sentences like "Mary hammered the nail into the wall," which implied that the nail was oriented horizontally. If readers constructed simulations to predict what the sentence meant, the simulation should have contained implicit perceptual information not mentioned in the sentence, such as object orientation. After reading the sentence, participants viewed a nail in either a horizontal or vertical orientation and named it. As predicted, participants were faster to name the nail in a horizontal position than in a vertical position, suggesting that they had simulated its orientation while comprehending the sentence (other participants showed the opposite pattern after reading sentences like "Mary pounded the nail into the floor"). Many similar experiments similarly demonstrate diverse perceptual matching effects, consistent with the view that comprehenders simulate situations to predict what sentences mean.

Much research has also shown that comprehenders use motor simulations to generate predictions about meaning. When participants comprehend the word for an action, the motor system represents its meaning (Pulvermüller, 2005). Specifically, verbs for head, arm, and leg actions produce head, arm, and leg simulations in the respective cortical areas. These simulations play causal roles in language processing, given that transcranial magnetic stimulation (TMS) over the relevant motor areas interferes with predicting meaning (e.g., Buccino et al., 2005; Pulvermüller, Hauk, Nikulin, & Ilmoniemi, 2005). Much behavioral research corroborates these results. For example, comprehension is facilitated when the action described in a sentence is consistent with the action to make a response (Glenberg & Kaschack, 2003; Zwaan & Taylor, 2006). Similarly, when reading about a sport, such as hockey, experts produce motor simulations absent in novices (Holt & Beilock, 2006). In all these experiments, participants use motor simulations to predict the meanings of words and sentences that describe action.

Other research shows that participants predict motion through space as they comprehend language. Richardson, Spivey, Barsalou, and McRae (2003) found that readers simulate horizontal and vertical paths to predict the meanings of concrete and abstract verbs (e.g., push vs. lift, argue vs. respect). Matlock (2004) found that implied motion in a sentence (e.g., The road *runs* through the valley) produces corresponding simulations of motion through space. Richardson and Matlock (2007) found that these simulations produce predictive eye movements.

Social Cognition

For decades, social psychologists have shown that bodily states predict relevant social situations, and conversely, that social situations predict relevant bodily states (Niedenthal, Barsalou, Winkielman, Krauth-Gruber, & Ric, 2005). For example, slumping posture is associated with negative affect and failure, whereas upright posture is associated with positive affect and success. Barsalou et al. (2003) proposed that situated conceptualizations represent these patterns of association, and that pattern completion inference produces extensive predictions from these patterns during social interaction. For example, knowing that a student failed an exam activates a situated conceptualization for this type of event, which in turn generates predictions that the individual will be slumped and unhappy. Conversely, seeing a slumped and unhappy student generates the prediction that the student might have failed an exam. In general, situated conceptualizations provide a powerful form of prediction in social cognition, with these predictions being conveyed via simulations during pattern completion inference.

CONCLUSION

Accumulating evidence suggests that simulators, simulations, and situated conceptualizations play central roles throughout cognition. Besides representing knowledge, these systems provide a powerful and ubiquitous source of prediction. Indeed, the entire brain can be viewed as a coordinated system that generates a continuous stream of multimodal predictions during situated action and social interaction (Barsalou, Breazeal, & Smith, 2007).

Perhaps the most pressing issue surrounding this area of work is the lack of well-specified computational accounts. Our understanding of simulators, simulations, situated conceptualizations, and pattern completion inference would be much deeper if computational accounts specified the underlying mechanisms. Increasingly grounding such accounts in neural mechanisms is obviously important as well, as is designing increasingly sophisticated experiments to assess and develop these accounts.

ACKNOWLEDGMENTS

I am grateful to Moshe Bar for helpful comments. This work was supported by National Science Foundation grants SBR-9421326, SBR-9796200, and BCS-0212134 to Lawrence W. Barsalou. Address correspondence to Lawrence W. Barsalou, Department of Psychology, Emory University, Atlanta, GA 30322 (barsalou@emory. edu), http://www.psychology.emory.edu/cogni tion/barsalou/index.html).

REFERENCES

Bar, M. (2004). Visual objects in context. *Nature Reviews: Neuroscience, 5,* 617–629.

Bar, M., & Ullman, S. (1996). Spatial context in recognition. *Perception, 25,* 343–352.

Barsalou, L. W. (1987). The instability of graded structure: Implications for the nature of concepts. In U. Neisser (Ed.), *Concepts and conceptual development: Ecological and intellectual factors in categorization* (pp. 101–140). Cambridge, England: Cambridge University Press.

Barsalou, L. W. (1989). Intraconcept similarity and its implications for interconcept similarity. In S. Vosniadou & A. Ortony (Eds.), *Similarity and analogical reasoning* (pp. 76–121). Cambridge, England: Cambridge University Press.

Barsalou, L. W. (1993). Structure, flexibility, and linguistic vagary in concepts: Manifestations of a compositional system of perceptual symbols. In A. C. Collins, S. E. Gathercole, & M. A. Conway (Eds.), *Theories of memory* (pp. 29–101). London: Lawrence Erlbaum Associates.

Barsalou, L. W. (1999). Perceptual symbol systems. *Behavioral and Brain Sciences, 22,* 577–660.

Barsalou, L. W. (2002). Being there conceptually: Simulating categories in preparation for situated action. In N. L. Stein, P. J. Bauer, & M. Rabinowitz (Eds.), *Representation, memory, and development: Essays in honor of Jean Mandler* (pp. 1–15). Mahwah, NJ: Erlbaum.

Barsalou, L. W. (2003a). Abstraction in perceptual symbol systems. *Philosophical Transactions of the Royal Society of London Part B: Biological Sciences, 358,* 1177–1187.

Barsalou, L. W. (2003b). Situated simulation in the human conceptual system. *Language and Cognitive Processes, 18,* 513–562.

Barsalou, L. W. (2005). Continuity of the conceptual system across species. *Trends in Cognitive Sciences, 9,* 309–311.

Barsalou, L. W. (2008). Grounded cognition. *Annual Review of Psychology, 59,* 617–645.

Barsalou, L. W., Breazeal, C., & Smith, L. B. (2007). Cognition as coordinated non-cognition. *Cognitive Processing, 8,* 79–91.

Barsalou, L. W., Niedenthal, P. M., Barbey, A., & Ruppert, J. (2003). Social embodiment. In B. Ross (Ed.), *The psychology of learning and motivation* (Vol. 43, pp. 43–92). San Diego, CA: Academic Press.

Barsalou, L. W., & Wiemer-Hastings, K. (2005). Situating abstract concepts. In D. Pecher & R. Zwaan (Eds.), *Grounding cognition: The role of perception and action in memory, language, and thought* (pp. 129–163). New York: Cambridge University Press.

Biederman, I. (1972). Perceiving real-world scenes. *Science, 177,* 77–80.

Biederman, I. (1981). On the semantics of a glance at a scene In M. Kubovy & J. R. Pomerantz (Eds.), *Perceptual organization* (pp. 213–253). Hillsdale, NJ: Erlbaum.

Bosbach, S., Cole., J., Prinz, W., & Knoblich, G. (2005). Inferring another's expectation from action: The role of peripheral sensation. *Nature Neuroscience, 8,* 1295–1297.

Bruner, J. S. (1957). Going beyond the information given. In J. S. Bruner, E. Brunswik, L. Festinger, F. Heider, K. F. Muenzinger, C. E. Osgood, & D. Rapaport, (Eds.), *Contemporary approaches to cognition* (pp. 41–69). Cambridge, MA: Harvard University Press.

Bub, D. N., Masson, M. E. J., & Cree, G. S. (2008). Evocation of functional and volumetric gestural knowledge by objects and words. *Cognition, 106,* 27–58.

Buccino, G., Riggio, L., Melli, G., Binkofski, F., Gallese, V., & Rizzolatti, G. (2005). Listening to action-related sentences modulates the activity of the motor system: A combined TMS and behavioral study. *Cognitive Brain Research, 24,* 355–363.

Chaigneau, S. E., Barsalou, L. W., & Zamani, M. (2009). Situational information contributes to object categorization and inference. *Acta Psychologica, 30,* 81–94.

Chao, L. L., & Martin A. (2000). Representation of manipulable man-made objects in the dorsal stream. *Neuroimage, 12,* 478–484.

Cree, G. S., & McRae, K. (2003). Analyzing the factors underlying the structure and computation of the meaning of chipmunk, cherry, chisel, cheese, and cello (and many other such concrete nouns). *Journal of Experimental Psychology: General, 132,* 163–201.

Damasio, A. R. (1989). Time-locked multiregional retroactivation: A systems-level proposal for the neural substrates of recall and recognition. *Cognition, 33,* 25–62.

Farah, M. J., & McClelland, J. L. (1991). A computational model of semantic memory impairment: Modality specificity and emergent category specificity. *Journal of Experimental Psychology: General, 120,* 339–357.

Finke, R. A. (1989). *Principles of mental imagery.* Cambridge, MA: MIT Press.

Freyd, J. J. (1987). Dynamic mental representations. *Psychological Review, 94,* 427–438.

Gibbs, R. W., Jr. (2006). *Embodiment and cognitive science.* New York: Cambridge University Press.

Glenberg, A. M., & Kaschak, M. P. (2003). The body's contribution to language. In B. Ross (Ed.), *The psychology of learning and motivation* (Vol. 43, pp. 93–126). New York: Academic Press.

Goldstone, R. L. (1995). Effects of categorization on color perception. *Psychological Science, 5,* 298–304.

Grèzes, J., & Decety, J. (2001). Functional anatomy of execution, mental simulation, observation, and verb generation of actions: A meta-analysis. *Human Brain Mapping, 12,* 1–19.

Grush, R. (2004). The emulation theory of representation: motor control, imagery, and perception. *Behavioral and Brain Sciences, 27* 377–442.

Halpern, A. R., Zatorre, R. J., Bouffard, M., & Johnson, J. A. (2004). Behavioral and neural correlates of perceived and imagined timbre. *Neuropsychologia, 42,* 1281–1292.

Hansen, T., Olkkonen, M., Walter, S., & Gegenfurtner, K. R. (2006). Memory modulates color appearance. *Nature Neuroscience, 9,* 1367–1368.

Helbig, H. B., Graf, M., & Kiefer, M. (2006). The role of action representations in visual object recognition. *Experimental Brain Research, 174,* 221–228.

Holt, L. E., & Beilock, S. L. (2006). Expertise and its embodiment: Examining the impact of sensorimotor skill expertise on the representation of action-related text. *Psychonomic Bulletin and Review, 13,* 694–701.

Jacoby, L. (1983). Remembering the data: Analyzing interactive processes in reading. *Journal of Verbal Learning and Verbal Behavior, 22,* 485–508.

Jacoby, L. L., & Hayman, C. A. G. (1987). Specific visual transfer in word identification. *Journal of Experimental Psychology: Learning, Memory, and Cognition, 13,* 456–463.

Jeannerod, M. (1995). Mental imagery in the motor context. *Neuropsychologia, 33,* 1419–1432.

Jolicoeur, P. (1985). The time to name disoriented natural objects. *Memory and Cognition, 13,* 289–303.

Kirsner, K., Dunn, J. C., Standen, P. (1989). Domain-specific resources in word recognition. In S. Lewandowsky, J. C. Dunn, & K. Kirsner (Eds.), *Implicit memory: Theoretical views* (pp. 99–122). Hillsdale, NJ: Erlbaum.

Kosslyn, S. M. (1980). *Image and mind.* Cambridge, MA: Harvard University Press.

Kosslyn, S. M. (1994). *Image and brain.* Cambridge, MA: MIT Press.

Lewis, J. W. (2006). Cortical networks related to human use of tools. *The Neuroscientist, 12,* 211–231.

Martin, A. (2001). Functional neuroimaging of semantic memory. In R. Cabeza & A. Kingstone (Eds.), *Handbook of functional neuroimaging of cognition* (pp. 153–186). Cambridge, MA: MIT Press.

Martin, A. (2007). The representation of object concepts in the brain. *Annual Review of Psychology, 58,* 25–45.

Matlock, T. (2004). Fictive motion as cognitive simulation. *Memory and Cognition, 32,* 1389–1400.

McGurk, H., & MacDonald, J. (1976). Hearing lips and seeing voices. *Nature, 264,* 756–748.

Medin, D. L., & Ross, B. H. (1989). The specific character of abstract thought: Categorization, problem-solving, and induction. In R. J. Sternberg (Ed.), *Advances in the psychology of human intelligence* (Vol. 5, pp. 189–223). Hillsdale, NJ: Erlbaum.

Niedenthal, P. M., Barsalou, L. W., Winkielman, P., Krauth-Gruber, S., & Ric, F. (2005). Embodiment in attitudes, social perception, and emotion. *Personality and Social Psychology Review, 9,* 184–211.

Palmer, S. (1975). The effects of contextual scenes on the identification of objects. *Memory and cognition, 3,* 519–526.

Parsons, L. M. (1987a). Imagined spatial transformations of one's body. *Journal of Experimental Psychology: General, 116,* 172–191.

Parsons, L. M. (1987b). Imagined spatial transformations of one's hands and feet. *Cognitive Psychology, 19,* 178–241.

Pecher, D., & Zwaan, R. (Eds.). (2005). *Grounding cognition: The role of perception and action in memory, language, and thought.* New York: Cambridge University Press.

Proffitt, D. R. (2006). Embodied perception and the economy of action. *Perspectives on Psychological Science, 1,* 110–122.

Pulvermüller, F. (1999). Words in the brain's language. *Behavioral and Brain Sciences, 22,* 253–336.

Pulvermüller, F. (2005). Brain mechanisms linking language and action. *Nature Reviews Neuroscience, 6,* 576–582.

Pulvermüller, F., Hauk, O., Nikulin, V. V., & Ilmoniemi, R. J. (2005). Functional links between motor and language systems. *European Journal of Neuroscience, 21,* 793–797.

Reed, C. L., & Vinson, N. G. (1996). Conceptual effects on representational momentum. *Journal of Experimental Psychology: Human Perception and Performance, 22,* 839–850.

Repp, B. H., & Knoblich, G. (2004). Perceiving action identity: How pianists recognize their own performances. *Psychological Science, 15,* 604–609.

Richardson, D. C., & Matlock, T. (2007). The integration of figurative language and static depictions: An eye movement study of fictive motion. *Cognition, 102,* 129–138.

Richardson, D. C., Spivey, M. J., Barsalou, L. W., & McRae, K. (2003). Spatial representations activated during real-time comprehension of verbs. *Cognitive Science, 27,* 767–780.

Richter, W., Somorjai, R., Summers, R., Jarmasz, M., Menon, R. S., Gati, J. S., et al. (2000). Motor area activity during mental rotation studied by time-resolved single-trial fMRI. *Journal of Cognitive Neuroscience, 12,* 310–320.

Robbins, P., & Aydede, M. (Eds.). (2008). *Cambridge handbook of situated cognition.* New York: Cambridge University Press.

Roediger, H. L., & Blaxton, T. A. (1987). Effects of varying modality, surface features, and retention interval on priming in word fragment completion. *Memory and Cognition, 15,* 379–388.

Roediger, H. L., & McDermott, K. B. (1993). Implicit memory in normal human subjects. In F. Boller & J. Grafman (Eds.), *Handbook of neuropsychology* (Vol. 8, pp. 63–131). Amsterdam: Elsevier.

Samuel, A. G. (1997). Lexical activation produces potent phonemic percepts. *Cognitive Psychology, 32,* 97–127.

Santos, A., Chaigneau, S. E., Simmons, W. K., & Barsalou, L. W. (2008). Word association and situated simulation in conceptual processing: Behavioral confirmation of neuroimaging findings. Under review.

Schacter, D. L., Dobbins, I. G., & Schnyer, D. M. (2004). Specificity of priming: A cognitive neuroscience perspective. *Nature Reviews Neuroscience, 5,* 853–862.

Schacter, D. L. & Graf, P. (1989). Modality specificity of implicit memory for new associations. *Journal of Experimental Psychology: Learning, Memory, and Cognition, 15,* 3–12.

Schyns, P. G., Goldstone, R. L., & Thibaut, J. P. (1998). The development of features in object concepts. *Behavioral and Brain Sciences, 21,* 1–54.

Semin, G. R., & Smith, E. R. (Eds.). (2008). *Embodied grounding: Social, cognitive, affective, and neuroscientific approaches.* New York: Cambridge University Press.

Shepard, R. N., & Cooper, L. A. (1982). *Mental images and their transformations.* New York: Cambridge University Press.

Shiffrar, M., & Freyd, J. J. (1990). Apparent motion of the human body. *Psychological Science, 4,* 257–264.

Shiffrar, M., & Freyd, J. J. (1993). Timing and apparent motion path choice with human body photographs. *Psychological Science, 6,* 379–384.

Simmons, W. K., & Barsalou, L. W. (2003). The similarity-in-topography principle: Reconciling theories of conceptual deficits. *Cognitive Neuropsychology, 20,* 451–486.

Simmons, W. K., Martin, A., & Barsalou, L. W. (2005). Pictures of appetizing foods activate gustatory cortices for taste and reward. *Cerebral Cortex, 15,* 1602–1608.

Smith, L. B. (2005). Cognition as a dynamic system: Principles from embodiment. *Developmental Review, 25,* 278–298.

Smith, L. B., & Gasser, M. (2005). The development of embodied cognition: Six lessons from babies. *Artificial Life, 11,* 13–30.

Stevens, J. A., Fonlupt, P., Shiffrar, M., & Decety, J. (2000). New aspects of motion perception: Selective neural encoding of apparent human movements. *NeuroReport, 11,* 109–115.

de Vega, M., Glenberg, A. M., & Graesser, A. C. (Eds.). (2008). *Symbols, embodiment, and meaning.* Oxford, England: Oxford University Press.

Thompson-Schill, S. L. (2003), Neuroimaging studies of semantic memory: Inferring "how" from "where." *Neurosychologia, 41,* 280–292.

Tucker, M., & Ellis, R. (2001). The potentiation of grasp types during visual object categorization. *Visual Cognition, 8,* 769–800.

Warren, R. M. (1970). Perceptual restoration of missing speech sounds. *Science, 167,* 392–393.

Wiemer-Hastings, K., Krug, J., & Xu, X. (2001). Imagery, context availability, contextual constraint, and abstractness. *Proceedings of the 23rd Annual Conference of the Cognitive Science Society,* 1134–1139. Mahwah, NJ: Erlbaum.

Wilson, M., & Knoblich, G. (2005). The case for motor involvement in perceiving conspecifics. *Psychological Bulletin, 131,* 460–473.

Wolpert, D. M., Ghahramani, Z., & Jordan, M. I. (1999). An internal model for sensorimotor integration. *Science, 269,* 1880–1882.

Wu, L., & Barsalou, L. W. (2008). Perceptual simulation in conceptual combination: Evidence from property generation. Manuscript under review.

Yeh, W., & Barsalou, L. W. (2006). The situated nature of concepts. *American Journal of Psychology, 119,* 349–384.

Zwaan, R. A., & Madden, C. J. (2005). Embodied sentence comprehension. In D. Pecher & R. Zwaan (Eds.), *Grounding cognition: The role of perception and action in memory, language, and thought* (pp. 224–245). New York: Cambridge University Press.

Zwaan, R. A., & Taylor, L. J. (2006). Seeing, acting, understanding: motor resonance in language comprehension. *Journal of Experimental Psychology: General, 135,* 1–11.

CHAPTER 4
Architecture of Counterfactual Thought in the Prefrontal Cortex

Aron K. Barbey, Frank Krueger, and Jordan Grafman

Remembering the past and predicting the future depend on the ability to shift from perceiving the immediate environment to an alternative, imagined perspective. Mental models of imagined past events or future outcomes not yet at hand support *counterfactual thinking* ("What would happen if X were performed in the past or enacted in the future?") (Byrne, 2002; Kahneman & Miller, 1986). The capacity for counterfactual thought enables learning from past experience (Byrne, 1997), supports planning and predicting future events (Barbey & Sloman, 2007; Brase & Barbey, 2006), provides the basis for creativity and insight (Costello & Keane, 2000; Sternberg & Gastel, 1989; Thomas, 1999), and gives rise to emotions and social ascriptions (e.g., guilt, regret, and blame) that are central for managing and regulating social behavior (Davis, Lehman, Wortman, Silver, & Thompson, 1995; Landman, 1987; Miller & Turnbull, 1990; Niedenthal, Tangney, & Gavanski, 1994; Zeelenberg, van der Pligt, & Manstead, 1998). The neural representation of counterfactual inference draws upon neural systems for constructing mental models of the past and future, incorporating prefrontal and medial temporal lobe structures (Fortin, Agster, & Eichenbaum, 2002; Tulving & Markowitsch, 1998). In this chapter, we develop an integrative cognitive neuroscience framework for understanding counterfactual reasoning on the basis of *structured event complexes* (SECs) in the human prefrontal cortex (PFC).

We begin by reviewing the biology and structure of the human PFC and introduce a cognitive neuroscience framework for the representation of event knowledge within the PFC. We then survey recent neuroscience evidence in support of the SEC framework and establish the role of distinct PFC subregions in the representation of specific forms of event knowledge. After reviewing the cognitive and neural foundations of the SEC framework, we show how this approach accounts for counterfactual reasoning. We identify three major categories of counterfactual inference (concerning action versus inaction, the self versus other, and upward versus downward thinking) and review neuroscience evidence for their representation within distinct regions of the medial PFC. We propose that mental models for goal-directed social behavior additionally recruit the lateral PFC, which represents behavior-guiding principles for counterfactual inference concerning obligatory, prohibited, and permissible courses of action. We survey recent evidence from the decision neuroscience literature to support the representation of behavior-guiding principles for counterfactual inference within distinct regions of the lateral PFC. Finally, we draw conclusions about the importance of SECs for learning from past experience, for planning and predicting future events, for creativity and insight, and for the management and regulation of social behavior.

Neurobiology of the human prefrontal cortex

Structured event complexes (SECs) are representations composed of goal-oriented sequences of events involved in executing, planning, and monitoring action. We briefly review the biology and structure of the human PFC, providing evidence to support our proposal that the PFC stores cognitive representations intimately concerned with goal-directed action.

The PFC can be divided into ventromedial and dorsolateral regions, each of which is associated with posterior and subcortical brain regions. The ventromedial PFC (vmPFC) has reciprocal connections with brain regions that are associated with emotional processing (amygdala), memory (hippocampus), and higher order sensory processing (temporal visual association areas), as well as with dorsolateral PFC (dlPFC). The dlPFC has reciprocal connections with brain regions that are associated with motor control (basal ganglia, premotor cortex, supplementary motor area), performance monitoring (cingulate cortex), and higher order sensory processing (association areas, parietal cortex). The vmPFC is well suited to support functions involving the integration of information about emotion, memory, and environmental stimuli, and the dlPFC is well suited to support the regulation of behavior and control of responses to environmental stimuli.

Prefrontal cortex neurons are particularly able to fire over extended periods of time (Levy & Goldman-Rakic, 2000) and across events (Bodner, Kroger, & Fuster, 1996; Fuster & Alexander, 1971). This indicates that the PFC can maintain stimulus representations across time, enabling a subject to engage in behavior to achieve long-term goals. In addition, pyramidal cells in the macaque PFC are more spinous—and therefore can handle more excitatory inputs—than other cortical pyramidal cells (Elston, 2000). This is one structural explanation for the PFC's ability to integrate inputs from many sources and to implement complex behaviors. The monkey's PFC contains cells that respond to both internally generated and observed

behaviors—these have been termed *mirror neurons* (Gallese et al., 1996). Similar regions have been shown to be activated in humans when observing and performing actions (Grafton, Arbib, Fadiga, & Rizzolatti, 1996). These data support a role for the PFC in the representation of action. Furthermore, Williams and colleagues have suggested that abnormal development of the PFC might lead to impaired social behavior (Williams, Whiten, Suddendorf, & Perret, 2001), which can also be caused by PFC damage later in life.

It is thought that the dlPFC evolved from motor regions and developed much later than the vmPFC (Fuster, 1997). Motor regions store motor programs; therefore, it seems reasonable that the functions of the "newer" PFC regions would be related to those of older PFC regions, providing a representational basis for goal-directed action.

In summary, the connectivity of PFC regions, physiological properties of its neurons, and evolutionary principles are strongly suggestive of its role in the integration of sensory and memory information and in the representation and control of actions and behavior. Along with the extended firing of neurons, specialized neural systems were developed that enabled the parsing and encoding of these behaviors into sequentially linked but individually recognizable events. At the broadest level, events are parsed into subcomponents consisting of an activity that signals the onset of the event, followed by a series of activities performed to achieve the desired goal, and a final activity resulting in event completion. Events are further characterized by their semantic content, temporal duration, and the number of component activities they entail (Zacks & Tversky, 2001; Zacks, Tversky, & Iyer, 2001).

We propose that the structure of event knowledge can be conceptualized as a "representation" or a unique form of knowledge that, when activated, corresponds to a dynamic brain state signified by the strength and pattern of neural activity in a local brain region. In this sense, over the course of evolution, the PFC became capable of representing knowledge of more complex behaviors. We label these representational units within the PFC *structured event complexes* (SECs).

Structured Event Complex Theory

A SEC represents event knowledge consisting of agents, objects, actions, mental states, and background settings that are temporally structured and semantically organized according to their causal roles (e.g., as cause, effect, enabler, or preventer). The SEC theory is a representational framework that motivates specific predictions regarding the properties and localization of SECs within the PFC (Fig. 4.1). We review principal elements of the SEC theory before turning to an assessment of its neurobiological predictions.

Neural Architecture

Structured event complexes are encoded and activated on the basis of simulation mechanisms (Barsalou, Niedenthal, Barbey, & Ruppert, 2003; Barsalou, Simmons, Barbey, & Wilson, 2003;

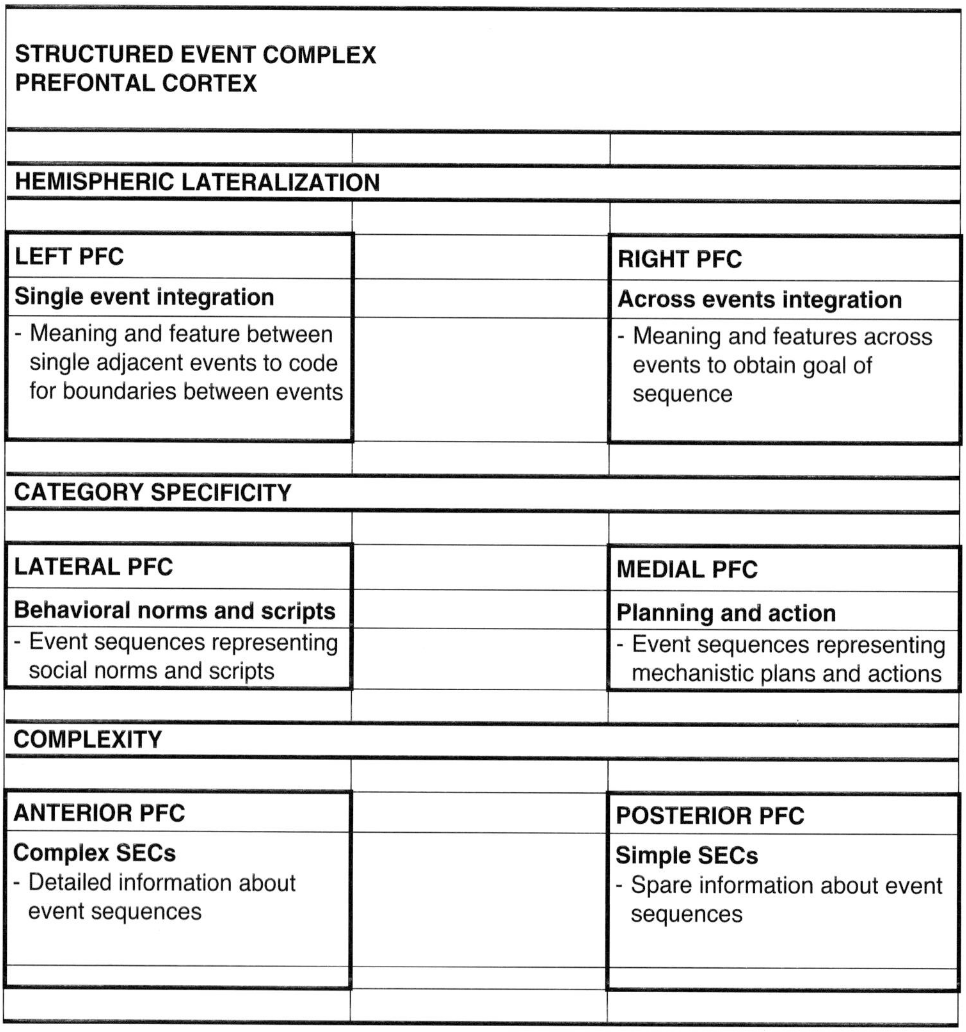

STRUCTURED EVENT COMPLEX PREFONTAL CORTEX		
HEMISPHERIC LATERALIZATION		
LEFT PFC		**RIGHT PFC**
Single event integration		**Across events integration**
- Meaning and feature between single adjacent events to code for boundaries between events		- Meaning and features across events to obtain goal of sequence
CATEGORY SPECIFICITY		
LATERAL PFC		**MEDIAL PFC**
Behavioral norms and scripts		**Planning and action**
- Event sequences representing social norms and scripts		- Event sequences representing mechanistic plans and actions
COMPLEXITY		
ANTERIOR PFC		**POSTERIOR PFC**
Complex SECs - Detailed information about event sequences		**Simple SECs** - Spare information about event sequences

Figure 4.1 SEC framework. The representational forms of the structured event complex (SEC) and their proposed localizations within the prefrontal cortex (PFC).

Damasio, 1989). A large body of neuroscience evidence demonstrates that experience in the physical and social world activates feature detectors in relevant features maps of the brain. During visual processing of a face, for example, some neurons fire for edges and planar surfaces, whereas others fire for color, configural properties, and movement. The global pattern of activation across this hierarchically organized distributed system represents the entity in vision (Palmer, 1999; Zeki, 1993). Analogous patterns of activation on other sensory modalities represent how the face might sound and feel. Activation in the motor system similarly represents responses to the face, such as the formation of a facial expression, and approach/avoidance behavior. A similar mechanism underlies the introspective states that arise while interacting with an entity. For example, activation patterns in the amygdala and orbitofrontal areas represent emotional reactions to social stimuli. Much neuroscience evidence documents the structure of feature maps across modalities and the states that arise in them.

When a pattern becomes active in a feature map during perception or action, conjunctive neurons in an association area capture the pattern for later cognitive use. For example, conjunctive neurons in the visual system capture the pattern active for a particular face. A population of conjunctive neurons together codes a particular pattern, with each individual neuron participating in the coding of many different patterns. Damasio (1989) called these association areas *convergence zones* and proposed that they exist at multiple hierarchical levels in the brain, ranging from posterior to anterior. Most locally, convergence zones near a modality capture activation patterns within it. Association areas near the visual system, for example, capture patterns there, whereas association areas near the motor system capture patterns in this local region. Downstream in more anterior regions, higher association areas, including temporal and frontal regions, integrate activation across modalities.

According to the SEC framework, event knowledge is represented by higher order convergence zones localized within particular regions of the PFC (see Fig. 4.1). Once a set of

conjunctive neurons within the PFC captures feature maps (representing components of event knowledge, social norms, ethical and moral rules, and temporal event boundaries), the set can later activate the pattern in the absence of bottom-up stimulation. For example, on entering a familiar situation and recognizing it, an SEC that represents the situation becomes active. Typically not all of the situation is perceived initially. A relevant person, setting, or event may be perceived, which then suggests that a particular situation is about to play out. It is in the agent's interests to anticipate what will happen next so that optimal actions can be executed. The agent must draw inferences that go beyond the information given (Griffin & Ross, 1991). The SEC that becomes active constitutes a rich source of social inference supporting the planning, execution, and monitoring of action. The SEC can be viewed as a distributed pattern representing components of event knowledge (i.e., as a complex configuration of multimodal components that represent the situation). Because part of this pattern matched the current situation initially, the larger pattern became active in memory. The remaining parts of the pattern—not yet observed in the situation—constitute inferences, namely educated guesses about what might occur next. Because the remaining parts co-occurred frequently with the perceived parts in previous situations, inferring the remaining parts from the perceived parts is reasonable. As a partially viewed situation activates an SEC, the SEC completes the pattern that the situation suggests.

To the extent that the SEC is entrenched in memory, pattern completion is likely to occur at least somewhat automatically. As a situation is experienced repeatedly, its simulated components and the associations linking them increase in potency. Thus, when one component is perceived initially, these strong associations complete the pattern automatically. Consider the example of meeting with a colleague. Her face, clothing, and bodily mannerisms initially match modality-specific simulations in one or more SECs that have become entrenched in memory. Once one of these wins the activation process, it provides inferences via pattern completion, such as actions that the colleague is likely to take, actions that the perceiver typically takes, affective states that are likely to result, and so forth. The unfolding of such inferences—realized as an SEC—produces social prediction (for a cognitive neuroscience review of simulation mechanisms in reasoning, see Barbey & Barsalou, in press; Barsalou, Barbey, Simmons, & Santos, 2005; Patterson & Barbey, in press).

Sequence Structure

Structured event complexes integrate modality-specific components of event knowledge, providing the semantic and temporal structure underlying goal-directed action. Components of event knowledge are integrated on the basis of their causal roles (e.g., as cause, effect, enabler, preventer). At the broadest level, SECs link event subcomponents consisting of an activity that signals the onset of the event (e.g., "hearing the morning alarm clock"), followed by a series of activities performed to achieve the desired goal (e.g., "waking up," "getting out of bed," etc.), and a final activity resulting in event completion (e.g., "arriving to work"). The temporal structure of SECs further obeys cultural and individual constraints, reflecting sociocultural norms of appropriate behavior (e.g., in the United States, people typically shower in the morning daily) and personal preferences concerning the temporal order and frequency of performed activities (e.g., the individual preference to shower in the morning and at night daily). The semantic and temporal structure of event knowledge supports goal-directed action in dynamic environments, enabling the on-line modification of specific activities (e.g., due to changing circumstances) and the simulation of only those event components necessary for goal achievement in the present context (e.g., beginning at various stages in the event sequence, returning to earlier stages, skipping unnecessary activities due to time pressure, etc.).

Goal Orientation

The semantic and temporal structure of SECs derives from event goals, which provide the basis for the selection, temporal ordering, and execution of activities underlying an event. Some SECs

are *well structured*, with clearly defined goals, and cognitive and behavioral action sequences that are available for goal achievement. For example, individuals with a well-structured SEC for "eating in a restaurant" are quite confident that once they have been seated at a table and have read the menu, someone will appear to take their order.

In contrast, some SECs are *ill structured*, requiring the individual to adapt to unpredictable circumstances by constructing novel or ad hoc goals, and selecting appropriate action sequences on-line (Barsalou, 1991). For example, if someone sees that a person entering a bank is wearing a ski-mask and carrying a gun, one can make sense of these events by completing the activated "bank robbery" SEC to access further components of event knowledge (concerning relevant agents, objects, actions, mental states, and background settings).

Binding

Multiple SECs are activated to support the events of our daily life; therefore, it is likely that these representations (like events within an SEC) can be activated in sequence, or additionally in a cascading or parallel manner. Event components interact and give rise to SECs through at least three binding mechanisms: sequential binding, proposed for linking multiple SECs within the PFC (Weingartner, Grafman, Boutelle, Kaye, & Martin, 1983); temporal binding among anatomically integrated regions representing event subcomponents in posterior cortex (Engel & Singer, 2001); and third-party binding of anatomical regions whose activity is synchronized via the hippocampus (O'Reilly & Rudy, 2000; Weingartner et al., 1983).

Hierarchical Structure

Given the slow development of the PFC during childhood, individual events are probably initially represented as independent memory units. For example, SECs associated with "kitchen" and "school cafeteria" cluster around the event "eat meal," whereas "car" and "school bus" cluster around the event "travel to new location." Later in development, these primitive SECs expand into large multievent units, based on repeated exposure and goal-directed action. In addition, the boundaries of event sequences become more firmly established, leading to a well-structured SEC. Thus, in adulthood, SECs will range from specific episodes to more abstract SECs that can be applied to a variety of situations (Barsalou & Wiemer-Hastings, 2005). For example, the domain "eat meal" includes specific episodes representing evenings at a particular restaurant, SECs representing the actions and themes of how to behave at different types of restaurants, in addition to more abstract SECs representing actions and themes related to "eating" that apply to a broad range of situations (e.g., at "restaurants," "parties," "picnics," "baseball games," etc.).

COUNTERFACTUAL THOUGHT

We propose that SECs provide the basis for counterfactual reasoning about past and future events and develop a process model of the regulatory functions these representations serve.

Counterfactual thinking involves mentally undoing the present state of affairs and imagining alternative realities "if only" different decisions were made or actions taken (Byrne, 2002; Kahneman & Miller, 1986). We propose that counterfactual thought depends on mental models of alternative possibilities represented in the form of SECs. For example, the counterfactual inference that "If we chose to sail the Mediterranean rather than continue writing, then you would not be reading this chapter" draws upon SEC knowledge, including the representation of relevant agents (e.g., the authors), objects (e.g., a sailboat), actions (e.g., sailing), mental states (e.g., freedom), and background settings (e.g., the Mediterranean Sea). Simulations of the representational elements of SEC knowledge provide the basis for evaluating the consequences of alternative courses of action, with the simulation of the authors "sailing the Mediterranean" resulting in the failure to complete this chapter.

A growing body of research demonstrates the importance of counterfactual inference for generating predictions about the future, supporting representations of unknown, future possibilities critical for planning and decision making (e.g., "How well would the Cubs perform next season if the manager would have acquired key players in the off season?") (Barbey & Sloman, 2007; Brase & Barbey, 2006). Predictions about the future are supported by modifying a factual event (e.g., "If the manager acquired key players in the off season…") and considering likely future consequences (e.g., "… would the team perform well next year?").

The SEC framework advocates a theory of *motivated thinking* (De Dreu, Beersma, Stroebe, & Euwema, 2006; Dunning, 1999), proposing that *drives*, *needs*, *desires*, *motives*, and *goals* structure and organize components of event knowledge and profoundly influence judgment and decision making. According to this framework, the primary role of counterfactual thought is to support emotions and social ascriptions that are central for managing and regulating social behavior. In particular, counterfactual reasoning enables the representation of guilt, regret, and blame, which are central for adaptive social behavior (Davis et al., 1995; Landman, 1987; Miller & Turnbull, 1990; Niedenthal et al., 1994; Zeelenberg et al., 1998). For example, the counterfactual inference that "The university would offer her a higher salary (in the past or future) if she were a man" gives rise to feelings of guilt and regret (for the observed gender inequity) that promote behavioral change and that enable the assessment of blame (held by university policy makers) to support planning and decision making (e.g., to apply for positions at other universities). Counterfactual inference therefore enables an assessment of the consequences of alternative decisions or actions sequences central for the representation of guilt, regret, and blame.

The neural representation of emotions and social ascriptions (e.g., guilt, regret, and blame) is distributed throughout the mPFC and is integrated with posterior knowledge networks via binding mechanisms in the medial temporal lobe (Fortin et al., 2002; Moll & de Oliveira-Souza, 2007; Tulving et al., 1998). This distributed pattern of multimodal information (e.g., representing agents, objects, actions, mental states, and background settings) gives rise to mental models for counterfactual inference.

Process Model

According to the SEC framework, counterfactual thought is deeply connected to drives, needs, desires, motives, and goals, and it provides the basis for regulatory mechanisms that keep behavior on track, particularly within social interactions. We propose that counterfactual thought depends on SEC representations and operates according to the following interactive process model (see Fig. 4.2).

i. Counterfactual thoughts are activated when a problem is encountered or anticipated in the future. Failure to achieve the desired goal or the anticipation of goal failure in the future typically initiates counterfactual thinking (e.g., due to negative emotions, the desire for rewards associated with goal achievement, etc.).

ii. Counterfactual thoughts are generated from causal implications represented by SECs in the form of events (agents, objects, actions, mental states, and background settings) that lead to a desired goal state (for a review of psychological theories of causal representation and reasoning, see Barbey & Wolff, 2006, 2007; submitted; Chaigneau & Barbey, 2008; Patterson & Barbey, in press; Sloman, Barbey, & Hotaling; in press).

iii. Structured event complexes activate corresponding behavioral intentions (e.g., to perform a particular action), mindsets (e.g., to focus on a particular class of events), motivations (e.g., to modulate one's desire for a particular outcome), and/or self-inferences (e.g., to monitor one's public image) that initiate corrective behavior.

To the extent that such behavior alleviates the original problem, this mechanism is effective in regulating behavior in terms of goal pursuit (for a review of medical health applications, see Gilbar & Heyroni, 2007; Wrosch, Bauer, Miller, & Lupien, 2007).

Categories of Counterfactual Inference

The proposed role of SECs in counterfactual thought motivates the prediction that this form of inference will depend on core elements of

A problem is encountered or anticipated in the future

Counterfactual thoughts are generated on the basis of SEC knowledge

SECs activate behavioral intentions, mind-sets, motivations, and self inferences to support adaptive behavior

Figure 4.2 A process model of the regulatory functions underlying counterfactual thought. SEC, structured event complex.

SECs, which fundamentally represent *actions* performed by *agents* leading to an observed *outcome*. The psychological literature on counterfactual thought supports this prediction, identifying three major categories of counterfactual inference corresponding to core components of SEC representations.

Action Knowledge

One broad distinction represents counterfactual thought about *action versus inaction*, or the addition versus subtraction of an action from the present state (Roese, Hur, & Pennington, 1999). For example, the counterfactual inference that "She should never go out the night before an exam" represents the addition of an action ("going out"), whereas the inference that "He should always read the instructions carefully" represents the removal of an action ("reading carefully"). This form of counterfactual thought is central for evaluating consequences of carrying out or failing to perform specific actions (in the past or future).

Agent Knowledge

A second major category of counterfactual inference represents reasoning about the *self versus other* (Mandel, 2003). For example, the counterfactual inference that "Problems would be avoided if I attended the meeting" represents features of the self, whereas the inference that "Your skills would improve if you played more often" embodies features of others. Counterfactual reasoning about the self versus other provides the basis for adaptive social behavior and inferring the connection between specific mental states and particular patterns of behavior (e.g., "She would not have left early if she wanted to talk with you").

Outcome Knowledge

A third major category represents the comparison of a current outcome to a *better or worse alternative* (Roese & Olson, 1995). For example, the counterfactual inference that "She should accept the job with the higher salary" represents an upward inference about a better alternative, whereas the observation that "Other people with her qualifications earn much less than she does" represents a downward inference about a worse alternative. Counterfactual reasoning about better versus worse outcomes is critical for learning from the past and assessing alternative courses of action in the future.

The reviewed categories of counterfactual inference embody core features of SEC knowledge, enabling adaptive social behavior on the basis of actions, agents, and event outcomes.

NEUROSCIENCE REVIEW

We review neuroscience findings in support of the SEC framework, providing evidence to confirm the representational role of the human PFC and to support the role of SECs in counterfactual thought. The representational aspects of SECs

and their proposed localizations within the PFC are summarized in Figure 4.1 (for a review of further evidence in support of the SEC framework, see Barbey & Grafman, in press; Krueger et al., 2009).

Category Specificity of the Prefrontal Cortex

The subdivision of the PFC into neuroanatomically distinct regions designed to process specific forms of knowledge supports the proposal that SEC representations are stored within particular regions of the PFC on a content-specific basis (see Fig. 4.1). Converging evidence is provided by lesion studies demonstrating selective impairments for social and reward-related behavior in vmPFC lesion patients (Dimitrov, Phipps, Zahn, & Grafman, 1999; Milne & Grafman, 2001), and impairments for mechanistic planning in dlPFC patients (Burgess, Veitch, de Lacy Costello, & Shallice, 2000; Goel & Grafman, 2000).

Our research group conducted a PET study providing further evidence to support the representation of domain-specific SECs for *nonemotional* versus *emotional* event knowledge within the PFC (Partiot, Grafman, Sadato, Wachs, & Hallett, 1995). The employed nonemotional task asked subjects to "imagine silently the sequence of events and feelings concerned with preparation and dressing before (their) mother comes over for dinner." In contrast, subjects in the emotional task were asked to "imagine silently the sequence of events and feelings concerned with preparation and dressing to go to (their) mother's funeral." Consistent with the domain-specific predictions of the SEC framework, distinct patterns of neural activity were observed when subjects assessed nonemotional versus emotional scripts. Nonemotional scripts activated the right superior frontal gyrus (Brodmann's area [BA] 8), bilateral middle frontal gyri (BA 8 and 9), and medial frontal gyri (BA 6 and 10), whereas emotional scripts recruited the left anterior cingulate (BA 24 and 32), bilateral medial frontal gyri (BA 8 and 9), and anterior medial temporal lobe (BA 21).

Employing fMRI, we further demonstrated that *social* versus *nonsocial* SECs depend on a distinct representational topography within the PFC (Wood, Romero, Makale, & Grafman, 2003). We applied a modified go/no-go paradigm in which subjects classified individual words (e.g., "menu," "order") or phrases (e.g., "read the menu," "order the food") according to one of two focal categories (social versus nonsocial). Social activities recruited the left superior frontal gyri (BA 8 and 9), whereas nonsocial activities engaged the right superior frontal gyrus (BA 8), left medial frontal gyrus (BA 6), and the bilateral anterior cingulate (BA 25). Despite the large body of evidence to support the role of the orbitofrontal cortex (OFC) in social processing (Fuster, 1997; Milne & Grafman, 2001), activation in this region was not observed. Further inspection of the functional images demonstrated signal dropout in the OFC, limiting conclusions drawn concerning the role of this region in the storage of social SECs.

To further investigate this issue, we conducted a lesion study in which patients with PFC lesions and matched controls performed the classification task of Wood et al. (2003; Wood, Tierney, Bidwell, & Grafman, 2005). Subjects classified individual words (e.g., "menu," "order") or phrases (e.g., "read the menu," "order the food") as representing social versus nonsocial events. Patients with damage to the right OFC demonstrated cognitive impairments in the accessibility of script and semantic representations of social (rather than nonsocial) activities, providing evidence to support the role of the OFC in social processes.

In a subsequent functional magnetic resonance imaging (fMRI) study, we applied multidimensional scaling to assess the psychological structure of event knowledge and its neural representation within particular regions of the PFC (Wood, Knutson, & Grafman, 2005). Multidimensional scaling revealed three psychological dimensions underlying event knowledge (engagement, social valence, and experience). To investigate the neural correlates of the identified psychological dimensions, we conducted an fMRI experiment in which subjects classified each event according to whether it represented a social activity. Parametric analyses of event-related fMRI data were conducted to investigate brain regions

whose activity was modulated by the three psychological components of event knowledge. The results demonstrated that the psychological structure of event knowledge is broadly organized along dimensions that are represented within distinct regions of the human PFC, with the experience dimension recruiting the medial PFC (BA 10), the engagement dimension activating the left OFC (BA 47), and the social valence dimension engaging the amygdala and right OFC (BA 11 and 47).

In summary, the reviewed studies provide evidence to support our proposal that category-specific SECs are stored within distinct regions of the PFC.

STRUCTURED EVENT COMPLEXES AND COUNTERFACTUAL THOUGHT

We propose that counterfactual thought depends on mental models represented in the form of SECs and review evidence demonstrating that SECs for counterfactual inference are functionally localized within distinct regions of the medial and lateral PFC.

Medial Prefrontal Cortex

Counterfactual reasoning is characterized by three major forms of inference that each recruit distinct regions of the mPFC (see Fig. 4.3). According to this framework, counterfactual thinking depends on category-specific SECs within the mPFC, which provide key representational elements within a larger network of anatomically connected prefrontal and posterior regions supporting counterfactual thought.

Action versus Inaction

According to the SEC framework, counterfactual reasoning about action versus inaction preferentially recruits the dorsomedial PFC (dmPFC). Several neuroscience studies have implicated the dmPFC in the continuous internal monitoring of action (Botvinick, Cohen, & Carter, 2004). Barch and colleagues (2001) report an extensive meta-analysis of functional imaging studies that included data from a broad range of action-monitoring tasks (e.g., involving the inhibition

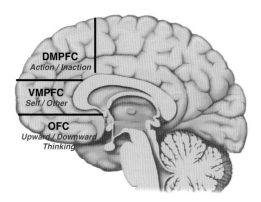

Figure 4.3 Neural predictions of the SEC theory of counterfactual thought. The dorsomedial prefrontal cortex (DMPFC) represents counterfactual reasoning about *action versus inaction*, the ventromedial prefrontal cortex (VMPFC) represents counterfactual thoughts directed toward the *self versus other*, and the orbitofrontal cortex (OFC) represents *upward versus downward* counterfactual thinking.

of prepotent responses) that recruited the dmPFC. Along the same lines, Walton, Devlin, and Rushworth (2004) observed activity in the dmPFC when participants monitored the outcome of self-selected actions. These finding suggest that the dmPFC is critical for monitoring the addition versus subtraction of actions for counterfactual reasoning.

Self versus Other

We propose that counterfactual thought involving the self versus others recruits the vmPFC. A large body of neuroscience evidence supports this proposal, demonstrating that the vmPFC represents components of self-knowledge, person knowledge, and mentalizing. Beldarrain et al. (2005) demonstrated impairments in self-generated counterfactual thought in vmPFC lesion patients. Converging evidence is provided by Macrae et al. (2004), who observed activation in the vmPFC when participants evaluated the self-relevance of specific personality traits. Ochsner et al. (2004) similarly found activation in the vmPFC when participants monitored their emotional states.

Recruitment of the vmPFC is also observed in studies that assess person knowledge more

broadly (applying to others as well as the self). Mitchell, Heatherton, and Macrae (2002) reported activation in this region when participants judged whether a presented adjective applied to a person (rather than an inanimate object). Consistent with these findings, Schmitz et al. (2004) observed activation in the vmPFC when participants thought about themselves or a close friend.

Finally, extensive neuroscience evidence implicates the vmPFC in the process of representing another person's psychological perspective (i.e., "mentalizing"). For example, Fletcher et al. (1995) and Goel et al. (1995) reported activation in the vmPFC when participants read social scripts in which the psychological perspectives of fictional characters were inferred.

Upward versus Downward Thinking

We propose that counterfactual reasoning about upward (better) versus downward (worse) outcomes recruits the OFC, which is widely implicated in the processing of event outcomes associated with rewards or penalties. Elliott, Dolan, and Frith (2000) propose that the OFC is involved in monitoring reward and serves to guide behavior in terms of the value of possible outcomes. Walton et al. (2004) found that the activity in the OFC was elicited by the need to monitor the outcomes of externally guided actions. Similarly, Coricelli et al. (2005) found that activity in the OFC correlated with the amount of anticipated regret associated with a decision. In sum, the reviewed findings suggest that the OFC provides the basis for counterfactual reasoning about upward (better) versus downward (worse) outcomes.

Lateral Prefrontal Cortex

It is likely that mental models for goal-directed social behavior involving future thinking additionally recruit the lateral PFC, which represents behavior-guiding principles for counterfactual inference concerning obligatory, prohibited, and permissible courses of action. Emerging evidence from the social and decision neuroscience literatures demonstrates *(1)* the involvement of the vlPFC when reasoning about necessary (obligatory or prohibited) courses of action, (2) the recruitment of the dlPFC for drawing inferences about possible (permissible) states of affairs, and (3) activation in the alPFC for higher order inferences that incorporate both categories of knowledge (Fig. 4.4). The simulation architecture underlying these forms of inference further predicts the recruitment of broadly distributed neural systems, incorporating medial prefrontal and posterior knowledge networks representing modality-specific components of experience.

Ventrolateral Prefrontal Cortex

An increasing number of social neuroscience studies have shown that social norms for necessary (obligatory or prohibited) courses of action are represented by the vlPFC (BA 44, 45, and 47; Fig. 4.4b). Fiddick, Spampinato, and Grafman (2005) observed activity within bilateral vlPFC (BA 47) for social exchange reasoning, employing stimuli consisting primarily of social norms for obligatory and prohibited courses of action.

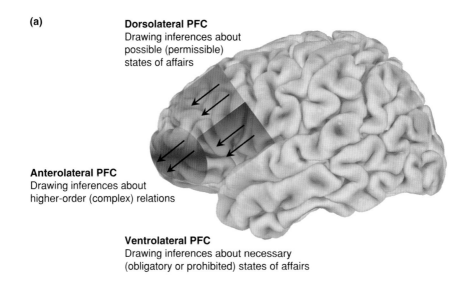

(a)

Dorsolateral PFC
Drawing inferences about possible (permissible) states of affairs

Anterolateral PFC
Drawing inferences about higher-order (complex) relations

Ventrolateral PFC
Drawing inferences about necessary (obligatory or prohibited) states of affairs

Drawing inferences about necessary states of affairs

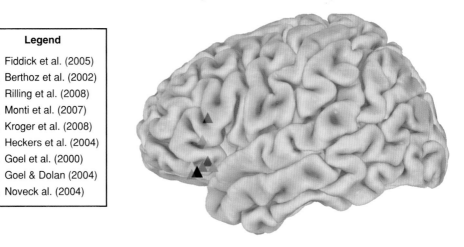

Legend

▲ Fiddick et al. (2005)
▲ Berthoz et al. (2002)
▲ Rilling et al. (2008)
▲ Monti et al. (2007)
▲ Kroger et al. (2008)
▲ Heckers et al. (2004)
▲ Goel et al. (2000)
▲ Goel & Dolan (2004)
▲ Noveck al. (2004)

Figure 4.4 An evolutionarily adaptive neural architecture for goal-directed social behavior. Panel *a* summarizes the functional organization of the lateral PFC, and panels *b*, *c*, and *d* illustrate supportive evidence.

(c) Drawing inferences about possible states of affairs

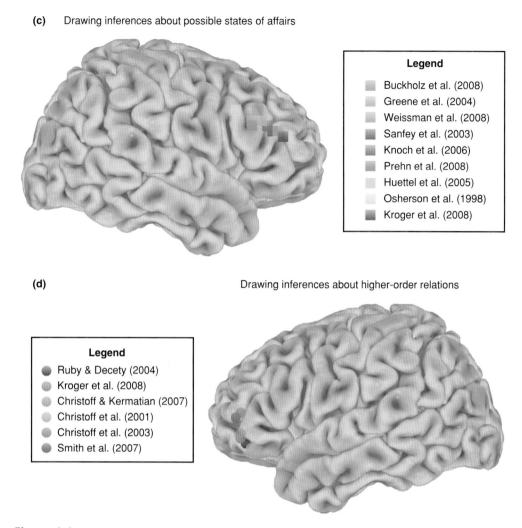

Legend
Buckholz et al. (2008)
Greene et al. (2004)
Weissman et al. (2008)
Sanfey et al. (2003)
Knoch et al. (2006)
Prehn et al. (2008)
Huettel et al. (2005)
Osherson et al. (1998)
Kroger et al. (2008)

(d) Drawing inferences about higher-order relations

Legend
Ruby & Decety (2004)
Kroger et al. (2008)
Christoff & Kermatian (2007)
Christoff et al. (2001)
Christoff et al. (2003)
Smith et al. (2007)

Figure 4.4 (*continued*)

Converging evidence is provided by Berthoz et al. (2002), who demonstrated recruitment of left vlPFC (BA 47) when participants detected violations of social norms stories representing obligatory and prohibited courses of action (e.g., the decision to "spit out food made by the host"). Similarly, Rilling et al. (2008) reported activation within left vlPFC (BA 47) when participants detected the violation of obligatory and prohibited norms of social exchange in a prisoner's dilemma game (i.e., the failure to cooperate).

The vlPFC is also involved when drawing conclusions that necessarily follow from the truth of the premises, that is, for *deductive inference*. Although a consensus has not yet been reached, an increasing number of studies report consistent findings when common sources of variability are controlled (regarding the linguistic content, linguistic complexity, and deductive complexity of reasoning problems). For example, a recent series of experiments by Monti et al. (2007) controlled for these sources of variability and provided evidence that the left vlPFC (BA 47) mediates representations of the logical structure of a deductive argument (e.g., If *P* or *Q*, then *Not-R*/*P*/Therefore, *Not-R*), supporting the representation of behavior-guiding principles for necessary forms of behavior within this region. Furthermore, a recent study by Kroger and colleagues (2008) controlled for the complexity and type of calculations that were performed and also observed activation within the left vlPFC (BA 44 and 45) for deductive reasoning (see also Heckers, Zalesak, Weiss, Ditman, & Titone, 2004). Converging evidence is provided by Goel and colleagues (Goel, Buchel, Frith, & Dolan, 2000; Goel & Dolan, 2004), who have consistently observed activation within the left vlPFC (BA 44 and 45) for deductive conclusions drawn from categorical syllogisms (e.g., All humans are mortal/Some animals are human/Therefore, some animals are mortal). Finally, Noveck, Goel, and Smith (2004) demonstrated recruitment of left vlPFC (BA 47) for drawing deductive conclusions from conditional statements (e.g., If *P* then *Q*/*P*/Therefore, *Q*), consistent with the role of this region for representing behavior-guiding principles in the form of a conditional. It is likely that such conditionals are utilized when charting future behavioral options.

Dorsolateral Prefrontal Cortex

Accumulating evidence demonstrates that the dlPFC (BA 46 and 9) represents behavior-guiding principles for evaluating the permissibility or fairness of observed behavior (Fig. 4.4c). An early study by Sanfey et al. (2003) reported activity within the right dlPFC (BA 46) when participants evaluated the fairness of an offer in an ultimatum game. Knoch et al. (2006) further demonstrated that deactivating this region with repetitive transcranial magnetic stimulation reduced participants' ability to reject unfair offers in the ultimatum game, suggesting that the dlPFC is central for guiding *future* behavior based on evaluations of fairness and permissibility. Converging evidence is provided by Buckholtz et al. (2008), who observed activity within the right dlPFC (BA 46) when participants assigned responsibility for crimes and made judgments about appropriate (e.g., equitable or fair) forms of punishment in a legal decision-making task. The work of Greene et al. (2004) further suggests that this region is involved in normative evaluations involving conflicting moral goals. These authors employed moral scenarios similar to the famous trolley problem (Thomson, 1976) and assessed trials in which

participants acted in the interest of greater aggregate welfare at the expense of personal moral standards. This contrast revealed reliable activation within the right dlPFC (BA 46), suggesting that this region is critical for evaluating the permissibility or fairness of behaviors that conflict with personal moral standards (for additional evidence, see Prehn et al., 2008; Weissman, Perkins, & Woldorff, 2008). Applying moral standards might be relevant if future planning demands a choice from among alternative courses of social action.

In contrast to deductive inference, conclusions about possible courses of action reflect uncertainty concerning the actions that "should" be taken and/or the consequences that "might" follow; these are referred to as *inductive inferences*. Volz et al. (2004) found that activation within the right dlPFC (BA 9) increased parametrically with the degree of uncertainty held by the participant (see also Huettel, Song, & McCarthy, 2005). Furthermore, Osherson et al. (1998) observed preferential recruitment of the right dlPFC (BA 46) when performance on an inductive reasoning task was directly compared to a matched deductive inference task, supporting the role of this region for reasoning about possible (rather than necessary) states of affairs.

Anterolateral Prefrontal Cortex

The alPFC (BA 10 and 11)—and the orbitofrontal cortex (OFC) more broadly—is central for social cognition (Fig. 4.4d). Studies of patients with lesions confined to the OFC have reported impairments in a wide range of social functions, including the regulation and control of social responses, the perception and integration of social cues, and perspective taking (Bechara et al., 2000; LoPresti et al., 2008; Rolls et al., 1994). Stone et al. (2002) further demonstrate that patients with orbitofrontal damage produced selective impairments in reasoning about social contracts, supporting the proposed role of the PFC in social exchange. Bechara et al. (2000) observed profound deficits in the ability of orbitofrontal patients to represent and integrate social and emotional knowledge in the service of decision making. Converging evidence is provided by LoPresti et al. (2008), who demonstrated that the left alPFC (BA 11) mediates the integration of multiple social cues (i.e., emotional expression and personal identity), further suggesting that this region supports the integration of multiple classes of social knowledge. Other fMRI evidence was provided by Moll and de Oliveira-Souza (2006), who reported bilateral recruitment of the OFC (BA 11) during a social decision-making task when participants had to evaluate the social contributions of a charitable organization and chose not to make a donation.

Progressively anterior subregions of the lateral PFC (BA 10 and 11) have also, more generally, been associated with higher order processing requirements for thought and action (Badre, 2008; Botvinick, 2008; Koechlin & Summerfield, 2007). Ramnani and Owen (2004) reviewed contemporary research and theory investigating the cognitive functions of the alPFC, concluding that this region is central for integrating the outcomes of multiple cognitive operations, consistent with the predicted role of the alPFC for representing higher order inferences that incorporate both necessary and possible states of affairs (for representative findings, see Christoff & Kermatian, 2007; Christoff et al., 2001; Christoff, Ream, Geddes, & Gabrieli, 2003; Kroger et al., 2008; Smith, Keramatian, & Christoff, 2007). Although future planning may simply require the application of an overlearned ritual or routine, it can also require the on-line explicit construction of an action series, albeit with different degrees of social involvement. In thinking about (or simulating) the future, the typical thought process would frequently include both counterfactual thinking and obligatory/permissive conditions that would eventually be integrated into the construction of the structured event complex used in the future to execute an activity.

CONCLUSION

We have introduced a "representational" theory of PFC function in accord with the structure, neurophysiology, and connectivity of the PFC, and the modern cognitive neuroscience view that elements of knowledge are represented within functionally localized brain regions. The reviewed evidence in support of the SEC framework confirms the importance and uniqueness of the human PFC for representing knowledge in the form of cognitive events and action sequences.

We have further advocated for the representational basis of SECs in counterfactual thought, reviewing evidence to support the role of specific regions of the medial and lateral PFC in the representation of particular forms of counterfactual inference. According to this framework, SECs in the mPFC represent components of event knowledge (agents, objects, actions, mental states, and background settings) that are essential for constructing mental models of past or future events and assessing the consequences of alternative courses of action (Fig. 4.3). We have also surveyed a broad range of neuroscience evidence demonstrating that the lateral PFC mediates behavior-guiding principles for specific classes of counterfactual inference, with the vlPFC recruited when drawing inferences about necessary (obligatory or prohibited) courses of action, engagement of the dlPFC when reasoning about possible (permissible) behavior, and the alPFC recruited when both categories of inference are utilized (Fig. 4.4).

Our findings underscore the importance of SECs for high-level cognition more broadly, supporting their role in the construction of mental models and the simulation of alternative possibilities for learning from past experience (Byrne, 1997), for planning and predicting future events (Barbey & Sloman, 2007; Brase & Barbey, 2006), for creativity and insight (Costello & Keane, 2000; Sternberg & Gastel, 1989; Thomas, 1999), and for adaptive social behavior (e.g., supported by regulatory mechanisms based on representations of guilt, regret, and blame; Davis et al., 1995; Landman, 1987; Miller & Turnbull, 1990; Niedenthal et al., 1994; Zeelenberg et al., 1998).

In conclusion, we believe SECs are the key to understanding the human ability to represent mental models of events, which guide the selection of goal-directed action sequences and the on-line updating of behavior based on past outcomes or anticipated future events. When stored as memories, SECs provide a link between past, current, and future activities, enabling explanatory and predictive inferences that enable adaptive behavior and issue significant advantages for our species. Our review demonstrates that there is now substantial evidence to suggest that studying the nature of SEC representations is a competitive and promising way to characterize the components of event knowledge stored within the human PFC. Although SECs must coordinate with representations and processes stored in other brain regions—requiring hippocampal and related structure binding processes for the sense of an episode to emerge in consciousness—the elusive scientific characterization of knowledge stored within the PFC remains the key missing part of the puzzle. We believe that the evidence collected so far has brought us one step closer to such an understanding of the contribution of the PFC to future planning.

Acknowledgment

The authors are supported by the NINDS Intramural Research Program.

References

Barch, D. M., Braver, T. S., Akbudak, E., Conturo, T., Ollinger, J., & Snyder, A. (2001). Anterior cingulate cortex and response conflict: Effects of response modality and processing domain. *Cerebral Cortex* 11, 837–848.

Barbey, A. K., & Barsalou, L. W. (in press). Reasoning and problem solving: models. In L. Squire, T. Albright, F. Bloom, F. Gage, & N. Spitzer (Eds.), *New encyclopedia of neuroscience*. Vol. 8, (pp. 35–43). Oxford, England: Elsevier.

Barbey, A. K., & Sloman, S. A. (2007). Base-rate respect: From ecological rationality to dual processes. *Behavioral and Brain Sciences*, 30, 241–297.

Barbey, A. K., & Wolff, P. (2006). Causal reasoning from forces. *Proceedings of the 28th Annual Conference of the Cognitive Science Society* (pp. 2439). Mahwah, NJ: Erlbaum.

Barbey, A. K., & Wolff, P. (2007). Learning causal structure from reasoning. *Proceedings of the 29th Annual Conference of the Cognitive Science Society* (pp. 713–718). Mahwah, NJ: Erlbaum.

Barbey, A. K., & Wolff, P. (submitted). Composing causal relations in force dynamics.

Barsalou, L. W. (1991). Deriving categories to achieve goals. In G. H. Bower (Ed.), *The psychology of learning and motivation: Advances in research and theory* (Vol. 27, pp. 1–64). San Diego, CA: Academic Press.

Barsalou, L. W., Barbey, A. K., Simmons, W. K., & Santos, A. (2005). Embodiment in religious knowledge. *Journal of Cognition and Culture*, 5, 14–57.

Barsalou, L. W., Niedenthal, P. M., Barbey, A. K., & Ruppert, J. (2003). Social embodiment. In B. Ross (Ed.), *The psychology of learning and motivation* (Vol. 43, pp. 43–92). San Diego, CA: Academic Press.

Barsalou, L. W., Simmons, W. K., Barbey, A. K., & Wilson, C. D. (2003). Grounding conceptual knowledge in modality-specific systems. *Trends in Cognitive Sciences*, 7, 84–91.

Barsalou, L. W., & Wiemer-Hastings, K. (2005). Situating abstract concepts. In D. Pecher & R. Zwaan (Eds.), *Grounding cognition: The role of perception and action in memory, language, and thought* (pp. 129–163). New York: Cambridge University Press.

Beldarrain, M., Garcia-Monco, J., Astigarraga, E., Gonzalez, A., & Grafman, J. (2005). Only spontaneous counterfactual thinking is impaired in patients with prefrontal cortex lesions. *Cognitive Brain Research*, 24, 723–726.

Berthoz, S., Armony, J. L., Blair, R. J. R., & Dolan, R. J. (2002). An fMRI study of intentional and unintentional (embarrassing) violations of social norms. *Brain*, 125, 1696–1708.

Bodner, M., Kroger, J., & Fuster, J. M. (1996). Auditory memory cells in dorsolateral prefrontal cortex. *Neuroreport*, 7, 1905–1908.

Botvinick, M. M., Cohen, J. D., & Carter, C. S. (2004). Conflict monitoring and anterior cingulate cortex: An update. *Trends in Cognitive Sciences*, 8, 539–546.

Brase, G., & Barbey, A. K. (2006). Mental representations of statistical information. In A. Columbus (Ed.), *Advances in psychological research* (Vol. 41, pp. 91–113). New York: Nova Science Publishers.

Buckholtz, J. W., Asplund, C. L., Dux, P. E., Zald, D. H., Gore, J. C., Jones, O. D., & Marois, R. (2008). The neural correlates of third-party punishment. *Neuron*, 60, 930–940.

Burgess, P. W., Veitch, E., de Lacy Costello, A., & Shallice, T. (2000). The cognitive and neuroanatomical correlates of multitasking. *Neuropsychologia*, 38, 848–863.

Byrne, R. M. J. (1997). Cognitive processes in counterfactual thinking about what might have been. In D. Medin (Ed.), *The psychology of learning and motivation, advances in research and theory* (Vol. 37, pp. 105–154). San Diego, CA: Academic Press.

Byrne, R. M. J. (2002). Mental models and counterfactual thinking. *Trends in Cognitive Sciences*, 6, 405–445.

Chaigneau, S., & Barbey, A. K. (2008). Assessing psychological theories of causal meaning and inference. In *Proceedings of the Thirtieth Annual Science Society*. Hillsdale, NJ: Erlbaum.

Christoff, K., & Keramatian, K. (2007). Abstraction of mental representations: Theoretical considerations and neuroscientific evidence. In S. A. Bunge & J. D. Wallis (Eds.), *The neuroscience of rule-guided behavior*. New York: Oxford University Press.

Christoff, K., Prabhakaran, V., Dorfman, J., Zhao, Z., Kroger, J. K., Holyoak, K. J., & Gabrieli, J. D. E. (2001). Rostrolateral prefrontal cortex involvement in relational integration during reasoning. *NeuroImage*, 14, 1136–1149.

Christoff, K., Ream, J. M., Geddes, L. P. T., & Gabrieli, J. D. E. (2003). Evaluating self-generated information: Anterior prefrontal contributions to human cognition. *Behavioral Neuroscience*, 117, 1161–1168.

Coricelli, G., Critchley, H. D., Joffily, M., O'Doherty, J. P., Sirigu, A., & Dolan, R. J. (2005). Regret and its avoidance: A neuroimaging study of choice behavior. *Nature Neuroscience*, 8, 1255–1262.

Costello, F. J., & Keane, M. T. (2000) Efficient creativity: Constraint guided conceptual combination. *Cognitive Science*, 24, 299–349.

Damasio, A. R. (1989). Time-locked multiregional retroactivation: A systems-level proposal for the neural substrates of recall and recognition. *Cognition*, 33, 25–62.

Davis, C. J., Lehman, D. R., Wortman, C. B., Silver, R. C., & Thompson, S. C. (1995). The undoing of traumatic life events. *Personality and Social Psychology Bulletin*, 21, 109–124.

De Dreu, C. K. W., Beersma, B., Stroebe, K., & Euwema, M. C. (2006). Motivated information processing, strategic choice, and the quality of negotiated agreement. *Journal of Personality and Social Psychology*, 6, 927–943.

Dimitrov M., Phipps M., Zahn T., & Grafman J. (1999). A thoroughly modern Gage. *Neurocase*, 5, 345–354.

Dunning, D. (1999). A newer look: Motivated social cognition and the schematic representation of social concepts. *Psychological Inquiry*, 10, 1–11.

Elliott, R., Dolan, R. J., & Frith, C. D. (2000). Dissociable functions in the medial and lateral orbitofrontal cortex: Evidence from human neuroimaging studies. *Cerebral Cortex*, 10, 308–317.

Elston, G. N. (2000). Pyramidal cells of the frontal lobe: All the more spinous to think with. *Journal of Neuroscience*, 20, RC95.

Engel, A. K., & Singer, W. (2001). Temporal binding and the neural correlates of sensory awareness. *Trends in Cognitive Sciences*, 5, 16–25.

Fiddick, L., Spampinato, M. V., & Grafman, J. (2005). Social contracts and precautions activate different neurological systems: An fMRI investigation of deontic reasoning. *NeuroImage*, 28, 778–786.

Fletcher, P. C., Happe, F., Frith, U., Baker, S. C., Dolan, R. J., Frackowiak, R. S. J., & Frith, C. D. (1995). Other minds in the brain: A functional imaging study of "theory of mind" in story comprehension. *Cognition*, 57, 109–128.

Fortin, N. J., Agster, K., & Eichenbaum, H. B. (2002). Critical role of the hippocampus in memory for sequences of events. *Nature Neuroscience*, 5, 458–562.

Fuster, J. M. (1997). *The prefrontal cortex: Anatomy, physiology, and neuropsychology of the frontal lobe*. New York: Raven.

Fuster, J. M., & Alexander, G. E. (1971). Neuron activity related to short-term memory. *Science*, 173, 652–654.

Gallese, V., Fadiga, L., Fogassi, L., & Rizzolatti, G. (1996). Action recognition in the premotor cortex. *Brain*, 119, 593–609.

Gilbar, O., & Hevroni, A. (2007). Counterfactuals, coping strategies and psychological distress among breast cancer patients. *Anxiety, Stress, and Coping*, 20, 382–392.

Goel, V., Buchel, C., Frith, C., & Dolan, R. (2000). Dissociation of mechanisms underlying syllogistic reasoning. *NeuroImage*, 12, 504–514.

Goel, V., & Dolan, R. J. (2004). Differential involvement of left prefrontal cortex in inductive and deductive reasoning. *Cognition*, 93, B109–B121.

Goel, V., & Grafman, J. (2000). The role of the right prefrontal cortex in ill-structured problem sovling. *Cognitive Neuropsychology*, 17, 415–436.

Goel, V., Grafman, J., Sadato, N., & Hallett, M. (1995). Modeling other minds. *Neuroreport*, 6, 1741–1746.

Grafton, S. T., Arbib, M. A., Fadiga, L., & Rizzolatti, G. (1996). Localization of grasp representations in humans by PET: II. Observation compared with imagination. *Experimental Brain Research, 112*, 103–111.

Greene, J. D., Nystrom, L. E., Engell, A. D., Darley, J. M., & Cohen, J. D. (2004). The neural bases of cognitive conflict and control in moral judgment. *Neuron, 44*, 389–400.

Griffin, D. W., & Ross, L. (1991). Subjective construal, social inference, and human misunderstanding. *Advances in Experimental Social Psychology, 24*, 319–359.

Heckers, S., Zalesak, M., Weiss, A. P., Ditman, T., & Titone, D. (2004). Hippocampal activation during transitive inference in humans. *Hippocampus, 14*, 153–162.

Huettel, S. A., Song, A. W., & McCarthy, G. (2005). Decisions under uncertainty: Probabilistic context influences activation of prefrontal and parietal cortices. *The Journal of Neuroscience, 25*, 3304–3311.

Kahneman, D., & Miller, D. T. (1986). Norm theory: Comparing reality to its alternatives. *Psychological Review, 93*, 136–153.

Knoch, D., Pascual-Leone, A., Meyer, K., Treyer, V., & Fehr, E. (2006). Diminishing reciprocal fairness by disrupting the right prefrontal cortex. *Science, 314*, 829–832.

Kroger, J. K., Nystrom, L. E., Cohen, J. D., & Johnson-Laird, P. N. (2008). Distinct neural substrates for deductive and mathematical processing. *Brain Research, 1243*, 86–103.

Krueger, F., Barbey, A. K., & Grafman, J. (in press). The medial prefrontal cortex represents social event knowledge. *Trends in Cognitive Sciences.*

Levy, R., & Goldman-Rakic, P. S. (2000). Segregation of working memory functions within the dorsolateral prefrontal cortex. *Experimental Brain Research, 133*, 23–32.

Macrae, C. N., Moran, J. M., Heatherton, T. F., Banfield, J. F., & Kelley, W. M. (2004). Medial prefrontal activity predicts memory for self. *Cerebral Cortex, 14*, 647–654.

Mandel, D. R. (2003). Counterfactuals, emotions, and context. *Cognition and Emotion, 17*, 139–159.

Miller, D. T., & Turnbull, W. (1990). The counterfactual fallacy: Confusing what might have been with what ought to have been. *Social Justice Research, 4*, 1–19.

Milne, E., & Grafman, J. (2001). Ventromedial prefrontal cortex lesions in humans eliminate implicit gender stereotyping. *Journal of Neuroscience, 21*, RC150 (1–6).

Mitchell, J. P., Heatherton, T. F., & Macrae, C. N. (2002). Distinct neural systems subserve person and object knowledge. *Proceedings of the National Academy of Sciences USA, 99*, 15238–15243.

Moll, J., & de Oliveira-Souza, R. (2007). Moral judgments, emotions, and the utilitarian brain. *Trends in Cognitive Sciences, 11*, 319–321.

Monti, M. M., Osherson, D. N., Martinez, M. J., & Parsons, L. M. (2007). Functional neuroanatomy of deductive inference: A language-independent distributed network. *NeuroImage, 37*, 1005–1016.

Niedenthal, P. M., Tangney, J. P., & Gavanski, I. (1994). "If only I weren't" versus "If only I hadn't": Distinguishing shame and guilt in counterfactual thinking. *Journal of Personality and Social Psychology, 67*, 585–595.

Noveck, I. A., Goel, V., & Smith, K. W. (2004). The neural basis of conditional reasoning with arbitrary content. *Cortex, 40*, 613–622.

Ochsner, K. N., Knierim, K., Ludlow, D. H., Hanelin, J., Ramachandran, T., Glover, G., & Mackey, S. C. (2004). Reflecting upon feelings: An fMRI study of neural systems supporting the attribution of emotion to self and other. *Journal of Cognitive Neuroscience, 16*, 1746–1772.

O'Reilly, R. C., & Rudy, J. W. (2000). Computational principles of learning in the neocortex and hippocampus. *Hippocampus, 10*, 389–397.

Osherson, D. N., Perani, D., Cappa, S., Schnur, T., Grassi, F., & Fazio, F. (1998). Distinct brain loci in deductive versus probabilistic reasoning. *Neuropsychologia, 36*, 369–376.

Palmer, S. E. (1999) *Vision science: Photons to phenomenology.* Cambridge, MA: MIT Press.

Ramnani, N., & Owen, A. M. (2004). Anterior prefrontal cortex: insights into function from anatomy and neuroimaging. *Nature Reviews Neuroscience, 5*, 184–194.

Partiot, A., Grafman, J., Sadato, N., Wachs, J., & Hallett, M. (1995). Brain activation during the generation of non-emotional and emotional plans. *Neuroreport, 6*, 1397–1400.

Patterson, R., & Barbey, A. K. (in press). Causal simulation theory: An integrative cognitive neuroscience framework for causal reasoning. In J. Grafman & F. Krueger (Eds.), *Neural basis of belief systems.* New York: Psychology Press.

Prehn, K., Wartenburger, I., Meriau, K., Scheibe, C., Goodenough, O. R., Villringer, A., van der Meer, E., & Heekeren, H. R. (2008). Individual differences in moral judgment competence influence neural correlates of socio-normative judgments.

Social Cognitive and Affective Neuroscience, 3, 33–46.

Rilling, J. K., Goldsmith, D. R., Glenn, A. L., Jairam, M. R., Elfenbein, H. A., Dagenais, J. E., Murdock, C. D., & Pagnoni, G. (2008). The neural correlates of the affective response to unreciprocated cooperation. *Neuropsychologia, 465,* 1256–1266.

Rizzolatti, G. (1996). Localization of grasp representations in humans by PET: I. Observation versus execution. *Experimental Brain Research, 111,* 246–252.

Roese, N. J., & Olson, J. M. (Eds.). (1995). *What might have been: The social psychology of counterfactual thinking.* Mahwah, NJ: Erlbaum.

Roese, N. J., Hur, T., & Pennington, G. L. (1999). Counterfactual thinking and regulatory focus: Implications for action versus inaction and sufficiency versus necessity. *Journal of Personality and Social Psychology, 77,* 1109–1120.

Sanfey, A. G., Rilling, J. K., Aronson, J. A., Nystrom, L. E., & Cohen, J. D. (2003). The neural basis of decision making in the ultimatum game. *Science, 300,* 1755–1758.

Schmitz, T. W., Kawahara-Baccus, T. N., & Johnson, S.C. (2004). Metacognitive evaluation self-relevance, and the right prefrontal cortex. *Neuroimage, 22,* 941–947.

Sloman, S., Barbey, A. K., & Hotalling, J. (2009). A causal model theory of the meaning of cause, enable, and prevent. *Cognitive Science, 33,* 21–50.

Smith, R., Keramatian, K., & Christoff, K. (2007). Localizing the rostrolateral prefrontal cortex at the individual level. *NeuroImage, 36,* 1387–1396.

Sternberg, R. J., & Gastel, J. (1989). If dancers ate their shoes: Inductive reasoning with factual and counterfactual premises. *Memory and Cognition, 17,* 1–10.

Stone, V. E., Cosmides, L., Tooby, J., Kroll, N., & Knight, R. T. Selective impairment of reasoning about social exchange in a patient with bilateral limbic damage. *Proceedings of the National Academy of Science of the USA, 17,* 11531–11536.

Thomas, N. J. T. (1999) Are theories of imagery theories of imagination? An active perception approach to conscious mental content. *Cognitive Science, 23,* 207–245.

Thomson, J. J. (1976). Killing, letting die, and the trolley problem. *Monist, 59,* 204–217.

Tulving, E., & Markowitsch, H. J. (1998). Episodic and declarative memory: Role of the hippocampus. *Hippocampus, 8,* 198–204.

Volz, K. G., Schubotz, R. I., & von Cramon, D. Y. (2004). Why am I unsure: Internal and external attributions of uncertainty dissociated by fMRI. *Neuroimage, 21,* 848–857.

Walton, M. E., Devlin, J. T., & Rushworth, M. F. (2004). Interactions between decision making and performance monitoring within prefrontal cortex. *Nature Neuroscience, 7,* 1259–1265.

Weingartner H., Grafman J., Boutelle W., Kaye W., & Martin P. R. (1983). Forms of memory failure. *Science, 221,* 380–382.

Weissman, D. H., Perkins, A. S., & Woldorff, M. G. (2008). Cognitive control in social situations: A role for the dorsolateral prefrontal cortex. *NeuroImage, 40,* 955–962.

Williams, J. H. G., Whiten, A., Suddendorf, T., & Perrett, D. I. (2001). Imitation, mirror neurons and autism. *Neuroscience and Biobehavioral Reviews, 25,* 287–295.

Wood, J. N., Knutson, K. M., & Grafman, J. (2005). Psychological structure and neural correlates of event knowledge. *Cerebral Cortex, 15,* 1155–1161.

Wood, J. N., Romero, S. G., Makale, M., & Grafman J. (2003). Category-specific representations of social and nonsocial knowledge in the human prefrontal cortex. *Journal of Cognitive Neurosciences, 15,* 236–248.

Wood, J. N., Tierney, M., Bidwell, L. A., & Grafman J. (2005). Neural correlates of script event knowledge: A neuropsychological study following prefrontal injury. *Cortex, 6,* 796–804.

Wrosch, C., Bauer, I., Miller, G. E., & Lupien, S. (2007). Regret intensity, diurnal cortisol secretion, and physical health in older individuals: Evidence for directional effects and protective factors. *Psychology and Aging, 22,* 319–330.

Zacks, J. M., & Tversky, B. (2001). Event structure in perception and conception. *Psychology Buletinl, 127,* 3–21.

Zacks, J. M., Tversky, B., & Iyer, G. (2001). Perceiving, remembering, and communicating structure in events. *Journal of Experimental Psychology: General, 130,* 29–58.

Zeki, S. (1993) *A vision of the brain.* Cambridge, MA: Blackwell Scientific Publications.

Zeelenberg, M., van der Pligt, J., & Manstead, A. S. R. (1998). Undoing regret on Dutch television: Apologizing for interpersonal regrets involving actions or inactions. *Personality and Social Psychology Bulletin, 24,* 1113–1119.

CHAPTER 5
On the Nature of Medial Temporal Lobe Contributions to the Constructive Simulation of Future Events

Daniel L. Schacter and Donna Rose Addis

Everyday experience suggests that predictions are about the future, whereas memory is about the past. From this perspective, the two phenomena run on parallel tracks in opposite temporal directions. For example, predictions about the future occur at varying different timescales, ranging from situations where one enters a new setting, such as a school or a museum, and tries to predict what might happen next (e.g., Bar, 2007), all the way to predicting how happy one might be years or decades in the future in a marriage or a job (Gilbert, 2006). Analogously, memory can operate on the very recent past, as when we use working memory to recall the last few words in a sentence, or the remote past, as when we recall our childhood experiences.

It is becoming increasingly clear, however, that predicting the future and remembering the past may be more closely related than everyday experience might suggest. For example, errors in predicting the future are often based on how we remember the past (for a review, see Gilbert & Wilson, 2007). In a related vein, remembering the past recruits many of the same cognitive processes as does imagining or simulating the occurrence of possible events in the future. Consider, for example, a study by D'Argembeau and van der Linden (2004), in which they asked subjects either to remember a specific event from their past or imagine a specific event that could plausibly happen to them in the future, and rate

various attributes of the event. Although remembered past events were associated with more vivid sensory and contextual details than were imagined future events, there were also strong commonalities between remembering the past and imagining the future. Positive past and future events were rated as more strongly experienced than negative past and future events; temporally close events in either the past or future were more strongly experienced, and included more sensory and contextual details, than did distant events; and participants were more likely to adopt a first-person than third-person perspective for temporally close than temporally distant events in both the past and future.

These commonalities in cognitive processes underlying past and future events are complemented by analogous similarities in brain activity: the same "core network" of brain regions is recruited when people remember the past and imagine the future, including medial prefrontal and frontopolar cortex, medial temporal lobe, lateral temporal and temporopolar cortex, medial parietal cortex including posterior cingulate and retrosplenial cortex, and lateral parietal cortex (for reviews, see, Buckner, Andrews, & Schacter, 2008; Schacter, Addis, & Buckner, 2007, 2008). For memory researchers, perhaps the most striking finding from this research is that the medial temporal lobe (MTL), a structure long known to play a critical role in remembering, appears to be similarly involved when individuals imagine or simulate events that might occur in their personal futures.

The purpose of the present chapter is to review recent evidence from our lab and others that links MTL activity to future event simulation, to consider alternative interpretations of these observations, and to discuss them in relation to other evidence concerning the medial temporal and constructive memory. Elsewhere, we have provided broad reviews concerning cognitive and neural aspects of future event simulation (Schacter et al., 2007, 2008). Here we focus instead on the contributions of two regions within the MTL: the hippocampus and parahippocampal cortex.

REMEMBERING THE PAST AND IMAGINING THE FUTURE: CONCEPTUAL ISSUES AND THE CONSTRUCTIVE EPISODIC SIMULATION HYPOTHESIS

When we use such terms as "episodic simulation" or "future event simulation," we refer to *imaginative constructions of hypothetical events or scenarios that might occur in one's personal future* (Schacter et al., 2008). Although we focus on the idea that simulation is critical for envisaging possible *future* events, we do not restrict our application of simulation to the future. People also engage in simulations of present and past events, a point that will be important to consider in relation to recent empirical observations and theoretical accounts.

Motivated in part by some of the striking commonalities noted earlier between remembering past events and simulating future ones, we advanced the *constructive episodic simulation* hypothesis (Schacter & Addis, 2007a, 2007b; for related views, see Buckner & Carroll, 2007; Hassabis & Maguire, 2007; Suddendorf & Corballis, 1997, 2007). By this view, past and future events draw on similar information stored in episodic memory and rely on similar underlying processes; episodic memory supports the construction of future events by extracting and recombining stored information into a simulation of a novel event. Indeed, we have suggested

that simulation of future events requires a system that can flexibly recombine details from past events.

Taking an adaptive perspective, we (Schacter & Addis, 2007a, 2007b) suggested that a critical function of a constructive memory is to make information available for simulation of future events. Episodic memory thus supports the construction of future events by flexibly recombining stored information into a simulation of a novel event. The adaptive value of such a system is that it enables past information to be used flexibly in simulating alternative future scenarios without engaging in actual behavior. A potential downside of such a system is that it is vulnerable to memory errors, such as misattribution and false recognition (for examples, see Schacter & Addis, 2007a, 2007b; see also Dudai & Carruthers, 2005; Suddendorf & Corballis, 1997).

With respect to the MTL, it has been suggested that the hippocampal region supports relational memory processes that link together disparate bits of information (e.g., Eichenbaum & Cohen, 2001). According to the constructive episodic simulation hypothesis, these processes are crucial for recombining stored information into future event simulations. Thus, our hypothesis posits an important link between hippocampal activity and the simulation of future events.

NEUROIMAGING OF PAST AND FUTURE EVENTS

A large number of neuroimaging studies have examined brain activity when people remember past autobiographical experiences (for reviews, see Cabeza & St Jacques, 2007; Svoboda, McKinnon, & Levine, 2006). In contrast, only a handful of studies have explored brain activity when people imagine future events. Okuda et al. (2003) reported the first such study. During scanning, participants talked freely for 60 seconds about either the near or distant past (last few days or years), or the near or distant future (the next few days or years). These critical conditions were compared with a semantic control task involving analysis of the meaning of words. Compared to the control condition, significant levels of activation were observed during both the past and future conditions in right hippocampus and bilateral parahippocampal cortex. Furthermore, two left parahippocampal areas showed greater activity when individuals were thinking about the future than about the past. Moreover, activity in a number of these MTL regions was modulated by temporal distance. Most of them showed the same neural response to temporal distance for both past and future events: either increasing or decreasing activity with increasing temporal distance. The only region that exhibited an interaction between temporal direction (i.e., past vs. future) and distance (i.e., near vs. distant) was an inferior region in left parahippocampus gyrus (Brodmann's area [BA] 36), one of the two areas noted earlier that showed greater activity for future than past events. In this region, Okuda et al. (2003) noted that the increase in brain activity from the near to distant future tasks was smaller than the increase in activity observed from the near to distant past tasks.

These observations are potentially important because they suggest that parahippocampal and hippocampal regions are at least as active during future event simulation as during remembering of past experiences. Note, however, that because Okuda et al. (2003) used a relatively unconstrained paradigm that did not probe participants about particular events, it is unclear whether these reports consisted of episodic memories/simulations (unique events specific in time and place), or general semantic information about an individual's past or future. More recent functional magnetic resonance imaging (fMRI) studies have used event-related designs to yield information regarding the neural bases of specific past and future events.

Addis, Wong, and Schacter (2007) used event-related fMRI to distinguish between an initial *construction* phase, where participants generated a specific past or future event in response to an event cue (e.g., "dress"), and making a button-press when they had an event in mind, and an *elaboration* phase during which participants generated as much detail as possible about the event. We compared activity during the past and future tasks with control tasks that required semantic and imagery processing, respectively.

We observed evidence of past- and future-related MTL activity during both the construction and elaboration phases. The construction phase was associated with common past-future activity in posterior left hippocampus, which we suggested might reflect the initial interaction between cues and hippocampally mediated pointers to memory traces. Similarly, the elaboration phase revealed evidence of common past-future activity in the left hippocampus, possibly reflecting the retrieval and/or integration of additional event details into the memorial or imaginal representations, as well as common past-future activity in bilateral parahippocampal cortex. There was also evidence for differential engagement of MTL activity in the future task: During the construction phase, a region of right hippocampus showed increased activity only in the future condition. We suggested that this future-specific hippocampal activity might reflect the novelty of future events and/or additional relational processing required when one must recombine disparate details into a coherent event.

Botzung, Denkova, and Manning (2008) reported fMRI data that contrast with the aforementioned results showing increased hippocampal activity for future events versus past events. One day prior to scanning, subjects described 20 past events from the last week and 20 future events planned for the next week. The subjects constructed cue words for these events that were then presented to them the next day during scanning, when they were instructed to think of past or future events to each cue. Although past and future events produced activation in a similar network to that reported by Addis et al. (2007) and Okuda et al. (2003), including bilateral MTL, Botzung et al. (2008) reported no evidence for increased activity in the future condition compared with the past condition. In fact, they noted that both right and left hippocampus showed greater activity in the past condition than in the future condition.

As we have pointed out elsewhere (Schacter et al., 2008), however, the fact that participants in the Botzung et al. (2008) study initially carried out their simulations of future events in a separate session prior to scanning and thus may have recalled their prior simulation during scanning, rather than constructing it for the first time, as subjects did in the earlier studies. Although Botzung et al. excluded those trials on which subjects stated that they produced an event from the pre-scan interview, it is unclear how reliably subjects can make the requested discrimination. And since subjects had previously encoded their future event simulation, rather than constructing it anew during scanning as in previous studies, there may have been less recruitment of processes involved in recombining details from past experiences. Similar findings have been reported in other studies examining the retrieval of previously constructed imaginary events (D'Argembeau, Xue, Lu, van der Linden, & Bechara, 2008; Hassabis, Kumaran, & Maguire, 2007a).

Two more recent studies from our laboratory have examined further the nature of hippocampal activations observed during the construction and elaboration stages of event remembering and simulation, respectively. Addis and Schacter (2008) analyzed further the elaboration-stage data reported initially by Addis et al. (2007), using parametric modulation analyses to examine MTL activity according to the amount of detail generated and the temporal distance of each event from the present usage. We suggested that *reintegrating* increasing amounts of detail for either a past or future event would be associated with increasing levels of hippocampal activity. However, future events should require more intensive *recombining* of disparate details into a coherent event, so the hippocampal response to increasing amounts of future event detail should be larger than that for past event detail. Consistent with these predictions, the analysis showed that the left posterior hippocampus was responsive to the amount of detail for both past and future events, likely reflecting the retrieval of details from episodic memory that is required for both tasks. In contrast, a distinct region in the left anterior hippocampus responded differentially to the amount of detail comprising future events, possibly reflecting the recombination of details into a novel future event.

The parametric modulation analysis of temporal distance revealed that the increasing recency of past events was associated with activity in the right parahippocampus gyrus (BA 35/36), while activity in bilateral hippocampus was associated with the increasing remoteness of future events. We proposed that the hippocampal response to the distance of future events reflects the increasing disparateness of details likely included in remote future events, and the intensive relational processing required for integrating such details into a coherent episodic simulation of the future. Overall, these results suggest that although MTL regions supporting past and future event simulation show impressive commonalities during event elaboration, they can be recruited in different ways depending on whether the generated event is in the past or future.

A study by Addis, Cheng, Roberts, and Schacter (in press) provides additional insight into the nature of MTL activity during the construction phase. Participants were cued to either remember specific past events or imagine specific future events, as in Addis et al. (2007). In addition, they were also cued to remember general, routine events (e.g., having brunch after attending church) or to imagine generic events that might occur in their personal futures (e.g., reading the newspaper each morning). We reasoned that in a region that is responsive to the amount of detail recombined into a coherent imagined episode, as we suggested with respect to the hippocampus (Addis & Schacter, 2008), more activity should be evident when constructing specific future events relative to general future events (as well as specific and generic past events). By contrast, if the hippocampal region is simply responsive to the prospective nature of future events, then it should be more engaged during the construction of both types of future events relative to past events, irrespective of specificity.

We replicated the aforementioned finding of greater right hippocampal activity for future than past event construction. Importantly, though, the increased right hippocampal activity was evident only for specific events; in fact, there was no evidence for right hippocampal activity during construction of generic future events. Thus, the results appear to provide evidence against the idea that right hippocampal activation for specific future events indicates a uniquely prospective function for this region.

An event-related fMRI study by Hassabis et al. (2007a) also provides data that call into question the idea that MTL activation during event simulation is tied specifically to thinking about events in one's future. Participants were asked to imagine novel, fictitious scenes, without explicit reference to whether those scenes should be placed in the past, present, or future. Subjects were then scanned in a subsequent session in which they were cued to remember the previously constructed fictitious scenes, construct additional novel fictitious scenes, or recall real episodic memories from their personal pasts. Hassabis et al. found that all three conditions were associated with activations in hippocampus, parahippocampal gyrus, and several other regions in the core network. The results thus indicate that activity in these regions is not restricted to conditions that explicitly require imagining future events.

Additional evidence on this point is provided by another recent study from our laboratory. Addis et al. (2009) approached the question of whether future event–related activity is specifically associated with prospective thinking, or with the more general demands of imagining an episodic event in either temporal direction, by instructing subjects to imagine events that might occur in their personal future or events that might have occurred in their personal pasts but did not. Prior to scanning, participants provided episodic memories of actual experiences that included details about a *person*, *object*, and *place* involved in that event. During scanning, the subjects were cued to recall some of the events that had actually occurred, and for the conditions in which they imagined events, the experimenters randomly recombined details concerning person, object, and place from separate episodes. Participants were thus presented with cues for a person, object, and place taken from multiple episodes and were instructed to imagine a single, novel episode that included the specified details.

With respect to the MTL, Addis et al. (2009) reported that both hippocampus and parahippocampal cortex were similarly engaged when participants imagined future and past events, suggesting that these regions (as well as others in the core network that showed the same pattern) can be used for event simulation regardless of the temporal location of the event.

This study also allowed us to address an issue that is particularly relevant to the constructive episodic simulation hypothesis discussed earlier, which emphasizes that future event simulations are built by flexibly recombining details from past experiences, likely engaging the relational processes supported by the hippocampus. However, our previous studies on imagining future events did not provide direct evidence that subjects recombine details from multiple past events into novel future simulations. An alternative possibility is that participants simply recast their memories of individual past experiences as imagined future events, especially when they are thinking about events that might plausibly occur in the near future. For example, when given the cue "car" and asked to imagine an event that might occur in the next few weeks involving a car, participants might simply recall a recent episode in which they saw a car run a red light, and imagine that such an incident might occur in the next few weeks. When this kind of recasting process occurs, there is little or no recombination of details of past events into imagined future scenarios. However, the finding that the hippocampus was robustly activated during event simulation when we experimentally recombined details concerning person, object, and place from different episodes provides evidence against this recasting hypothesis. Although we would not rule out the possibility that recasting occurs on some test trials, the finding of hippocampal activation in this paradigm, which should minimize or eliminate recasting, is consistent with the claim from the constructive episodic simulation hypothesis that activity in the hippocampus during event simulation reflects the recombination of details from different episodes.

One feature common to the neuroimaging studies reviewed so far is that each one provided some evidence for activity in both hippocampal and parahipppocampal regions in conditions designed to elicit future event simulation (Addis et al., 2007, 2009; Botzung et al., 2008; Okuda et al., 2003) or imagination (Hassabis et al., 2007a). Szpunar, Watson, and McDermott (2007) reported a contrasting pattern of results. In their fMRI study, instructed participants were given event cues, such as *past birthday* or *retirement party*, and were instructed to remember specific events from their personal pasts, imagine specific events that might reasonably occur in their personal futures, or imagine specific events that could involve a familiar individual (Bill Clinton). Compared with the latter condition, remembering one's personal past or simulating one's personal future was associated with significant and comparable levels of activity in bilateral parahippocampal cortex, as well as other regions activated in other studies, including other posterior regions such as posterior cingulate and anterior regions such as frontopolar cortex. By contrast, no evidence for hippocampal activation was reported in the personal past or future conditions relative to the "Bill Clinton" control. We will return to this observation later when considering theoretical implications of the aforementioned results.

Szpunar et al. (2009) sought to characterize the nature of activity they had observed in the parahippocampal and related posterior regions. They noted previous work from Bar and Aminoff (2003) suggesting that the parahippocampal cortex and posterior cingulate are involved in processing contextual associations, thus suggesting that these regions may be responsible for generating the familiar contexts in which future event simulations are situated (Addis et al., 2007; Szpunar et al., 2007). To test the idea, Szpunar et al. asked participants to imagine themselves in future scenarios involving either a familiar or an unfamiliar context; they also asked participants to remember past experiences involving familiar contexts. They carried out region-of-interest analyses focused on the areas within bilateral parahippocampal cortex and posterior cingulate that had been activated in their previous study. Consistent with the hypothesis that these regions are important for instantiating contextual information, both regions showed robust activity in

the past and future conditions that required generating familiar context, and significantly less activity in the future condition that required generating an unfamiliar context.

STUDIES OF AMNESIC PATIENTS AND OLDER ADULTS

Although most of the evidence linking future event simulation with MTL activity comes from neuroimaging studies, additional evidence is provided by studies of amnesic patients, who exhibit an impairment in the ability to remember past experiences as a result of bilateral damage to the medial temporal lobes and related structures. Tulving (1985) reported that the severely amnesic patient K. C., who cannot remember any specific episodes from his past (for a review of K. C., see Rosenbaum et al., 2005), exhibits similar problems envisioning any specific episodes in his future. K. C. is characterized by bilateral MTL damage, but he also has extensive damage in prefrontal and other regions (see Rosenbaum et al., 2005), so it is unclear whether his problems imagining the future are associated specifically with MTL. A similar caveat applies to a more recent study concerning patient D. B., who became amnesic as a result of cardiac arrest and consequent anoxia (Klein, Loftus, & Kihlstrom, 2002). D. B. showed clear deficits on a 10-item questionnaire probing past and future personal events that were matched for temporal distance from the present. However, even though anoxia is typically associated with MTL damage, no neuroanatomical findings were reported concerning patient D. B.

Hassabis et al. (2007b) examined the ability of five patients with documented bilateral hippocampal amnesia to imagine novel experiences, such as "Imagine you're lying on a white sandy beach in a beautiful tropical bay." The experimenters scored the constructions of patients and controls based on the content, spatial coherence, and subjective qualities of the imagined scenarios. Four of the five hippocampal patients produced constructions that were significantly reduced in richness and content, and especially the spatial coherence of the scenarios, relative to scenarios constructed by controls. The single patient who performed normally on the imaginary scene task maintained some residual hippocampal tissue. Because the lesions in the other cases appear to be restricted to hippocampal formation, this study strengthens the link between event simulation and hippocampal function.

We also note that a recent study by Addis, Wong, and Schacter (2008) provides evidence that future event simulation is impaired in older adults, who also exhibit memory impairments, albeit considerably milder than those seen in amnesic patients. Young and older participants generated memories of past events and simulations of future events in response to individual word cues, and transcriptions of the events were segmented into distinct details that were classified as either internal (episodic) or external (semantic; Levine, Svoboda, Hay, Winocur, & Moscovitch, 2002). The key finding was that older adults generated fewer internal (but not external) details than younger adults; importantly, this effect was observed to the same extent for future events as for past events. Although there is no direct evidence from this study linking the age-related deficits to MTL dysfunction, two kinds of indirect evidence suggest that such a link may exist. First, we reported that the internal (but not external) detail score in older adults correlated significantly with a measure of relational memory (paired-associate learning) that is known to be dependent on the hippocampus. Second, hippocampal atrophy has been documented in older adults (e.g., Driscoll et al., 2003).

The medial temporal lobe and future event simulation: summary, extensions, and theoretical implications

The studies reviewed in the preceding sections are broadly consistent with the idea that regions within the MTL are associated with constructing simulations of future events. We discuss now a number of points regarding these studies and related research that has characterized MTL function in different domains.

Consider first the neuroimaging studies that we reviewed. On balance, the most consistent feature of the neuroimaging data is that both hippocampus and parahippocampal cortex are similarly active during the simulation of future events and the remembering of past events, in agreement with a meta-analysis by Spreng, Mar, and Kim (2009). In addition, however, it is clear that this common activation of hippocampus and parahippocampus is not restricted to conditions requiring prospective event simulation: The same regions are engaged when individuals are instructed to simulate events that might have occurred in their pasts (Addis et al., 2009) or when asked to imagine scenes without a specific temporal reference (Hassabis et al., 2007a). This latter finding fits well with the related observations that both regions show similarly increased activity during tasks involving spatial navigation (for review, see Buckner & Carroll 2007; Spreng et al. 2009) and under some conditions, during tasks requiring theory of mind judgments, which commonly activate medial prefrontal and parietal regions of the core network (Buckner & Carroll 2007; Spreng et al., 2009; but these structures are likely not necessary for some theory of mind tasks, on which amnesic patients perform well; see Rosenbaum, Stuss, Levine, & Tulving, 2007).

Even though more evidence is required given the relatively small database, in general extant results support the view that hippocampal and parahippocampal regions are engaged when individuals build simulations of events located in the future, past, or present. Thus, although our focus in this chapter remains on the simulation of future events, it seems likely that ideas concerning the role of MTL regions apply more broadly to other kinds of simulations.

Another issue raised by neuroimaging studies concerns the evidence that hippocampal and parahippocampal regions can be differentially engaged by tasks requiring future event simulation compared with autobiographical remembering. Addis et al. (2007) reported that right hippocampus shows greater activity during construction of future than past events, a finding that we subsequently replicated when demonstrating that the effect occurs for specific but not general future events. In contrast, Okuda et al. (2003) reported greater future than past activity for two areas within left parahippocampal gyrus. The contrasting results suggest that interpretive caution must be exercised regarding possible difference between hippocampal and parahippocampal regions in this respect, but given that the right hippocampal effect has been replicated, and the methodological concerns noted earlier regarding the Okuda et al. (2003) study, we are inclined to assign more weight at the present time to the hippocampal than the parahippocampal finding.

We have suggested that the future greater than past activity in right hippocampus could reflect the more intensive constructive activity associated with recombining details of past events to generate a novel future event (Addis et al., 2007). Note that this effect was observed in right *anterior* hippocampus (Talairach xyz coordinate for peak voxel in Addis et al., 2007 = 40 –22 –11). This idea fits nicely with our thinking about the finding reported by Addis and Schacter (2008) during event elaboration, where activity in a left anterior hippocampal region (xyz = –20 –22 –6) correlated with the amount of detail in future but not past events, while left posterior hippocampal activity (xyz = –18 –34 1) correlated with both future and past details. This latter region is quite close to the posterior hippocampal region associated with the amount of retrieved detail in an earlier study of autobiographical memory (xyz = –20, –37, 0; Addis, Moscovitch, Crawley, & McAndrews, 2004). These observations led us to propose that the anterior hippocampal region is specifically involved in recombining details from past events, converging with our account of the future greater than past activity during construction in anterior right hippocampus.

These ideas also fit with findings from other memory paradigms. In a meta-analysis of MTL activations during encoding and retrieval, Schacter and Wagner (1999) noted evidence linking anterior hippocampal activity with relational or associative processing at both encoding and retrieval. Subsequent research has been largely consistent with this observation, as anterior regions of the hippocampus shown preferential activation in conditions requiring relational processing at both encoding (e.g., Chua, Schacter, Rand-Giovanelli, & Sperling, 2007; Giovanello, Schnyer, & Verfaellie, 2004; Jackson & Schacter, 2004; Kirwan & Stark, 2004) and retrieval (Giovanello et al., 2004; Kirwan & Stark, 2004). Recent work using functional connectivity analyses of rest fMRI data suggest that anterior and posterior hippocampus are connected with distinct cortical systems (Kahn, Andrews-Hanna, Vincent, Snyder, & Buckner, 2008).

Findings reported by Preston et al. (2004; see also Heckers, Zalesak, Weiss, Ditman, & Titone, 2004) point toward an even further possible refinement of the foregoing ideas, suggesting that left anterior hippocampal activity ($y = -22$) is associated specifically with recombining elements from previously learned associations. They used a transitive inference design in which participants first learned to associate specific faces (stimuli A) with specific houses (stimuli B), and then learned to associate another set of faces (stimuli C) with the same houses (stimuli B). Critically, the A and C faces were not shown together during training, but were related to one another through their overlapping associations with the same house (B). During scanning, correctly recognizing that the A-C face pair contained related elements significantly engaged the left anterior hippocampus relative to all other recognition conditions, including successful recognition of A-B and B-C face-house pairs as "old." By contrast, a region of left posterior hippocampus ($y = 30$) was engaged by all tasks requiring the retrieval of relational information (i.e., correct recognition of A-B, B-C, and A-C pairs). Linking these observations with the aforementioned data from Addis and Schacter (2008), perhaps both past and future events require the retrieval of some form of relational information (i.e., details that were encoded as part of a complex autobiographical memory) and commonly engage posterior hippocampus, whereas only future events require recombining such details, and thus, as in Preston et al.'s study, recruit anterior hippocampus.

The foregoing observations might be useful in thinking about one of the puzzling findings from neuroimaging research noted earlier: In contrast to other studies, Szpunar et al. (2007) did not report evidence of hippocampal activation when individuals simulated events in their personal futures, compared with when they imagined Bill Clinton participating in similar kinds of events. We suggested that both of these tasks likely involve the kind of relational processing and recombining of event details thought to elicit hippocampal activation. If so, significant hippocampal activation during each task would not be evident in a comparison between tasks.

Of course, the question of whether hippocampal regions are *necessary* for simulating future events cannot be answered by neuroimaging studies alone, which are necessarily correlational in nature. Moreover, the imaging evidence leaves open the question of whether hippocampal activity during future event simulation reflects retrieval and/or recombination of event details, as we have suggested, versus the encoding and storage of novel information. As we have stressed, future event simulations involve the constructions of novel scenarios, and the hippocampus appears to play a role in the encoding of novel events (e.g. Ranganath & Rainer, 2003). Evidence reviewed earlier indicates that impaired future event simulation in amnesic patients is consistent with the idea that the hippocampal region is indeed necessary for retrieving and/or recombining event details into a representation that supports simulation of the future. However, further studies of amnesic patients are required to understand more fully the nature and extent of their simulation deficits.

Intriguingly, several recent studies of rodents have shown that hippocampal neurons code for prospective information concerning where the rat needs to go in the immediate future (e.g., Ferbinteanu & Shapiro, 2003; Foster & Wilson, 2007; Johnson & Redish, 2007). For instance, Johnson and Redish (2007) recorded from ensembles of neurons with place fields in the CA3 region of hippocampus, allowing them to analyze activity during choices made by rats in a spatial decision task. On some trials, the spatial representation reconstructed from the neural ensemble appeared to indicate possible future paths, leading Johnson and Redish to suggest that the hippocampus may be a source of prospective memory signals. It will be important to investigate whether and to what extent such

findings are related to the observations on future event simulation in humans considered here.

Let us also consider the role of the parahippocampal region in future event simulation. As we have seen, this region is activated consistently in neuroimaging studies as part of a more general core network. Although hippocampal and parahippocampal regions generally show similar activity patterns, there are reasons to posit that they play different roles within the network. Evidence discussed earlier from Szpunar et al. (2009) suggests that the parahippocampal region (along with posterior cingulate) is important for generating familiar contexts that contribute to future event simulations. This idea fits well with the previously mentioned studies of Bar and Aminoff (2003; see also Bar, 2007), which have independently implicated the parahippocampal cortex (and posterior cingulate/retrosplenial cortex) in contextual processing. Strong evidence that the parahippocampal region contributes specifically to the generation of contextual associations comes from a recent study by Bar, Aminoff, and Schacter (2008), who showed that it responds more strongly to scenes with strong contextual associations (e.g., scenes involving objects such as a traffic light, which are strongly associated to a particular context) compared with scenes that are matched with respect to visual qualities but have weaker contextual associations (e.g., scenes involving objects such as a water bottle, which are not strongly associated with a particular context). It therefore makes both theoretical and empirical sense to suggest that the parahippocampal region may allow access to contextual associations that are recombined by the hippocampus with other kinds of event details to create a full-blown episodic simulation.

Finally, we note that the research considered here also raises important issues regarding *reality monitoring* processes that allow us to distinguish between remembered and imagined events (Johnson & Raye, 1981). If, as we have seen, remembering past events and imagining future or novel events recruit largely overlapping brain networks, including the MTL, then how do individuals distinguish mental simulations from memories of real events? There is likely no simple answer to this question (for a recent discussion, see Hassabis et al., 2007a), but we think there is a role for the well-known idea from research on reality monitoring that remembering events that one has actually experienced is associated with greater sensory and perceptual details than remembering previously imagined events (e.g., Johnson & Raye, 1981). This idea has received support from behavioral studies (e.g., Johnson, Foley, Suengas, & Raye, 1988) as well as neuroimaging research (Kensinger & Schacter, 2006; see also Slotnick & Schacter, 2004).

More directly related to the present concerns, in our previously discussed study using experimental recombination of event details (Addis et al., 2009), we found evidence suggesting the existence of distinct remembering and imagining subsystems within the core network. Remembering actual autobiographical events was preferentially associated with activity in parahippocampal cortex and posterior visual regions, whereas imagining future or past events was preferentially associated with a subsystem including anterior hippocampus. In our study, remembered events were rated as significantly more detailed than imagined events, so it would make sense from the perspective of the reality monitoring framework that regions associated with processing of sensory and contextual details would show greater activity for real than imagined events.

Although much work remains to be done, we believe that the research considered here has the potential to enrich, broaden, and perhaps alter our ideas about the nature and functions of memory, as well as our thinking about how the MTL allows us to stay connected with both the past and the future.

ACKNOWLEDGMENTS

Preparation of this chapter was support by grants from the NIMH and NIA. We thank Adrian Gilmore for help with preparation of the manuscript.

REFERENCES

Addis, D. R., Cheng, T., Roberts, R., & Schacter, D. L. (in press), Hippocampal contributions to the episodic simulation of specific and general future events. *Hippocampus.*

Addis, D. R., Moscovitch, M., Crawley, A. P., & McAndrews, M. P. (2004). Recollective qualities modulate hippocampal activation during autobiographical memory retrieval. *Hippocampus* 14, 752–762.

Addis, D. R., Pan, L., Vu, M. A., Laiser, N., & Schacter, D. L. (2009). Constructive episodic simulation of the future and the past: Distinct subsystems of a core brain network mediate imagining and remembering. *Neuropsychologia*, 47, 2222–2238.

Addis, D. R., & Schacter, D. L. (2008). Constructive episodic simulation: Temporal distance and detail of past and future events modulate hippocampal engagement. *Hippocampus*, 18, 227–237.

Addis, D. R., Wong, A. T., & Schacter, D. L. (2007). Remembering the past and imagining the future: Common and distinct neural substrates during event construction and elaboration. *Neuropsychologia*, 45, 1363–1377.

Addis, D. R., Wong, A. T., & Schacter, D. L. (2008). Age-related changes in the episodic simulation of future events. *Psychological Science*, 19, 33–41.

Bar, M. (2007). The proactive brain: Using analogies and associations to generate predictions. *Trends in Cognitive Sciences*, 11, 280–289.

Bar, M., & Aminoff, E. (2003). Cortical analysis of visual context. *Neuron*, 38, 347–358.

Bar, M., Aminoff, E., & Schacter, D. L. (2008). Scenes unseen: The parahippocampal cortex intrinsically subserves contextual associations, not scenes or places per se. *Journal of Neuroscience*, 28, 8539–8544.

Botzung, A., Denkova, E., & Manning, L. (2008). Experiencing past and future personal events: Functional neuroimaging evidence on the neural bases of mental time travel. *Brain and Cognition*, 66, 202–212.

Buckner, R. L., Andrews, J. R., & Schacter, D. L. (2008). The brain's default network: Anatomy, function, and relevance to disease. *Annals of the New York Academy of Sciences*, 1124, 1–38.

Buckner, R. L., & Carroll, D. C. (2007). Self-projection and the brain. *Trends in Cognitive Sciences*, 11, 49–57.

Cabeza, R., & St Jacques, P. (2007). Functional neuroimaging of autobiographical memory. *Trends in Cognitive Sciences*, 11, 219–227.

Chua, E. F., Schacter, D. L., Rand-Giovanelli, E., & Sperling, R. A. (2007). Evidence for a specific role of the anterior hippocampal region in successful associative encoding. *Hippocampus, 17*, 1071–1080.

D'Argembeau, A., & Van der Linden, M. (2004). Phenomenal characteristics associated with projecting oneself back into the past and forward into the future: Influence of valence and temporal distance. *Consciousness and Cognition, 13*, 844–858.

D'Argembeau, A., Xue, G., Lu, Z. L., Van der Linden, M., & Bechara, A. (2008). Neural correlates of envisioning emotional events in the near and far future. *Neuroimage, 40*, 398–407.

Driscoll, I., Hamilton, D. A., Petropoulos, H., Yeo, R. A., Brooks, W. M., Baumgarter, R. N., et al. (2003). The aging hippocampus: Cognitive, biochemical, and structural findings. *Cerebral Cortex, 13*, 1344–1351.

Dudai, Y., & Carruthers, M. (2005). The Janus face of mnemosyne. *Nature, 434*, 823–824.

Eichenbaum, H., & Cohen, N. J. (2001). *From conditioning to conscious recollection: Memory systems of the brain.* New York: Oxford University Press.

Ferbinteanu, J., & Shapiro, M. L. (2003). Prospective and retrospective memory coding in the hippocampus. *Neuron, 40*, 1227–1239.

Foster, D. J., & Wilson, M. A. (2007). Hippocampal theta sequences. *Hippocampus, 17*, 1093–1099.

Gilbert, D. T. (2006). *Stumbling on happiness.* New York: Alfred A. Knopf.

Gilbert, D. T., & Wilson, T. (2007). Prospection: Experiencing the future. *Science, 317*, 1351–1354.

Giovanello, K. S., Schnyer, D. M., & Verfaellie, M. (2004). A critical role for the anterior hippocampus in relational memory: Evidence from an fMRI study comparing associative and item recognition. *Hippocampus, 14*, 5–8.

Hassabis, D., Kumaran, D., & Maguire, E. A. (2007a). Using imagination to understand the neural basis of episodic memory. *Journal of Neuroscience, 27*, 14365–14374.

Hassabis, D., Kumaran, D., Vann, S. D., & Maguire, E. A. (2007b). Patients with hippocampal amnesia cannot imagine new experiences. *Proceedings of the National Academy of Sciences USA, 104*, 1726–1731.

Hassabis, D., & Maguire, E. A. (2007). Deconstructing episodic memory with construction. *Trends in Cognitive Sciences, 11*, 299–306.

Heckers, S., Zalesak, M., Weiss, A.P., Ditman, T., & Titone, D. (2004). Hippocampal activation during transitive inference in humans. *Hippocampus, 14*, 153–162.

Jackson, O., & Schacter, D. L. (2004). Encoding activity in anterior medial temporal lobe supports associative recognition. *Neuroimage, 21*, 456–464.

Johnson, A., & Redish, A. D. (2007). Neural ensembles in CA3 transiently encode paths forward of the animal at a decision point. *Journal of Neuroscience, 27*, 12176–12189.

Johnson, M. K., Foley, M. A., Suengas, A. G., & Raye, C. L. (1988). Phenomenal characteristics of memories for perceived and imagined autobiographical events. *Journal of Experimental Psychology: General, 117*, 371–376.

Johnson, M. K., & Raye, C. L. (1981). Reality monitoring. *Psychological Review, 88*, 67–85.

Kahn, I., Andrews-Hanna, J. R., Vincent, J. L., Snyder, A. Z., & Buckner, R. L. (2008). Distinct cortical anatomy linked to subregions of the medial temporal lobe revealed by intrinsic functional connectivity. *Journal of Neurophysiology, 100*, 129–139.

Kensinger, E. A., & Schacter, D. L. (2006). Neural processes underlying memory attribution on a reality-monitoring task. *Cerebral Cortex, 16*, 1126–1133.

Kirwan, C. B., & Stark, C. E. (2004). Medial temporal lobe activation during encoding and retrieval of novel face-name pairs. *Hippocampus, 14*, 919–930.

Klein, S. B., Loftus, J., & Kihlstrom, J. F. (2002). Memory and temporal experience: The effects of episodic memory loss in an amnesic patient's ability to remember the past and imagine the future. *Social Cognition, 20*, 353–379.

Levine, B., Svoboda, E., Hay, J. F., Winocur, G., & Moscovitch, M. (2002). Aging and autobiographical memory: Dissociating episodic from semantic retrieval. *Psychology of Aging, 17*, 677–689.

Okuda, J., Fujii, T., Ohtake, H., Tsukiura, T., Tanji, K., Suzuki, K., et al. (2003). Thinking of the future and the past: The roles of the frontal pole and the medial temporal lobes. *Neuroimage, 19*, 1369–1380.

Preston, A. R., Shrager, Y., Dudukovic, N. M., & Gabrieli, J. D. (2004). Hippocampal contribution to the novel use of relational information in declarative memory. *Hippocampus, 14*, 148–152.

Ranganath, C., & Rainer, G. (2003). Neural mechanisms for detecting and remembering novel events. *Nature Reviews Neuroscience, 4*, 193–202.

Rosenbaum, R. S., Kohler, S., Schacter, D. L., Moscovitch, M., Westmacott, R., Black, S. E., et al. (2005). The case of K.C.: Contributions of a memory-impaired person to memory theory. *Neuropsychologia*, *43*, 989–1021.

Rosenbaum, R. S., Stuss, D. T., Levine, B., & Tulving, E. (2007). Theory of mind is independent of episodic memory. *Science*, *318*, 1257.

Schacter, D. L., & Addis, D. R. (2007a). The cognitive neuroscience of constructive memory: Remembering the past and imagining the future. *Philosophical Transactions of the Royal Society B: Biological Sciences*, *362*, 773–786.

Schacter, D. L., & Addis, D. R. (2007b). The ghosts of past and future. *Nature*, *445*, 27.

Schacter, D. L., Addis, D. R., & Buckner, R. L. (2007). Remembering the past to imagine the future: The prospective brain. *National Review of Neuroscience*, *8*, 657–661.

Schacter, D. L., Addis, D. R., & Buckner, R. L. (2008). Episodic simulation of future events: Concepts, data, and applications. *Annals of the New York Academy of Science*, *1124*, 39–60.

Schacter, D. L., & Wagner, A. D. (1999). Medial temporal lobe activations in fMRI and PET studies of episodic encoding and retrieval. *Hippocampus*, *9*, 7–24.

Slotnick, S. D., & Schacter, D. L. (2004). A sensory signature that distinguishes true from false memories. *Nature Neuroscience*, *7*, 664–672.

Spreng, R. N., Mar, R. A., & Kim, A. S. N. (2009). The common neural basis of autobiographical memory, prospection, navigation, theory of mind, and the default mode: A quantitative meta-analysis. *Journal of Cognitive Neuroscience*, *21*, 489–510.

Suddendorf, T., & Corballis, M. C. (1997). Mental time travel and the evolution of the human mind. *Genetic, Social, and General Psychology Monographs*, *123*, 133–167.

Suddendorf, T., & Corballis, M. C. (2007). The evolution of foresight: What is mental time travel and is it unique to humans? *Behavioral and Brain Science*, *30*, 299–313.

Svoboda, E., McKinnon, M. C., & Levine, B. (2006). The functional neuroanatomy of autobiographical memory: A meta-analysis. *Neuropsychologia*, *44*, 2189–2208.

Szpunar, K. K., Chan, C. K., & McDermott, K. B. (2009). Contextual processing in episodic future thought. *Cerebral Cortex*, *19*, 1539–1548.

Szpunar, K. K., Watson, J. M., & McDermott, K. B. (2007). Neural substrates of envisioning the future. *Proceedings of the National Academy of Sciences USA*, *104*, 642–647.

Tulving, E. (1985). Memory and consciousness. *Canadian Psychologist*, *26*, 1–12.

CHAPTER 6
The Construction System of the Brain

Demis Hassabis and Eleanor A. Maguire

The recollection of episodic memories is widely accepted to be a reconstructive process as opposed to the simple retrieval of a perfect holistic record (Bartlett, 1932; Conway & Pleydell-Pearce, 2000; Hassabis & Maguire, 2007; Rubin, Schrauf, & Greenberg, 2003; Schacter, Addis, & Buckner, 2008; Schacter, Norman, & Koutstaal, 1998). Recollection relies on a number of component processes. These include a sense of subjective time (Tulving, 2002), connection to the self (Conway & Pleydell-Pearce, 2000; Gallagher, 2000), narrative structure (Rubin et al., 2003), retrieval of relevant semantic information (Gottfried, Smith, Rugg, & Dolan, 2004; Wheeler, Petersen, & Buckner, 2000; Wheeler, Stuss, & Tulving, 1997), feelings of familiarity (Wagner et al., 2005), and rich multimodal re-experiencing of the event (Tulving, 2002) in a coherent spatial context (Bird & Burgess, 2008; Byrne, Becker, & Burgess, 2007; Hassabis, Kumaran, Vann, & Maguire, 2007b; Hassabis & Maguire, 2007). From functional magnetic resonance imaging (fMRI) studies we also know that a distributed and highly consistent network of brain regions supports memory for past experiences. This comprises dorsal and ventromedial prefrontal cortex (PFC), lateral prefrontal cortex, the hippocampus, parahippocampal gyrus, lateral temporal cortices, temporo-parietal junction, thalamus, retrosplenial cortex (RSC), posterior cingulate cortex (PCC), precuneus, and cerebellum (Cabeza & St Jacques, 2007; Hassabis, Kumaran, & Maguire, 2007a; Maguire, 2001a; Maguire & Frith, 2003; Svoboda, McKinnon, & Levine, 2006)

(see Fig. 6.1). Despite over a decade of activating this network, however, surprisingly little is understood about the contributions individual brain areas make to the overall recollective experience (Hassabis & Maguire, 2007).

Taking a different approach, several recent fMRI studies compared recall of autobiographical memories with predicting possible personally relevant future events (known as episodic future thinking [EFT]; Atance & O'Neill, 2001) and found near-complete overlap in the brain networks activated (Botzung, Denkova, & Manning, 2008; Okuda et al., 2003; Szpunar, Watson, & McDermott, 2007; but see Addis, Wong, & Schacter, 2007). In terms of characterizing underlying processes and their mapping to specific brain regions, however, it is clear from these studies that only limited further progress can be made by using EFT as a comparison task because it engages all of the same processes as episodic memory and to a similar degree (Schacter, Addis, & Buckner, 2007; Suddendorf & Corballis, 1997). Here we suggest that in the context of real-world experiences, a productive way to investigate recollection of the past and prediction of the future is, ironically, not to study the past or the future at all. We argue that because the core processes underlying prediction of the future can be co-opted by a range of other atemporal cognitive functions, these processes may be best isolated and understood in the context of paradigms where time is not an explicit factor, such as imagining fictitious experiences. We believe that time does not merit elevation to the level of an

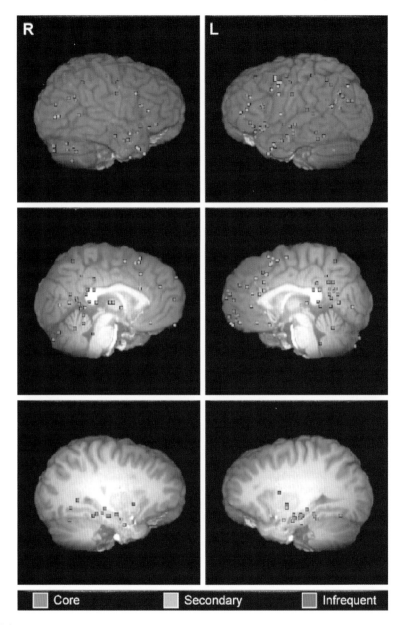

Figure 6.1 The episodic memory network. Significant peaks of activity from a meta-analysis of 24 neuroimaging studies of autobiographical memory (Svoboda et al., 2006). The classic core episodic memory network can be seen in red and includes the hippocampus bilaterally, parahippocampal gyrus, retrosplenial, posterior cingulate and posterior parietal cortices, and medial prefrontal cortex. Activations in core, secondary, and infrequently reported regions are depicted across right and left, lateral, medial, and subcortical planes. (Reprinted from Svoboda et al., 2006, with permission from Elsevier.)

independent process with a distinct neural signature. Instead we view the timestamp of an event (whether future or past) as simply the result of a content or goal difference rather than a change in the fundamental processes involved (see Hassabis & Maguire, 2007). To test this idea, it has been necessary to develop novel experimental paradigms.

Using imagination

Recently, one important tool in the development of novel tasks has been imagination (Hassabis & Maguire, 2007). In many ways imagining new experiences can be regarded as the purest expression of construction. All healthy volunteers can effortlessly use their imagination to a basic degree (indeed humans have told stories and delighted in fiction and narrative for thousands of years), and verbally induced imagination of scenes has been shown to be possible and useful in the neuropsychological context (Bisiach & Luzzatti, 1978). Experiences constructed by the imagination, while having much in common with episodic memories, have the advantage of being easier to systematize and experimentally manipulate (Hassabis & Maguire, 2007). For example, participants can be asked to construct the same fictitious situations, and their performances can be compared and contrasted more directly than would be possible in a standard episodic memory recall paradigm (Hassabis et al., 2007b).

Crucially, tasks involving imagined scenarios can be designed to de-emphasize key features, allowing insights to be gained into the neural substrates of these features when compared with episodic memories (Hassabis et al., 2007a). For example, participants can be asked to construct fictitious experiences in their imagination that are atemporal (i.e., not set in the past or in the future) and with a low connection to the self. Figure 6.2a shows a description of one such imagined experience (Hassabis et al., 2007a). It is interesting to contrast this transcript with one from an fMRI study involving plans for a future personal experience (Addis et al., 2007) (Fig. 6.2b). Clearly the imagined scenario is set in the present and in this case does not have the same

involvement with the imaginer's self-schema as the personal future event (Conway & Pleydell-Pearce, 2000; Gallagher, 2000) although both types of scenario involve the adoption of an egocentric viewpoint on the part of the imaginer (Burgess, 2006). Being able to manipulate factors such as the level of self-relevance/involvement and the degree of overlap between memories and imagined experiences has the potential to progress our understanding of the core processes and brain areas involved (Hassabis & Maguire, 2007).

To this end we designed a novel imagination task that involved participants richly imagining new fictitious experiences (Hassabis et al., 2007b). We reasoned that if episodic memory recall was truly a reconstructive process (Bartlett, 1932; Schacter et al., 1998), with a memory reassembled from its stored constituent components, then some of these integrative processes should also be co-opted by a purely constructive task involving imagination (Hassabis et al., 2007b). We tested patients with primary damage to the hippocampus bilaterally as this structure is well known to be critical in supporting episodic memory (Scoville & Milner, 1957). We found that, as well as being impaired at recalling the past, the patients were not able to richly imagine new experiences. This was the case for EFT scenarios (see also Klein, Loftus, & Kihlstrom, 2002; Rosenbaum et al., 2005) and, crucially, for constructions that were atemporal and low in self-relevance. Even when all the components necessary to construct a fictitious experience were supplied in the form of visual elements, sounds, and smells, patients' performance did not improve (Hassabis et al., 2007b). The source of their deficit was an inability to integrate the imagined experience into a coherent whole manifesting itself most obviously in the discontinuity of the spatial context. We concluded that the hippocampus plays a critical role in imagination by binding together the disparate elements of an event or scene (Cohen & Eichenbaum, 1993; O'Keefe & Nadel, 1978).

If the hippocampus plays a critical integrative role in a constructive process such as imagination, it seems plausible that it might also have a similar role in supporting the rich recollection of

---

(a) Imagined fictitious experience

Cue: Imagine standing by a small stream somewhere deep in a forest

"It's a pine forest. What I can see on the ground all around me are patches of pine needles and brown earth with nothing really growing. The tree trunks are quite narrow. Overhead are the spikes of the green pines and you can only just see the sky. There's a pine needle smell but down towards the stream there's a slightly rotting smell. It's quite a narrow stream with stones in it and dark water rushing round them causing little white water eddies. There's not much life around the stream and the banks are quite steep sloping down to the stream. It's peaceful and quiet..."

(b) Episodic future thinking

Timescale: 5 years in future; Cue: Dress

"My sister will be finishing... her undergraduate education, I imagine some neat place, Ivy League private school... it would be a very nice spring day and my mom and my dad will be there, my dad with the camcorder as usual, and my mom with the camera as usual. My sister will be in the crowd and they'd be calling everyone's name... I can see her having a different hair style by then, maybe instead of straight, very curly with lots of volume. She would be wearing contacts by then and heels of course. And I can see myself sitting in some kind of sundress, like yellow, and under some trees... the reception either before or after and it would be really nice summer food, like salads and fruits, and maybe some sweets, and cold drinks that are chilled but have no ice. And my sister would be sitting off with her friends, you know, talking with them about graduating, and they'd probably get emotional."

Figure 6.2 Descriptions of experiences. Representative examples of participant transcripts when cued to describe (*a*) an imagined fictitious experience (data from Hassabis et al., 2007a) and (*b*) a personally relevant future experience (data from Addis et al., 2007). Note the absence of explicit temporal and self-relevant statements in (*a*) that are commonplace in (*b*), such as "I will be" and "my sister is there."

episodic memories and in predicting the future (Hassabis et al., 2007b). It has long been known that the hippocampus is required to initially encode the memory of an ongoing event (Scoville & Milner, 1957). The traditional view of memory posits that over time these memories are consolidated to the neocortex, which is then able to support the recall of remote memories independently from the hippocampus (Squire, Stark, & Clark, 2004). Conversely, other accounts (Cipolotti et al., 2001; Maguire, Nannery, & Spiers, 2006; Moscovitch et al., 2005; Murray & Bussey, 2001; Sanders & Warrington, 1971), supported by the results of the majority of fMRI studies on episodic memory (Maguire, 2001a; Svoboda et al., 2006), have suggested that the hippocampus is always required for rich episodic memory recall irrespective of memory age. Various patient studies have been unable to arbitrate between these two positions largely due to disparate testing protocols, patient etiologies, and scoring systems (Kirwan, Bayley, Galvan, & Squire, 2008;

Levine, Svoboda, Hay, Winocur, & Moscovitch, 2002; Moscovitch et al., 2005). It has been suggested that discrepancies between studies of remote episodic memory in hippocampal-damaged patients (Bayley, Hopkins, & Squire, 2003) might be accounted for by differences in the quality or richness of the recollective experience (Gilboa, Winocur, Grady, Hevenor, & Moscovitch, 2004), a feature that is not always captured by existing scoring systems (Hassabis, Kumaran, Vann, & Maguire, 2007b; Kopelman, Wilson, & Baddeley, 1989).

Considering the aforementioned extant literature and now also the findings from our imagination study (Hassabis et al., 2007b), we suggest that the hippocampus may have two distinct functions in episodic memory recall. Furthermore, we propose that such a dual role may help to resolve the long-standing debate about the timescale of hippocampal involvement in episodic memory. First, the hippocampus may be the initial location for the memory index

(Marr, 1971), which reinstantiates the active set of contextual details (Polyn & Kahana, 2008; Polyn, Natu, Cohen, & Norman, 2005; Wheeler et al., 2000) and later might be consolidated out of the hippocampus (Squire et al., 2004). Second, the hippocampus may have another role as an online integrator supporting the binding of these reactivated components into a coherent whole to facilitate the rich recollection of a past episodic memory, regardless of its age. Such a function would be of great use also for imagination, navigation, and predicting the future.

Further empirical evidence hinting at a two-process function of the hippocampus comes from structural MRI studies of expert navigators (London taxi drivers) who show increased gray matter volume in posterior hippocampus seemingly at the expense of reduced gray matter volume in anterior hippocampus (Maguire, Woollett, & Spiers, 2006). Moreover, their increased spatial knowledge appears to come at a cost to the acquisition of new visual associative information (Maguire, Woollett, et al., 2006; Woollett & Maguire, 2009). The hippocampus is ideally placed to support these two roles both in terms of the diversity of its multisensory inputs and its specific anatomical properties (Andersen, Morris, Amaral, Bliss, & O'Keefe, 2007), such as the high number of recurrent connections, although clearly more work is required to categorically ascertain whether the hippocampus is performing more than one function in episodic memory recall.

THE CONSTRUCTION SYSTEM

Although critically reliant on the hippocampus, the (re)constructive process is not supported by it alone. We sought to characterize the entire construction network by using fMRI to compare imagination with episodic memory recall (Hassabis et al., 2007a). Healthy participants engaged in three tasks while in the scanner: *(1)* vivid recall of recent real memories, *(2)* vivid recall of previously created imaginary experiences, and *(3)* construction of new imaginary experiences for the first time in the scanner. Recall of recent autobiographical memories activated the now classic network shown

in Figure 6.1 (Maguire, 2001a; Svoboda et al., 2006). Interestingly, imagined experiences were associated with increased activity in many of the same brain areas (Fig. 6.3). A conjunction analysis was performed to examine the brain regions activated in common by the three conditions. A distributed brain network was implicated involving the hippocampus, parahippocampal gyrus, RSC, posterior parietal cortices, middle temporal cortices, and ventromedial PFC (Fig. 6.4). This construction network can not only account for a large part of the episodic memory recall network (Fig. 6.1) and EFT (Addis et al., 2007; Botzung, Denkova, & Manning, 2008; Szpunar et al., 2007), but it also bears a striking resemblance to networks activated by navigation (Burgess, Maguire, & O'Keefe, 2002; Maguire, 2001b), spatial (Kumaran & Maguire, 2005; Maguire, Valentine, Wilding, & Kapur, 2003), and place tasks (Epstein & Kanwisher, 1998; Sugiura, Shah, Zilles, & Fink, 2005) as well as those associated with mind wandering (Mason et al., 2007) and the default network (Buckner, Andrews-Hanna, & Schacter, 2008; Raichle et al., 2001). This suggests there may be a set of key component processes underlying all of these cognitive functions (Buckner & Carroll, 2007; Hassabis & Maguire, 2007; Spreng, Mar, & Kim, 2009).

We have suggested that these common processes can be characterized by the concept of scene construction (Hassabis & Maguire, 2007). Scene or event construction involves the mental generation and maintenance of a complex and coherent scene or event. This is achieved by the reactivation, retrieval, and integration of relevant semantic, contextual, and sensory components, stored in their modality-specific cortical areas (Wheeler et al., 2000), the product of which has a coherent spatial context (Hassabis et al., 2007b) and can then later be manipulated and visualized. In fact, scene construction is a specific example of "associative construction," which involves visual imagery, binding, and also disparate multimodal elements that, when bound together, (re-)create an event as a whole. This includes contextual details such as sounds and smells in addition to visual inputs, people, objects, entities, and their actions.

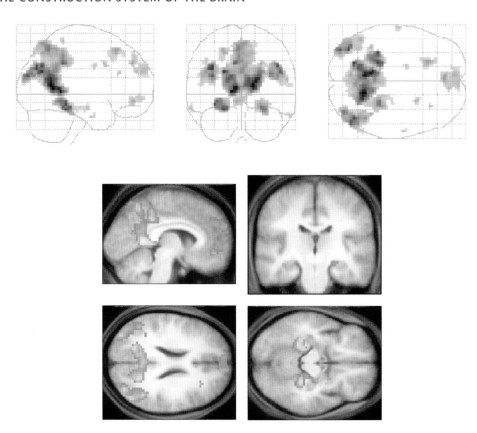

Figure 6.3 The imagination network. Brain regions active when recalling imagined fictitious experiences that were previously created in a prescan interview included the hippocampus, parahippocampal gyrus, retrosplenial and posterior parietal cortices, and medial prefrontal cortex. The top panels show sagittal, coronal, and axial images from a "glass brain," which enables one to appreciate activations in all locations and levels in the brain simultaneously. The bottom panels show activations on a selection of relevant sagittal, coronal, and axial sections from the averaged structural magnetic resonance image (MRI) scan of the 21 study participants at a threshold of $p < 0.001$ uncorrected (data from Hassabis et al., 2007a).

Scene construction differs markedly from "simple" visual imagery such as that for single objects (Kosslyn, Gannis, & Thompson, 2001) in that it requires the flexible association and integration of many scene elements. Our fMRI study also included tasks requiring vivid visualization of acontextual single objects as a baseline task (Hassabis et al., 2007a). Recalling previously seen or previously imagined objects, or imagining objects for the first time in the scanner, resulted in activation of brain areas associated with supporting object representations and manipulations, namely lateral occipital complex and intraparietal sulcus (e.g. Sugiura et al., 2005)

(see Fig. 6.5). Moreover, there was no overlap between this simple object network (Sugiura et al., 2005) and that of complex scene construction (Hassabis et al., 2007a), suggesting they represent dissociable cognitive processes with distinct neural bases. Nevertheless, complex scenes and experiences are clearly constructed out of simpler elements (Summerfield, Hassabis, & Maguire 2010). It has been suggested that past and future experiences draw on information stored in episodic memory (Schacter et al., 2007; Schacter et al., 2008). However, we argue that the component elements of constructions are not simply fragments of past events; rather, they can

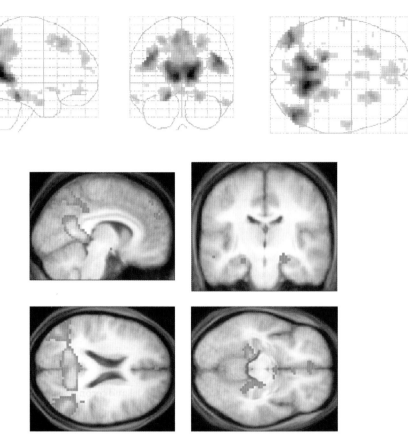

Figure 6.4 The construction system. This conjunction analysis shows the brain regions activated in common by three tasks: recall of recent real memories, recall of previously imagined experiences, and the construction of imaginary scenarios for the first time in the scanner. This network of areas is likely involved in scene or event construction, the primary process these three conditions have in common. This construction network included hippocampus bilaterally, parahippocampal gyrus, retrospenial and posterior parietal cortices, middle temporal cortices, and medial prefrontal cortex. Views of this distributed brain network are also shown in the lower panels on a selection of relevant sagittal, coronal, and axial sections from the averaged structural MRI scan of the 21 study participants at a threshold of $p < 0.001$ uncorrected (data from Hassabis et al. 2007a).

comprise elements that are more abstracted and semantic, such as the sound of ocean waves crashing on the shore or the face of your best friend, and potentially learned over and shared across multiple episodic memories.

Alternatives to scene construction have been proposed (Buckner & Carroll, 2007; Schacter & Addis, 2007; Schacter et al., 2008). Like scene construction, the process of "self-projection" (Buckner & Carroll, 2007) defined as "the shifting of the self to alternative perspectives in time or space" has been posited as an underlying

process common to a set of disparate cognitive functions, including episodic memory recall, EFT, and navigation. However, while self-projection is clearly an important concept, it conflates several distinct component processes, including scene construction (Hassabis & Maguire, 2007) and theory of mind (Amodio & Frith, 2006). For the purposes of teasing apart the various component processes underpinning episodic memory, we suggest it is advantageous to consider constituent processes in as reduced a form as possible. Thus, we believe the construction network is

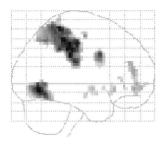
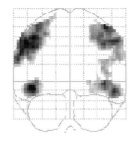
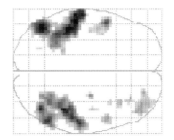
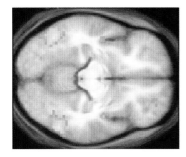
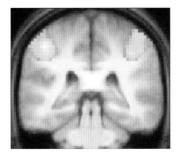

Figure 6.5 **Neural correlates of recalling single objects. These are the brain areas activated more for recalling (real or imagined) single objects than for complex experiences, and they include the lateral occipital complex bilaterally, intraparietal sulcus bilaterally, and right lateral prefrontal cortex. Views of these brain regions are also shown in the lower panels on axial and coronal sections from the averaged structural MRI scan of the 21 subjects, at a threshold of $p < 0.001$ uncorrected (data from Hassabis et al., 2007a).**

most accurately characterized as being invoked whenever attention is directed away from the current external situation and instead focused inward toward a rich internal representation of an event, whether real or imagined. Processes such as theory of mind are only engaged if required, that is, in the case of EFT or episodic memory recall but not necessarily in imagination or navigation. This may explain why the construction network has a similar pattern of activity to that associated with the default network (Buckner et al., 2008; Raichle et al., 2001) and mind wandering (Mason et al., 2007), cognitive functions that involve minimal external stimuli combined with introspection and rich internal imagery. These constructed scenes or events, created and maintained by the construction network, can then be manipulated further by other processes, such as theory of mind, to allow shifting of the self to alternative perspectives in space or subjective

time (Arzy, Molnar-Szakacs, & Blanke, 2008; Buckner & Carroll, 2007).

ADD-ONS TO THE CONSTRUCTION SYSTEM

We have demonstrated that scene construction is a dissociable set of processes supporting the episodic memory system (Hassabis et al., 2007a), both past and future, but what are some of the other processes that together with the construction system underpin the special properties of episodic memory? We addressed this question using our fMRI imagination paradigm by contrasting the recall of real memories to the recall of previously created imaginary memories matched for difficulty, age, detail, and vividness, thus partialling out the effects of the common construction network (Hassabis et al., 2007a). Three distinct areas were more active for real compared to imaginary memories, the anterior medial PFC, PCC, and the precuneus (Fig. 6.6).

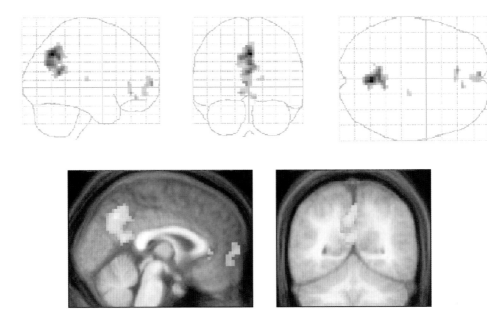

Figure 6.6 Comparison of real and imagined memories. Contrast showing brain regions more active for the recall of real memories compared to the recall of imaginary memories matched for difficulty, age, vividness, and detail. This revealed three well-defined regions preferentially engaged for real memories: precuneus, posterior cingulate cortex, and anterior medial prefrontal cortex (Brodmann's area 10). Views of these brain regions are also shown in the lower panels on a sagittal and coronal section from the averaged structural MRI scan of the 21 study participants at a threshold of *p* < 0.001 uncorrected (data from Hassabis et al., 2007a).

The precuneus has been implicated in studies of recognition memory with increased activity in response to familiar items (Hornberger, Rugg, & Henson, 2006; Rugg, Otten, & Henson, 2002; Vincent et al., 2006; Wagner, Shannon, Kahn, & Buckner, 2005). Therefore, the increased precuneus activity here likely reflects the relatively greater familiarity of the visualized experience for real memories over more novel imaginary memories, given that we controlled for vividness. Activation in anterior medial PFC and PCC is consistent with studies of self-reflection (Johnson et al., 2002) and theory of mind (Amodio & Frith, 2006; Kumaran & Maguire, 2005), suggesting that these two regions support processes related to the self. Together, then, we suggest that during episodic memory retrieval, the interaction or cooperation between the self-processing and familiarity functions performed by the anterior medial PFC/PCC and precuneus, respectively, may be sufficient to distinguish between

real and fictitious memories. Further work examining these brain areas and their roles in supporting the "selfness" and "realness" of memories and constructions are clearly required and are beginning to emerge (Abraham, von Cramon, & Schubotz, 2008; Summerfield, Hassabis, & Maguire, 2009). It should be noted that while we have proposed that intact self-reflection and theory of mind processes are also recruited in addition to scene construction to support episodic memory, this does not imply that the episodic memory system as a whole is required for the operation of any individual component process. This erroneous logic was applied recently in a study showing, not surprisingly, that a patient with amnesia retained intact theory of mind abilities (Rosenbaum, Stuss, Levine, & Tulving, 2007).

In summary, as a first approximation at the process level, episodic memory and prediction of self-relevant future events rely on scene construction, self-connection, and familiarity processes, supported by at least two sets of distinct and dissociable brain networks, in addition to general attentional and control/monitoring processes performed by parietal and frontal regions, respectively.

CONCLUSION

The scene construction network highlighted here supports the construction system of the brain allowing for the internal rehearsal of events or scenes. Scene construction underpins the process of creating a setting in which a simulated event can unfold whether past, present, future, atemporal, or hypothetical. Undoubtedly we still have a long way to go to understand exactly how scenes and events are constructed, as well as the precise role of each brain area in the system. Nevertheless, it is clear that the ability to pre-experience hypothetical events confers an evolutionary advantage in planning for the future. Consider an organism that, in its present situation, is confronted by several choices of what to do next. Being able to accurately and richly enact possible future states mentally before making a decision would help to evaluate the desirability of different outcomes and also the planning processes needed to make them happen.

In humans the utilization of this constructive process goes far beyond simply predicting the future, to the general evaluation of fitness for purpose. For example, a scriptwriter or novelist who is writing a passage in a film or book may play out the whole scene using his or her construction system, not with the idea of predicting the future, but instead for the purpose of evaluating its aesthetic suitability. Similarly an engineer might approach the problem of designing the features of a new household product by envisaging how it would be used by someone in the home. Again, the use of construction is not for future prediction per se but to facilitate evaluation judgments of general fitness for purpose of a tool. The construction process, the ability to flexibly recombine stored information in novel ways, in conjunction with evaluation functions attuned to assess fitness and possibly mediated in some instances by the emotional system (D'Argembeau, Xue, Lu, Van der Linden, & Bechara, 2008; Gilbert & Wilson, 2007; Sharot, Riccardi, Raio, & Phelps, 2007), arguably sits near the apex of human intellectual abilities. This allows humans to be limitlessly creative and inventive, even though constrained by a basic set of raw component elements gleaned over a lifetime of experiences.

ACKNOWLEDGMENTS

This work was supported by the Wellcome Trust and the Brain Research Trust.

REFERENCES

Abraham, A., von Cramon, D. Y., & Schubotz, R. I. (2008). Meeting George Bush versus meeting Cinderella: The neural response when telling apart what is real from what is fictional in the context of our reality. *Journal of Cognitive Neuroscience, 20,* 965–976.

Addis, D. R., Wong, A. T., & Schacter, D. L. (2007). Remembering the past and imagining the future: Common and distinct neural substrates during event construction and elaboration. *Neuropsychologia, 45,* 1363–1377.

Amodio, D. M., & Frith, C. D. (2006). Meeting of minds: The medial frontal cortex and social cognition. *Nature Reviews Neuroscience, 7,* 268–277.

Andersen, P., Morris, R., Amaral, D. G., Bliss, T., & O'Keefe, J. (2007). *The hippocampus book.* New York: Oxford University Press.

Arzy, S., Molnar-Szakacs, I., & Blanke, O. (2008). Self in time: Imagined self-location influences neural activity related to mental time travel. *Journal of Neuroscience, 28,* 6502–6507.

Atance, C. M., & O'Neill, D. K. (2001). Episodic future thinking. *Trends in Cognitive Sciences, 5,* 533–539.

Bartlett, F. C. (1932). *Remembering.* Cambridge, England: Cambridge University Press.

Bayley, P. J., Hopkins, R. O., & Squire, L. R. (2003). Successful recollection of remote autobiographical memories by amnesic patients with medial temporal lobe lesions. *Neuron, 38,* 135–144.

Bird, C. M., & Burgess, N. (2008). The hippocampus and memory: Insights from spatial processing. *Nature Reviews Neuroscience, 9,* 182–194.

Bisiach, E., & Luzzatti, C. (1978). Unilateral neglect of representational space. *Cortex, 14,* 129–133.

Botzung, A., Denkova, E., & Manning, L. (2008). Experiencing past and future personal events: Functional neuroimaging evidence on the neural bases of mental time travel. *Brain and Cognition, 66,* 202–212.

Buckner, R. L., Andrews-Hanna, J. R., & Schacter, D. L. (2008). The brain's default network: Anatomy, function, and relevance to disease. *Annals of the New York Academy of Science, 1124,* 1–38.

Buckner, R. L., & Carroll, D. C. (2007). Self-projection and the brain. *Trends in Cognitive Sciences, 11,* 49–57.

Burgess, N. (2006). Spatial memory: How egocentric and allocentric combine. *Trends in Cognitive Sciences, 10,* 551–557.

Burgess, N., Maguire, E. A., & O'Keefe, J. (2002). The human hippocampus and spatial and episodic memory. *Neuron, 35,* 625–641.

Byrne, P., Becker, S., & Burgess, N. (2007). Remembering the past and imagining the future: A neural model of spatial memory and imagery. *Psychological Review, 114,* 340–375.

Cabeza, R., & St Jacques, P. (2007). Functional neuroimaging of autobiographical memory. *Trends in Cognitive Sciences, 11,* 219–227.

Cipolotti, L., Shallice, T., Chan, D., Fox, N., Scahill, R., Harrison, G., Stevens, J., & Rudge, P. (2001). Long-term retrograde amnesia: The crucial role of the hippocampus. *Neuropsychologia, 39,* 151–172.

Cohen, N. J., & Eichenbaum, H. (1993). *Memory, amnesia and the hippocampal system.* Cambridge, MA: MIT Press.

Conway, M. A., & Pleydell-Pearce, C. W. (2000). The construction of autobiographical memories in the self-memory system. *Psychological Review, 107,* 261–288.

D'Argembeau, A., Xue, G., Lu, Z. L., Van der Linden, M., & Bechara, A. (2008). Neural correlates of envisioning emotional events in the near and far future. *Neuroimage, 40,* 398–407.

Epstein, R., & Kanwisher, N. (1998). A cortical representation of the local visual environment. *Nature, 392,* 598–601.

Gallagher, S. (2000). Philosophical conceptions of the self: implications for cognitive science. *Trends in Cognitive Sciences, 4,* 14–21.

Gilbert, D. T., & Wilson, T. D. (2007). Prospection: Experiencing the future. *Science, 317,* 1351–1354.

Gilboa, A., Winocur, G., Grady, C. L., Hevenor, S. J., & Moscovitch, M. (2004). Remembering our past: Functional neuroanatomy of recollection of recent and very remote personal events. *Cerebral Cortex, 14,* 1214–1225.

Gottfried, J. A., Smith, A. P., Rugg, M. D., & Dolan, R. J. (2004). Remembrance of odors past: Human olfactory cortex in cross-modal recognition memory. *Neuron, 42,* 687–695.

Hassabis, D., Kumaran, D., & Maguire, E. A. (2007a). Using imagination to understand the neural basis of episodic memory. *Journal of Neuroscience, 27,* 14365–14374.

Hassabis, D., Kumaran, D., Vann, S. D., & Maguire, E. A. (2007b). Patients with hippocampal amnesia cannot imagine new experiences. *Proceedings of the National Academy of Sciences USA, 104,* 1726–1731.

Hassabis, D., & Maguire, E. A. (2007). Deconstructing episodic memory with construction. *Trends in Cognitive Sciences, 11,* 299–306.

Hornberger, M., Rugg, M. D., & Henson, R. N. (2006). fMRI correlates of retrieval orientation. *Neuropsychologia, 44,* 1425–1436.

Johnson, S. C., Baxter, L. C., Wilder, L. S., Pipe, J. G., Heiserman, J. E., & Prigatano, G. P. (2002). Neural correlates of self-reflection. *Brain, 125,* 1808–1814.

Kirwan, C. B., Bayley, P. J., Galvan, V. V., & Squire, L. R. (2008). Detailed recollection of remote autobiographical memory after damage to the medial temporal lobe. *Proceedings of the National Academy of Sciences USA, 105,* 2676–2680.

Klein, S. B., Loftus, J., & Kihlstrom, J. F. (2002). Memory and temporal experience: The effects of episodic memory loss on an amnesic patient's ability to remember the past and imagine the future. *Social Cognition, 20,* 353–379.

Kopelman, M. D., Wilson, B. A., & Baddeley, A. D. (1989). The autobiographical memory interview: A new assessment of autobiographical and personal semantic memory in amnesic patients. *Journal of Clinical and Experimental Neuropsychology, 11,* 724–744.

Kosslyn, S. M., Ganis, G., & Thompson, W. L. (2001). Neural foundations of imagery. *Nature Reviews Neuroscience, 2,* 635–642.

Kumaran, D., & Maguire, E. A. (2005). The human hippocampus: Cognitive maps or relational memory? *Journal of Neuroscience, 25,* 7254–7259.

Levine, B., Svoboda, E., Hay, J. F., Winocur, G., & Moscovitch, M. (2002). Aging and autobiographical memory: Dissociating episodic from semantic retrieval. *Psychology and Aging, 17,* 677–689.

Maguire, E. A. (2001a). Neuroimaging studies of autobiographical event memory. *Philosophical Transactions of the Royal Society London B: Biological Sciences, 356*, 1441–1451.

Maguire, E. A. (2001b). The retrosplenial contribution to human navigation: A review of lesion and neuroimaging findings. *Scandinavian Journal of Psychology, 42*, 225–238.

Maguire, E. A., & Frith, C. D. (2003). Aging affects the engagement of the hippocampus during autobiographical memory retrieval. *Brain, 126*, 1511–1523.

Maguire, E. A., Nannery, R., & Spiers, H. J. (2006). Navigation around London by a taxi driver with bilateral hippocampal lesions. *Brain, 129*, 2894–2907.

Maguire, E. A., Valentine, E. R., Wilding, J. M., & Kapur, N. (2003). Routes to remembering: The brains behind superior memory. *Nature Neuroscience, 6*, 90–95.

Maguire, E. A., Woollett, K., & Spiers, H. J. (2006). London taxi drivers and bus drivers: A structural MRI and neuropsychological analysis. *Hippocampus, 16*, 1091–1101.

Marr, D. (1971). Simple memory: A theory for archicortex. *Philosophical Transactions of the Royal Society of London B: Biological Sciences, 262*, 23–81.

Mason, M. F., Norton, M. I., Van Horn, J. D., Wegner, D. M., Grafton, S. T., & Macrae, C. N. (2007). Wandering minds: The default network and stimulus-independent thought. *Science, 315*, 393–395.

Moscovitch, M., Rosenbaum, R. S., Gilboa, A., Addis, D. R., Westmacott, R., Grady, C., McAndrews, M. P., Levine, B., Black, S., Winocur, G., & Nadel, L. (2005). Functional neuroanatomy of remote episodic, semantic and spatial memory: A unified account based on multiple trace theory. *Journal of Anatomy, 207*, 35–66.

Murray, E. A., & Bussey, T. J. (2001). Consolidation and the medial temporal lobe revisited: Methodological considerations. *Hippocampus, 11*, 1–7.

O'Keefe, J., & Nadel, L. (1978). *The hippocampus as a cognitive map*. Oxford, England: Oxford University Press.

Okuda, J., Fujii, T., Ohtake, H., Tsukiura, T., Tanji, K., Suzuki, K., Kawashima, R., Fukuda, H., Itoh, M., & Yamadori, A. (2003). Thinking of the future and past: The roles of the frontal pole and the medial temporal lobes. *Neuroimage, 19*, 1369–1380.

Polyn, S. M., & Kahana, M. J. (2008). Memory search and the neural representation of context. *Trends in Cognitive Sciences, 12*, 24–30.

Polyn, S. M., Natu, V. S., Cohen, J. D., & Norman, K. A. (2005). Category-specific cortical activity precedes retrieval during memory search. *Science, 310*, 1963–1966.

Raichle, M. E., MacLeod, A. M., Snyder, A. Z., Powers, W. J., Gusnard, D. A., & Shulman, G. L. (2001). A default mode of brain function. *Proceedings of the National Academy of Sciences USA, 98*, 676–682.

Rosenbaum, R. S., Kohler, S., Schacter, D. L., Moscovitch, M., Westmacott, R., Black, S. E., Gao, F., & Tulving, E. (2005). The case of K. C.: Contributions of a memory-impaired person to memory theory. *Neuropsychologia, 43*, 989–1021.

Rosenbaum, R. S., Stuss, D. T., Levine, B., & Tulving, E. (2007). Theory of mind is independent of episodic memory. *Science, 318*, 1257.

Rubin, D. C., Schrauf, R. W., & Greenberg, D. L. (2003). Belief and recollection of autobiographical memories. *Memory and Cognition, 31*, 887–901.

Rugg, M. D., Otten, L. J., & Henson, R. N. (2002). The neural basis of episodic memory: Evidence from functional neuroimaging. *Philosophical Transactions of the Royal Society of London B: Biological Sciences, 357*, 1097–1110.

Sanders, H. I., & Warrington, E. K. (1971). Memory for remote events in amnesic patients. *Brain, 94*, 661–668.

Schacter, D. L., & Addis, D. R. (2007). The cognitive neuroscience of constructive memory: Remembering the past and imagining the future. *Philosophical Transactions of the Royal Society of London B: Biological Sciences, 362*, 773–786.

Schacter, D. L., Addis, D. R., & Buckner, R. L. (2007). Remembering the past to imagine the future: The prospective brain. *Nature Reviews Neuroscience, 8*, 657–661.

Schacter, D. L., Addis, D. R., & Buckner, R. L. (2008). Episodic simulation of future events: Concepts, data, and applications. *Annals of the New York Academy of Science, 1124*, 39–60.

Schacter, D. L., Norman, K. A., & Koutstaal, W. (1998). The cognitive neuroscience of constructive memory. *Annual Review of Psychology, 49*, 289–318.

Scoville, W. B., & Milner, B. (1957). Loss of recent memory after bilateral hippocampal lesions. *Journal of Neurology, Neurosurgery and Psychiatry, 20*, 11–21.

Sharot, T., Riccardi, A. M., Raio, C. M., & Phelps, E. A. (2007). Neural mechanisms mediating optimism bias. *Nature, 450,* 102–105.

Spreng, R. N., Mar, R. A., & Kim, A. S. (2009). The common neural basis of autobiographical memory, prospection, navigation, theory of mind and the default mode: A quantitative meta-analysis. *Journal of Cognitive Neuroscience, 21,* 489–510.

Squire, L. R., Stark, C. E., & Clark, R. E. (2004). The medial temporal lobe. *Annual Review of Neuroscience, 27,* 279–306.

Suddendorf, T., & Corballis, M. C. (1997). Mental time travel and the evolution of the human mind. *Genetic, Social, and General Psychology Monographs, 123,* 133–167.

Sugiura, M., Shah, N. J., Zilles, K., & Fink, G. R. (2005). Cortical representations of personally familiar objects and places: Functional organization of the human posterior cingulate cortex. *Journal of Cognitive Neuroscience, 17,* 183–198.

Summerfield, J. J., Hassabis, D., & Maguire, E. A. (2009). Cortical midline involvement in autobiographical memory. *Neuroimage, 44,* 1188–1200.

Summerfield, J.J., Hassabis, D., & Maguire, E.A. (2010). Differential engagement of brain regions within a 'core' network during scene construction. *Neuropsychologia, 48,* 1501-1509.

Svoboda, E., McKinnon, M. C., & Levine, B. (2006). The functional neuroanatomy of autobiographical memory: A meta-analysis. *Neuropsychologia, 44,* 2189–2208.

Szpunar, K. K., Watson, J. M., & McDermott, K. B. (2007). Neural substrates of envisioning the future. *Proceedings of the National Academy of Sciences USA, 104,* 642–647.

Tulving, E. (2002). Episodic memory: From mind to brain. *Annual Review of Psychology, 53,* 1–25.

Vincent, J. L., Snyder, A. Z., Fox, M. D., Shannon, B. J., Andrews, J. R., Raichle, M. E., & Buckner, R. L. (2006). Coherent spontaneous activity identifies a hippocampal-parietal memory network. *Journal of Neurophysiology, 96,* 3517–3531.

Wagner, A. D., Shannon, B. J., Kahn, I., & Buckner, R. L. (2005). Parietal lobe contributions to episodic memory retrieval. *Trends in Cognitive Sciences, 9,* 445–453.

Wheeler, M. A., Stuss, D. T., & Tulving, E. (1997). Toward a theory of episodic memory: The frontal lobes and autonoetic consciousness. *Psychological Bulletin, 121,* 331–354.

Wheeler, M. E., Petersen, S. E., & Buckner, R. L. (2000). Memory's echo: Vivid remembering reactivates sensory-specific cortex. *Proceedings of the National Academy of Sciences USA, 97,* 11125–11129.

Woollett, K., & Maguire, E. A. (2009). Navigation expertise may compromise anterograde associative memory. *Neuropsychologia, 47,* 1088-1095.

CHAPTER 7
Similarities in Episodic Future Thought and Remembering: The Importance of Contextual Setting

Kathleen B. McDermott, Karl K. Szpunar, and Kathleen M. Arnold

The diversity of entries in this volume speaks to the wide variety of "predictive" capacities of the brain that are currently under experimental investigation. The present contribution focuses on one specific type of future-oriented thinking that has received a considerable amount of attention with respect to human cognition, namely episodic future thought. Indeed, a number of reviews related to this topic have appeared recently (Schacter, Addis, & Buckner, 2007, 2008; Szpunar, 2010). In this chapter, we take a novel approach and present a personal story of how our own thinking about episodic future thought has evolved over time and how our own ideas have fit in with the larger picture that has developed around this rapidly emerging line of research (see Chapter 5).

The first order of business is to define "episodic future thought." Although the basic concept was first considered as a potentially important topic of inquiry in relation to brain function approximately 30 years ago (see Ingvar 1979, 1985; Tulving, 1985), the term itself was proposed only recently by Atance and O'Neil (2001), who defined episodic future thought as "a projection of the self into the future to pre-experience an event" (p. 533). Szpunar (2010) has expanded upon this definition to refer to simulation of "specific personal episodes that may potentially occur in the future" (p. 2).

For example, can you envision an event that could plausibly take place on Thanksgiving Day in the coming year? How about an event that could unfold over an upcoming vacation? These plausible, personal episodes are common examples of episodic future thought. Note this capacity differs from planning and is focused on the (pre)-experience of an episode, not the steps necessary to ensure the future-oriented image becomes reality (see Chapter 1). We also note that the term *episodic future thought* is roughly synonymous with other terms that have been recently used, including *prospection* (Buckner & Carroll, 2006; Gilbert & Wilson, 2007), *pre-experiencing* (Botzung, Denkova, & Manning, 2008), *simulation* (Schacter et al., 2007), and *projection* (Okuda et al., 2003). In part due to its close ties with the concept and term *episodic memory* (Szpunar & McDermott, 2008b; Tulving, 1983, 2002b), we prefer the term *episodic future thought* to the alternatives and will use it throughout this chapter.

The organization of the chapter is as follows. First, we consider the theoretical motivation behind the study of episodic future thought. We next consider initial attempts from our own laboratory aimed at identifying neural correlates of episodic future thought and how they compare to those underlying retrieval of episodes from one's past. After considering some of the initial results, which demonstrate a high level of similarity in the neural substrates of autobiographical remembering and episodic future thinking, we discuss a few early theoretical accounts of this state of affairs. To preview, most such accounts center on the basic conclusion that episodic future thought is accomplished by drawing upon memory and recombining elements of these memories into novel (future-oriented) scenarios (Schacter & Addis, 2007). We then consider some recent behavioral research that grew out of this conceptualization. Finally, we discuss a neuroimaging study designed to test directly the hypothesis that memory for previously experienced contextual settings (e.g., places) is an important component in understanding the similarities between remembering and episodic future thought.

BACKGROUND

Our work took as its starting point the hypothesis offered by Endel Tulving in 1985 that recollection and episodic future thought are two sides of the same core cognitive capacity, which he termed "autonoetic (self-knowing) consciousness." The hypothesis emerged from Tulving's interactions with neuropsychological patient KC (referred to in earlier articles as NN), who could neither recollect his past nor envision his personal future in any detail. This profound deficit is poignantly captured by the following introspections made by KC when trying to envision his future: "It's like being in a room with nothing there and having a guy tell you to go find a chair, and there's nothing there" (Tulving, 1985, p. 4). On another occasion he described it as "like swimming in the middle of a lake. There's nothing there to hold you up or do anything with" (p. 4.) And when asked to compare his state of mind when trying to think about tomorrow and trying to think about yesterday, he observed that it's the "same kind of blankness" (p. 4).

On the basis of these observations, Tulving (1985; see also Tulving, 2002a; Wheeler, Stuss, & Tulving, 1997) posited that the ability to remember events from one's personal life and the ability to engage in episodic future thinking were made possible by a single cognitive capacity: autonoetic consciousness. He further postulated that this capacity for autonoetic consciousness (and the related concept of *mental time travel*) is uniquely human; that aspect of autonoetic consciousness will not be considered here but has provoked interesting debate (Suddendorf & Corballis, 2007).

Over the years, Tulving has built the case for the claim that there exists a close relation between remembering and episodic future thought, but with a few exceptions direct empirical research on this question did not develop until recently. In the text that follows we discuss some of our attempts to inform the question, with a focus on functional magnetic resonance imaging (fMRI) studies.

THE METHODOLOGICAL APPROACH: DIRECT COMPARISON OF REMEMBERING AND EPISODIC FUTURE THOUGHT

Our first experiment in this domain was an exploratory investigation designed to examine the degree to which episodic future thought and remembering exhibited similarities and differences in neural activation as measured by fMRI. The basic experimental design borrowed directly from the autobiographical memory literature. Specifically, a variation of the Galton-Crovitz word-cueing technique (Crovitz & Schiffman, 1974; Galton, 1879) was adopted, whereby people are given a cue (e.g., "birthday") and asked to use this cue as a starting point for recollecting a single event from their life. The event can be loosely related to the cue; the important point is that the cue directs the subject to a single discrete episode. Szpunar, Watson, and McDermott (2007) gave participants 10 seconds for each trial and asked them to spend the entire time trying to recollect that single event as vividly as possible (see Fig. 7.1, left panel).

This condition was contrasted with one that involved episodic future thought—vividly envisioning a specific, plausible episode that might occur in one's personal future. A similar cue was presented, with subjects instructed to use it as a starting point to envision some specific future episode (for 10 seconds). Subjects were instructed to play out their future scenarios for the entire 10 second period and not to just think about a static image.

To the extent that Tulving's (1985) hypothesis was correct, we would expect regions important for these tasks—regions that underlie autonoetic consciousness—to exhibit identical activity for episodic future thought and remembering. To pinpoint these regions, we sought out a third

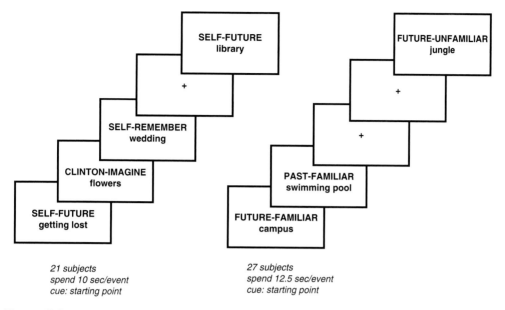

Figure 7.1 Schematic of the design of Szpunar et al. (2007, *left*) and Szpunar et al. (2009, *right*). Subjects were asked to spend 10 seconds per event remembering (or envisioning) in as much detail as possible, using the cue as a starting point to recollect (or imagine) a specific episode, discrete in time. The intertrial interval was variable.

condition, one that would contain many elements of the same core processes but that would not involve thinking about oneself in time. Having a case in which people envisioned personal life events in the temporal present did not turn out to be a logistical possibility (e.g., imagine having a birthday party or shopping in the immediate environment while lying in the scanner), so we asked subjects to envision another, well-known person that they could imagine in a wide variety of situations. Specifically, we chose a person subjects reported being able to flexibly imagine using a variety of cues: former U.S. President Bill Clinton.

INITIAL RESULTS

Our first finding was that no regions were more active for remembering than for envisioning the future (Szpunar et al., 2007). This finding was particularly surprising to us at the time; clearly, there is a profound phenomenological difference between the two situations, and memory and imagination are not typically confused with one another (Johnson, Hashtroudi, & Lindsay, 1993). Was it possible that the regions consistently activated during autobiographical memory did not manifest greater activity for remembering than for episodic future thought? One of us (KS) gave a talk on this work in July 2006 at the International Conference on Memory in Sydney, after which Dan Schacter and Donna Addis mentioned having recently analyzed a similar experiment, with similar results in that no regions were preferentially active for remembering relative to episodic future thought. Hence, this result seemed stable if not immediately interpretable. Furthermore, since this time, the two other articles reporting whole-brain analyses comparing episodic future thought and remembering have also failed to find any regions more active for remembering (Botzung et al., 2008; Szpunar, Chan, & McDermott, 2009).[1]

[1] In a study at least somewhat similar to these, Okada et al. (2003) assessed free-form future thought and compared it to remembering. The tasks used were fairly unconstrained (i.e., think about "during the next few years" for 1 minute). An examination of the subjects'

Although no regions emerged as showing more activity for remembering than episodic future thought, the converse pattern was indeed seen: Regions (mostly in left frontal cortex and right cerebellum) showed greater activity for episodic future thought. Might that pattern arise because episodic future thought is more generative than remembering? In essence, could we think of remembering as being a "primed" task in which the component elements are more readily assembled than the less constrained generation of potential future scenarios (Szpunar et al., 2007)? At this point, it is unclear how to think of this pattern, but that is one possibility. Admittedly, though, this interpretation seems somewhat unsatisfactory in that phenomenologically remembering does not "feel like" only a facilitated construction of an image; it subjectively feels like something additional is taking place during the experience we think of as recollection.[2]

A third important pattern of results emerged in a set of regions that showed activity indistinguishable for remembering the past and envisioning the future but that differed from the control condition of imagining another person. A representative sample of those regions and the time course of blood oxygen level–dependent (BOLD) activity that led to the identification of those regions is shown in the top row of Figure 7.2. This pattern of results is the basis for the work that follows in most of the remainder of the chapter.

Specifically, this pattern emerged in regions within bilateral parahippocampal cortex, posterior cingulate, and left superior occipital gyrus (and also others in frontal cortex and cerebellum; see Table 2 of Szpunar et al., 2007 for details). That is, these regions demonstrated statistically indistinguishable activity for the two conditions instantiating autonoetic consciousness and greater activity for those two conditions than for the imagery control condition.

What might we conclude from this study, especially with respect to the equivalencies between episodic future thought and remembering within these posterior cortical regions (i.e., the results in Fig. 7.2, top panel)? Several possibilities exist; Szpunar and colleagues (2007) favored one conclusion over the others, but we mention briefly some of the possibilities.

First, it is possible that a Type II error is responsible for the failure to identify regions more active for remembering than future thought. This idea seemed unlikely to us in that differences in other directions did occur, and the null effects were particularly convincing (across time courses, across regions). Nonetheless, it is statistically impossible to prove the null hypothesis.

A second potential explanation is that the crucial difference among the three conditions was whether the task was self-referential. That is, both the remember and future thought conditions required thinking about oneself (at a time other than the present), whereas the third condition involved thinking about another person. For now, we put aside this explanation, but we will demonstrate later why this explanation does not seem to capture the full picture.

A third potential conclusion is that these regions underlie the mental set of attempting to remember and attempting to envision the future (i.e., retrieval mode and its corresponding mental set for future thought). This conclusion, while intriguing, seemed unlikely for a couple of reasons. First, such control processes would seem most likely to occur within frontal cortex (Tulving, 2002b; Wheeler et al., 1997). Second, the regions we identified appear qualitatively similar to those consistently seen in the literature

reports about the thoughts they generated demonstrated that very few of their future thoughts were episodic (14% or 20%, depending upon condition), whereas most of their past-oriented thoughts were episodic. As a result, we conclude that this study is not directly relevant to episodic future thought (in that most of the future thoughts did not refer to a discrete episode); nonetheless, the study deserves mention and is quite interesting in its own right.

[2] Interestingly, a recent study by Addis et al. (2009) has presented data suggesting that neural regions associated with vivid recollection of past events (e.g., occipital regions) may emerge in comparison to future thinking tasks provided that sufficiently sensitive statistical techniques are used. Given that this intriguing set of results has yet to be replicated, we mention them with some caution.

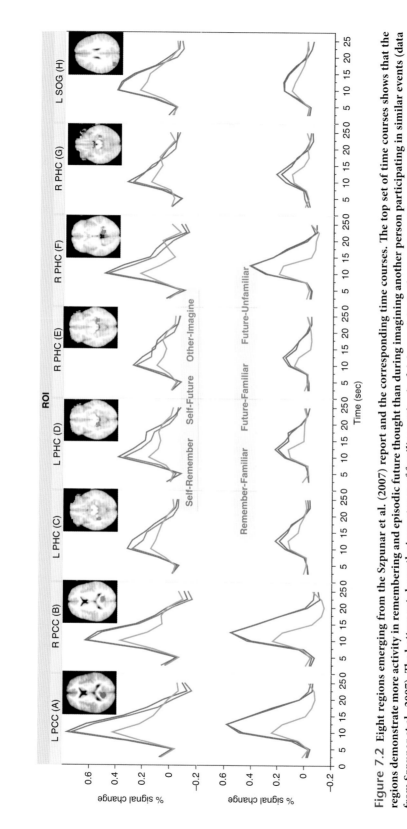

Figure 7.2 Eight regions emerging from the Szpunar et al. (2007) report and the corresponding time courses. The top set of time courses shows that the regions demonstrate more activity in remembering and episodic future thought than during imagining another person participating in similar events (data from Szpunar et al., 2007). The bottom set shows the importance of familiar setting in driving activity in these regions; here, all conditions were self-referential and involved a time other than the present, and the critical factor was familiarity of the contextual setting (data from Szpunar et al., 2009). L, left; R, right; PCC, posterior cingulate cortex; PHC, parahippocampal cortex; SOG, superior occipital gyrus.

on mental navigation of familiar routes (Ghaem et al., 1997; Mellet et al., 2000; Rosenbaum, Ziegler, Winocur, Grady, & Moscovitch, 2004) and autobiographical memory (Maguire, 2001; Svoboda, McKinnon, & Levine, 2006). Mental navigation would not necessitate any willful attempt to perform "mental time travel" (Tulving, 2002a) to recollect specific past episodes.

To appreciate the similarity in activity across comparisons, consider Figure 7.3, where the top row shows regions that demonstrated equivalent activity for remembering and episodic future thought (but more activity in these conditions than the imagery control condition) in the Szpunar et al. (2007) study. The center panel shows results of a meta-analysis using the activation likelihood estimation procedure (Turkeltaub, Eden, Jones, & Zeffiro, 2002) to identify voxels that consistently activate ($p < .05$)

in the literature when an autobiographical memory task is compared to a control condition (for details, see McDermott, Szpunar, & Christ, 2009). The point here is that at a qualitative level, anyway, there appears to be great overlap between the two maps, especially in the cortical midline regions, including posterior cingulate and parahippocampal cortex.

This observation, along with some behavioral observations (discussed later in the chapter), led us to speculate that the pattern seen in these regions could be attributable to episodic future thought drawing upon memory (specifically, memory for known locations). Specifically, we concluded that "We propose, as others have (Ingvar, 1985; Okuda et al., 2003), that to effectively generate a plausible image of the future, subjects reactivate images (e.g., visual-spatial context) stored in posterior cortical regions" (p. 645).

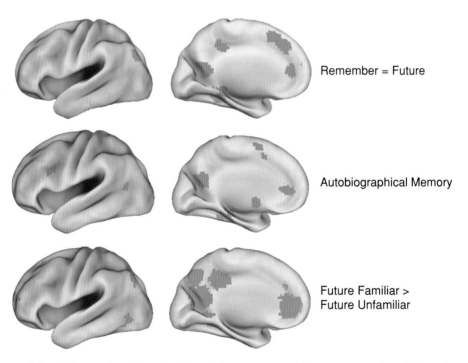

Remember = Future

Autobiographical Memory

Future Familiar > Future Unfamiliar

Figure 7.3 Left hemisphere lateral and medial projections of brain regions identified as showing equivalent activity for remembering and episodic future thought (Szpunar et al., 2007); those identified as being consistently active in studies of autobiographical memory (McDermott et al., 2009); and more active during episodic future thought taking place in familiar relative to unfamiliar locations (Szpunar et al., 2009).

EMERGING THEORIES AND REVIEWS

At roughly the same time as publication of Szpunar et al. (2007), two other highly related empirical papers came out. One was a neuroimaging study by Addis, Wong, and Schacter (2007), which was very consistent with the results just discussed. The Galton-Crovitz word-cueing task was adapted for this study, too. During the initial construction and subsequent elaboration of episodic future thoughts and the retrieval of memories, no regions were preferentially activated for remembering (see also Botzung et al., 2008). Moreover, the latter, elaboration phase was "characterized by remarkable overlap in regions comprising the autobiographical memory retrieval network, attributable to the common processes engaged during elaboration, including self-referential processing, contextual and episodic imagery" (Addis et al., 2007, p. 1363). Some regions did show preferential activation for future thought relative to remembering, especially during the initial construction phase (e.g., left middle frontal gyrus and precuneus, both consistent with the results of Szpunar et al., 2007).

The other related article was a neuropsychological study of five patients with amnesia resulting from medial temporal lobe damage (Hassabis, Kumaran, Vann, & Maguire, 2007b). Hassabis et al. asked their subjects to imagine themselves in a situation not currently experienced. Some such scenarios involved plausible future episodes, whereas others were atemporal (e.g., "imagine you're lying on a white sandy beach in a beautiful tropical bay"). The scene descriptions produced by amnesic patients were fragmentary and less spatially coherent than those given by control subjects. This observation held both when participants were asked to imagine the scenes without specification of time and when asked to envision them in the future. Hence, one of the contributions of medial temporal lobe structures to memory, imagination, and episodic future thought may be to contribute to the spatial context of the scene.

Within a very short span of time after publication of these articles (and in one case, even while these articles were still in press), several reviews and theoretical perspectives were offered (Buckner & Carroll, 2006; Hassabis & Maguire, 2007; Schacter & Addis, 2007; Schacter et al., 2007). We focus here primarily on the one that has thus far received the most attention: the *constructive episodic simulation* hypothesis forward by Schacter, Addis, and colleagues (Addis, Pan, Vu, Laiser, & Schacter, 2009; Addis & Schacter, 2008; Schacter et al., 2008). The basic suggestion here is that episodic future thinking draws upon remembering. That is, people accomplish episodic future thought by drawing upon a neurocognitive system that "flexibly extracts and recombines elements of previous experiences" (p. 773). Hence, the "constructive" nature of memory—that recollection involves inferences, elaboration, and construction (Bartlett, 1932; Roediger & McDermott, 2000)—can be thought of as enabling one to piece together fragments from memory in the service of imagining potential future scenarios.

A couple of the other hypotheses forwarded could be considered to be variations on the same idea (although perhaps less formalized than the constructive episodic simulation hypothesis). One such proposal was that "scene construction" is the key common element linking these two capacities (Hassabis, Kumaran, & Maguire, 2007a; Hassabis et al., 2007b; Hassabis & Maguire, 2007). On the basis of their study of amnesic patients, Hassabis and Maguire (2007) concluded that "scene construction provides the stage on which the remembered event is played or the 'where' for the 'what' to occur in" (p. 304). Elsewhere, they suggest that "The hippocampus…may make a critical contribution to the creation of new experiences by providing the spatial context into which the disparate elements of an experience can be bound" (Hassabis et al., 2007, p. 1726). This conceptualization is probably the most similar to our own suggestion that "similarities in activity for these two tasks are attributed to the reactivation of previously experienced visual–spatial contexts" (Szpunar et al., 2007, p. 642).

Finally, another suggestion, qualitatively different from the three mentioned earlier, is that "self-projection" is a key element linking these capacities and other related abilities: episodic future thought, episodic memory, theory of mind, and mental navigation (Buckner & Carroll, 2006). The idea here is that these capacities rely upon a common core network (although see Rosenbaum, Stuss, Levine, & Tulving, 2007 for evidence that theory of mind is independent of episodic memory).

We return now to the proposals (considered to be roughly equivalent here but likely amenable to empirical differentiation) that episodic future thought relies upon memory, and that the specific locations and contextual settings of one's life represent one of the main contributions of memory to episodic future thought. The discussion that follows will tend to focus on the role of "context" (i.e., known visual-spatial settings and their associations), but our results can also be accommodated quite readily by the related theoretical points of view (constructive episodic simulation and scene construction).

Behavioral characteristics of episodic future thought are in line with what one would predict if memory is sampled

To the extent that episodic future thought is accomplished by drawing upon remembered elements from the past, it would be reasonable to expect that memory-based manipulations could be used to influence the qualities of episodic future thought. Specifically, Szpunar and McDermott (2008a) examined the impact of manipulating the visual contextual setting envisioned on the accompanying phenomenological characteristics.

Subjects were asked to envision a novel plausible episode that could occur within the next week. They were asked to do so in both familiar settings (e.g., friend's apartment) and unfamiliar settings (e.g., jungle). After spending 1 minute envisioning the event, subjects used 7-point scales to rate the characteristics of that image with respect to eight questions. Specifically, following D'Argembeau and Van der Linden (2004, 2006), three measures were combined to form a sensorial details index (visual details, sounds, smell/taste: 1 = none, 7 = a lot), three measures were combined to form a clarity of context index

(clarity of location, clarity of spatial arrangement of objects, clarity of spatial arrangement of people; 1 = vague, 7 = clear), and two measures to form an index of the subjective experience (feeling of experiencing the event, feeling of mental projection: 1 = none, 7 = a lot).

As can be seen in Figure 7.4, those future thoughts imagined in familiar settings were experienced with greater vividness, higher clarity of context, and greater subjective experience than those envisioned in unfamiliar contextual settings. These results are consistent with the idea that memory is sampled when constructing future scenarios; when memory is less able to support the construction of a future thought, the resulting image is less vivid.

Similarly, when subjects were asked to envision future events (within the next week) that could occur within recently experienced settings (e.g., university campus), they reported greater sensorial detail, clarity of context, and subjective experience than when they envisioned future events in settings that were well known but not as recently experienced (e.g., high school; see Fig. 7.4). Because contextual settings experienced on a daily basis are reported to have greater perceptual detail than settings from one's past (Brewer, 1986), these results, too, are consistent with the idea that variables that affect the characteristics of one's memory exert similar influence on the characteristics of future thought (as would be expected if memory forms the basis of episodic future thought).

More recent work from our lab (Arnold, McDermott, & Szpunar, 2010) has taken a similar approach by manipulating temporal distance from the present for both episodic future thought and memory. As temporal distance from the present increases, the vividness of the imagined event decreases both for episodic future thought and for memory (Arnold et al., 2010; D'Argembeau & Van der Linden, 2004). That vividness declines with increasing remoteness is perhaps not surprising for remembering. But why should such a finding appear for events that one has not experienced? All imagined future events are constructions of novel future scenarios. Therefore, why should an event imagined to occur in the far future be less clear than an event

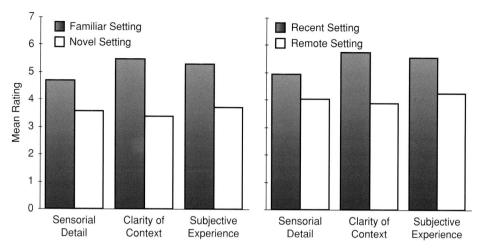

Figure 7.4 Episodic future thoughts vary as a function of the memorial representations upon which they are based. (Adapted from Szpunar & McDermot, 2008.)

imagined to occur in the near future? Arnold et al. (2010) demonstrate that the clarity of the imagined location is a key factor: As temporal distance from the present increased (from 1 day to 1 week, 1 year, 5 years, to 10 years), the mean ratings for the "clarity of location" decreased both for remembering and future thought, but the decrease was much more pronounced for episodic future thought. Furthermore, when people were asked directly about the locations they chose for their future thoughts, they were much more likely to report placing near than far future events in known locations. Far future events, it seems, are less vivid than near future events because there is less memory to draw upon when constructing the locations of far future events. In short, contextual setting appears to be one of the big contributors to the similarities between episodic future thought and remembering. Our personal "places" appear to be a key element of the link between episodic memory and episodic future thought.

CONTEXTUAL ASSOCIATIONS

If places and contextual associations are key to understanding the link between episodic future thought and memory, how are we to understand the finding that these two sets of processes elicit greater activity than imagining another person

(specifically, Bill Clinton) engaged in similar activities (Szpunar et al., 2007)? As a reminder, subjects were given cues (e.g., *birthday, wedding, getting sick*) and asked to use the cue as a starting point to remember some specific episode from their lives, envision a plausible episode that could occur in their future, or imagine an event involving another person (Szpunar et al., 2007).

An examination of postexperiment questionnaires with this study, other behavioral protocols from our lab, and the existing literature (D'Argembeau & Van der Linden, 2004, 2006) suggests that when envisioning the future, subjects tend to place the images in the context of familiar places and familiar people. In contrast, when asked to imagine Clinton participating in similar events, our subjects tended to rely upon more semantic knowledge and not place him in their well-known personal settings.

To appreciate this difference, consider the following two examples. When given the cues *Self-Remember: Birthday* one participant said, "It is my 13th birthday. My 20 best friends and I are at a swimming pool located by my high school. My mom baked 2 heart-shaped cakes because my birthday is so close to Valentine's Day. Some of my friends got up on the pool deck and made a dance routine to Backstreet Boys. Some of us played water basketball. Everyone still wore 1-piece bathing suits." Contrast this scene with the following description of the scene imagined to the cue *Clinton-Imagine: Birthday*. This subject describes, "I imagine him in the oval office and his cabinet/advisors/other people that work w/him bringing in a cake to him and Hilary comes in. He is just sitting down at his desk. They sing to him, he gets a lil' embarrassed, stands up and blows out the candle, then they socialize a lil' and slowly people leave."

We therefore designed a study to address directly the hypothesis that regions within posterior cingulate and medial temporal cortex reinstate familiar context during episodic future thought, and that it is this aspect that drives the equivalent neural activity in the two conditions (Szpunar et al., 2009). To this end, we devised three instructional conditions (to match cues similar to those used in the prior study). In one case, subjects were to remember an event taking place in a familiar contextual setting (e.g., the house in which one grew up; a friend's apartment). In the second case, subjects were to envision a plausible future event taking place in a familiar context. In the third condition, they were asked to envision a plausible future event taking place in an unfamiliar contextual setting. To assist in doing this third task, the cues were changed to be relatively unfamiliar. Examples of the cueing conditions would be *Past-Familiar: Friend's Apartment*; *Future-Familiar: Campus*; *Future-Unfamiliar: Jungle*. The procedure is represented on the right side of Figure 7.1.

Importantly, all three conditions are self-referential, and all involve mental time travel (i.e., thinking about an event occurring in the past or the future). The rationale was that if contextual setting mediates the activity in the regions of parahippocampal cortex and posterior cingulate, we would expect that the two conditions involving familiar context should elicit equivalent activity, which exceeds that in the condition involving unfamiliar context.

The primary finding from this study is that the two conditions requiring one to reinvoke familiar contextual associations led to equivalent activity (and greater activity than the third condition, which explicitly did not require thinking about known contexts) in these regions (see Fig. 7.2 for time course data and Fig. 7.3,

bottom panel, for a depiction of some of the regions emerging from a whole-brain analysis of this contrast). The data shown in Figure 7.2 offer a replication of the past/future equivalence for known contextual settings (i.e., the Past-Familiar and Future-Familiar conditions could be thought of as conceptual replications of the Self-Remember and Self-Future conditions from the Szpunar et al., 2007 dataset). Critically, these new data demonstrate that mental time travel and self-relevance are not the deciding factor behind activity in these regions. Hence, it is not remembering and future thought per se that drive this equivalence but the drawing upon known contextual settings. When episodic future thought was elicited for unfamiliar settings, less activation emerged within these regions (as can be seen in the bottom row of Fig. 7.2; the degree to which familiar, known locations are invoked drives activity in these regions).

Of course, contextual processing is a broad term (Bar, 2007; Bar & Aminoff, 2003) and future work will need to further clarify the aforementioned results. For instance, although context (or setting) appears to play an important role in episodic future thought, it is also possible that people have associated more items in memory with familiar contexts (than with unfamiliar contexts), and the role of these more tangential associations will need to be seriously considered (Bar, Aminoff, & Schacter, 2008). Furthermore, the separate regions are likely not contributing identical subprocesses. Nonetheless, this study represents an advance in understanding the processes contributing to the similarities in episodic future thought and remembering. The results are also broadly consistent with the Maguire/Hassabis framework of scene construction and the constructive episodic simulation hypothesis of Schacter and Addis.

Summary

The last several years have witnessed a remarkable surge of interest with respect to episodic future thought and related capacities. Although there is still much to be learned, already a fairly consistent story is emerging from the data, at least with respect to pinpointing the aspects of memory most critical for episodic future thought. Here we have presented the story for how this evidence emerged in our own thinking and research approach. Our data have converged nicely with those emerging from various other laboratories. As it stands, there is a general consensus among researchers that personal "places" rich in contextual associations play an important role in the capacity to imagine personal future scenarios.

References

Addis, D. R., Pan, L., Vu, M. A., Laiser, N., & Schacter, D. L. (2009). Constructive episodic simulation of the future and the past: Distinct subsystems of a core brain network mediate imagining and remembering. *Neuropsychologia*, *47*, 2222–2238.

Addis, D. R., & Schacter, D. L. (2008). Constructive episodic simulation: Temporal distance and detail of past and future events modulate hippocampal engagement. *Hippocampus*, *18*, 227–237.

Addis, D. R., Wong, A. T., & Schacter, D. L. (2007). Remembering the past and imagining the future: Common and distinct neural substrates during event construction and elaboration. *Neuropsychologia*, *45*, 1363–1377.

Arnold, K. M., McDermott, K. B., & Szpunar, K. K. (2010). The influence of temporal distance on phenomenological characteristics of episodic memory and episodic future thought. *Manuscript under review*.

Bar, M. (2007). The proactive brain: Using analogies and associations to generate predictions. *Trends in Cognitive Sciences*, *11*, 280–289.

Bar, M., & Aminoff, E. (2003). Cortical analysis of context. *Neuron*, *38*, 347–358.

Bar, M., Aminoff, E., & Schacter, D.L. (2008). Scenes unseen: The parahippocampal cortex intrinsically subserves contextual associations, not scenes or places per se. *Journal of Neuroscience*, *28*, 8539–8544.

Bartlett, F. C. (1932). *Remembering: A study in experimental and social psychology*. New York: Macmillan.

Botzung, A., Denkova, E., & Manning, L. (2008). Experiencing past and future personal events: Functional neuroimaging evidence on the neural basis of mental time travel. *Brain and Cognition*, *66*, 202–212.

Brewer, W. F. (1986). What is autobiographical memory? In D. C. Rubin (Ed.), *Autobiographical memory* (pp. 25–49). Cambridge, England: Cambridge University Press.

Buckner, R. L., & Carroll, D. C. (2006). Self-projection and the brain. *Trends in Cognitive Sciences*, *11*(2), 49–57.

Crovitz, H. F., & Schiffman, H. (1974). Frequency of episodic memories as a function of their age. *Bulletin of the Psychonomic Society*, *4*(5B), 517–518.

D'Argembeau, A., & Van der Linden, M. (2004). Phenomenal characteristics associated with projecting oneself back into the past and forward into the future: Influence of valence and temporal distance. *Consciousness and Cognition*, *13*, 844–858.

D'Argembeau, A., & Van der Linden, M. (2006). Individual differences in the phenomenology of mental time travel: The effect of vivid visual imagery and emotion regulation strategies. *Consciousness and Cognition*, *15*(2), 342–350.

Galton, F. (1879). Psychometric experiments. *Brain*, *2*, 149–162.

Ghaem, O., Mellet, E., Crivello, F., Tzourio, N., Mazoyer, B., Berthoz, A., et al. (1997). Mental navigation along memorized routes activates the hippocampus, precuneus, and insula. *NeuroReport.*, *8*, 739–744.

Gilbert, D. T., & Wilson, T. D. (2007). Prospection: Experiencing the future. *Science*, *317*, 1351–1354.

Hassabis, D., Kumaran, D., & Maguire, E. A. (2007). Using imagination to understand the neural basis of episodic memory. *The Journal of Neuroscience*, *27*(52), 14365–14374.

Hassabis, D., Kumaran, D., Vann, S. D., & Maguire, E. A. (2007). Patients with hippocampal amnesia cannot imagine new experiences. *Proceedings of the National Academy of Sciences USA*, *104*(5), 1726–1731.

Hassabis, D., & Maguire, E. A. (2007). Deconstructing episodic memory with construction. *Trends in Cognitive Sciences*, *11*, 299–306.

Ingvar, D. H. (1985). "Memory of the future": An essay on temporal organization of conscious awareness. *Human Neurobiology*, *4*(3), 127–136.

Ingvar, D.H. (1979). "Hyperfrontal" distribution of the general grey matter flow in resting wakefulness: on the functional anatomy of the conscious state. *Acta Neurologica Scandinavica*, *60*, 12–25.

Johnson, M. K., Hashtroudi, S., & Lindsay, D. S. (1993). Source monitoring. *Psychological Bulletin*, *114*, 3–28.

Maguire, E. A. (2001). Neuroimaging studies of autobiographical event memory. *Philosophical Transactions of the Royal Society of London B: Biological Sciences, 356*(1413), 1441–1451.

McDermott, K. B., Szpunar, K. K., & Christ, S. E. (2009). Laboratory-based and autobiographical retrieval tasks differ substantially in their neural substrates. *Neuropsychologia, 47*, 2290–2298.

Mellet, E., Bricogne, S., Tzourio-Mazoyer, N., Ghaem, O., Petit, L., Zago, O., et al. (2000). Neural correlates of topographic mental exploration: The impact of route versus survey perspective learning. *NeuroImage, 12*, 588–600.

Okuda, J., Fujii, T., Ohtake, H., Tsukiura, T., Tanji, K., Suzuki, K., et al. (2003). Thinking of the future and past: The roles of the frontal pole and the medial temporal lobes. *Neuroimage, 19*, 1369–1380.

Roediger, H. L., & McDermott, K. B. (2000). Distortions of memory. In E. Tulving & F. I. M. Craik (Eds.), *The Oxford handbook of memory* (pp. 149–162). Oxford, England: Oxford University Press.

Rosenbaum, R. S., Stuss, D. T., Levine, B., & Tulving, E. (2007). Theory of mind is independent of episodic memory. *Science, 318*, 1257.

Rosenbaum, R. S., Ziegler, M., Winocur, G., Grady, C. L., & Moscovitch, M. (2004). I have often walked down this street before: fMRI studies on the hippocampus and other structures during mental navigation of an old environment. *Hippocampus, 14*(7), 826–835.

Schacter, D. L., & Addis, D. R. (2007). The cognitive neuroscience of constructive memory: Remembering the past and imagining the future. *Philosophical Transactions of the Royal Society B: Biological Sciences, 362*, 773–786.

Schacter, D. L., Addis, D. R., & Buckner, R. L. (2007). Remembering the past to imagine the future: The prospective brain. *Nature Reviews Neuroscience, 8*, 657–661.

Schacter, D. L., Addis, D. R., & Buckner, R. L. (2008). Episodic simulation of future events: Concepts, data, and application [Special Theme Issue]. *Annals of the New York Academy of Sciences, 1124*, 39–60.

Suddendorf, T., & Corballis, M. C. (2007). The evolution of foresight: What is mental time travel and is it unique to humans? *Behavioral and Brain Sciences, 30*, 299–313.

Svoboda, E., McKinnon, M. C., & Levine, B. (2006). The functional neuroanatomy of autobiographical memory: A meta-analysis. *Neuropsychologia, 44*, 2189–2208.

Szpunar, K. K. (2010). Episodic future thought: An emerging concept. *Perspectives on Psychological Science, 5*, 142–162.

Szpunar, K. K., Chan, J. C. K., & McDermott, K. B. (2009). Contextual processing in episodic future thought. *Cerebral Cortex, 19*, 1539–1548.

Szpunar, K. K., & McDermott, K. B. (2008a). Episodic future thought and its relation to remembering: Evidence from ratings of subjective experience. *Consciousness and Cognition, 17*, 330–334.

Szpunar, K. K., & McDermott, K. B. (2008b). Episodic memory: An evolving concept. In H. L. Roediger (Ed.), *Learning and memory: A comprehensive reference* (Vol. 2, pp. 491–509). Oxford, England: Elsevier.

Szpunar, K. K., Watson, J. M., & McDermott, K. B. (2007). Neural substrates of envisioning the future. *Proceedings of the National Academy of Sciences USA, 104*, 642–647.

Tulving, E. (1983). *Elements of episodic memory.* New York: Oxford University Press.

Tulving, E. (1985). Memory and consciousness. *Canadian Psychologist, 26*, 1–12.

Tulving, E. (2002a). Chronesthesia: Awareness of subjective time. In D. T. Stuss & R. C. Knight (Eds.), *Principles of frontal lobe function* (pp. 311–325). New York: Oxford University Press.

Tulving, E. (2002b). Episodic memory: From mind to brain. *Annual Review of Psychology, 53*, 1–25.

Turkeltaub, P. E., Eden, G. F., Jones, K. M., & Zeffiro, T. A. (2002). Meta-analysis of the functional neuroanatomy of single-word reading: Method and validation. *NeuroImage, 16*, 765–780.

Wheeler, M. A., Stuss, D. T., & Tulving, E. (1997). Toward a theory of episodic memory: The frontal lobes and autonoetic consciousness. *Psychological Bulletin, 121*, 331–354.

CHAPTER 8
Imagining Predictions: Mental Imagery as Mental Emulation

Samuel T. Moulton and Stephen M. Kosslyn

For cognitive scientists, the term *mental imagery* typically first brings to mind either the protracted debate over the nature of the representations used in imagery or the role of imagery as a mnemonic (see Kosslyn, Thompson, & Ganis, 2006; Paivio, 1971, 1986). The "imagery debate" frequently overshadows the question of the everyday functions of mental imagery, which are at least as important as the questions that have received the most attention. However, research on this topic has often been hobbled by a key problem, namely the sparse stimuli and artificial tasks that imagery researchers contrive for their experiments (e.g., the rotation of geometric shapes; Shepard & Metzler, 1971). The minimalist character of the sorts of imagery evoked in most laboratory studies may obscure the vivid, rich character of everyday imagery.

In this chapter we move beyond questions such as "What is imagery?" and "Can imagery enhance memory?" to ask, "What is the primary psychological function of imagery?" In doing so, we argue that mental imagery affords us more than the mental rotation of stacked cubes—it allows us to simulate reality at will, and, because of this, allows us to predict what we would experience in a specific situation or after we perform a specific action. This ability not only allows us to reconstruct the past but also to anticipate what may occur in the near and distant future.

MENTAL IMAGERY: LEVELS OF ANALYSIS

Mental imagery occurs "when a representation of the type created during the initial phases of perception is present but the stimulus is not actually being perceived; such representations preserve the perceptible properties of the stimulus and ultimately give rise to the subjective experience of perception" (Kosslyn et al., 2006, p. 4). Critically, this characterization of mental imagery implies that multiple forms of imagery exist: Every type of perception should have a corresponding type of imagery. And, in fact, there is evidence for distinct object-based imagery (e.g., of shapes and colors) versus spatial imagery (e.g., of locations; Smith et al., 1995; Tresch, Sinnamon, & Seamon, 1993); there is evidence for auditory imagery (e.g., Zatorre, Halpern, Perry, Meyer, & Evans, 1996) and for what is commonly called "motor imagery" (which actually appears to be proprioceptive or kinesthetic imagery—one experiences the bodily sensations of movement, not the movement commands themselves; Jeannerod, 1994).

Although this characterization captures essential features of mental imagery, it does not explain how imagery works or what it does. In his seminal analysis of vision, Marr (1982) argued compellingly that to understand fully an information processing system, researchers must analyze it from three distinct levels: the computational level (which focuses on *what* the system is designed to accomplish), the algorithmic level (which focuses on the system's structures and processes and *how* they are drawn upon to perform specific computations), and the implementation level (which focuses on the system's physical substrate). As Kosslyn and Maljkovic (1990) pointed out, Marr's levels of analysis are interdependent, not independent: Theory and research focused exclusively on one level of analysis constrain theories and inform research focused on other levels of analysis.

In an effort to characterize mental imagery more completely as an information processing system, we consider it next using Marr's levels of analysis.

Computation: The Functions of Mental Imagery

When we consider the computational level, we are led to ask first and foremost: What is the function or functions of mental imagery? In our view, the primary function of mental imagery is to allow us to generate specific predictions based upon past experience. Imagery allows us to answer "what if" questions by making explicit and accessible the likely consequences of being in a specific situation or performing a specific action. For example, imagery can allow us to predict the path of a projectile, the consequences of a chess move, the scariness of a snake, and the feelings of a friend.

We want to make a very strong claim, namely that *all* imagery allows us to generate specific predictions based upon past experience. Consider the most trivial example of imagery: Close your eyes and imagine[1] a dot. What did your dot look like? Round, we hope. Because a dot is by definition round, however, the roundness of your image hardly predicts anything. Now, what color was your dot? A dot is not defined as having a specified color; it can be an

---

[1] The term "imagine" is ambiguous, meaning either "suppose" or "image" (as in "visualize," which is imaging in the visual modality). The fact that the same word is used for the two meanings is telling; we often "suppose" by creating mental images. In this chapter, we will use the term "imagine" to mean "image," with the implication that such imagery is being used in the service of supposing.

infinite number of colors, from fire-engine red to burnt umber. In all likelihood, however, your imagined dot was black, not fire-engine red. The reason is simple: Most dots you have previously experienced (e.g., the periods on this page) were black, and imagery draws automatically on this past experience. Thus, even the bare image of a dot transforms past experience into explicit, specific predictions: In this instance, you used imagery to predict the undefined color of the dot we asked you to visualize; put differently, you used imagery to predict the color of a typical dot.

Mental imagery not only allows us to predict the imminent or distant future but also to consider many possible futures—or even many possible worlds. For example, when deciding the best way to drive home from a friend's house, you might imagine several alternative routes and compare the likely traffic patterns, the number of stoplights, and so on. Moreover, we can use imagery to predict events that we may never actually experience in the future (e.g., Einstein's imagery of traveling at light speed) or events in the counterfactual present (e.g., imagining life as a lottery winner). This same mental machinery allows us to revisit events that have already occurred (e.g., the images of a murder scene formed by someone who witnessed the crime). In our view, the oft-cited role of imagery in memory (e.g., Kosslyn, 1980; Paivio, 1971) is in fact an application of a more general function, namely the ability to simulate what one would perceive in a specific situation.

Algorithm: Representations and Processes Used in Imagery

Considering imagery at the algorithmic level leads us to focus on how it accomplishes its computational functions. Specifically, at this level, we ask: What mental structures and processes does imagery engage? Many empirical investigations attest to the fact that imagery relies on many of the same representations that give rise to perception. There is good evidence that, at least in some circumstances, imagery recruits mechanisms used in early phases of perceptual processing. Such mechanisms rely in part on depictive representations, where configurations of densely arranged points (with size, intensity, and color) in a coordinate space are arranged so that the pattern "resembles" the appearance of the referent (see Kosslyn et al., 2006).

Because imagery relies on perceptual representations, it makes explicit and accessible the same types of information that are registered by the senses during perception (including proprioception and kinesthetic information). In visual imagery, for instance, depictive representations make available all types of visual information (i.e., size, intensity, and color values for each point included in the image). Critically, the information made explicit and accessible by perceptual representations during imagery supports its computational functions. For instance, if asked the shape of a cat's ears, most people will visualize the feline and "look" at the shape—which they had never considered explicitly before but which is implicit in the representation.

However, we must note that representations by themselves do no work. They must be processed in some way, or they may as well not exist. Imagery invokes at least four distinct types of processes. First, memorial processes must retrieve and later encode episodic information (e.g., to imagine telling a risqué joke during a toast at your wedding, you would retrieve memories of past weddings; furthermore, you then encode your imagined episode of wedding imagery). Much evidence supports this interplay between memory and imagery. For example, neuroimaging studies have revealed that most of the perceptual regions activated by mental imagery also become active during episodic retrieval, and do so in a modality-specific manner (for reviews, see Buckner & Wheeler, 2001; Cabeza & Nyberg, 2000; Mellet, Petit, Mazoyer, Denis, & Tzourio, 1998; Wagner, Shannon, Kahn, & Buckner, 2005). Furthermore, neuropsychological evidence suggests that this overlap is not merely correlational: Amnesic patients often exhibit severe deficits in their imagery (e.g., Hassabis, Kumaran, Vann, & Maguire, 2007; O'Connor, Butters, Miliotis, Eslinger, & Cermak, 1992; Ogden, 1993; for review, see Rubin & Greenberg, 1998; see also

Rosenbaum, McKinnon, Levine, & Moscovitch, 2004).

Second, imagery processes must draw on retrieved episodic information to generate explicit, accessible representations in working memory (e.g., an auditory image of yourself telling the joke and a visual image of your attentive bride; for reviews, see Kosslyn, 1980, 1994; Kosslyn et al., 2006).

Third, automatic associative processes must guide the imagery realistically, both in terms of providing new content (e.g., a look of horror on your bride's face upon hearing the punch line) and generating affective or physiological responses (e.g., a feeling of embarrassment, a racing heart). Just as a percept can bring to mind associated images and memories (as evidenced by innumerable studies of ways that linguistic prompts can prime visual processing), so can an image. Furthermore, just as a percept can induce associated affective and physiological events (e.g., Watson & Rayner, 1920), so can a mental image. For example, victims of childhood sexual abuse report greater negative affect and undergo greater physiological stress when imagining scenarios of abuse than when imagining neutral scenarios (Shin et al., 1999).

Finally, top-down executive processes must direct the processes that initiate, inspect, manipulate, and terminate the imagery when it has allowed you to accomplish your goal (e.g., upon embarrassment, ending the imagery or re-imagining the toast with a different joke). Substantial evidence supports the role of top-down processing in imagery (for review, see Kosslyn et al., 2006).

Implementation: Core Network

At the level of the implementation we are led to ask: How is imagery realized physically in the brain? As with perception, the neural mechanisms that underlie imagery surely depend on the content and purpose of particular instances. Nevertheless, we make three strong claims. First, because it relies on perceptual representations, imagery should activate perceptual cortices in a predictably specific manner. For example, whereas individuals who imagine preparing a banana split should reliably activate their visual cortex (and possibly motor cortex), individuals who imagine the sensation of eating a banana split should reliably activate their gustatory cortex (and possibly motor cortex). Indeed, much evidence supports this claim. Visual imagery activates the visual cortices, including—in some cases—the earliest cortex (e.g., Kosslyn & Thompson, 2003), auditory imagery activates the auditory cortices (e.g., Zatorre et al., 1996), motor imagery activates motor cortices (e.g., Porro et al., 1996), and gustatory imagery activates gustatory cortices (e.g., Kobayashi et al., 2004).

Second, because of the complex and temporally extended nature of imagery, it should activate a broad and diverse set of brain regions. More specifically, imagery should activate—in addition to perceptual cortices—regions involved in episodic memory retrieval (e.g., the hippocampus), top-down processing (e.g., prefrontal cortices), and associative processing (e.g., the retrosplenial complex). Considerable evidence supports these claims (for review, see Cabeza & Nyberg, 2000), although baseline conditions in many neuroimaging studies—in conjunction with the sparse stimuli often used by researchers—frequently obscure the full range and degree of brain activation elicited by mental imagery. In a noteworthy recent study, Hassabis, Kumaran, and Maguire (2007) investigated which brain areas become active during the sort of rich imagery individuals use in everyday life, using a simple imagery task as baseline; their results revealed a broad network that included the ventromedial prefrontal cortex, hippocampus, retrospenial complex, and posterior parietal cortex.

Finally, the activation of these distinct regions should unfold temporally in a pattern that mirrors the temporal sequence of imagery processing. For example, the prefrontal activation associated with top-down control should precede the hippocampal activation associated with episodic memory retrieval which, in turn, should precede the perceptual activation associated with perceptual representation. Because neuroscientists are just beginning to track the temporal-spatial unfolding of mental imagery (e.g., Sack et al., 2008), this hypothesis has yet to be tested.

The network of regions implicated in imagery often resembles the "core network" (for review, see Buckner, Andrews-Hanna, & Schacter, 2008), which is also sometimes called the "default network" because of its association with task-unrelated thought. The core network supports processing for a set of imagery-dependent tasks such a navigation, episodic recall, and perspective taking (see Buckner & Carroll, 2007; Hassabis & Maguire, 2007), and it has been characterized as a distinct network after researchers observed that seemingly dissimilar tasks activate strikingly similar brain regions.

That said, we note that some of the brain areas that are sometimes activated during visual mental imagery are not activated in the core network, particularly areas in the medial occipital lobe (for a summary, see Kosslyn et al., 2006). To a large degree, this difference may reflect the baseline conditions researchers tend to employ in their neuroimaging contrasts. Imagery researchers typically use baselines conditions that do not require visual processing or require minimal visual processing (e.g., Slotnick, Thompson, & Kosslyn, 2005), whereas researchers who investigate the core network typically use baseline conditions that do require visual processing (e.g., Addis, McIntosh, Moscovitch, Crawley, & McAndrews, 2004). When contrasted with target conditions that involve imagery, such baseline conditions surely mask activation in the lowest level sensory cortices. Furthermore, medial occipital areas are not activated during all types of imagery (such as spatial imagery). Moreover, even during visual mental imagery, these areas tend to be activated only when high-resolution representations are required to perform the task (see Kosslyn & Thompson, 2003); if a task does not require making fine-grained judgments about shape, these areas tend not to be activated.

Thus, baseline problems aside, we cannot identify a single "imagery network"; the areas that are activated depend, to some extent, both on the specific type of imagery (e.g., of objects versus spatial relations) and on the requirements of the task. Nonetheless, the core network is very similar to the network of areas that is activated during many imagery tasks, particularly those that do not require making subtle judgments about shape.

MENTAL IMAGERY, MENTAL SIMULATION, AND MENTAL EMULATION

Mental imagery may best be understood in the context of mental simulation, specifically as a kind of mental emulation. As a psychological construct, mental simulation has been considered theoretically and researched empirically in many different contexts: self-regulation (e.g., Taylor, Pham, Rivkin, & Armor, 1998), memory (e.g., Ingvar, 1979), mental practice (e.g., Driskell, Copper, & Moran, 1994), decision making (e.g., Kahneman & Tversky, 1982), mechanical reasoning (e.g., Hegarty, 2004), consciousness (e.g., Hesslow, 2002), creativity (Clement, 2008), social cognition (e.g., Gordon, 1986), affective regulation (e.g., Gilbert & Wilson, 2007), and mental imagery (e.g., Kosslyn, 2008).

Nearly all of these differing treatments of simulation converge on the two essential features of mental simulations. First, simulations are, in the words of Fisher (2006), "epistemic devices" (p. 419). In other words, they make available or generate knowledge. For example, in simulating the sound of a police siren you can access stored information about its acoustical properties to answer questions such as "Does a police siren have a constant pitch?" In addition, mental simulations can be used to generate knowledge, allowing you to answer presumably novel questions such as "How does a police siren differ from an ambulance siren?" However, we note that many mental processes other than simulation make available or generate knowledge (e.g., perception, deduction), and hence this feature cannot by itself define simulation.

Second, simulations operate by sequential analogy. That is, the steps of the simulation mimic the corresponding steps of the represented situation. Mental simulations are "run" such that intermediate steps in the process correspond to intermediate states in the event being simulated. This correspondence is not necessarily one to one (i.e., an isomorphism; see Goldman, 1995); not every step in the event must correspond to a distinct step in processing. But each of the intermediate states of the simulation must approximate an intermediate state of the to-be-simulated event (see Fisher, 2006). For example,

in simulating the drive from one location to another, one need not simulate every turn of the steering wheel or curve of the road; instead, one can merely simulate a sequence of key turns. Importantly, this loose correspondence in intermediate states is a necessary but not sufficient condition of simulation: The ordering of intermediate states in the simulation must also mirror the ordering of the corresponding process or event. In the navigation example, therefore, the sequence of simulated turns must correspond to the sequence of turns in the actual journey.

Furthermore, the sequence of states is functional, not epiphenomenal: Each step generates or makes accessible information that critically constrains succeeding steps. A simple example is mental rotation: As an object rotates, each intermediate orientation represents an intermediate orientation of the corresponding object. Or, to take a richer example, when visualizing how far one could hit a ping-pong ball with a baseball bat, one does not engage in simulation by merely imagining the ball at some distance from its initial position; instead, one must also imagine the initial setup, the swing of the baseball bat, and the full trajectory of the ball. Furthermore, the swing of the baseball bat depends on the initial setup, the trajectory of the ball depends on the swing and the initial setup, and the final resting place of the ball depends on the initial setup, the swing, and the trajectory. Any process that lacks a functionally dependent sequence does not qualify as a mental simulation. Thus, in sum, we define mental simulation as an epistemic device that operates by sequential analogy.[2]

Critically, we can distinguish between two fundamentally different types of simulations: *instrumental simulations* and *emulative simulations*. In the former, the algorithms that transform between successive states in the simulation differ categorically from the processes that transform successive states in the simulated event. For example, you could simulate a social conversation by using conceptual knowledge or hypotheses of the participants to approximate

---

[2] Although we limit this definition to mental simulation and not simulation in general, it may very well apply to the latter as well.

their dialogue. Although this simulation generates knowledge via sequential analogy, the explicit third-person theorizing that drives the simulation bears little resemblance to the first-person socializing that would characterize the actual encounter. These simulations are instrumental in the sense that their algorithms serve merely as the means to produce successive states (and a final outcome) given a set of initial parameters.

In contrast to instrumental simulations, emulative simulations (or, simply, "emulations") mimic not only the intermediate states of the simulated event, but they also rely on algorithms that mimic the processes that transform successive states of that event. To simulate a conversation via emulation, for example, you could place yourself in the "mental shoes" of those conversing, predicting their dialogue based upon how you would respond (based on your emotions and the associations that are triggered) in their respective situations. Unlike instrumental simulations, the processes that generate successive states of emulative simulations are not merely instruments used to produce these successive states—they also function as a second layer of simulation. Put differently, whereas instrumental simulations can be thought of as first-order simulation (in that they imitate content), emulations can be thought of as second-order simulations (in that they imitate the processes that change content as well as the content itself).

In defining mental emulation as a type of simulation in which the psychological processes that drive the simulation mimic the processes involved in the simulated event, we imply a close connection to mental imagery. Images, by definition, mimic what we perceive, and hence images can easily capture a sequence of states that underlie an event. Others imply such a connection between imagery and simulation, too, oftentimes without clarifying explicitly the relationship between the two concepts. For example, Roese (1997) defines simulation as "imaginative mental construction" (p. 134), Buckner, Andrews-Hanna, and Schacter (2008) define it as "imaginative constructions of hypothetical events or scenarios" (p. 20), and Taylor and colleagues (1998) define it as "imitative representation of some event or series of events" (p. 430). But how tight

is the relation between mental emulation and mental imagery? Could they be one and the same? Or might mental emulation merely sometimes draw on imagery? Or might there be no functional connection between the two?

Similarities between Imagery and Mental Emulation

On all three levels of analysis—computation, algorithm, and implementation—imagery and mental emulation are fundamentally similar. In fact, based on the evidence reviewed next, we argue that although all mental emulations may not involve imagery, all imagery is mental emulation.

Predictive Function

Because all mental simulations make available or generate knowledge about specific events, they make specific predictions. Thus, in terms of computational function, imagery and mental simulation (instrumental and emulative) are fundamentally similar. Indeed, the fact that the terms "simulation" and "imagery" can often be used interchangeably reveals their functional similarity. For example, if we asked you to "imagine a cat's head on a dog's body" and "simulate a cat's head on a dog's body" you, in all likelihood, would understand the task similarly, if not identically. In fact, many experiments that ostensibly investigate mental simulation explicitly instruct their participants to engage in imagery. For example, Bruzzo, Geslerich, and Wohlschläger (2008) studied the "mechanisms underlying mental simulation" (p. 145) by asking participants to "imagine" movements, and Green, Applebaum, and Tong (2006) studied "how mental simulation alters the impact of previously presented arguments" (p. 32) by asking participants to "imagine a future state of affairs" (p. 38). Clearly, imagery and simulation can be used interchangeably to instruct research participants, which implies that the terms often have comparable meanings.

Perceptual Representation

Much evidence supports the claim that many forms of mental simulation rely on perceptual representations and, in doing so, connects mental emulation with mental imagery. For starters, individuals engaged in simulation often report the defining phenomenological feature of imagery: "seeing with their mind's eye" (e.g., Clement, 1994). However, even if we take such reports at face value, the co-occurrence of mental imagery and mental simulation does not imply that the latter requires the former: Mental imagery may play an epiphenomenal role in simulation, just as the trajectory of a projectile visualized on a computer monitor plays no functional role in the underlying simulation.

Interference and individual differences paradigms provide evidence that many forms of mental simulation depend on perceptual representations. For example, Sims and Hegarty (1997) found that a visuospatial task (compared to an equally difficult verbal task) selectively interfered with participants' ability to simulate mechanical motion. And using an individual differences approach, Hegarty and Sims (1994) found that performance on mechanical simulation tasks correlated strongly with performance on spatial imagery tasks. If these forms of simulation did not depend on perceptual representations, one could not explain easily either of these findings.

Moreover, neuroscientific evidence also implicates perceptual representations in many types of mental simulation. On the whole, the perceptual regions associated with actual movement are also associated with simulated movement (for review, see Grezes & Decety, 2001; Jeannerod, 2001). Furthermore, simulated movement reduces the amount of transcranial magnetic stimulation (TMS) required to induce actual motion (Fadiga et al., 1999; Hashimoto & Rothwell, 1999), which is just as expected if the simulated movements engage the same neural structures that are stimulated by TMS—and hence boost the effects of TMS.

The forms of simulation investigated in the aforementioned studies are all, arguably, examples of mental emulation. The "mental witnessing" of mechanical motion and experiencing of bodily motion, for example, rely fundamentally on perceptual processes. Whereas emulative simulations of these events apparently rely on

perceptual representations, instrumental simulations of the same events do not.

Neural Implementation

In addition to activating perceptual cortices, mental simulation activates all other regions of the core network, as noted earlier. In fact, in coining the term "core network," Buckner and Carroll (2007) describe its unifying function in terms of simulation: "the processes of the network are characterized by a personal, internal mode of mental simulation" (p. 49).

Thus, from the perspective of the brain, mental simulation and mental imagery are similar. Again, we argue that this similarity applies specifically to emulative simulations. Only with emulations would one expect such a strong overlap between the neural correlates of mental imagery (which mimics perception) and simulation, as well as the overlap between simulation (e.g., in episodic memory) and perception (e.g., Wheeler, Petersen, & Buckner, 2000).

Differences between Imagery and Emulation

Given the fundamental similarities between mental emulation and imagery, one could be tempted to conclude that they are not merely overlapping constructs, but instead are identical. However, before making this leap, we must reflect on several potential distinctions between emulation and imagery. The following distinctions have been raised in the literature.

Simple versus Complex

Schacter, Addis, and Buckner (2008) define simulation as the "imaginative constructions of hypothetical events or scenarios…that involves more than simple imagery" (p. 42). Whether simulation differs qualitatively from "simple imagery" in their view, however, remains unclear, as does their notion of simple imagery. But even if it does, there may be no difference between complex imagery and simulation (cf. Hassabis, Kumaran, & Maguire, 2007).

Along similar lines, Hegarty (2004) argues that simulation does not simply involve visual representations. Her argument is based on evidence that concurrent motion and body position affect simulation. As far as we know, however, no one has claimed that mental simulation involves exclusively visual representations, and for good reason: Even performance on apparently simple tasks of "visual" imagery (e.g., mental rotation) often relies on motor representations (e.g., Ganis, Keenan, Kosslyn, & Pascual-Leone, 2000) and is affected by body position (Mast, Ganis, Christie, & Kosslyn, 2003).

Holistic versus Piecemeal Generation

Citing evidence that individuals construct mental simulations of mechanical systems in a piecemeal fashion, Hegarty (2004) claims that simulation differs from imagery. She argues that if individuals used imagery to simulate mechanical motion, they could create and inspect holistic images of mechanical motion, and they would not need to build up their simulations piece by piece. However, she ignores evidence that individuals construct images, like simulations, in stages. For example, individuals generate images of novel patterns serially based upon the sequence in which they originally encoded the parts into memory, and they generate images of block letters serially based upon writing sequence (Kosslyn, Cave, Provost, & von Gierke, 1988). Depending on the image, sequential image generation probably reflects a variety of constraints, including limited attentional resources, the "refresh rate" of co-opted perceptual hardware, the encoding of object parts (rather than entire objects), and the reliance on relative (rather than absolute) spatial information (see Kosslyn, 1994).

Conscious versus Unconscious

Barsalou (2008) draws a clear distinction between imagery and the broader concept of simulation: "Whereas mental imagery typically results from deliberate attempts to construct conscious representations in working memory, other forms of simulation often appear to become active automatically and unconsciously outside working memory" (p. 619). Kent and Lamberts (2008) echo this distinction, arguing that whereas explicit simulation involves mental imagery, implicit simulation requires neither "consciously

experienced analogue reasoning or explicit episodic recall" (p. 93). Relying on this same explicit-implicit/deliberate-automatic distinction, Gallese (2003) argues that imagery and simulation are wholly distinct constructs and goes so far as to claim that all simulations are implicit and automatic.

However, the distinction between instrumental simulation and emulative simulation is pertinent here. It is possible that only emulations necessarily rely on working memory. Indeed, ample evidence indicates that people are aware of at least some simulations, and that they intentionally use such simulations (e.g., Clement, 1994). Thus, we can easily reject the idea that all simulations are implicit and automatic.[3] We cannot reject as easily, however, the possibility that some implicit simulations exist in implicit memory—specifically simulations that underlie high-level perception, sensorimotor coordination, conceptual knowledge (Barsalou, 1999, 2003, 2008), language comprehension (Pulvermuller, 2005), and social cognition (Gallese, 2003).

However, to qualify as simulation, and thereby serve as an epistemic device, a simulation must feed into processes used in working memory. Even if an implicit process were to operate via sequential analogy, it would not qualify as an emulation unless it produces consciously accessible information. As Fisher (2006) states, "a simulation is supposed to work by providing an epistemically available process that reflects the relevant aspects of some process that is not so epistemically available " (p. 419).

In short, we are led to conclude that *all* mental imagery is mental emulation. However, we do not assert that all mental emulation (or simulation) necessarily must be mental imagery; we leave open the possibility that implicit simulation exists, and that it does not rely on imagery.

Advantages of Imagery-Based Mental Emulation

Mental emulation via mental imagery offers several functional advantages over instrumental

---

[3] In stark contrast to Gallese's (2003) argument that all simulation is implicit and automatic, Hesslow (2002) argues that all conscious thought is simulation.

simulation and implicit emulation (if such processing in fact exists).

For one, because imagery mimics perception (including the perception of movement, both of the body and of objects), it evokes similar associations (including emotional responses), and, in turn, can generate accurate predictions (see Kosslyn, 2008). Thus, one can try out alternative scenarios, varying key aspects of an anticipated situation (e.g., the person to whom one asks specific questions). Implicit simulation is by definition rigid: It is a response to a specific stimulus, and it cannot be varied at will.

In addition, imagery can reveal conceptual knowledge that informs prediction. For example, one can recover information stored tacitly in memory and use that information to guide future behavior. One example is our ability to visualize spatial layouts and then to use this information to plan routes. Furthermore, because imagery-based predictions are mediated by working memory (and hence we are aware of them), they can be explicitly reported, shared, remembered, and violated.

Finally, imagery can aid prediction by creating or modifying implicit memories. As Bar (2007) notes, "We simulate, plan and combine past and future in our thoughts, and the result might be 'written' in memory for future use" (p. 286). In fact, imagery can actually build in conditioned responses (Dadds, Bovbjerg, Redd, & Cutmore, 1997).

CONCLUDING REMARKS

In this brief chapter we have made the case that mental imagery plays a key role in many forms of mental simulation, specifically in emulative simulations. We have by necessity only skimmed the surface. We have not considered, for example, the circumstances in which such mental emulations rely on different forms of imagery, such as object versus spatial. Nor have we considered the alternatives to imagery-based simulation in detail or reviewed the abundant evidence that imagery-based simulation underlies episodic memory, episodic future thinking, counterfactual thinking, spontaneous cognition, and mentalizing. We leave the door open to the possibility

that some simulations rely on implicit, nonimagery processes, but we argue strongly that whenever imagery is used, it is used in the service of simulation. One uses imagery to simulate what one would perceive if one were in a specific situation; this is as true of imagery used to retrieve memories as it is of imagery used to predict the future. Mental images are a way to move the world into the head and then to "run" models to observe possible implications for the actual world. As such, imagery and simulation are joined at the hip and should be studied together.

ACKNOWLEDGMENTS

Correspondence concerning this chapter should be sent to Sam Moulton (moulton@wjh.harvard.edu). Preparation of this chapter was supported by National Institutes of Mental Health grant R01 MH060734 to S. M. Kosslyn. Any opinions, findings, and conclusions or recommendations expressed in this material are those of the authors and do not necessarily reflect the views of the National Institutes of Mental Health. We thank Fenna M. Krienen for her insightful comments on an earlier draft of this manuscript.

REFERENCES

Addis, D. R., McIntosh, A. R., Moscovitch, M., Crawley, A. P., & McAndrews, M. P. (2004). Characterizing spatial and temporal features of autobiographical memory retrieval networks: A partial least squares approach. *NeuroImage, 23,* 1460–1471.

Bar, M. (2007). The proactive brain: using analogies and associations to generate predictions. *Trends in Cognitive Sciences, 11,* 280–289.

Barsalou, L. W. (1999). Perceptual symbol systems. *Behavioral and Brain Sciences, 22,* 577–609.

Barsalou, L. W. (2003). Situated simulation in the human conceptual system. *Language and Cognitive Processes, 18,* 513–562.

Barsalou, L. W. (2008). Grounded cognition. *Annual Review of Psychology, 59,* 617–645.

Bruzzo, A., Gesierich, B., & Wohlschlaeger, A. (2008). Simulating biological and non-biological motion. *Brain and Cognition, 66,* 145–149.

Buckner, R. L., Andrews-Hanna, J. R., & Schacter, D. L. (2008). The brain's default network—Anatomy, function, and relevance to disease [Special issue]. *Annals of the New York Academy of Sciences,, 1124*, 1–38.

Buckner, R. L., & Carroll, D. C. (2007). Self-projection and the brain. *Trends in Cognitive Sciences, 11*, 49–57.

Buckner, R. L., & Wheeler, M. E. (2001). The cognitive neuroscience of remembering. *Nature Reviews Neuroscience, 2*, 624–634.

Cabeza, R., & Nyberg, L. (2000). Imaging cognition II: An empirical review of 275 PET and fMRI studies. *Journal of Cognitive Neuroscience, 12*, 1–47.

Clement, J. (1994). Use of physical intuition and imagistic simulation in expert problem solving. In D. Tirosh (Ed.), *Implicit and explicit knowledge: An educational approach* (pp. 204-244). Norwood, NJ: Ablex.

Clement, J. (2008). *Creative model construction in scientists and students: The role of imagery, analogy, and mental simulation.* Amherst, MA: Springer.

Dadds, M. R., Bovbjerg, D. H., Redd, W. H., & Cutmore, T. R. H. (1997). Imagery in human classical conditioning. *Psychological Bulletin, 122*, 89–103.

Driskell, J. E., Copper, C., & Moran, A. (1994). Does mental practice enhance performance? *Journal of Applied Psychology, 79*, 481–492.

Fadiga, L., Buccino, G., Craighero, L., Fogassi, L., Gallese, V., & Pavesi, G. (1999). Corticospinal excitability is specifically modulated by motor imagery: A magnetic stimulation study. *Neuropsychologia, 37*, 147–158.

Fisher, J. C. (2006). Does simulation theory really involve simulation? *Philosophical Psychology, 19*, 417–432.

Gallese, V. (2003). The manifold nature of interpersonal relations: The quest for a common mechanism. *Philosophical Transactions of the Royal Society of London B: Biological Sciences, 358*, 517–528.

Ganis, G., Keenan, J. P., Kosslyn, S. M., & Pascual-Leone, A. (2000). Transcranial magnetic stimulation of primary motor cortex affects mental rotation. *Cerebral Cortex, 10*, 175–180.

Gilbert, D. T., & Wilson, T. D. (2007). Prospection: Experiencing the future. *Science, 317*, 1351–1354.

Gordon, R. M. (1986). Folk psychology as simulation. *Mind and Language, 1*, 158–171.

Green, D. W., Applebaum, R., & Tong, S. (2006). Mental simulation and argument. *Thinking and Reasoning, 12*, 31–61.

Grezes, J., & Decety, J. (2001). Functional anatomy of execution, mental simulation, observation, and verb generation of actions: A meta-analysis. *Human Brain Mapping, 12*, 1–19.

Hashimoto, R., & Rothwell, J. C. (1999). Dynamic changes in corticospinal excitability during motor imagery. *Experimental Brain Research, 125*, 75–81.

Hassabis, D., Kumaran, D., & Maguire, E. A. (2007). Using imagination to understand the neural basis of episodic memory. *The Journal of Neuroscience, 27*, 14365–14374.

Hassabis, D., Kumaran, D., Vann, S. D., & Maguire, E. A. (2007). Patients with hippocampal amnesia cannot imagine new experiences. *Proceedings of the National Academy of Sciences USA, 104*, 1726–1731.

Hassabis, D., & Maguire, E. A. (2007). Deconstructing episodic memory with construction. *Trends in Cognitive Sciences, 11*, 299–306.

Hegarty, M. (2004). Mechanical reasoning by mental simulation. *Trends in Cognitive Sciences, 8*, 280–285.

Hegarty, M., & Sims, V. K. (1994). Individual differences in mental animation during mechanical simulation. *Memory and Cognition, 22*, 411–430.

Hesslow, G. (2002). Conscious thought as simulation of behaviour and perception. *Trends in Cognitive Sciences, 6*, 242–247.

Ingvar, D. H. (1979). Hyper-frontal distribution of the cerebral grey-matter flow in resting wakefulness: On the functional-anatomy of the conscious state. *Acta Neurologica Scandinavica, 60*, 12–25.

Jeannerod, M. (1994). The representing brain: Neural correlates of motor intention and imagery. *Behavioral and Brain Sciences, 17*, 187–202.

Jeannerod, M. (2001). Neural simulation of action: A unifying mechanism for motor cognition. *NeuroImage, 14*, S103–S109.

Kahneman, D., & Tversky, A. (1982). The simulation heuristic. In D. Kahneman, P. Slovic, & A. Tversky (Eds.), *Judgment under uncertainty* (pp. 201–208). Cambridge, England: Cambridge University Press.

Kent, C., & Lamberts, K. (2008). The encoding-retrieval relationship: Retrieval as mental simulation. *Trends in Cognitive Sciences, 12*, 92–98.

Kobayashi, M., Takeda, M., Hattori, N., Fukunaga, M., Sasabe, T., Inoue, N., Nagai, Y., Sawada, T.,

Sadato, N., & Watanabe, Y. (2004). Functional imaging of gustatory perception and imagery: "top-down" processing of gustatory signals. *NeuroImage, 23*, 1271–1282.

Kosslyn, S. M. (1980). *Image and mind*. Cambridge, MA: Harvard University Press.

Kosslyn, S. M. (1994). *Image and brain: The resolution of the imagery debate*. Cambridge, MA: MIT Press.

Kosslyn, S. M. (2008). Remembering images. In M. A. Gluck, J. R. Anderson, & S. M. Kosslyn (Eds.), *Memory and mind: A festschrift for Gordon H. Bower* (pp. 93-110). New York: Erlbaum.

Kosslyn, S. M., Cave, C. B., Provost, D. A., & von Gierke, S. M. (1988). Sequential processes in image generation. *Cognitive Psychology, 20*, 319–343.

Kosslyn, S. M., & Maljkovic, V. (1990). Marr's metatheory revisited. *Concepts in Neuroscience, 1*, 239–251.

Kosslyn, S. M., & Thompson, W. L. (2003). When is early visual cortex activated during visual mental imagery? *Psychological Bulletin, 129*, 723–746.

Kosslyn, S. M., Thompson, W. L., & Ganis, G. (2006). *The case for mental imagery*. New York: Oxford University Press.

Marr, D. (1982). *Vision: A computational approach*. San Francisco: Freeman & Company.

Mast, F. W., Ganis, G., Christie, S., & Kosslyn, S. M. (2003). Four types of visual mental imagery processing in upright and tilted observers. *Cognitive Brain Research, 17*, 238–247.

Mellet, E., Petit, L., Mazoyer, B., Denis, M., & Tzourio, N. (1998). Reopening the mental imagery debate: Lessons from functional anatomy. *NeuroImage, 8*, 129–139.

O'Connor, M., Butters, N., Miliotis, P., Eslinger, P., & Cermak, L. S. (1992). The dissociation of anterograde and retrograde-amnesia in a patient with herpes encephalitis. *Journal of Clinical and Experimental Neuropsychology, 14*, 159–178.

Ogden, J. A. (1993). Visual object agnosia, prosopagnosia, achromatopsia, loss of visual-imagery, and autobiographical amnesia following recovery from cortical blindness: Case MH. *Neuro-psychologia, 31*, 571–589.

Paivio, A. (1971). *Imagery and verbal processes*. Oxford, England: Holt, Rinehart, & Winston.

Paivio, A. (1986). *Mental representations: A dual coding approach*. Oxford, England: Oxford University Press.

Porro, C. A., Francescato, M. P., Cettolo, V., Diamond, M. E., Baraldi, P., Zuiani, C., Bazzocchi, M., & di Prampero, P. E. (1996). Primary motor and sensory cortex activation during motor performance and motor imagery: A functional magnetic resonance imaging study. *Journal of Neuroscience, 16*, 7688–7698.

Pulvermuller, F. (2005). Brain mechanisms linking language and action. *Nature Reviews Neuroscience, 6*, 576–582.

Roese, N. J. (1997). Counterfactual thinking. *Psychological Bulletin, 121*, 133–148.

Rosenbaum, R. S., McKinnon, M. C., Levine, B., & Moscovitch, M. (2004). Visual imagery deficits, impaired strategic retrieval, or memory loss: Disentangling the nature of an amnesic person's autobiographical memory deficit. *Neuropsychologia, 42*, 1619–1635.

Rubin, D. C., & Greenberg, D. L. (1998). Visual memory-deficit amnesia: A distinct amnesic presentation and etiology. *Proceedings of the National Academy of Sciences USA, 95*, 5413–5416.

Sack, A. T., Jacobs, C., De Martino, F., Staeren, N., Goebel, R., & Formisano, E. (2008). Dynamic premotor-to-parietal interactions during spatial imagery. *Journal of Neuroscience, 28*, 8417–8429.

Schacter, D. L., Addis, D. R., & Buckner, R. L. (2008). Episodic simulation of future events—concepts, data, and applications [Special isssue]. *Cognitive Neuroscience, 1124*, 39–60.

Shepard, R. N., & Metzler, J. (1971). Mental rotation of three-dimensional objects. *Science, 171*, 701–703.

Shin, L. M., McNally, R. J., Kosslyn, S. M., Thompson, W. L., Rauch, S. L., Alpert, N. M., et al. (1999). Regional cerebral blood flow during script-driven imagery in childhood sexual abuse-related PTSD: A PET investigation. *American Journal of Psychiatry, 156*, 575–584.

Sims, V. K., & Hegarty, M. (1997). Mental animation in the visuospatial sketchpad: Evidence from dual-task studies. *Memory and Cognition, 25*, 321–332.

Slotnick, S. D., Thompson, W. L., & Kosslyn, S. M. (2005). Visual mental imagery induces retinotopically organized activation of early visual areas. *Cerebral Cortex, 15*, 1570–1583.

Smith, E. E., Jonides, J., Koeppe, R. A., Awh, E., Schumacher, E. H., & Minoshima, S. (1995). Spatial versus object working-memory: PET investigations. *Journal of Cognitive Neuroscience, 7*, 337–356.

Taylor, S. E., Pham, L. B., Rivkin, I. D., & Armor, D. A. (1998). Harnessing the imagination—Mental simulation, self-regulation, and coping. *American Psychologist*, *53*, 429–439.

Tresch, M. C., Sinnamon, H. M., & Seamon, J. G. (1993). Double dissociation of spatial and object visual memory: Evidence from selective interference in intact human subjects. *Neuropsychologia*, *31*, 211–219.

Wagner, A. D., Shannon, B. J., Kahn, I., & Buckner, R. L. (2005). Parietal lobe contributions to episodic memory retrieval. *Trends in Cognitive Sciences*, *9*, 445–453.

Watson, J. B., & Rayner, R. (1920). Conditional emotional reactions. *Journal of Experimental Psychology*, *3*, 1–14.

Wheeler, M. E., Petersen, S. E., & Buckner, R. L. (2000). Memory's echo: Vivid remembering reactivates sensory-specific cortex. *Proceedings of the National Academy of Sciences USA*, *97*, 11125–11129.

Zatorre, R. J., Halpern, A. R., Perry, D. W., Meyer, E., & Evans, A. C. (1996). Hearing in the mind's ear: A PET investigation of musical imagery and perception. *Journal of Cognitive Neuroscience*, *8*, 29–46.

CHAPTER 9
See It with Feeling: Affective Predictions during Object Perception

Lisa Feldman Barrett and Moshe Bar

Michael May lost the ability to see when he was 3 years old, after an accident destroyed his left eye and damaged his right cornea. Some 40 years later, Mr. May received a corneal transplant that restored his brain's ability to absorb normal visual input from the world (Fine et al., 2003). With the hardware finally working, Mr. May saw only simple movements, colors, and shapes rather than, as most people do, a world of faces and objects and scenes. It was as though he lived in two different worlds: one where sound, touch, smell, and taste were all integrated, and a second world of vision that stood apart. His visual sensations seemed foreign, like a language he was just learning to speak. As time passed, and Mr. May gained experience with the visual world in context, he slowly became fluent in vision. Two years after his surgery, Mr. May commented, "*The difference between today and over 2 years ago is that I can better guess at what I am seeing. What is the same is that I am still guessing*" (p. 916, italics in the original).

What Mr. May did not know is that sighted people automatically make the guesses he was forced to make with effort. From birth, the human brain captures statistical regularities in sensory-motor patterns and stores them as internal representations. The brain then uses these stored representations, on a regular basis and almost instantaneously, to predict continuously and unintentionally what incoming visual sensations stand for in the world (Bar, 2003, 2007; Kveraga, Ghuman, & Bar, 2007a, b; see also Chapter 2).

When the brain receives new sensory input from the world in the present, it generates a hypothesis based on what it knows from the past to guide recognition and action in the immediate future. This is how people learn that the sounds of a voice come from moving lips on a face, that the red and green blotches on a round Macintosh apple are associated with a certain tartness of taste, and that the snowy white petals of an English rose have a velvety texture and hold a certain fragrance.

External sensations do not occur in a vacuum. They occur in a context of internal sensations from the body that holds the brain. The sensory-motor patterns being stored for future use include sensations from organs, muscles, and joints (or "interoceptive" sensations), as well as representations of sights, sounds, smells, tastes, and touch ("exteroceptive" sensations). Although bodily sensations are rarely experienced consciously or with perfect fidelity (Barrett, Quigley, Bliss-Moreau, & Aronson, 2004), they are continually detected and internally represented (Craig, 2002). Psychology refers to these internal bodily changes as "affective." In addition to directly experiencing changes in their breathing, muscle tension, or stomach motility, people routinely experience bodily changes as more diffuse feelings of pleasure or discomfort, feeling worked up or slowed down. Therefore, in addition to learning that the sounds of a voice come from moving lips, people also learn whether they liked the sound of the voice (Bliss-Moreau, Owren, & Barrett, 2010) and the person that it belongs to (Bliss-Moreau, Barrett, & Wright, 2008); they learn that they enjoy tartly flavored red and green (Macintosh) apples or the milder tasting yellow apples (Golden Delicious); and they learn whether they prefer the strong fragrance of white English roses over the milder smell of a deep red American Beauty, or even the smell of roses over lilies. When the brain detects visual sensations from the eye in the present moment, and tries to interpret them by generating a prediction about what those visual sensations refer to or stand for in the world, it uses not only previously encountered patterns of sound, touch, smell, and tastes, or stored conceptual knowledge. It also uses affective representations—prior experiences of how those external sensations have influenced internal sensations from the body. Often these representations reach subjective awareness and are experienced as affective feelings, but they need not (for a recent discussion, see Barrett & Bliss-Moreau, in 2009). Guessing at what an object is, in part, requires knowing its value.

In this chapter, we explore the hypothesis that the brain routinely makes affective predictions during visual recognition. We suggest that the brain's prediction about the meaning of visual sensations of the present includes some representation of the affective impact of those (or similar) sensations in the past. An affective prediction, in effect, allows the brain to anticipate and prepare to act on those sensations in the future. Furthermore, we hypothesize that affective predictions are made quickly and efficiently, only milliseconds after visual sensations register on the retina. From this perspective, sensations from the body are a dimension of knowledge—they help people to identify what an object is when upon encountering it, based in part on past reactions. If this hypothesis is correct, then affective responses signaling an object's salience, relevance, or value, do not occur as a separate step after the object is identified—affective response assists in seeing an object as what it is from the very moment that visual stimulation begins. Regardless of whether he was aware of it, Mr. May's predictions about the visual world probably became more effective, in part, as his body became more responsive to his visual sensations.

Learning to see meant experiencing visual sensations as value added. Whether experienced consciously or not, a pleasant or unpleasant affective change in response to visual stimulation might have helped Mr. May (as it helps all of us) to recognize moving lips as a particular person speaking, a blotch of red and green as an apple, or white silky petals as a rose.

Affect defined

In English, the word *affect* means "to produce a change." To be affected by something is to be influenced by it. In psychology, "affect" refers to a specific kind of influence—something's ability to influence a person's body state. Sometimes, the resulting bodily sensations in the core of the body are experienced as physical symptoms (such as being wound up from drinking too much coffee, fatigued from not enough sleep, or energetic from exercise). Much of the time, sensations from the body are experienced as simple feelings of pleasure or displeasure with some degree of activation, either alone, or as an emotion (see Fig. 9.1; see Barrett & Bliss-Moreau, 2009; Russell & Barrett, 1999). At still other times, bodily changes are too subtle to be consciously experienced at all. Whether consciously felt or not, an object is said to have affective "value" if it has the capacity to influence a person's breathing, heart rate, hormonal secretions, and so on. In fact, objects are said to be "positive" or "negative" by virtue of their capacity to influence a person's body state (just as objects are said to be "red" if they reflect light at 600 nm).

When affect is experienced so that it is reportable, it can be in the background or foreground of consciousness. When in the background, it is perceived as a property of the world, rather than as the person's reaction to it. "Unconscious affect" (as it is called) is why a drink tastes delicious or is unappetizing (e.g., Berridge & Winkielman, 2003; Koenigs & Tranel, 2008; Winkielman, Berridge, & Wilbarger, 2005); why some people are nice and others as mean (Li, Moallem, Paller, & Gottfried, 2007); and why some paintings are beautiful while others are ugly (for discussion of affect and preferences, see Clore & Storbeck, 2006). When in the foreground, it is perceived as

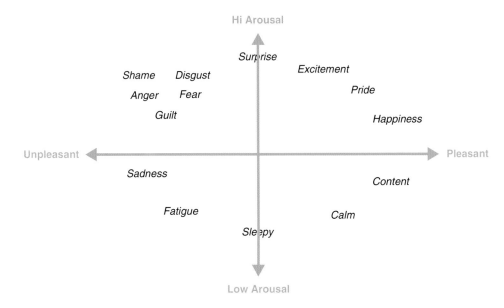

Figure 9.1 A descriptive map of core affect.

a personal reaction to the world: People like or dislike a drink, a person, or a painting. Affect can be experienced as emotional (such as being anxious at an uncertain outcome, depressed from a loss, or happy at a reward; Barrett, 2006 a, b).

AFFECT AND PERCEPTION

For centuries, philosophers have believed that every moment of waking life is to some degree pleasant or unpleasant with some degree of arousal, so that affect is a basic ingredient of mental life. This idea continues to be incorporated into contemporary perspectives on consciousness, including Damasio's somatic marker hypothesis (Damasio, 1999), Edelman's theory of neural Darwinism (Edelman, 1987; Edelman & Tononi, 2000), Searle's theory of consciousness (Searle, 1992, 2004), and Humphrey's theory of conscious sensation (Humphrey, 2006). This idea can also be found in early psychological writing of Spencer (1855), James (1890), Sully (1892), and Wundt (1998/1897). During the behaviorist era in psychology, scientists no longer regarded affect as central to psychology, and this trend continued as psychology emerged into the cognitive revolution. Affective responses were ignored in cognitive science altogether and questions about affect were relegated to the study of emotion, where it was assumed that affect occurred after object perception and in reaction to it (e.g., Arnold, 1960). First, a red, round, hard object is perceived as an apple, and only then is the object related to past experiences of enjoying the crunchy sweetness of the first bite, or to a breezy trip to the farm for apple picking on a fine autumn afternoon.

As it turns out, philosophers and early psychologists were right, at least when it comes to the place of affect in mental life. We contend that prior affective reactions to apples might actually help the brain to predict that visual sensations refer to an apple in the first place. Not only does the brain draft the prediction of an apple into a conscious perception of an apple, but the resulting affective response may also become conscious, so that the apple is experienced as pleasant or perceivers experience themselves as reacting with a pleasant, mild state of arousal.

It is easy to see evidence for this logic by referring briefly to the neuronal workspace that realizes affective responses (presented in Fig. 9.2).

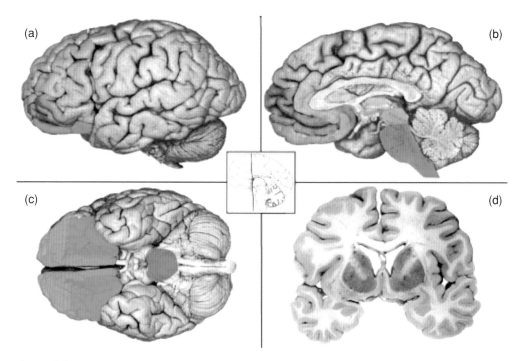

Figure 9.2 The affective workspace. The neural workspace for core affect includes a broadly distributed set of interconnected cortical and subcortical brain areas that are not functionally specific to affect, but that realize affective responses as a network (for imaging evidence, see Barrett, Mesquita, Ochsner, & Gross, 2007; Kringelbach & Rolls, 2004; Wager et al., 2008; for a discussion, see Barrett & Bliss-Moreau, in press). Some areas are traditionally considered to be "emotional," such as the amygdala (rose) and ventral striatum (green). Other areas were (until recently) considered "cognitive" (Duncan & Barrett, 2007; for a similar view, see Pessoa, 2008), such as the orbitofrontal cortex (OFC; blue, purple). Typically, researchers use the term "orbitofrontal cortex" to refer to anywhere within the orbital sector of prefrontal cortex. This includes the lateral parts (blue) that are bounded by ventrolateral prefrontal cortex (vlPFC) and agranular insula (yellow), as well as the medial portions that wrap to include ventromedial prefrontal cortex (vmPFC; purple) extending back to the sub/pregenual portions of the anterior cingulate cortex (ACC; brown and gold). Other components of this workspace include the hypothalamus (light green) and autonomic control centers in the midbrain and brain stem (turquoise, maroon). This neural reference space for affect is meant to be non-specific without sounding vague, in that different assemblies of neurons across these areas realize momentary representations of value (Barbas et al., 2003; Ghashghaei & Barbas, 2002) Photographs taken from DeArmond, Fusco, & Dewey (1989, p. 5, 7, 8, and 43).

The centerpiece of this circuitry is the orbitofrontal cortex (OFC). In this chapter, we use the acronym OFC to refer to the entire orbital sector of prefrontal cortex. The OFC is a heteromodal association area that integrates sensory input from the world and the body (i.e., from extrapersonal and intrapersonal space) to create a contextually sensitive, multimodal representation of the world and its value to the person at a particular moment in time (Barbas 1993, 2000; Carmichael & Price 1995; McDonald 1998;

Cavada et al. 2000; Ghashghaei & Barbas 2002; Mesulam 2000). The OFC plays a role in representing reward and threat (e.g., Kringelbach & Rolls, 2004) as well as hedonic experience (Kringelbach, 2005; Wager et al., 2008), but it also plays a role in processing olfactory, auditory, and visual information (see Figure 6 in Kringelbach, 2005; also see Price, 2007). The OFC's ongoing integration of sensory information from the external world with sensory information from the body strongly supports the idea that conscious percepts are intrinsically infused with affective value, so that the affective salience or significance of an object is not computed after the fact. As it turns out, the OFC plays a crucial role in forming the predictions that support object perception. This suggests the hypothesis that the predictions generated during object perception carry affective value as a necessary and normal part of visual experience.

EVIDENCE FOR AFFECTIVE PREDICTIONS

To formulate the affective prediction hypothesis, it is important to consider a more general aspect about the way the brain seems to formulate predictions during visual perception. There is accumulating evidence that during object perception, the brain quickly makes an initial prediction about the "gist" of the scene or object to which visual sensations refer (Bar et al., 2003, 2006; Oliva & Torralba, 2001; Schyns & Oliva, 1994; Torralba & Oliva, 2003). Like a Dutch artist from the sixteenth or seventeenth century, the brain uses low spatial frequency visual information available from the object in context to produce a rough sketch of an object, and then begins to fill in the details using information from memory (for a review, see Bar, 2004, 2007; also see Chapter 2). Effectively, the brain is performing a basic-level categorization that serves as a gist-level prediction about the class to which the object belongs.

With back-and-forth between visual cortex and areas of prefrontal cortex (via the direct projections that connect them), a finer level of categorization is achieved until a precise representation of the object is finally constructed. Like an artist who successively creates a representation of objects by applying smaller and smaller pieces of paint to represent light of different colors and intensities, the brain gradually adds high spatial frequency information until a specific object is consciously seen.

As the brain generates its initial prediction about an object, it uses information from the OFC, supporting the hypothesis that affect is a key ingredient of prediction. Studies that precisely measure the timing of neuronal activity indicate that information about an object is instantly propagated to the front of the brain. Activation of the OFC has been observed between 80 and 130 ms after stimulus onset (when objects are presented in isolation; e.g., for a review, see Bullier, 2001; Lamme & Roelfsema, 2000; also see Bar et al., 2006; Rudrauf et al., 2008; Thorpe, Rolls, & Maddison, 1983). Two studies indicate that this early activity is driven by low spatial frequency and magnocellular visual input characteristic of early stage prediction (Bar et al., 2006; Kveraga et al., 2007). This propagation of neuronal firing is sometimes called a "feedforward sweep" (Lamme & Roelfsema, 2000), where sensory information from the world is projected rapidly from the back to the front of the brain after an image is presented to the visual system (Bar, 2007, Bar et al., 2006). Many of these same studies show another wave of OFC activity between 200 and 450 ms, which might represent the refinement of initial affective predictions.

Similar findings are reported in the face perception literature. Early event-related potentials (ERPs) in frontal regions begin around 80 ms, but are typically observed between 120 and 180 ms after stimulus onset (depending on whether the face is presented foveally or parafoveally). These early components reflect the categorization of the face as a face (vs. a non-face) or as generally affective (neutral vs. valenced), as valenced (e.g., happy vs. sad), or as portraying some degree of arousal (for reviews, see Eimer & Holmes, 2007; Palermo & Rhodes, 2007; Vuilleumier & Pourtois, 2007). Later ERP components between 200 and 350 ms correspond to the conscious perception of fear, disgust, sadness, and anger (for a review, see Barrett, Lindquist, & Gendron, 2007).

THE CIRCUITRY FOR SEEING WITH FEELING

Neuroanatomical evidence provides the strongest support for the notion that affect informs visual perception and allows the affective prediction hypothesis to be further specified. The two functionally related circuits within the OFC (see Fig. 9.3; for reviews, see Barbas & Pandya, 1989; Carmichael & Price, 1996; Ongur & Price, 2000; Ongur, Ferry, & Price, 2003) are differentially connected to the dorsal "where is it" visual stream

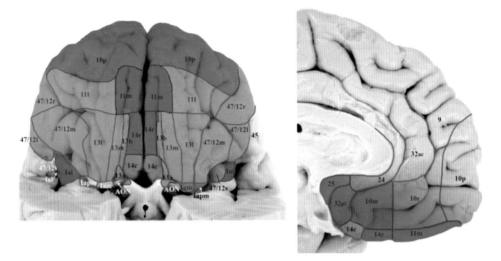

Figure 9.3 Medial and lateral networks of the orbitofrontal cortex (OFC). Orbital and medial views of the brain are shown. The medial network is shown in blue and has robust reciprocal connections to all limbic areas (including many nuclei within the amygdala, and the ventral striatum), as well as to the hypothalamus, midbrain, brain stem, and spinal cord areas that are involved in internal state regulation. Medial OFC has few direct connections to sensory cortices. The lateral network is shown in purple and has robust connections with unimodal sensory association areas as well as the cortical aspects of the amygdala (including the basolateral complex, which also receives sensory input from unimodal association areas. The lateral OFC has few direct projections to autonomic and endocrine control centers in the hypothalamus, midbrain, and brain stem but has some influence on those autonomic centers via projections to the intercalated masses within the amygdala that have the net effect of disinhibiting (i.e., activating) these nuclei. Areas that connect the two networks are shown in rose. (Adapted from Ongur et al. [2003] based on evidence from Barbas [1993, 2000], Carmichael & Price [1995], Cavada et al. [2000], Ghashghaei & Barbas [2002], McDonald [1998], and Stefanacci & Amaral [2002]).

and the ventral "what is it" stream (Fig. 9.4), suggesting two different roles for affect during object perception.

In the next section, we describe how medial parts of the OFC are connected to the dorsal "where" visual stream, and help to generate the brain's gist-level prediction by providing initial affective information about what an object might mean for a person's well-being. With gist-level visual information about an object, the medial OFC modulates the internal bodily changes that are needed to guide subsequent actions on that object in context. The ability to reach for a round object and pick it up for a bite depends on the prediction that it is an apple and that it will enhance one's well-being in the immediate future because it has done so in the past.

While the medial OFC is directing the body to prepare a physical response (or what might be

called "crafting an initial affective response"), the lateral parts of the OFC are integrating the sensory feedback from this bodily state with cues from the five external senses. Based on the anatomical connections to lateral OFC, we hypothesize that the resulting multimodal representation helps to create a unified experience of specific objects in context. The ability to consciously see a particular apple might not only require integration of information from the five senses; it might also require that this information is integrated with the "sixth sense" of affect (e.g., that apples are delicious).

BASIC-LEVEL AFFECTIVE PREDICTIONS IN OBJECT PERCEPTION

Medial OFC has strong reciprocal connections to lateral parietal areas (MT and MST) within the dorsal "where is it" visual stream (Barbas, 1988, 1995; Carmichael & Price, 1995; Cavada, Company, Tejedor, Cruz-Rizzolo, & Reinsos-Suarez, 2000; Kondo et al., 2003) (Fig. 9.4). The dorsal stream carries achromatic visual information of low spatial and fast temporal resolution through posterior parietal cortex, processing spatial information and visual motion, and providing the basis for spatial localization (Ungerleider & Miskin, 1982) and visually guided action (Milner & Goodale, 1992). Via largely magnocellular pathways, medial OFC receives this low spatial frequency visual information (Kveraga et al., 2007a, b), devoid of specific visual detail, that is used to create a basic-level category representation about the object's identity (Bar, 2003, 2007).

The medial portions of OFC guide autonomic, endocrine, and behavioral responses to an object (Barbas & De Olmos, 1990; Barbas, Saha, Rempel-Clower, & Ghashghaie, 2003; Carmichael & Price, 1995, 1996; Ghashghaei & Barbas, 2002; Ongur et al., 1998; Price, 2007; Rempel-Clower & Barbas, 1998) and is sometimes referred to as a visceromotor control area. Via strong projections to hypothalamic, midbrain, brain stem, and spinal column control centers, the medial OFC uses low spatial frequency visual information from the dorsal visual stream to modify the perceiver's bodily state to re-create the affective context in which the object was experienced in the past (to allow subsequent behavior in the immediate future).

Based on its neuroanatomical connections to the lateral parietal cortex, we hypothesize that the OFC's representation of these autonomic and endocrine changes is relayed back to the dorsal "where is it" stream as an initial estimate of the affective value and motivational relevance. With bidirectional processing between the medial OFC and the lateral parietal cortex, a person's physiological and behavioral response is coordinated with information about the spatial location of the object. This prediction is part of the brain's preparation to respond to an object (based on this gist-level prediction) even before the object is consciously perceived.

There is some additional neuroimaging evidence to support our hypothesis that affective changes are part of a basic "gist" prediction during object perception. Areas in the medial OFC, including ventromedial prefrontal cortex (vmPFC) and the portion of the rostral anterior cingulate cortex (ACC) beneath the corpus callosum, typically show increased activity during processing of contextual associations, where an object triggers cortical representations of other objects that have predicted relevance in a particular situation (Bar, 2004; Bar & Aminoff, 2003; Bar, Aminoff, Mason, & Fenske, 2007). For example, a picture of a traffic light activates visual representations of other objects that typically

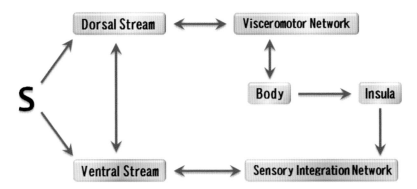

Figure 9.4 Connections between orbitofrontal cortex (OFC) and visual networks. "S" represents visual information that reaches the dorsal "where" stream and ventral "what" stream both from early visual areas and from the thalamus directly. The medial OFC is part of a "visceromotor" network that helps to control internal body state. The lateral OFC is part of a "sensory integration network" that joins together sensory representations from outside and inside the body.

share a "street" context, such as cars, pedestrians, and so on. These findings suggest that an object has the capacity to reinstate the context with which it has been associated in prior experience. Given that vmPFC and rostral ACC project directly to autonomic and endocrine output centers in the hypothalamus, midbrain, brain stem, and spinal cord, it is likely that this reinstatement includes reconstituting the internal affective context that is associated with past exposures to the object. The internal world of the body may be one element in the "context frame" that facilitates object recognition (for a discussion of context frames, see Bar, 2004).

AFFECTIVE PREDICTIONS IN VISUAL CONSCIOUSNESS

Lateral OFC has robust reciprocal connections to the inferior temporal areas (TEO, TE, and temporal pole) of the ventral "what" visual stream (Fig. 9.4; Barbas, 1988, 1995; Carmichael & Price, 1995; Cavada et al., 2000; Kondo et al., 2003; Rolls & Deco, 2002). The ventral stream carries higher resolution visual details (including color) through interior temporal cortex that gives rise to the experience of seeing. Via largely parvocellular pathways, the lateral OFC receives this high spatial frequency visual information full of rich detail about the visual features of objects used to create a specific representation of an object. Many neurons within the lateral OFC are multimodal and respond to a variety of different sensory inputs (Kringelbach & Rolls, 2004). In addition to receiving visual (and other exteroceptive sensory) information, the lateral portions of OFC also receive information about the nuanced body changes (via the insula) that occur as the result of gist-level affective predictions. Lateral OFC then integrates this bodily context information with sensory information from the world to establish an experience-dependent representation of an object in context. In addition, the internal sensory information received from anterior insula are important for the conscious experience of affect (Craig, 2002). The resulting multimodal representation then influences processing in the ventral "what" stream, and with additional back and forth, a

specific, polysensory, contextually relevant representation of the object is generated. This conscious percept includes the affective value of the object. Sometimes this value is represented as a property of the object, and at other times it is represented as a person's reaction to that object.

COORDINATING AFFECTIVE PREDICTIONS IN THE BRAIN

On the basis of neuroanatomical evidence, we have thus far proposed that affect plays two related roles in object perception. The medial OFC estimates the value of gist-level representations. A small, round, object might be an apple if it is resting in a bowl on a kitchen counter, associated with an unpleasant affective response if the perceiver does not enjoy the taste of apples, a pleasant affective response if he or she is an apple lover and is hungry, and even no real affective change in an apple lover who is already satiated. The medial OFC not only realizes the affective significance of the apple, but it also prepares the perceiver to act—to turn away from the apple, to pick it up and bite, or to ignore it, respectively. The lateral OFC integrates sensory information from this bodily context information with information from other sensory modalities, as well as more detailed visual information, producing the visual experience of a specific apple, ball, or balloon. These two aspects of affective prediction do not occur in stages per se, but there might be slight differences in the time at which the two are computed.

Autonomic, hormonal, or muscular changes in the body that are generated as part of a gist-level prediction via the medial OFC might be initiated before and incorporated into the multimodal representation of the world that is represented in the lateral OFC. Visual information arrives more quickly to the medial OFC owing to a "magnocellular advantage" in visual processing (term by Laylock, Crewther, & Crewther, 2007). Magnocellular neurons projecting from the lateral geniculate nucleus (in the thalamus) rapidly conduct low spatial frequency visual information to V1 and the dorsal "where" stream areas (compared with the parvocelluar neurons that carry highly specific and detailed visual information to V1 and to the ventral "what" stream). In humans, magnocellular neurons in V1 fire from 25 ms (Klistorner, Crewther, & Crewether, 1997) to 40 ms (Paulus, Korinth, Wischer, & Tergau, 1999) earlier than parvocellular neurons in V1. Even more strikingly, under certain conditions some neurons within the dorsal stream that receive input directly from the lateral geniculate nucleus (e.g., V5/MT; Sincich, Park, Wohlgemuth, & Horton, 2004) become active even before V1 (Buchner et al., 1997; Ffytche, Guy, & Zeki, 1995). As a result, low spatial frequency visual information about an object arrives to the medial OFC before high spatial frequency visual information arrives to the lateral OFC. Consistent with this view, Foxe and Simpson (2002) found that neurons in prefrontal cortex became active approximately 10 ms after neurons in the dorsal "where" stream but coincident with activation in the ventral "what" stream.

A magnocellular advantage extending to the medial OFC would help to resolve the debate over how the brain processes affective value of objects and faces when they are unattended or presented outside of visual awareness (either because of experimental procedures or brain damage). Some researchers argue for a subcortical route by which low spatial frequency visual information about objects and faces can bypass V1 via the amygdala to represent affective value in the body and behavior (e.g., Catani, Jones, Donato, & Ffytche, 2003; LeDoux, 1996; Morris, Ohman, & Dolan, 1998; Rudrauf et al., 2008; Weiskrantz, 1996), whereas others argue that such a circuit is not functional in primates (Pessoa & Ungerleider, 2004; Rolls, 2000). Either way, affective predictions do not necessarily require a purely subcortical route. Nor is a subcortical route necessary to explain how objects presented outside of visual awareness influence the body and behavior, how blindsighted patients can respond to the affective tone of a stimulus despite damage to V1, or why patients with amygdala damage have deficits in face perception. And because OFC lesions have been linked to memory deficits (for a discussion, see Frey & Petrides, 2000), the absence of a magnocellular advantage may also help to explain why people

suffering from agnosia can experience deficits in affective responses to visual stimulation but not to other sensory stimuli (Bauer, 1982; Damasio, Damasio, & van Hoesen, 1982; Habib, 1986; Sierra, Lopera, Lambert, Phillips, & David, 2002). The amygdala's importance in object and face processing (for a review, see Vuilleumier & Pourtois, 2007) may refer as much (if not more) to its participation in affective predictions than to its ability to work around early cortical processing in perception. These findings also suggest that the enhanced activity observed in fusiform gyrus in response to unattended emotional faces (e.g., Vuilleumeir, Armony, Driver, & Dolan, 2001) might be influenced, in part, by the OFC (which is strongly connected to the amygdala) in addition to the amygdala per se.

That being said, there is other evidence to suggest that both components of affective prediction happen more or less simultaneously. There is something like a parvocellular advantage in visual processing, in that visual information reaches the ventral "what" stream very quickly, and like the input to the dorsal "where" stream, arrives without the benefit of cortical processing in early visual cortex. The lateral geniculate nucleus not only projects directly to the dorsal stream, but it also appears to project directly to anterior temporal lobe areas that are connected to the ventral stream (including the parahippocampal gyrus and amygdala; Catani et al., 2003). As a consequence, upon the presentation of a stimulus, some of the neurons in anterior temporal cortex fire almost coincidently with those in occipital cortex (e.g., 47 vs. 45 ms, respectively; Wilson, Babb, Halgren, & Crandall, 1983). Without further study, however, it is difficult to say whether these are magno- or parvocellular connections.

Taken together, these findings indicate that it may be more appropriate to describe the affective predictions generated by the medial and lateral OFC as phases in a single affective prediction evolving over time, rather than as two separate "types" of affective predictions (with one informing the other). This interpretation is supported by the observation that the medial and lateral OFC are strongly connected by intermediate areas (see Fig. 9.3); in addition, lateral OFC receives some low spatial frequency visual information and medial OFC some high spatial frequency information; and, magnocellular and parvocellular projections are not as strongly anatomically segregated as was first believed (for a review, see Laylock et al., 2007). Furthermore, there are strong connections throughout the dorsal "where" and ventral "what" streams at all levels of processing (Chen et al., 2007; Merigan & Maunsell, 1993). Finally, the OFC has widespread connections to a variety of thalamic nuclei that receive highly processed visual input and therefore can not be treated as solely bottom-up structures in visual processing.[1] As a result of these interconnections, the timing differences in medial and lateral OFC affective predictions will be small and perhaps difficult to measure with current technology, even if they prove to be functionally significant in the time course of object perception.

IMPLICATIONS

A tremendous amount of research has now established that object recognition is a complex process that relies on many different sources of information from the world (e.g., contrast, color, texture, low spatial frequency cues, etc.). In this paper, we suggest that object recognition uses another source of information: sensory cues from the body that represent the object's value in a particular context. We have laid the foundation for the hypothesis that people do not wait to evaluate an object for its personal significance until after they know what the object is. Rather, an affective reaction is one component of the prediction that helps a person see the object in the first place. Specifically, we hypothesize that very shortly after being exposed to objects, the brain predicts their value for the person's well-being based on prior experiences with those objects, and these affective representations shape the person's visual experience and guide action

in the immediate future. When the brain effortlessly guesses an object's identity, that guess is partially based on how the person feels.

Our ideas about affective prediction suggest that people do not come to know the world exclusively through their senses; rather, their affective states influence the processing of sensory stimulation from the very moment an object is encountered. These ideas also suggest the intriguing possibility that exposure to visual sensations alone is not sufficient for visual experience. And even more exciting, plasticity in visual cortex areas might require, at least to some extent, the formation of connections between visual processing areas in the back of the brain and affective circuitry in the front. This suggests that affective predictions may not be produced by feedback from OFC alone. As unlikely as it may seem, affective predictions might also influence plasticity in the visual system so that visual processing is changed from the bottom up.

This, of course, brings us back to Mr. May. Even several years after his surgery, Mr. May's brain did not have a sufficiently complex and nuanced cache of multimodal representations involving visual sensations to allow him to easily predict the meaning of novel input from the visual world around him. Said a different way, his paucity of knowledge about the visual world forced him to think through every guess. Our hypothesis is that the guessing became easier, and more automatic, as Mr. May's visual sensations took on affective value. He went from having what the philosopher Nicolas Humphrey (2006) called "affectless vision" (p. 67) to seeing with feeling.

Mr. May was lucky. Even though he construed visual sensations as a world that stood apart, he experienced that visual world with a sense of excitement and wonder. His visual sensations were the vehicle for discovering something new, rather than discovering that something was missing. Not everyone who recovers from blindness is so fortunate. The patient HD was functionally blind from the age of 3 until she had the cataracts removed from her eyes at the age of 27 (Ackroyd, Humphrey, & Warrington, 1974). Once her vision was restored, she, like Mr. May, could successfully navigate and avoid obstacles

---

[1] For example, the midbrain's superior colliculus and thalamic nuclei such as the pulviar and mediodorsal receive cortically processed visual input from V1, the ventral visual stream (area IT), and the sensory integration network in OFC (Abramson & Chalupa, 1985; Casanova, 1993; Webster, Bachevalier, & Ungerleider, 1993, 1995).

such as curbs on the street, and could point towards and even grasp objects with neither prompting nor instruction. But she did not report having any conscious visual experience of these objects. It seems that her vision lacked the affective quality that makes a percept feel personal, as if it were her own. HD knew that objects were there, but experienced them as if somebody else were describing them to her. Just as people with certain agnosias lack the functional connections between visual and affective areas, people with affectless vision don't see the world differently – they simply fail to see it. Eventually, HD returned to wearing dark glasses because vision without affective quality was more disturbing than no vision at all.

Conclusions

We have proposed that a person's affective state has a top-down influence in normal object perception. Specifically, we have proposed that the medial OFC participates in an initial phase of affective prediction ("what is the relevance of this class of objects for me?"), whereas the lateral OFC provides more subordinate-level and contextually relevant affective prediction ("what is the relevance of this particular object in this particular context for me at this particular moment in time?"). If this view is correct, then personal relevance and salience are not computed after an object is already identified; they may be part of object perception itself.

Acknowledgments

Thanks to Eliza Bliss-Moreau, Krysal Yu, and Jasmine Boshyan who helped with figure preparation. Thanks also to Daniel Gilbert and members of the Barrett and Bar labs who made helpful comments on previous drafts of this manuscript. Preparation of this paper was supported by NIH grant R01NS050615 to Moshe Bar, and an National Institutes of Health Director's Pioneer Award (DP1OD003312), grants from the National Institute of Aging (AG030311) and the National Science Foundation (BCS 0721260; BCS 0527440), and a contract with the Army Research Institute (W91WAW), as well as by a Cattell Award and a Fellowship from the American Philosophical Society to Lisa Feldman Barrett. Correspondence should be addressed to Lisa Feldman Barrett at the Department of Psychology, Northeastern University. E-mail: l.barrett@neu.edu.

References

Abramson, B. P., & Chalupa, L. M. (1985). The laminar distribution of cortical connections with the tecto- and cortico-recipient zones in the cat's lateral posterior nucleus. *Neuroscience, 15*(1), 81–95.

Alechsieff, N. (1907). Die Grundformen der Gefühle. *Psychologische Studien, 3*, 156–271.

Amaral, D. G., Behniea, H., & Kelly J. L. (2003). Topographical organization of projections from the amygdala to the visual cortex in the Macaque monkey. *Neuroscience, 118*, 1099–1120.

Arnold, M. B. (1960). *Emotion and personality.* New York: Columbia University Press.

Bar, M. (2003). A cortical mechanism for triggering top-down facilitation in visual object recognition. *Journal of Cognitive Neuroscience, 15*, 600–609.

Bar, M. (2007). The proactive brain: Using analogies and associations to generate predictions. *Trends in Cognitive Sciences, 11*(7), 280–289.

Bar, M., Kassam, K. S., Ghuman, A. S., Boshyan, J., Schmidt, A. M., Dale, A. M. Hamalainen, M. S., Marinkovic, K., Schacter, D. L., Rosen, B. R., & Halgren, E. (2006). Top-down facilitation of visual recognition. *Proceedings of the National Academy of Science, 103*(2), 449–454.

Bar, M., Tootell, R. B., Schacter, D. L., Greve, D. N., Fischl, B., Mendola, J. D., et al. (2001). Cortical mechanisms specific to explicit visual object recognition. *Neuron, 29*, 529–535.

Barbas, H. (1988). Anatomic organization of basoventral and mediodorsal visual recipient prefrontal regions in the rhesus monkey. *Journal of Comparative Neurology, 276*, 313–342.

Barbas, H. (1993). Organization of cortical afferent input to orbitofrontal areas in the rhesus monkey. *Neuroscience, 56*, 841–864.

Barbas, H. (1995). Anatomic basis of cognitive-emotional interactions in the primate prefrontal cortex. *Neuroscience and Biobehavioral Reviews, 19*, 499–510.

Barbas, H. (2000). Connections underlying the synthesis of cognition, memory, and emotion in primate prefrontal cortices. *Brain Research Bulletin, 52*, 319–330.

Barbas, H., & De Olmos, J. (1990). Projections from the amygdala to basoventral and mediodorsal prefrontal regions in the rhesus monkey. *Journal of Comparative Neurology, 300*(4), 549–571.

Barbas, H., & Pandya, D. N. (1989). Architecture and intrinsic connections of the prefrontal cortex in the rhesus monkey. *Journal of Comparative Neurology, 286*, 353–375.

Barbas, H., & Zikopoulos, B. (2007). The prefrontal cortex and flexible behavior. *Neuroscientist, 13*, 532–545.

Barbas, H., Saha, S., Rempel-Clower, N., & Ghashghaei, T. (2003). Serial pathways from primate prefrontal cortex to autonomic areas may influence emotional expression. *BMC Neuroscience, 4*, 25–37.

Barrett, L. F., Quigley, K., Bliss-Moreau, E., & Aronson, K. R. (2004). Arousal focus and interoceptive sensitivity. *Journal of Personality and Social Psychology, 87*, 684–687.

Barrett, L. F. (2006a). Solving the emotion paradox: Categorization and the experience of emotion. *Personality and Social Psychology Review, 10*, 20–46.

Barrett, L. F. (2006b). Valence as a basic building block of emotional life. *Journal of Research in Personality, 40*, 35–55.

Barrett, L. F., & Bliss-Moreau, E. (2009). Affect as a psychological primitive. *Advances in Experimental Social Psychology, 41*. 167–218.

Barrett, L. F., Lindquist, K., & Gendron, M. (2007). Language as a context for emotion perception. *Trends in Cognitive Sciences, 11*, 327–332.

Barrett, L. F., Mesquita, B., Ochsner, K. N., & Gross, J. J. (2007). The experience of emotion. *Annual Review of Psychology, 58*, 373–403.

Bauer, R. M. (1982). Visual hypoemotionality as a symptom of visual-limbic disconnection in man. *Archives of Neurology, 39*, 702–708.

Bliss-Moreau, E., Owren, M. & Barrett, L.F. (2010). I like the sound of your voice: Affective learning about the human voice. *Journal of Experimental Social Psychology, 46*, 557–563.

Buchner, H., Gobbele, R., Wagner, M., Fuchs, M., Waberski, T. D., & Beckmann, R. (1997). Fast visual evoked potential input into human area V5. *Neuroreport, 8*, 2419–2422.

Bullier, J. (2001). Integrated model of visual processing. *Brain Research Reviews, 36*, 96–107.

Carmichael, S. T., & Price, J. L. (1995). Limbic connections of the orbital and medial prefrontal cortex in macaque monkeys. *Journal of Comparative Neurology, 363*(4), 615–641.

Carmichael, S. T., & Price, J. L. (1996). Connectional networks within the orbital and medial prefrontal cortex of macaque monkeys. *Journal of Comparative Neurology, 371*, 179–207.

Casanova, C. (1993). Response properties of neurons in area 17 projecting to the striate-recipient zone of the cat's lateralis posterior-pulvinar complex: Comparison with cortico-tectal cells. *Experimental Brain Research, 96*(2), 247–259.

Catani, M., Jones, D. K., Donato, R., & Ffytche, D. H. (2003). Occipito-temporal connections in the human brain. *Brain, 126*, 2093–2107.

Cavada, C., Company, T., Tejedor, J., Cruz-Rizzolo, R. J., & Reinsos-Suarez, F. (2000). The anatomical connections of the Macaque monkey orbitofrontal cortex: A review. *Cerebral Cortex, 10*, 220–242.

Chen, C. M., Lakatos, P., Shah, A. S., Mehta, A. D., Givre, S. J., Javitt, D. C., & Schroeder, C. E. (2007). Functional anatomy and interaction of fast and slow visual pathways in Macaque monkeys. *Cerebral Cortex, 17*, 1561–1569.

Craig, A. D. (2002). Opinion: How do you feel? Interoception: The sense of the physiological condition of the body. *Nature Reviews: Neuroscience, 3*, 655–666.

Damasio, A. (1999). *The feeling of what happens: Body and emotion in the making of consciousness*. TX: Harcourt College.

Damasio, A. R., Damasio, H., & van Hoesen, G. W. (1982). Prosopagnosia: Anatomic basis and behavioral mechanisms. *American Academy of Neurology, 32*, 331–341.

DeArmond, S. J., Fusco, M. M., & Dewey, M. M. (1989). Structure of the human brain: A photographic atlas. 3rd Ed. New York: University Press.

Duncan, S., & Barrett, L. F. (2007). Affect as a form of cognition: A neurobiological analysis. *Cognition and Emotion, 21*, 1184–1211.

Edelman, G. M. (1987). *Neural Darwinism: The theory of neuronal group selection*. New York: Basic Books.

Edelman, G. M., & Tononi, G. (2000). *A universe of consciousness: How matter becomes imagination*. New York: Basic Books.

Eimer, M., & Holmes, A. (2007). Event-related brain potential correlates of emotional face processing. *Neuropsychologia, 45*, 15–31

Feldman, L. A. (1995a). Variations in the circumplex structure of emotion. *Personality and Social Psychology Bulletin, 21*, 806–817.

Feldman, L. A. (1995b). Valence focus and arousal focus: Individual differences in the structure of affective experience. *Journal of Personality and Social Psychology*, 69, 153–166.

Ffytche, D. H., Guy, C. N., & Zeki, S. (1995). The parallel visual motion inputs into areas V1 and V5 of human cerebral cortex. *Brain*, 118, 1375–1394.

Fine, I., Wade, A. R., Brewer, A. A., May, M. G., Goodman, D. F., Boynton, G. M., Wendell, B. A. & MacLeod, D. I. A. (2003). Long-term deprivation affects visual perception and cortex. *Nature Neuroscience*, 6, 915–916.

Foxe, J. J., & Simpson, G. V. (2002). Flow of activation from V1 to frontal cortex in humans. A framework for defining "early" visual processing. *Experimental Brain Research*, 142, 139–150.

Freese, J. L., & Amaral, D. G. (2005). The organization of projections from the amygdala to visual cortical areas TE and V1 in the Macaque monkey. *Journal of Comparative Neurology*, 486, 295–317.

Freese, J. L., & Amaral, D.G. (2006). Synaptic organization of projections from the amygdala to visual cortical areas TE and V1 in the macaque monkey. *Journal of Comparative Neurology*, 496, 655–667.

Frey, S., & Petrides, M. (2000). Orbitofrontal cortex: A key prefrontal region for encoding information. *Proceedings of the National Academy of Sciences*, 97, 8723–8727.

Ghashghaei, H. T., & Barbas, H. (2002). Pathways for emotion: Interactions of prefrontal and anterior temporal pathways in the amygdala of the rhesus monkey. *Neuroscience*, 115, 1261–1279

Goodale, M. A., & Milner, A. D. (1992). Separate visual pathways for perception and action. *Trends in Neuroscience*, 15, 20–25.

Habib, M. (1986). Visual hypo-emotionality and prosopagnosia associated with right temporal lobe isolation. *Neuropsychologia*, 24, 577–582.

Holmes, A., Winston, J. S., & Eimer, M. (2005). The role of spatial frequency information for ERP components sensitive to faces and emotional facial expression. *Cognitive Brain Research*, 25, 508–520.

Humphrey, N. (2006). *Seeing red: A study in consciousness*. Cambridge, MA: Harvard University Press.

James, W. (1890). *The principals of psychology*. New York: Holt.

Klistorner, A., Crewther, D. P., & Crewther, S. G. (1997). Separate magnocellular and parvocellular contributions from temporal analysis of the multifocal VEP. *Vision Research*, 37, 2161–2169.

Koenigs, M., & Tranel, D. (2008). Prefrontal cortex damage abolishes brand-cued changes in cola preference. *Social, Cognitive, and Affective Neuroscience*, 3, 1–6.

Kringelbach, M. L. (2005). Linking reward to hedonic experience. *Nature Reviews Neuroscience*, 6, 691–702.

Kringelbach, M. L., & Rolls, E. T. (2004). The functional neuroanatomy of the human orbitofrontal cortex: Evidence from neuroimaging and neuropsychology. *Progress in Neurobiology*, 72, 341–372.

Kveraga, K., Boshyan, J., & Bar, M. (2007). Magnocellular projections as the trigger of top-down facilitation in recognition. *Journal of Neuroscience*, 27, 13232–13240.

Kveraga, K., Ghuman, A. S., & Bar, M. (2007) Top-down predictions in the cognitive brain. *Brain and Cognition*, 65, 145–168.

Lamme, V. A., & Roelfsema, P. R. (2000). The distinct modes of vision offered by feedforward and recurrent processing. *Trends in Neurosciences*, 23, 571–579.

Laylock, R., Crewther, S. G., & Crewther, D. P. (2007). A role for the "magnocellular advantage" in visual impairments in neurodevelopmental and psychiatric disorders. *Neuroscience and Biobehavioral Reviews*, 31, 363–376.

LeDoux, J. E. (2000). Emotion circuits in the brain. *Annual Review of Neuroscience*, 23, 155–184.

Li, W., Moallem, I., Paller, K. A., & Gottfried, J. A. (2007). Subliminal smells can guide social preferences. *Psychological Science*, 18, 1044–1049.

Martinez, A., Hillyard, S. A., Dias, E. C., Hagler, D. J., Butler, P. D., Guilfoyle, D. N., Jalbrzikowski, M., Silipo, G., & Javitt, D. (2008). Magnocellular pathway impairments in schizophrenia: Evidence from functional magnetic resonance imaging. *The Journal of Neuroscience*, 28, 7492–7500.

McDonald, A. J. (1998). Cortical pathways to the mammalian amygdala. *Progress in Neurobiology*, 55, 257–332

Merigan, W. H., & Maunsell, J. H. R., (1993). How parallel are the primate visual pathways? *Annual Review of Neuroscience*, 16, 369–402.

Mesulam, M. (2000). Behavioral neuroanatomy: Large-scale networks, association cortex, frontal syndromes, the limbic system, and hemispheric specializations. In M. Mesulam (Ed.), *Principles of behavioral and cognitive neurology* (2nd ed., pp. 1–120). New York: Oxford University Press

Morris, J. S., Ohman, A., & Dolan, R. J. (1998). A subcortical pathway to the right amygdala mediating "unseen" fear. *Proceedings of the National Academy of Sciences USA, 96,* 1680–1685.

Nauta, W. (1971). The problem of the frontal lobe: A reinterpretation. *Journal of Psychiatric Research, 8,* 167–187.

Oliva, A., & Torralba, A. (2001). Modeling the shape of a scene: A holistic representation of the spatial envelope. *International Journal of Computer Vision, 42,* 145–175.

Ongur, D., & Price, J. L. (2000). The organization of networks within the orbital and medial prefrontal cortex of rats, monkeys and humans. *Cerebral Cortex, 10,* 206–219.

Ongur, D., Ferry, A. T., & Price, J. L. (2003). Architectonic subdivision of the human orbital and medial prefrontal cortex. *Journal of Comparative Neurology, 460,* 425–449.

Palermo, R., & Rhodes, G. (2007). Are you always on my mind? A review of how face perception and attention interact. *Neuropsychologia, 45,* 75–92.

Paulus, W., Korinth, S., Wischer, S., & Tergau, F. (1999). Differential inhibition of chromatic and achromatic perception by transcranial magnetic stimulation of the human visual cortex. *Neuroreport 10,* 1245–1248.

Pessoa, L. (2008). On the relationship between emotion and cognition. *Nature Reviews Neuroscience, 2,* 148–158.

Pessoa, L., & Ungerleider, L. G. (2004). Neuroimaging studies of attention and the processing of emotion-laden stimuli. *Progress in Brain Research, 144,* 171–182.

Pessoa, L., Japee, S., Sturman, D., & Ungerleider, L. G. (2006). Target visibility and visual awareness modulate amygdala responses to fearful faces. *Cerebral Cortex, 16,* 366–375.

Price, J. L. (2007). Connections of orbital cortex. In D. H. Zald & S. L. Rauch (Eds.), *The orbitofrontal cortex* (p. 38–56). New York: Oxford University Press.

Rempel-Clower, N. L., & Barbas, H. (1998). Topographic organization of connections between the hypothalamus and prefrontal cortex in the rhesus monkey. *Journal of Comparitive Neurology, 398,* 393–419.

Rolls, E. T. (2000). Précis of "The brain and emotion." *Behavioral and Brain Sciences, 23,* 177–191.

Rudrauf, D., David, O., Lachaux, J-P., Kovach, C. K., Martinerie, J., Renault, B., & Damasio, A. (2008). Rapid interactions between the ventral visual stream and emotion-related structures rely on a two-pathway architecture. *The Journal of Neuroscience, 28,* 2796–2803.

Russell, J. A. (2003). Core affect and the psychological construction of emotion. *Psychological Review, 110,* 145–172.

Russell, J. A., & Barrett, L. F. (1999). Core affect, prototypical emotional episodes, and other things called emotion: Dissecting the elephant. *Journal of Personality and Social Psychology, 76,* 805–819.

Schyns, P. G., & Oliva, A. (1994). From blobs to boundary edges: Evidence for time- and spatial-dependent scene recognition. *Psychological Science, 5*(4), 195–200.

Searle, J. (1992). *The rediscovery of the mind.* Cambridge, MA: MIT Press.

Searle, J. (2004). *Mind: A brief introduction.* New York: Cambridge University Press.

Sierra, M., Lopera, F., Lambert, M. V., Phillips, M. L., & David, A. S. (2002). Separating depersonalisation and derealisation: The relevance of the "lesion method." *Journal of Neurology, Neurosurgery and Psychiatry, 72,* 530–532.

Sincich, L. C., Park, K. F., Wohlgemuth, M. J., & Horton, J. C. (2004). Bypassing V1: A direct geniculate input to area MT. *Nature Neuroscience, 7,* 1123–1128.

Spencer, H. (1855). *Principles of psychology.* London: Longman, Brown, Green, and Longmans.

Stefanacci, L., & Amaral, D. G. (2002). Some observations on cortical inputs to the Macaque monkey amygdala: An anterograde tracing study. *Journal of Comparative Neurology, 451,* 301–323.

Sully, J. (1892). *Outlines of psychology* (Vol. 2). New York: D. Appleton and Company.

Torralba, A., & Oliva, A. (2003). Statistics of natural image categories. *Network, 14*(3), 391–412.

Thorpe, S. J., Rolls, E. T., & Maddison, S. (1983). The orbitofrontal cortex: Neuronal activity in the behaving monkey. *Experimental Brain Research, 49,* 93–115.

Ungerleider, L. G., & Mishkin, M. (1982). Two cortical visual systems. In D. A. Ingle, M. A. Goodale, & R. J. W. Mansfield (Eds.), *Analysis of visual behavior* (pp. 549–586). Cambridge, MA: MIT Press.

Vuilleumier, P., & Pourtois, G. (2007). Distributed and interactive brain mechanisms during emotion face perception: Evidence from functional neuroimaging. *Neuropsychologia, 45,* 174–194

Vuilleumier, P., Armony, J. L., Driver, J., & Dolan, R. J. (2001). Effects of attention and emotion on face processing in the human brain: An event-related fMRI study. *Neuron, 30,* 829–841.

Wager, T. D., Barrett, L. F., Bliss-Moreau, E., Lindquist, K., Duncan, S., Kober, H., Joseph, J., Davidson, M., & Mize, J. (2008). The neuroimaging of emotion. In M. Lewis, J. M. Haviland-Jones, & L. F. Barrett (Eds.), *The handbook of emotion* (3rd ed., pp. 249–271). New York: Guilford.

Webster, M. J., Bachevalier, J., & Ungerleider, L. G. (1993). Subcortical connections of inferior temporal areas TE and TEO in macaque monkeys. *Journal of Comparative Neurology, 335(1)*, 73–91.

Webster, M. J., Bachevalier, J., & Ungerleider, L. G. (1995). Transient subcortical connections of inferior temporal areas TE and TEO in infant macaque monkeys. *Journal of Comparative Neurology, 352(2)*, 213–226.

Weiskrantz, L. (1996). Blindsight revisited. *Current Opinion in Neurobiology, 6(2)*, 215–220.

Wilson, C. L., Babb, T. L., Halgren, E., & Crandall, P. H. (1983). Visual receptive fields and response properties of neurons in human temporal lobe and visual pathways. *Brain, 106*, 473–502.

Wundt, W. (1998). *Outlines of psychology* (C. H. Judd, Trans.). Bristol, England: Thoemmes Press. (Original work published 1897).

CHAPTER 10
The Somatic Marker Hypothesis and Its Neural Basis: Using Past Experiences to Forecast the Future in Decision Making

Antoine Bechara

The terms *ventromedial prefrontal cortex* (vmPFC) and *orbitofrontal cortex* (OFC) are often used interchangeably in the literature, even though these do not refer to identical regions. For this reason, it is necessary to clarify exactly what we mean when we use these terms. The OFC is the entire cortex occupying the ventral surface of the frontal lobe, dorsal to the orbital plate of the frontal bone. We have used the term *vmPFC* to designate a region that encompasses medial portions of the OFC along with ventral portions of the medial prefrontal cortex. The vmPFC is an anatomical designation that has arisen because lesions that occur in the basal portions of the anterior fossa, which include meningiomas of the cribriform plate and falx cerebri, and aneurysms of the anterior communicating and anterior cerebral arteries, frequently lead to damage in this area. Often this damage is bilateral. With respect to the cytoarchitectonic fields identified in the human orbitofrontal and medial prefrontal cortices by Price and colleagues (Ongur & Price, 2000), the vmPFC comprises Brodmann area (BA) 14 and medial portions of BA 11 and 13 on the orbital surface and BA 25, 32, and caudal portions of BA 10 on the mesial surface. The vmPFC excludes lateral portions of the OFC, namely BA 47/12, as well as more dorsal and posterior regions of BA 24 and 32 of the medial prefrontal cortex. The vmPFC is thus a relatively large and heterogenous area.

One of the first and most famous cases of the so-called frontal lobe syndrome was the patient Phineas Gage, a railroad construction worker who survived an explosion that blasted an iron tamping bar through the front of his head (Harlow, 1848). Before the accident, Gage was a man of normal intelligence, energetic, and persistent in executing his plans of operation. He was responsible, sociable, and popular among peers and friends. After the accident, his medical recovery was remarkable. He survived the accident with normal intelligence, memory, speech, sensation, and movement. However, his behavior changed completely. He became irresponsible, untrustworthy, and impatient of restraint or advice when it conflicted with his desires. Using modern neuroimaging techniques, Damasio and colleagues have reconstituted the accident by relying on measurements taken from Gage's skull (Damasio, Grabowski, Frank, Galburda, & Damasio, 1994). The key finding of this neuroimaging study was that the most likely placement of Gage's lesion included the vmPFC region, bilaterally.

The case of Phineas Gage paved the way for the notion that the frontal lobes were linked to social conduct, judgement, decision making, and personality. A number of instances similar to the case of Phineas Gage have since appeared in the literature (Ackerly & Benton, 1948; Brickner, 1932; Welt, 1888). Interestingly, all these cases received little attention for many years. Over the years, we have studied numerous patients with this type of lesion. Such patients with damage to the vmPFC develop severe impairments in personal and social decision making, in spite of otherwise largely preserved intellectual abilities. These patients had normal intelligence and creativity before their brain damage. After the damage, they begin to have difficulties planning their work day and future, and difficulties in choosing friends, partners, and activities. The actions they elect to pursue often lead to losses of diverse order, for example, financial losses, losses in social standing, and losses of family and friends. The choices they make are no longer advantageous and are remarkably different from the kinds of choices they were known to make in the premorbid period. These patients often decide against their best interests. They are unable to learn from previous mistakes as reflected by repeated engagement in decisions that lead to negative consequences. In striking contrast to this real-life decision-making impairment, problem-solving abilities in laboratory settings remain largely normal. As noted, the patients have normal intellect, as measured by a variety of conventional neuropsychological tests (Bechara, Damasio, Tranel, & Anderson, 1998; Damasio, Tranel, & Damasio, 1990; Eslinger & Damasio, 1985; Saver & Damasio, 1991).

The question then arose as to whether the decision-making deficits caused by vmPFC damage were related to its visceromotor functions. Nauta had by then proposed that the guidance of behavior by the frontal lobes was linked to the interoceptive and visceromotor functions of this area (Nauta, 1971). Specifically, he proposed that the prefrontal cortex, broadly defined, functioned to compare the affective responses evoked by the various choices for behavior and to select the option that "passed censure by an interoceptive sensorium." According to Nauta, the "interoceptive agnosia" suffered by patients with frontal lobe damage could explain their impairments in real life, as well as their poor performance on various tests of executive function, including the Wisconsin Card Sort Task. This model was meant to explain the function of the prefrontal cortex as a whole. Furthermore, it was meant as a broad

explanation of executive function deficits, not of a specific deficit in decision making within the social and personal domains. However, the deficits of patients with damage in the vmPFC were limited to the personal and social domains; patients with focal vmPFC damage showed marked impairments in their real-life personal and social functioning, but they had intact intelligence. Indeed, these patients performed normally on standard laboratory tests of executive function such as the Wisconsin Card Sort Task.

This background helped to shape a more specific formulation, deemed the "somatic marker hypothesis" (Damasio, 1994; Damasio, Tranel, & Damasio, 1991). According to this hypothesis, patients with damage in the vmPFC make poor decisions in part because they are unable to elicit somatic (visceral) responses that "mark" the consequences of their actions as positive or negative. In this framework, the vmPFC functions to elicit visceral responses that reflect the anticipated value of the choices. Though this function is specific to the vmPFC, it draws upon information about the external world that is represented in multiple higher order sensory cortices. Furthermore, this function is limited to specific types of decision making, in particular, those situations where the meaning of events is implied and the consequences of behavior are uncertain. These are situations, such as social interactions and decisions about one's personal and financial life, where the consequences of behavior have emotional value, that is, they can be experienced as subjective feelings and can also increase or decrease the likelihood of similar behavior in the future (they are rewarding or punishing). Furthermore, these are situations where the rules of behavior are not explicit, but yet require some form of mental deliberation in real time to navigate them successfully. This form of reasoning is distinct from reasoning that does not require the weighing of positive and negative consequences, or in which the outcomes of decisions are known with a high degree of certainty.

Thus, the somatic marker hypothesis proposed by Antonio R. Damasio attributes the inability of certain patients with frontal lobe damage to make advantageous decisions in real life to a defect in an emotional (somatic) mechanism that rapidly signals the prospective consequences of an action, and accordingly assists in the selection of an advantageous response option. However, this somatic marker signal is actually derived from a prior life experience with reward and/or punishment. As such, the "affective" or "emotional" past is actually used to anticipate or forecast the future.

Outline of the Somatic Marker Hypothesis

Several neural structures have been shown to be key components of the neural circuitry underlying somatic state activation. The amygdala as well as the medial orbitofrontal cortex/ventromedial prefrontal cortex region are critical structures for triggering somatic states, but the amygdala seems more important for triggering somatic states from emotional events that occur in the environment (that is, primary inducers), whereas the medial orbitofrontal cortex/ventromedial prefrontal cortex region seems more important for triggering somatic states from memories, knowledge, and cognition (that is, secondary inducers) (Bechara & Damasio, 2005). Decision making is a complex process that relies on the integrity of at least two sets of neural systems: *(1)* one set is important for memory (e.g., the hippocampus), especially working memory (e.g., the dorsolateral prefrontal cortex), to bring online knowledge and information used during the deliberation of a decision; *(2)* another set is important for triggering emotional responses. This set includes effector structures such as the hypothalamus and autonomic brainstem nuclei that produce changes in internal milieu and visceral structures along with other effector structures such as the ventral striatum, periacqueductal gray, and other brainstem nuclei, which produce changes in facial expression and specific approach or withdrawal behaviors. It also includes cortical structures that receive afferent input from the viscera and internal milieu, such as the insular cortex and the posterior cingulate gyrus (and adjacent retrosplenial cortex), and precuneus region (i.e., medial area of the parietal cortex) (Fig. 10.1).

During the process of pondering decisions, the immediate prospects of an option may be

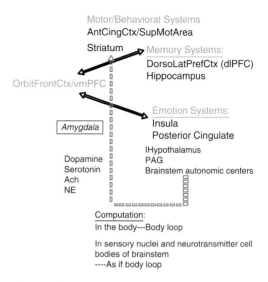

Figure 10.1 A schematic of all the brain regions involved in decision making according to the somatic marker hypothesis. Ach, acetylcholine; NE, noreadrenaline; PAG, periaqueductal gray; vmPFC, ventromedial prefrontal cortex.

driven by more subcortical mechanisms (e.g., via the amygdala) that do not require a prefrontal cortex. However, weighing the future consequences requires a prefrontal cortex for triggering somatic responses about possible future consequences. Specifically, when pondering the decision, the immediate and future prospects of an option may trigger numerous somatic responses that conflict with each other (i.e., positive and negative somatic responses). The end result, though, is that an overall positive or negative signal emerges (a "go" or "stop" signal, as it were). There is a debate as to where this overall somatic state may be computed. We have argued that this computation occurs in the body proper (via the so-called body loop), but it can also occur in the brain itself, in areas that represent "body" states such as the dorsal tegmentum of the midbrain, or areas such as the insula and posterior cingulate (via the so-called as-if body loop). The controversy has largely been in relation to the body loop, with certain investigators arguing that decision making is not necessarily dependent on "somatic markers" expressed in the body (e.g., see Maia & McClelland, 2004—but also see Bechara, Damasio, Tranel, & Damasio, 2005, and

Persaud, McLeod, & Cowey, 2007 for counter arguments). Irrespective of whether this computation occurs in the body itself, or within the brain, we have proposed that the emergence of this overall somatic state is consistent with the principles of natural selection. In other words, numerous and conflicting signals may be triggered simultaneously, but stronger ones gain selective advantage over weaker ones, until a winner takes all emerges, a positive or negative somatic state that consequently biases the decision one way or the other (Bechara & Damasio, 2005).

In order for somatic signals to influence cognition and behavior, they must act on the appropriate neural systems. One target for somatic state action is the striatum. A large number of channels convey body information (that is, somatic signals) to the central nervous system (e.g., spinal cord, vagus nerve, and humoral signals). Evidence suggests that the vagal route is especially critical for relaying somatic signals (Martin, Denburg, Tranel, Granner, & Bechara, 2004). Furthermore, it was proposed that the next link in this body–brain channel involves neurotransmitter systems (Bechara & Damasio, 2005; Damasio, 1994, 1996). Indeed, the cell bodies of the neurotransmitter dopamine, serotonin, noradrenaline, and acetylcholine are located in the brain stem; the axon terminals of these neurotransmitter neurons synapse on cells and/or terminals all over the cortex and striatum (Blessing, 1997). When somatic state signals are transmitted to the cell bodies of dopamine or serotonin neurons, for example, the signaling influences the pattern of dopamine or serotonin release at the terminals. In turn, changes in dopamine or serotonin release will modulate synaptic activities of neurons subserving behavior and cognition within the cortex. This chain of neural mechanisms provides a way for somatic states to exert a biasing effect on decisions. At the cellular, and more recently the functional neuroimaging, level, the pioneering work of Schultz, Dayan, and Montague (1997) on the role of dopamine in reward processing and error prediction provides a strong validity for the proposed neural framework. Thus, all the work related to dopamine and the ventral striatum is consistent with the somatic

marker framework. The key difference is that the dopamine mechanism addresses only one specific component of a larger neural network that is important for implementing decisions. The somatic marker hypothesis is a neural framework that incorporates all the different neural steps involved in decision making, including the dopamine link, such as the one initially studied by Schultz et al. (1997).

We note that one of the clear predictions of the somatic marker hypothesis is that working memory (and other executive processes of working memory such as response inhibition and reversal learning) is a key process in decision making. Consequently, damage to neural structures that impair working memory, such as the dorsolateral prefrontal cortex, also lead to impaired decision making. Nonetheless, some criticisms of the theory were made on the basis that deficits in decision making as measured by the Iowa Gambling Task may not be specific to the ventromedial prefrontal cortex (Manes et al., 2002), or it may be explained by deficits in other processes, such as reversal learning (Fellows & Farah, 2003). However, research has demonstrated that the relationship between decision making on one hand and working memory or reversal learning on the other hand are asymmetrical in nature (e.g., see Bechara, 2004; Bechara & Damasio, 2005, for reviews). In other words, working memory and/or reversal learning are not dependent on the intactness of decision making (that is, subjects can have normal working memory and normal reversal learning in the presence or absence of deficits in decision making). Some patients with ventromedial prefrontal cortex lesions who were severely impaired in decision making (that is, abnormal in the Iowa Gambling Task) had superior working memory and are perfectly normal on simple reversal learning tasks. In contrast, decision making seems to be influenced by the intactness or impairment of working memory and/or reversal learning (that is, decision making is worse in the presence of abnormal working memory and/or poor reversal learning). Patients with right dorsolateral prefrontal cortex lesions and severe working memory impairments showed low normal results in the Iowa Gambling Task

(Bechara et al., 1998). Patients with damage to the more posterior sector of the ventromedial prefrontal cortex (which includes the basal forebrain), such as the patients who were included in the study by Fellows and Farah (2003), showed impairments on reversal learning tasks, but similar patients with similar lesions also showed poor performance on the Iowa Gambling Task (Bechara et al., 1998).

THE NOW: TESTING THE SOMATIC MARKER HYPOTHESIS

At the core of somatic marker hypothesis lays the insight that decision makers encode the consequences of alternative choices affectively. For many years, these vmPFC patients presented a puzzling defect. Although the decision-making impairment was obvious in the real-world behavior of these patients, there was no effective laboratory probe to detect and measure this impairment. Bechara's development of what became known as the Iowa Gambling Task enabled the detection of these patients' elusive impairment in the laboratory for the first time, measure it, and investigate its possible causes (Bechara, Damasio, Damasio, & Anderson, 1994). Such work using the Iowa Gambling Task has provided the key empirical support for the proposal that somatic markers significantly influence decision making (Bechara & Damasio, 2005).

1. *The Iowa Gambling Task (IGT)* (Bechara et al., 1994; Bechara, Tranel, & Damasio, 2000). The IGT closely mimics real-life decisions. The task is carried out in real time and it resembles real-world contingencies. It factors reward and punishment (i.e., winning and losing money) in such a way that it creates a conflict between an immediate, luring reward and a delayed, probabilistic punishment. Therefore, the task engages the subject in a quest to make advantageous choices. As in real-life choices, the task offers choices that may be risky, and there is no obvious explanation of how, when, or what to choose. Each choice is full of uncertainty because a precise calculation or prediction of the outcome of a

given choice is not possible. The way that one can do well on this task is to follow one's "hunches" and "gut feelings."

More specifically, this task involves four decks of cards. The goal in the task is to maximize profit on a loan of play money. Subjects are required to make a series of 100 card selections. However, they are not told ahead of time how many card selections they are going to make. Subjects can select one card at a time from any deck they choose, and they are free to switch from any deck to another at any time, and as often as they wish. However, the subject's decision to select from one deck versus another is largely influenced by various schedules of immediate reward and future punishment. These schedules are pre-programmed and known to the examiner, but not to the subject, and they entail the following principles: every time the subject selects a card from two decks (decks A and B), the subject gets $100. Every time the subject selects a card from the two other decks (C or D), the subject gets $50. However, in each of the four decks, subjects encounter unpredictable punishments (money loss). The punishment is set to be higher in the high-paying decks A and B, and lower in the low-paying decks C and D. For example, if 10 cards were picked from deck A, one would earn $1,000. However, in those 10 card picks, 5 unpredictable punishments would be encountered, ranging from $150 to $350, bringing a total cost of $1,250. Deck B is similar: every 10 cards that were picked from deck B would earn $1,000; however, these 10 card picks would encounter one high punishment of $1,250. On the other hand, every 10 cards from deck C or D earn only $500, but only cost $250 in punishment. Hence, decks A and B are disadvantageous because they cost more in the long run; that is, one loses $250 every 10 cards. Decks C and D are advantageous because they result in an overall gain in the long run; that is, one wins $250 every 10 cards.

2. *Lesions in the vmPFC disrupt visceral responses during the Iowa Gambling Task (IGT)*. In light of the finding that the IGT is an instrument that detects the decision-making impairment of vmPFC patients in the laboratory, we went on to address the next question of whether

the impairment is linked to a failure in somatic signaling (Bechara, Tranel, Damasio, & Damasio, 1996).

3. *Visceral responses that signal the correct strategy do not need to be conscious.* According to the somatic marker hypothesis, the vmPFC mediates an implicit representation of the anticipated value of choices that is distinct from an explicit awareness of the correct strategy. To test this idea, we performed a study (Bechara et al., 1997) examining the development of skin conductance responses (SCR) over time in relation to subjects' knowledge of the advantageous strategy in the IGT. In this study, the IGT was administered as before, but this time, the task was interrupted at regular intervals and the subjects were asked to describe their knowledge about "what was going on" in the task and about their "feelings" about the task. Here, it was shown that normal subjects began to choose preferentially from the advantageous decks before they were able to report why these decks were preferred over the disadvantageous decks. They then began to form "hunches" about the correct strategy, which corresponded to their choosing more from the advantageous decks than from the disadvantageous decks. Finally, some subjects reached a "conceptual" stage, where they possessed explicit knowledge about the correct strategy (i.e., to choose from decks C and D because they pay less but also result in less punishment). As before, normal subjects developed SCRs preceding their choices that were larger for the disadvantageous decks than for the advantageous decks. This time, it was also found that the SCR discrimination between advantageous and disadvantageous decks preceded the development of conceptual knowledge of the correct strategy. In fact, the SCR discrimination between advantageous and disadvantageous decks even preceded the development of hunches about the correct strategy. In contrast to the normal subjects, subjects with damage in the vmPFC failed to switch from the disadvantageous decks to the advantageous decks, as was previously shown. In addition, as previously shown, subjects in this group failed to develop anticipatory responses that discriminated between the disadvantageous and advantageous decks. Furthermore, patients with vmPFC damage never developed "hunches" about the correct strategy. Together, they suggest that anticipatory visceral responses that are governed by the vmPFC precede emergence of advantageous choice behavior, which itself precedes explicit knowledge of the advantageous strategy. This suggests that signals generated by the vmPFC, reflected in visceral states, may function as a nonconscious bias toward the advantageous strategy.

More recently, other investigators have questioned whether it is necessary to invoke visceral responses as constituting nonconscious biasing signals (Maia & McClelland, 2004). By using more detailed questions to probe subjects' awareness of the attributes of each of the decks in the IGT, this study showed that subjects possess explicit knowledge of the advantageous strategy at an earlier stage in the task than was shown in the Bechara et al. (1997) study. Furthermore, the Maia and McClelland study found that subjects began to make advantageous choices at around the same time that they reported knowledge of the correct strategy. Based on these findings, it was argued that nonconscious somatic marker processes are not *required* to explain how decision making occurs.

A response to this study has been published elsewhere (Bechara et al., 2005), along with a rebuttal by Maia and McClelland (2005). Two points bear discussion here. Firstly, since this study did not measure visceral responses nor examined the effects of brain damage, it does not disprove the hypothesis that somatic markers mediated by the vmPFC play a role in decision making; it only shows that conscious awareness of the correct strategy occurs at around the same time as advantageous decision making. Secondly, both the Bechara et al. (1997) study and the Maia and McClelland (2005) study found that some subjects continue to make disadvantageous choices despite being able to report the correct strategy. This pattern bears an uncanny resemblance to the way in which subjects with lesions in the vmPFC are able to report the correct strategies for personal and social decision making, despite their severe deficits in the actual execution of personal and social behavior in real life. Indeed, this clinical observation provided the initial impetus to hypothesize a role for covert biasing processes in decision making in the first place. This indicates that, in both the IGT and in real life, conscious knowledge of the correct strategy may not be enough to guide advantageous decision making.

Thus, some process that operates independently of conscious knowledge of the correct strategy (i.e., somatic markers) must be invoked to explain fully how individuals make advantageous decisions. Indeed, it seems likely that this process can sometimes bias behavior that goes against what a person consciously thinks to be the correct strategy. That nonconscious biasing processes may not precede conscious knowledge in time is potentially an important finding, but it does not provide a basis for rejection of the fundamental role of somatic markers as nonconscious biases of behavior.

4. *The biological nature of these "somatic markers" is related to neurotransmitters systems in the brain.* Somatic states do not cause or produce behavior; they only bias or modulate behavior through changes in neurotransmitter release. A preliminary study supports this basic notion that decisions made during the IGT are influenced by manipulations of these neurotransmitter systems with agonist/antagonist drugs. We studied normal subjects under a serotonin manipulation with either: *(1)* a placebo (Vitamin C); *(2)* a selective serotonin reuptake inhibitor (fluvoxamine); or *(3)* a serotonin 5HT2A receptor antagonist (cyproheptadine) with H1 histamine receptor antagonist properties. We studied other normal subjects under a dopamine manipulation involving the use of either *(1)* a placebo; *(2)* a psychostimulant (dextroamphetamine) resulting in a net increase in dopaminergic neurotransmission; or *(3)* a dopamine D2-like receptor antagonist (haloperidol). For each drug condition, the subjects were tested with a different version of the IGT for assessing decision making, with the order of the three drug conditions counterbalanced within each group. The blockade of both dopamine and serotonin interfered with the selection of advantageous choices, but the dopamine effect seemed restricted to the earlier part of the IGT, when decisions are still guided by covert knowledge. The stimulation of both dopamine and serotonin improved the selection of advantageous choices, but only in specific parts of the task. Serotonin improved only the latter part of the task, when decisions are guided by conscious knowledge of which choices are good or bad. By contrast, dopamine improved only the early part of the task when guidance is covert. The results suggest that covert biasing of decisions might be dopaminergic, whereas overt biasing might be serotonergic. This also suggests that different types of decision making (e.g., risk versus ambiguity) can be manipulated by different pharmacological mechanisms. It is more difficult to manipulate noreadrenaline and acetylcholine in similar laboratory settings, but unquestionably these neurotransmitters do play a role in decision making, which remains to be determined.

5. *Functional neuroimaging support of the somatic marker hypothesis.* Studies that have looked at neural activation while participants performed the Iowa Gambling Task remain relatively scarce. One study had individuals perform the Iowa Gambling Task while situated in a positron emission tomography (PET) scanner (Ernst et al., 2002). The control task in this experiment involved the examiner signaling the participant to select cards from the four decks in a specified order, instead of allowing the participant to actually select decks. A predominantly right-sided network of prefrontal and posterior cortical regions was activated, which included the medial orbitofrontal cortex/ventromedial prefrontal cortex region, adjacent anterior cingulate cortex, dorsolateral prefrontal cortex, insula, and adjacent inferior parietal cortex (Ernst et al., 2002). This neural network overlaps considerably with that known from lesion studies to interfere with Iowa Gambling Task performance, as outlined earlier.

Similar neural correlates underlying Iowa Gambling Task performance were revealed using functional magnetic resonance imaging (fMRI). Fifteen healthy volunteers performed the Iowa Gambling Task while having their brain activity scanned using event-related fMRI (Fukui, Murai, Fukuyama, Hayashi, & Hanakawa, 2005). When the neural activity occurring during selections from the advantageous decks was compared with the neural activity occurring during selections from the disadvantageous decks, it was found that activity during the anticipatory period (that is, the time spent pondering which deck to choose) engaged the superior part of the anterior cingulate and the neighboring medial frontal gyrus. This activity occurred in an area that is relatively superior to the medial orbitofrontal cortex/ventromedial prefrontal cortex area, though it still lies within the overall region known for housing decision-making impairments in patients with prefrontal cortex lesions. It is unclear whether the medial orbitofrontal cortex/ventromedial prefrontal cortex area was precluded in this fMRI study because of signal dropout due to distortion artifacts.

Northoff et al. (2006) analyzed the relationship between the ventromedial prefrontal cortex, emotionally accentuated affective judgment (that is, unexpected), cognitively accentuated affective judgment (that is, expected), and performance on the Iowa Gambling Task. Neuronal activity in the ventromedial prefrontal cortex during unexpected affective judgment significantly correlated with Iowa Gambling Task performance. The authors posit that the degree to which subjects recruit the ventromedial prefrontal cortex during affective judgments is related to beneficial performance on the Iowa Gambling Task (Northoff et al., 2006). These findings support the claim of somatic marker theory that not only cognitive but also affective mechanisms are crucial for decision making. Since affective judgments require an interaction between affective and cognitive components, it might be considered a key process in decision making that has been linked to neural activity in the ventromedial prefrontal cortex.

Research by Windmann et al. (2006) used the original and inverted versions of the Iowa Gambling Task in healthy controls and suggested that the tendency to choose from the bad decks for longer in the original, relative to the inverted, task activated the medial orbitofrontal cortex more, which is consistent with the notion that the medial orbitofrontal cortex is involved in maintaining a behavioral strategy. Conversely, the inverted task activated more the lateral orbitofrontal cortex subregions, consistent with the notion that the ability to shift from the initially preferred choice option to alternative options is the relevant variable determining lateral orbitofrontal cortex activation, as well as performance on the Iowa Gambling Task, and not the ability to look into the future.

Finally, Lawrence et al. (2009) utilized the Iowa Gambling Task to analyze decision making under initially ambiguous circumstances. Using a version of the Iowa Gambling Task that was modified for event-related fMRI, the authors find involvement of several prefrontal cortical regions in task performance. Decision making in healthy subjects resulted in ventromedial prefrontal cortex activation. The findings of this study not only replicate but also add to prior research in that they disclose that deciding advantageously under initially ambiguous circumstances may require both continuous and dynamic processes involving the ventral and dorsal prefrontal cortex (Lawrence, 2009). As such, this research adds more validity to the Iowa Gambling Task in terms of eliciting dorsal and ventral prefrontal cortex activation.

In summary, the ventromedial prefrontal cortex, the dorsolateral prefrontal cortex, the medial orbitofrontal cortex, and the amygdala emerge as key brain areas related to emotion and decision making from the aforementioned research and, as such, form the neuroanatomical basis of the somatic marker framework.

THE FUTURE: HIERARCHICAL ORGANIZATION OF THE PREFRONTAL CORTEX

We have proposed a neural framework for how some of the factors affecting decision-making may be implemented in the vmPFC (Bechara and Damasio, 2005). The major advancement in the size, complexity, and connectivity of the frontal lobes in humans has occurred in relation to Brodmann area (BA) 10, i.e., the frontal pole, and not so much to the more posterior areas of the vmPFC (Semendeferi et al., 2001; Semendeferi et al., 2002). We have proposed that information conveying delay in the future (or distance in the past) depends on the integrity of more anterior vmPFC cortices (i.e., frontal pole) in order for a delayed outcome to exert an influence on behavior. If those anterior regions (frontal pole) are damaged, decision-making shifts towards shorter time horizons (i.e., the decision-making process becomes more influenced by more immediate, or more recent, outcomes). As the damage extends to the more posterior vmPFC regions (including the anterior cingulate cortex, basal forebrain, and nucleus accumbens), the shortening of this time horizon (or high recency) becomes more severe (Bechara and Damasio, 2005). Anatomically, the more posterior areas of the vmPFC (e.g., BA 25) are directly connected to brain structures involved in triggering (autonomic, neurotransmitter nuclei), or representing (sensory nuclei in the brainstem, insular, and somatosensory cortices) affective states, while access of more anterior areas is polysynaptic and indirect (Ongur and Price, 2000). It follows that coupling of information to representations of somatic states via posterior vmPFC is associated with relatively fast, effortless, and strong somatic signals, while the signaling via more anterior vmPFC is relatively slowed, effortful, and weak. Consistent with this framework, we suggested that humans have developed greater capacity to decide according to outcomes that are far more distant in the future (or past). This capacity places even normal individuals at a disadvantage because nearer events possess stronger somatic states, so that they tend to bias decisions in their favor. However, damage to the vmPFC tends to curb this capacity to a much greater extent.

Empirical evidence for this theoretical framework remains lacking, although there are several clinical observations and studies that are consistent with this notion. The first comes from clinical observations that patients with damage to the vmPFC have shortened time horizons, and have been described as having myopia for future consequences (Damasio, 1994). However, the first experimental evidence in support of this notion was found by Fellows and Farah (Fellows and Farah, 2005). Patients with damage to the vmPFC, but not dorsolateral prefrontal cortex (DLPC), demonstrated a severe shortening in their personal future time perspective, i.e., short-sightedness in their self-defined future (Fellows and Farah, 2005). Other studies have shown that these patients also have severe impairments in their prospective feeling-of-knowing judgments (Schnyer et al., 2004). Although time processing has been studied extensively in animal experiments (Nichelli, 2002), only recently neuroscientists have begun to address this issue in functional neuroimaging (McClure et al., 2004) and human lesion studies (Fellows and Farah, 2005). Using a complex decision-making task, such as the Iowa Gambling Task, which relies on information of outcomes that occurred more recently, or in the distant past, vmPFC lesion patients are especially impaired in the "recency" parameter of a cognitive model described below, in that they base their next choice on the most recent outcome, as opposed to integrating the outcomes from several past trials (Yechiam et al., 2005). However, the knowledge so far in this regard has not been sufficient, and evidence for how time may be processed across the anterior-posterior axis of the ventromedial prefrontal cortex remains lacking, until more recently (Hochman et al., 2010). We assessed the brain substrates implicated in two decision making dimensions in a sample of prefrontal cortex patients: (a) the tendency to differently weigh recent compared to past experience; and (b) the tendency to differently weigh gains compared to loss. The participants performed the Iowa Gambling Task, a complex experience-based decision-making task (Bechara, Damasio, Damasio, & Anderson, 1994), which was analyzed with a formal cognitive model (the Expectancy-Valance model – Busemeyer & Stout, 2002). The results indicated that decisions become influenced by most recent, as opposed to older, events when the damage reaches the posterior sectors of the ventromedial prefrontal cortex. Furthermore, the degree of this recency deficit is related to the size of the lesion. These results suggest that time delay plays a key role in decision-making, and that time may be processed in relative, not absolute, terms within the prefrontal cortex, such that the posterior regions of the ventromedial prefrontal cortex are concerned with the processing of information that is closer in time, while the anterior sectors respond to information that is relatively further in time (Hochman et al., 2010).

ACKNOWLEDGMENTS

The research of this study was supported by the following grants from the National Institute on Drug Abuse (NIDA): DA11779, DA12487, and DA16708; by the National Science Foundation (NSF) grant IIS 04-42586; and by NINDS Program project grant P01 NS19632.

REFERENCES

Ackerly, S. S., & Benton, A. L. (1948). Report of a case of bilateral frontal lobe defect. *Proceedings of the Association for Research in Nervous and Mental Disease (Baltimore), 27*, 479–504.

Bechara, A. (2004). The role of emotion in decision-making: Evidence from neurological patients with orbitofrontal damage. *Brain and Cognition, 55*, 30–40.

Bechara, A., & Damasio, A. (2005). The somatic marker hypothesis: a neural theory of economic decision. *Games and Economic Behavior, 52*(2), 336–372.

Bechara, A., Damasio, A. R., Damasio, H., & Anderson, S. W. (1994). Insensitivity to future consequences following damage to human prefrontal cortex. *Cognition, 50*, 7–15.

Bechara, A., Damasio, H., Tranel, D., & Anderson, S. W. (1998). Dissociation of working memory from decision making within the human prefrontal cortex. *The Journal of Neuroscience, 18*, 428–437.

Bechara, A., Damasio, H., Tranel, D., & Damasio, A. R. (1997). Deciding advantageously before knowing the advantageous strategy. *Science, 275*, 1293–1295.

Bechara, A., Damasio, H., Tranel, D., & Damasio, A. R. (2005). The Iowa gambling task (IGT) and the somatic marker hypothesis (SMH): Some questions and answers. *Trends in Cognitive Sciences, 9*(4), 159–162.

Bechara, A., Dolan, S., & Hindes, A. (2002). Decision-making and addiction (Part II): Myopia for the future or hypersensitivity to reward? *Neuropsychologia, 40*(10), 1690–1705.

Bechara, A., Tranel, D., & Damasio, H. (2000). Characterization of the decision-making impairment of patients with bilateral lesions of the ventromedial prefrontal cortex. *Brain, 123*, 2189–2202.

Bechara, A., Tranel, D., Damasio, H., & Damasio, A. R. (1996). Failure to respond autonomically to anticipated future outcomes following damage to prefrontal cortex. *Cerebral Cortex, 6*, 215–225.

Blessing, W. W. (1997). Anatomy of the lower brainstem. In (Ed.), *The lower brainstem and bodily homeostasis* (pp. 29–99). New York: Oxford University Press.

Brickner, R. M. (1932). An interpretation of frontal lobe function based upon the study of a case of partial bilateral frontal lobectomy. Localization of function in the cerebral cortex. *Proceedings of the Association for Research in Nervous and Mental Disease (Baltimore), 13*, 259–351.

Cacioppo, J., Berntson, G., Larsen, J., Poehlmann, K., & Ito, T. (2000). The psychophysiology of emotion. In M. Lewis & J. Haviland-Jones (Eds.), *The handbook of emotion* (2nd ed., pp. 173–191). New York: Guilford Press.

Cacioppo, J., Klein, D. J., Berntson, G. G., & Hatfield, E. (1993). The psychophysiology of emotion. In M. Lewis & J. M. Haviland (Eds.), *The handbook of emotion* (1st ed., pp. 119–148). New York: Guilford Press.

Damasio, A. R. (1994). Descartes' error: Emotion, reason, and the human brain. New York: Grosset/Putnam.

Damasio, A. R. (1996). The somatic marker hypothesis and the possible functions of the prefrontal cortex. *Philosophical Transactions of the Royal Society of London (Biology), 351*, 1413–1420.

Damasio, A. R., Tranel, D., & Damasio, H. (1990). Individuals with sociopathic behavior caused by frontal damage fail to respond autonomically to social stimuli. *Behavioral Brain Research, 41*, 81–94.

Damasio, A. R., Tranel, D., & Damasio, H. (1991). Somatic markers and the guidance of behavior: Theory and preliminary testing. In H. S. Levin, H. M. Eisenberg & A. L. Benton (Eds.), *Frontal lobe function and dysfunction* (pp. 217–229). New York: Oxford University Press.

Damasio, H., Grabowski, T., Frank, R., Galburda, A. M., & Damasio, A. R. (1994). The return of Phineas Gage: Clues about the brain from the skull of a famous patient. *Science, 264*, 1102–1104.

Ernst, M., Bolla, K., Moratidis, M., Contoreggi, C. S., Matochick, J. A., Kurian, V., et al. (2002). Decision-making in a risk taking task. *Neuropsychopharmacology, 26*, 682–691.

Eslinger, P. J., & Damasio, A. R. (1985). Severe disturbance of higher cognition after bilateral frontal lobe ablation: Patient EVR. *Neurology, 35*, 1731–1741.

Fellows, L. K., & Farah, M. J. (2003). Ventromedial frontal cortex mediates affective shifting in humans: Evidence from a reversal learning paradigm. *Brain, 126*, 1830–1837.

Fellows, L. K., & Farah, M. J, (2005), Dissociable elements of human foresight: a role for the ventromedial frontal lobes in framing the future, but not in discounting future rewards. *Neuropsychologia, 43*, 1214–1221.

Fukui, H., Murai, T., Fukuyama, H., Hayashi, T., & Hanakawa, T. (2005). Functional activity related to risk anticipation during performance of the Iowa Gambling Task. *Neuroimage, 24*, 253–259.

Harlow, J. M. (1848). Passage of an iron bar through the head. *Boston Medical and Surgical Journal, 39*, 389–393.

Hochman, G., Yechiam, E., & Bechara, A. (2010). Recency gets larger as lesions move from anterior to posterior locations within the ventromedial prefrontal cortex. *Behav Brain Res 213*, 27–34.

Lang, P. J., Bradley, M. M., Cuthbert, B. N., & Patrick, C. J. (1993). Emotion and psychopathology: A startle probe analysis. In L. J. Chapman, J. P. Chapman, & D. C. Fowles (Eds.), *Experimental personality and psychopathology research* (Vol. 16, pp. 163–199). New York: Spring Publishing Co.

Lawrence, N. (2009). edit edit. *Cerebral Cortex*.

Maia, T. V., & McClelland, J. L. (2004). A reexamination of the evidence for the somatic marker hypothesis: What participants really know in the Iowa Gambling Task. *Proceedings of the National Academy of Science, 101*, 16075–16080.

Maia, T. V., & McClelland, J. L. (2005). The somatic marker hypothesis: Still many questions but no answers: Response to Bechara et al. *Trends in Cognitive Sciences, 9*(4), 162–164.

Manes, F., Sahakian, B., Clark, L., Rogers, R., Antoun, N., Aitken, M., et al. (2002). Decision-making processes following damage to the prefrontal cortex. *Brain, 125*, 624–639.

Martin, C., Denburg, N., Tranel, D., Granner, M., & Bechara, A. (2004). The effects of vagal nerve stimulation on decision-making. *Cortex, 40*, 1–8.

McClure, S. M., Laibson, D. I., Loewenstein, G., & Cohen, J. D. (2004). Separate neural systems value immediate and delayed monetary rewards. *Science 306*, 503–507.

Nauta, W. J. H. (1971). The problem of the frontal lobes: A reinterpretation. *Journal of Psychiatric Research, 8*, 167–187.

Nichelli P (2002) The processing of temporal information in the frontal lobe. In: Handbook of Neuropsychology: Frontal Lobes, 2nd Edition (Grafman J, ed), pp 175–193. Amsterdam: Elsevier.

Northoff, G., Grimm, S., Boeker, H., Schmidt, C., Bermpohl, F., Heinzel, A., et al. (2006). Affective judgment and beneficial decision making: Ventromedial prefrontal activity correlates with performance in the Iowa Gambling Task. *Human Brain Mapping, 27*, 572–587.

Ongur, D., & Price, J. L. (2000). The organization of networks within the orbital and medial prefrontal cortex of rats, monkeys and humans. *Cerebral Cortex, 10*(3), 206–219.

Persaud, N., McLeod, P., & Cowey, A. (2007). Post-decision wagering objectively measures awareness. *Nature Neuroscience, 10*(2), 257–261.

Rainville, P., Bechara, A., Naqvi, N., Virasith, A., Bilodeau, M., & Damasio, A. R. (2006). Basic emotions are associated with distinct patterns of cardiorespiratory activity. *International Journal of Psychophysiology, 61*(1), 5–18.

Saver, J. L., & Damasio, A. R. (1991). Preserved access and processing of social knowledge in a patient with acquired sociopathy due to ventromedial frontal damage. *Neuropsychologia, 29*, 1241–1249.

Schultz, W., Dayan, P., & Montague, P. R. (1997). A neural substrate of prediction and reward. *Science, 275*, 1593–1599.

Schnyer, D.M., Verfaellie, M., Alexander, M.P., LaFleche. G., Nicholls. L., & Kaszniak, A.W. (2004). A role for right medial prefrontal cortex in accurate feeling-of-knowing judgments: Evidence from patients with lesions to frontal cortex. *Neuropsychologia 42*, 957–966.

Semendeferi, K., Lu, A., Schenker, N., & Damasio, H. (2002). Humans and great apes share a large frontal cortex. *Nature Neuroscience 5*, 272–276.

Semendeferi, K., Armstrong, E., Schleicher, A., Zilles, K., Van Hoesen, G.W. (2001). Prefrontal cortex in humans and apes: A comparative study of area 10. *American Journal of Physical Anthropology 114*, 224–241.

Tomb, I., Hauser, M., Deldin, P., & Caramazza, A. (2002). Do somatic markers mediate decisions on the gambling task? *Nature Neuroscience*, 5(11), 1103–1104.

Welt, L. (1888). Uber Charaktervaranderungen des Menschen infoldge von Lasionen des Stirnhirns []. *Dtsch. Arch. Klin. Med.*, 42, 339–390.

Windmann, S., Kirsch, P., Mier, D., Stark, R., Walter, B., Gunturkun, O., et al. (2006). On framing effects in decision making: Linking lateral versus medial orbitofrontal cortex activation to choice outcome processing. *Journal of Cognitive Neuroscience*, 18(7), 1198–1211.

Yechiam, E., Busemeyer, J., Stout, J., Bechara, A. (2005). Using cognitive models to map relations between neuropsychological disorders and human decision-making deficits. *Psychological Science 16*, 973–978.

CHAPTER 11
Envisioning the Future and Self-Regulation

Shelley E. Taylor

A vital skill that humans possess is the ability to envision the future. By creating imagined scenarios of future events, people are able to regulate their behaviors and emotions so as to bring about future events, adjust to inevitable difficult situations, or manage their reactions to ongoing events. People conjure up images, stories, and projections of things not currently present on the basis of what they want to have happen or what they think is likely and use those projections for entertaining the self, planning for the future, and performing other basis tasks of self-regulation.

Our program of research on mental simulation was spearheaded by several disappointing trips to the bookstore. Before Amazon existed, I used to prowl the psychology shelves and was invariably disappointed and annoyed to find them overpopulated by self-help books. A quotation from a self-help book written by Patrick Fanning (1994) best captures the source of this annoyance:

> See yourself enjoying favorite activities in your new-found leisure, running, dancing, swimming, or whatever you would like to do. See yourself surrounded by loved ones and friends, popular and relaxed, having a good time. See yourself wearing stylish clothes, driving a new car, playing with a new tennis racquet, or skiing on new skis. (p. 21)

This quotation and many others like it suggest that merely by envisioning the outcome one wants to achieve, one will make progress toward that goal. We doubted that this was the case and set out to test the idea (Taylor, Pham, Rivkin, & Armor, 1998).

We conducted a program of research on mental simulation, which we define as the imitative representation of some event or series of events. Mental simulation can address a number of purposes. They include rehearsals of future events, such as envisioning the activities of an upcoming wedding; replays of past events, such as going over the events of a failed relationship to determine what went wrong; fantasies, such as imagining what one will do when one has won the lottery; and mixtures of real and hypothetical events, such as mentally replaying a real argument with an imaginary "what I should have said" resolution.

Our research focuses primarily on planning for future events. Mental simulations can be valuable for anticipating and managing future events because they address the two main tasks of coping: the need to come up with plans for forthcoming events or solutions for anticipated problems and the need to manage emotional reactions to future events or problems (Lazarus & Folkman, 1984).

ATTRIBUTES OF MENTAL SIMULATIONS

There are several intrinsic qualities of mental simulations that make them useful for anticipating the future, solving problems, reaching goals, and coping with stressful events. First, mental simulations make events seem real (e.g., Koehler, 1991 for a review). When people run a set of events through in their minds and imagine them in concrete form, it can make those events seem true. One may have the experience of imagining a conversation with someone, and later not been altogether sure as to whether the conversation actually took place. (Unhappily, this particular problem only gets worse with age.)

One reason why mental simulations make events seem true is that they are typically constrained by reality (Kahneman & Miller, 1986). That is, mental simulations may be imaginary, but they are typically not magical. For example, one of the most common fantasies that people have is suddenly becoming wealthy. But even a fantasy about acquiring wealth typically begins with an unexpected inheritance or winning a lottery, rather than with a large cloud opening up and dumping the money in the front yard. This is an intriguing characteristic of mental simulations because, after all, it is your fantasy, and you can have the cloud dump the money in the front yard if you want to. But people rarely do. Instead, most mental simulations are constrained by what is possible, if not always plausible, and this constraint can make them useful for anticipating the future.

Mental simulations prompt problem-solving activities (e.g., Hayes-Roth & Hayes-Roth, 1979). Usually when we imagine events that are going to occur, we imagine them in the way that social reality actually transpires. The events occur in their logical order with the characters one expects to encounter. Like reality, a simulation involves a sequence of successive interdependent actions and the organization of those actions can yield a plan. Consider Peter Lynch, the legendary former manager of the multi-billion dollar Fidelity Magellan Fund. In his books (e.g., Lynch, 1989), Lynch provides highly entertaining accounts of the stories he mentally generated for making decisions about what stocks to buy. For example, one day Lynch's wife, Caroline, brought home a pair of L'Eggs pantyhose from the supermarket. This caught Lynch's attention because pantyhose had not before been sold in a supermarket. Lynch was able to envision the large numbers of working women who needed pantyhose on a regular basis but who had very little time to go to a department store. At the time, women typically

went to a department store once every 3 weeks, but they went to the grocery store on average a couple of times a week. Lynch's recognition that they could pop this product into their grocery cart with the cereal and coffee led him to make a very timely and lucrative investment.

Mentally imagining events evokes emotions (e.g., Wright & Mischel, 1982). For example, if one thinks of a particularly sad event, this thinking may so completely evoke the original sadness that it is experienced all over again. Or remembering a wonderful event from the past, such as one's child winning a prize or graduating from school, can fully bring back the warm glow that experience generated initially. Mentally imagining events reliably evokes these emotional states and their physiological consequences, such as changes in heart rate, blood pressure, and skin conductivity (e.g., Lyman, Bernardin, & Thomas, 1980).

A fifth important characteristic of mental simulations is that they produce links to action by virtue of the self-regulatory benefits they provide. At least two important literatures illustrate this valuable link between thought and action. The first is a large literature from sports psychology on mental practice effects, much of it with elite athletes (Cratty, 1984). Mental practice refers to using mental imagery or simulation to improve performance. For example, Jack Nicklaus (1976) used this method to succeed at golf tournaments.

> Before every shot I go to the movies inside my head. Here is what I see. First, I see the ball where I want it to finish, nice and white and sitting up high on the bright green grass. Then, I see the ball going there; its path and trajectory and even its behavior on landing. The next scene shows me making the kind of swing that will turn the previous image into reality. These home movies are a key to my concentration and to my positive approach to every shot. (p. 45)

Many athletes remark that they can actually feel the muscle twinges associated with their actions as they imagine themselves executing a dive or a service in tennis. Linda Thom, an Olympic medalist in shooting, reported that one day while she was in line at the bank to cash a check, she was mentally rehearsing her shot and discovered that she had raised the barrel of an imaginary gun and was pointing it directly at the head of a very startled bank teller. Formal investigation of mental practice effects with athletes typically find that mental practice of an athletic skill enhances performance, although not as much as real practice (Feltz & Landers, 1983).

A second literature illustrating how mental simulation produces links to action is research from cognitive behavior therapy on relapse prevention. Most people who try to break bad habits have relapses, and so preventing permanent relapse is important. Alan Marlatt and others (e.g., Marlatt & Gordon, 1985) have shown how mental rehearsal of high-risk-for-relapse situations can help to maintain abstinence from health-compromising behaviors such as smoking and excessive drinking. For example, a man trying to overcome a drinking problem might mentally rehearse exactly how he will handle Superbowl Sunday with his friends, so he can refrain from drinking during the afternoon. Through such rehearsals and formal training, people develop specific coping skills that will help them avoid these temptations.

TYPES OF MENTAL SIMULATIONS

The sports psychology literature and the relapse prevention literature illustrate a particular type of mental simulation. The critical component is an emphasis on simulating the process needed for reaching a goal. According to this viewpoint, one sets a goal and then mentally rehearses the steps required to reach it, which leads one to make the appropriate changes in behavior, increasing the likelihood that the goal will be obtained.

Why would simulation of a process be an effective way of regulating behavior? Rehearsal of the process forces a person to organize the steps involved in mind, which in turn can yield a plan. At the same time, as one is mentally moving through these activities, the emotions involved may be evoked, at least modestly, such that one can anticipate and control what these emotional reactions will be.

An alternative viewpoint, namely outcome simulation, has been a staple of the self-help

movement and is embodied in the Fanning quote, with which this chapter opened. This approach maintains that if one actively focuses on an outcome one wants to achieve, it will help to bring it about. A quotation by Norman Vincent Peale (1982) illustrates essentially the same point of view:

> Hold the image of yourself succeeding, visualize it so vividly, that when the desire[d] success comes, it seems to be merely echoing a reality that has already existed in your mind. (p. 15)

The self-help literature has not for the most part explained why a focus on the outcome one wants to achieve would be successful. Drawing on the distinction made early between emotion regulation and problem-solving activities, one might assume that outcome simulation would be particularly effective in engaging emotional responses to help people muster the motivation to achieve their goals.

PROCESS VERSUS OUTCOME SIMULATIONS: EMPIRICAL TESTS

The Planning Fallacy

In a program of research conducted with Lien Pham, Inna Rivkin, and David Armor (1998), we examined how effective process versus outcome simulations are for bringing about desired outcomes. We began with an investigation of something that people do not seem to do very well, namely planning.

The planning fallacy is a charming problem identified by Buehler, Griffin, and Ross (1994) embodied by the dilemma experienced by anyone who has ever been involved in a construction project. It refers to the fact that people invariably underestimate the amount of time and resources such as money that will be required to finish a project and overestimate how easily it can be done. Anyone who has spent 6 months waiting for a kitchen that was supposed to take 3 months to complete or 1.5 years for a home addition that was supposed to be done in 6 months knows this experience firsthand. In fact, construction is one of the most notorious examples of the planning fallacy. The Sydney Opera House, begun in 1957, was initially expected to be completed by 1963 at a cost of $7 million. In reality, a greatly scaled-down version was completed in 1973, and it cost $192 million. More recent examples include the Chunnel connecting England and France, the Denver airport, and the largely nonexistent Los Angeles subway system.

The planning fallacy also exists at an individual level. It is embodied in the daily "to do" list, which many people create in a fit of unrealistic optimism at the beginning of each day, only to find that at least half the items are left undone at the end of the day. But each day, a new list is created, just as overly optimistic as the old one. Or if it has been a really bad day, one simply crosses out the day at the top of the page "Wednesday" and puts the next day, "Thursday." This goes on day after day. We seem to be oblivious to the feedback our own behavior should provide. Individuals appear to be as vulnerable to the planning fallacy as group projects. Accordingly, in our research, we used the process–outcome distinction to see if process simulations would enable people to plan projects more effectively.

In this investigation (Taylor et al., 1998), we recruited students and asked them to describe a school-related project that had to be completed during the subsequent week. We told them to pick a project that required some time and effort, such as a lab report or a short paper. Students in our control group were told simply to monitor their progress on the assignment each day. Students in the process simulation condition were told to envision themselves gathering the materials or resources they would need for the completion of the project and to see themselves getting organized and beginning work on the assignment. A third group was told to perform an outcome simulation each day that involved envisioning how pleased they would be by the final result. They were told to see themselves packing up the project and taking it to class, confident that they had done well.

We first addressed whether the planning fallacy asserts itself in the form of procrastination, in the form of not finishing on time, or both. Overall, the evidence suggests that it is both. Only 21% of participants began their projects when they said they would, and only 30% finished when they said they would. We then examined how the different mental simulation conditions affected these processes. The control condition behaved abysmally: Only 14% of the students began their projects when they expected to, and only 14% finished them when they expected to. The process simulation group fared somewhat better. They started somewhat closer to the time that they estimated (24%), and they were significantly more likely to finish when they said they would (41%). The outcome simulation had similar effects: 26% started on time, and 33% finished on time. The outcome simulation may have facilitated progress because it kept an inevitable assignment in mind. However, there was no assessment of the quality of the product, which, as will shortly be seen, turns out to be an important measure.

People who practice outcome simulations report that it is quite motivating and inspiring. We were therefore concerned that people who are asked to mentally rehearse process simulations instead might find them to be a bit depressing. It is much more fun to think about how great a project will be when it is completed than to think about the steps along the way. Consequently, we examined whether the process simulation undermined enjoyment. What we found surprised us. People who used the process simulation found the assignment they had to complete to be easier than people in either the control condition or the outcome simulation condition, who reported that the assignment was slightly harder than they had expected it to be. It appears that, because they had thought through the steps they would need to go through during their mental simulations, the people who practiced the process simulation had a plan which made completion of the project easier. Thus, although the process simulation may not be quite as much fun to practice as the outcome simulation is, the effects on overall ease of the project may offset these rather modest costs.

The Exam Studies

To further our understanding of the relative benefits and liabilities of process and outcome simulations, we conducted an intervention with Introductory Psychology students at UCLA,

who were studying for their first midterm examination (Pham & Taylor, 1999b). We contacted
them a week before their midterm exam and
explained that we were evaluating the success of
different ways of managing the stress of forthcoming exams. Students instructed in the process simulation intervention were told to visualize
themselves studying for the exam in a way that
would lead them to obtain their desired grade.
They were told how important it was to see themselves studying and to hold that picture in their
minds. They were given some sample details,
such as visualizing themselves sitting at their
desk or bed and studying the chapters and going
over the lecture notes. After they had practiced
the mental simulation in the lab, they were told
to do it for each of the next 5 to 7 days before the
exam took place, for 5 to 7 minutes each day.

Participants in the outcome simulation condition were told to imagine themselves getting
the high grade they desired. They were told to see
themselves standing in front of the glass case
where the midterm exam grades were posted,
holding their breath, moving their gaze horizontally to find their score, finding out that they got
the grade they wanted, beaming with joy, and
feeling confident and proud. They were also told
to practice this mental simulation for several
minutes each day for the 5 to 7 days prior to the
exam. Participants in the control condition simply monitored their studying over the same time
period. The night before the exam, we recon-
tacted all participants by phone. We asked them
how many hours they had studied, when they
had started studying, and the number of times
they had reviewed each chapter.

The students who had mentally rehearsed the
process of studying for the exam benefited substantially from this mental simulation. They
started studying early and spent more hours
studying for the exam. They also added several
points to their exam score. The students who had
rehearsed the outcome simulation, however,
were not for the most part benefited by its practice. There were negligible effects on how much
they studied for the exam, and they performed
significantly more poorly than students who
practiced the process simulation. Indeed, the
only beneficial effect of the outcome simulation

was that these students said that they were highly
motivated to study for the exam, more so than
was true in the other conditions. Apparently, the
outcome simulation got them cranked up, but
they failed to translate that feeling into effective
action.

These findings are similar to findings reported
by Oettingen (1995), who has found that positive
fantasies and daydreams can undermine future
achievement because they lead to anticipatory
consummation of success. Like the fantasies
studied by Oettingen, outcome simulations may
make people feel good without providing a basis
for achieving the desired outcome in the future.

We did a second study and replicated what we
had found in the first study, except the results
were worse. Participants who practiced the process simulation did quite well on the exam,
whereas those who focused on the outcome they
wanted to achieve did significantly worse than
both the process simulation participants and the
control condition. In this second study, we had
also included a condition that combined the process and outcome simulations. The basis for this
intervention was the mental practice literature: It
appears that athletes often move back and forth
between the outcome they want to achieve and
the process needed to achieve it, and so we created a mental simulation that attempted to mirror this process. It was unsuccessful. Although
students faithfully practiced the process and outcome simulations individually, they were less
likely to practice the simulation that combined
the two. Moreover, exam scores for those in the
combined condition were more similar to those
of the students rehearsing the outcome simulation than those practicing the process simulation
condition. We have not repeated these interventions, inasmuch as we now know that outcome
simulations not only do not consistently help
people but can actually harm performance.

What is responsible for the adverse effects of
outcome simulations and the beneficial effects of
process simulations on performance? We conducted structural equation analyses to identify
the underlying mechanisms. Those results suggested that students who had practiced the outcome simulation rehearsed the excitement that
they would experience over the high grade but

failed to study more. Over time, they reduced their aspirations, with a detrimental effect on performance. When we asked them what grade they thought they would get, they had lowered their desired grade by a full letter grade by the night before the exam, compared to the initial grade they had told us they were striving to obtain, and they had studied fewer hours. By contrast, those who practiced the process simulation had studied more, had lower anxiety, and appeared to have planned their study time better, which increased the grade they strove for. Specifically, the impact of the process simulation on planning and reduced anxiety appear to be the critical determinants of the better exam performance this condition created (Castaño, Sujan, Kacker, & Sujan, 2008). As noted, problem solving and emotion regulation are two vital components of coping, and they appear to account for the beneficial effects of process simulation in the exam studies.

COPING WITH STRESS

The fact that mental simulations appear to achieve their beneficial effects by facilitating planning and emotion regulation provides an implicit link to a large and growing coping literature, which maintains that these are the central tasks of coping (Lazarus & Folkman, 1984). In the next study, we made those connections explicit.

We (Rivkin & Taylor, 1999) asked college students to designate a stressful event they were currently going through and gave them examples of academic or interpersonal stressors they might name. One group of participants was asked to visualize the process surrounding the stressor, including how the problem arose, what happened step by step, the actions they had undertaken or might undertake, the circumstances surrounding the event, and the feelings they experienced. A second group of participants completed an outcome simulation and was asked to imagine the problem beginning to resolve itself, to imagine their relief that the problem was no longer bothering them, and to experience satisfaction in having dealt successfully with the problem. A control group did not perform a

mental simulation. Following the initial practice of the mental simulation and then again 1 week later, after participants had had the opportunity to practice the simulation during the intervening week, they reported on their emotional responses to the stressful event, the coping activities they planned to use (immediately after practicing the mental simulation), and the ones they had actually used (1 week later) to deal with the problem.

The students who had mentally simulated the ongoing process reported more positive affect, compared to the outcome simulation group and control groups, immediately after performing the simulation, and 1 week later, this positive effect on mood persisted. In addition, the participants in the process simulation condition reported having used more positive reinterpretation and social support for emotional solace as coping techniques, compared with participants in the outcome simulation and control conditions.

The intervention uncovered significant changes in problem-solving activities as well. Those who had practiced the process simulation reported, 1 week later, that they had used more active coping and had sought more instrumental social support, relative to the outcome simulation condition and the control group. The outcome simulation had no significant impact on either the intended use of active coping strategies or the reported use of active coping strategies, relative to the process simulation condition or to the control condition. When people are coping with ongoing stressful events, then, a mental simulation that focuses their attention on the unfolding processes surrounding those events can have both emotion-regulation benefits as well as problem-solving benefits, especially with respect to active coping and use of social support.

The students had been asked to characterize the stressful event they had selected, and serendipitously, these events split evenly into academic problems, which were initially conceived of as quite controllable, and interpersonal problems, which were initially seen as less controllable. In the past, research has found that controllable problems are especially amenable to coping via problem-solving activities, whereas uncontrollable problems are more amenable to coping via emotion-regulation (e.g., Vitaliano et al., 1990). An intriguing pattern emerged regarding changes in the perceptions of these problems following practice of the process simulation. Interpersonal stressors came to be seen as more amenable to active coping strategies among those who had practiced the process mental simulation, whereas the reverse was true for academic problems: The process simulation led participants to perceive that emotion-regulation strategies, including acceptance, could help with the management of academic stressful events as well.

These patterns fit very well with the extant coping literature, emphasizing problem-solving and emotion-regulation efforts as critical to successful coping. They suggest that process mental simulations can have beneficial effects on self-regulation, by helping people to regulate their emotions effectively and engage in problem-solving activities. In particular, stressors for which active coping efforts are not immediately obvious solutions (interpersonal stressors) and those for which emotion-regulation coping efforts may not be immediately obvious solutions (e.g., academic stressors) may be especially benefited by this kind of process simulation.

Other studies have replicated these findings in other life domains. For example, Armitage and Reidy (2008) found that process, but not outcome, simulations led people to change health cognitions related to health behaviors, in their case, donating blood. Health behaviors, such as exercise and diet, may be altered through interventions that include process simulations as well (Cameron & Chan, 2008). Process simulations are not always more successful than outcome simulations: In some high involvement situations (Escalas & Luce, 2004) or when people are making difficult decisions (Thompson, Hamilton, & Petrova, 2009), process simulations can interfere with effective performance. Moreover, for simple goals, outcome simulations may be effective as well (Pham & Taylor, 1999a). However, for stressors and self-regulatory tasks of moderate complexity, on balance, process simulations appear to be more effective.

BRAIN MECHANISMS LINKING MENTAL SIMULATIONS TO PERFORMANCE

The research just described was completed more than a decade ago, and in recent years, psychologists have uncovered some of the neural bases for effects such as these. Among the most important insights gained is the realization that memory is used not only to retain and recall past experiences but also to permit people to imagine future events, by drawing on representations in memory and knowledge of likely future events. In particular, episodic memory is crucially implicated in the ability to imagine nonexistent events and simulate future ones (Schacter, Addis, & Buckner, 2007). Imagining future events evokes activity in the prefrontal cortex and parts of the medial temporal lobe, specifically the hippocampus and the parahippocampal gyrus. Related investigations have also implicated a posterior midline region near the precuneus. Replication across multiple studies (Okuda et al., 2003; Szpunar, Watson, & McDermott, 2007) indicates that the process of imagining the future evokes activation of a specific core brain system, including medial prefrontal regions, posterior regions in the medial and lateral parietal cortex (extending into the precuneus and the retrosplenial cortex), the lateral temporal cortex, and the medial temporal lobe.

The fact that mental simulations often produce links to action suggests that brain regions implicated in motor behavior or its anticipation would also be activated during mental simulations. Studies with monkeys who observed other monkeys performing actions found brain activations especially in premotor cortical regions and also in motor cortical regions that parallel activations associated with actual performance (e.g., Cisek & Kalaska, 2004; Raos, Evangeliou, & Savaki, 2007), consistent with this prediction. One might therefore predict that a successful mental simulation, that is, one that leads to effective action, would be more likely to be associated with activation in brain regions implicated in relevant motor activity than would be an ineffective mental simulation. Given the distinction between process and outcome simulations described earlier and the fact that process simulations appear to more reliably evoke goal-related actions, one might expect to see more premotor and motor region activation during process than outcome simulations.

The coping literature generates hypotheses regarding what brain regions may be involved in mental simulations of different kinds as well. As noted, imagining how events will transpire in the future appears to achieve its effects on behavior primarily by enabling people to develop plans and to assess or manage their emotional reactions to unfolding events. Regions of the brain that have been consistently implicated in planning include the prefrontal cortex, and regions implicated in the management of emotional reactions to events include the right ventrolateral prefrontal cortex and the amygdala. On this last point, a number of studies reveal that when coping efforts are successful in down-regulating emotions related to fear, threat, or uncertainty, heightened activity in the ventrolateral prefrontal cortex and corresponding lower activity in the amygdala are often found (e.g., Hariri, Bookheimer, & Mazziotta, 2000; Ochsner et al., 2004; Taylor et al., 2008). Thus, one might expect that to the extent that a mental simulation, such as the process simulation described earlier, helps people control their emotional responses to events, lower amygdala and higher right ventrolateral prefrontal cortex activity would be found.

As noted, Oettingen (1995) raised intriguing arguments regarding why mental simulations that involve focusing on the outcomes one wants to achieve often fail to produce goal-directed action. She concluded that outcome simulations represent the symbolic consummation of rewards in advance of their actual occurrence. Accordingly, during outcome simulations, one might expect to see activity in brain regions related to reward, such as the ventral striatum and orbitofrontal cortex, with lesser activity in prefrontal regions devoted to planning. Whether a focus on reward leads to heightened activation in reward-related brain regions that may in turn be related to lower activity in the prefrontal cortex is a hypothesis, but it is a potentially intriguing one that would fit the evidence to date.

A fifth potential line of empirical inquiry related to mental simulations derives from brain research which identifies the underpinnings of behavioral intentions. In a recent study (Gilbert, Gollwitzer, Cohen, Burgess, & Oettingen, 2009), researchers distinguished between goal intentions, which are representations of things people want to achieve, similar perhaps to outcome simulations, and implementation intentions, which are representations of how, when, and where one will implement a particular action plan, similar, perhaps, to process simulations. Implementation intentions are characterized as representations of specific environmental events which cue behavioral responses that may bring about a desired goal state. Goal intentions, by contrast, are more abstract, and thus do not necessarily engage specific behavioral responses, because they are less reliant on intention-related actions and instead are more dependent on spontaneous action.

In the Gilbert et al. (2009) study, participants were given two prospective memory tasks to perform and told either to respond to the task using the cues indicated (analogous to implementation intentions), or, in the second condition, they were given the option of responding spontaneously (more characteristic of goal intentions). Consistent with the process versus outcome distinction reviewed earlier, the authors predicted that participants would respond more efficiently in the cued condition than in the spontaneous condition. These predictions were supported.

Previous studies have suggested that activity in the rostral prefrontal cortex approximating Brodmann's area 10 (BA 10) plays an important role in attending to both internally and externally represented information, such as intentions for future action. Gilbert et al. (2009) predicted that if the cued condition prompts more efficient external coding of behavior, activity in medial BA 10 should be evoked, because this region is involved in environmentally triggered behavior. By contrast, in the spontaneous condition, which involves self-initiated behavior, activity in lateral BA 10 would be implicated. As predicted, the cued condition was associated with greater activation in medial area 10, whereas the spontaneous condition was associated with greater activation in lateral area 10. The difference in activity between these two conditions in left lateral area 10 was mirrored in performance differences, with greater activity in lateral area 10 tied to poorer performance.

The spontaneous condition was associated with activation in a predominantly frontoparietal network, whereas the cued condition was not associated with significant activity in any region. It may be that implementation intentions, or planning as generated by a process simulation, allows behavior to proceed relatively automatically in response to environmental cues, whereas goal intentions, or a focus on the outcome, may be more dependent on self-initiated behavior, and thus lead to greater brain activation and poorer performance (Gollwitzer & Sheeran, 2006). Whether these lines of investigation inform each other is currently not definitive, but the parallels are intriguing.

Conclusions

What do we conclude from these and the other investigations of mental simulation? Mental simulations can help people manage potential problems and reach goals that might otherwise be more difficult. Such activities as health behavior change (Cameron & Chan, 2008), achievement of personal goals (Gollwitzer & Sheeran, 2006), and consumer decision making (Castaño et al., 2008) can all be benefitted by mental simulations. Although imagining either the outcome one wishes to achieve or the process required to achieve it can be helpful (e.g., Greitemeyer & Würz, 2006), on the whole, the evidence supporting the value of process simulations, namely envisioning the steps needed to achieve a goal, is more consistent. Process simulations appear to aid performance primarily by helping people come up with specific plans and steps that they can take to solve problems or further their goals, and by helping people manage their emotions effectively. As such, the range of behaviors to which process simulations might profitably be directed could be enlarged. Current developments in neuroscience hold promise for revealing the brain mechanisms that underlie these effects.

Acknowledgment

This research was supported by a grant from the National Institute on Aging (AG030309).

References

Armitage, C. J., & Reidy, J. G. (2008). Use of mental simulations to change theory of planned behavior variables. *British Journal of Health Psychology*, *13*, 513–524.

Buehler, R., Griffin, D., & Ross, M. (1994). Exploring the planning fallacy: Why people underestimate their task completion times. *Journal of Personality and Social Psychology*, *67*, 366–381.

Cameron, L. D., & Chan, C. K. Y. (2008). Designing health communications: Harnessing the power of affect, imagery, and self-regulation. *Social and Personality Psychology Compass*, *2*, 262–282.

Castaño, R., Sujan, M., Kacker, M., & Sujan, H. (2008). Managing consumer uncertainty in the adoption of new products: Temporal distance and mental simulation. *Journal of Marketing Research*, *45*, 320–336.

Cisek, P., & Kalaska, J. F. (2004). Neural correlates of mental rehearsal in dorsal premotor cortex. *Nature*, *431*, 993–996.

Cratty, B. J. (1984). *Psychological preparation and athletic excellence*. Ithaca, NY: Mouvement.

Escalas, J. E., & Luce, M. F. (2004). Understanding the effects of process-focused versus outcome-focused thought in response to advertising. *Journal of Consumer Research*, *31*, 274–285.

Fanning, P. (1994). *Visualization for change* (2nd ed.). Oakland, CA: New Harbinger.

Feltz, D. L., & Landers, D. M. (1983). The effects of mental practice on motor skill learning and performance: A meta-analysis. *Journal of Sports Psychology*, *5*, 25–57.

Gilbert, S. J., Gollwitzer, P. M., Cohen, A., Burgess, P. W., & Oettingen, G. (2009). Separable brain systems supporting cued versus self-initiated realization of delayed intentions. *Journal of Experimental Psychology: Learning, Memory and Cognition*, *35*, 905–915.

Gollwitzer, P. M., & Sheeran, P. (2006). Implementation intentions and goal achievement: A meta-analysis of effects and processes. *Advances in Experimental Social Psychology*, *38*, 69–119.

Greitemeyer, T., & Würz, D. (2006). Mental simulation and the achievement of health goals: The role of goal difficulty. *Imagination, Cognition, and Personality*, *25*, 239–251.

Hariri, A. R., Bookheimer, S. Y., & Mazziotta, J. C. (2000). Modulating emotional responses: Effects of a neocortical network on the limbic system. *NeuroReport, 11,* 43–48.

Hayes-Roth, B., & Hayes-Roth, F. (1979). A cognitive model of planning. *Cognitive Science, 3,* 275–310.

Kahneman, D., & Miller, D. T. (1986). Norm theory: Comparing reality to its alternatives. *Psychological Review, 93,* 136–153.

Koehler, D. J. (1991). Explanation, imagination, and confidence in judgment. *Psychological Bulletin, 110,* 499–519.

Lazarus, R. S., & Folkman, S. (1984). *Stress, appraisal, and coping.* New York: Springer.

Lyman, B., Bernardin, S., & Thomas, S. (1980). Frequency of imagery in emotional experience. *Perceptual and Motor Skills, 50,* 1159–1162.

Lynch, P. (1989). *One up on Wall Street.* New York: Simon & Schuster.

Marlatt, G. A., & Gordon, J. R. (1985). *Relapse prevention: Maintenance strategies in the treatment of addictive behaviors.* New York: Guilford Press.

Nicklaus, J. (1976). *Play better golf.* New York: King Features.

Oettingen, G. (1995). Positive fantasy and motivation. In P. M. Gollwitzer & J. A. Bargh (Eds.), *The psychology of action: Linking cognition and motivation to behavior* (pp. 219–235). New York: Guilford Press.

Okuda, J., Fujii, T., Ohtake, H., Tsukiura, T., Tanji, K., Suzuki, K., et al. (2003). Thinking of the future and the past: The roles of the frontal pole and the medial temporal lobes. *NeuroImage, 19,* 1369–1380.

Ochsner, K. N., Ray, R. D., Cooper, J. C., Robertson, E. R. Chopra, S., Gabrieli, J. D. E., et al. (2004). For better or for worse: Neural systems supporting the cognitive down-and-up-regulation of negative emotion. *NeuroImage, 23,* 483–499.

Peale, N. V. (1982). *Positive imaging: The powerful way to change your life.* New York: Fawcett Crest.

Pham, L. B., & Taylor, S. E. (1999a). The effect of mental simulation on goal-directed performance. *Imagination, Cognition and Personality, 18,* 253–268.

Pham, L. B., & Taylor, S. E. (1999b). From thought to action: Effects of process- versus outcome-based mental simulations on performance. *Personality and Social Psychology Bulletin, 25,* 250–260.

Raos, V., Evangeliou, M. N., & Savaki, H. E. (2007). Mental simulation of action in the service of action perception. *Journal of Neuroscience, 27,* 12675–12683.

Rivkin, I. D., & Taylor, S. E. (1999). The effects of mental simulation on coping with controllable stressful events. *Personality and Social Psychology Bulletin, 25,* 1451–1462.

Schacter, D. L., Addis, D. R., & Buckner, R. L. (2007). Remembering the past to imagine the future: The prospective brain. *Nature Reviews Neuroscience, 8,* 657–661.

Szpunar, K. K., Watson, J. M., & McDermott, K. B. (2007). Neural substrates of envisioning the future. *Proceedings of the National Academy of Sciences USA, 104,* 642–647.

Taylor, S. E., Burklund, L. J., Eisenberger, N. I., Lehman, B. J., Hilmert, C. J., & Lieberman, M. D. (2008). Neural bases of moderation of cortisol stress responses by psychosocial resources. *Journal of Personality and Social Psychology, 95,* 197–211.

Taylor, S. E., Pham, L. B., Rivkin, I., & Armor, D. A. (1998). Harnessing the imagination: Mental simulation and self-regulation of behavior. *American Psychologist, 53,* 429–439.

Thompson, D. V., Hamilton, R. W., & Petrova, P. K. (2009). When mental simulation hinders behavior: The effects of process-oriented thinking on decision difficulty and performance. *Journal of Consumer Research, 36.* Retrieved August 15, 2009, from http://www.journals.uchicago.edu/doi/abs/10.1086/599325

Vitaliano, P. P., Maiuro, R. D., Russo, J., Katon, W., DeWolfe, D., & Hall, G. (1990). Coping profiles associated with psychiatric, physical health, work, and family problems. *Health Psychology, 9,* 348–376.

Wright, J., & Mischel, W. (1982). Influence of affect on cognitive social learning person variables. *Journal of Personality and Social Psychology, 43,* 901–914.

CHAPTER 12
Prediction: A Construal-Level Theory Perspective

Nira Liberman, Yaacov Trope, and SoYon Rim

Predicting the future is indispensible for our functioning. We need to predict tomorrow's weather, the condition of our food in a week's time, or the reaction of our partner to our suggestion to move to another town. Yet we experience only the present. To predict the future, we use present and past experiences, and in that sense, predictions build a bridge between the experienced past and the unknown future.

How do we make predictions? Consider two extreme views on the viability of prediction. One states that things always change and thus remain fundamentally unpredictable: "You cannot step twice into the same river; for fresh waters are ever flowing in upon you" (Heraclitus). The other view is that nothing is new: "What has been will be again, what has been done will be done again; there is nothing new under the sun" (Ecclesiastes 1:9). Both views are valid in that if you apply narrow enough categories ("a specific configuration of light, temperature, wind and smell"), then everything is new and prediction is impossible, whereas if you apply broad enough categories (this is just another day), then everything is old, utterly predictable, yet uninformative. These extreme views exemplify the basic trade-off in any prediction: the trade-off between informativeness, which is achieved by applying specific, narrow categories, and accuracy, which is achieved by applying general, abstract categories. Ideally, we would like to predict the future in minute detail, yet in practice, details are too variable and unpredictable, and we, therefore, resort to abstraction, sacrificing detail to achieve stability and predictability.

We contend that abstraction has evolved in the service of prediction. We use construal-level theory (CLT) to examine how people bridge the past and the future by means of abstraction, or, in other words, how people make predictions by using abstract mental construals. In the framework of CLT, prediction, or bridging over time, is akin to mentally bridging over other psychological distances: understanding another person's perspective (bridging over social distance), constructing alternate worlds (bridging over hypotheticality), or understanding other places and taking a different spatial perspective (mentally bridging over spatial distance). We thus use the word *prediction* in this broad sense, as referring to the act of imagining a situation that is distal not only in time (the common definition of prediction) but also in space, social perspective, or one that is hypothetical. We first introduce CLT and then describe relevant research on prediction, also pointing, along the way, to open questions for further research. Finally, we examine the commonalities among predictions over different types of distance.

CONSTRUAL-LEVEL THEORY OF PSYCHOLOGICAL DISTANCE

Psychological Distance

We directly experience only ourselves, here and now. Anything that will happen in the future, things that happen in different, remote places, or other people's experiences and hypothetical alternatives (what could have been) can be predicted but cannot be directly experienced. In CLT, time, space, social perspectives, and hypotheticality constitute the four dimensions of psychological distance, as they comprise the different ways in which an object might be removed from the self in the here and now. Research within the framework of CLT has shown that the different dimensions of psychological distance are mentally associated (Bar-Anan, Liberman, Trope, & Algom, 2007) and affect each other (Stephan, Liberman, & Trope, 2010).

For a theory of prediction, this view suggests that the processes that underlie prediction of future events might be similar to the processes that underlie imagining events that are distant in other ways—taking the perspective of other people, imagining a different spatial perspective, and envisioning alternatives to an existing state of affairs. It might be the case that similar challenges are set by the need to make predictions across these various distance dimensions. Therefore, it is possible that insights from research on interpersonal perspective taking or spatial perspective taking could be used to understand prediction over time. We will explore this idea in the third section of our chapter.

It is interesting to note that human evolution, the history of human civilization, and human development are all associated with making predictions or building bridges across larger psychological distances. For example, the turning points of human evolution include developing tools, which required constructing hypothetical alternative scenarios of future events and planning for the future; developing language, which enabled forming larger and more complex social groups and relations; and domestication of animals and plants, which required an extended temporal perspective (Flinn, Geary, & Ward, 2005). Human history, likewise, is associated with crossing greater spatial distances (e.g., discovering new continents, space travel), forming larger social groups (families vs. cities vs. states vs. global institutions), planning and investing in the more distant future, and reaching farther back into the past. Human development involves acquiring the ability to plan for the distant future, considering possibilities that are not-present, and taking the perspective of other people

(from self-centeredness to acknowledging others, from immediate social environment to larger social groups). Although evolution, history, and child development have different time scales, we propose that all of them entail prediction over expanding temporal, spatial, and social distances, and considering increasingly remote alternative worlds. We further propose that all of these types of predictions require and are enabled by the human capacity for abstract mental construal.

Level of Construal

Construal-level theory builds on the notion that mental construals vary in levels of abstractness. Specifically, we argue that the same event or object can be represented at a low or high level of construal. Low-level construals are relatively unstructured, contextualized representations that include subordinate and incidental features of events. High-level construals are schematic, decontextualized representations that extract the gist from the available information, emphasizing superordinate, core features of events, and omitting incidental features—features that may vary without significantly changing the meaning of events. For example, by moving from representing an object as a "cellular phone" to representing it as "a communication device," we omit information about size; moving from representing an activity as "learning to drive a car" to representing it as "advancing one's independence" we omit the car. Concrete representations typically lend themselves to multiple abstractions. For example, a cellular phone could also be construed as a "small object," and "learning to drive a car" could be construed as "operating a machine." An abstract representation is selected according to its relevance to one's goals. Thus, if one's goal is to contact a friend, then "a communication device" is relevant but size is not. If, however, one's goal is to pickpocket a valuable object, then size is a relevant attribute, and function is of less relevance. Like irrelevant details, details that are inconsistent with the chosen abstract representation are omitted from the representation or assimilated into it. For example, the detail that one is taking a driving lesson would be omitted or modified once the activity is represented as "advancing one's independence." As a result, abstract representations tend to be simpler, less ambiguous, more coherent, more schematic, and more prototypical than concrete representations.

It is important to note, however, that higher level construals are not simply more impoverished or vague than lower level construals. They often convey additional information about the value of the stimulus and its relations to other stimuli. For example, "advancing one's independence" entails many characteristics that are not an obvious part of "learning to drive a car" (e.g., relevance to personal and cultural values) and places the activity within a broader context by specifying its relations to other concepts (e.g., getting a job). Thus, the process of abstraction involves not only a loss of specific, idiosyncratic, and incidental information but also an ascription of new meaning deduced from stored knowledge and organized in structured representations.

High-Level Construal as a Bridge across Distances

Construal-level theory posits that we transcend current direct experience and build bridges across time, space, social perspectives, and hypothetical worlds by using high-level construals, or abstract mental representations. This is because high-level construals are more likely than low-level construals to remain unchanged as one gets closer to an object or farther away from it. For example, the higher level goal to contact a friend is more stable over time and space than the more concrete goal to send her an e-mail, because an Internet connection might be unavailable when one is actually trying to contact the friend. From a temporally and spatially distant perspective, it is therefore more useful to represent the goal at a higher level. The same holds for social distance and hypotheticality. For example, most people use communication devices but not necessarily e-mail; therefore, the former construal is more useful for predicting actions of socially distant individuals or those in hypothetical worlds.

At the same time as being abstract, high-level construals, being driven by goals, preserve informativeness. To return to our previous example,

if one's goal is to call a friend, then a cell phone might be construed abstractly as a communication device. An even more abstract representation (e.g., a human artifact), although bridging to more distal times, places, social groups, and alternative worlds, does not serve the goal, because it does not distinguish between objects that are conducive of goal attainment (e.g., a cell phone, an Internet connection) and those that are not (e.g., a carpet, a jar).

The goal-driven nature of the process of forming higher level construals is distinct from retrieval of preexisting abstract categories from long-term memory. For example, a child wishing to play with another child's ball may have to appreciate the way her actions would be seen by the owner of the ball (that is, to bridge across social distance, or predict another person's actions). The goal-relevant higher level construal of the ball (e.g., as "an object that belongs to another kid") is an abstraction that is not necessarily part of the semantic meaning of "ball," but is rather constructed in the current context.

Psychological Distance and Level of Construal Are Associated

It follows from the former discussion of the relation between distance and level of construal that the greater the psychological distance from an event, the more likely is the event to be represented abstractly. Distant events are likely to be represented in terms of few general features that convey the relatively invariant essence of the events, rather than in terms of concrete, more incidental, and potentially changeable details of the events. Indeed, a considerable amount of research has shown that distant activities are described in terms of superordinate goals, whereas near activities are described in terms of subordinate goals (Fujita, Henderson, Eng, Trope, & Liberman, 2006; Liberman & Trope, 1998; Liviatan, Trope, & Liberman, 2008; Wakslak, Trope, Liberman, & Alony, 2006). Distant objects are classified into few broad categories, whereas near objects are classified into a relatively large number of narrow categories (Henderson, Fujita, Trope, & Liberman, 2006; Liberman, Sagristano, & Trope, 2002; Wakslak et al., 2006). A simpler, more coherent structure thus underlies people's responses to distant events than to near events (Liberman et al., 2002).

According to CLT, high-level construals serve the function of prediction, that is, bridging between the experienced me, here and now, and events that are distal in that they lie beyond direct experience. Indeed, research has shown that construing objects and events at a higher level makes people think of more distal times, places, and people and about less likely events. For example, thinking about an activity in high-level, "why" terms rather than low-level, "how" terms led participants to expect more temporally distant instantiations of the activity (Liberman, Trope, McCrea, & Sherman, 2007). Similarly, thinking about events in terms of their defining properties rather than their incidental details made them seem less likely to occur (Wakslak et al., 2006).

Importantly, the tendency to construe more distal objects in higher level terms does not depend on whether people actually happen to possess specific, low-level knowledge about distal objects and whether they believe that with increasing distance these low-level details would change. Construal-level theory contends that because of a frequent association between distance and high level of construal, people tend to use high-level construals when they think of distant objects and low-level construals when they think of proximal objects even if they have no reason to believe that things will change with distance. For example, a researcher may know well in advance that low-level random factors might contaminate the results of her research and have no reason to believe that these factors change over time. Nevertheless, CLT contends that this researcher will underweight the effect of such random factors when making predictions for the more distant future, for a more spatially remote laboratory, for research conducted by a colleague rather than herself, and for research that is less likely to be carried out.

In sum, psychological distance is a subjective experience that something is close or far away from the self, here and now. Psychological distance is thus egocentric, that is, its reference point is the self here and now, and the different ways in which an object might be removed from that point—in time, space, social distance, and hypotheticality—constitute different distance dimensions. Moving beyond one's direct experience is the essence of making predictions, and it is both advantageous and indispensable for human self-regulation. Prediction is achieved by construing goal-relevant abstractions, and farther removed objects on any distance dimension are construed at a higher (more abstract) level. In the following section we turn to research examining the implications of the association between distance and level of construal for prediction.

LARGER DISTANCES FOSTER MORE SCHEMATIC PREDICTIONS

As argued earlier, the function of high-level construals is to enable people to mentally transcend the here and now by forming a representation of distal objects that consists of the invariant features of the available information. Predictions of future experiences would therefore be more schematic than the actual experiences, giving rise to a variety of prediction biases that stem from underweighting contextual and incidental features (Gilbert & Wilson, 2007; Kahneman, Krueger, Schkade, Schwarz, & Stone, 2006; Wilson & Gilbert, 2003). For example, people tend to predict that they will react more extremely to positive events (e.g., getting tenure) and negative events (e.g., a rejected paper) than they actually do. This misprediction stems from underweighting the effect of diluting low-level circumstances (Wilson, Wheatley, Meyers, Gilbert, & Axsom, 2000). This research on prediction biases compares predictions and actual outcomes. In contrast, CLT research compares predictions of distal versus proximal outcomes, and it examines effects that cannot be accounted for by differences in knowledge. According to CLT, the prediction biases uncovered by previous research should be accentuated by distance because predicting more distal events should direct attention to more invariant, schematic features of those events and away from low-level situational details, even if these latter details are known.

Theories versus Noise

The French anthropologist Claude Levi-Strauss once noted that in the Western sciences, the most distal topics (e.g., astronomy and geography) developed first, whereas those that look at more proximal entities (e.g., psychology) were last to develop (Levi-Strauss, 1963). We would like to propose, consistent with this observation, that in scientific prediction, high-level construals reflect the theory, which fosters confidence, whereas low-level construals include noise, which might undermine confidence. As a result, theories better apply to distant events than to proximal events.

A study by Nussbaum, Liberman, and Trope (2006, Study 1) examined the confidence of advanced psychology students in replicating classic findings in psychology in either the near future or the distant future. For example, participants imagined entering a class at the university, either the next day or a year later (depending on the experimental condition), handing the students a list of words to memorize, and then testing how well they remember it after moving some of the students to a different room. Participants estimated how likely it is that those tested in the same room would outperform, on average, those that were moved to a different room, thus replicating the encoding specificity effect. Participants were more confident that they would replicate this effect when they imagined conducting the experiment in the distant future than in the near future, especially when reminded of the theory underlying prediction. The same pattern of results was obtained with other classic findings in social, cognitive, and developmental psychology.

It is possible that experts, too, would be more confident in predicting distal outcomes than proximal outcomes. For example, economic theory posits that increasing interest rates causes the stock market to decline; from the perspective of this theory, other factors that also affect the stock market constitute noise. According to CLT, psychological distancing would promote confidence in predicting based on theories such as this, when making predictions about more geographically distant markets, when making forecasts about the investments of other people, and when the predictions concern a hypothetical or unlikely scenario.

Global Trends versus Local Deviations

In some prediction situations, time series data are available (e.g., stock prices over time), which allows looking at both global trends over extended periods of time, and local deviations from these trends. For example, in inspecting the fluctuations of stock prices in the United States during the years of the great recession, between the years 1929–1932, one can observe a global downward trend along with local movements upward. On March 1, 1931, observing a recent recovery in stock prices, would one predict a continued plunge (consistent with the global trend) or a continued recovery (consistent with the local trend)? In terms of CLT, global trends convey a high-level construal, whereas deviations, being local exceptions, convey a low-level construal.

In a study that investigated the effect of spatial distance on the tendency to base predictions on global rather than local information (Henderson et al., 2006), New York University (NYU) participants viewed a series of graphs depicting information from the years 1999–2004 (e.g., average number of photocopies per student). The information was said to pertain to the NYU campus in Manhattan (spatially near condition) or to the NYU campus in Florence, Italy (spatially distant condition). Each graph showed either an upward or downward trend, with the final year (2004) always deviating from that global trend. Participants estimated the likelihood that the year 2005 would be consistent with the general trend or with the more recent local deviation. Consistent with CLT's predictions, spatial distance enhanced the tendency to predict on the basis of the global trend rather than the local deviation.

Other distances, too, may be expected to shift the weight toward considering global trends and ignoring local deviations. For example, it might be easier to appreciate global trends and ignore local deviations when making predictions for someone other than oneself, for an unlikely scenario, and for a more temporally distant event. Thus, looking 70 years back, it might be easier to appreciate the global downward trend of the stock market than it was back in 1932. Let us consider more specifically the case of prediction over past temporal distance, or hindsight.

Hindsight: The Case of Past Temporal Distance

How does confidence about past events change over time? Bearing on this question is research on the hindsight bias—namely, people's tendency to exaggerate their past estimated likelihoods of an event after it has occurred (Fischhoff, 1975, for a review see Christensen-Szalanski & Willham, 1991). For example, after January 1, 2000 (post-Y2K, when people realized that no major incidents had occurred with the advent of year 2000), people reported lower estimated likelihoods of disasters happening than the estimates they actually gave before that date (Pease, McCabe, Brannon, & Tagler, 2003). Interestingly, one of the explanations for the hindsight bias is akin to mental construal: People construct a theory to explain the outcome (e.g., 9/11 events were foreseeable given the frustration of the Muslim world), which makes the outcome seem inevitable.

Construal-level theory predicts that the hindsight bias and, more generally, theory-driven confidence in the inevitability of past events will increase over time. Supporting this prediction, Bryant and Guilbault (2002) found that hindsight about Ex-President Clinton's acquittal in the Monica Lewinski case increased from 4 days after the verdict to 11 days after the verdict. Obviously, more research is needed to examine this hypothesis in more detail and to specify the conditions under which it would occur. For example, it would be interesting to examine whether confidence in the inevitability of historical events increases over large time spans (e.g., how inevitable were the events of 9/11/2001 vs. how inevitable was World War II) and whether an increase in confidence is associated with holding general theories that explain those events. It would also be interesting to manipulate the salience of local, low-level theories (e.g., 9/11

happened because the FBI failed to arrest the suicide pilots) as opposed to global, high-level theories (e.g., the Muslim world felt outraged toward the United States), and examine whether greater salience of the latter would make the effect of hindsight increase over temporal distance. Such results, if obtained, would suggest that past events that are attributed to global and abstract (vs. specific and low-level) events seem increasingly inevitable over the course of time. In other words, the more global one's theories, the more the distant past would seem inevitable, and the distant future seem foreseeable.

Personal Dispositions versus Situational Constraints

Social psychological theories of personal perception assume that people seek to infer others' personal dispositions (e.g., personality traits, values, attitudes) from their behavior to better predict their future behavior (Gilbert & Malone, 1995; Heider, 1958; Jones & Nisbett, 1987; Trope, 1986). For example, knowing that a person is introverted makes it possible to predict his or her behavior at a party, and knowing that a friend is conservative makes it possible to predict his or her taste in music. Dispositions are mini-theories of personality, and like other theories, the predictions they make might be undermined by situation-specific, incidental factors, as a considerable amount of research has shown (see Gilbert & Malone, 1995; Jones, 1979).

In terms of CLT, inferring dispositions from behavior reflects a high-level construal of behavior in abstract, decontextualized terms (see Fiedler, Semin, Finkenauer, & Berkel, 1995; Semin & Fiedler, 1988; Semin & Smith, 1999; Trope, 1986; Trope & Gaunt, 1999). According to CLT, this tendency, like any tendency to apply theory and disregard situational variations, would increase with psychological distance. Research on dispositional inferences by actors and observers provides considerable evidence in support of this idea. This research has shown that people emphasize the role of concrete situational factors when observing their own behavior (e.g., I stepped on your toe because the bus was crowded) and the role of stable, general dispositional properties of the actor when observing others' behaviors (he stepped on my toe because he is clumsy). Such self–other differences might reflect differences in knowledge (people know more about themselves and the variability of their behavior over situations than about others) and differences in the salience of behaviors versus situations (the latter is more salient from one's own perspective, the former from the observer's perspective). These explanations, however, do not hold for differences in perspective. For example, personal memories of behaviors that were recalled from a third-person perspective (e.g., "Try to remember your first day at school, as if you are now watching the kid you were") rather than from a first-person perspective (e.g., "Try to remember your first day at school, as if you are a kid again") tended to use dispositional (as opposed to situational) terms (Frank & Gilovich, 1989; Nigro & Neisser, 1983). Moreover, Pronin and Ross (2006) showed that taking a third-person (vs. first-person) perspective on one's own behavior promoted attribution of the behavior to personality traits rather than to specific situational factors.

Other distances also increase the tendency to draw dispositional inferences from behavior. Henderson et al. (2006) found that student participants drew stronger corresponding attitude inferences from situationally constrained behavior when the behavior was believed to have occurred in a spatially remote location (vs. a near location). Rim, Uleman, and Trope (2009) used the rate of false recognition of traits (e.g., "clever") that are implied by (but not present in) behavior descriptions (e.g., "The secretary solved the mystery halfway through the book") as a measure of dispositional inference. They found that NYU participants inferred more such traits from behaviors when led to believe that actors were in a distant location (Florence, Italy) or were from the relatively distant past (year 1997), as compared to a proximal location (Manhattan) or the more recent past (year 2007).

The preceding research shows that people draw stronger dispositional inferences from distant than near behavior. More important here, there is research showing that people are more likely to rely on dispositional information and underweight situational constraints when predicting others' distant future than near future behavior. For example, in Nussbaum, Trope, and Liberman's (2003) study (conducted a few months before Israel's withdrawal from Lebanon in June 2000), participants from Tel-Aviv University read an essay arguing in favor of Israel's withdrawal from Lebanon. They were told that the essay was written by a student who had been instructed either to express her own opinion (unconstrained condition) or to argue in favor of withdrawal (situationally constrained condition). Participants were asked to estimate the likelihood that the writer would express pro-withdrawal attitudes in a variety of near future (next day) or distant future (a year later) situations (e.g., in a conversation with friends, attend a pro-withdrawal rally). The results showed that the judged likelihoods of essay-consistent (pro-withdrawal) behavior in the near future were moderated in view of the situational constraints, whereas the judged likelihoods for the more distant future were high regardless of situational constraints. Thus, near future predictions showed substantial situational discounting, whereas distant future predictions showed little or none.

As a result of relying on personal dispositions for predicting distant future behaviors, people should predict others to behave more consistently across different situations in the distant future than in the near future. Nussbaum et al. (2003, Study 2) tested this hypothesis by asking participants to predict an acquaintance's behavior in four different situations (e.g., a birthday party, waiting in line at the supermarket) in the near or distant future. Participants predicted the extent to which their acquaintances would display 15 traits (e.g., friendly vs. unfriendly) representative of the Big Five personality dimensions (extraversion, agreeableness, conscientiousness, emotional stability, and intellect). Cross-situational consistency was assessed by computing, for each of the 15 traits, the variance in predicted behavior across the four situations and the correlations among the predicted behaviors in the four situations. As hypothesized, the results showed that participants expected others to behave more consistently across distant future than near future situations. This was manifested in both lower cross-situational variance and higher cross-situational correlations for distant (vs. near) future behavior predictions.

Similar findings were obtained with the self as the target. Wakslak, Nussbaum, Liberman, and Trope (2008) asked participants to imagine themselves in different situations either in the near or distant future, and to indicate the extent to which their behavior in those situations would reflect each of the Big Five traits. As with describing other people, it was found that in the distant future participants expected themselves to exhibit traits more consistently across situations. This study suggests, in line with CLT, that people are more likely to use abstract, decontextualized trait concepts in predicting distant future than near future behaviors of both other people and themselves.

Values and Ideologies versus Extenuating Circumstances

Values are commonly viewed as abstract structures that provide continuity and meaning under changing circumstances (Feather, 1995), as stable meaning-producing superordinate cognitive structures (Rohan, 2000), and as trans-situational guides for action (Schwartz & Bilsky, 1987). Based on CLT, we propose that values, because of their relatively abstract and decontextualized nature, will be more readily applied to psychologically distant situations. Evidence for this proposal has been recently obtained by Eyal, Sagristano, Trope, Liberman, and Chaiken (2009). One study used Schwartz's (1992) value questionnaire to assess the importance participants assigned to a wide range of values (e.g., power, benevolence, hedonism) Then participants were asked to imagine 30 behaviors (e.g., rest as much as I can) and to indicate the likelihood of performing each behavior either in the near or distant future. Eyal et al. (2009) correlated the rated importance of each value and the mean likelihood of performing the behaviors corresponding to that value. As expected, these correlations were higher when the behaviors were planned for the distant rather than the near future, suggesting that people's values are better reflected in their behavioral intentions for the distant future. For example, being high (vs. low) in hedonism might mean planning hedonic activities for the distant future, but not necessarily for the upcoming week. Interestingly, Eyal et al. (2009) also found that while values predicted participants' intentions for the distant future, feasibility concerns were more predictive of their intentions for the near future. For example, the number of hours participants volunteered in the distant future condition was predicted by their benevolence values, but not by the convenience of the timing. In contrast, the number of hours participants volunteered in the near future condition was not predicted by their benevolence values, and instead depended on the convenience of the timing.

Eyal, Liberman, and Trope (2008) argued that people judge immoral acts as more offensive and moral acts as more virtuous when the acts are psychologically distant than near. They showed that transgressions against core values that are deemed harmless due to extenuating circumstances (e.g., eating one's dead dog) were judged more severely when imagined from a more distant temporal or social perspective. Conversely, moral acts that might have had ulterior motives (e.g., adopting a disabled child when a government pays high adoption pensions) are judged more positively from temporal distance. The findings suggest that moral criteria are more likely to guide people's judgments of distant rather than proximal behaviors.

Our attitudes shift, often outside of our awareness, in response to other people in our local social context, including communication partners, significant others, and even total strangers (Baldwin & Holmes, 1987; Davis & Rusbult, 2001; Higgins & Rholes, 1978; Kawakami, Dovidio, & Dijksterhuis, 2003; Lowery, Hardin, & Sinclair, 2001). Construal-level theory predicts that when an attitude object is psychologically near, evaluations will be attuned to a particular social context and therefore more likely to be affected by incidental attitudes of others in the social situation rather than by one's ideology. Conversely, when the attitude object is psychologically distant, it will be abstracted away from its local context, and evaluation will therefore be less affected by the incidental attitudes of salient others and, instead, reflect one's ideology.

A series of studies by Ledgerwood, Trope, and Chaiken (2009) tested the hypothesis that attitudes will align with those of another person in the local social context more when psychological distance is low (vs. high). Using an anticipated interaction paradigm, participants read about a policy that would increase the deportation of illegal immigrants starting either next week (near future) or next year (distant future), and learned that their discussion partner was either in favor of or against deporting illegal immigrants. They then privately reported how likely they would be to vote in favor of the policy. Participants' voting intentions shifted toward the interaction partner's attitude when the policy was set to be implemented in the near (vs. distant) future, but voting intentions more strongly reflected participants' previously assessed ideological values when the policy was to be implemented in the distant (vs. near) future.

Predicting One's Own Performance: Knowledge versus Task Format

Nussbaum et al. (2006) examined participants' confidence in predicting their own performance on a general knowledge quiz expected to take place either on the same day or 2 months later (Nussbaum et al., 2006, Studies 3 and 4). The questions were the same, but in either a relatively easy (multiple choice) or hard (open-ended) question format, which is a low-level aspect of the quiz, as compared to the content of the quiz. In another study, the quiz consisted of questions with either two response alternatives (relatively easy) or four response alternatives (relatively hard). The researchers also assessed participants' perceived ability in each knowledge domain (e.g., how knowledgeable you are in geography, history, etc.). The results showed that the more difficult question format appropriately reduced confidence in near, but not distant, future performance. Furthermore, participants' perceived knowledge in each domain was a better predictor of how confident they were in predicting their performance in that domain in the distant future as compared to the near future. To summarize, question format, which constitutes a low-level aspect of the quiz, affected confidence

in near future predictions, and beliefs about knowledge, which constitutes a high-level aspect of the quiz, predicted confidence in distant future predictions.

Notably, participants were not simply more optimistic about more distant future performance. Rather, optimism increased only when it stemmed from high-level features of the situation (domains in which the participants had more knowledge) but not when it stemmed from low-level features (easy task format).

In sum, psychological distances increase the impact of high-level information (e.g., theories, dispositions, self beliefs, general trends) and decrease the impact of low-level information (e.g., irregular outcomes, specific situational and task characteristics) on prediction. Thus, two complementary processes may contribute to the unwarrantedly higher confidence levels associated with predictions about psychologically distant events: underweighting of the uncertainty associated with low-level information and overweighting of the certainty associated with high-level information. Although we may know less about distant than near situations, our greater reliance on high-level construals in predicting the more distant situations may lead us to make more confident predictions about distant than near situations. Moreover, according to CLT, the tendency to make clearer, more confident predictions about more distal events is a natural consequence of the very same property of the human mental system that allowed it to effectively make predictions.

PREDICTION OVER TIME AND PERSPECTIVE TAKING

As noted earlier, CLT assumes that prediction over time is akin to prediction over other distances. In the present sections we discuss some commonalities between prediction over time and prediction over social and spatial distances (perspective taking). Spatial perspective taking refers to understanding what might be seen from a different spatial perspective (see Kozhevnikov & Hegarty, 2001; Shelton & McNamara, 2004; for experimental paradigms of spatial perspective taking). Mental perspective taking refers to understanding another person's state of mind. For example, a writer of a scientific paper needs to understand that the reader does not know the details of the studies conducted in his or her lab (see Chandler, 1973; Epley, Keysar, Van Boven, & Gilovich, 2004; for experimental paradigms of theory of mind).

Theory versus Simulation

How do people take perspective? Two prominent approaches offer distinct answers: According to the theory approach, people use rules or theories to draw inferences about other people and/or other spatial locations. According to the simulation approach, people simulate being the other person or simulate being at (or moving to) another spatial location (e.g., Stich & Nichols, 1992). For example, imagine that a friend of yours won an important award and is to give a speech at a crowded ceremony. In predicting her behavior at the ceremony, one could resort to a general theory (she is an introvert, introverts dislike crowds), or one might imagine oneself in the friend's place. Likewise, in predicting how an object might look from an opposite perspective, one can use a theory (everything on the left side will be on the right), or one could imagine rotating the object.

In theories of prediction, likewise, simulation processes have been proposed. Specifically, the theories of constructive simulation (Schacter & Addis, 2007) and embodied cognition (Barsalou, 1999; Niedenthal, Barsalou, Winkielman, Krauth-Gruber, & Ric, 2005; Winkielman, Niedenthal, & Oberman, 2008) suggest that episodic memory enables prospection through a constructive process of mentally simulating future episodes. Such simulations are analogical and multimodal and serve to guide choice and action with respect to the future (Barsalou, 2008). For example, in predicting tomorrow's meeting with a friend, a person could imagine the friend's voice and the taste of the beer he will drink in the bar. Of course, theory-based prediction is also possible, when, for example, one applies general knowledge (tomorrow is a World Cup soccer game and the bar is likely to be empty).

In both prediction and perspective taking literature, there has been much debate over the question of whether theory-based or simulation-based predictions predominate and whether it is possible, in a specific instance of prediction, to defend one alternative and rule out the other. A different question, more germane to CLT, is when and how predictions would be based on theories versus simulations. A few possibilities arise. First, it is possible that simulations would vary in level of construal, ranging from multimodal simulations that are rich in contextual detail and resemble the kind of analogical representation identified by embodied cognition researchers to general, gist-based simulations that retain common elements and omit incidental detail. Construal-level theory predicts that the latter, higher level simulations would be used more with increasing distance of the past episodes on which predictions are based, of the target situation which is being predicted. For example, a simulation of a future meeting with a friend is likely to be more abstract (i.e., contain less detail on the tone of her voice and the look of the room in which the meeting would take place) to the extent that *(1)* it is constructed from meetings held with that friend in the relatively distant past or distant location, *(2)* the meeting is expected in the relatively distant future or location, *(3)* the friend is more socially distant, and *(4)* the meeting is less likely to take place. Indeed, there is some research to support this prediction; D'Argembeau and Van der Linden (2004) found that temporal distance (both past and future) decreased the amount of sensorial and contextual detail in people's representations of events. Similarly, Szpunar and McDermott (2004) showed that simulations of events occurring in a familiar (i.e., psychologically proximal) versus novel (i.e., psychologically distal) location contained more perceptual details.

Second, it is possible that as distance increases, prospection is increasingly more likely to be based on theory and propositional representations (rather than analogical simulations). For example, a representation of a more distant future meeting with a friend that works in a high-tech company may refer more to semantic knowledge about layoffs in the high-tech industry and include less detail related to perceptual properties, such as the tone of her voice. The research showing that people switch from pictorial to linguistic representations of objects as distance from the object increases is consistent with this possibility (Amit, Algom, & Trope, 2009).

Third, symbolic representations might also differ in abstraction, ranging from broad abstractions (she is a woman) to more narrowly applied knowledge (she is a single mother to four and a high-tech manager who is afraid to lose her job). In sum, according to CLT both simulations and theories might vary in level of construal. Distance may determine whether a simulation or a theory is applied to make predictions, and the level of abstractness at which both theories and simulations will be constructed. These predictions await testing in future research.

Accuracy in Prediction and Perspective Taking

How good are people at making predictions? What mental abilities promote accurate predictions? These questions, too, were raised with respect to prediction of future events, spatial perspective taking, social perspective taking, and the ability to consider alternatives to reality. It would be interesting to examine in future research whether these abilities have a common core. For example, do they have a similar developmental trajectory? Does practicing one skill enhance the others? For example, does learning interpersonal perspective taking help people better predict future outcomes? Do these tasks procedurally prime each other? For example, does practicing spatial perspective taking enhance subsequent interpersonal perspective taking?

Another interesting question is whether prediction is assisted or hindered by psychological distance and high levels of construal. We think that the answer to this question is complex. On the one hand, prediction requires using high-level construals to ignore the here and now and to connect to a distal time, point in space, person, or alternative. On the other hand, a low-level construal is needed to understand the details of the distal situation. For example, to take the perspective of a young child whose toy was taken, I need to abandon my egocentric view of the toy as a useless, cheap plastic object and

reconstrue it as an object one occupies oneself with (a high-level construal). I then need to immerse myself in the specific situation of the child: the sensation in her hands of the toy being taken away, the surprise and frustration of not knowing what to do (low-level construal). It is possible, then, that both high-level and low-level construals of the situations are needed for effective prediction, just like a bridge needs not only to leave the current location and go over distance (for which a high-level construal is required) but also to be firmly grounded in the specific target destination (for which a low-level construal is needed). Again, further research is needed to explore these ideas in more depth.

Common Brain Systems

Are predictions across different distances supported by common brain systems? A growing body of research suggests that such structures may actually exist. For example, recent research suggests that a common brain network involving the prefrontal cortex and the medial temporal lobe is implicated in prospection, retrospection, and taking another person's perspective (e.g., Buckner & Carroll, 2007; Mitchell, Macrae, & Banaji, 2006; Schacter & Addis, 2007, 2008; Suddendorf & Corballis, 2007). Related to social distance, Mitchell et al. (2006) found that predictions about a similar other engage a ventral region of the mPFC, whereas predictions about a dissimilar other engage more dorsal subregions of the mPFC. Moreover, recent research by Mitchell, Schirmer, Ames, and Gilbert (2010) observed an association in the brain between social distance and temporal distance. Specifically, the ventral mPFC was implicated in predicting similar others and the present self, whereas the dorsal mPFC was implicated in predicting dissimilar others and the future self.

There is also a large amount of research showing that the brain is hierarchically organized, with higher points in the cortical hierarchy representing increasingly more abstract aspects of stimuli (Grill-Spector & Malach, 2004; Lieberman, Gaunt, Gilbert, & Trope, 2002). For example, progressively anterior subregions of the prefrontal cortex have been found to be associated with more abstract representations (Badre & D'Esposito, 2007; Koechlin & Summerfield, 2007; Ramnani & Owen, 2004). Possibly, this organization of information in the brain might be related to distance from stimuli, such that activation systematically progresses to higher points in the hierarchy as psychological distance from the stimuli increases. Furthermore, Marsolek and colleagues conducted divided visual field experiments (i.e., where input stimuli are presented to one cerebral hemisphere at a time to detect hemispheric asymmetries in processing) and found that the left hemisphere is associated with abstract, categorical processing and the right hemisphere with specific, exemplar processing (Marsolek, 1995, 1999; Marsolek & Burgund, 2008; Marsolek, Schacter, & Nicholas, 1996, Marsolek, Squire, Kosslyn, & Lulenski, 1994). In addition to general hemispheric differences, Garoff, Slotnick, and Schacter (2005) used a subsequent memory paradigm and found that encoding-related activity in the left fusiform cortex is associated with nonspecific, gist-based memory for previously studied pictorial objects, whereas encoding-related activity in the right fusiform cortex is associated with specific memory. In sum, there may be a "construal axis" in brain systems that maps onto a "distance axis." Brain systems that process high-level construal information may be biased toward distal prediction, and brain systems that process low-level construal information may be biased toward proximal prediction.

Conclusion

We have proposed that people must be able to predict and plan both within and outside the immediate situation. To do so, they rely on mental construals that can integrate across available information in two different ways. Low-level construals serve to guide predictions and plans for the here and now by integrating specific details of the present context. They can therefore fluidly incorporate variable aspects of the situation, enabling people to flexibly respond to local concerns. Conversely, high-level construals enable individuals to transcend the here and now to predict and plan the "there and then."

These construals abstract what is consistent about an object across multiple contexts, allowing people to transcend the particularities of the present situation and act according to their global concerns. The different levels of mental construal may thus help expand and contract the temporal, spatial, and social scope of human plans.

References

Amit, E., Algom, D., Trope, Y. (2009). Distance-dependent processing of pictures and words. *Journal of Experimental Psychology: General, 138*, 400–415.

Badre, D., & D'Esposito, M. (2007). fMRI evidence for a hierarchical organization of the prefrontal cortex. *Journal of Cognitive Neuroscience, 19*, 2082–2099.

Baldwin, M. W., & Holmes, J. G. (1987). Salient private audiences and awareness of the self. *Journal of Personality and Social Psychology, 52*, 1087–1098.

Bar-Anan, Y., Liberman, N., Trope, Y., & Algom, D. (2007). Automatic processing of psychological distance: Evidence from a Stroop task. *Journal of Experimental Psychology: General, 136*, 610–622.

Barsalou, L. W. (1999). Perceptual symbol system. *Behavioral and Brain Sciences, 22*, 577–660.

Barsalou, L. W. (2008). Grounded cognition. *Annual Review of Psychology, 59*, 617–645.

Bryant, F. B., & Guilbault, R. L. (2002). "I knew it all along" eventually: The development of hindsight bias in reaction to the Clinton impeachment verdict. *Basic and Applied Social Psychology, 24*, 27–41.

Buckner, R. L., & Carroll, D. C. (2007). Self-projection and the brain. *Trends in Cognitive Sciences, 11*, 49–57.

Chandler, M. J. (1973). Egocentrism and antisocial behavior: The assessment and training of social perspective-taking skills. *Developmental Psychology, 9*, 326–332.

Christensen-Szalanski, J. J., & Willham, C. F. (1991). The hindsight bias: A meta-analysis. *Organizational Behavior and Human Decision Processes, 48*, 147–168.

D'Argembeau, A., & Van der Linden, M. (2004). Phenomenal characteristics associated with projecting oneself back into the past and forward into the future: Influence of valence and temporal distance. *Consciousness and Cognition: An International Journal, 13*, 844–858.

Davis, J. L., & Rusbult, C. E. (2001). Attitude alignment in close relationships. *Journal of Personality and Social Psychology, 81*, 65–84.

Epley, N., Keysar, B., Van Boven, L., & Gilovich, T. (2004). Perspective taking as egocentric anchoring and adjustment. *Journal of Personality and Social Psychology, 87*, 327–339.

Eyal, T., Liberman, N., & Trope, Y. (2008). Judging near and distant virtue and vice. *Journal of Experimental Social Psychology, 44*, 1204–1209.

Eyal, T., Sagristano, M. D., Trope, Y., Liberman, N., & Chaiken, S. (2009). When values matter: Expressing values in behavioral intentions for the near vs. distant future. *Journal of Experimental Social Psychology, 45*, 35–43.

Feather, N. T. (1995). Values, valences, and choice: The influence of values on the perceived attractiveness and choice of alternatives. *Journal of Personality and Social Psychology, 68*, 1135–1151.

Fiedler, K., Semin, G. R., Finkenauer, C., & Berkel, I. (1995). Actor–observer bias in close relationships: The role of self–knowledge and self–related language. *Personality and Social Psychology Bulletin, 21*, 525–538.

Fischhoff, B. (1975). Hindsight is not equal to foresight: The effect of outcome knowledge on judgment under uncertainty. *Journal of Experimental Psychology: Human Perception and Performance, 1*, 288–299.

Flinn, M., Geary, D., & Ward, C. (2005). Ecological dominance, social competition, and coalitionary arms races: Why humans evolved extraordinary intelligence. *Evolution and Human Behavior, 26*, 10–46.

Frank, M. G., & Gilovich, T. (1989). Effect of memory perspective on retrospective causal attributions. *Journal of Personality and Social Psychology, 5*, 399–403.

Fujita, K., Henderson, M., Eng, J., Trope, Y., & Liberman, N. (2006). Spatial distance and mental construal of social events. *Psychological Science, 17*, 278–282.

Garoff, R. J., Slotnick, S. D., & Schacter, D. L. (2005). The neural origins of specific and general memory: The role of the fusiform cortex. *Neuropsychologia, 43*, 847–859.

Gilbert, D. T., & Malone, P. S. (1995). The correspondence bias. *Psychological Bulletin, 117*, 21–38.

Gilbert, D. T., & Wilson, T. D. (2007). Prospection: Experiencing the future. *Science, 317*, 1351–1354.

Grill-Spector, K., & Malach, R. (2004). The human visual cortex. *Annual Review of Neuroscience, 27*, 649–677.

Heider, F. (1958). *The psychology of interpersonal relations.* Hoboken, NJ: John Wiley & Sons, Inc.

Henderson, M. D., Fujita, K., Trope, Y., & Liberman, N. (2006). Transcending the "here": The effect of spatial distance on social judgment. *Journal of Personality and Social Psychology, 91*, 845–856.

Higgins, E. T., & Rholes, W. S. (1978). "Saying is believing": Effects of message modification on memory and liking for the person. *Journal of Experimental Social Psychology, 14*, 363–378.

Jones, E. E. (1979). The rocky road from acts to dispositions. *American Psychologist, 34*, 107–117.

Jones, E. E., & Nisbett, R. E. (1987). The actor and the observer: Divergent perceptions of the causes of behavior. In E. E. Jones, D. E. Kanouse, H. H. Kelley, R. E. Nisbett, S. Valins, & B. Weiner (Eds.), *Attribution: Perceiving the causes of behavior* (pp. 79–94). Hillsdale, NJ: Erlbaum.

Kahneman, D., Krueger, A. B., Schkade, D., Schwarz, N., & Stone, A. A. (2006). Would you be happier if you were richer? A focusing illusion. *Science, 312*, 1908–1910.

Kawakami, K., Dovidio, J. F., & Dijksterhuis, A. (2003). Effect of social category priming on personal attitudes. *Psychological Science, 14*, 315–319.

Koechlin, E., & Summerfield, C. (2007). An information theoretical approach to prefrontal executive function. *Trends in Cognitive Sciences, 11*, 229–235.

Kozhevnikov, M., & Hegarty, M. (2001). A dissociation between object manipulation spatial ability and spatial orientation ability. *Memory and Cognition, 29*, 745–756.

Ledgerwood, A., Trope, Y., & Chaiken, C. (2010). Flexibility Now, Consistency Later: Psychological distance and construal shape evaluative responding. *Journal of Personality and Social Psychology, 99*, 32–51.

Levi-Strauss, C. (1963). *Structural anthropology.* New York: Basic Books.

Liberman, N., Sagristano, M., & Trope, Y. (2002). The effect of temporal distance on level of construal. *Journal of Experimental Social Psychology, 38*, 523–535.

Liberman, N., & Trope, Y. (1998). The role of feasibility and desirability considerations in near and distant future decisions: A test of temporal construal theory. *Journal of Personality and Social Psychology, 75*, 5–18.

Liberman, N., Trope, Y., McCrea, S. M., & Sherman, S. J. (2007). The effect of level of construal on temporal distance. *Journal of Experimental Social Psychology, 43*, 143–149.

Lieberman, M. D., Gaunt, R., Gilbert, D. T., & Trope, Y. (2002). Reflection and reflexion: A social cognitive neuroscience approach to attributional inference. In M. P. Zanna (Ed.), *Advances in experimental social psychology* (Vol. 34, pp. 199–249). San Diego, CA: Academic Press.

Liviatan, I., Trope, Y., & Liberman, N. (2008). Interpersonal similarity as a social distance dimension: Implications for perception of others' actions. *Journal of Experimental Social Psychology, 44*, 1256–1269.

Lowery, B. S., Hardin, C. D., & Sinclair, S. (2001). Social influence effects on automatic racial prejudice. *Journal of Personality and Social Psychology, 81*, 842–855.

Marsolek, C. J. (1995). Abstract visual-form representations in the left cerebral hemisphere. *Journal of Experimental Psychology: Human Perception and Performance, 21*, 375–386.

Marsolek, C. J. (1999). Dissociable neural subsystems underlie abstract and specific object recognition. *Psychological Science, 10*, 111–118.

Marsolek, C. J., & Burgund, E. D. (2008). Dissociable neural subsystems underlie visual working memory for abstract categories and specific exemplars. *Cognitive, Affective, and Behavioral Neuroscience, 8*, 17–24.

Marsolek, C. J., Schacter, D. L., & Nicholas, C. D. (1996). Form-specific visual priming for new associations in the right cerebral hemisphere. *Memory and Cognition, 24*, 539–556.

Marsolek, C. J., Squire, L. R., Kosslyn, S. M., & Lulenski, M. E. (1994). Form-specific explicit and implicit memory in the right cerebral hemisphere. *Neuropsychology, 8*, 588–597.

Mitchell, J., Schirmer, J., Ames, D. L., & Gilbert, D. T. (in press). Medial prefrontal cortex predicts intertemporal choice. *Journal of Cognitive Neuroscience*.

Mitchell, J. P., Macrae, C. N., Banaji, M. R. (2006). Dissociable medial prefrontal contributions to judgments of similar and dissimilar others. *Neuron, 50*, 655–663.

Niedenthal, P. M., Barsalou, L., Winkielman, P., Krauth-Gruber, S., & Ric, F. (2005). Embodiment in attitudes, social perception, and emotion. *Personality and Social Psychology Review, 9*, 184–211.

Nigro, G., & Neisser, U. (1983). Point of view in personal memories. *Cognitive Psychology, 15*, 467–482.

Nussbaum, S., Liberman, N., & Trope, Y. (2006). Predicting the near and distant future. *Journal of Experimental Psychology: General, 135*, 152–161.

Nussbaum, S., Trope, Y., & Liberman, N. (2003). Creeping dispositionism: The temporal dynamics of behavior prediction. *Journal of Personality and Social Psychology, 84*, 485–497.

Pease, M. E., McCabe, A. E., Brannon, L. A., & Tagler, M. J. (2003). Memory distortions for pre-Y2K expectancies: A demonstration of the hindsight bias. *Journal of Psychology: Interdisciplinary and Applied, 137*, 397–399.

Pronin, E., & Ross, L. (2006). Temporal differences in trait self ascription: When the self is seen as an other. *Journal of Personality and Social Psychology, 90*, 197–209.

Ramnani, N., & Owen, A. M. (2004). Anterior prefrontal cortex: Insights into function from anatomy and neuroimaging. *Nature Reviews Neuroscience, 5*, 184–194.

Rim, S., Uleman, J. S., & Trope, Y. (2009). Spontaneous trait inference and construal level theory: Psychological distance increases nonconscious trait thinking. *Journal of Experimental Social Psychology, 45*, 1088–1097.

Rohan, M. J. (2000). A rose by any name? The values construct. *Personality and Social Psychology Review, 4*, 255–277.

Schacter, D. L., & Addis, D. R. (2007). The cognitive neuroscience of constructive memory: Remembering the past and imagining the future. *Philosophical Transactions of the Royal Society of London, 362*, 773–786.

Schacter, D. L., & Addis, D. R. (2008). The cognitive neuroscience of constructive memory: Remembering the past and imagining the future. In J. Driver, P. Haggard, & T. Shallice (Eds.), *Mental processes in the human brain. Philisophical Transactions of the Royal Society of London B: Biological Sciences* (pp. 27–47). New York: Oxford University Press.

Schwartz, S. H. (1992). Universals in the content and structure of values: Theoretical advances and empirical tests in 20 countries. In M. P. Zanna (Ed.), *Advances in experimental social psychology* (Vol. 25, pp. 1–65). New York: Academic Press.

Schwartz, S. H., & Bilsky, W. (1987). Toward a universal psychological structure of human values.

Journal of Personality and Social Psychology, 53, 550–562.

Semin, G. R., & Fiedler, K. (1988). The cognitive functions of linguistic categories in describing persons: Social cognition and language. *Journal of Personality and Social Psychology, 54,* 558–568.

Semin, G. R., & Smith, E. R. (1999). Revisiting the past and back to the future: Memory systems and the linguistic representation of social events. *Journal of Personality and Social Psychology, 76,* 877–892.

Shelton, A. L., & McNamara, T. P. (2004). Orientation and perspective dependence in route and survey learning. *Journal of Experimental Psychology: Learning, Memory, and Cognition, 30,* 158–170.

Stephan, E., Liberman, N., & Trope, Y. (2010). Politeness and social distance: A construal level perspective. *Journal of Personality and Social Psychology, 98,* 268–280.

Stich, S., & Nichols, S. (1992). Folk psychology: Simulation or tacit theory? [Special Issue] *Mind and Language, 7,* 35–71.

Suddendorf, T., & Corballis, M. C. (2007). The evolution of foresight: What is mental time travel, and is it unique to humans? *Behavioral Brain Science, 30,* 299–313.

Szpunar, K. K., & McDermott, K. B. (2004). Episodic future thought and its relation to remembering: Evidence from ratings of subjective experience. *Consciousness and Cognition, 17,* 330–334.

Trope, Y. (1986). Identification and inferential processes in dispositional attribution. *Psychological Review, 93,* 239–257.

Trope, Y., & Gaunt, R. (1999). A dual-process model of overconfident attributional inferences. In S. Chaiken & Y. Trope (Eds.), *Dual-process theories in social psychology* (pp. 161–178). New York: Guilford Press.

Wakslak, C. J., Nussbaum, S., Liberman, N., & Trope, Y. (2008). Representations of the self in the near and distant future. *Journal of Personality and Social Psychology, 95,* 757–773.

Wakslak, C. J., Trope, Y., Liberman, N., & Alony, R (2006). Seeing the forest when entry is unlikely: Probability and the mental representation of events. *Journal of Experimental Psychology: General, 135,* 641–653.

Wilson, T. D., & Gilbert, D. T. (2003). Affective forecasting. In M. P. Zanna (Ed.), *Advances in experimental social psychology* (Vol. 35, pp. 345–411). San Diego, CA: Academic Press.

Wilson, T. D., Wheatley, T., Meyers, J. M., Gilbert, D. T., & Axsom, D. (2000). Focalism: A source of durability bias in affective forecasting. *Journal of Personality and Social Psychology, 78,* 821–836.

Winkielman, P., Niedenthal, P., & Oberman, L. (2008). The embodied emotional mind. In G. R. Semin & E. R. Smith (Eds.), *Embodied grounding: Social, cognitive, affective, and neuroscientific approaches* (pp. 263–288). New York: Cambridge University Press.

CHAPTER 13
Previews, Premotions, and Predictions

Daniel T. Gilbert and Timothy D. Wilson

Mark Twain worked hard to be funny. One of his editors reported that before every speech, Twain "mused his words to an imagined audience... He studied every tone and every gesture and he forecast the result with the real audience from its result with that imagined audience" (Twain, 1910, p. 11). Twain tested new material on an imaginary focus group and assumed that if the people in his head laughed at a punch line then people in the theatre would do the same. This technique may seem unremarkable, but in fact, there is something decidedly odd about it. After all, Mark Twain was testing jokes on the people in his head, but the people in his head were all... well, Mark Twain. That is, the person who was telling the joke and the people who were reacting to the joke were all inventions of the same brain—so why did that brain need to go through an elaborate ritual of telling and listening just to find out whether its own jokes were funny?

If the brain were a single unified system, then this ritual would be puzzling. But the brain is not a single unified system. Rather, it is a collection of independent systems that specialize in receiving, processing, producing, and transmitting different kinds of information. The parts of Mark Twain's brain that produced jokes were not the same parts that produced laughter, so to determine whether a joke was funny, the joke-production system had to tell the joke to the laughter-production system and then take note of its reaction. As it turns out, this ritual is one

that most of us perform every day—not just to find out if our jokes are funny, but to make the predictions by which we guide our lives.

FROM PREVIEW TO PREMOTION TO PREDICTION

Organisms remember the past so they can predict the future. If a bird can remember that the appearance of a cat followed the tinkling of a bell, the bird can thereafter use the sound of the bell to predict the cat's arrival. This is a valuable skill because a bird that can predict the future can act so as to preclude the futures in which it plays the role of the entrée. The memory of the co-occurrence of the cat and the bell allows the bird to transcend the normal restrictions of linear time, reacting to a future cat instead of a present cat. The brain specializes in memory because memory enables prediction, and prediction gives organisms a head start. Unfortunately, these sorts of memory-based predictions require past experience—a bird can predict the appearance of a cat from the sound of a bell only if those two stimuli have co-occurred in the past—which means that a bird can act preemptively only after having had at least one close encounter of the feline kind. Because such encounters are a potentially expensive way to gain the power of prognostication, human beings have developed a different and more sophisticated technique that allows them to make predictions about future events that they have never experienced.

For example, when asked how much they would enjoy learning that they had pancreatic cancer, most people can reliably produce the correct answer, which is some version of "not so much." They do not produce this answer by remembering how it felt to receive such news in the past, but by quickly simulating the event and then noting their emotional reaction to that simulation. Just as Mark Twain assumed that feeling amused by an imaginary joke meant that he would be amused by the real thing, most of us assume that if we feel anxious when we imagine bad news then we would feel even more anxious upon receiving it. In essence, we generate mental simulations or *previews* of future events, which cause us to have affective reactions or *premotions*, which we then use as a basis for our forecasts or *predictions* about the event's likely emotional consequences (Berns et al., 2006; Breiter, Aharon, Kahneman, Anders, & Shizgal, 2001; Damasio, 1994; Gilbert, 2006; Gilbert & Wilson, 2007; Schwarz & Strack, 1999). We know which future events will feel good and which will feel bad because we feel good or bad when we simulate them.

ERRORS IN EMOTIONAL PREDICTION

Previews and premotions are the building blocks of prediction, and neuroscientists have recently begun to investigate them. For example, research suggests that previews of future events are produced in large part by the frontal regions of the brain (Fellows & Farah, 2005; Ingvar, 1985; Wheeler, Stuss, & Tulving, 1997), which are especially active when people are asked to simulate the future (Addis, Wong, & Schacter, 2007; Buckner & Carroll, 2007; Schacter, Addis, & Buckner, 2007; Szpunar, Watson, & McDermott, 2007). Patients with damage to these regions are often unable to simulate future events (Klein, Loftus, & Kihlstrom, 2002; Tulving, 1985; Tulving, Schacter, McLachlan, & Moscovitch, 1988) and are typically described as being "bound to present stimuli" (Melges, 1990) and "locked into immediate space and time" (Faglioni, 1999). The premotions that these previews produce appear to depend specifically on the ventromedial prefrontal cortex, as people with damage to this area

find it difficult to predict their emotional reactions to the events they are previewing (Bechara & Damasio, 2005; Shiv, Loewenstein, Bechara, Damasio, & Damasion, 2005).

But long before neuroscientists began investigating the neural substrates of previews and premotions, psychologists were investigating how people use them to make emotional predictions (for a recent review, see Gilbert & Wilson, 2007). This research suggests a simple way of thinking about the sources of error in emotional prediction. If we assume that (a) people's premotions are influenced by the *content* of their previews (i.e., those features of the future event that appear in people's mental simulations) and by the *context* of their previews (i.e., features of the situation in which people are generating mental simulation) and (b) people's emotions are influenced by the content and the context of their views, then (c) it follows that premotions will be good predictors of emotions when the content and context of a preview are similar to the content and context of a view. For example, if one sunny day a man was on his way to his favorite cafe and imagined eating a piece of chocolate cake, he would probably experience a positive premotion and expect to enjoy eating the cake when he arrived. If he arrived while the sun was still shining and ate the chocolate cake he had imagined, there is every reason to believe that he would enjoy the experience just as he predicted (see Fig. 13.1). On the other hand, if he arrived at the café only to find that (a) the chocolate cake was gone and mincemeat pie was being served in its place (see Fig. 13.2), or (b) the weather had turned cold and nasty (see Fig. 13.3), then he might not enjoy his experience as much as he expected to. The point is that premotions will accurately predict emotions *when the content and context of the preview are similar to the content and context of the view*. Errors in emotional prediction occur when these two criteria go unmet, and we shall now explore each in turn.

The Problem of Dissimilar Content

Events do not always unfold precisely as we imagine them. No matter how hard we try, we can never know everything there is to know

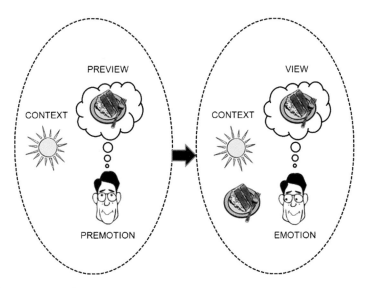

Figure 13.1 Accurate prediction.

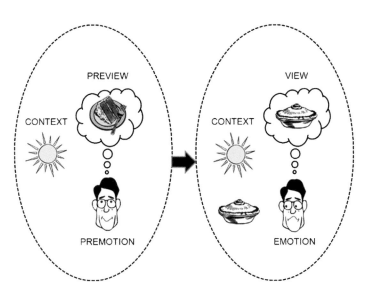

Figure 13.2 Unreliable previews lead to inaccurate predictions.

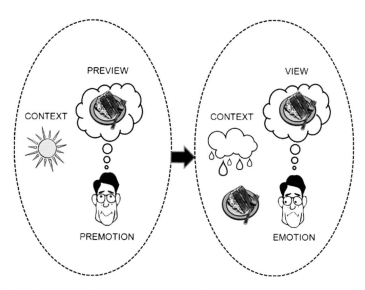

Figure 13.3 Unstable contexts lead to inaccurate predictions.

about the cakes and cafes that populate our tomorrows, and even our best guesses are nothing more than that. The inherent uncertainty of the future means that previews and views often have dissimilar content. But research shows that the problem of dissimilar content is caused by several other factors as well.

Previews Are Unrepresentative

People who have difficulty remembering the past often have difficulty predicting the future (Hassabis, Kumaran, Vann, & Maguire, 2007; Klein et al., 2002; Tulving, 1985). When we generate previews of a future event, we draw on a vast network of information about similar events that have happened in the past (Addis et al., 2007; Buckner & Carroll, 2007; Dudai & Carruthers, 2005; Hawkins & Blakeslee, 2004), and thus our previews are only as good as the memories on which they are based. Ideally, a preview of a future event should be based on memories of very similar past events—but given that we cannot know precisely how a future event will unfold, how can we know which past events are most similar to it? The statistically sensible

solution to this problem is to base our previews on those past events that are most representative or typical of their class. For instance, we may not know precisely what our next dental appointment will be like, but we do know that most past dental appointments have involved cleaning and not extraction, and thus our preview of the next visit has a better chance of being accurate if it is based on memories of flossing and buffing rather than on memories of injecting and drilling.

But research shows that we tend to base our previews on those memories that are most available rather than most typical and that, ironically enough, our most available memories are often of the *least* typical events. For example, in one study, commuters who were waiting on a platform were asked to imagine how they would feel if they missed their train that day (Morewedge, Gilbert, & Wilson, 2005). Before making this prediction, some of the commuters (*the any-memory group*) were asked to remember and describe "a time you missed your train." Other commuters (*the worst-memory group*) were asked to remember and describe "the worst time you missed your train." The results showed that commuters in the any-memory group remembered a past episode that was every bit as bad as the episode remembered by commuters in the worst-memory group. Apparently, disastrous but atypical instances of train-missing came more readily to mind than did less disastrous but more typical instances. As such, when commuters in the any-memory group were asked to predict how they would feel if they missed their train *that day*, they expected to feel terrible—and that prediction turned out to be wrong. Commuters based their predictions on the premotions that their previews produced, but because these previews were based on atypical memories, they provided a poor basis for prediction.

Like atypical experiences, recent experiences are especially available and are thus likely to become the building blocks of our previews. Participants in one study (Kahneman, Fredrickson, Schreiber, & Redelmeier, 1993) were asked to submerge their hands in ice water while using an electronic rating scale to report their moment-to-moment discomfort. All participants performed a short trial and a long trial. On the short trial, participants submerged their hands for 60 seconds in a water bath that was 57°F. On the long trial, participants submerged their hands for 90 seconds in a water bath that was 57°F for the first 60 seconds and then surreptitiously warmed to 59°F over the course of the remaining 30 seconds. The short trial thus consisted of 60 cold seconds, and the long trial consisted of the same 60 cold seconds with an additional 30 less-cold seconds. Although the participants' moment-to-moment reports revealed that they experienced equal discomfort for the first 60 seconds on both trials but much more discomfort in the next 30 seconds on the long trials, they *remembered* the long trial as less painful than the short trials because it had a less painful ending. When participants were then asked which of the two trials they would prefer to repeat (a question that required them to preview those future events and predict how painful they would be), 69% chose to repeat the long trial.

One reason why previews provide a poor basis for prediction, then, is that they tend to be based on memories that are not representative of the future events that those previews were meant to simulate.

Previews Are Essentialized

If previews contained every detail of the views they were meant to simulate, then imagining a dental appointment would take precisely as long as the appointment itself. But it does not, and that is because previews generally contain only the essential features that define an event and omit the features that are merely incidental to it. When we preview a dental appointment, we imagine sitting in the dentist's chair or having our teeth inspected, but not parking the car or leafing through magazines in the waiting room. The benefit of omitting these incidental features from our previews is that we can preview a 30-minute appointment in 15 seconds. The cost of omitting these incidental features is that although they do not define the event, they can have a significant influence on our emotional reactions to it.

Most events have a small set of extremely positive or extremely negative features that define them and a much larger set of mildly positive and mildly negative features that are incidental to them. Having someone work on our teeth is the defining feature of a dental appointment, and for most of us this feature is quite negative. On the other hand, parking the car and reading magazines are incidental features of the event and these features may be mildly positive (free parking) or mildly negative (old magazines). Our emotional reaction to the actual dental appointment will be a weighted sum of its defining and incidental features. The defining features are likely to be more powerful than the incidental features, of course, but the fact that there are so many incidental features means that they too may have a considerable combined impact. Because some of these incidental features are likely to have a valence opposite to the valence of the defining features, these incidental features are likely to dilute the power of the defining features. In other words, we imagine the unpleasant features of going to the dentist because these features are what going to the dentist is all about, and we fail to imagine the pleasant features of going to the dentist because they are incidental to the purpose of our visit. Anyone who has ever expected to enjoy a gourmet meal at a famous restaurant and instead spent the evening being irritated by the interminable wait and the imperious waiter has experienced this phenomenon. *Blanquette de veau* may define a gastronomic experience and waits and waiters may be incidental to it, but the latter features are likely to have some impact on one's experience of the event.

Studies confirm that our failure to preview the incidental features of future events can lead us to mispredict our emotional reactions to them. For example, participants in one study (Wilson, Wheatley, Meyers, Gilbert, & Axsom, 2000) were asked to predict how they would feel the day after their favorite football team won or lost a game against its arch rival. Before making these predictions, some participants were asked to describe the day's activities in great detail— that is, to preview the incidental features of the event. Other participants were not asked to preview the incidental features. The results showed that participants who were not asked to preview the incidental features of the event expected to be very happy if their team won and very unhappy if their team lost, but that those who were instructed to preview the incidental features of the event made much more moderate emotional predictions—and these more moderate predictions turned out to be more accurate. Similar studies have shown that people overestimate how happy they would be if they moved to California (Schkade & Kahneman, 1998) or became wealthy (Kahneman, Krueger, Schkade, Schwarz, & Stone, 2006) because their previews of these events include defining features such as sunshine and money, but fail to include incidental features such as traffic and taxes.

Our tendency to omit incidental features from our previews of future events is especially pronounced when the events are temporally distant (Trope & Liberman, 2003; Vallacher & Wegner, 1985). Participants in one study (Liberman & Trope, 1998) were told that in a year there would be a lecture on an interesting topic at an inconvenient location and a lecture on a boring topic at a convenient location. Participants were asked to predict which lecture they would attend. Because their previews contained the defining feature of the event (e.g., the topic) but lacked the incidental feature (e.g., the location), participants predicted that they would attend the more interesting lecture, presumably because they expected to enjoy that experience more than its alternative. But participants who were told that the same lecture was taking place tomorrow instead of next year were more likely to include the incidental feature of the event in their previews, and were thus more likely to predict that they would attend the lecture that was boring but convenient.

One reason why previews and views differ, then, is that previews tend to omit features that are incidental to the event but that nonetheless may have a significant impact on our emotional reactions to it.

Previews Are Truncated

Just as previews tend to emphasize the defining rather than the incidental features of future events, so do they tend to emphasize the event's early-occurring rather than late-occurring moments. For example, in one study(Forrin & Dunn, 2007), people were asked to predict how much they would enjoy an experience that involved putting their hand in an ice water bath for a few minutes (which is painful) and receiving a massage (which is pleasant). Participants in the *good beginning* condition were asked to predict how much they would like the experience if the massage preceded the ice water bath, and participants in the *bad beginning* condition were asked to predict how much they would like the experience if the ice water bath preceded the massage. Results showed that participants in the good beginning condition expected to like the experience more than did participants in the bad beginning condition when, in fact, the order of the two components had no influence on how much participants actually liked the experience. Just as people represent past events by their endings, they appear to represent future events by their beginnings.

One important consequence of emphasizing early-occurring moments is that previews take little account of adaptation. For many reasons, emotions tend to dissipate over time, which means that previews tend to emphasize precisely those moments that evoke the most intense emotion. This leads to one of the most pervasive errors of emotional prediction—the *impact bias*—which is the tendency for predicted emotions to be more extreme than actual emotions (Wilson & Gilbert, 2003). For example, when people are asked to imagine how they would feel some time after a negative event (such as failing to get tenure or breaking up with a romantic partner) or a positive event (such as getting tenure or beginning a new romantic relationship), they typically overestimate how bad or good they will feel because they fail to simulate their adaptation to the event (Gilbert, Pinel, Wilson, Blumberg, & Wheatley, 1998; Hoerger, Quirk, Lucas, & Carr, 2009). Similarly, research shows that healthy people consistently overestimate how unhappy they would be in various states of ill health (Menzel, Dolan, Richardson, & Olsen, 2002; Riis et al., 2005; Ubel, Loewenstein, & Jepson, 2003) in part because their previews of illness emphasize the early moments in which they are making the difficult transition from being healthy to being ill, but not the more numerous moments that follow, in which they have adapted to their new state. People imagine *becoming* disabled rather than *being* disabled (Kahneman et al., 2006), and becoming is much worse than being because over time most people adapt at least partially to disability (Lucas, 2007; Oswald & Powdthavee, 2008).

Because previews tend to ignore adaptation, they tend to be insensitive to those features of an event that might promote or inhibit it (Gilbert & Ebert, 2002; Gilbert, Lieberman, Morewedge, & Wilson, 2004; Gilbert, Morewedge, Risen, & Wilson, 2004; Gilbert et al., 1998). For example, research has established that people adapt to events more quickly when they understand why those events happened than when they do not (Wilson & Gilbert, 2008). When participants in one study (Wilson, Centerbar, Kermer, & Gilbert, 2005) were approached at a library and given $1, those who received an explanation for the gift

were less happy a few minutes later than were those who received no explanation. But when asked to preview these two incidents, a similar group of participants predicted that they would be happier if they received the gift with an explanation rather than without one. Because their previews did not include the event's late-occurring moments, people who were asked to preview receiving a gift with an explanation were unable to foresee their own adaptation. Similarly, research has established that people adapt to events more quickly when they cannot undo them than when they can. Participants in one study (Gilbert & Ebert, 2002) were more satisfied with a gift when they did not have the opportunity to exchange it than when they did; yet a similar group of participants who were asked to preview these two incidents were insensitive to the opportunity for exchange and expected to be just as happy in both instances. Because their previews did not include the event's late-occurring moments, participants who were asked to preview receiving a gift that they could not exchange were unable to foresee their own adaptation.

One reason why previews and views differ, then, is that they tend to emphasize the early-occurring moments of the event in which emotions are likely to be most intense.

Previews Are Comparative

How would it feel to buy a lottery ticket that paid $50 if one's friend bought a ticket that paid $80? Many of us have the compelling intuition that we would be slightly unhappy, and that we might actually be happier if we had won only $40 and our friend had won only $10 (Solnick & Hemenway, 1998; Tversky & Griffin, 1991). The reason we make this prediction is that we imagine comparing our $60 to our friend's $80, which makes our winnings seem paltry by contrast. But research suggests that in a wide range of circumstances, people are less likely to make such comparisons than they imagine (Hsee & Zhang, 2004; Novemsky & Ratner, 2003). For example, in one study (Morewedge, Gilbert, Myrseth, Kassam, & Wilson, 2010), participants were either asked to eat or to imagine eating a potato chip in the presence of a superior food (chocolate) or an inferior food (sardines). Participants who imagined eating the chip predicted that they would enjoy it more when it was eaten in the presence of sardines than in the presence of chocolate. In other words, these participants mentally compared the food they would be eating with the food they would not be eating. But participants who actually ate the chip enjoyed it just as much when it was eaten in presence of chocolate as when it was eaten in presence of sardines. Similarly, students in another study (Golub, Gilbert, & Wilson, 2009) who imagined receiving a poor grade on their midterm exam predicted that they would feel worse if they had been expecting a good grade than if they had been expecting a bad grade. In other words, they believed that they would compare the grade they received to the grade they had expected to receive. In actuality, however, students who received a poor grade felt equally bad regardless of their prior expectations. In both of these studies, people's previews included comparisons that their views did not.

Just as our previews omit incidental features that ultimately impact our emotional reactions, they tend to include comparative features that ultimately do not impact our emotional reactions. Although we think we will compare what we got with what others got, with what we thought we would get, with what we could have gotten, or with what we have gotten in the past, the fact is that real outcomes command our attention and thus attenuate such comparisons. When we imagine eating chips in the presence of chocolate, we naturally compare the two; but when we actually have a mouthful of crunchy, salty, greasy, fried potatoes, the experience we are having is much more salient than the one we are not having, which makes comparison less likely. Imaginary chips are readily compared to imaginary sardines, but real chips are not. One reason why previews and views differ, then, is that previews include comparisons that views do not.

The Problem of Dissimilar Context

Accurate predictions require that the content of our previews be similar to the content of our views, and as the studies reviewed earlier suggest, this is not always the case. But accurate predictions also require that the context in which previewing occurs be similar to the context in which viewing occurs, and as it turns out, this is not always the case either. Why do contexts matter? Premotions are not just reactions to previews; they are reactions to previews *and* to the context in which those previews are generated. That is why we feel happier when we preview chocolate cake while we are lying on a comfortable couch than on a bed of nails, or when we are hungry rather than sated. When viewing immediately follows previewing—for example, when we see a doughnut, buy it, and pop it into our mouths—the contexts in which these two operations were carried out are likely to be similar. But when previewing precedes viewing by a substantial interval—for example, when we see a doughnut, buy it, take it home, and eat it for breakfast the next morning—the two contexts are likely to differ. When this happens, the premotions we experienced at the bakery may be unreliable indicators of the emotions we will experience when we eat the doughnut at home the next day.

All of this seems elementary, but research shows that people often fail to realize just how easily differences in the contexts of previewing and viewing can derail emotional prediction (Loewenstein, O'Donoghue, & Rabin, 2003). For example, in one study (Gilbert, Gill, & Wilson, 2002) hungry and sated people were asked to predict how much they would enjoy eating a bite of spaghetti with meat sauce for dinner the next day or for breakfast the next day. The results showed that people's current level of hunger strongly influenced their predictions and that the time of day at which they would be eating the spaghetti did not. In other words, hungry people mistakenly expected to like eating spaghetti for breakfast the next day and sated people mistakenly expected to dislike eating spaghetti for dinner the next day. In a related study (van Boven & Loewenstein, 2003), people who were working out at a gym were asked to predict how much they would want food and water if they were lost in the woods. Those who had just finished exercising predicted that they would want water more than food, but those who were just about to exercise predicted that they would want food more than water. In both of these studies, people failed to realize that the context in which they were generating their previews was having a strong influence on their premotions, and that because the previewing context was different than the viewing context, their premotions would not match their emotions.

Conclusion

Emotional prediction is the process by which we discover what we already know. We evolved to have emotional reactions to events in the present, and so to find out how we will react to events in the future, we simply pretend those events are happening now. But the system that does the reacting (often called System 1) and the system that does the pretending (often called System 2) are not the same systems (Stanovich, 1999). System 2 generates simulations of dentists and doughnuts and System 1 reacts to those simulations. Because System 2 does not know how System 1 will react to an event, it tells System 1 a story—sometimes enthralling, sometimes frightening—and then monitors its reactions. System 2 uses System 1 as a test audience, assuming that if System 1 reacts with pleasure to a simulated event, then it will react with pleasure to the event itself. In essence, System 2 learns how System 1 will react to a real event in the future by tricking it into reacting to a simulated event in the present.

This ritual of pretending and reacting is an inventive way to make emotional predictions, but it suffers from two shortcomings. First, the simulations that System 2 generates are not perfect facsimiles of real events. Compared to real events, simulated events are *unrepresentative* (i.e., they are based on past events that are not typical of their class), *essentialized* (i.e., they omit features that are incidental to the event but that influence emotional reactions to it), *truncated* (i.e., they emphasize early-occurring moments in which emotions are most intense, and ignore late-occurring moments in which adaptation occurs), and *comparative* (i.e., they include comparisons that are not unlikely to be made during viewing). Second, both the premotional and emotional reactions that System 1 generates are influenced by the contexts in which they occur, and these contexts are not necessarily the same. For both of these reasons, our premotional reactions to simulated events often differ from our emotional reactions to the events themselves, rendering our predictions inaccurate. When the human brain interrogates itself, it does not always learn the truth.

Acknowledgments

We gratefully acknowledge the support of research grant BCS-0722132 from the National Science Foundation to Daniel T. Gilbert and Timothy D. Wilson. We thank Lisa Feldman-Barrett for comments on an earlier version of this paper.

References

Addis, D. R., Wong, A. T., & Schacter, D. L. (2007). Remembering the past and imagining the future: Common and distinct neural substrates during event search and elaboration. *Neuropsychologia*, 45, 1363–1377.

Bechara, A., & Damasio, A. R. (2005). The somatic marker hypothesis: A neural theory of economic decision. *Games and Economic Behavior*, 52, 336–372.

Berns, G. S., Chappelow, J., Cekic, M., Zink, C. F., Pagnoni, G., & Martin-Skurski, M. E. (2006). Neurobiological substrates of dread. *Science*, 312, 754–758.

Breiter, H. C., Aharon, I., Kahneman, D., Anders, D., & Shizgal, P. (2001). Functional imaging of neural responses to expectancy and experience of monetary gains and losses. *Neuron*, 30, 619–639.

Buckner, R. L., & Carroll, D. C. (2007). Self-projection and the brain. *Trends in Cognitive Sciences*, 11, 49–57.

Damasio, A. R. (1994). *Descartes' error, emotion, reason and the human brain*. New York: Avon Books.

Dudai, Y., & Carruthers, M. (2005). The Janus face of mnemosyne. *Nature*, 434, 823–824.

Forrin, N. D. & Dunn, E. W. (2007). *In defense of having dessert first: The importance of startpoints*. Poster presented at the annual meeting of the Society for Personality and Social Psychology. Palm Springs, CA.

Faglioni, P. (1999). The frontal lobes. In G. Denes & L. Pizzamiglio (Eds.), *The handbook of clinical and experimental neuropsychology* (pp. 525–569). East Sussex, England: Psychology Press.

Fellows, L. K., & Farah, M. J. (2005). Dissociable elements of human foresight: A role for the ventromedial frontal lobes in framing the future, but not in discounting future rewards. *Neuropsychologia*, *43*, 1214–1221.

Gilbert, D. T. (2006). *Stumbling on happiness*. New York: Knopf.

Gilbert, D. T., & Ebert, J. E. J. (2002). Decisions and revisions: The affective forecasting of changeable outcomes. *Journal of Personality and Social Psychology*, *82*, 503–514.

Gilbert, D. T., Gill, M. J., & Wilson, T. D. (2002). The future is now: Temporal correction in affective forecasting. *Organizational Behavior and Human Decision Processes*, *88*, 430–444.

Gilbert, D. T., Lieberman, M. D., Morewedge, C. K., & Wilson, T. D. (2004). The peculiar longevity of things not so bad. *Psychological Science*, *15*, 14–19.

Gilbert, D. T., Morewedge, C. K., Risen, J. L., & Wilson, T. D. (2004). Looking forward to looking backward: The misprediction of regret. *Psychological Science*, *15*(5), 346–350.

Gilbert, D. T., Pinel, E. C., Wilson, T. D., Blumberg, S. J., & Wheatley, T. P. (1998). Immune neglect: A source of durability bias in affective forecasting. *Journal of Personality and Social Psychology*, *75*, 617–638.

Gilbert, D. T., & Wilson, T. D. (2007). Prospection: Experiencing the future. *Science*, *317*, 1351–1354.

Golub, S. A., Gilbert, D. T., & Wilson, T. D. (2009). Anticipating one's troubles: The costs and benefits of negative expectations. *Emotion*, *9*, 277–281.

Hassabis, D., Kumaran, D., Vann, S. D., & Maguire, E. A. (2007). Patients with hippocampal amnesia cannot imagine new experiences. *Proceedings of the National Academy of Sciences*, *104*(5), 1726–1731.

Hawkins, J., & Blakeslee, S. (2004). *On intelligence*. New York: Times Books.

Hoerger, M., Quirk, S. W., Lucas, R. E., & Carr, T. H. (2009). Immune neglect in affective forecasting. *Journal of Research in Personality*, *43*, 91–94.

Hsee, C. K., & Zhang, J. (2004). Distinction bias: Misprediction and mischoice due to joint evaluation. *Journal of Personality and Social Psychology*, *86*(5), 680–695.

Ingvar, D. H. (1985). Memory of the future: An essay on the temporal organization of conscious awareness. *Human Neurobiology*, *4*, 127–136.

Kahneman, D., Fredrickson, B. L., Schreiber, C. A., & Redelmeier, D. A. (1993). When more pain is preferred to less: Adding a better ending. *Psychological Science*, *4*, 401–405.

Kahneman, D., Krueger, A. B., Schkade, D., Schwarz, N., & Stone, A. A. (2006). Would you be happier if you were richer? A focusing illusion. *Science*, *312*, 1908–1910.

Klein, S. B., Loftus, J., & Kihlstrom, J. F. (2002). Memory and temporal experience: The effects of episodic memory loss on an amnesic patient's ability to remember the past and imagine the future. *Social Cognition*, *20*, 353–380.

Liberman, N., & Trope, Y. (1998). The role of feasibility and desirability considerations in near and distant future decisions: A test of temporal construal theory. *Journal of Personality and Social Psychology*, *75*, 5–18.

Loewenstein, G., O'Donoghue, T., & Rabin, M. (2003). Projection bias in predicting future utility. *The Quarterly Journal of Economics*, *118*, 1209–1248.

Lucas, R. E. (2007). Adaptation and the set-point model of subjective well-being: Does happiness change after major life events? *Current Directions in Psychological Science*, *16*(2), 75–79.

Melges, F. T. (1990). Identity and temporal perspective. In R. A. Block (Ed.), *Cognitive models of psychological time* (pp. 255–266). Hillsdale, NJ: Erlbaum.

Menzel, P., Dolan, P., Richardson, J., & Olsen, J. A. (2002). The role of adaptation to disability and disease in health state valuation: A preliminary normative analysis. *Social Science and Medicine*, *55*, 2149–2158.

Morewedge, C. K., Gilbert, D. T., Myrseth, K. O. R., Kassam, K. S., & Wilson, T. D. (2010). Consuming experience: Why affective forecasters overestimate comparative value. *Journal of Experimental Social Psychology*, *46*, 986–992.

Morewedge, C. K., Gilbert, D. T., & Wilson, T. D. (2005). The least likely of times: How memory for past events biases the prediction of future events. *Psychological Science*, *16*, 626–630.

Novemsky, N., & Ratner, R. K. (2003). The time course and impact of consumers' erroneous beliefs about hedonic contrast effects. *Journal of Consumer Research*, *29*(4), 507–516.

Oswald, A. J., & Powdthavee, N. (2008). Does happiness adapt? A longitudinal study of disability with implications for economists and judges. *Journal of Public Economics*, *92*, 1061–1077.

Riis, J., Loewenstein, G., Baron, J., Jepson, C., Fagerlin, A., & Ubel, P. A. (2005). Ignorance of hedonic adaptation to hemo-dialysis: A study using ecological momentary assessment. *Journal of Experimental Psychology: General, 134*, 3–9.

Schacter, D. L., Addis, D. R., & Buckner, R. L. (2007). Remembering the past to imagine the future: The prospective brain *Nature Reviews Neuroscience, 8*, 657–661.

Schkade, D. A., & Kahneman, D. (1998). Does living in California make people happy? A focusing illusion in judgments of life satisfaction. *Psychological Science, 9*, 340–346.

Schwarz, N., & Strack, F. (1999). Reports of subjective well-being: Judgmental processes and their methodological implications. In D. Kahneman, E. Diener, & N. Schwarz (Eds.), *Well-being: The foundations of hedonic psychology* (pp. 61–84). New York: Russell Sage Foundation.

Shiv, B., Loewenstein, G., Bechara, A., Damasio, H., & Damasion, A. R. (2005). Investment behavior and the negative side of emotion. *Psychological Science, 16*, 435–439.

Solnick, S. J., & Hemenway, D. (1998). Is more always better? A survey on positional concerns. *Journal of Economic Behavior and Organization, 37*(3), 373–383.

Stanovich, K. E. (1999). *Who is rational? Studies of individual differences in reasoning.* Mahwah, NJ: Erlbaum.

Szpunar, K. K., Watson, J. M., & McDermott, K. B. (2007). Neural substrates of envisioning the future. *Proceedings of the National Academy of Sciences USA, 104*(2), 642–647.

Trope, Y., & Liberman, N. (2003). Temporal construal. *Psychological Review, 110*, 403–421.

Tulving, E. (1985). Memory and consciousness. *Canadian Psychology, 26*, 1–12.

Tulving, E., Schacter, D. L., McLachlan, D. R., & Moscovitch, M. (1988). Priming of semantic autobiographical knowledge: A case study of retrograde amnesia. *Brain and Cognition, 8*, 3–20.

Tversky, A., & Griffin, D. (1991). Endowment and contrast in judgments of well-being. In F. Strack, M. Argyle, & N. Schwarz (Eds.), *Subjective well-being: An interdisciplinary perspective* (Vol. 21, pp. 101–118). New York: Pergamon Press.

Twain, M. (1910). *Speeches.* New York: Harper & Brothers.

Ubel, P. A., Loewenstein, G., & Jepson, C. (2003). Whose quality of life? A commentary exploring discrepancies between health state evaluations of patients and the general public. *Quality of Life Research, 12*(6), 599–607.

Vallacher, R. R., & Wegner, D. M. (1985). *A theory of action identification.* Hillsdale, NJ: Erlbaum.

van Boven, L., & Loewenstein, G. (2003). Social projection of transient drive states. *Personality and Social Psychology Bulletin, 29*, 1159–1168.

Wheeler, M. A., Stuss, D. T., & Tulving, E. (1997). Toward a general theory of episodic memory: The frontal lobes and autonoetic consciousness. *Psychological Bulletin, 121*, 331–354.

Wilson, T. D., Centerbar, D. B., Kermer, D. A., & Gilbert, D. T. (2005). The pleasures of uncertainty: Prolonging positive moods in ways people do not anticipate. *Journal of Personality and Social Psychology, 88*, 5–21.

Wilson, T. D., & Gilbert, D. T. (2003). Affective forecasting. In M. Zanna (Ed.), *Advances in experimental social psychology* (Vol. 35, pp. 345–411). New York: Elsevier.

Wilson, T. D., & Gilbert, D. T. (2008). Explaining away: A model of affective adaptation. *Perspectives on Psychological Science, 3*(5), 370–386.

Wilson, T. D., Wheatley, T. P., Meyers, J., Gilbert, D. T., & Axsom, D. (2000). Focalism: A source of durability bias in affective forecasting. *Journal of Personality and Social Psychology, 78*, 821–836.

CHAPTER 14
On Look-Ahead in Language: Navigating a Multitude of Familiar Paths

Shimon Edelman

Do I understand this sentence? Do I understand it just as I should if I heard it in the course of a narrative? If it were set down in isolation I should say, I don't know what it's about. But all the same I should know how this sentence might perhaps be used; I could myself invent a context for it. (A multitude of familiar paths lead off from these words in every direction.)

—Wittgenstein (1958, §525, p. 142)

WHAT IS THE TITLE OF THIS . . .?

Language is a rewarding field if you are in the prediction business. A reader who is fluent in English and who knows how academic papers are typically structured will readily come up with several possible guesses as to where the title of this section could have gone, had it not been cut short by the ellipsis. Indeed, in the more natural setting of spoken language, anticipatory processing is a must: performance of machine systems for speech interpretation depends critically on the availability of a good predictive model of how utterances unfold in time (Baker, 1975; Goodman, 2001; Jelinek, 1990), and there is strong evidence that prospective uncertainty affects human sentence processing, too (Hale, 2006; Jurafsky, 2003; Levy, 2008).

The human ability to predict where the current utterance is likely to be going is just another adaptation to the general pressure to anticipate the future (Craik, 1943; Dewey, 1910; Hume, 1748), be it in perception, thinking, or action, which is exerted on all cognitive systems by evolution (Dennett, 2003). Look-ahead in language

is, however, special in one key respect: language is a medium for communication, and in communication the most interesting (that is, informative) parts of the utterance that the speaker is working through are those that cannot be predicted by the listener ahead of time.

That certain parts of an utterance or some of the aspects of its structure are unpredictable in a given context does not imply that they can all be entirely novel, that is, never before encountered by the listener in any other context; if too many of them were, communication would have been just as impossible as with completely predictable signals.[1]

In theorizing about how language mediates communication, it is tempting to make the opposite assumption, namely, that both the structures and the parts (lexicon) are fully shared between the interlocutors, with only the assignment of parts to slots in structures being unexpected in the present context and hence informative. This temptation, however, must be firmly resisted; as Quine (1961, p. 259) put it, "the narrowly linguistic habits of vocabulary and syntax are imported by each speaker from his unknown past." It is certainly convenient to assume, as the

---

[1] In this connection, we may consider the debunking by Pereira (2000) of Chomsky's claim of irrelevance of statistics to language that is based on his famous "colorless green ideas sleep furiously" example: a simple corpus-based statistical model of language handily labeled this sentence as 200,000 times more probable than its scrambled version.

so-called generative tradition in linguistics does,[2] that all humans share an innately specified universal grammar that defines all and only structures that a listener need ever contemplate while processing a speaker's output. Unfortunately, this assumption runs counter to empirical findings even for adults, let alone for infants who are just learning to make sense of the hubbub that surrounds them, and who, in doing so, only gradually overcome the vast mismatch in structural and conceptual knowledge that initially exists between them and their caregivers (Edelman & Waterfall, 2007).

The individual differences among language users, being the rule rather than an exception in language (Chipere, 2001; Dabrowska & Street, 2006), cause structural and conceptual interpretation gaps to open between interlocutors. To understand how linguistic communication is at all possible, we should integrate insights and theories from language development (which lays down the foundation for an individual's linguistic ability), processing (which initially overcomes formidable difficulties; Thal & Flores, 2001; Von Berger, Wulfeck, Bates, & Fink, 1996), and generation (the capacity for which builds up gradually, as the brain matures and assimilates more and more experience; Bates & Goodman, 1999; Bates, Thal, Finlay, & Clancy, 1999; Bloom, 1970; Diessel, 2004). Only such an integrated approach, grounded in abundant and realistic behavioral data (rather than in an intuitive analysis of hand-picked cases), can lead to an understanding both of the nature of the knowledge that is shared by language users and of their idiosyncrasies.

The order of business for the remainder of this chapter is, therefore, as follows. In the next section I propose a computational framework that seems particularly suitable for the representation and processing of experience data. I then consider such data in search of cues that may be helping infants learn language reliably and efficiently by turning experience into a kind of grammar and outline a hypothesis regarding the possible brain mechanisms for acquiring and maintaining linguistic knowledge that fit within the proposed computational framework. Finally, I suggest how the proposed approach may advance the development of new models of language acquisition and processing. As we shall see, prediction—that is, projection of the past experience into the immediate future—figures prominently in all these settings.

THE STRUCTURE OF SENSORIMOTOR EXPERIENCE

The idea of grammar—a formal system that codifies the well-formedness of a class of utterances to the exclusion of others—as the repository of the knowledge of a language arises from the textbook answer to the fundamental question of linguistics: what does it mean to know a language? This answer, however, is only valid if one assumes a priori that a person's knowledge of language depends entirely on an ability to tell apart well-formed ("grammatical") sentences from ill-formed ones (Chomsky, 1957).[3] Although this assumption underlies a tremendous amount of work in the linguistic tradition that has been termed "formalist," it is not the only game in town: there is a complementary, functionalist, view, which focuses on language *use* (Newmeyer, 1998). From the functionalist standpoint, to know a language means, roughly, to be able to conceptualize what you hear and to be ready to prove that you do by generating an appropriate reply or action, given what you just heard, what you know, and what you are thinking. Correspondingly, to learn a language is to

---

[2] Although the "generative" label has been traditionally associated exclusively with the Chomskian brand of linguistics, in reality it applies to any approach that calls for learning a generative probabilistic model of a data set—an empiricist notion par excellence (Goldsmith, 2007) and the only universally valid way of dealing with data that afford generalization (Bishop, 2006). For an outline of an empirical generative framework for understanding language acquisition, see Waterfall et al. (2010).

[3] An early expression of the conviction that "syntax" is an independent level that, moreover, cannot be side-stepped is offered by Chomsky (1957, p. 87): "What we are suggesting is that the notion of 'understanding a sentence' be explained in part in terms of the notion of 'linguistic level.' To understand a sentence, then, it is first necessary to reconstruct its analysis on each linguistic level." The supposed "autonomy of syntax" has been recently reaffirmed by Chomsky (2004, p. 138).

learn to communicate with those who already speak it.

What gets communicated through the use of language is, of course, meaning—a tantalizingly intuitive concept that is easy to make precise (in a number of mathematically clever ways), but hard to make precise using formal tools that are *(1)* psychologically relevant, *(2)* neurobiologically plausible, and *(3)* most importantly, learnable from experience.[4] Not surprisingly, lowered expectations rule the day in semantics: "At least for now, the way to study meaning is by supposing that our publicly available sentences have meanings—and then trying to say how various features of sentences contribute to sentential meanings" (Pietroski, 2003).

Infants over the course of their development perceptibly progress from being, linguistically speaking, noncommunicators to being experts at bending others to their will, in a gradual process whose rate and eventual degree of success depend critically on their sensorimotor activity and social environment (Goldstein et al., 2010). It makes sense, therefore, to ask how the "features of sentences" that contribute to their meanings can be learned from sensorimotor experience, *as a matter of principle*; in other words, what cues for learning to communicate are available in the raw data.[5]

To find that out, one must begin by subjecting the raw data—the utterances in some realistic corpus of experience, along with as many extralinguistic cues as are available—to a particular manipulation. In fact, what is called for here is precisely the same manipulation that constitutes

the only possible basis for the discovery of any kind of structure in sequential data: the *alignment* of utterances to one another (that is, of the stream of data to shifted versions of itself) for the purposes of *comparison* (Edelman & Waterfall, 2007; Goldstein et al., 2010; Harris, 1946, 1991; Solan, Horn, Ruppin, & Edelman, 2005). Insofar as the raw data that are being subjected to this procedure are a record of embodied and physically and socially situated language use (and not just the "sound track" of the interaction), what a learner can glean from it are proper patterns of use—pragmatics and semantics, as it were, and not just syntax.

The data structure that best fits this notion of a record of experience and of how it should be processed is a kind of graph (Edelman, 2008a, p. 274; Solan et al., 2005). Semi-formally, a graph is a discrete structure that consists of a set of vertices and a table that specifies which pairs of vertices are interconnected by edges. The set of discrete vertices in the present case may be found, for instance, in the phonemes of the language, whose sequence imposes a temporal order on all the rest of the information in a record of experience. Because the phonemes themselves can be extracted from raw speech data through alignment and comparison (Harris, 1946, 1952; see the review in Edelman, 2008a, ch. 7), and because babies easily learn "words" formed by statistically stable patterns of phonemes (Saffran, Aslin, & Newport, 1996; Werker & Yeung, 2005), we may assume without loss of generality that the graph of experience is defined over words.[6]

The edges in this graph are directed: they are determined by the order of words in the utterances that comprise the corpus. The graph is heavily annotated by the various aspects of experience that label its vertices and edges: prosodic contours, pointers to the listener's conceptual structures, pointers to visual and other sensory information about the surrounding scene, social markers (including joint attention with and contingent feedback from the interlocutor[s]),

---

[4] Some progress has been made in modeling human processing of meaning in various circumscribed situations, such as dealing with simple logical problems (Stenning & van Lambalgen, 2008). In computational linguistics, the learning of semantics is either heavily supervised (e.g., the wide-coverage semantic parser of Bos et al. [2004] works from very detailed semantic knowledge that's built into its lexicon-grammar) or else works for highly simplified situations (e.g., Eisenstein, Clarke, Goldwasser, and Roth, 2009).

[5] This formulation of the question stresses that it pertains to what Marr and Poggio (1977) termed the abstract computational level. Note that the popular trick of declaring it all innate amounts to dodging the question rather than answering it (Putnam, 1967).

[6] At the level that matters, language is "digital" (that is, defined over a set of discrete primitives) for reasons of computational tractability (Edelman, 2008b).

records of motor acts, and so on (see Goldstein et al., 2010 for a discussion of the importance of those cues in language acquisition).

This, then, is the fundamental structure of experience (minimally processed so as to impart to it a discrete sequential "backbone"), with which any cognitive agent (human, robotic, or alien) that sets out to learn to communicate with humans must contend. Such a graph structure can afford the system that harbors it only a minimal "look-ahead" capability: the full range of documented continuations of a given utterance prefix is encoded in the graph, but the probability distribution over such continuations is still implicit. Moreover, the raw graph can support only limited comprehension (as in the mapping of a finite set of fully spelled-out utterances to conceptual or motor structures) and no productivity at all (no generation of novel utterances). In other words, merely committing experience to memory would allow the learner, at best, to act in some respects like a dog and in others like a parrot.

To go beyond one's own immediate experience and exhibit combinatorially open-ended comprehension and productivity, the listener must process and modify the graph. One way to do so is by recursively seeking partially alignable bundles of paths through it, thereby learning collocations, equivalences, and other statistical dependency patterns, which are assigned their own labeled vertices and are wired back into the graph. The result may be thought of as a kind of probabilistic "grammar" of sensorimotor experience, distilled from the original data. Solan et al. (2005) showed that such grammars learned automatically from raw transcripts of speech can be precise and productive—surprisingly so, given the highly impoverished nature of text-only data.

A much more concise and therefore powerful representation for a grammar of experience is a *higraph*—a directed graph in which subsets of the set of vertices may serve as vertices in their own right, edges may connect arbitrary tuples (rather than just pairs) of vertices, and Cartesian products of vertex sets are directly represented (Harel, 1988). A programming formalism for reactive systems based on higraphs, called *statecharts*, has proved to be widely applicable in computer science (Harel, 2007). It may help the reader to observe that a statechart bears the same relationship to a finite-state automaton as a higraph does to a graph, the former being exponentially more expressive; in other words, a finite-state machine whose behavior is equivalent to that of a given statechart may need exponentially more states (vertices).[7] A simple example of possible use of statecharts for integrated representation of speech and action—that is, syntax along with situated semantics—appears in Figure 14.1.

Computationally, the task of using sensorimotor experience to learn to communicate reduces, therefore, to the problem of distilling a statechart from a labeled graph that represents the raw data (a record of the learner's experience), subject to certain constraints, which must be specified as a part of the learning algorithm. Interestingly, statecharts have recently been taken up by game programmers, who use this formalism to specify patterns of discourse and behavior for computer game characters (Brusk, 2008). Within the present conceptual framework, this is an entirely expected turn. A game character's predicament resembles that of an infant in that it must make the best use of its limited experience and bounded computational resources to respond—preferably, on the basis of partial information, hence in an anticipatory manner—to the locutions and actions of the other characters, most importantly human players. Unfortunately, unsupervised algorithms for learning a statechart machine from samples of its intended behavior do not yet exist (except perhaps in babies' brains).[8] In developing such algorithms, every little helps. What we must consider next, then, is information

---

[7] For once, Chomsky (2004, p. 92) gets it right: "It is obvious, in some sense, that processing systems are going to be represented by finite state transducers. That has got to be the case [. . .] But that leaves quite open the question of what is the internal organization of the system of knowledge."

[8] In one of the existing algorithms, a teacher (the designer) serves as an oracle that evaluates pieces of generated behavior and decides the fate of the rules that gave rise to them (Mäkinen & Systä, 2002). In another work, statecharts are synthesized from scenario-based requirements, themselves stated in a formal language (Harel, Kugler, & Pnueli, 2005).

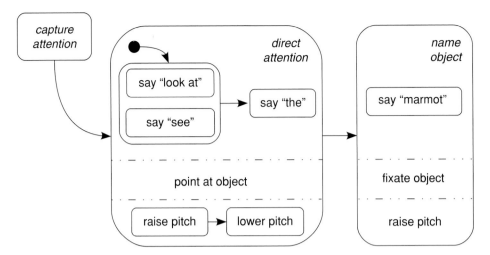

Figure 14.1 Statecharts are a powerful formalism for describing (or prescribing, if used generatively) behavior, which is based on the higraph notation (Harel, 1988). Informally, statecharts are state diagrams endowed with representational depth, orthogonality, and broadcast communication. The simple statechart in this example represents a routine for pointing out an object to a baby. It begins on the left with the capture of the baby's attention and proceeds simultaneously on three independent (orthogonal) tracks: lexical content (*top*), actions (*middle*), and prosody (*bottom*). The default entry point to the top of the *direct attention* node is at either of the two phrases, "look at" and "see," which are mutually exclusive. In the *name object* node, the label "marmot" can be replaced with any member of the appropriate equivalence class (see Fig. 14.2). For mathematical details, many illuminating examples, and pointers to literature where the syntax and the semantics of statecharts are rigorously defined, see Harel (1988).

that infants have at their disposal that helps them turn experience into practical, executable knowledge.

THE RICHNESS OF THE STIMULUS

The problem of inferring a statechart (or any other kind of grammar) from samples of the behavior that it needs to generate is an instance of the wider problem of learning a (probabilistic) generative model for a set of (random-variable) data (Bishop, 2006; Hinton, 2007). Only very few unsupervised algorithms exist that are capable of working with raw transcribed language from large-scale realistic corpora, such as those in the CHILDES collection (MacWhinney, 2000); these are ADIOS (Solan et al., 2005), UDOP (Bod, 2009), and ConText (Waterfall, Sandbank, Onnis, & Edelman, 2010). The performance of the grammars inferred by these algorithms cannot yet compete with that of human learners. There is no doubt that this is due in part to the sparse

sampling of language data that are available for learning (the conversations recorded in CHILDES are few and far apart, relatively to the density and total amount of speech to which a typical child is exposed). It would be instructive, however, to consider what characteristics of a child's language experience, apart from sheer volume, are not yet utilized by the state of the art learning algorithms.[9]

Quite tellingly, Smith and Gasser (2005), who offer "six lessons from babies" to those who seek to understand and perhaps emulate cognitive

[9] Cf. Bates et al. (1999): "Consider the following statistics: assuming a taciturn Calvinist family in which an English-speaking child hears approximately 5 hours of speech input per day, at a mean rate of 225 words per minute, the average 10-year-old child has heard 1,034,775,000 English phonemes (at an average of 25,869,375 trials per phoneme). She has heard just under 250 million words (including 17,246,250 renditions of the most common function words) and 28 million sentences [. . .]."

development, put language last: "starting as a baby grounded in a physical, social and linguistic world is crucial to the development of the flexible and inventive intelligence that characterizes humankind." In what follows, I briefly discuss three sources of cues, only one of which is linguistic, that likely assist development. These are the suprasentential structure of discourse, the multimodal sensorimotor context that accompanies speech, and the dynamical social setting in which human linguistic interaction takes place.

Cross-Sentential Cues

In everyday child-directed speech, a large proportion of utterances come in the form of *variation sets*—runs of two or more sentences that share at least one lexical element (Küntay & Slobin, 1996; Waterfall, 2006; see Figure 14.2a, top). A recent survey of the caregivers' parts of eight naturalistic interaction corpora from the English collection in CHILDES revealed this to be a pervasive phenomenon: Over 20% of the utterances in the corpus occur within variation sets that contain at least two words in common. If a gap of up to two intervening sentences is allowed between two consecutive members of a variation set, this proportion rises to over 40% (when variation sets are defined by a single-word overlap, these figures rise to over 50% and 80%, respectively). Moreover, the lexical elements shared by the members of a typical variation set are not just some common function words: Over 25% of unique words in the corpus participate in defining variation sets. These statistics apply to languages that are as different as Turkish, English, and Mandarin (Küntay & Slobin, 1996; Waterfall & Edelman, 2009).

Because of the partial lexical overlap, sentences in a variation set can be aligned, affording a natural way to compare them. Such comparison can yield informative and statistically reliable evidence of syntactic structure (Waterfall et al., 2010), and indeed longitudinal studies show that infants are better at structurally appropriate use of nouns and verbs that had occurred in their caregivers' speech within variation sets, compared to those that did not (Waterfall, 2006; Hoff-Ginsberg, 1986, 1990; Nelson, 1977).

An artificial grammar study with adult subjects confirmed the effectiveness of variation sets in making word segmentation and phrase structure easier to learn (Onnis, Waterfall, & Edelman, 2008).

Most importantly for infant language acquisition, however, the manner in which variation sets bring out structure is local: the mechanisms of alignment and comparison need only span a few seconds' worth of the baby's attention, because the members of a variation set are, by definition, never far apart from each other in time. Given how prevalent variation sets are, it is as if child-directed speech sets the baby up with an expectation of a partial repetition—and with it a morsel of certifiable structural knowledge about language—that is constantly renewed: each successive utterance is highly likely either to be continuing an already open variation set or to start a new one.

In its reliance on the anticipation of a partially familiar input, learning from variation sets takes advantage of predictive processing, a function which, as I pointed out in the opening section, language shares with other cognitive systems. Although variation sets become less prominent in caregivers' speech as the child grows older (Waterfall, 2006), partial overlap between utterances that occur in temporal proximity to each other in a conversation—that is, in naturally coordinated speech generated by two or more interlocutors—is extremely common (Du Bois, 2003; Szmrecsanyi, 2005). This realization, as well as abundant data on so-called syntactic priming (Bock, 1986; Bock, Dell, Chang, & Onishi, 2007), led researchers to speculate about the possible mechanisms that keep the participants in a conversation in tune with each other (Pickering & Garrod, 2004).

Multimodal Cues

In addition to partial overlap between nearby chunks of speech, the statistical significance of patterns that emerge from data can be boosted by a convergence of multiple cues that join forces to highlight the same candidate structure. Such convergence is the first of the six principles of learning listed by Smith and Gasser (2005): "Babies' experience of the world is profoundly

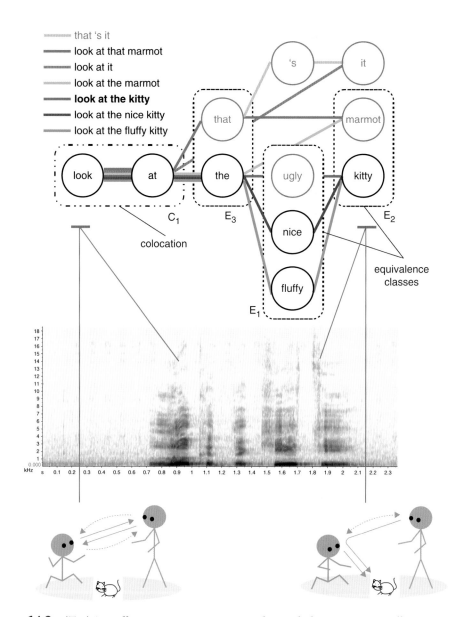

Figure 14.2a (*Top*) A small, seven-utterance corpus and a graph that represents it, illustrating a *cross-sentential* (statistically significant alignment) cue to structure and meaning. (*Middle*) A spectrogram of one of the utterances ("look at the kitty"), illustrating a *multimodal* (prosody + content) cue to structure and meaning. (*Bottom*) Eye fixation patterns, illustrating a *social* (joint attention) cue to structure and meaning. *Cross-sentential* cues. The seven utterances in this example, which is typical of child-directed speech, form a variation set. The way they overlap when aligned highlights certain statistical facts about this corpus, for example, that "look at" is a collocation, C_1 and that "nice" and "fluffy" form an equivalence class. E_1, in the specific context shown (a separate bout of experience may indicate to the child that "ugly" belongs to E_1 too). *Multimodal* cues. The significance of these structures is boosted by the parallel stream of prosodic information (e.g., the rising pitch at "look" and at "kitty"). *Social* cues. Joint attention combines with alignment and prosody to single out the label "kitty" and to fix its situational reference (i.e., the cat, which the baby and the caregiver both end up looking at; the drawings are courtesy of Hideki Kozima, Miyagi University, Japan).

multi-modal. We propose that multiple overlapping and time-locked sensory systems enable the developing system to educate itself—without defined external tasks or teachers—just by perceiving and acting in the world." What William James (1890, p. 488) described as an unruly mob of stimuli that beset the developing organism's senses ("the baby, assailed by eye, ear, nose, skin and entrails at once, feels it all as one great blooming, buzzing confusion") is in fact more like a well-organized circus parade in which troupes of mutually consistent cues reinforce each other and help the learner infer structure and impose order on its sensory experience (Goldstein et al., 2010).

The simplest example of such convergence in action can be found in word learning. As famously noted by Quine (1960), a mapping between a novel word and the object, if any, that it stands for cannot be inferred with complete confidence by mere observation. However, consistent cross-situational statistics do allow infants to learn a word-object pairing after encountering just a few "coincidences" the timing of each of which if taken in isolation is insufficiently precise (Smith & Yu, 2008). The power of such statistical learning is further increased when additional cues, such as the speaker's prosody and joint attention between the speaker and the listener, are utilized (Fig. 14.2a, middle and bottom; Yu & Ballard, 2007). The use of multiple cues does not, of course, cease in adulthood: there is now massive evidence to the effect that language processing during comprehension is incremental and relies heavily on a plethora of perceptual cues assisting each other's interpretation through cross-modal expectations (Crocker, Knoeferle, & Mayberry, 2010).

Social Cues

Being a key component of the human "interactional engine" (Levinson, 2006), language is closely intertwined with other social communication mechanisms that are available to people. It obviously facilitates social cognition, and just about every other kind of cognition as well, thereby serving as a scaffolding for the growth of the human civilization (Clark, 1998). It is becoming increasingly clear that this facilitation is bidirectional. As argued by Herrmann and colleagues (2007), the distinctly human social traits, many of which are exhibited already by prelinguistic babies, may have been essential for the emergence of human language, whose evolution proceeds at a much faster pace than the evolution of its host species (Christiansen & Chater, 2008). It stands to reason, therefore, that social factors should shape language development, and indeed they do (Hoff, 2006).

The social origin of many of the multimodal cues mentioned earlier, such as the characteristic prosody of child-directed speech (Pereira, Smith, & Yu, 2008; Yu & Ballard, 2007), is but one aspect of this influence. A much more powerful mechanism through which caregivers can shape and facilitate learning is social feedback that is contingent on the baby's own actions. As my colleagues and I have argued elsewhere (Goldstein et al., 2010), such social interaction allows candidate linguistic structures to stand out from a continuous stream of experience by passing two kinds of significance tests.

The first of these tests is intrinsic to the speech data; it applies, for example, when partially alignable chunks of utterances in a variation set highlight a structure that may be worth learning (as noted earlier in this section). The second test is socially situated: by definition for a communication system, "interesting" structures must be behaviorally significant, as indicated by cues that are extrinsic to the stream of speech. There is growing evidence that socially guided learning that relies on both tests provides a powerful early impetus to the language acquisition process (Goldstein et al., 2003; Goldstein & Schwade, 2008).[10] In this connection, we may observe that social feedback works by facilitating the delivery of information precisely when the baby *expects* it (and is therefore self-motivated to give it due processing diligence).

---

[10] Social guidance also helps robots learn to solve puzzles (Thomaz & Breazeal, 2008).

SENSORIMOTOR EXPERIENCE AND THE BRAIN

In this chapter, I have already deviated twice from the usual practice of formalist linguistics of approaching the study of language with a firm preconception of what the answers to the big questions should look like. First, I identified an open inquiry into the informational structure of experience, of which speech is but one strand, as a prerequisite for any study of "grammar," conceived of properly as a distillation of experience

(Figure 14.2b). Second, by focusing on the information that is made available to infants by their caregivers and environment, I noted three clusters of properties that can facilitate the distillation of experience into a vehicle of anticipation (in listening) and eventual purposeful production (in speaking).

For good measure, I shall now commit a third transgression: instead of acquiescing to the textbook assertion that there exists in the brain a language module whose evolutionary origins,

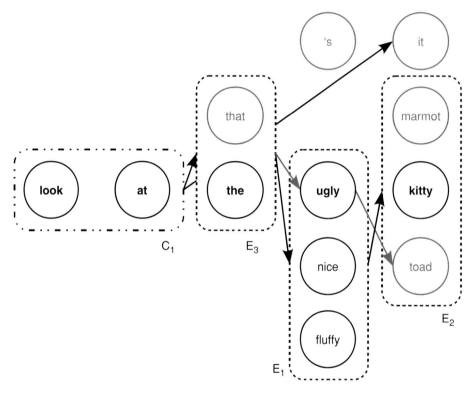

Figure 14.2b The graph in (a), top, can be distilled into this compressed form (conceptual and other extralinguistic annotations, without which the grammar would be worthless as a guide for behavior, have been omitted for clarity). Observe that one arrow connects E_3 to E_1 (that is, to any of its members) and another connects it just to "ugly" (which thereby is distinguished from other members of E_3). This representation affords productivity: It can generate the utterance "look at the ugly marmot" that the learner may never have encountered. A formalism that includes this and several other, much more powerful, representational tools is statecharts (see the section "The Structure of Sensorimotor Experience"). The statechart notation may seem overly complicated compared to the standard one (e.g., $S \rightarrow C_1E_3E_1E_2$; this slightly too lax rule would ensue if the distinction between the contextual expectations of "ugly" on the one hand and "nice" and "fluffy" on the other hand were dropped). However, speech is situated not on a book page but in the world (which has no place in the standard notation), and it starts not with the empty symbol S but rather with an activation of some concepts, such as *look* and *kitty*, which then spreads through the graph until an utterance is ready for output. The statechart formalism fits these requirements to the T.

developmental trajectory, and neurocomputational circuitry can all be left safely and conveniently opaque,[11] I shall line up and discuss, necessarily briefly, a series of insights and findings from brain science that language theorists can ill afford to ignore. The main thrust of the discussion will be to argue that language acquisition and use involve certain general-purpose (i.e., not exclusively linguistic) functions of the "language" areas in the frontal lobe of the cortex and, more importantly, of certain subcortical structures (Lieberman, 2002; Muller & Basho, 2004; Ullman, 2006).

The Hippocampus

Let us first consider the hippocampus, a subcortical structure that resides in the medial temporal lobe (MTL) of the brain. Classical studies in rats, beginning with O'Keefe and Dostrovsky (1971), led to the common view of the hippocampus as a cognitive map. Subsequent research showed that its function is predictive (Muller & Kubie, 1989) and that it is map-like in that it integrates a wide range of episodic information about spatially anchored events (Eichenbaum, Dudchenko, Wood, Shapiro, & Tanila, 1999). More recently, it became apparent that memory traces for *sequences* of events are laid down in the hippocampus and that both the events and their ordering may be abstract rather than spatial (Buzsaki, 2005; Fortin, Agster, & Eichenbaum, 2002; Levy, 1996; Levy, Hocking, & Wu, 2005). The role of the hippocampus in learning sequence-structured data is especially important *(1)* when the sequences partially overlap, so that each distinct prefix of a common subsequence determines its respective distinct suffix (Levy, 1996) and *(2)* when a substantial amount of time may elapse between successive items in a sequence (Agster, Fortin, & Eichenbaum, 2002).

The view of the hippocampus that emerges from the animal studies is that of a computational tool that is honed to process multimodal (sensorimotor plus abstract) graph-structured data, which would make it well suited to handle the distillation of experience into a probabilistic statechart grammar. This notion does not really contradict the established view of the role of the hippocampal formation in humans, which holds it to be essential for explicit memory and for long-term memory consolidation: what is language learning if not a massive exercise in memory consolidation? Once we begin seeing the hippocampus in this light, several pieces of the puzzle fall into place.

First, the hippocampus is presumably a key brain structure that makes space matter in discourse. Just as rats learn better when the data are presented to them in a spatially consistent manner, human infants are better at word learning when location is used consistently to anchor word reference (Hockema & Smith, 2009). This developmental finding complements the results of behavioral studies with adults that show similarly strong effects of space serving as a scaffolding for building up bundles of episodic information (Richardson & Spivey, 2000) and as a medium for dynamic social coordination between interlocutors (Richardson & Dale, 2005).

Second, the hippocampus is involved in language processing. This is suggested by its role in implicit sequence learning, of the kind that psychologists test with small artificial grammars. The expectation that such tests should be relevant to the processing of real language is borne out both by electroencephalography (EEG) and by functional magnetic resonance imaging (fMRI) results (Meyer et al., 2005; Schendan, Searl, Melrose, & Stern, 2003). Furthermore, imaging studies show that hippocampal activity distinguishes between good and poor learners of sequence tasks (Breitenstein et al., 2005). Individual variability in implicit sequence learning also correlates with performance in the processing of sequential context in spoken language (Conway & Pisoni, 2008).

Third, the hippocampus appears to be indispensable for language acquisition. Thus, partial lesions of the hippocampus result in developmental amnesia, in which the patient exhibits in particular a reduced ability to recall sequentially

---

[11] Chomsky (2004, p. 56): "I think a linguist can do a perfectly good work in generative grammar without ever caring about questions of physical realism or what his work has to do with the structure of the mind."

structured information after a 24-hour delay (Adlam, Vargha-Khadem, Mishkin, & de Haan, 2005). Early left hippocampal pathology results in abnormal language lateralization (Weber et al., 2006). Most tellingly, infants who suffer from extensive bilateral hippocampal sclerosis early in life fail to acquire language (or lose attained language) or to develop social and adaptive skills, despite adequate sensorimotor functioning (DeLong & Heinz, 1997).

The Basal Ganglia

Extraordinary feats of memory require extraordinary motivation, as well as proper coordination between data compression,[12] sequencing, and associative storage mechanisms. One would expect that the social cues that highlight complex sequential structure in the stream of experience would also help motivate learning, and that mechanisms of motivated sequence learning could be shared between all the tasks that need them (Lashley, 1951). This is indeed the case; in addition to areas in the medial temporal lobe (the hippocampus and the entorhinal cortex), in the frontal lobe, and in the thalamus, the system in question includes, most significantly, the basal ganglia.

Behavioral and neuropsychological findings in humans show that the basal ganglia interact with the hippocampus and with cortical areas in supporting learning and execution of a wide variety of cognitive tasks that require flexible coordination of sequential structure processing and working memory (Seger, 2006), including language (Lieberman, 2002, pp. 116–119). Ullman (2006, p. 482) suggests that "the basal ganglia may play a particularly important role in the acquisition of grammatical and other procedural knowledge, whose use eventually depends largely on the posterior portion of Broca's area." Moreover, the basal ganglia circuits also handle the social-motivational aspects of complex learning, in all species that are capable of it (Syal & Finlay, 2009). Although this system receives

much attention from neuroscientists and from computational modelers (Cohen & Frank, 2009; Dominey, 2005; Dominey & Hoen, 2006; O'Reilly & Frank, 2006),[13] the social computing role of basal ganglia is rarely mentioned. Given how important this system is, one hopes that before long "researchers in early language development turn their attention from the storage device, the cortex, to the neuroanatomy which provide[s] the motivational structure for behavior, the basal forebrain and striatum" (Syal & Finlay, 2009).

All Together Now

In mammals, the hippocampus sits at the functional apex of three converging bidirectional streams of information, which are channeled by somatosensory-motor, visual, and auditory isocortical hierarchies, respectively (Merker, 2004). Furthermore, the hippocampus and the basal ganglia have bidirectional functional links to the prefrontal cortex (Okanoya & Merker, 2007, fig. 22.4), an arrangement that is starting to attract modeling efforts (O'Reilly, 2006; O'Reilly & Norman, 2002).[14] Coordination among all these brain structures is required for learning sequential behaviors, for exerting control over their production, and for committing them to long-term memory (Shapiro, 2009).

The mechanisms of this coordination are being thoroughly studied in animals. For instance, there is much evidence for replay of maze traversal experience during sleep in rats (Lee & Wilson, 2002), which is analogous to song replay during sleep in songbirds (Dave & Margoliash, 2000). Such replay, whose unfolding is coordinated between the hippocampus and the cortex (visual and prefrontal; Ji & Wilson, 2007; Peyrache, Khamassi, Benchenane,

[12] Data compression is critically important not only because of capacity limitations: without compression, there can be no generalization and therefore no prediction ability (Grunwald, 1994).

[13] An entire special issue of *Behavioural Brain Research* (volume 199, number 1, 2009) was devoted to the role of basal ganglia in learning and memory.

[14] The isocortical and especially the frontal areas, are, of course, much more extensive in humans than in other mammals, which explains, in part, why not all species that have the "standard" machinery in place for processing sequences (thalamus, basal ganglia, hippocampus, prefrontal cortex) can learn to play the violin or engage in conversation. Merker and Okanoya (2007) relate the emergence of language to encephalization in humans.

Wiener, & Battaglia, 2009) is thought to underlie memory consolidation. The coordination is mediated by oscillatory activity (Jones & Wilson, 2005), whose frequency and phase relationships across regions are tightly controlled (Buzsaki, 2010). Imaging evidence is becoming available that favors the existence in the human brain of an analogous system for sequence learning, consolidation, and production (Albouy et al., 2008; Schendan et al., 2003; Seger & Cincotta, 2006).[15]

LANGUAGE ACQUISITION RELOADED

The mosaic of behavioral, electrophysiological, and imaging findings surveyed in the previous sections is consistent with the theoretical framework that I outlined earlier that addresses the initial representation of experience and its eventual distillation into a form of generative grammar that in humans supports all complex, hierarchically structured, sequential behaviors, including language. Much work remains to be done, both in integrating the wealth of experimental findings and in developing a viable neurocomputational approach to statechart learning that would draw on the integrated empirical data.[16] The open issues that remain cannot even be all listed, let alone resolved, here, which is why I shall offer merely a sample of one question each on the problem, algorithm, and mechanism levels.

The Big Statechart in the Sky

The first question pertains to the scope of the statechart grammar that a situated language user is expected to require. As implied by a theorem proved by Conant and Ashby (1970), a cognitive system that aims to control its fate must maintain an internal model of its environment. This model, as noted earlier, must be probabilistic and generative, to better deal with the ubiquitous and unavoidable uncertainties. In a society of cognitive agents, of which a linguistic community is a special case, an individual's internal model must, therefore, include both the shared environment and other agents.[17]

The methodological virtues of this approach have been discussed by Syal and Finlay (2009), who conclude: "In the avian species that display learned vocal behavior, the learning environment is an integrated system, viewed best when the entire infant bird, its tutor, the interaction between the two, and the effect of each actor on its own, and the other's nervous system, are considered." In humans, arguments for socially shared representations have been put forward by Decety and Sommerville (2003); in the case of language, it is hypothesized that such representations involve emulating the other speaker in a dialogue (Pickering & Garrod, 2007) (for a survey of the available evidence and computational arguments, see Edelman, 2008a, chs. 6, 7). The statechart formalism, which has been developed to model reactive systems and which has powerful means for representing combinatorially complex, nested relationships, is well suited for capturing grammars that involve multiple interacting agents.

---

[15] In what must count as an understatement of the year, Albouy et al. (2008) write: "Motor sequences constitute an integral part of a number of everyday life activities such as writing, typing, speaking, knitting, or playing a musical instrument."

[16] The idea of a "grammar of behavior" is related to the notion of action schemata, which has been entertained by psychologists for some decades now (Arbib, 2006; Lashley, 1951). Houghton and Hartley (1996) offer a particularly cogent discussion of the obstacles that any neurocomputational implementation of serially and hierarchically structured schemata must overcome.

[17] In modeling other agents, one must beware of too deep a recursion, as illustrated by the following excerpt from the script of *The Princess Bride* by William Goldman:

MAN IN BLACK

All right: where is the poison? The battle of wits has begun. It ends when you decide and we both drink, and find out who is right and who is dead.

VIZZINI

But it's so simple. All I have to do is divine from what I know of you. Are you the sort of man who would put the poison into his own goblet, or his enemy's? Now, a clever man would put the poison into his own goblet, because he would know that only a great fool would reach for what he was given. I'm not a great fool, so I can clearly not choose the wine in front of you. But you must have known I was not a great fool; you would have counted on it, so I can clearly not choose the wine in front of me.

(This goes on for a bit longer before one of them dies.)

The Ace of Bayes?

The second question is how to learn such grammars from records of experience. I believe that the answer to this question will be Bayesian. A Bayesian foundation for word learning has been described by Frank, Goodman, and Tenenbaum (2009), who showed that considering simultaneously word reference fixation and the speaker's referential intention is more effective than treating each problem separately. More generally, Bayesian cue integration is also the proper approach to multimodal perception (Kersten & Yuille, 2003) and, indeed, to any kind of learning and inference from data in cognition (Chater, Tenenbaum, & Yuille, 2006; Edelman, 2008a).

In the ADIOS algorithm for distilling a grammar from a graph representing a corpus of language (Solan et al., 2005), the criterion for rewiring the graph relied on a simple binomial significance test for vertex connectivity. Clearly, we must do better than that. A hint as to how a Bayesian approach could be made to work for this problem can be found in recent computational analysis of experience-based modification of the hippocampal network by Levy et al. (2005, p. 1252), who noted that the use of Bayesian "inversion" allows the active graph formed by the CA3-entorhinal loop to estimate forward-looking dependencies—that is, formulate predictions—as a part of its processing of past experiences.

A very general abstract Bayesian model for learning graphs (or any other structural representations) from relational data has been recently proposed by Kemp and Tenenbaum (2008). The worked examples they offer begin with writing down a multivariate Gaussian with a dimension for each node in the graph to parametrize the generative model, and proceed by performing a greedy search, guided by the Bayes formula, in the resulting parameter space. Although in principle this approach can be applied as is to the problem of statechart learning, scaling is bound to become a problem with realistic corpora of experience. An intriguing possibility for resolving the scaling issue is to try to isolate "islands" in the statechart grammar where learning can

be made effectively local, perhaps under the influence of variation sets and other local cues in the data.

Time and Again

In the cortex, which is where the distilled grammar would be anchored in long-term memory according to the present framework (Ullman, 2006, p. 482), the dynamic representation of a particular sequence of states (say, the phonemes that form a word) may take the form of a synfire chain—an orderly propagation of activity between designated cliques of neurons (Abeles, 1982; Bienenstock, 1992). Evidence for the existence of such chains of activity in the primary visual cortex (Ikegaya et al., 2004) indicates that synfire-based representations are biologically feasible. Indeed, synfire activity arises spontaneously (Izhikevich, 2006), or in response to input patterns (Hosaka, Araki, & Ikeguchi, 2008), in recurrent networks of simulated spiking neurons that learn from the statistics of their own firing experience via a spike timing-dependent plasticity (STDP) synaptic modification rule.[18]

A pressing implementational issue that needs to be resolved for STDP to provide an explanation of the synaptic mechanism of learning language is that of timing (Wallenstein, Eichenbaum, & Hasselmo, 1998, p. 318). Spike timing-dependent plasticity operates on the time scale of tens of milliseconds at most; in comparison, language (and human behavior in general) unfolds on the time scale of seconds, while social and other cues that are contingent on one's utterance or act may not come until much later. Izhikevich (2007) showed that this issue can be addressed through combined action of a fast STDP mechanism that "marks" the relevant synapses and a subsequent slow process of stabilizing the change, which depends on reward-related release of dopamine—a neurotransmitter that mediates learning in the loops connecting the basal ganglia with the cortex (Da Cunha et al., 2009).

---

[18] Spike timing-dependent plasticity is a Hebbian learning rule (Caporale & Dan, 2008), which has interesting connections to Bayesian inference (Deneve, 2008).

A similar issue arises in understanding memory replay in the rat (Ji & Wilson, 2007). The replay, which presumably happens to allow STDP-based consolidation, is much faster than the animal's running speed, indicating that some form of time compression takes place (Davidson et al., 2009; Jensen & Lisman, 2005). Interestingly, the manner in which time compression in memory replay works may hold a hint as to how the hippocampus-cortex-striatum network can learn and generate long sequences that are formed by various combinations of shorter ones. Replay in the rat hippocampus coincides with high-frequency "ripple" oscillations, which do not last long enough to represent long treks through the rat's environment, but, as shown by Davidson, Kloosterman, and Wilson, (2009), are composed combinatorially, thus altering the behavioral meaning of the entire event.[19] Moreover, Davidson et al. (2009, p. 504) noted that "replayed trajectories represent the set of possible future or past paths linked to the animal's current position rather than the actual paths." Add to this capability a modicum of recursion (by allowing some subsequences to be nested within others, up to a point), and you have a biological substrate for complex behavior, including language.

Conclusion

I have now come full circle to the beginning of this chapter—back to the twin notions that, first, mastering language must have something to do with getting *meaning* in and out of it and, second, that meaning must have something to do with the way language is *used* as part of behavior.

[19] Henson and Burgess (1997) hypothesized that sequential information could be represented in the brain by a collection of oscillators operating at different frequencies. Specifically, they showed that a sequence can be coded by the oscillator whose half-period best fits its length, with the position of each item in the sequence being signaled by the phase of the oscillator at the point in time when that item was presented. In addition to accounting for a range of behavioral data on memory for sequences (Henson, 1999), this model fits well with the recent findings on the interplay of various oscillatory regimes in the hippocampus (Davidson et al., 2009).

In doing so, I could not help noticing some intriguing parallels between a computational analysis of the nature of linguistic experience and the deep insights into this very same matter that are to be found in the work of Ludwig Wittgenstein—a philosopher whose construal of meaning is usually condensed to the maxim "meaning is use," which has been misused to the point of meaninglessness.

A better idea of what Wittgenstein may have had in mind can be obtained by considering three extraordinary passages from *Philosophical Investigations*. The first one, which I used as the motto for this chapter, broaches the possibility that a record of linguistic experience may look like a graph ("A multitude of familiar paths lead off from these words in every direction"). The second one reiterates this view of language and connects it to both vision and action:

> Phrased *like this*, emphasized like this, heard in this way, this sentence is the first of a series in which a transition is made to *these* sentences, pictures, actions. (A multitude of familiar paths lead off from these words in every direction.) (Wittgenstein (1958, §534, p. 142)

Finally, in the third passage Wittgenstein rounds off his observation with some memorable metaphors:

> Suppose someone said: every familiar word, in a book for example, actually carries an atmosphere with it in our minds, a 'corona' of lightly indicated uses.—Just as if each figure in a painting were surrounded by delicate shadowy drawings of scenes, as it were in another dimension, and in them we saw the figures in different contexts. (Wittgenstein (1958, II:VI, p. 181)

What a language user relies upon in looking ahead to the successive instalments of the incoming utterance, or in constructing a sequence of words to be uttered, is a probabilistically annotated graph-like record of experience—the "multitude of familiar paths" along with the "'corona' of lightly indicated uses"—which has been incorporated into the general "grammar" that drives behavior. Developing biologically relevant algorithms that can distill multimodal experience in this manner is the great challenge that the research program I sketched here will have to tackle next.

Acknowledgments

The idea of representing a corpus of language in the form of a graph arose in a series of conversations that I had with Zach Solan in 2001–2003. The final form of the section "Sensorimotor Experience and the Brain" was influenced by discussions I participated in at the Ernst Strungmann Forum on Dynamic Coordination in the Brain, held in August 2009 at the Frankfurt Institute for Advanced Studies. I thank Barb Finlay, Mike Goldstein, David Harel, David Horn, Björn Merker, Luca Onnis, Geoff Pullum, Eytan Ruppin, Ben Sandbank, Jen Schwade, Aaron Sloman, Mark Steedman, Heidi Waterfall, and Matt Wilson for comments on various aspects of this project.

References

Abeles, M. (1982). Role of cortical neuron: Integrator or coincidence detector? *Israel Journal of Medical Sciences, 18*, 83–92.

Adlam, A-L. R., Vargha-Khadem, F., Mishkin, M., & de Haan, M. (2005). Deferred imitation of action sequences in developmental amnesia. *Journal of Cognitive Neuroscience, 17*, 240–248.

Agster, K. L., Fortin, N. J., & Eichenbaum, H. (2002). The hippocampus and disambiguation of overlapping sequences. *The Journal of Neuroscience, 22*, 5760–5768.

Albouy, G., Sterpenich, V., Balteau, E., Vandewalle, G., Desseilles, M., Dang-Vu, T., Darsaud, A., Ruby, P., Luppi, P-H., Degueldre, C., Peigneux, P., Luxen, A., & Maquet, P. (2008). Both the hippocampus and striatum are involved in consolidation of motor sequence memory. *Neuron, 58*, 261–272.

Arbib, M. A. (2006). A sentence is to speech as what is to action? *Cortex, 42*, 507–514.

Baker, J. K. (1975). Stochastic modeling for automatic speech understanding. In R. Reddy (Ed.), *Speech recognition* (pp. 521–542). New York: Academic Press.

Bates, E., & Goodman, J. C. (1999). On the emergence of grammar from the lexicon. In B. MacWhinney (Ed.), *Emergence of language* (pp. 29–79). Hillsdale, NJ: Erlbaum.

Bates, E., Thal, D., Finlay, B. L., & Clancy, B. (2003). Early language development and its neural correlates. In I. Rapin & S. Segalowitz (Eds.), *Handbook of neuropsychology* (2nd ed., Vol. 8, pp. 525–592. Amsterdam: Elsevier.

Bienenstock, E. (1992). Suggestions for a neurobiological approach to syntax. In D. Andler, E. Bienenstock, & B. Laks (Eds.), *Proceedings of Second Interdisciplinary Workshop on Compositionality in Cognition and Neural Networks* (pp. 13–21). Abbaye de Royaumont, France.

Bishop, C. M. (2006). *Pattern recognition and machine learning.* Berlin: Springer.

Bloom, L. (1970). *Language development: form and function in emerging grammars.* Cambridge, MA: MIT Press.

Bock, J. K. (1986). Syntactic priming in language production. *Cognitive Psychology, 18*, 355–387.

Bock, K., Dell, G. S., Chang, F., & Onishi, K. H. (2007). Persistent structural priming from language comprehension to language production. *Cognition, 104*, 437–458.

Bod, R. (2009). From exemplar to grammar: A probabilistic analogy-based model of language learning. *Cognitive Science, 33*, 752–793.

Bos, J., Clark, S., Curran, J. R., Hockenmaier, J., & Steedman, M. (2004). Wide-coverage semantic representations from a CCG parser. In *Proceedings of the 20th International Conference on Computational Linguistics (COLING '04)*, Geneva, Switzerland. Association for Computational Linguistics, Morristown, NJ.

Breitenstein, C., Jansen, A., Deppe, M., Foerster, A-F., Sommer, J., Wolbers, T., & Knecht, S. (2005). Hippocampus activity differentiates good from poor learners of a novel lexicon. *NeuroImage, 25*, 958–968.

Brusk, J. (2008). Dialogue management for social game characters using statecharts. In *Proceedings of the 2008 International Conference on Advances in Computer Entertainment Technology* (pp. 219–222). Yokohama, Japan:

Buzsaki, G. (2005). Theta rhythm of navigation: Link between path integration and landmark navigation, episodic and semantic memory. *Hippocampus, 15*, 827–840.

Buzsáki, G., & K. Diba (2010). Oscillation-supported information processing and transfer in the hippocampus-entorhinal-neocortical interface. In C. von der Malsburg, W. A. Phillips, & W. Singer (Eds.), *Strungmann Forum Report: Vol. 5, Chapter 7. Dynamic coordination in the brain: From neurons to mind* (pp. xx–xx). Cambridge, MA: MIT Press.

Caporale, N., & Dan, Y. (2008). Spike timing-dependent plasticity: A Hebbian learning rule. *Annual Review of Neuroscience, 31*, 25–46.

Chater, N., Tenenbaum, J. B., & Yuille, A. (2006). Probabilistic models of cognition: Conceptual foundations. *Trends in Cognitive Sciences, 10*, 287–291.

Chipere, N. (2001). Native speaker variations in syntactic competence: Implications for first language teaching. *Language Awareness, 10*, 107–124.

Chomsky, N. (1957). *Syntactic structures.* The Hague, Netherlands: Mouton.

Chomsky, N. (2004). *The generative enterprise revisited.* Berlin: Mouton de Gruyter.

Christiansen, M. H., & Chater, N. (2008). Language as shaped by the brain. *Behavioral and Brain Sciences, 31*, 489–509.

Clark, A. (1998). Magic words: How language augments human computation. In P. Carruthers & J. Boucher (Eds.), *Language and thought: Interdisciplinary themes* (pp. 162–183). Cambridge, England: Cambridge University Press.

Cohen, M. X., & Frank, M. J., (2009). Neuro-computational models of basal ganglia function in learning, memory and choice. *Behavioural Brain Research, 199*, 141–156.

Conant, R. C., & Ashby, W. R. (1970). Every good regulator of a system must be a model of that system. *International Journal of Systems Science, 1*, 89–97.

Conway, C. M., & Pisoni, D. B. (2008). Neuro-cognitive basis of implicit learning of sequential structure and its relation to language processing. *Annals of the New York Academy of Science, 1145*, 113–131.

Craik, K. J. W. (1943). *The nature of explanation.* Cambridge, England: Cambridge University Press.

Crocker, M. W., Knoeferle, P., & Mayberry, M. R. (2010). Situated sentence processing: The coordinated interplay account and a neurobehavioral model. *Brain and Language, 112*, 189–201.

Da Cunha, C., Wietzikoski, E. C., Dombrowski, P., Bortolanza, M., Santos, L. M., Boschen, S. L. & Miyoshi, E. (2009). Learning processing in the basal ganglia: A mosaic of broken mirrors. *Behavioural Brain Research, 199*, 157–170.

Dabrowska, E., & Street, J. (2006). Individual differences in language attainment: Comprehension of passive sentences by native and non-native

English speakers. *Language Sciences, 28*, 604–615.

Dave, A. S., & Margoliash, D. (2000). Song replay during sleep and computational rules for sensorimotor vocal learning. *Science, 290*, 812–816.

Davidson, T. J., Kloosterman, F., & Wilson, M. A. (2009). Hippocampal replay of extended experience. *Neuron, 63*, 497–507.

Decety, J., & Sommerville, J. A. (2003). Shared representations between self and other: A social cognitive neuroscience view. *Trends in Cognitive Sciences, 7*, 527–533.

DeLong, G. R., & Heinz, E. R. (1997). The clinical syndrome of early-life bilateral hippocampal sclerosis. *Annals of Neurology, 42*, 11–17.

Deneve, S. (2008). Bayesian spiking neurons I: Inference. *Neural Computation, 20*, 91–117.

Dennett, D. C. (2003). *Freedom evolves.* New York: Viking.

Dewey, J. (1910). *How we think.* Lexington, MA: D. C. Heath.

Diessel, H. (2004). *Cambridge studies in linguistics: Vol. 105. The acquisition of complex sentences, .* Cambridge, England: Cambridge University Press.

Dominey, P. F. (2005). From sensorimotor sequence to grammatical construction: Evidence from simulation and neurophysiology. *Adaptive Behavior, 13*, 347–361.

Dominey, P. F., & Hoen, M. (2006). Structure mapping and semantic integration in a construction-based neurolinguistic model of sentence processing. *Cortex, 42*, 476–479.

Du Bois, J. W. (2003). Argument structure: Grammar in use. In J. W. Du Bois, L. E. Kumpf, & W. J. Ashby (Eds.), *Preferred argument structure. Grammar as architecture for function* (pp. 11–60). Amsterdam, Netherlands: John Benjamins.

Edelman, S. (2008a). *Computing the mind: How the mind really works.* New York: Oxford University Press.

Edelman, S. (2008b). On the nature of minds, or: Truth and consequences. *Journal of Experimental and Theoretical AI, 20*, 181–196.

Edelman, S., & Waterfall, H. R. (2007). Behavioral and computational aspects of language and its acquisition. *Physics of Life Reviews, 4*, 253–277.

Eichenbaum, H., Dudchenko, P., Wood, E., Shapiro, M., & Tanila, H. (1999). The hippocampus, memory and place cells: Is it spatial memory or memory space? *Neuron, 23*, 209–226.

Eisenstein, J., Clarke, J., Goldwasser, D., & Roth, D. (2009). Reading to learn: Constructing features from semantic abstracts. In *Proceedings of the Conference on Empirical Methods in Natural Language Processing (EMNLP-2009)*, Singapore.

Fortin, N. J., Agster, K. L., & Eichenbaum, H. B. (2002). Critical role of the hippocampus in memory for sequences of events. *Nature Neuroscience, 5*, 458–462.

Frank, M. C., Goodman, N. D., & Tenenbaum, J. B. (2009). Using speakers' referential intentions to model early cross-situational word learning. *Psychological Science, 20*, 578–585.

Goldsmith, J. A. (2007). Towards a new empiricism. In J. B. de Carvalho (Ed.), *Recherches linguistiques à Vincennes* (Vol. 36).

Goldstein, M. H., King, A. P., & West, M. J. (2003). Social interaction shapes babbling: Testing parallels between birdsong and speech. *Proceedings of the National Academy of Sciences USA, 100*, 8030–8035.

Goldstein, M. H., & Schwade, J. A. (2008). Social feedback to infants' babbling facilitates rapid phonological learning. *Psychological Science, 19*, 515–523.

Goldstein, M. H., Waterfall, H. R., Lotem, A., Halpern, J., Schwade, J., Onnis, L., & Edelman, S. (2010). General cognitive principles for learning structure in time and space. Trends in Cognitive Sciences, 14, 249–258.

Goodman, J. T. (2001). A bit of progress in language modeling. *Computer Speech and Language, 15*, 403–434.

Grünwald, P. (1994). A minimum description length approach to grammar inference. In G. Scheler, S. Wernter, & E. Riloff (Eds.), *Lecture Notes in AI: Vol. 1004, Connectionist, statistical and symbolic approaches to learning for natural language* (pp. 203–216). Berlin: Springer Verlag.

Hale, J. (2006). Uncertainty about the rest of the sentence. *Cognitive Science, 30*, 643–672.

Harel, D. (1988). On visual formalisms. *Communications of the ACM, 31*, 514–530.

Harel, D. (2007). Statecharts in the making: A personal account. In *HOPL III: Proceedings of the Third ACM SIGPLAN Conference on History of Programming Languages* (pp. 5-1–5-43). New York: ACM.

Harel, D., Kugler, H., & Pnueli, A. (2005). Synthesis revisited: Generating statechart models from scenario-based requirements. In *Lecture notes in computer science* (Vol. 3393, pp. 309–324). London: Springer-Verlag.

Harris, Z. S. (1946). From morpheme to utterance. *Language, 22*, 161–183.

Harris, Z. S. (1952). Discourse analysis. *Language, 28*, 1–30.

Harris, Z. S. (1991). *A theory of language and information*. Oxford, England: Clarendon Press.

Henson, R. N. A. (1999). Coding position in short-term memory. *International Journal of Psychology, 34*, 403–409.

Henson, R. N. A., & Burgess, N. (1997). Representations of serial order. In J. A. Bullinaria, D. W. Glasspool, & G. Houghton (Eds.), *4th Neural Computation and Psychology Workshop* (pp. 283–300). London: Springer.

Herrmann, E., Call, J., Lloreda, M., Hare, B., & Tomasello, M. (2007). Humans have evolved specialized skills of social cognition: The cultural intelligence hypothesis. *Science, 317*, 1360–1366.

Hinton, G. E. (2007). Learning multiple layers of representation. *Trends in Cognitive Sciences, 11*, 428–434.

Hockema, S. A., & Smith, L. B. (2009). Learning your language, outside-in and inside-out. *Linguistics, 47*, 453–479.

Hoff, E. (2006). How social contexts support and shape language development. *Developmental Review, 26*, 55–88.

Hoff-Ginsberg, E. (1986). Function and structure in maternal speech: Their relation to the child's development of syntax. *Developmental Psychology, 22*, 155–163.

Hoff-Ginsberg, E. (1990). Maternal speech and the child's development of syntax: A further look. *Journal of Child Language, 17*, 85–99.

Hosaka, R., Araki, O., & Ikeguchi, T. (2008). STDP provides the substrate for igniting synfire chains by spatiotemporal input patterns. *Neural Computation, 20*, 415–435.

Houghton, G., & Hartley, T. (1996). Parallels models of serial behaviour: Lashley revisited. *Psyche 2*(25).

Hume, D. (1748). *An enquiry concerning human understanding*. Retrieved June 30, 2010, from http://eserver.org/18th/hume-enquiry.html.

Ikegaya, Y., Aaron, G., Cossart, R., Aronov, D., Lampl, I., Ferster, D., & Yuste, R. (2004). Synfire chains and cortical songs: Temporal modules of cortical activity. *Science, 304*, 559–564.

Izhikevich, E. M. (2006). Polychronization: Computation with spikes. *Neural Computation, 18*, 245–282.

Izhikevich, E. M. (2007). Solving the distal reward problem through linkage of STDP and dopamine signaling. *Cerebral Cortex*, *17*, 2443–2452.

James, W. (1890). *The principles of psychology*. Retrieved June 30, 2010, from http://psychclassics.yorku.ca/James/Principles/.

Jelinek, F. (1990). Self-organized language modeling for speech recognition. In A. Waibel & K-F. Lee (Eds.), *Readings in speech recognition* (pp. 450–506). San Mateo, CA: Morgan Kaufmann. (Originally published as an IBM internal report, November 1982)

Jensen, O., & Lisman, J. E. (2005). Hippocampal sequence-encoding driven by a cortical multi-item working memory buffer. *Trends in Neurosciences*, *28*, 67–72.

Ji, D., & Wilson, M. A. (2007). Coordinated memory replay in the visual cortex and hippocampus during sleep. *Nature Neuroscience*, *10*, 100–107.

Jones, M. W., & Wilson, M. A. (2005). Theta rhythms coordinate hippocampal-prefrontal interactions in a spatial memory task. *PLoS Biology*, *3*, 2187–2199.

Jurafsky, D. (2003). Probabilistic modeling in psycholinguistics: Linguistic comprehension and production. In R. Bod, J. Hay, & S. Jannedy (Eds.), *Probabilistic linguistics* (pp. 39–96). Cambridge, MA: MIT Press.

Kemp, C., & Tenenbaum, J. B. (2008). The discovery of structural form. *Proceedings of the National Academy of Sciences USA*, *105*, 10687–10692.

Kersten, D., & Yuille, A. (2003). Bayesian models of object perception. *Current Opinion in Neurobiology*, *13*, 1–9.

Kuntay, A., & Slobin, D. (1996). Listening to a Turkish mother: Some puzzles for acquisition. In D. Slobin & J. Gerhardt (Eds.), *Social interaction, social context, and language: Essays in honor of Susan Ervin-Tripp* (pp. 265–286). Hillsdale, NJ: Erlbaum.

Lashley, K. S. (1951). The problem of serial order in behavior. In L. A. Jeffress (Ed.), *Cerebral mechanisms in behavior* (pp. 112–146). New York: Wiley.

Lee, A. K., & Wilson, M. A. (2002). Memory of sequential experience in the hippocampus during slow wave sleep. *Neuron*, *36*, 1183–1194.

Levinson, S. C. (2006). On the human interactional engine. In N. Enfield & S. C. Levinson (Eds.), *Roots of human sociality* (pp. 39–69). Oxford, England: Berg.

Levy, R. (2008). Expectation-based syntactic comprehension. *Cognition*, *106*, 1126–1177.

Levy, W. B. (1996). A sequence predicting CA3 is a flexible associator that learns and uses context to solve hippocampal-like tasks. *Hippocampus*, *6*, 579–590.

Levy, W. B., Hocking, A. B., & Wu, X. (2005). Interpreting hippocampal function as recoding and forecasting. *Neural Networks*, *18*, 1242–1264.

Lieberman, P. (2002). *Human language and our reptilian brain: The subcortical bases of speech, syntax, and thought*. Cambridge, MA: Harvard University Press.

MacWhinney, B. (2000). *The CHILDES Project: Tools for analyzing talk* (*Vols. 1–2*). Mahwah, NJ: Erlbaum.

Makinen, E., & Systa, T. (2002). Minimally adequate teacher synthesizes statechart diagrams. *Acta Informatica*, *38*, 235–259.

Marr, D., & Poggio, T. (1977). From understanding computation to understanding neural circuitry. *Neurosciences Research Progress Bulletin*, *15*, 470–488.

Merker, B. (2004). Cortex, countercurrent context, and dimensional integration of lifetime memory. *Cortex*, *40*, 559–576.

Merker, B., & Okanoya, K. (2007). The natural history of human language: Bridging the gaps without magic. In C. Lyon, C. L. Nehaniv, & A. Cangelosi (Eds.), *Emergence of communication and language* (pp. 403–420). London: Springer-Verlag.

Meyer, P., Mecklinger, A., Grunwald, T., Fell, J., Elger, C. E., & Friederici, A. D. (2005). Language processing within the human medial temporal lobe. *Hippocampus*, *15*, 451–459.

Müller, R-A., & Basho, S. (2004). Are nonlinguistic functions in "Broca's area" prerequisites for language acquisition? fMRI findings from an ontogenetic viewpoint. *Brain and Language*, *89*, 329–336.

Muller, R. U., & Kubie, J. L. (1989). The firing of hippocampal place cells predicts the future position of freely moving rats. *Journal of Neuroscience*, *9*, 4101–4110.

Nelson, K. (1977). Facilitating children's syntax acquisition. *Developmental Psychology*, *13*, 101–107.

Newmeyer, F. (1998). *Language form and language function*. Cambridge, MA: MIT Press.

Okanoya, K., & Merker, B. (2007). Neural substrates for string-context mutual segmentation: A path to human language. In C. Lyon, C. L. Nehaniv, & A. Cangelosi (Eds.), *Emergence of communication and language* (pp. 421–434). London: Springer-Verlag.

O'Keefe, J., & Dostrovsky, J. (1971). The hippocampus as a spatial map: Preliminary evidence from unit activity in the freely moving rat. *Brain Research, 34,* 171–175.

Onnis, L., Waterfall, H. R., & Edelman, S. (2008). Learn locally, act globally: Learning language from variation set cues. *Cognition, 109,* 423–430.

O'Reilly, R. C. (2006). Biologically based computational models of high-level cognition. *Science, 314,* 91–94.

O'Reilly, R. C., & Frank, M. J. (2006). Making working memory work: A computational model of learning in the frontal cortex and basal ganglia. *Neural Computation, 18,* 283–328.

O'Reilly, R. C., & Norman, K. A. (2002). Hippocampal and neocortical contributions to memory: Advances in the complementary learning systems framework. *Trends in Cognitive Sciences, 6,* 505–510.

Pereira, A. F., Smith, L. B., & Yu, C. (2008). Social coordination in toddler's word learning: Interacting systems of perception and action. *Connection Science, 20,* 73–89.

Pereira, F. (2000). Formal grammar and information theory: Together again? *Philosophical Transactions of the Royal Society of London, 358*(1769), 1239–1253.

Peyrache, A., Khamassi, M., Benchenane, K., Wiener, S. I., & Battaglia, F. P. (2009). Replay of rule-learning related neural patterns in the prefrontal cortex during sleep. *Nature Neuroscience, 12,* 919–929.

Pickering, M. J., & Garrod, S. (2004). Toward a mechanistic psychology of dialogue. *Behavioral and Brain Sciences, 27,* 169–225.

Pickering, M. J., & Garrod, S. (2007). Do people use language production to make predictions during comprehension? *Trends in Cognitive Sciences, 11,* 105–110.

Pietroski, P. M. (2003). The character of natural language semantics. In A. Barber (Ed.), *Epistemology of language* (pp. 217–256). Oxford, England: Oxford University Press.

Putnam, H. (1967). The "innateness hypothesis" and explanatory models in linguistics. *Synthese, 17,* 12–22.

Quine, W. V. (1961). The problem of meaning in linguistics. In S. Saporta (Ed.), *Psycholinguistics: a book of readings* (pp. 251–261). New York: Holt, Rinehart and Winston.

Quine, W. V. O. (1960). *Word and object.* Cambridge, MA: MIT Press.

Richardson, D. C., & Dale, R. A. (2005). Looking to understand: The coupling between speakers' and listeners' eye movements and its relationship to discourse comprehension. *Cognitive Science, 29,* 39–54.

Richardson, D. C., & Spivey, M. J. (2000). Representation, space and Hollywood Squares: Looking at things that aren't there anymore. *Cognition, 76,* 269–295.

Saffran, J. R., Aslin, R. N., & Newport, E. L. (1996). Statistical learning by 8-month-old infants. *Science, 274,* 1926–1928.

Schendan, H. E., Searl, M. M., Melrose, R. J., & Stern, C. E. (2003). An fMRI study of the role of the medial temporal lobe in implicit and explicit sequence learning. *Neuron, 37,* 1013–1025.

Seger, C. A. (2006). The basal ganglia in human learning. *The Neuroscientist, 12,* 285–290.

Seger, C. A., & Cincotta, C. M. (2006). Dynamics of frontal, striatal, and hippocampal systems in rule learning. *Cerebral Cortex, 16,* 1546–1555.

Shapiro, M. (2009). Memory networks: Answering the call of the hippocampus. *Current Biology, 19,* R329–R330.

Smith, L. B., & Gasser, M. (2005). The development of embodied cognition: Six lessons from babies. *Artificial Life, 11,* 13–30.

Smith, L. B., & Yu, C. (2008). Infants rapidly learn word-referent mappings via cross-situational statistics. *Cognition, 106,* 333–338.

Solan, Z., Horn, D., Ruppin, E., & Edelman, S. (2005). Unsupervised learning of natural languages. *Proceedings of the National Academy of Sciences USA, 102,* 11629–11634.

Stenning, K., & van Lambalgen, M. (2008). *Human reasoning and cognitive science.* Cambridge, MA: MIT Press.

Syal, S., & Finlay, B. L. (2009). Motivating language learning: Thinking outside the cortex. Developmental Science, in press.

Szmrecsanyi, B. (2005). Language users as creatures of habit: A corpus-based analysis of persistence in spoken English. *Corpus Linguistics and Linguistic Theory, 1,* 113–149.

Thal, D. J., & Flores, M. (2001). Development of sentence interpretation strategies by typically developing and late-talking toddlers. *Journal of Child Language, 28,* 173–193.

Thomaz, A. L., & Breazeal, C. (2008). Experiments in socially guided exploration: Lessons learned in building robots that learn with and without human teachers [Special Issue]. *Connection Science, 20,* 91–110.

Ullman, M. T. (2006). Is Broca's area part of a basal ganglia thalamocortical circuit? *Cortex*, *42*, 480–485.

Von Berger, E., Wulfeck, B., Bates, E., & Fink, N. (1996). Developmental changes in real-time sentence processing. *First Language*, *16*, 193–222.

Wallenstein, G. V., Eichenbaum, H., & Hasselmo, M. E. (1998). The hippocampus as an associator of discontiguous events. *Trends in Neurosciences*, *21*, 317–323.

Waterfall, H. R. (2006). *A little change is a good thing: Feature theory, language acquisition and variation sets*. Unpublished Ph.D. dissertation. University of Chicago.

Waterfall, H. R., & Edelman, S. (2009). The neglected universals: Learnability constraints and discourse cues. *Behavioral and Brain Sciences*, *32*, 471–472.

Waterfall, H. R., Sandbank, B., Onnis, L., & Edelman, S. (2010). An empirical generative framework for computational modeling of language acquisition. *Journal of Child Language*, *37*, 671–703.

Weber, B., Wellmer, J., Reuber, M., Mormann, F., Weis, S., Urbach, H., Ruhlmann, J., Elger, C. E., & Fernandez, G. (2006). Left hippocampal pathology is associated with atypical language lateralization in patients with focal epilepsy. *Brain*, *129*, 346–351.

Werker, J. F., & Yeung, H. H. (2005). Infant speech perception bootstraps word learning. *Trends in Cognitive Sciences*, *9*, 519–527.

Wittgenstein, L. (1958). *Philosophical investigations* (G. E. M. Anscombe, Trans., 3rd ed.). Englewood Cliffs, NJ: Prentice Hall.

Yu, C., & Ballard, D. (2007). A unified model of word learning: Integrating statistical and social cues. *Neurocomputing*, *70*, 2149–2165.

CHAPTER 15
A Look around at What Lies Ahead: Prediction and Predictability in Language Processing

Marta Kutas, Katherine A. DeLong, and Nathaniel J. Smith

Traditionally, prediction has been considered an inefficient and cognitively expensive processing mechanism in the domain of language comprehension, where there are many possible ways for relaying a single thought, meaning or desire and the chances of mispredicting are accordingly high. Predictive linguistic processing, however, does not seem untenable given its similarity to other neural processing domains that are contextually grounded and appear to implement knowledge- and experience-based mental representations anticipatorily. Here, we examine linguistic prediction from multiple perspectives, ranging from theoretical models that analyze predictability at the level of ambiguity resolution, to experimental evidence primarily from event-related brain potentials (ERPs) that supports a "strong" model of prediction in which items are not just incrementally integrated, but are wholly or featurally pre-activated via accruing mental sentential representations. We also explore possible consequences of a neural language parser (aka, brain) that may be prone to mispredicting, and what electrophysiological evidence for such processing may look like. We conclude by arguing for the importance of investigating such linguistic effects as yet another example of a neural system in which probability estimation is inherent, with a proposal to move beyond the debate of *whether* there is linguistic prediction, toward focusing research efforts on *how* pre-activation may occur and *what* is pre-activated.

POTENTIAL BENEFITS OF LINGUISTIC PREDICTION

Within a variety of neural domains, perhaps including some described in other chapters of this volume, the understanding of how predictive processing benefits a system may be relatively straightforward. With the study of language processing, however, such benefits could be various and perhaps not immediately clear. Linguistic comprehension requires processing a noisy sensory input to recognize complex structures (e.g., phonemes, syllables, words, syntax) and integrating these structures with physical and social contexts, with general/world knowledge, and with each other, to construct meaning. Amazingly, this whole process occurs over mere hundreds of milliseconds. As such, there are a number of ways that linguistic comprehension could be facilitated by predicting upcoming material.

Given the time constraints under which comprehension operates, one clear benefit of being able to predict upcoming material is that it may allow a listener or reader to produce an overt response more quickly, without waiting for the material itself to become available. For instance, Marslen-Wilson (1973) argued that experimental participants performing verbal shadowing (i.e., listening to a stream of speech and simultaneously repeating it aloud) were—given the form of the shadowers' speech errors in which they supplied structurally appropriate, semantically and syntactically congruent continuations—using predictions about upcoming speech to achieve faster response latencies. Similarly, Sacks, Schegloff, and Jefferson (1974) observed that during ordinary dialogue, one interlocutor commonly begins to talk precisely at the moment that the previous speaker finishes, and they argued that listeners must be predicting the timing of such "transition-relevance places" to properly time their own responses.

Another potential benefit to linguistic prediction relates to a challenge faced by the linguistic processor: The appropriate interpretation of the current input often depends on future input. Consider the classic "garden-path" sentence, "*The horse raced past the barn fell*" (Bever, 1970). When the processor has encountered only part of this sentence—"*The horse raced past…*"—then it is ambiguous whether *raced* is the sentence's main verb (referring to what the horse did), or the beginning of a relative clause (describing the horse). In principle, the language processor should therefore wait until the end of the sentence to interpret *raced*. Only when it reaches *fell* would it discover that the relative clause reading ("*The horse, (that was) raced past the barn, fell*") is correct, but by this point, most people have already committed to a main verb reading and thus are at least briefly stymied. This early commitment can be seen as a prediction about the form of the remainder of the sentence, and the confusion the result of an inaccurate prediction. But garden-path sentences are relatively rare in real life, and when this early prediction is accurate, it should allow substantial benefits in speed of processing, reduced memory load, and so forth. In this sense, any language processor that proceeds incrementally, without waiting for the end of each utterance before beginning its work, could be seen as inherently predictive. However, this does not mean that such a processor is forming explicit expectations about upcoming material. Many classic models of such effects instead rely on various bottom-up heuristics that—as a kind of happy coincidence, from the processor's point of view—often result in choices that later turn out to have been correct (e.g., Frazier & Fodor, 1978).

The difficulties caused by garden-path sentences can also be seen as a special case of a more general problem in language comprehension: the problem of ambiguity. In addition to the temporary ambiguity created by temporal sequencing, there is ambiguity created by (at least) sensory noise (*letter* and *ladder* may be acoustically indistinguishable in a noisy room, or compare "*wreck a nice*" and *recognize*), lexical items with multiple senses (*palms*, the tree versus the body part), and syntactic ambiguity ("*I saw the girl in the park with the telescope*"—who had the telescope?). Just as comprehenders might resolve temporary ambiguities by predicting upcoming input, they may resolve these more durable ambiguities by "predicting" the speaker's intent. While such cases are, on a surface level, quite different from prediction as it is usually understood, these two kinds of ambiguity resolution are unified in probabilistic models of language comprehension, where both reduce to the problem of picking the most likely interpretation (Jurafsky, 1996).

A final possible role for prediction in language is that, by forming explicit predictions of upcoming material, the parser may not only ease the processing of current material (as described earlier), but get a head start on future material, leading to increased efficiency if this anticipatory processing turns out to be accurate (though it undoubtedly will not always be). Broadly construed, then, this "strongly" predictive view of language comprehension posits that comprehenders utilize a variety of sources of constraint as they become available to pre-activate upcoming items and/or their features, with aspects of linguistic input being processed both incrementally and in parallel. This type of presumably rapid, online pre-activation that most likely does not reach the level of consciousness has (until recently) been difficult to tap into experimentally, and thus, it has historically also been the most controversial.

HISTORICAL OPPOSITION TO PREDICTIVE LANGUAGE PROCESSING

Despite general considerations about biological continuity, informal intuitions stemming from our experiences "taking the words out of" a speaker's mouth, and evidence from specialized tasks or instances (such as the shadowing proce-dure and garden-path sentences described earlier), prediction has played a relatively minor role in theories of language processing. The idea that individuals might predict linguistic features or content has not been part of the generative grammar tradition. Indeed, linguists and psy-cholinguists alike (e.g., Jackendoff, 2002; Morris, 2006) have argued that with infinite options available as each new word of an unfolding sen-tence is encountered, predicting what comes next is not just improbable but nonviable as a strategy, except perhaps on the rare occasions when contextual constraint is unusually high (Stanovich & West, 1979).

Results from controlled experiments seem to support this proposal: When participants are asked to continue a phrase or complete a sen-tence, their responses routinely converge on the same word when contextual constraint is strong but show greater variance under weak constraints (e.g., Bloom & Fischler, 1980; Schwanenflugel, 1986). In off-line language tasks, then, it is widely acknowledged that with *sufficient time* individu-als do use sentential context to select the most probable linguistic completions. Most language, however, is not so highly constrained. In either case, there is a question as to whether this more deliberate, conscious (post-lexical) offline strat-egy translates to the rapid, less conscious processing that seems to characterize real-time language comprehension. Or is the real-time use of contextual constraint of a qualitatively differ-ent nature? Indeed, a major outstanding question in the sentence processing literature has been whether information about particular words or their features gets pre-activated during on-line sentence processing as a result of top-down con-textual processing, or whether word processing is stimulus driven (bottom up), triggered by the input, that is, initiated only *after* the physical stimulus has been received. Perhaps surprisingly to some, there is no clear consensus. In fact, most theories of sentence processing have not addressed this issue directly, even though some stance about linguistic prediction is often implicit.

Why the paucity of research on this question? As already mentioned, natural language is not

considered to be very constraining, certainly not constraining enough for a predictive system to be accurate a majority of the time. In principle, such errors should result in processing costs, but such costs have rarely been evidenced (Gough, Alford, & Holley-Wilcox, 1981). Even those who grant some word-level prediction from senten-tial context argue that word recognition can only benefit from context under special circumstances such as when the target input is degraded, when targets are temporally offset with respect to the context (allowing time for prediction), or when readers are unskilled, and thus slow (Mitchell, 1982). Furthermore, the ecological validity of the paradigms from which much of the existing evi-dence for prediction comes has been questioned. Rayner, Ashby, Pollatsek, and Reichle (2004), for example, point to the typically nonnaturalistic stimulus presentation rates (e.g., artificial timing of sentences or context-target word delays), which they believe provide readers with ample time to form conscious predictions, and thus bear little resemblance to natural language. We suggest that a more insidious (and perhaps unconscious) component to anti-prediction biases in language research may have to do with the long history of modular views of language processing (e.g., Fodor, 1983; Forster, 1979) and their inherently bottom-up emphasis. On the view that language comprehension is a context-invariant, data-driven process, with information from one neural domain unlikely to preemp-tively influence processing in another, antici-pation of upcoming input based on contextual cues would seem untenable. In sum, some com-bination of these reasons, among others, has likely contributed to the general lack of explora-tion of anticipatory comprehension in language historically.

Fortunately, the tides are changing, and in the following sections we review evidence demon-strating that both incremental processing and estimation of linguistic probabilities are perva-sive. Building on this work, we then present recent results which argue that the language pro-cessor implements even the "strong form" of prediction, regularly pre-activating material in an anticipatory fashion. In this discussion, we pro-vide some evidence for how such anticipatory processing may be instantiated in the brain as well as examine potential consequences of predicting incorrectly.

FROM BUFFERING TO INCREMENTALITY

Early models of sentence processing included some form of memory buffer by which sentential elements were temporarily stored for later integration at phrasal, clausal, or sentence boundaries (Abney, 1989; Carroll & Bever, 1978; Daneman & Carpenter, 1983; Just & Carpenter, 1980; Kintsch & van Dijk, 1978; Mitchell & Green, 1978; Pritchett, 1991). Eventually, such delayed processing models became difficult to reconcile with accumulating evidence for context updating on a word-by-word basis. Notions of buffering gradually gave way to the more widely held view that words are incorporated successively into the sentential context as they are received and identified, with gradual accretion of meaning in the mind of the comprehender—a more *incremental* view (e.g., Altmann & Steedman, 1988; Boland, Tanenhaus, Garnsey, & Carlson, 1995; Eberhard, Spivey-Knowlton, Sedivy, & Tanenhaus, 1995; Kutas & Hillyard, 1983; Marslen-Wilson, 1975; Marslen-Wilson & Tyler, 1980; Pickering, 1994; Steedman, 1989; Tanenhaus, Spivey-Knowlton, Eberhard, & Sedivy, 1995; Traxler, Bybee, & Pickering, 1997; Tyler & Marslen-Wilson, 1977).

The view that language comprehension is largely incremental is rooted in evidence from a wide variety of studies with different methodologies, including off-line and on-line techniques. For instance, Boland et al. (1995) asked readers to indicate via a button press when a sentence stopped making sense. Presented with identically structured "*wh*"-questions such as "*Which military base did Hank deliver the machine guns to last week?*" vs. "*Which preschool did Hank deliver the machine guns to last week?*" participants pushed the button at *machine guns* in the *preschool* version but not in the *military base* version. These results indicate that the thematic role of the questioned element (*military base/preschool*), displaced from its location in a declarative sentence (e.g., *Hank delivered the machine guns to which military base/preschool*), is assigned as soon as the verb (*deliver*) is encountered, rather

than buffered for interpretation at sentence end; in other words, it is processed incrementally. Using a different behavioral method, Marslen-Wilson (1975) showed that so-called fast shadowers—individuals that repeated back recorded speech with very little delay (sometimes as short as 250 ms)—corrected pronunciation errors in the recorded speech signal, indicating that they were processing the shadowed text at a semantic level, *as* it was received.

Though clear evidence for incrementality has emerged from such behavioral work, the strongest evidence to date comes from investigations of real-time language processing using techniques like eye-tracking and event-related brain potentials (ERPs) that *(a)* do not require additional tasks (e.g., button presses or spoken responses) other than listening or reading, and *(b)* are able to continuously track sentence processing with high temporal resolution throughout the course of a sentence, thereby making it easier to isolate the precise processing stage implicated. In eye-tracking studies, for instance, the time-locked characteristics of eye movements provide information about the processes that underlie spoken language comprehension. In the visual world paradigm, for example, individuals' eye movements are monitored as they look at a visual scene while simultaneously listening to a sentence or set of instructions that refers to objects in that scene (Tanenhaus et al., 1995). Many such studies have found that participants make saccadic eye movements to depicted objects without delay upon hearing the relevant input (often prior to the referent word itself), supporting models of word-by-word integration (e.g., Allopenna, Magnuson, & Tanenhaus, 1998; Sedivy, Tanenhaus, Chambers, & Carlson, 1999; Spivey, Tanenhaus, Eberhard, & Sedivy, 2002).

Similarly, ERPs—scalp recordings of the synaptic potentials generated primarily by synchronously firing multiple pyramidal cells in the neocortex—also afford a continuous but time-stamped look at ongoing neural activity during written and spoken language processing. Kutas and Hillyard (1980), for example, showed that a semantically anomalous word within a certain context elicits an enhanced ERP component known as the N400 at the point at which it is encountered—indeed, within 200 ms of the word's onset—relative to a semantically congruent continuation in the same context. The N400, as a neural response to any potentially meaningful item, has sometimes been considered to index semantic fit of an item in a particular context, and as such, provides additional evidence for context updating before the end of an utterance. Thus, these and other studies (e.g., van Berkum, Brown, & Hagoort, 1999; van Berkum, Koornneef, Otten, & Nieuwland, 2007; van Berkum, Zwitserlood, Hagoort, & Brown, 2003; Van Petten & Kutas, 1990) indicate that sentence processing is incremental.

ANTICIPATORY LANGUAGE PROCESSING

In the past decade or so, however, there has been a wave of both empirical and modeling work suggesting that language processing may not *just* be incremental; instead, evidence from various sources has supported the view that sentential constraint begins to exert its influence *before* words have been uniquely identified. We might even consider this somewhat of a "revival," since a few early language processing models argued specifically for more anticipatory processing in which available contextual factors are used to activate words in advance of receiving them (McClelland & Elman, 1986; McClelland & Rumelhart, 1981). More recent investigations of anticipatory processing have been spurred, in part, by interest in questions of how generalized prediction might be, what it might be used for, what information is available to predictive processing, and what aspects of upcoming input are being predicted.

Eye-tracking methods, for instance, have successfully employed the visual world paradigm to detect preferential looks to visual targets before complete auditory information is available. As an example, Eberhard et al. (1995) found that when participants were given an instruction "*Pick up the candle*," they not only immediately initiated a saccade to an actual candle in front of them, but did so before the second syllable of *candle* had been fully articulated. Furthermore, this predictive process was sensitive to visual

context; when the same instruction was given to participants whose work area contained both a candle and candy, so that the first syllable *can-* was no longer sufficient to identify the reference, the average saccade initiation occurred only after the disambiguating second syllable was spoken.

Other visual world studies have demonstrated looks to candidate entities that entirely preceded the relevant input (e.g., Altmann & Kamide, 1999; 2007; Kamide, 2008; Kamide, Scheepers & Altmann, 2003; Kamide, Scheepers, Altmann, & Crocker, 2002; Knoeferle, Crocker, Scheepers, & Pickering, 2005; Sussman & Sedivy, 2003). For instance, upon hearing a sentence fragment such as "*The girl will ride the…*" while viewing a scene depicting a man, a girl, a motorcycle, and a carousel, comprehenders looked toward the depiction of the carousel during the verb *ride*; conversely, upon hearing "*The man will ride the…*," they looked toward the motorcycle during the verb *ride* (Kamide, Altmann, & Haywood, 2003). Based on such research, we can conclude that the language parser is capable of combining visual context with noun/verb semantics to quickly narrow the possibilities for upcoming input.

Studies like these demonstrate one approach to examining prediction, although it might be argued that this is prediction in a very restricted sense (where candidates for upcoming input are limited, visually present, and highly constrained). We therefore turn our attention to studies using written stimuli, which—while forgoing the visual world paradigm's naturalistic environment— allow the examination of a broad range of linguistic structures beyond concrete referential phrases.

EFFECTS OF PREDICTABILITY

In our discussion so far, we have been careful to use the word *prediction* only for cases in which upcoming, unseen input in some way alters current processing. There is also, however, a substantial literature on the effects of "predictability" on linguistic processing. The basic intuition here is that some words could be predicted in advance from context; and even if the brain does not make this predict*ion* in advance, once the word is encountered it might still be processed differently depending on its predict*ability*—how well it *could* have been predicted from context. Obviously, if the brain does make an explicit prediction in advance, then that may well alter its processing in a way that later creates predictability effects; but other mechanisms that do not involve prediction per se are also possible, and several have been proposed. In this section we briefly review theoretical and experimental evidence for predictability effects, as well as the potential mechanisms underlying them.

In the context of language, the most compelling theoretical reason for the brain to compute predictabilities is, as mentioned earlier, for use in disambiguation. Ambiguities of various sorts are pervasive in language, and resolving them requires combining evidence from semantic, syntactic, and other sources; experiments show that comprehenders are able to quickly bring all of these to bear (Hanna & Tanenhaus, 2004; MacDonald, 1993; MacDonald, Pearlmutter, & Seidenberg, 1994; McRae, Spivey-Knowlton, & Tanenhaus, 1998; Spivey et al., 2002; Tanenhaus et al., 1995; Trueswell, Tanenhaus, & Garnsey, 1994). This requires a common mechanism for evidence combination across different parts of the linguistic processing system, and probability theory (with Bayes' rule) is a natural, even optimal, fit (Jurafsky, 1996). In general, the system must presumably be flexible about what probabilities it can compute; picking the most likely sense of a word has different requirements from, for instance, picking the most likely parse of a sentence. For our discussion of prediction, the most relevant computation would be of the probabilities of current or upcoming individual words. But are these among the probabilities that the brain computes? Arguably, yes. Work on automatic speech recognition has shown that such single-word probabilities are exactly what are needed to accurately decode the noisy (thus ambiguous) acoustic speech signal.

Furthermore, experimental evidence shows that the processor is sensitive to such single-word probabilities. In ERP studies, the N400 component to semantically congruous words shows a graded sensitivity to those words' predictability

in context (Kutas & Hillyard, 1984), while the P600 component responds differentially to high- versus low-likelihood syntactic forms (even when those forms are all acceptable; Hsu, 2009; Kaan, Harris, Gibson, & Holcomb, 2000; Osterhout, Holcomb, & Swinney, 1994), and even earlier effects of context on lexical access may be present as well (Sereno, Brewer, & O'Donnell, 2003). Such effects could potentially be glimpses of different aspects of the system described earlier at work. We return to the question of whether the N400's sensitivity to predict*ability* is truly predict*ive* in a later section.

Reading time studies are another source of evidence that the brain is sensitive to predictability. Less predictable words—those with lower probability given context—are read more slowly (Ehrlich & Rayner, 1981). This effect is sensitive to both semantic (Bicknell, Elman, Hare, McRae, & Kutas, 2008; Duffy, Henderson, & Morris, 1989; Garnsey, Pearlmutter, Myers, & Lotocky, 1997; Hare, McRae, & Elman, 2003; Morris, 1994) and syntactic (Levy, 2008; Staub & Clifton, 2006; Trueswell, Tanenhaus, & Kello, 1993) manipulations of predictability, and its underlying cause is not yet clear. For instance, Norris (2006) suggests that the reading time effect may arise in the sensory system, as a side effect of decoding noisy visual input. The idea is that to recognize words that have less top-down support (relative to their visual competitors), the brain must acquire more bottom-up sensory evidence before it can reach an acceptable level of certainty that the word has been correctly identified, and gathering more evidence requires looking longer. Levy (2008), on the other hand, proposes that the reading time effect arises because as each word is processed, each potential whole-sentence interpretation has some shift in likelihood, becoming more or less supported by the available data. If there is a cost to shifting the internal representation of these likelihoods, as measured in reading time, then words which cause a greater total likelihood shift will take longer to read. Finally, he shows mathematically that the size of this shift (measured in KL divergence; Kullback & Leibler, 1951) is determined by the word's predictability. These two theories are nonpredictive accounts of predictability effects: All of the affected processing takes place after the word itself is seen.

Another approach is to model the linguistic processor as maintaining a sorted, limited size list of candidate whole-sentence parses; then, increased reading time may occur either when it turns out that the appropriate parse was pruned from the list for having too low probability (Jurafsky, 1996; Narayanan & Jurafsky, 1998), or when new evidence turns a less preferred parse into the most likely possibility, triggering a shift in attention (Crocker & Brants, 2000; Narayanan & Jurafsky, 2002). Such models are weakly predictive in the sense that they explicitly marginalize over potential continuations to determine which parses are most likely and which can be pruned to reduce memory load. However, pruning can only explain effects in somewhat special cases (i.e., garden-path sentences), while attention shifts only occur at some relatively special points in a sentence.

Smith and Levy (2008), however, demonstrate predictability effects on reading time at arbitrary points in naturalistic text, and they argue that sensory factors (as per Norris) cannot explain all variations in processing time (Rayner, Liversedge, White, & Vergilino-Perez, 2003). They propose instead a motor control–inspired model of "optimal preparation," in which the processor does a graded amount of anticipatory processing for each potential continuation; the actual amount of processing is determined as a trade-off between the resources spent on this anticipatory processing (preparing to process a word quickly is costly) versus the increased processing efficiency achieved if this continuation is actually encountered (sometimes preparation is worth it). Such a model naturally expends more effort on preparing for those continuations which are more likely to be encountered, thus explaining the predictability effect on the subsequent reading time of the continuation. By our classifications, this is a strongly predictive model, but one with little direct evidence to support it—we cannot observe this postulated anticipatory processing directly via behavioral measures. We therefore turn to discussion of recent electrophysiological work that bears on this question.

EVENT-RELATED POTENTIAL EVIDENCE FOR A "STRONG" FORM OF PREDICTION

As should be evident from the previous sections, linguistic prediction and predictability can be identified in a variety of ways. We will now present evidence for the "strong" form of prediction—that is, experimental evidence showing that specific linguistic items or their features are pre-activated at some time point prior to encountering the confirmatory bottom-up input. Such evidence turns out to be somewhat tricky to obtain, due to the challenge of identifying processing related to an item that has not yet occurred. In particular, one difficulty centers on the *prediction/integration* debate—in other words, the challenge of distinguishing facilitation effects at a target word as being due to that word being predicted versus it being simply easier to integrate upon receipt. A case in point is the N400 ERP component. N400 amplitude is sensitive to a variety of factors—including word frequency, repetition, concreteness, and orthographic neighborhood size, among others—and is especially large to nouns that do not semantically fit with their preceding context (e.g., the word *dog* in "*I take my coffee with cream and dog*"; Kutas & Hillyard, 1980). N400s are also evident in responses to all but the most highly expected of nouns, even when they do fit with a prior sentence context. However, despite the sensitivity of the N400 to offline semantic expectancy, it is impossible to determine whether variation in N400 amplitude to the eliciting word during online sentence processing means that readers are using context to generate expectancies for that upcoming item (*prediction* view) or whether they are forced by the word itself to devote more or fewer resources to integrating the word into the existing sentence representation (*integration* view). Clearly, an argument for information getting pre-activated would be strengthened if it could be demonstrated that predictions were being formulated prior to target words.

In one of the earlier ERP studies to argue for predictive language comprehension, Federmeier and Kutas (1999a) found that in highly constraining contexts (e.g., "*He caught the pass and scored another touchdown. There was nothing he enjoyed more than a good game of…*"), unexpected and implausible target nouns (e.g., *baseball*) that were categorically related to the contextually expected target endings (e.g., *football*) were processed more similarly at a semantic level (as reflected in N400 amplitudes) to the expected endings than they were to categorically unrelated unexpected nouns (e.g., *monopoly*). *Baseball* and *monopoly* are equally implausible endings in this context, and yet the brain response to these two endings in the N400 region (200–500 ms post-target onset) is different. Critically, this facilitation decreases as sentential constraint becomes weaker even as the plausibility of these categorically related anomalies increases, for example, "*Eleanor wanted to fix her visitor some coffee. Then she realized she did not have a clean cup/bowl/fork.*" Why might the within category violation (*baseball*) behave like a more plausible ending, eliciting a brain response closer to the expected ending? Federmeier and Kutas argue that it is because the language processing system is predicting in the strong sense; in other words, pre-activating perceptual-conceptual features of the expected ending, which is more likely to share these features with the within category violation (*baseball*) than the between category one (*monopoly*). Thus, while norming shows that these words are equally incongruous with the linguistic context, *baseball* is more congruous with the brain's predictions. Importantly, similar results obtain whether the sentences were read one word at a time at relatively slow rates or presented as natural speech (Federmeier, McLennan, De Ochoa, & Kutas, 2002).

Van Petten, Coulson, Plante, Rubin, and Parks (1999) also found N400-based evidence for prediction during naturalistic speech processing in a study designed to determine whether semantic integration processes began before or only after complete identification of a spoken word. To that end, participants listened to sentences (e.g., "*It was a pleasant surprise to find that the car repair bill was only seventeen…*") that were completed by a highly constrained, expected, congruous completion (*dollars*), a semantically incongruous word that began with the same initial sound (phonemic similarity) as the expected congruous completion (*dolphins*), and a semantically

incongruous word (*scholars*) that ended with the same final sound and thus rhymed with the expected congruous completion. The critical contrast is between the N400s elicited by the two incongruous endings, which are equally nonsensical in the sentence context. Although equivalent in amplitude, the N400s differed in their latencies, with the N400 to the incongruous rhyming endings (*scholars*) diverging much earlier from the relative positivity to the congruous ending (*dollars*) than the incongruous ending with an overlapping initial sound (*dolphins*). Moreover, the effect of context preceded a word's isolation point—that is, before sufficient acoustic information had accrued to determine the word's identity (by about 200 ms). This demonstrates that not only do listeners use context to disambiguate partial auditory input—confirming the visual world results described earlier—but, in addition, their N400 response to incongruity begins when they detect the deviation from the expected word, potentially before the incongruous word could be identified.

Results from these studies are difficult to reconcile with a purely integrative model of comprehension, implicating some form of neural pre-activation instead. In all these cases, however, the observed ERP effects were evident at the target words of interest, leaving them at least superficially open to the "oh, it's just integration" criticism. Perhaps more compelling evidence of pre-activation comes from designs in which the electrophysiological sign of prediction precedes the target word that was presumably being predicted. For instance, work by Wicha and colleagues (Wicha, Bates, Moreno, & Kutas, 2003; Wicha, Moreno, & Kutas, 2003; Wicha, Moreno, & Kutas, 2004) investigated linguistic expectation in a series of studies with Spanish sentences by focusing on ERPs to gender-marked articles preceding target nouns of particular gender classes. In separate experiments, native Spanish speakers either listened to or read moderately to highly constraining sentences that contained a gender-marked article followed by either a written word or an embedded line drawing. The word or line drawing target was either the expected (highly probable) continuation or a semantically incongruent continuation of the same gender class as the expected continuation. In half of the sentences, the gender of the article mismatched the gender of the following noun or picture, although participants were not explicitly informed about this. A set of sample Spanish stimuli with their English glosses follows:

> *Caperucita Roja llevaba la comida para su abuela en…(una/un) canasta/corona …*
> Little Red Riding Hood carried the food for her grandmother in a…basket/crown …
>
> (a) …*una*[feminine] *CANASTA*[feminine] … (gender match/semantically congruous)
> (b) …*una*[feminine] *CORONA*[feminine] … (gender match/semantically incongruous)
> (c) …*un*[masculine] *CANASTA*[feminine] … (gender mismatch/semantically congruous)
> (d) …*un*[masculine] *CORONA*[feminine] … (gender mismatch/semantically incongruous)

It is important to note that in the experimental sentences there was always a reasonable word continuation regardless of the grammatical gender of the (manipulated) article; in this case, *una CANASTA*(feminine)/BASKET vs. *un COSTAL*(masculine)/SACK. The interpretation of any ERP effect in response to the article hinges on the fact that there was nothing semantically or syntactically wrong with an article of either gender. Accordingly, if any article ERP effect was obtained, it must have reflected the language system's discord at receiving an article of one gender when it was expecting a noun (and accompanying article) of the other gender. The pattern of ERPs for both word and picture targets clearly confirmed this hypothesis, even if the specifics of the ERP effects for words and pictures differed. The language processing system had expectations, and noncompliance with those was reflected in a differential ERP pattern for the articles of one gender versus the other.

van Berkum, Brown, Zwitserlood, Kooijman, and Hagoort (2005) sought evidence of prediction for spoken words in Dutch with similar logic by manipulating gender marking (neuter or common) on prenominal adjectives—a feature controlled by the gender of the upcoming noun. Participants heard sentences with moderately predictable noun continuations, such as "*The burglar had no trouble at all locating the secret family safe. Of course, it was situated behind a*

big[noun-appropriate gender marking] but rather unobtrusive painting[neuter]/*bookcase*[common]." The gender-marked inflectional suffixes on the target adjectives were either congruent with the gender of the more expected target noun or were not, being instead of the opposite gender category and then followed by a less expected but still semantically congruent noun. In contrast to the Wicha studies, they did not include any gender mismatches between adjectives and their upcoming nouns. Within high constraint contexts, there was a differential ERP effect for adjectives with versus without the expected gender, which emerged at the point the predicted and unpredicted inflectional suffixes of the adjectives first diverged from each other (e.g., the Dutch word for "big" marked with neuter gender is *groot* vs. with common gender *grote*; the ERP effect began when their pronunciations begin to diverge). They concluded that the ERP effect at the gender-marked adjectives was primarily a syntactic one, and as this study and other work by their group (e.g., Otten, Nieuwland, & Van Berkum, 2007; Otten & van Berkum, 2008, 2009) attest, comprehenders do indeed use sentence context to form predictions.

DeLong, Urbach, and Kutas (2005) employed a logically similar experimental design in English to test for prediction of yet another feature of language. Their design took advantage of a phonological feature of the English language in which different indefinite articles, *a* and *an*, are used depending on the initial phoneme of the immediately following word. Devoid of gender, case marking, and specific semantic content, English indefinite articles offer a means for exploring linguistic prediction at the level of phonological word forms. Participants read sentences that ranged in constraint and were continued by a range of more or less expected indefinite article/noun pairings; for example, "*The day was breezy so the boy went outside to fly…a kite/an airplane…in the park*" in which *a kite* is highly expected and *an airplane*, although plausible, is less so. The primary focus, as in the Wicha et al. and van Berkum et al. studies, was not on the nouns but on the prenominal words—in this case, the articles. As expected based on the literature, there was a significant inverse correlation between N400 amplitudes in the ERPs to the target nouns (*kite/airplane*) and their offline cloze probabilities (with cloze defined as the percentage of respondents supplying a particular continuation for a context in an offline norming task; Taylor, 1953): the higher a word's cloze probability, the smaller its N400 amplitude. This correlation, however, is equally consistent with theoretical accounts based on integration difficulty or prediction. The same pattern of reliable inverse correlations in the N400 region of the ERP to the articles, however, is less theoretically accommodating. Although the article correlations were slightly lower (maximal *r*-values in high –.60's to low –.70's at posterior electrode sites), they could only be explained by a predictive account. Otherwise, would the brain respond differentially to *a* versus *an*? Certainly, they mean the same thing, and they are in principle equally easy to integrate with respect to the ongoing context. What they differ in is their phonological form and critically what that says about the initial sound of the upcoming noun. We maintain that these correlations demonstrate that readers were anticipating the most likely noun given the prior context (e.g., *kite*), and encountering the phonologically wrong article (*an*) for that noun affected ongoing sentence processing.

Similar to the nouns, the maximum N400 article-cloze correlations were not randomly distributed, but rather were clustered over the posterior regions of the head where N400 effects are typically the largest. So over these scalp sites, a large percentage of the variance of brain activity (N400 amplitude) for the indefinite articles was accounted for by the average probability that individuals would continue the sentence context with that article. In short, these data are clear evidence of prediction in language at a phonological level. These results indicate that people do use sentence context to form graded predications for specific upcoming words, and not just in highly constraining contexts. Even in moderately constraining sentence contexts at least one and perhaps multiple items seem to be pre-activated albeit to varying degrees.

Studies of ERPs in written and spoken language, then, have offered up relatively strong evidence for linguistic prediction at featural and lexical levels. Arguably even more striking findings about linguistic prediction have come from studies in which ERPs are recorded in combination with the visual hemifield technique. In the visual hemifield technique, target stimuli are presented a few degrees to the right or left of subject's fixation to expose only the contralateral hemisphere to that stimulus for the first approximately 10 ms (Banich, 2003). This mode of presentation provides the receiving hemisphere a brief head start that remarkably results in temporally extended lateralized processing differences in the two hemispheres, which by inference has been taken to reflect the different ways in which the two hemispheres deal with various linguistic factors. In studies of this type, Federmeier and colleagues (e.g., Federmeier, 2007; Federmeier & Kutas, 1999b, 2002; Wlotko & Federmeier, 2007) found that only with right visual field presentations (when target words were initially presented to the left hemisphere, or LH) did the pattern of ERPs resemble those with central visual presentation; ERP patterns with left visual field presentations (when targets were initially presented to the right hemisphere) resulted in a different ERP pattern. These results thus led them to propose that left hemisphere processing was biased toward semantic feature pre-activation (i.e., prediction) via top-down cues, whereas right hemisphere (RH) processing was characterized by more bottom-up processing in combination with a wait-and-see approach, operating via integration with working memory. These findings dovetail nicely with a longstanding and more general view of the LH functioning as the brain's "interpreter" (sometimes "confabulator"), hypothesizing patterns even when there are none; in contrast, the RH maintains a more veridical record of the world it perceives (Gazzaniga, 1985; Metcalfe, Funnell, & Gazzaniga, 1995; Wolford, Miller & Gazzaniga, 2000). The idea that the LH may respond more to perceived event probabilities (even if the event's occurrence is not immediate), while the RH may be less likely to generalize away from the input (Gazzaniga, 2000), is one that undoubtedly requires more exploration within the domain of linguistic pre-activation. It is of particular relevance if one takes the view that comprehension does not employ a special language processor, but rather is a "new machine built of old parts" (Bates & Goodman, 1997).

Taken together, these electrophysiological studies argue for the "strong" form of prediction by implicating a neural language parser that triggers word features (e.g., syntactic, conceptual, semantic) and forms in advance of their input. This work demonstrates that linguistic expectancies can emerge from contextual operators on semantic memory as sentential context accrues, in cases where candidate entities (or their depictions) are not physically present to aid the brain in narrowing the possibilities for likely continuations. And most importantly, these experiments are sensitive to the key factor for demonstrating that prediction is a routine part of real-time linguistic processing—that is, the pre-target *timing* of such effects.

POSSIBLE CONSEQUENCES TO LINGUISTIC PREDICTION

A flip side to anticipating upcoming language input is that there could (though according to some models, there needn't!) be some type of processing consequence—or even a landscape of processing consequences—for not encountering highly probable material. A possible example of such an effect, Federmeier, Wlotko, De Ochoa-Dewald, and Kutas (2007) observed a late positive (LP) ERP to low probability congruous sentence endings (relative to high probability ones) that completed highly but not weakly constraining contexts (e.g., "*He bought her a pearl necklace for her collection*" vs. "*He looked worried because he might have broken his collection.*") From these results they argued for a cost—perhaps reflecting inhibition or revision—upon encountering an unlikely, but plausible, word in a strongly predictive context. Similarly, DeLong, Urbach, and Kutas (2007) also observed a prolonged, late frontal positivity (500–1200 ms) to unexpected relative to expected nouns (e.g., *airplane* in "*The day was breezy so the boy went outside to fly…a kite/an airplane…*"). Moreover, they demonstrated that this graded late positivity to unexpected nouns varied as a function of the strength of expectancy (constraint) for the most

predictable items. Taken together, these findings of late positive ERPs to unexpected nouns that increase with the degree of constraint violation strongly support the idea that when highly pre-activated input is not received, some form of additional processing may be called for.

In contrast, there has been little behavioral evidence over the years for such sentence processing "costs" in terms of naming/lexical decision time latencies, a detail which has served for some as an important argument against linguistic prediction (e.g., Gough et al., 1981). However, a general problem with studies basing their "no prediction" arguments on "no cost" findings (e.g., a lack of an inhibitory effect) relates to the baseline conditions of comparison, that is, the supposedly "neutral" conditions against which the "cost" conditions are contrasted (e.g., Stanovich & West, 1983). The difficulty (if not impossibility) in determining what constitutes an appropriately neutral context, brings into question the weight of such conclusions, and indeed the specific binary contrasts typical of such studies may not be the only (or best) way to go about testing for "cost."

Comprehension theories that have included some type of processing "costs" have mainly posited them in terms of syntactic predictions. For instance, in Gibson's Dependency Locality Theory (Gibson, 1998) grammatical complexity in sentences is modeled in terms of memory and integration costs that arise from predictions generated by previous items, with such costs being a function of the distance between syntactically dependent elements. Additionally, various electrophysiological studies have proposed that at a minimum, the P600 (a late occurring positive-going ERP component) has an amplitude that increases as various syntactic aspects of sentence processing become more difficult (e.g., for syntactic disambiguation, Osterhout & Mobley, 1995; syntactic revision, Osterhout & Holcomb, 1992; syntactic integration difficulty, Kaan et al., 2000; or syntactic reanalysis, Hagoort, Brown, & Groothusen, 1993). Although "cost" may not be the right way of thinking about this component, it is certainly a different situation than, say, the N400 whose amplitude *decreases* as contextual facilitation from preceding semantic information increases.

Another hint that the P600 might be related to some sort of prediction violation comes from a number of recent studies that have found modulations of this ERP component to more semantic experimental manipulations. These "semantic P600s" have alternately been linked to costs for thematic role assignments (e.g., Hoeks, Stowe, & Doedens, 2004), detections of conflicts between semantic plausibility and syntactic requirements (e.g., Van Herten, Chwilla, & Kolk, 2006), and conflicting processing streams, including syntax versus semantics (e.g., Kuperberg, 2007). Though none of these lines of research directly implicates violation of general linguistic prediction as the possible source of such ERP patterns, an intriguing possibility is that these effects could potentially be related to those observed in the Federmeier et al. (2007) and DeLong et al. (2007) studies described earlier—an idea that undoubtedly warrants further investigation.

Whether referred to as a processing "cost" or a processing "consequence," we believe what is relevant in considering such ideas is that the brain may need to engage in some form of "extra" processing when, on the basis of constraint-based predictive comprehension, an accruing contextual representation must be overridden, revised, inhibited, or reanalyzed—at least, if not only, in cases where there is a strong lexical candidate that does not materialize. "Cost" also might not be the most apt term if an unexpected item triggers updating in a learning signal, where probability likelihoods are being adjusted for the future. Such learning might be considered a "cost" in the short term, but in the longer term, the comprehender would benefit by gaining an accurate model of their linguistic environment.

Our interpretation of a "misprediction consequence" is compatible with theories suggesting that such effects may be best accounted for in terms of cognitive control and conflict monitoring. Kolk and colleagues (Kolk, Chwilla, van Herten, & Oor, 2003; van Herten et al., 2006; Vissers, Kolk, van de Meerendonk, & Chwilla, 2008), for instance, have suggested that when conflicts emerge between incompatible sentential representations, reanalysis is initiated to check whether the conflict is due to processing error. Novick, Trueswell, and Thompson-Schill

(2005) and Thompson-Schill (2005) suggest that such reanalysis might stem from the selection among competing representations based on task demands. Although none of these authors frame a hypothesis specifically in terms of pre-activation or prediction violation, we believe that our results, and others, are compatible with this proposal. Moreover, we propose that the relevant "conflicts" need not be ones of syntactic or even semantic violation, arising even when items or their features are pre-activated to varying degrees, and then disconfirmed by the actual (physical) input. This more domain-general proposal is also consistent with the view that the cognitive control mechanisms involved in sentence comprehension may be similar to those employed in more general conflict tasks like the Stroop task (e.g., Novick et al., 2005; Thompson-Schill, 2005; Ye & Zhou, 2008). In addition, the observation of the generally more frontal scalp distribution of Federmeier et al.'s and DeLong et al.'s LP effect is roughly consistent with imaging data implicating various frontal and prefrontal cortical areas in inhibition (e.g., Aron, Robbins, & Poldrack, 2004), error detection (e.g., Rubia, Smith, Brammer, & Taylor, 2003), and suppression of interfering memories (e.g., Anderson et al., 2004). While ERP patterns at the scalp do not allow for direct mappings to specific brain areas, these distributional similarities are nonetheless suggestive.

CONCLUSIONS

In this chapter, we have offered some evidence for implicit, probabilistic anticipatory language processing, which we have argued may be cost incurring when continuations are highly anticipated but not received. These findings stand in contrast to a more classical view of language comprehension, and brain processing in general, as being essentially bottom up, waiting for sensory input that is processed and eventually recruited for action. The research reviewed herein is more compatible with the new wave of neural models proposing that a unifying principle for brain operation is one of being more "proactive," "prospective," or "pre-experiencing" (Bar, 2007; Gilbert & Wilson, 2007; Schacter,

Addis, & Buckner, 2007;). Under active brain accounts like these, neural processors are assumed to constantly be predicting upcoming input and monitoring the consistency of the anticipated and actual outcomes. This default mode of operation is proposed to occur across all domains, at sensory, motor, and cognitive levels. With respect to a more cognitive domain, Schacter and Addis (2007) have proposed that a crucial function of memory is to make information available for simulating future events. Under this model, it is unclear what the exact role of a semantic component is in constructing future scenarios; however, it seems that prediction in language processing fits nicely with models of predicting upcoming language input based on our stored mental representations in combination with contextual factors. And co-opting another idea from vision research (Enns & Lleras, 2008), it seems possible that some recent findings indicating a "cost" for pre-activation may be compatible with the idea of processing information that is inconsistent with some prevailing, pre-activated schema or expectation; in turn, the information triggering such discrepancies may ultimately be processed relatively slowly because the parser must start over restructuring a new contextual representation. These few examples highlight our belief that as we "look ahead" to continued exploration of prediction issues in the language domain, it will also be beneficial to "look around" and let our research be informed, shaped, and spurred by examinations within a larger framework of general brain processing, incorporating proposals of prediction from theories of human motor control (so-called forward models), from a variety of aspects of vision research, from judgment and decision making, and from episodic and semantic memory studies; indeed, scientists within these various domains are already doing just this! Without denying the uniqueness and seeming specialization of the human brain for comprehending and producing language, it seems that the door has been cracked wider for investigations of how predictive linguistic processing might better be understood in terms of how the brain more generally predicts. We maintain that the studies we have described here have served to tip the scale,

such that anticipatory processing should no longer be considered a lingering question in the literature, but rather should be understood as a natural part of the way language is comprehended, with future investigations targeting the nature and consequences of linguistic pre-activation.

Acknowledgments

This work was supported by NIH grants HD-22614 and AG-08313 to M. K. and by a Center for Research in Language Training Fellowship to N. J. S. We thank Kara Federmeier and Roger Levy for their helpful comments on earlier drafts; as ever, we are influenced by and grateful for thought-provoking discussions with Jeff Elman.

References

Abney, S. P. (1989). A computational model of human parsing [Special issue]. *Journal of Psycholinguistic Research*, *18*(1), 129–144.

Allopenna, P. D., Magnuson, J. S., & Tanenhaus, M. K. (1998). Tracking the time course of spoken word recognition using eye movements: Evidence for continuous mapping models. *Journal of Memory and Language*, *38*(4), 419–439.

Altmann, G. T. M., & Kamide, Y. (1999). Incremental interpretation at verbs: Restricting the domain of subsequent reference. *Cognition*, *73*, 247–264.

Altmann, G. T. M., & Kamide, Y. (2007). The real-time mediation of visual attention by language and world knowledge: Linking anticipatory (and other) eye movements to linguistic processing. *Journal of Memory and Language*, *57*(4), 502–518.

Altmann, G. T. M., & Steedman, M. J. (1988). Interaction with context during human sentence processing. *Cognition*, *30*, 191–238.

Anderson, M. C., Ochsner, K. N., Kuhl, B., Cooper, J., Robertson, E., Gabrieli, S. W., et al. (2004). Neural systems underlying the suppression of unwanted memories. *Science*, *303*(5655), 232–235.

Aron, A. R., Robbins, T. W., & Poldrack, R. A. (2004). Inhibition and the right inferior frontal cortex. *Trends in Cognitive Sciences*, *8*(4), 170–177.

Banich, M. T. (2003). Interaction between the hemispheres and its implications for the processing capacity of the brain. In K. Hugdahl & R. J. Davidson (Eds.), *The asymmetrical brain* (pp. 261–302). Cambridge, MA: MIT Press.

Bar, M. (2007). The proactive brain: Using analogies and associations to generate predictions. *Trends in Cognitive Sciences, 11*(7), 280–289.

Bates, E., & Goodman, J. C. (1997). On the inseparability of grammar and the lexicon: Evidence from acquisition, aphasia and real-time processing. *Language and Cognitive Processes, 12,* 507–584.

Bever, T. G. (1970). The cognitive basis for linguistic structures. In J. R. Hayes (Ed.), *Cognition and the development of language* (pp. xx–xx). New York: John Wiley & Sons.

Bicknell, K., Elman, J. L., Hare, M., McRae, K., & Kutas, M. (2008). Online expectations for verbal arguments conditional on event knowledge. In B. C. Love, K. McRae, & V. M. Sloutsky (Eds.), *Proceedings of the 30th Annual Conference of the Cognitive Science Society* (pp. 2220–2225). Austin, TX: Cognitive Science Society.

Bloom, P. A., & Fischler, I. (1980). Completion norms for 329 sentence contexts. *Memory and Cognition, 8,* 631–642.

Boland, J. E., Tanenhaus, M. K., Garnsey, S. M., & Carlson, G. N. (1995). Verb argument structure in parsing and interpretation: Evidence from wh-questions. *Journal of Memory and Language, 34,* 774–806.

Carroll, J., & Bever, T. (1978). The perception of relations: A case study in the relation of knowledge and perception. In E. Carterette & M. Friedman (Eds.), *Handbook of perception: Vol. 7. Speech and language.* New York: Academic Press.

Crocker, M. W., & Brants, T. (2000). Wide-coverage probabilistic sentence processing. *Journal of Psycholinguistic Research, 29*(6), 647–669.

Daneman, M., & Carpenter, P. A. (1983). Individual differences in integrating information between and within sentences. *Journal of Experimental Psychology: Learning, Memory, and Cognition, 9,* 561–584.

DeLong, K. A., Urbach, T. P., & Kutas, M. (2005). Probabilistic word pre-activation during language comprehension inferred from electrical brain activity. *Nature Neuroscience, 8*(8), 1117–1121.

DeLong, K. A., Urbach, T. P., & Kutas, M. (2007, March 29-31). *A cost to mispredicting: Effects of sentential constraint violations.* Poster presented at the 20th Annual CUNY Conference on Human Sentence Processing, La Jolla, CA.

Duffy, S. A., Henderson, J. M., & Morris, R. K. (1989). The semantic facilitation of lexical access during sentence processing. *Journal of Experimental Psychology: Learning, Memory, and Cognition, 15,* 791–801.

Eberhard, K. M., Spivey-Knowlton, M. J., Sedivy, J. C., & Tanenhaus, M. K. (1995). Eye movements as a window into real-time spoken language comprehension in natural contexts. *Journal of Psycholinguistic Research, 24,* 409–436.

Ehrlich, S. F., & Rayner, K. (1981). Contextual effects on word perception and eye movements during reading. *Journal of Verbal Learning and Verbal Behavior, 20*(6), 641–655.

Enns, J. T., & Lleras, A. (2008). What's next? New evidence for prediction in human vision. *Trends in Cognitive Sciences, 12*(9), 327–333.

Federmeier, K. D. (2007). Thinking ahead: The role and roots of prediction in language comprehension. *Psychophysiology, 44*(4), 491–505.

Federmeier, K. D., & Kutas, M. (1999a). A rose by any other name: Long-term memory structure and sentence processing. *Journal of Memory and Language, 41,* 469–495.

Federmeier, K. D., & Kutas, M. (1999b). Right words and left words: Electrophysiological evidence for hemispheric differences in meaning processing. *Cognitive Brain Research, 8*(3), 373–392.

Federmeier, K. D., & Kutas, M. (2002). Picture the difference: Electrophysiological investigations of picture processing in the two cerebral hemispheres. *Neuropsychologia, 40*(7), 730–747.

Federmeier, K. D., Mclennan, D. B., De Ochoa, E., & Kutas, M. (2002). The impact of semantic memory organization and sentence context information on spoken language processing by younger and older adults: An ERP study. *Psychophysiology, 39*(2), 133–146.

Federmeier, K. D., Wlotko, E. W., De Ochoa-Dewald, E., & Kutas, M. (2007). Multiple effects of sentential constraint on word processing [Special issue]. *Brain Research, 1146,* 75–84.

Fodor, J. A. (1983). *The modularity of mind.* Cambridge, MA: MIT Press.

Forster, K. I. (1979). Levels of processing and the structure of the language processor. In W. Cooper & E. Walker (Eds.), *Sentence processing* (pp. xx–xx). Hillsdale, NJ: Erlbaum.

Frazier, L., & Fodor, J. D. (1978). The sausage machine: A new two-stage parsing model. *Cognition, 6*(4), 291–325.

Garnsey, S. M., Pearlmutter, N. J., Myers, E., & Lotocky, M. A. (1997). The contributions of verb bias and plausibility to the comprehension of temporarily ambiguous sentences. *Journal of Memory and Language*, *37*(1), 58–93.

Gazzaniga, M. S. (1985).*The social brain*. New York: Basic Books.

Gazzaniga, M. S. (2000). Cerebral specialization and interhemispheric communication: Does the corpus callosum enable the human condition? *Brain*, *123*(7), 1293–1326.

Gibson, E. (1998). Linguistic complexity: Locality of syntactic dependencies. *Cognition*, *68*(1), 1–76.

Gilbert, D. T., & Wilson, T. D. (2007). Prospection: Experiencing the future. *Science*, *317*(5843), 1351–1354.

Gough, P. B., Alford, J. A., & Holley-Wilcox, P. (1981). Words and contexts. In O. J. L. Tzeng & H. Singer (Eds.), *Perception of print: Reading research in experimental psychology* (pp. 85–102). Hillsdale, NJ: Erlbaum.

Hagoort, P., Brown, C., & Groothusen, J. (1993). The syntactic positive shift (SPS) as an ERP measure of syntactic processing [Special issue]. *Language and Cognitive Processes*, *8*(4), 439–483.

Hanna, J. E., & Tanenhaus, M. K. (2004). Pragmatic effects on reference resolution in a collaborative task: Evidence from eye movements. *Cognitive Science*, *28*(1), 105–115.

Hare, M., McRae, K., & Elman, J. L. (2003). Sense and structure: Meaning as a determinant of verb subcategorization preferences. *Journal of Memory and Language*, *48*(2), 281–303.

Hoeks, J. C. J., Stowe, L. A., & Doedens, G. (2004). Seeing words in context: The interaction of lexical and sentence level information during reading. *Cognitive Brain Research*, *19*(1), 59–73.

Hsu, H. (2009). A neurophysiological study on probabilistic grammatical learning and sentence processing (Doctoral dissertation). Retrieved July 1, 2010, from http://ir.uiowa.edu/etd/243.

Jackendoff, R. (2002). *Foundations of language: Brain, meaning, grammar, evolution*. Oxford University Press.

Jurafsky, D. (1996). A probabilistic model of lexical and syntactic access and disambiguation. *Cognitive Science: A Multidisciplinary Journal*, *20*(2), 137–194.

Just, M. A., & Carpenter, P. A. (1980). A theory of reading: From eye fixations to comprehension. *Psychological Review*, *87*, 329–354.

Kaan, E., Harris, A., Gibson, E., & Holcomb, P. (2000). The P600 as an index of syntactic integration difficulty. *Language and Cognitive Processes*, *15*(2), 159–201.

Kamide, Y. (2008). Anticipatory processes in sentence processing. *Language and Linguistics Compass*, *2*(4), 647–670.

Kamide, Y., Altmann, G. T. M., & Haywood, S. L. (2003). The time-course of prediction in incremental sentence processing: Evidence from anticipatory eye movements. *Journal of Memory and Language*, *49*(1), 133–156.

Kamide, Y., Scheepers, C., & Altmann, G. T. M. (2003). Integration of syntactic and semantic information in predictive processing: Cross-linguistic evidence from German and English. *Journal of Psycholinguistic Research*, *32*(1), 37–55.

Kamide, Y., Scheepers, C., Altmann, G. T. M., & Crocker, M. W. (2002, March). *Integration of syntactic and semantic information in predictive processing: Anticipatory eye-movements in German*. Paper presented at the 14th Annual CUNY Conference on Human Sentence Processing, New York.

Kintsch, W., & van Dijk, T. A. (1978). Towards a model of text comprehension and productions. *Psychological Review*, *85*, 363–394.

Knoeferle, P., Crocker, M. W., Scheepers, C., & Pickering, M. J. (2005). The influence of the immediate visual context on incremental thematic role-assignment: Evidence from eye-movements in depicted events. *Cognition*, *95*(1), 95–127.

Kolk, H. H. J., Chwilla, D. J., van Herten, M., & Oor, P. J. W. (2003). Structure and limited capacity in verbal working memory: A study with event-related potentials. *Brain and Language*, *85*(1), 1–36.

Kullback, S., & Leibler, R. A. (1951). On information and sufficiency. *The Annals of Mathematical Statistics*, *22*(1), 79–86.

Kuperberg, G. R. (2007). Neural mechanisms of language comprehension: Challenges to syntax [Special issue]. *Brain Research*, *1146*, 23–49.

Kutas, M., & Hillyard, S. A. (1980). Reading senseless sentences: Brain potentials reflect semantic incongruity. *Science*, *207*(4427), 203–205.

Kutas, M., & Hillyard, S. A. (1983). Event-related brain potentials to grammatical errors and semantic anomalies. *Memory and Cognition*, *11*, 539–550.

Kutas, M., & Hillyard, S. A. (1984). Brain potentials during reading reflect word expectancy and semantic association. *Nature, 307*(5947), 161–163.

Levy, R. (2008). Expectation-based syntactic comprehension. *Cognition, 106*(3), 1126–1177.

MacDonald, M. C. (1993). The interaction of lexical and syntactic ambiguity. *Journal of Memory and Language, 32*, 692–692.

MacDonald, M. C., Pearlmutter, N. J., & Seidenberg, M. S. (1994). Lexical nature of syntactic ambiguity resolution. *Psychological Review, 101*(4), 676–703.

Marslen-Wilson, W. (1973). Linguistic structure and speech shadowing at very short latencies. *Nature, 244*, 522–523.

Marslen-Wilson, W. D. (1975). Sentence perception as an interactive parallel process. *Science, 189*, 226–228.

Marslen-Wilson, W. D., & Tyler, L. K. (1980). The temporal structure of spoken language understanding. *Cognition, 8*, 1–71.

McClelland, J. L., & Elman, J. L. (1986). The TRACE model of speech perception. *Cognitive Psychology, 18*(1), 1–86.

McClelland, J. L., & Rumelhart, D. E. (1981). An interactive activation model of context effects in letter perception: I. An account of basic findings. *Psychological Review, 88*, 375–407.

McRae, K., Spivey-Knowlton, M. J., & Tanenhaus, M. K. (1998). Modeling the influence of thematic fit (and other constraints) in on-line sentence comprehension. *Journal of Memory and Language, 38*(3), 283–312.

Metcalfe, J., Funnell, M., & Gazzaniga, M. S. (1995). Right-hemisphere memory superiority: Studies of a split-brain patient. *Psychological Science, 6*(3), 157–164.

Mitchell, D. C. (1982). *The process of reading: A cognitive analysis of fluent reading and learning to read*. New York: Wiley.

Mitchell, D. C., & Green, D. W. (1978). The effects of context and content on immediate processing in reading. *Quarterly Journal of Experimental Psychology, 30*, 609–636.

Morris, R. K. (1994). Lexical and message-level sentence context effects on fixation times in reading. *Journal of Experimental Psychology: Learning, Memory, and Cognition, 20*(1), 92–103.

Morris, R. K. (2006). Lexical processing and sentence context effects. In M. J. Traxler & M. A. Gernsbacher (Eds.), *Handbook of psycholinguistics* (2nd ed., pp. 377–402).

Narayanan S., & Jurafsky, D. (1998). Bayesian models of human sentence processing. In *Proceedings of the 20th Cognitive Science Society Conference* (pp. 84–90).

Narayanan, S., & Jurafsky, D. (2002). A Bayesian model predicts human parse preference and reading time in sentence processing. In S. B. T. G. Dietterich & Z. Ghahramani (Eds.), *Advances in neural information processing systems 14* (pp. 59–65). Cambridge, MA: MIT Press.

Norris, D. (2006). The Bayesian reader: Explaining word recognition as an optimal Bayesian decision process. *Psychological Review, 113*(2), 327–357.

Novick, J. M., Trueswell, J. C., & Thompson-Schill, S. L. (2005). Cognitive control and parsing: Reexamining the role of Broca's area in sentence comprehension. *Cognitive, Affective and Behavioral Neuroscience, 5*(3), 263–281.

Osterhout, L., & Holcomb, P. J. (1992). Event-related brain potentials elicited by syntactic anomaly. *Journal of Memory and Language, 31*(6), 785–806.

Osterhout, L., Holcomb, P. J., & Swinney, D. A. (1994). Brain potentials elicited by garden-path sentences: Evidence of the application of verb information during parsing. *Journal of Experimental Psychology: Learning, Memory, and Cognition, 20*(4), 786–803.

Osterhout, L., & Mobley, L. A. (1995). Event-related brain potentials elicited by failure to agree. *Journal of Memory and Language, 34*(6), 739–773.

Otten, M., Nieuwland, M., & van Berkum, J. (2007). Great expectations: Specific lexical anticipation influences the processing of spoken language. *BMC Neuroscience, 8*(1), 89.

Otten, M., & van Berkum, J. J. A. (2008). Discourse-based word anticipation during language processing: Prediction or priming? *Discourse Processes, 45*(6), 464–496.

Otten, M., & van Berkum, J. J. A. (2009). Does working memory capacity affect the ability to predict upcoming words in discourse? *Brain Research, 1291*, 92–101.

Pickering, M. J. (1994). Processing local and unbounded dependencies: A unified account. *Journal of Psycholinguistic Research, 23*, 323–352.

Pritchett, B. L. (1991). Head position and parsing ambiguity [Special issue]. *Journal of Psycholinguistic Research, 20*(3), 251–270.

Rayner, K., Ashby, J., Pollatsek, A., & Reichle, E. D. (2004). The effects of frequency and predictability on eye fixations in reading: Implications for the E-Z reader model. *Journal of Experimental Psychology: Human Perception and Performance, 30*(4), 720–732.

Rayner, K., Liversedge, S. P., White, S. J., & Vergilino-Perez, D. (2003). Reading disappearing text: Cognitive control of eye movements. *Psychological Science, 14*, 385–389.

Rubia, K., Smith, A. B., Brammer, M. J., & Taylor, E. (2003). Right inferior prefrontal cortex mediates response inhibition while mesial prefrontal cortex is responsible for error detection. *NeuroImage, 20*(1), 351–358.

Sacks, H., Schegloff, E. A., & Jefferson, G. (1974). A simplest systematics for the organization of turn-taking for conversation. *Language, 50*(4, Part 1), 696–735.

Schacter, D. L., & Addis, D. R. (2007). On the constructive episodic simulation of past and future events. *Behavioral and Brain Sciences, 30*(3), 331–332.

Schacter, D. L., Addis, D. R., & Buckner, R. L. (2007). Remembering the past to imagine the future: The prospective brain. *Nature Reviews Neuroscience, 8*(9), 657–661.

Schwanenflugel, P. J. (1986). Completion norms for final words of sentences using a multiple production measure. *Behavior Research Methods, Instrumentation, and Computers, 18*, 363–371.

Sedivy, J. C., Tanenhaus, M. K., Chambers, C. G., & Carlson, G. N. (1999). Achieving incremental semantic interpretation through contextual representation. *Cognition, 71*, 109–148.

Sereno, S. C., Brewer, C. C., & O'Donnell, P. J. (2003). Context effects in word recognition: Evidence for early interactive processing. *Psychological Science, 14*(4), 328–333.

Smith, N. J., & Levy, R. (2008, June 23–26). *Optimal processing times in reading: A formal model and empirical investigation.* Paper presented at the 30th Annual Meeting of the Cognitive Science Society, Washington, DC.

Spivey, M. J., Tanenhaus, M. K., Eberhard, K. M., & Sedivy, J. C. (2002). Eye movements and spoken language comprehension: Effects of visual context on syntactic ambiguity resolution. *Cognitive Psychology, 45*(4), 447–481.

Stanovich, K. E., & West, R. F. (1979). Mechanisms of sentence context effects in reading: Automatic activation and conscious attention. *Memory and Cognition, 7*(2), 77–85.

Stanovich, K. E., & West, R. F. (1983). On priming by a sentence context. *Journal of Experimental Psychology: General, 112*(1), 1–36.

Staub, A., & Clifton, C., Jr. (2006). Syntactic prediction in language comprehension: Evidence from either…or. *Journal of Experimental Psychology: Learning, Memory, and Cognition, 32*(2), 425–436.

Steedman, M. (1989). Grammar, interpretation, and processing from the lexicon. In W. Marslen-Wilson (Ed.), *Lexical representation and process.* Cambridge, MA: MIT Press.

Sussman, R. S., & Sedivy, J. C. (2003). The time-course of processing syntactic dependencies: Evidence from eye movements. *Language and Cognitive Processes, 18*(2), 143–161.

Tanenhaus, M., Spivey-Knowlton, M., Eberhard, K., & Sedivy, J. (1995). Integration of visual and linguistic information during spoken language comprehension. *Science, 268*, 1632–1634.

Taylor, W. L. (1953). "Cloze procedure": A new tool for measuring readability. *Journalism Quarterly, 30*, 415–433.

Thompson-Schill, S. L. (2005). Dissecting the language organ: A new look at the role of Broca's area in language processing. In A. Cutler (Ed.), *Twenty-first century psycholinguistics: Four cornerstones.* (pp. 173–189). Mahwah, NJ: Erlbaum.

Traxler, M., Bybee, M., & Pickering, M. (1997). Influence of connectives on language comprehension: Eye-tracking evidence for incremental interpretation. *Quarterly Journal of Experimental Psychology A, 50*(3), 481–497.

Trueswell, J. C., Tanenhaus, M. K., & Garnsey, S. M. (1994). Semantic influences on parsing: Use of thematic role information in syntactic ambiguity resolution. *Journal of Memory and Language, 33*(3), 285–318.

Trueswell, J. C., Tanenhaus, M. K., & Kello, C. (1993). Verb-specific constraints in sentence processing: Separating effects of lexical preference from garden-paths. *Journal of Experimental Psychology: Learning, Memory, and Cognition, 19*, 528–528.

Tyler, L. K., & Marslen-Wilson, W. D. (1977). The on-line effects of semantic context on syntactic processing. *Journal of Verbal Learning and Verbal Behavior, 16*, 683–692.

van Berkum, J. J. A., Brown, C. M., & Hagoort, P. (1999). Early referential context effects in sentence processing: Evidence from event-related brain potentials. *Journal of Memory and Language*, *41*(2), 147–182.

van Berkum, J. J. A., Brown, C. M., Zwitserlood, P., Kooijman, V., & Hagoort, P. (2005). Anticipating upcoming words in discourse: Evidence from ERPs and reading times. *Journal of Experimental Psychology: Learning, Memory, and Cognition*, *31*(3), 443–467.

van Berkum, J. J. A., Koornneef, A. W., Otten, M., & Nieuwland, M. S. (2007). Establishing reference in language comprehension: An electrophysiological perspective. *Brain Research*, *1146*, 158–171.

van Berkum, J. J. A., Zwitserlood, P., Hagoort, P., & Brown, C. M. (2003). When and how do listeners relate a sentence to the wider discourse? Evidence from the N400 effect. *Cognitive Brain Research*, *17*(3), 701–718.

van Herten, M., Chwilla, D. J., & Kolk, H. H. J. (2006). When heuristics clash with parsing routines: ERP evidence for conflict monitoring in sentence perception. *Journal of Cognitive Neuroscience*, *18*(7), 1181–1197.

Van Petten, C., & Kutas, M. (1990). Interactions between sentence context and word frequency in event-related brain potentials. *Memory and Cognition*, *18*(4), 380–393.

Van Petten, C., Coulson, S., Plante, E., Rubin, S., & Parks, M. (1999). Timecourse of word identification and semantic integration in spoken language. *Journal of Experimental Psychology: Learning, Memory, and Cognition*, *25*(2), 394–417.

Vissers, C. T. W. M., Kolk, H. H. J., van de Meerendonk, N., & Chwilla, D. J. (2008). Monitoring in language perception: Evidence from ERPs in a picture-sentence matching task. *Neuropsychologia*, *46*(4), 967–982.

Wicha, N. Y. Y., Bates, E., Moreno, E. M., & Kutas, M. (2003). Potatoes not Pope: Human brain potentials to gender expectation and agreement in Spanish spoken sentences. *Neuroscience Letters*, *346*, 165–168.

Wicha, N. Y., Moreno, E. M., & Kutas, M. (2003). Expecting gender: An event related brain potential study on the role of grammatical gender in comprehending a line drawing within a written sentence in Spanish. *Cortex*, *39*, 483–508.

Wicha, N. Y. Y., Moreno, E., & Kutas, M. (2004). Anticipating words and their gender: An event-related brain potential study of semantic integration, gender expectancy, and gender agreement in Spanish sentence reading. *Journal of Cognitive Neuroscience*, *16*(7), 1272–1288.

Wlotko, E. W., & Federmeier, K. D. (2007). Finding the right word: Hemispheric asymmetries in the use of sentence context information. *Neuropsychologia*, *45*(13), 3001–3014.

Wolford, G., Miller, M. B., & Gazzaniga, M. (2000). The left hemisphere's role in hypothesis formation. *Journal of Neuroscience*, *20*(6), RC64.

Ye, Z., & Zhou, X. (2008). Involvement of cognitive control in sentence comprehension: Evidence from ERPs. *Brain Research*, *1203*(8), 103–115.

CHAPTER 16
Cortical and Subcortical Predictive Dynamics and Learning during Perception, Cognition, Emotion, and Action

Stephen Grossberg

1. Introduction: learning and prediction by complementary cortical processing streams

Advanced brains have an extraordinary capacity to autonomously learn in real time from changing environmental conditions. Such learning includes both perceptual/cognitive and spatial/motor processes. Accumulating experimental and theoretical evidence shows that perceptual/cognitive and spatial/motor processes both need predictive mechanisms to control learning. Thus, there is an intimate connection between learning and predictive dynamics in the brain. However, neural models of these processes have proposed, and many experiments have supported, the hypothesis that perceptual/cognitive and spatial/motor processes use different types of predictive mechanisms to regulate the learning that they carry out.

The need for different predictive mechanisms is clarified by accumulating theoretical and empirical evidence that brain specialization is governed by computationally *complementary* cortical processing streams that embody different predictive and learning mechanisms (Grossberg, 2000b). As summarized in Figure 16.1, perceptual/cognitive processes in the What ventral cortical processing stream often use *excitatory matching* and *match-based learning* to create predictive representations of objects and events in the world. Match-based learning can occur quickly without causing catastrophic forgetting,

much as we quickly learn new faces without forcing rapid forgetting of familiar faces. Complementary spatial/motor processes in the Where dorsal cortical processing stream often use *inhibitory matching* and *mismatch-based learning* to continually update spatial maps and sensory-motor gains as our bodily parameters change through time. As noted in more detail in the following text, these What and Where processes need to work together. For example, the What stream learns spatially invariant object categories, whereas the Where stream learns spatial maps and movement gains. What-Where interstream interactions enable spatially invariant object representations to control actions toward desired goals in space. Because of their different types of matching and learning, perceptual and cognitive learning provide a self-stabilizing front end to control the more labile spatial and motor learning that enables changing bodies to effectively act upon recognized objects in the world. The present chapter reviews and synthesizes data and models of these processes and outlines a unified theory of predictive brain processing.

2. Learning of invariant recognition categories in the What cortical stream

As noted in Figure 16.1, learning in the What cortical stream leads to recognition categories that tend to be increasingly independent of object size and position at higher cortical levels. The anterior inferotemporal cortex exhibits such invariance (Bar et al., 2001; Sigala & Logothetis, 2002; Tanaka, Saito, Fukada, & Moriya, 1991). Although how this occurs needs careful discussion (e.g., Zoccolan, Kouh, Poggio, & DiCarlo, 2007), such object invariance prevents a combinatorial explosion in memory of object representations that could otherwise occur at every perceived size and position. Such categorization processes have been predicted to achieve fast learning without experiencing catastrophic forgetting (Fig. 16.1). How is this accomplished? Adaptive Resonance Theory (ART) predicts how What stream categorization processes integrate properties of consciousness, learning, expectation, attention, resonance, and synchrony (CLEARS, Grossberg, 1980). Subsequent experiments have supported this prediction; see Grossberg (2003) and Grossberg and Versace (2008) for reviews.

Predictive ART matching uses a top-down learned expectation that causes an excitatory resonance when it *matches* consistent bottom-up input patterns (Figs. 16.1 and 16.2). The match focuses attention upon a *critical feature pattern* of matched object features that resonates synchronously with the recognition category that reads out the top-down expectation. The resonance leads to a sustained focus of object attention and drives fast learning that incorporates the critical feature pattern into the emerging prototype of the corresponding recognition category. This link between prediction and learning hereby joins excitatory matching, resonance, synchrony, attention, and match-based learning,

These processes together solve the *stability-plasticity dilemma* (Grossberg, 1980); namely, they enable the brain to learn quickly without experiencing catastrophic forgetting. They also clarify why many animals are intentional beings who pay attention to salient objects, why *all conscious states are resonant states,* and how brains can learn both *many-to-one maps* (representations whereby many object views, positions, and sizes all activate the same invariant object category; see Section 15) and *one-to-many maps* (representations that enable us to expertly know many things about individual objects and events); see Carpenter and Grossberg (1992).

Adaptive Resonance Theory predicts that all brain representations that solve the stability-plasticity dilemma use variations of CLEARS mechanisms (Grossberg, 1978a, 1980, 2007). Synchronous resonances are therefore expected to occur between multiple cortical and subcortical areas. Recent data support this prediction; for example, see Buschman and Miller (2007),

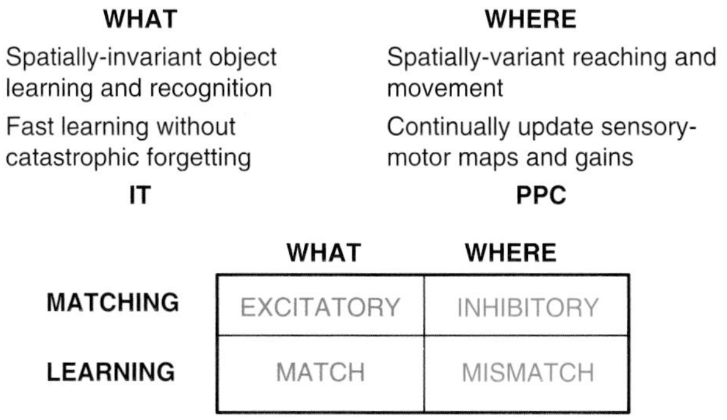

	WHAT	WHERE
	Spatially-invariant object learning and recognition	Spatially-variant reaching and movement
	Fast learning without catastrophic forgetting	Continually update sensory-motor maps and gains
	IT	PPC

	WHAT	WHERE
MATCHING	EXCITATORY	INHIBITORY
LEARNING	MATCH	MISMATCH

Figure 16.1 Complementary What and Where cortical processing streams for spatially invariant object recognition and spatially variant spatial representation and action, respectively. Perceptual and recognition learning use top-down excitatory matching and match-based learning that achieves fast learning without catastrophic forgetting. Spatial and motor learning use inhibitory matching and mismatch-based learning that enable rapid adaptation to changing bodily parameters. IT, inferotemporal cortex; PPC, posterior parietal cortex. See text for details.

Engel, Fries, and Singer (2001), Grossberg (2009), and Pollen (1999).

3. EXPECTATIONS AND BIASED COMPETITION: MODULATORY ON-CENTER, OFF-SURROUND NETWORK

How are What-stream top-down expectations computed? How do they focus attention on expected combinations of features? Carpenter and Grossberg (1987) mathematically proved that the simplest network that solves the stability-plasticity dilemma is a *top-down, modulatory on-center, off-surround network*, which provides excitatory priming of features in the on-center, and driving inhibition in the off-surround. The modulatory on-center emerges from a balance between top-down excitation and inhibition. Subsequent modeling studies of varied biological data clarify how such a circuit can participate in many different types of brain processes (e.g., Dranias, Grossberg, & Bullock, 2008; Gove, Grossberg, & Mingolla, 1995; Grossberg, Govindarajan, Wyse, & Cohen, 2004; Grossberg & Myers, 2000), and laminar cortical models predict identified cell types (Grossberg, 1999; Grossberg & Pearson, 2008; Grossberg & Versace, 2008; Raizada & Grossberg, 2003). Many anatomical and neurophysiological experiments have provided support for this prediction (e.g., Bullier, Hupé, James, & Girard, 1996; Caputo & Guerra, 1998; Downing, 1988; Hupé, Jame, Girard, & Bullier, 1997; Mounts, 2000; Reynolds, Chelazzi, & Desimone, 1999; Sillito, Jones, Gerstein, & West, 1994; Smith, Singh, & Greenlee, 2000; Somers, Dale, Seiffert, & Tootell, 1999; Steinman, Steinman, & Lehmkuhle, 1995; Vanduffel, Tootell, & Orban, 2000), which is more qualitatively called the "biased competition" model of attention (Desimone, 1998; Kastner & Ungerleider, 2001).

4. IMAGINING AND PLANNING AHEAD: PREDICTION WITHOUT ACTION

A top-down expectation is not always modulatory. The excitatory/inhibitory balance in the modulatory on-center of a top-down expectation can be modified by volitional control from the basal ganglia. If, for example, volitional signals inhibit inhibitory interneurons in the on-center, then readout of a top-down expectation from a recognition category can fire cells in the on-center prototype. Such volitional control has been predicted to control mental imagery and the ability to think and plan ahead without external action, a crucial type of predictive competence in humans and other mammals. If these volitional signals become tonically hyperactive, then top-down expectations can fire without overt intention, leading to properties like schizophrenic hallucinations (Grossberg, 2000a). The ability to imagine and think thus risks having hallucinations. All of these properties are, in turn, traced to the fundamental ability to learn quickly throughout life without catastrophic forgetting by using top-down expectations to stabilize learned memories.

5. COMPLEMENTARY ATTENTIONAL AND ORIENTING SYSTEMS: EXPECTED VERSUS UNEXPECTED EVENTS

To adapt autonomously to a changing world, an individual needs to process and learn about unfamiliar and unexpected events. How does a brain learn to balance between expected and unexpected events? How does a brain learn to incorporate unexpected and unfamiliar events within the corpus of previously learned events, and do so without causing catastrophic forgetting? Within ART, this is achieved by a memory search, or hypothesis testing, process that discovers the recognition category that best matches an event or object. Figure 16.2 illustrates how this is predicted to happen in a simple two-level example.

A bottom-up input pattern I activates an activity pattern X across feature detectors of processing stage F_1. For example, the "features" of a visual scene may be 3D boundary and surface representations. Vector I represents the relative importance of different features. In Figure 16.2a, the pattern peaks represent more active feature detector cells, the troughs less activated feature detectors. This feature pattern sends signals S through an adaptive filter to the level F_2 at which a recognition category Y is activated

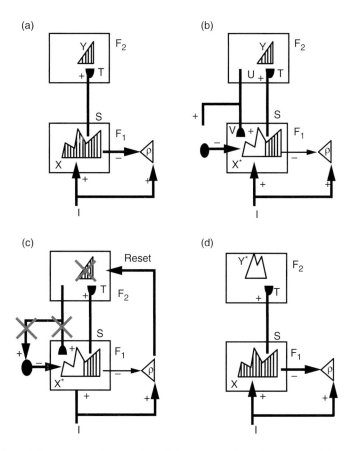

Figure 16.2 Search for a recognition code within an ART learning circuit: (*a*) Input pattern I is instated across feature detectors at level F_1 as an activity pattern X, while it nonspecifically activates the orienting system *A* with gain ρ, which is called the *vigilance* parameter. Output signals from activity pattern X inhibit *A* and generate output pattern S. S is multiplied by learned adaptive weights to form the input pattern T. T activates category cells Y at level F_2. (*b*) Y generates the top-down signals U, which are multiplied by adaptive weights and added at F_1 cells to form a *prototype* V that encodes the learned expectation of active F_2 categories. If V mismatches I at F_1, then a new STM activity pattern X* (the hatched pattern) is selected at F_1. X* is active at I features that are confirmed by V. Mismatched features (white area) are inhibited. When X changes to X*, total inhibition decreases from F_1 to A. (*c*) If inhibition decreases sufficiently so that the total inhibition due to X* is less than the total excitation due to I multiplied by the vigilance parameter ρ, then A is activated and releases a nonspecific arousal burst to F_2; that is, "novel events are arousing." Arousal resets F_2 by inhibiting Y. (*d*) After Y is inhibited, X is reinstated and Y stays inhibited as X activates a different activity pattern Y*. Search for better F_2 category continues until a better matching or novel category is selected. When the search ends, an attentive resonance triggers learning of the attended data. (Adapted with permission from Carpenter and Grossberg, 1993.)

by the distributed input T. Input T is computed by multiplying S by bottom-up adaptive weights that are altered by learning. The activity pattern Y is derived by contrast-enhancing T using recurrent inhibitory interactions across F_2 that allow only a small subset of the most strongly

activated category cells to remain active in response to T. The pattern Y in the figure indicates that a small number of category cells may be activated to different degrees. Active category cells send top-down signals U to F_1 (Fig. 16.2b). U is converted into the top-down expectation

V by being multiplied by top-down adaptive weights. This is the "predictive" process during the search. At F_1, matching between the input vector I and V selects that subset X∗ of features within the modulatory on-center of the top-down expectation that are "expected" by Y. These features define the emerging "attentional focus."

If the match is good enough, then the pattern X∗ of attended features reactivates category Y, which, in turn, reactivates X∗ and locks the network into a synchronous resonant state that dynamically links, or binds, attended features across X∗ with their category Y and enables fast learning to occur. If the match is not good enough, search for a novel or better matching category continues (see Figs. 16.2c and 16.2d). How good a match is required for resonance, attention, and learning to occur is determined by the gain ρ of the excitatory inputs I that attempt to activate the orienting system A (see Fig. 16.2). Varying vigilance can cause learning of concrete categories (high vigilance) or abstract categories (low vigilance) because a larger vigilance value requires a better match for resonance and learning to occur.

This *match-based learning* process stabilizes learned memories both in the bottom-up adaptive filters that activate recognition categories and in the top-down expectations that are matched against feature patterns. It embodies a fundamental form of prediction that can be activated either bottom-up by input data, or top-down by an expectation that predictively primes a class of events whose future occurrence is sought. Match-based learning allows memories to change only when input from the external world is close enough to internal expectations, or when something completely new occurs.

6. SPIKES, SYNCHRONY, AND ATTENTIVE LEARNING IN LAMINAR THALAMOCORTICAL CIRCUITS

The SMART model (Fig. 16.3) predicts how finer details about CLEARS processes may be realized by multiple levels of brain organization. SMART provides a unified functional explanation of single-cell properties, such as spiking dynamics,

spike-timing-dependent plasticity (STDP), and acetylcholine modulation; detailed laminar thalamic and cortical circuit designs and their interactions; aggregate cell recordings, such as current-source densities and local field potentials; and single-cell and large-scale interareal oscillations in the gamma and beta frequency domains.

Figure 16.3 summarizes how these circuits embody the ART matching rule and thereby allow laminar circuits of multiple cortical and thalamic areas to carry out attentive visual learning and information processing. In particular, ART top-down modulatory on-center, off-surround networks occur in both corticocortical and corticothalamic circuits. For example, layer 6^{II} of cortical area V2 sends top-down outputs to cortical area V1 via layer 1, where they activate apical dendrites of layer 5 cells. Layer 5, in turn, activates layer 6^I, which sends modulatory on-center, off-surround signals to layer 4. In addition, layer 5 cells activate layer 6^{II}, which sends top-down modulatory on-center off-surround signals to LGN. These pathways help to regulate stable learning in laminar thalamo-cortical circuits. The generality of learned recognition codes is proposed to be controlled by a vigilance process (see Fig. 16.2) that is mediated by acetylcholine.

7. GAMMA AND BETA OSCILLATIONS DURING RESONANT LEARNING AND MISMATCH RESET

One of the new SMART predictions concerns how brain oscillations contribute to predictive learning. SMART predicts that *matches* cause gamma oscillations that support attention, resonance, learning, and consciousness, whereas *mismatches* inhibit learning by causing slower beta oscillations while triggering attentional reset and hypothesis testing operations (Fig. 16.2) that are initiated in the deeper cortical layers. Three kinds of recent data support this prediction:

(1) Buffalo, Fries, and Desimone (2004) have reported beta oscillations in deeper layers of visual cortex.

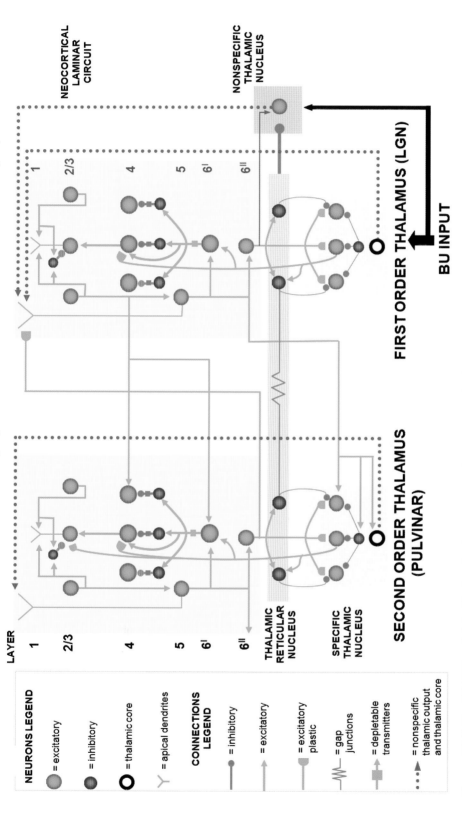

Figure 16.3 The SMART model clarifies how laminar neocortical circuits in multiple cortical areas interact with specific and nonspecific thalamic nuclei to regulate learning on multiple organizational levels, ranging from spikes to cognitive dynamics. The thalamus is subdivided into specific first-order and sec

(continued)

Figure 16.3 (continued) ond-order nuclei, nonspecific nucleus, and thalamic reticular nucleus (TRN). The first-order thalamic matrix cells (shown as an open ring) provide nonspecific excitatory priming to layer 1 in response to bottom-up input, priming layer 5 cells and allowing them to respond to layer 2/3 input. This allows layer 5 to close the intracortical loop and activate the pulvinar (PULV). V1 layer 4 receives inputs from two parallel bottom-up thalamocortical pathways: a direct LGN$\rightarrow$4 excitatory input, and a $6^{I} \rightarrow 4$ modulatory on-center, off-surround network that contrast-normalizes the pattern of layer 4 activation via the recurrent $4 \rightarrow 2/3 \rightarrow 5 \rightarrow 6^{I} \rightarrow 4$ loop. V1 activates the bottom-up $V1 \rightarrow V2$ corticocortical pathways from V1 layer 2/3 to V2 layers 6^{I} and 4, as well as the bottom-up corticothalamocortical pathway from V1 layer 5 to the PULV, which projects to V2 layers 6^{I} and 4. In V2, as in V1, the layer $6^{I} \rightarrow 4$ pathway provides divisive contrast normalization to V2 layer 4 cells. Corticocortical feedback from V2 layer 6^{II} reaches V1 layer 1, where it activates apical dendrites of layer 5 cells. Layer 5 cells, in turn, activate the modulatory $6^{I} \rightarrow 4$ pathway in V1, which projects a V1 top-down expectation to the LGN. TRN cells of the two thalamic sectors are linked via gap junctions, which synchronize activation across the two thalamocortical sectors when processing bottom-up stimuli. The nonspecific thalamic nucleus receives convergent bottom-up excitatory input from specific thalamic nuclei and inhibition from the TRN, and it projects to layer 1 of the laminar cortical circuit, where it regulates mismatch-activated reset and hypothesis testing in the cortical circuit. Corticocortical feedback connections from layer 6^{II} of the higher cortical area terminate in layer 1 of the lower cortical area, whereas corticothalamic feedback from layer 6^{II} terminates in its specific thalamus and on the TRN. This corticothalamic feedback is matched against bottom-up input in the specific thalamus. (Reprinted with permission from Grossberg and Versace, 2008.)

(2) Buschman and Miller (2009) have reported beta oscillations during spatial attention shifts in frontal eye fields.

(3) Berke and colleagues (2008) have reported beta oscillations during hippocampal place cell learning in novel environments.

Place cells can develop within seconds to minutes and can remain stable for months (Frank, Stanley, & Brown, 2004; Muller, 1996; Thompson & Best, 1990; Wilson & McNaughton, 1993). Place cell learning thus seems to have solved the stability-plasticity dilemma. How place cells are formed has attracted even more interest since the remarkable discovery of grid cells (Hafting, Fyhn, Molden, Moser, & Moser, 2005) within entorhinal cortical circuits that project to the hippocampus. Are place cells learned using ART dynamics? The Berke et al. (2008) data are consistent with this hypothesis: Paradoxically, beta power was very low as a mouse traversed a lap for the first time, grew to full strength on the second and third laps, became low again after 2 minutes of exploration, and remained low on subsequent days. Beta oscillation power also correlated with the rate at which place cells became spatially selective, and it did not correlate with theta oscillations. Given the rapidity with which

place cell learning occurred, and the sharp increase in beta activity during the second exposure to the environment, it would seem that a highly selective learning mechanism is at work.

These data can be explained as follows (Grossberg, 2008): Gorchetchnikov and Grossberg (2007) modeled how place cell receptive fields may be learned in an ART system wherein hippocampal place cells are spatial category cells that arise from multiple scales of entorhinal grid cells (Hafting et al., 2005). In any ART system, top-down adaptive weights are broadly distributed before learning occurs, so that they can match whatever input pattern first initiates learning of a new category (Carpenter & Grossberg, 1987). Such top-down weights are then pruned on subsequent learning trials to match the emerging critical feature pattern during mismatch-based reset events. The low beta power on the first lap of exploration can be explained by the initial top-down match. Beta power on subsequent laps can be explained by mismatch reset events that correlate with the rate at which place cells become spatially selective.

Given the possibility that place cells are spatial categories in an ART system from entorhinal grid cells to hippocampal place cells, how is the striking hexagonal pattern of grid cell firing itself learned? Mhatre, Gorchetchnikov, and Grossberg (2009, 2010) propose that grid cells also arise through a self-organizing map process in response to linear velocity and angular velocity path integration signals. Thus, a hierarchy of self-organizing maps seems to learn both grid cell and place cell receptive fields, whose memory may be stabilized by top-down attentive feedback from hippocampus (CA1) to entorhinal cortex.

Experimental data are consistent with this predicted role of attention in hippocampal learning. For example, Kentros and colleagues (2004) showed that "conditions that maximize place field stability greatly increase orientation to novel cues. This suggests that storage and retrieval of place cells is modulated by a top-down cognitive process resembling attention and that place cells are neural correlates of spatial memory" (p. 283). In like manner, it has been proposed that learning of place cell receptive fields reflects an "automatic recording of attended experience" (Morris & Frey, 1997, p. 1489). These experiments clarify that cognitive processes like attention play a role in hippocampal learning and memory stability, and they interact with NMDA receptors to mediate long-lasting hippocampal place field memory in novel environments (Kentros et al., 1998).

8. Cognitive–emotional interactions endow predictions with value constraints

Invariant recognition categories can be activated when objects are experienced, but they do not reflect the emotional value of these objects. An *invariant* object category can, however, be readily associated through reinforcement learning with one or more drive representations, which are brain sites that represent internal drive states and emotions. Activation of a drive representation by an invariant object category can trigger emotional reactions and motivational decisions that can motivationally modulate the ability of object representations to generate behavioral outputs. Because a single invariant object category can be activated by a wide range of input exemplars, all these input exemplars

can, via the invariant category, trigger choice and release of actions that realize valued goals in a context-sensitive way. Recognized objects can hereby trigger choice and release of actions that realize valued goals in a context-sensitive way.

In Figures 16.4a and 16.4b, visually perceived objects are called conditioned stimuli (CS_i). The invariant object categories that they activate are called sensory representations (S_{CSi}), which, in turn, activate drive representations (D). Figure 16.4a summarizes how predictive behavior can be constrained by such external sensory options and internal emotional and motivational requirements.

The amygdala is a drive representation (e.g., Aggleton, 1993; LeDoux, 1993). Reinforcement learning (Figs. 16.4a and 16.4b) can convert the event or object (say CS_1) that activates an invariant object category ($S_{CS_1}^{(1)}$) into a *conditioned reinforcer* by strengthening associative links from the category to the drive representation (D); for example, learning in inferotemporal-to-amygdala pathways. The invariant object category can also send excitatory projections to regions of prefrontal cortex ($S_{CS_2}^{(1)}$), such as orbitofrontal cortex. The amygdala (D) also sends projections to orbitofrontal cortex (Barbas, 1995; Grossberg, 1975, 1982). Reinforcement learning can hereby strengthen amygdala-to-orbitofrontal pathways, which provide *incentive motivation* to the orbitofrontal representations. Orbitofrontal representations fire most vigorously when they receive convergent inputs from inferotemporal categories and amygdala incentive motivation (Baxter, Parker, Lindner, Izquierdo, & Murray, 2000; Schoenbaum, Setlow, Saddoris, & Gallagher, 2003). The incentive outputs from the amygdala are sensitive to the drive state of the individual and become desensitized when the corresponding drive is satisfied. In this way, an object that represents a valued goal object can vigorously activate its orbitofrontal representation through the combination of direct inferotemporal-to-orbitofrontal connections and indirect inferotemporal-to-amygdala-to-orbitofrontal connections. The latter connections withdraw their support of orbitofrontal firing when the corresponding amygdala drive state is satisfied.

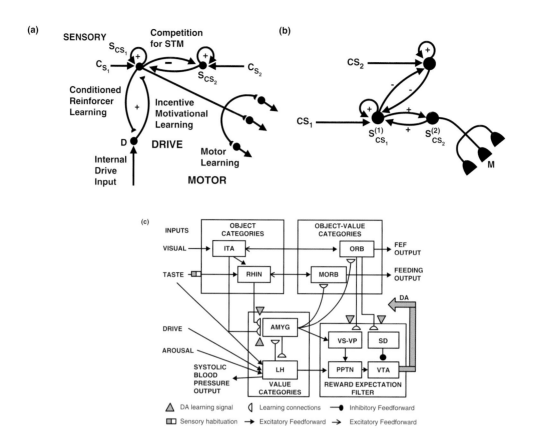

Figure 16.4 (*a*) CogEM model: Three types of interacting representations (sensory, drive, and motor) control three types of learning (conditioned reinforcer, incentive motivational, and motor) during reinforcement learning. Sensory representations S temporarily store internal representations of sensory events in working memory. Drive representations D are sites where reinforcing and homeostatic, or drive, cues converge to activate emotional responses. Motor representations M control readout of actions. Conditioned reinforcer learning enables sensory events to activate emotional reactions at drive representations. Incentive motivational learning enables emotions to generate a motivational set that biases the system to process information consistent with that emotion. Motor learning allows sensory and cognitive representations to generate actions. (*b*) To work well, a sensory representation S must have (at least) two successive stages, $S^{(1)}$ and $S^{(2)}$, so that sensory events cannot release actions that are motivationally inappropriate. (Reprinted with permission from Grossberg and Seidman, 2006.) (*c*) MOTIVATOR model: Brain areas in the MOTIVATOR circuit can be divided into four regions that process information about conditioned stimuli (CSs) and unconditioned stimuli (USs). Object Categories represent visual or gustatory inputs, in anterior inferotemporal (ITA) and rhinal (RHIN) cortices. Value Categories represent the value of anticipated outcomes on the basis of hunger and satiety inputs, in amygdala (AMYG) and lateral hypothalamus (LH). Object-Value Categories resolve the value of competing perceptual stimuli in medial (MORB) and lateral (ORB) orbitofrontal cortex. The Reward Expectation Filter involves basal ganglia circuitry that responds to unexpected rewards. (Reprinted with permission from Dranias, Grossberg, and Bullock, 2008.)

Orbitofrontal cells ($S_{CS_2}^{(1)}$) send top-down feedback to sensory cortex ($S_{CS_1}^{(1)}$) to enhance sensory representations that are motivationally salient (Fig. 16.4b). Competition among inferotemporal categories chooses those with the best combination of sensory and motivational support. An inferotemporal-amygdala-orbitofrontal feedback loop triggers a cognitive-emotional resonance that supports core consciousness of goals and feelings (Damasio, 1999; Grossberg, 1975, 2000a) and releases learned action commands from prefrontal cortex via downstream circuitry ($S_{CS_2}^{(1)} \rightarrow M$) to achieve valued goals.

The CogEM, or Cognitive-Emotional-Motor, model that is schematized in Figures 16.4a and 16.4b predicted and functionally explained these processes with increasing precision and predictive range since its introduction by Grossberg (1972a, 1972b, 1975, 1982). CogEM top-down prefrontal-to-sensory cortex feedback is another example of ART matching, one that clarifies data about attentional blocking and unblocking (Grossberg, 1975; Grossberg & Levine, 1987; Kamin, 1969; Pavlov, 1927). When this CogEM circuit functions improperly, symptoms of various mental disorders result. For example, hypoactivity of the amygdala or orbitofrontal cortex can cause failures in Theory of Mind processes that may occur in both autism and schizophrenia (Grossberg, 2000c; Grossberg & Seidman, 2006). In addition, as noted earlier, when top-down predictive matching processes become driving rather than modulatory, say due to abnormal tonic basal ganglia activity, schizophrenic hallucinations can occur (Grossberg, 2000a).

The MOTIVATOR model (Dranias et al., 2008; Grossberg, Bullock, & Dranias, 2008) further develops the CogEM model, just as SMART further develops ART (see Figure 16.4c). The MOTIVATOR model unifies the CogEM and TELOS models (Brown, Bullock, & Grossberg, 1999, 2004). TELOS proposes how the basal ganglia trigger reinforcement learning in response to unexpected rewards (Schultz, 1998), and it gates selection and release of plans and actions that are learned through reinforcement learning, In vivo, the basal ganglia and amygdala work together to provide motivational support, focus

attention, and release contextually appropriate actions to achieve valued goals. MOTIVATOR clarifies how this interaction happens.

MOTIVATOR describes cognitive–emotional interactions between higher order sensory cortices and an evaluative neuraxis composed of the hypothalamus, amygdala, basal ganglia, and orbitofrontal cortex. Given a conditioned stimulus (CS), the model amygdala and lateral hypothalamus interact to calculate the expected current value of the subjective outcome that the CS predicts, constrained by the current state of deprivation or satiation. The amygdala relays the expected value information to orbitofrontal cells that receive inputs from anterior inferotemporal cells, and medial orbitofrontal cells that receive inputs from rhinal cortex. The activations of these orbitofrontal cells code the subjective values of objects. These values guide behavioral choices. The model basal ganglia detect errors in CS-specific predictions of the value and timing of rewards. Excitatory inputs from the pedunculopontine nucleus interact with timed inhibitory inputs from model striosomes in the ventral striatum to regulate dopamine burst and dip responses from cells in the substantia nigra pars compacta and ventral tegmental area. Learning in cortical and striatal regions is strongly modulated by dopamine.

The model has been used to simulate tasks that examine food-specific satiety, Pavlovian conditioning, reinforcer devaluation, and simultaneous visual discrimination. Model simulations successfully reproduce discharge dynamics of known cell types, including signals that predict saccadic reaction times and CS-dependent changes in systolic blood pressure. The model hereby illustrates how cognitive processes in prefrontal cortex can influence both bodily processes such as blood pressure and actions such as eye movements toward a valued goal object.

9. ADAPTIVELY TIMED PREDICTIONS: DISTINGUISHING EXPECTED VERSUS UNEXPECTED DISCONFIRMATIONS

Reinforcement learning must be adaptively timed, since rewards are often delayed in time relative to actions aimed at acquiring them.

On the one hand, if an animal or human could not inhibit its exploratory behavior, then it could starve to death by restlessly moving from place to place, unable to remain in one place long enough to obtain delayed rewards there, such as food. On the other hand, if an animal inhibited its exploratory behavior for too long while waiting for an expected reward, such as food, then it could starve to death if food was not forthcoming. Being able to predict *when* desired consequences occur is often as important as predicting *that* they will occur. Indeed, to control predictive action, the brain needs to coordinate the What, Why, When, Where, and How of desired consequences by combining recognition learning, reinforcement learning, adaptively timed learning, spatial learning, and sensory-motor learning, respectively. Thus, the survival of a human or animal may depend on its ability to accurately time the delay of a goal object based upon its previous experiences in a given situation.

Adaptive timing requires balancing between *exploratory* behavior, which may discover novel sources of reward, and *consummatory* behavior, which may acquire expected sources of reward. A human or animal needs to suppress exploratory behavior and focus attention upon an expected source of reward when the reward is expected. The Spectral Timing model (Brown et al., 1999; Fiala, Grossberg, & Bullock, 1996; Grossberg & Merrill, 1992, 1996; Grossberg & Schmajuk, 1989) accomplishes this by predicting how the brain distinguishes *expected nonoccurrences*, or *disconfirmations*, of rewards, which should not interfere with acquiring the delayed goal, from *unexpected nonoccurrences*, or *disconfirmations*, of rewards, which can trigger consequences of predictive failure, including reset of working memory, attention shifts, emotional rebounds, and exploratory behaviors.

10. Spectral timing and spectral spacing in the hippocampus

The name *spectral timing* signifies that a population "spectrum" of cells, or cell sites, with different reaction rates can learn to match the statistical distribution of expected delays in reinforcement over time. Although each of these cells, or cell sites, reacts briefly at different times, their population response as a whole can bridge a much longer time interval, ranging from hundreds of milliseconds to seconds, that can be tuned by learning to match external experimental contingencies. Gorchetchnikov and Grossberg (2007) have proposed that the spectral timing mechanisms within the hippocampus which respond to conditioned stimuli use circuits which are homologous to those by which entorhinal grid cells give rise to hippocampal place cells. In the former case, a spectrum of small time scales can be combined to generate much longer and behaviorally relevant times. In the latter case, a "spectrum" of small grid cell spatial scales can be combined to generate much larger and behavioral relevant spaces. This homology has led to the name *spectral spacing* for the mechanism whereby grid cells give rise to place cells. The Spectral Timing model reflects the part of entorhinal-hippocampal dynamics that is devoted to representing objects and events; for example, from lateral entorhinal cortex; the Spectral Spacing model reflects a complementary part of entorhinal-hippocampal dynamics that is devoted to representing spatial representations, for example, from medial entorhinal cortex, with both types joined in the hippocampus to support both spatial navigation and episodic learning and memory (Eichenbaum & Lipton, 2008).

11. Spectral timing in cerebellum and hippocampus: timed action, attention, and autism

The Spectral Timing model clarifies many different aspects of adaptively timed learning. These behaviors range from adaptively timed reinforcement learning, motivated attention, and action, via circuits involving basal ganglia, hippocampus, and cerebellum, to how various individuals with autism experience failures of adaptive timing. In the latter case, these individuals prematurely display behaviors in a context-inappropriate manner that can prevent the behaviors from being rewarded (Grossberg & Seidman, 2006; Sears, Finn, & Steinmetz, 1994).

Evidence for adaptive timing occurs during several types of reinforcement learning. For example, classical conditioning is optimal at a range of positive interstimulus intervals (ISIs) between the conditioned stimulus (CS) and unconditioned stimulus (US) that are characteristic of the animal and the task, and it is greatly attenuated at zero and long ISIs. Within this range, learned responses are timed to match the statistics of the learning environment (Smith, 1968). Although the amygdala is a primary site for emotion and stimulus–reward association, the hippocampus and cerebellum have also been implicated in adaptively timed processing of cognitive-emotional interactions. For example, Thompson et al. (1987) distinguished two types of learning that go on during conditioning of the rabbit Nictitating Membrane Response: Adaptively timed "conditioned fear" learning that is linked to the hippocampus, and adaptively timed "learning of the discrete adaptive response" that is linked to the cerebellum.

A unified explanation of why both hippocampus and cerebellum use adaptively timed learning is given by the START (Spectrally Timed ART) model (Fig. 16.5a), which unifies the ART and CogEM models (Fiala et al., 1996; Grossberg & Merrill, 1992, 1996; Grossberg & Schmajuk, 1987). CogEM predicts how salient conditioned cues can rapidly focus attention upon their sensory categories (S) via a cognitive-emotional resonance with their associated drive (D) representations (Fig. 16.4). However, what then prevents the actions (M) that they control from being prematurely released?

In particular, suppose that a conditioned stimulus (CS), say via the motor output pathway M in Figures 4a and 4b, activates pathways to both a subcortical cerebellar nucleus and to cerebellar cortex parallel fibers that synapse on Purkinje cells with a spectrum of differently timed intracellular processes (Fig. 16.5b). Unconditioned stimulus–activated climbing fibers provide a teaching signal that also converges upon the parallel fiber/Purkinje cell synapses. This teaching signal causes the active synapses within the parallel fiber spectrum to become weaker (long-term depression) if they are activated by the CS when the US teaching signal becomes active. Synapses whose spectral activity does not overlap the climbing fiber signals become stronger (long-term potentiation). Because the Purkinje cells tonically inhibit their subcortical target cells, their adaptively timed inhibition by the CS disinhibits the effect of tonic Purkinje cell outputs on cerebellar nuclear cells. In other words, a timed gate opens and allows the subcortical cells to fire. The model proposes that climbing fibers also control learning of adaptive gains along subcortical pathways through the nuclear cells. Thus, when the adaptively timed Purkinje cell gate opens, the learned gains can be expressed at the correct time and with the correct amplitude to cause a correctly calibrated motor response.

Fiala, Grossberg, and Bullock (1996) have developed and simulated a detailed model of cerebellar adaptive timing. This model links biochemistry, neurophysiology, neuroanatomy, and behavior, and it predicts how the metabotropic glutamate (mGluR) receptor system may create a spectrum of delays during cerebellar adaptively timed learning, as well as, by extension, in other brain regions with adaptively timed cell responses, such as the hippocampus and basal ganglia (Brown et al., 1999; Grossberg & Merrill, 1992, 1996). Subsequent experiments confirmed a role for calcium signaling and mGluR in cerebellar adaptive timing (Finch & Augustine, 1998; Ichise et al., 2000; Miyata et al., 2000; Takechi, Eilers, & Konnerth, 1998). This model simulates both normal adaptively timed conditioning data and premature responding when cerebellar cortex is lesioned (Perrett, Ruiz, & Mauk, 1993). Cerebellar adaptive timing hereby reconciles two potentially conflicting behavioral properties: fast allocation of attention to motivationally salient events via cortico-amydala feedback versus adaptively timed responses to these events via cortico-cerebellar adaptively timed responding. Indeed, various individuals with autism, who are known to have cerebellar deficiencies, also perform short-latency responses in the eye-blink paradigm (Grossberg & Seidman, 2006; Sears et al., 1994). The Spectral Timing model provides a way to understand how such adaptive timing deficits occur. Its prediction of a key role of mGluR in

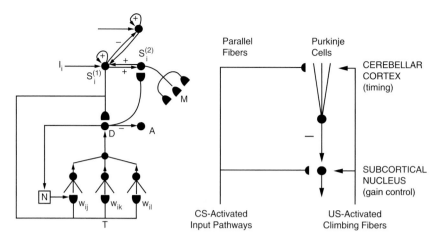

Figure 16.5 START model: Adaptively timed learning maintains motivated attention (pathway $D \rightarrow S_i^{(2)} \rightarrow S_i^{(1)} \rightarrow I$**) while it inhibits activation of the orienting system (pathway** $D \rightarrow A$**). See text for details. (Reprinted with permission from Grossberg and Merrill, 1992.)**

adaptively timed learning also points to new experiments or tests that can be done with autistic individuals to determine whether, indeed, the mGluR system is not functioning normally in them.

For adaptively timed responding to be effective, motivated attention needs to persist long enough to support the readout of adaptively timed motor commands and to prevent irrelevant events from prematurely resetting these commands. The START model (Grossberg & Merrill, 1992, 1996) proposes how hippocampal dentate-CA3 circuits that are capable of adaptively timed learning can modulate the responses of ART and CogEM circuits that have already been summarized (Fig. 16.5a). Without these hippocampal mechanisms, a novel event could easily reset motor commands prematurely. Indeed, if a top-down prototype and bottom-up sensory input mismatch too much for resonance to occur, then the orienting system can be activated and reset active categories (Fig. 16.2). The hippocampal system and nonspecific thalamus are proposed to be part of this mismatch-activated orienting system A. The thalamocortical and corticocortical mismatches that activate hippocampus or nonspecific thalamus are not, however, sensitive to whether the novel event that caused the mismatch is task relevant. The START model clarifies how mismatches may be

modulated by task relevance in an adaptively timed way.

In particular, Figure 16.5a suggests how adaptively timed learning within the dentate-CA3 circuits (T in Fig. 16.5a) of the hippocampus is proposed to inhibit the activation of the orienting system A during an interval wherein a valued and predictable goal is being acted upon. Indeed, hippocampal dentate-CA3 cell firing reflects the learned delays observed during the rabbit nictitating membrane response (Berger, Berry, & Thompson, 1986). The START model hereby proposes how adaptively timed inhibition of the hippocampal orienting system (Fig. 16.5a) and adaptively timed disinhibition of cerebellar nuclear cells (Fig. 16.5b) may be coordinated to enable motivated attention to be maintained on a goal while adaptively timed predictive responses are released to obtain the goal.

Processing stages $S^{(2)}$ and $S^{(2)}$ in Figure 16.5a play the role of sensory cortex and prefrontal cortex, respectively, in the CogEM model circuit of Figure 16.4a. Stage D is an emotional center, or drive representation, like the amygdala. Stage M schematizes motor output pathways. The feedback pathways $D \rightarrow S^{(2)} \rightarrow S^{(1)}$ from a particular drive representation to sensory representations are capable of focusing attention on motivationally consistent events in the world. The excitatory pathways from $S^{(1)} \rightarrow D$ learn the conditioned reinforcer properties of a sensory cue, such as a CS, whereas the pathways $D \to S^{(2)}$ learn the incentive motivational properties of cues. Representations in $S^{(2)}$ can fire vigorously only if they receive convergent signals from $S^{(1)}$ and D, corresponding to the sensitivity of orbitofrontal cortex to both sensory and reinforcing properties of cues. Then they deliver positive feedback to $S^{(1)}$ and bias the competition among sensory representations to focus attention on their respective features and to attentionally block inhibited features.

Prior to conditioning, a CS can be stored at $S^{(1)}$ and can prime D and $S^{(2)}$ without supraliminally firing these representations. After conditioning, the CS can trigger strong conditioned $S^{(1)} \to D \to S^{(2)} \to S^{(1)}$ feedback and rapidly draw attention to itself as it activates the emotional representations and motivational pathways controlled by D. Representation D can also inhibit the orienting system A as it focuses attention upon motivationally valued sensory events. Thus, here is one way in which the CogEm and ART models interact: Emotionally salient goal objects can inhibit the orienting system and thus prevent irrelevant distractors from attracting attention when there is an ART mismatch.

This inhibition of the orienting system becomes adaptively timed as follows: The sensory representations $S^{(1)}$ send pathways to a spectral timing circuit T, assumed to be in the dentate-CA3 region of the hippocampus, whose adaptive weights w are trained by a Now Print, or teaching signal, N. The teaching signal N is transiently activated by changes in the activity of the drive representation D that occur when a reinforcing event activates D. After conditioning of T takes place, adaptively timed readout from T can maintain attention on task-relevant cues by amplifying their cortical representations $S^{(2)}$ while inhibiting the orienting system A for an adaptively timed duration. In Figure 16.5a, the simplest such inhibitory path is depicted, directly from T to D and thereupon to A. A more complex set of pathways exists in vivo.

Many data have been rationalized using these circuits, including data from delayed nonmatch to sample (DNMS) experiments wherein both temporal delays and novelty-sensitive recognition processes are involved (Gaffan, 1974; Mishkin & Delacour, 1975). In summary, the START model enables three key properties to simultaneously coexist:

- *Fast motivated attention.* Rapid focusing of attention on motivationally salient cues occurs from regions like the amygdala to prefrontal cortex (pathway $D \to S^{(2)}$ in Fig. 16.5a). Without further processing, fast activation of the CS-activated $S^{(2)}$ sensory representations could prematurely release motor behaviors (pathway $S^{(2)} \to M$ in Fig. 16.5).
- *Adaptively timed responding.* Adaptively timed readout of responses via cerebellar circuits (pathway M in Fig. 16.5b) enables learned responses to be released at task-appropriate times, despite the fact that CS cortical representations can be quickly activated by fast motivated attention.
- *Adaptively timed duration of motivated attention and inhibition of orienting responses.* Premature reset of active CS representations by irrelevant cues during task-specific delays is prevented by adaptively timed inhibition of mismatch-sensitive cells in the orienting system of the hippocampus (pathway $T \to D \to A$ in Fig. 16.5a). This inhibition is part of the competition between consummatory and orienting behaviors (Staddon, 1983). Adaptively timed incentive motivational feedback ($D \to S^{(2)} \to S^{(1)}$ in Fig. 16.5a) simultaneously maintains CS activation in short-term memory, so that the CS can continue to read out adaptively timed responses until they are complete. The contingent negative variation (CNV), event-related potential is predicted to be a neural marker of adaptively timed motivational feedback. Many additional data have been explained using these circuits, including data from delayed nonmatch to sample (DNMS) experiments wherein both temporal delays and novelty-sensitive recognition processes are involved (Gaffan, 1974; Mishkin & Delacour, 1975). Similar adaptive timing mechanisms seem to operate in basal ganglia (Brown et al., 1999).

12. Laminar cortical dynamics of working memory, list chunking, and performance

The aforementioned mechanisms do not explain how the brain responds selectively to *sequences* of events. Predictive behavior depends upon the capacity to think about, plan, execute, and evaluate such event sequences. In particular, multiple events in a specific temporal order can be stored temporarily in *working memory*. As event sequences are temporarily stored, they are grouped, or chunked, through learning into unitized plans, or list chunks, and can later be performed at variable rates under volitional control. Here, the term *working memory* is used to describe brain processes that temporarily store the *temporal order of several events*, not merely persistence of individual events.

Grossberg (1978a, 1978b) introduced a model of working memory and list chunking, which proposed how working memories are designed to enable list chunks to be stably learned and remembered. Inputs to this working memory are unitized item categories of individual events or objects (see Section 2) that have enough adaptively timed, incentive motivational support (see Section 7) to be persistently stored and transferred into working memory. Item representations are stored in working memory as a temporally evolving spatial pattern of activity across working memory cells. The relative activity of different cell populations codes the temporal order in which the items will be rehearsed, with the largest activities rehearsed earliest; hence, the name Item and Order working memory for this class of models. A more recent name is competitive queuing (Houghton, 1990). The LIST PARSE model (Grossberg & Pearson, 2008) built on this foundation to predict how laminar circuits in ventrolateral prefrontal cortex embody a cognitive working memory and list chunk learning network that interacts with a motor working memory in dorsolateral prefrontal cortex and a basal ganglia adaptively timed volitional control system.

Accumulating neurobiological data support the view that visual and verbal object categories may be learned in temporal and ventromedial prefrontal (e.g., orbitofrontal) cortex, with the latter responding to combined item and motivational signals, followed by the loading of these item representations into a sequential working memory that codes temporal order information in ventrolateral and/or dorsolateral prefrontal cortex (e.g., Barbas, 2000; Goldman-Rakic, 1987; Petrides, 2005; Ranganath & D'Esposito, 2005). These temporally evolving working memory patterns are, in turn, categorized by list chunks, or sequential plans, which can be used to predict subsequent expected events.

A full review of the LIST PARSE model goes beyond the scope of this chapter. Here it suffices to note that LIST PARSE unifies the explanation of cognitive, neurophysiological, and anatomical data from humans and monkeys concerning how predictive, sequentially organized behaviors are controlled. Its laminar cognitive prefrontal circuits are variations of laminar circuits in visual cortex (see Section 6). Thus, both vision and cognition seem to use variations of a shared laminar cortical design to rapidly learn and stably remember, using ART top-down matching mechanisms, categories with which to predict a changing world. In particular, LIST PARSE quantitatively simulates human cognitive data about immediate *serial* recall and immediate, delayed, and continuous-distracter *free* recall, as well as monkey neurophysiological data from the prefrontal cortex obtained during sequential sensory-motor imitation and planned performance. It hereby clarifies how both spatial and nonspatial working memories may share the same laminar cortical circuit design.

13. Balancing reactive versus planned behaviors: basal ganglia gating

Complementary orienting versus attentional systems search for and learn new recognition codes (see Section 5). They are subsumed by a larger complementary brain system that balances reactive versus planned behaviors. Rapid reactive movements, such as orienting movements, facilitate survival in response to unexpected dangers. Planned movements, which involve focused attention, often take longer to select and release. How does the brain prevent premature reactive movements toward objects in situations where a more slowly occurring planned movement is more adaptive?

Movement gates (see Section 10) can inhibit a reactive movement command until a planned movement can effectively compete with it. Then a planned command can open its gate and launch its movement. The basal ganglia carry out such a gating function. Movement gates overcome a potentially devastating problem: A movement gate must be opened to release any movement. Given that a movement gate needs to be opened to release even a reactive movement, how does the brain know that a plan is being selected, before it is selected, so that it can inhibit the gate-opening process that would otherwise have released the faster reactive movement? The TELOS model (Brown et al., 2004) predicts how frontal–parietal interactions prevent a reactive movement command from opening its gate before a planned movement command is ready, yet also allow a reactive movement command to open its gate quickly when no planned movement command is being formed. In particular, the model predicted that a frontal-parietal resonance occurs when this competition is resolved. Such a resonance has recently been reported (Buschman & Miller, 2007). This resonance is predicted to signal attentive consistency between a finally selected movement plan and available movement targets, and to thereby enable the appropriate basal ganglia movement gate to open. Pasupathy and Miller (2002) have reported the expected timing of frontal and basal ganglia interactions during this process.

14. SPATIALLY INVARIANT RECOGNITION CODES CONTROL SPATIALLY PRECISE ACTIONS

Conditional movements toward valued goal objects cannot be made until goal objects are recognized and selected and their spatial locations specified. As noted in section 1 and 3, and Figure 16.1, the What stream learns object representations that are increasingly independent of object position and size, whereas the Where stream represents object positions and how to move. What-Where interstream interactions overcome these complementary informational deficiencies to generate movements toward recognized objects.

Whereas object representations in posterior inferotemporal cortex (ITp) combine feature and positional information, object representations in anterior inferotemporal cortex (ITa) are more positionally invariant. These two types of representations are linked by reciprocal learned connections, as described by ART. ITp representations also project to the posterior parietal cortex (PPC) as target locations of an object. Consider what happens when multiple objects in a scene all try to activate their corresponding ITp and ITa representations. Suppose that a particular ITa category represents a valued goal object in that situation. As noted in the Section 8, the ITa representation can get amplified by an inferotemporal-amygdala-orbitofrontal resonance. When this happens, the amplified ITa representation can better compete for object attention, and it can send larger top-down priming signals to its ITp representations. The ITp representation that corresponds to the valued object is thereby selectively amplified and sends an amplified signal to the parietal cortex, where its target location can win the competition for where the next movement will go. See Figure 16.6. This scheme can help to solve the Where's Waldo problem, or the rapid discovery of a desired goal object in a cluttered scene.

15. LEARNING VIEW- AND POSITION-INVARIANT OBJECT CATEGORIES USING ATTENTIONAL SHROUDS

How are position-invariant and view-invariant categories learned by the brain? To understand how this happens, several basic questions need to be answered: What is an object? How does the brain learn what an object is under both unsupervised and supervised learning conditions? How does the brain learn to bind multiple views of an object into a view-invariant and position-invariant object category while scanning its parts with eye movements?

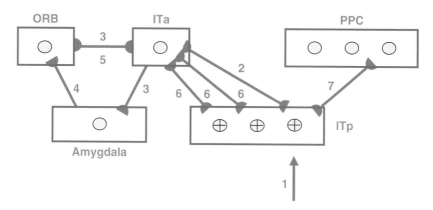

Figure 16.6 Linking What stream recognition to Where stream action: Interactions between cortical areas ITp, ITa, amygdala, orbitofrontal cortex (ORB), and posterior parietal cortex (PPC) can bridge the gap between invariant ITa categories and parietal target locations. The numbers indicate the order of pathway activations. If there are two numbers, the larger one represents the stage when feedback activates that pathway. See text for details.

To answer these questions, one also needs to solve the following problem: As eyes scan a scene, two successive eye movements may focus on different parts of the same object or on different objects. How does the brain avoid erroneously classifying views of different objects together, even before the brain knows what the object is? One cannot say that the brain does this by knowing that some views belong together whereas others do not, because this can happen even before the brain has a concept of what the object is. Indeed, such scanning eye movements may be used to learn the object concept in the first place.

The ARTSCAN model (Fig. 16.7) clarifies how the brain uses scanning saccadic eye movements to learn view-invariant object categories (Fazl, Grossberg, & Mingolla, 2009). The earlier discussion about ART considered only object attention (Posner, 1980) in the What cortical stream. ARTSCAN explains how object attention works with spatial attention (Duncan, 1984) in the Where cortical stream to direct eye movements that explore object surfaces. As the eyes move around an object surface, multiple view-specific categories are learned of the object (e.g., in ITp) and are associated with an emerging view-invariant object category (e.g., in ITa).

How does the brain know which view-specific categories should be associated with a given view-invariant category?

ARTSCAN predicts that a *pre-attentively* formed surface representation activates an *attentional shroud* (Tyler & Kontsevich, 1995), or form-fitting distribution of spatial attention, even before the brain can recognize the surface as representing a particular object. This shroud persists within the Where stream during active scanning of an object. The shroud protects the view-invariant category from getting reset, even while view-specific categories are reset, as the eyes explore an object. The shroud does this by inhibiting the ITa reset mechanism (Fig. 16.7).

How does the shroud persist during active scanning of an object? A *surface-shroud resonance* arises due to feedback interactions between a surface representation (e.g., in area V4) and spatial attention (e.g., in posterior parietal cortex), and it focuses spatial attention upon the object to be learned. When the shroud collapses as the eyes move to another surface, its view-invariant object category is reset as well. Many paradoxical data are explained by these concepts, including how spatial attention can increase the perceived brightness of a surface (Carrasco, Penpeci-Talgar, & Eckstein, 2000; Reynolds & Desimone, 2003),

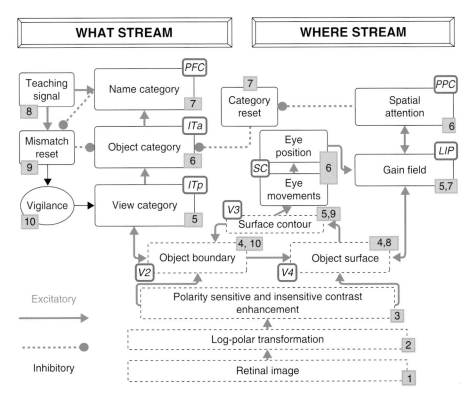

Figure 16.7 **ARTSCAN model: An active attentional shroud in PPC inhibits otherwise tonically active Category Reset inhibition. This enables the emerging view-invariant object category in ITa to stay active while view-specific categories in ITp are associated with it as the eyes scan a scene. Interactions between object boundaries and surfaces via a surface contour process are proposed to control eye movements on a surface whose shroud amplifies the corresponding object surface. (Reprinted with permission from Fazl, Grossberg, and Mingolla, 2009.)**

and what sort of category invariance can be learned (Zoccolan et al., 2007).

A recent experiment of Chiu and Yantis (2009) provides evidence for the ARTSCAN prediction of how a shroud protects an emerging view-invariant category from being prematurely reset when each of the view-specific categories that are associated with it is reset. These authors found that a shift of spatial attention evokes a transient signal in the medial superior parietal lobule that corresponds to a shift in categorization rules. In ARTSCAN, collapse of an attentional shroud (spatial attention shift) disinhibits the parietal reset mechanism (transient signal) that leads to collapse of the previous view-invariant object category and instatement of a new one (shift in categorization rules)

16. INHIBITORY MATCHING AND MISMATCH LEARNING OF SENSORY-MOTOR MAPS AND GAINS

As noted in the Section 2, learning of object representations in the What stream uses excitatory matching and match-based learning to solve the stability-plasticity dilemma. Where stream learning, in contrast, often uses inhibitory matching and mismatch-based learning. Inhibitory matching is often between brain representations of a target position and the present position of a motor effector. Inhibitory matching computes a difference vector that represents the distance and direction of an intended movement. The difference vector is volitionally gated (See section 12) by a basal ganglia GO signal that determines when and how fast the movement will occur (Bullock, Cisek, & Grossberg, 1998; Bullock & Grossberg, 1988). During motor learning, a difference vector can also generate error signals when the same target position and present position are encoded but not properly calibrated. These error signals eliminate the source of the mismatch through time by recalibrating system maps and gains. Neural models predict how mismatch learning may tune spatial representations and adaptive motor gains in basal ganglia, cerebellum, motor cortex, parietal cortex, and prefrontal cortex (Brown et al., 1999, 2004; Fiala et al., 1996; Grossberg & Paine, 2000; Guenther, Bullock, Greve, & Grossberg, 1994).

Inhibitory matching and mismatch learning exhibit catastrophic forgetting. However, catastrophic forgetting is a good property for learning sensory-motor maps and gains. In particular, it would be maladaptive to remember for life the maps and gains whereby our brains controlled our infant limbs. Continual recalibration of maps and gains is adaptive in response to corresponding changes in our bodies. These recalibrated maps and gains are capable of generating predictive commands that our bodies can then accurately obey.

In summary, perceptual/cognitive processes often use excitatory matching and match-based learning to create stable predictive representations of objects and events in the world. Complementary spatial/motor processes often use inhibitory matching and mismatch-based learning to continually update spatial maps and sensory-motor gains. Together these complementary predictive and learning mechanisms create a self-stabilizing perceptual/cognitive front end for activating the more labile spatial/motor processes that control our changing bodies as they act upon objects in the world.

ACKNOWLEDGMENTS

Supported in part by CELEST, a National Science Foundation Science of Learning Center (SBE-0354378), and by the SyNAPSE program of DARPA (HR0011-09-C-0001).

REFERENCES

Aggleton, J. P. (1993). The contribution of the amygdala to normal and abnormal emotional states. *Trends in Neurosciences, 16*, 328–333.

Bar, M., Tootell, R. B. H., Schacter, D. L., Greve, D. N., Fischl, B., Mendola, J. D., Rosen, B. R., & Dale, A. M. (2001). Cortical mechanisms specific to explicit object recognition. *Neuron, 29*, 529–535.

Barbas, H. (1995). Anatomic basis of cognitive-emotional interactions in the primate prefrontal cortex. *Neuroscience and Biobehavioral Reviews, 19*, 499–510.

Barbas, H. (2000). Connections underlying the synthesis of cognition, memory and emotion in primate prefrontal cortices. *Brain Research Bulletin, 52*, 319–330.

Baxter, M. G., Parker, A., Lindner, C. C. C., Izquierdo, A. D., & Murray, E. A. (2000). Control of response selection by reinforcer value requires interaction of amygdala and orbital prefrontal cortex. *Journal of Neuroscience, 20*, 4311–4319.

Berger, T.W., Berry, S.D., & Thompson, R.F. (1986). Role of the hippocampus in classical conditioning of aversive and appetitive behaviors. In R.L. Isaacson & K.H. Pribram (Eds). *The Hippocampus, Volume 4*. (pp. 203–239) New York: Plenum Press.

Berke, J. D., Hetrick, V., Breck, J., & Greene, R. W. (2008). Transient 23-30 Hz oscillations in mouse hippocampus during exploration of novel environments. *Hippocampus, 18*, 519–529.

Brown, J. W., Bullock, D., & Grossberg, S. (1999). How the basal ganglia use parallel excitatory and inhibitory learning pathways to selectively respond to unexpected rewarding cues. *Journal of Neuroscience, 19*, 10502–10511.

Brown, J. W., Bullock, D., & Grossberg, S. (2004). How laminar frontal cortex and basal ganglia circuits interact to control planned and reactive saccades. *Neural Networks, 17*, 471–510.

Buffalo, E. A., Fries, P., & Desimone, R. (2004). Layer-specific attentional modulation in early visual areas. *Society for Neuroscience Abstracts, 30*, 717–716.

Bullier, J., Hupé, J. M., James, A., & Girard, P. (1996). Functional interactions between areas V1 and V2 in the monkey. *Journal of Physiology (Paris), 90*, 217–220.

Bullock, D., & Grossberg, S. (1988). Neural dynamics of planned arm movements: Emergent invariants and speed-accuracy properties during trajectory formation. *Psychological Review, 95,* 49–90.

Bullock, D., Cisek, P., & Grossberg, S. (1998). Cortical networks for control of voluntary arm movements under variable force conditions. *Cerebral Cortex, 8,* 48–62.

Buschman, T. J., & Miller, E. K. (2007). Top-down versus bottom-up control of attention in the prefrontal and posterior parietal cortices. *Science, 315,* 1860–1862.

Buschman, T. J., & Miller, E. K. (2009). Serial, covert shifts of attention during visual search are reflected by the frontal eye fields and correlated with population oscillations. *Neuron, 63,* 386–396.

Caputo, G., & Guerra, S. (1998). Attentional selection by distractor suppression. *Vision Research, 38,* 669–689.

Carpenter, G. A., & Grossberg, S. (1987). A massively parallel architecture for a self-organizing neural pattern-recognition machine. *Computer Vision Graphics and Image Processing, 37,* 54–115.

Carpenter, G. A., & Grossberg, S. (1992). A self-organizing neural network for supervised learning, recognition, and prediction. *IEEE Communications Magazine, 30,* 38–49.

Carpenter, G.A. & Grossberg, S. (1993). Normal and amnesic learning, recognition, and memory by a neural model of cortico-hippocampal interactions. *Trends in Neurosciences, 16,* 131–137.

Carrasco, M., Penpeci-Talgar, C., & Eckstein, M. (2000). Spatial covert attention increases contrast sensitivity across the CSF: Support for signal enhancement. *Vision Research, 40,* 1203–1215.

Chiu, Y-C., & Yantis, S. (2009). A domain-independent source of cognitive control for task sets: Shifting spatial attention and switching categorization rules. *The Journal of Neuroscience, 29,* 3930–3938.

Damasio, A. R. (1999). *The feeling of what happens: Body and emotion in the making of consciousness.* New York: Harcourt Brace.

Desimone, R. (1998). Visual attention mediated by biased competition in extrastriate visual cortex. *Philosophical Transactions of the Royal Society of London, 353,* 1245–1255.

Downing, C. J. (1988). Expectancy and visual-spatial attention: Effects on perceptual quality. *Journal of Experimental Psychology: Human Perception and Performance, 14,* 188–202.

Dranias, M. R., Grossberg, S., & Bullock, D. (2008). Dopaminergic and non-dopaminergic value systems in conditioning and outcome-specific revaluation. *Brain Research, 1238,* 239–287.

Duncan, J. (1984). Selective attention and the organization of visual information. *Journal of Experimental Psychology: General, 113,* 501–517.

Eichenbaum, H., & Lipton, P. A. (2008). Towards a functional organization of the medial temporal lobe memory system: Role of the parahippocampal and medial entorhinal cortical areas. *Hippocampus, 18,* 1314–1324.

Engel, A. K., Fries, P., & Singer, W. (2001). Dynamics predictions: Oscillations and synchrony in top-down processing. *Nature Reviews Neuroscience, 2,* 704–716.

Fazl, A., Grossberg, S., & Mingolla, E. (2009). View-invariant object category learning, recognition, and search: How spatial and object attention are coordinated using surface-based attentional shrouds. *Cognitive Psychology, 58,* 1–48.

Fiala, J. C., Grossberg, S., & Bullock, D. (1996). Metabotropic glutamate receptor activation in cerebellar Purkinje cells as substrate for adaptive timing of the classically conditioned eye blink response. *Journal of Neuroscience, 16,* 3760–3774.

Finch, E. A., & Augustine, G. J. (1998). Local calcium signalling by inositol-1,4,5-triphosphate in Purkinje cell dendrites. *Nature, 396,* 753–756.

Frank, L. M., Stanley, G. B., & Brown, E. N. (2004). Hippocampal plasticity across multiple days of exposure to novel environments. *Journal of Neuroscience, 24,* 7681–7689.

Gaffan, D. (1974). Recognition impaired and association intact in the memory of monkeys after transection of the fornix. *Journal of Comparative and Physiological Psychology, 86,* 1100–1109.

Goldman-Rakic, P. S. (1987). Circuitry of primate prefrontal cortex and regulation of behavior by representational memory. In F. Plum & V. Mountcastle (Eds.), *Handbook of physiology* (Vol. 5, pp. 373–417). Bethesda, MD: American Physiological Society.

Gorchetchnikov, A., & Grossberg, S. (2007). Space, time, and learning in the hippocampus: How fine spatial and temporal scales are expanded into population codes for behavioral control. *Neural Networks, 20,* 182–193.

Gove, A., Grossberg, S., & Mingolla, E. (1995). Brightness perception, illusory contours, and corticogeniculate feedback. *Visual Neuroscience, 12,* 1027–1052.

Grossberg, S. (1972a). A neural theory of punishment and avoidance, I: Qualitative theory. *Mathematical Biosciences*, *15*, 39–67.

Grossberg, S. (1972b). A neural theory of punishment and avoidance, II: Quantitative theory. *Mathematical Biosciences*, *15*, 253–285.

Grossberg, S. (1975). A neural model of attention, reinforcement, and discrimination learning. *International Review of Neurobiology*, *18*, 263–327.

Grossberg, S. (1978a). A theory of human memory: self-organization and performance of sensory-motor codes, maps, and plans. In B. Rosen & F. Snell (Eds.), *Progress in theoretical biology* (Vol. 5, pp. 233–374). New York: Academic Press. (Reprinted in Grossberg, S. [1982]. *Studies of Mind and Brain* [pp. 500–639]. Boston: Reidel.)

Grossberg, S. (1978b). Behavioral contrast in short-term memory: Serial binary memory models or parallel continuous memory models? *Journal of Mathematical Psychology*, *17*, 199–219.

Grossberg, S. (1980). How does a brain build a cognitive code? *Psychological Review*, *87*, 1–51.

Grossberg, S. (1982). Processing of expected and unexpected events during conditioning and attention: A psychophysiological theory. *Psychological Review*, *89*, 529–572.

Grossberg, S. (1999). How does the cerebral cortex work? Learning, attention and grouping by the laminar circuits of visual cortex. *Spatial Vision*, *12*, 163–186.

Grossberg, S. (2000a). How hallucinations may arise from brain mechanisms of learning, attention, and volition. *Journal of the International Neuropsychological Society*, *6*, 579–588.

Grossberg, S. (2000b). The complementary brain: Unifying brain dynamics and modularity. *Trends in Cognitive Sciences*, *4*, 233–246.

Grossberg, S. (2000c). The imbalanced brain: From normal behavior to schizophrenia. *Biological Psychiatry*, *48*, 81–98.

Grossberg, S. (2007). Consciousness CLEARS the mind. *Neural Networks*, *20*, 1040–1053.

Grossberg, S. (2009). Beta oscillations and hippocampal place cell learning during exploration of novel environments. *Hippocampus*, *19*, 881–885.

Grossberg, S., Bullock, D., & Dranias, M. R. (2008). Neural dynamics underlying impaired autonomic and conditioned responses following amygdala and orbitofrontal lesions. *Behavioral Neuroscience*, *122*, 1100–1125.

Grossberg, S., Govindarajan, K. K., Wyse, L. L., & Cohen, M. A. (2004). ARTSTREAM: A neural network model of auditory scene analysis and source segregation. *Neural Networks*, *17*, 511–536.

Grossberg, S., & Levine, D. S. (1987). Neural dynamics of attentionally modulated Pavlovian conditioning: Blocking, inter-stimulus interval, and secondary reinforcement. *Applied Optics*, *26*, 5015–5030.

Grossberg, S., & Merrill, J. W. L. (1992). A neural network model of adaptively timed reinforcement learning and hippocampal dynamics. *Cognitive Brain Research*, *1*, 3–38.

Grossberg, S., & Merrill, J. W. L. (1996). The hippocampus and cerebellum in adaptively timed learning, recognition, and movement. *Journal of Cognitive Neuroscience*, *8*, 257–277.

Grossberg, S., & Myers, C. W. (2000). The resonant dynamics of speech perception: Interword integration and duration-dependent backward effects. *Psychological Review*, *107*, 735–767.

Grossberg, S., & Paine, R. W. (2000). A neural model of corticocerebellar interactions during attentive imitation and predictive learning of sequential handwriting movements. *Neural Networks*, *13*, 999–1046.

Grossberg, S., & Pearson, L. (2008). Laminar cortical dynamics of cognitive and motor working memory, sequence learning and performance: Toward a unified theory of how the cerebral cortex works. *Psychological Review*, *115*, 677–732.

Grossberg, S., & Schmajuk, N. A. (1987). Neural dynamics of attentionally-modulated Pavlovian conditioning: Conditioned reinforcement, inhibition, and opponent processing. *Psychobiology*, *15*, 195–240.

Grossberg, S., & Schmajuk, N.A. (1989). Neural dynamics of adaptive timing and temporal discrimination during associative learning. *Neural Networks*, *2*, 79–102.

Grossberg, S., & Seidman, D. (2006). Neural dynamics of autistic behaviors: Cognitive, emotional, and timing substrates. *Psychological Review*, *113*, 483–525.

Grossberg, S., & Versace, M. (2008). Spikes, synchrony, and attentive learning by laminar thalamocortical circuits. *Brain Research*, *1218*, 278–312.

Guenther, F. H., Bullock, D., Greve, D., & Grossberg, S. (1994). Neural representations for sensory-motor control, III: Learning a body-centered representation of 3-D target position. *Journal of Cognitive Neuroscience*, *6*, 341–358.

Hafting, T., Fyhn, M., Molden, S., Moser, M. B., & Moser, E. (2005). Microstructure of the spatial map in the entorhinal cortex. *Nature*, *436*, 801–806.

Houghton, G. (1990). The problem of serial order: A neural network model of sequence learning and recall. In R. Dale, C. Mellish, & M. Zock (Eds.), *Current research in natural language generation* (pp. 287–319). London: Academic Press.

Hupé, J. M., James, A. C., Girard, D. C., & Bullier, J. (1997). Feedback connections from V2 modulate intrinsic connectivity within V1. *Society for Neuroscience Abstracts*, *406*(15), 1031.

Ichise, T., Kano, M., Hashimoto, K., Yangihara, D., Nakao, K., Shigemoto, R., Katsuki, M., & Aiba, A. (2000). mGluR1 in cerebellar Purkinje cells essential for long-term depression, synapse elimination, and motor coordination. *Science*, *288*, 1832–1835.

Kamin, L. J. (1969). Predictability, surprise, attention and conditioning. In B. A. Campbell & R. M. Church (Eds.), *Punishment and aversive behavior* (pp. 279–296.). New York: Appleton-Century-Crofts.

Kastner, S., & Ungerleider, L. G. (2001). The neural basis of biased competition in human visual cortex. *Neuropsychologia*, *39*, 1263–1276.

Kentros, C. G., Agnihotri, N. T., Streater, S., Kawkins, R. D., & Kandel, E. R. (2004). Increased attention to spatial context increases both place field stability and spatial memory. *Neuron*, *42*, 283–295.

Kentros, C., Hargreaves, E., Hawkins, R. D., Kandel, E. R., Shapiro, M., & Muller, R. V. (1998). Abolition of long-term stability of new hippocampal place cell maps by NMDA receptor blockade. *Science*, *280*, 2121–2126.

LeDoux, J. E. (1993). Emotional memory systems in the brain. *Behavioural Brain Research*, *58*, 69–79.

Mhatre, H., Gorchetchnikov, A., & Grossberg, S. (2009). Hexagonal structure of grid cells formed by fast self-organized learning within the entorhinal cortex. *Society for Neuroscience Abstracts*, *679*, 6.

Mhatre, H., Gorchetchnikov, A., & Grossberg, S. (2010). Grid cell hexagonal patterns formed by fast self-organized learning within entorhinal cortex.. *Hippocampus*, in press.

Mishkin, M., & Delacour, J. (1975). An analysis of short-term visual memory in the monkey. *Journal of Experimental Psychology: Animal Behavior Processes*, *1*, 326–334.

Miyata, M., Finch, E. A., Khiroug, L., Hashimoto, K., Hayasaka, S., Oda, S. I., Inouye, M., Takagishi, Y., Augustine, G. J., & Kano, M. (2000). Local calcium release in dendritic spines required for long-term synaptic depression. *Neuron*, *28*, 233–244.

Morris, R. G. & Frey, U. (1997). Hippocampal synaptic plasticity_role in spatial learning or the automatic recording of attended experience? *Philosophical Transactions of the Royal Society of London B: Biological Sciences*, *352*, 1489–1503.

Mounts, J. R. W. (2000). Evidence for suppressive mechanisms in attentional selection: Feature singletons produce inhibitory surrounds. *Perception and Psychophysics*, *62*, 969–983.

Muller, R.A. (1996). A quarter of a century of place cells. *Neuron*, *17*, 813–822.

Pasupathy, A., & Miller, E. K. (2002). Different time courses of learning-related activity in the prefrontal cortex and striatum. *Nature*, *433*, 873–876.

Pavlov, I. P. (1927). *Conditioned reflexes*. Oxford, England: Oxford University Press.

Perret, S. P., Ruiz, B. P., & Mauk, M. D. (1993). Cerebellar cortex lesions disrupt learning-dependent timing of conditioned eyelid responses. *Journal of Neuroscience*, *13*, 1708–1718.

Petrides, M. (2005). Lateral prefrontal cortex: architectonic and functional organization. *Philosophical Transactions of the Society of London B Biological Science*, *360*(1456), 781–795.

Pollen, D. A. (1999). On the neural correlates of visual perception. *Cerebral Cortex*, *9*, 4–19.

Posner, M. I. (1980). Orienting of attention. *Quarterly Journal of Experimental Psychology*, *32*, 3–25.

Raizada, R., & Grossberg, S. (2003). Towards a theory of the laminar architecture of cerebral cortex: Computational clues from the visual system. *Cerebral Cortex*, *13*, 100–113.

Ranganath, C., & D'Esposito, M. (2005). Directing the mind's eye: Prefrontal, inferior and medial temporal mechanisms for visual working memory. *Current Opinion in Neurobiology*, *15*, 175–182.

Reynolds, J., Chelazzi, L., & Desimone, R. (1999). Competitive mechanisms subserve attention in macaque areas V2 and V4. *The Journal of Neuroscience*, *19*, 1736–1753.

Reynolds, J. H., & Desimone, R. (2003). Interacting roles of attention and visual salience in V4. *Neuron*, *37*, 853–863.

Schoenbaum, G., Setlow, B., Saddoris, M. P., & Gallagher, M. (2003). Encoding predicted outcome and acquired value in orbitofrontal cortex during cue sampling depends upon input from basolateral amygdala. *Neuron*, *39*, 855–867.

Schultz, W. (1998). Predictive reward signals of dopamine neurons. *Journal of Neurophysiology*, *80*, 1–27.

Sears, L. L., Finn, P. R., & Steinmetz, J. E. (1994). Abnormal classical eye-blink conditioning in autism. *Journal of Autism and Developmental Disorders*, *24*, 737–751.

Sigala, N., & Logothetis, N. K. (2002). Visual categorization shapes feature selectivity in the primate temporal cortex. *Nature*, *415*, 318–320.

Sillito, A. M., Jones, H. E., Gerstein, G. L., & West, D. C. (1994). Feature-linked synchronization of thalamic relay cell firing induced by feedback from the visual cortex. *Nature*, *369*, 479–482.

Smith, E. L., Chino, Y., Ni, J., & Cheng, H. (1997). Binocular combination of contrast signals by striate cortical neurons in the monkey. *Journal of Neurophysiology*, *78*, 366–382.

Smith, M. C. (1968). CS-US interval and US intensity in classical conditioning of the rabbit's nictitating membrane response. *Journal of Comparative and Physiological Psychology*, *3*, 678–687.

Smith, A.T., Singh, K.D., & Greenlee, M.W. (2000). Attentional suppression of activity in the human visual cortex. *Neuroreport*, *11*, 271–277.

Somers, D. C., Dale, A. M., Seiffert, A. E., & Tootell, R. B. (1999). Functional MRI reveals spatially specific attentional modulation in human primary visual cortex. *Proceedings of the National Academy of Sciences USA*, *96*, 1663–1668.

Staddon, J. E. R. (1983). *Adaptive behavior and learning*. New York: Cambridge University Press.

Steinman, B. A., Steinman, S. B., & Lehmkuhle, S. (1995). Visual attention mechanisms show a center-surround organization. *Vision Research*, *35*, 1859–1869.

Takechi, H., Eilers, J., & Konnerth, A. (1998). A new class of synaptic response involving calcium release in dendritic spines. *Nature*, *396*, 757–760.

Tanaka, K., Saito, H., Fukada, Y., & Moriya, M. (1991). Coding visual images of objects in the inferotemporal cortex of the macaque monkey. *Journal of Neurophysiology*, *66*, 170–189.

Thompson, L. T., & Best, P. J. (1990). Long-term stability of the place-field activity of single units recorded from the dorsal hippocampus of freely behaving rats. *Brain Research*, *509*, 299–308.

Thompson, R. F., Clark, G. A., Donegan, N. H., Lavond, G. A., Lincoln, D. G., Maddon, J., Mamounas, L. A., Mauk, M. D., & McCormick, D. A. (1987). Neuronal substrates of discrete, defensive conditioned reflexes, conditioned fear states, and their interactions in the rabbit. In I. Gormenzano, W. F. Prokasy, & R. F. Thompson (Eds.), *Classical conditioning* (3rd ed., pp. 371–399). Hillsdale, NJ: Erlbaum.

Tyler, C. W., & Kontsevich, L. L. (1995). Mechanisms of stereoscopic processing: Stereoattention and surface perception in depth reconstruction. *Perception*, *24*, 127–153.

Vanduffel, W., Tootell, R. B., & Orban, G. A. (2000). Attention-dependent suppression of meta bolic activity in the early stages of the macaque visual system. *Cerebral Cortex*, *10*, 109–126.

Wilson, M. A., & McNaughton, B. L. (1993). Dynamics of the hippocampal ensemble code for space. *Science*, *261*, 1055–1058.

Zoccolan, C., Kouh, M., Poggio, T., & DiCarlo, J. J. (2007). Trade-off between object selectivity and tolerance in monkey inferotemporal cortex. *Journal of Neuroscience*, *27*, 12292–12307.

CHAPTER 17
Predictive Coding: A Free-Energy Formulation

Karl J. Friston and Stefan Kiebel

This chapter looks at prediction from the point of view of perception; namely, the fitting or inversion of internal models of sensory data by the brain. Critically, the nature of this inversion lends itself to a relatively simple neural network implementation that shares many formal similarities with real cortical hierarchies in the brain. The basic idea that the brain uses hierarchical inference has been described in a series of papers (Friston, 2005; Friston, Kilner, & Harrison, 2006; Munford, 1992; Rao & Ballard, 1998), which entertain the notion that the brain uses empirical Bayes for inference about its sensory input, given the hierarchical organization of cortical systems. Here, we focus on how neural networks could be configured to invert these models and deconvolve sensory causes from sensory input.

This chapter comprises four sections. In the first, we introduce hierarchical dynamic models. Hierarchies induce empirical priors that provide constraints, which are exploited during inversion. In the second section, we consider model inversion in statistical terms. This summarizes the material in Friston et al. (2008). In the third section, we show how this inversion can be formulated as a simple gradient ascent using neuronal networks and, in the final section, we consider how evoked brain responses might be understood in terms of inference under hierarchical dynamic models of sensory input.

HIERARCHICAL DYNAMIC MODELS

Hierarchical dynamic models are probabilistic generative models $p(y, \vartheta) = p(y \mid \vartheta) p(\vartheta)$ based on state-space models. They entail the likelihood, $p(y \mid \vartheta)$, of getting some sensory data, y, given some parameters $\vartheta = \{x, v, \theta\}$ and priors on those parameters, $p(\vartheta)$. We will see that the parameters subsume different quantities, some of which change with time and some which do not. A dynamic model can be written as

$$
\begin{aligned}
y &= g(x, v) + z \\
\dot{x} &= f(x, v) + w
\end{aligned}
\tag{1}
$$

The continuous nonlinear functions f and g of the states are parameterized by θ. The states $v(t)$ can be deterministic, stochastic, or both. They are referred to as inputs, sources, or causes. The states $x(t)$ mediate the influence of the input on the output and endow the system with memory. They are often referred to as hidden states because they are seldom observed directly. We assume the stochastic innovations (i.e., observation noise) $z(t)$ are analytic, such that the covariance of $\tilde{z} = [z, z', z'', \ldots]^T$ is well defined; similarly for the system or state noise, $w(t)$, which represents random fluctuations on the motion of the hidden states. Under local linearity assumptions, the generalized response, $\tilde{y} = [y, y', y'', \ldots]^T$, comprising the position, velocity, acceleration jerk, and so on, is given by

$$
\begin{array}{ll}
y = g(x, v) + z & \dot{x} = x' = f(x, v) + w \\
y' = g_x x' + g_v v' + z' & \dot{x}' = x'' = f_x x' + f_v v' + w' \\
y'' = g_x x'' + g_v v'' + z'' & \dot{x}'' = x''' = f_x x'' + f_v v'' + w''
\end{array}
\tag{2}
$$

The first (observer) equations show that the generalized states $u = [\tilde{v}, \tilde{x},]^T$ are needed to generate a generalized response. The second (state) equations enforce a coupling between orders of motion of the hidden states and confer memory on the system. We can write these equations compactly as

$$\tilde{y} = \tilde{g} + \tilde{z}$$
$$D\tilde{x} = \tilde{f} + \tilde{w}$$

3

where $\tilde{g}$ and $\tilde{f}$ are the predicted response and motion, respectively, and D is a block-matrix derivative operator, whose first diagonal contains identity matrices. Gaussian assumptions about the fluctuations $p(\tilde{z}) = N(\tilde{z}:0,\Sigma^v)$ provide the likelihood, $p(\tilde{y}\,|\,\tilde{x},\tilde{v})$. Similarly, Gaussian assumptions about state-noise $p(\tilde{w}) = N(\tilde{w}:0,\Sigma^x)$ furnish empirical priors, $p(\tilde{x}\,|\,\tilde{v})$ in terms of predicted motion

$$p(\tilde{y},\tilde{x},\tilde{v}) = p(\tilde{y}\,|\,\tilde{x},\tilde{v})p(\tilde{x},\tilde{v})$$
$$p(\tilde{y}\,|\,\tilde{x},\tilde{v}) = N(\tilde{y}:\tilde{g},\Sigma^v)$$

4

$$p(\tilde{x},\tilde{v}) = p(\tilde{x}\,|\,\tilde{v})p(\tilde{v})$$
$$p(\tilde{x}\,|\,\tilde{v}) = N(D\tilde{x}:\tilde{f},\Sigma^x)$$

The density on the hidden states $p(\tilde{x}\,|\,\tilde{v})$ is part of the prior on quantities needed to evaluate the likelihood of the sensory data. It is these constraints that can be exploited by the brain and are accessed through plausible assumptions about noise. These assumptions are encoded by their covariances $\tilde{\Sigma}^v$ and $\tilde{\Sigma}^x$ or inverses $\tilde{\Pi}^v$ and $\tilde{\Pi}^x$ (known as precisions).

Hierarchical dynamic models have the following form, which generalizes the $(m = 1)$ model above

$$y = g(x^{(1)},v^{(1)}) + z^{(1)}$$
$$\dot{x}^{(1)} = f(x^{(1)},v^{(1)}) + w^{(1)}$$
$$\vdots$$
$$v^{(i-1)} = g(x^{(i)},v^{(i)}) + z^{(i)}$$
$$\dot{x}^{(i)} = f(x^{(i)},v^{(i)}) + w^{(i)}$$
$$\vdots$$

5

Again, $f^{(i)} = f(x^{(i)},v^{(i)})$ and $g^{(i)} = g(x^{(i)},v^{(i)})$ are continuous nonlinear functions of the states.

The innovations $z^{(i)}$ and $w^{(i)}$ are conditionally independent fluctuations that enter each level of the hierarchy. These play the role of observation error or noise at the first level and induce random fluctuations in the states at higher levels. The causal states $v = [v^{(1)},\ldots,v^{(m)}]^T$ link levels, whereas the hidden states $x = [x^{(1)},\ldots,x^{(m)}]^T$ link dynamics over time. In hierarchical form, the output of one level acts as an input to the next. Inputs from higher levels can enter nonlinearly into the state equations and can be regarded as changing its control parameters to produce complicated convolutions with "deep" (i.e., hierarchical) structure.

The conditional independence of the fluctuations means that these models have a Markov property over levels (Empirical Bayes; Efron, & Morris, 1973), which simplifies the architecture of attending inference schemes. See Kass and Steffey (1989) for a discussion of approximate Bayesian inference models of static data and Friston (2008) for dynamic models. In short, a hierarchical form endows models with the ability to construct their own priors. For example, the prediction $\tilde{g}^{(i)} = \tilde{g}(\tilde{x}^{(i)},\tilde{v}^{(i)})$ plays the role of a prior expectation on $\tilde{v}^{(i-1)}$, yet it has to be estimated in terms of $(\tilde{x}^{(i)},\tilde{v}^{(i)})$. This feature is central to many inference and estimation procedures, ranging from mixed-effects analyses in classical covariance component analysis to automatic relevance determination in machine learning.

Summary

This section has introduced hierarchical dynamic models in generalized coordinates of motion. These models are about as complicated as one could imagine; they comprise causal and hidden states, whose dynamics can be coupled with arbitrary (analytic) nonlinear functions. Furthermore, these states can have random fluctuations with unknown amplitude and arbitrary (analytic) autocorrelation functions. A key aspect of these models is their hierarchical structure, which induces empirical priors on the causes. These complement the constraints on hidden states, furnished by empirical priors on their motion or dynamics. Later, we will examine the roles of these structural and dynamical priors in perception. We now consider how these models are inverted to disclose the unknown states generating observed sensory data.

MODEL INVERSION AND VARIATIONAL BAYES

This section considers model inversion and provides a heuristic summary of the material in Friston et al. (2008). It uses variational Bayes, which is a generic approach to model inversion that approximates the conditional density $p(\vartheta \mid \tilde{y}, m)$ on some model parameters, ϑ, given a model m and data $\tilde{y}$. This is achieved by optimizing the sufficient statistics of a recognition density $q(\vartheta)$ with respect to a lower bound on the evidence $p(\tilde{y} \mid m)$ of the model itself (Feynman, 1972; Friston et al., 2007; Hinton & von Camp, 1993; MacKay, 1995; Neal & Hinton, 1998). The log-evidence can be expressed in terms of a free-energy and divergence term

$$\ln p(\tilde{y} \mid m) = F + K(q(\vartheta) \| p(\vartheta \mid \tilde{y}, m)) \Rightarrow$$

6

$$F = \langle \ln p(\tilde{y}, \vartheta) \rangle_q - \langle \ln q(\vartheta) \rangle_q$$

The free-energy comprises an energy term, corresponding to a Gibb's energy, $U(\tilde{y}, \vartheta) := \ln p(\tilde{y}, \vartheta)$ expected under the recognition density $q(\vartheta)$ and its entropy. Equation 6 shows that $F(\tilde{y}, q)$ is a lower-bound on the log-evidence because the divergence, $K \geq 0$, is always positive. The objective is to optimize the sufficient statistics of $q(\vartheta)$ by maximising the free-energy and minimizing the divergence. This ensures $q(\vartheta) \approx p(\vartheta \mid \tilde{y}, m)$ becomes an approximate posterior density.[1]

Invoking the recognition density, $q(\vartheta)$, converts a difficult integration problem (inherent in computing the evidence) into an easier optimization problem. This rests on inducing a bound that can be optimized with respect to $q(\vartheta)$. To finesse optimization, one usually assumes $q(\vartheta)$ factorizes over a partition of the parameters. In statistical physics, this is called a mean-field

[1] By convention, the free energy in machine learning is usually the negative of the free energy in physics. This means the free energy increases with log-evidence and has to be maximized.

approximation. We will assume $q(\vartheta) = q(u)q(\theta)$, where $u(t) = [\tilde{x}, \tilde{v}]^T$ are time-varying generalized states and θ are all other unknown time-invariant parameters. We now seek $q(u)$ that maximizes the free energy at each point in time. It is fairly easy to show (Friston et al., 2008) that this is proportional to $\exp(V)$, where $V(t)$ is called the variational energy; this is the Gibbs energy expected under the conditional density of the parameters. In what follows, we will assume the parameters are known and focus on the states. In this case, the variational and Gibbs energy are the same thing: $V(t) = U(t) = \ln p(\tilde{y}, u)$. To further simplify things, we will assume the brain uses something called the Laplace approximation. This enables us to focus on a single quantity for each unknown state, the conditional expectation or mean.

Under the Laplace approximation, the conditional density assumes a fixed Gaussian form $q(u) = N(u : \tilde{\mu}, C)$ with sufficient statistics $\tilde{\mu}$ and C, corresponding to the conditional mean and covariance of the unknown states. The advantage of the Laplace approximation is that the conditional precision is a function of the mean (the curvature of the Gibbs energy at the mean). This means we can reduce model inversion to optimizing one sufficient statistic; namely, the conditional mean. This is the solution to

$$\dot{\tilde{\mu}} - D\tilde{\mu} = \partial_u V$$

7

Here, $\dot{\tilde{\mu}} - D\tilde{\mu}$ can be regarded as motion in a frame of reference that moves along the trajectory encoded in generalized coordinates. Critically, the stationary solution (in this moving frame of reference) maximizes variational energy and implicitly free energy. This can be seen easily by noting $\dot{\tilde{\mu}} - D\tilde{\mu} = 0$ means the gradient of the variational energy is zero. At this point the mean of the motion becomes the motion of the mean, $\dot{\tilde{\mu}} = D\tilde{\mu}$.

Summary

In this section, we have seen how the inversion of dynamic models can be formulated as an optimization of free energy. By assuming a fixed-form (Laplace) approximation to the conditional density, one can reduce optimization to finding the conditional means of unknown quantities. For the states, this entails finding a path or trajectory that maximizes variational energy at all times. This can found by making the motion of the generalized mean perform a gradient ascent in a frame of reference that moves with the mean of the generalized motion. The only thing we need to implement this recognition scheme is the Gibbs energy, $U(t) = \ln p(\tilde{y}, u)$. This is specified by the generative model of the previous section (Equation 4). In the next section, we look at what this scheme might look like in the brain.

HIERARCHICAL MODELS IN THE BRAIN

A key architectural principle of the brain is its hierarchical organization (Felleman & van Essen, 1991; Maunsell & van Essen, 1983; Mesulam, 1998; Zeki & Shipp, 1988). This has been established most thoroughly in the visual system, where lower (primary) areas receive sensory input and higher areas adopt a multimodal or associational role. The neurobiological notion of a hierarchy rests upon the distinction between forward and backward connections (Angelucci et al., 2002; Felleman & Van Essen, 1991; Murphy & Sillito, 1987; Rockland & Pandya, 1979; Sherman & Guillery, 1998). This distinction is based upon the specificity of cortical layers that are the predominant sources and origins of extrinsic connections. Forward connections arise largely in superficial pyramidal cells, in supra-granular layers, and terminate on spiny stellate cells of layer four in higher cortical areas (DeFelipe, Alonso-Nanclares, & Arellano, 2002; Felleman & Van Essen, 1991). Conversely, backward connections arise largely from deep pyramidal cells in infra-granular layers and target cells in the infra and supra-granular layers of lower cortical areas. Intrinsic connections mediate lateral interactions between neurons that are a few millimeters away. There is a key functional asymmetry between forward and backward connections that renders backward connections more modulatory or nonlinear in their effects on neuronal responses (e.g., Sherman & Guillery, 1998; see also Hupe et al., 1998).

This is consistent with the deployment of voltage-sensitive NMDA receptors in the supra-granular layers that are targeted by backward connections (Rosier, Arekens, Orban, & Vandesande, 1993). Typically, the synaptic dynamics of backward connections have slower time constants. This has led to the notion that forward connections are driving and elicit obligatory responses in higher levels, whereas backward connections have both driving and modulatory effects and operate over larger spatial and temporal scales.

The hierarchical structure of the brain speaks to hierarchical models of sensory input. We now consider how this functional architecture can be understood under the inversion of hierarchical models by the brain. If we assume that the activity of neurons encodes the conditional mean of states, then Equation 7 specifies the neuronal dynamics entailed by perception or recognizing states of the world from sensory data. In Friston et al. (2008) we show how these dynamics can be expressed simply in terms of auxiliary variables

$$\varepsilon^v = \begin{bmatrix} y \\ v^{(1)} \\ \vdots \\ v^{(m)} \end{bmatrix} - \begin{bmatrix} g^{(1)} \\ g^{(2)} \\ \vdots \\ 0 \end{bmatrix} \quad \varepsilon^x = \begin{bmatrix} Dx^{(1)} \\ \vdots \\ Dx^{(m)} \end{bmatrix} - \begin{bmatrix} f^{(1)} \\ \vdots \\ f^{(m)} \end{bmatrix}$$

$$\tilde{\varepsilon} = \begin{bmatrix} \tilde{\varepsilon}^v \\ \tilde{\varepsilon}^x \end{bmatrix} \qquad\qquad 8$$

These correspond to prediction errors on the causes and motion of the hidden states. Using these errors, we can write Equation 7 as

$$\dot{\tilde{\mu}} = \partial_u V + D\tilde{\mu}$$
$$= D\tilde{\mu} - (\partial_u \tilde{\varepsilon})^T \xi$$

$$\qquad\qquad 9$$

$$\xi = \Pi \tilde{\varepsilon} = \tilde{\varepsilon} - \Lambda \xi$$

$$\Pi = \begin{bmatrix} \Pi^v & \\ & \Pi^x \end{bmatrix}$$

Equation 9 describes how neuronal states self-organize, when exposed to sensory input. Its form is quite revealing and suggests two distinct populations of neurons: causal or hidden *state-units* whose activity encodes $\tilde{\mu}(t)$ and *error-units* encoding precision-weighted prediction error, $\xi = \tilde{\Pi}\tilde{\varepsilon}$, with one error-unit for each state. Furthermore, the activities of error-units are a function of the states, and the dynamics of state-units are a function of prediction error. This means the two populations pass messages to each other and to themselves. The messages passed within the states, $D\tilde{\mu}$, mediate empirical priors on their motion, while $-\Lambda\xi$ decorrelate the error-units. The matrix $\Lambda = \tilde{\Sigma}-1$ can be thought of as lateral connections among error-units that mediate winner-take-all like interactions and increase with higher levels of noise or uncertainty.

If we unpack these equations, we can see the hierarchical nature of this message passing

$$\dot{\tilde{\mu}}^{(i)v} = D\tilde{\mu}^{(i)v} - (\partial_v \tilde{\varepsilon}^{(i)})^T \xi^{(i)} - \xi^{(i+1)v}$$

$$\dot{\tilde{\mu}}^{(i)x} = D\tilde{\mu}^{(i)x} - (\partial_x \tilde{\varepsilon}^{(i)})^T \xi^{(i)}$$

15

$$\xi^{(i)v} = \tilde{\mu}^{(i-1)v} - \tilde{g}(\tilde{\mu}^{(i)}) - \Lambda^{(i)v}\xi^{(i)v}$$

$$\xi^{(i)x} = D\tilde{\mu}^{(i)x} - \tilde{f}(\tilde{\mu}^{(i)}) - \Lambda^{(i)x}\xi^{(i)x}$$

This shows that error-units receive messages from the states in the same level and the level above, whereas states are driven by error-units in the same level and the level below (see Fig. 17.1). Critically, inference requires only the prediction error from the lower level, $\xi^{(i)}$, and the level in question, $\xi^{(i+1)}$. These provide bottom-up and lateral messages that drive conditional expectations $\tilde{\mu}^{(i)}$ toward a better prediction, to explain away the prediction error in the level below. These top-down and lateral predictions correspond to $\tilde{g}^{(i)}$ and $\tilde{f}^{(i)}$. This is the essence of recurrent message passing between hierarchical levels to optimize free energy or suppress prediction error, that is, recognition dynamics. In summary, all connections between error and state-units are reciprocal, where the only connections that link levels are forward connections conveying prediction error to state-units and reciprocal backward connections that mediate predictions.

We can identify error-units with superficial pyramidal cells, because the only messages that pass up the hierarchy are prediction errors and superficial pyramidal cells originate forward connections in the brain. This is useful because it is these cells that are primarily responsible for electroencephalographic (EEG) signals that can be measured noninvasively. Similarly, the only messages that are passed down the hierarchy are the predictions from state-units that are necessary to form prediction errors in lower levels. The sources of extrinsic backward connections are the deep pyramidal cells, and one might deduce that these encode the expected causes of sensory states (see Mumford, 1992 and Fig. 17.1). Critically, the motion of each state-unit is a linear mixture of bottom-up prediction error (Equation 9). This is exactly what is observed physiologically, in that bottom-up driving inputs elicit obligatory responses that do not depend on other bottom-up inputs. The prediction error itself is formed by predictions conveyed by backward and lateral connections. These influences embody the nonlinearities implicit in $\tilde{g}^{(i)}$ and $\tilde{f}^{(i)}$. Again, this is entirely consistent with the nonlinear or modulatory characteristics of backward connections.

Summary

In summary, we have seen how the inversion of a generic hierarchical and dynamical model of sensory inputs can be transcribed onto neuronal quantities that optimize a variational bound on the evidence for that model. This optimization corresponds, under some simplifying assumptions, to suppression of prediction error at all levels in a cortical hierarchy. This suppression rests upon a balance between bottom-up (prediction error) influences and top-down (empirical prior) influences. In the final section, we use this scheme to simulate neuronal responses. Specifically, we pursue the electrophysiological correlates of prediction error and ask whether we can understand some common phenomena in event-related potential (ERP) research in terms of the free-energy principle and message passing in the brain.

BIRDSONG AND ATTRACTORS

In this section, we examine the emergent properties of a system that uses hierarchical dynamics

Message passing in neuronal hierarchies

$$\xi^{(i)v} = \tilde{\mu}^{(i-1)v} - \tilde{g}(\tilde{\mu}^{(i)}) - \Lambda^{(i)v}\xi^{(i)v}$$
$$\xi^{(i)x} = D\tilde{\mu}^{(i)x} - \tilde{f}(\tilde{\mu}^{(i)}) - \Lambda^{(i)x}\xi^{(i)x}$$

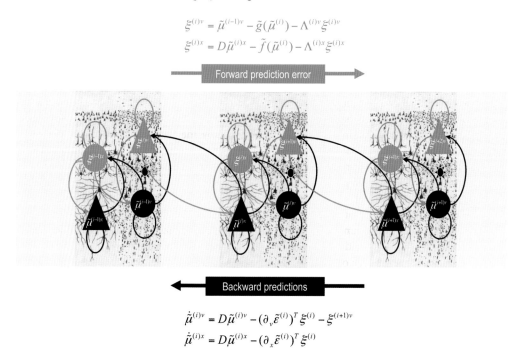

$$\dot{\tilde{\mu}}^{(i)v} = D\tilde{\mu}^{(i)v} - (\partial_v\tilde{\varepsilon}^{(i)})^T\xi^{(i)} - \xi^{(i+1)v}$$
$$\dot{\tilde{\mu}}^{(i)x} = D\tilde{\mu}^{(i)x} - (\partial_x\tilde{\varepsilon}^{(i)})^T\xi^{(i)}$$

Figure 17.1 Schematic detailing the neuronal architectures that encode an ensemble density on the states of a hierarchical model. This schematic shows the speculative cells of origin of forward-driving connections that convey prediction error from a lower area to a higher area and the backward connections that are used to construct predictions. These predictions try to explain away input from lower areas by suppressing prediction error. In this scheme, the sources of forward connections are the superficial pyramidal cell population, and the sources of backward connections are the deep pyramidal cell population. The differential equations relate to the optimization scheme detailed in the main text. The state-units and their efferents are in black and the error-units in red, with causes on the right and hidden states on the left. For simplicity, we have assumed the output of each level is a function of, and only of, the hidden states. This induces a hierarchy over levels and, within each level, a hierarchical relationship between states, where causes predict hidden states. This schematic shows how the neuronal populations may be deployed hierarchically within three cortical areas (or macro-columns).

or attractors as generative models of sensory input. The example we use is birdsong, and the empirical measures we focus on are local field potentials (LFPs) or evoked (ERP) responses that can be recorded noninvasively. Our aim is to show that canonical features of empirical electrophysiological responses can be reproduced easily under attractor models of sensory input. Furthermore, in a hierarchical setting, the use of dynamic models has some interesting implications for perceptual infrastructures (Kiebel, Daumizeau, & Friston, 2008).

We first describe the model of birdsong and demonstrate the nature and form of this model through simulated lesion experiments. We will then use simplified versions of this model to show how attractors can be used to categorize sequences of stimuli quickly and efficiently. Throughout this section, we will exploit the fact that superficial pyramidal cells are the major contributors to observed LFP and ERP signals, which means we can ascribe these signals to prediction error because the superficial pyramidal cells are the source of bottom-up messages in the brain (see Fig. 17.1)

Attractors in the Brain

The basic idea here is that the environment unfolds as an ordered sequence of spatiotemporal dynamics, whose equations of motion entail attractor manifolds that contain sensory trajectories. Critically, the shape of the manifold generating sensory data is itself changed by other dynamical systems that could have their own attractors. If we consider the brain has a generative model of these coupled dynamical systems, then we would expect to see attractors in neuronal dynamics that are trying to predict sensory input. In a hierarchical setting, the states of a high-level attractor enter the equations of motion of a low-level attractor in a nonlinear way, to change the shape of its manifold. This form of generative model has a number of sensible and appealing characteristics.

First, at any level the model can generate and therefore encode structured sequences of events, as the states flow over different parts of the manifold. These sequences can be simple, such as the quasi-periodic attractors of central pattern generators (McCrea & Rybak, 2008) or can exhibit complicated sequences of the sort associated with chaotic and itinerant dynamics (e.g., Breakspear & Stam, 2005; Canolty et al., 2006; Friston, 1997; Haken, Kelso, Fuchs, & Pandya, 1990; Jirsa, Fuchs, & Kelso, 1998; Kopell, Ermentrout, Whittington, & Traub, 2000; Rabinovich, Huerta, & Laurent, 2008). The notion of attractors as the basis of generative models extends the notion of generalized coordinates, encoding trajectories, to families of trajectories that lie on the attractor manifold; that is, paths that are contained in the flow-field specified by the control parameters provided by the states of the level above.

Second, hierarchically deployed attractors enable the brain to generate and therefore predict or represent different categories of sequences. This is because any low-level attractor embodies a family of trajectories that correspond to a structured sequence. The neuronal activity encoding the particular state at any one time determines where the current dynamics are within the sequence, while the shape of the attractor manifold determines which sequence is currently being expressed. In other words, the attractor manifold encodes *what* is being perceived and the neuronal activity encodes *where* the current percept is located on the manifold or within the sequence.

Third, if the state of a higher attractor changes the manifold of a subordinate attractor, then the states of the higher attractor come to encode the category of the sequence or dynamics represented by the lower attractor. This means it is possible to generate and represent sequences of sequences and, by induction, sequences of sequences of sequences, and so on. This rests upon the states of neuronal attractors at any cortical level providing control parameters for attractor dynamics at the level below. This necessarily entails a nonlinear interaction between the top-down effects of the higher attractor and the states of the recipient attractor. Again, this is entirely consistent with the known functional asymmetries between forward and backward connections and speaks to the nonlinear effects of top-down connections in the real brain.

Finally, this particular model has implications for the temporal structure of perception. Put simply, the dynamics of high-level representations unfold more slowly than the dynamics of lower level representations. This is because the state of a higher attractor prescribes a manifold that guides the flow of lower states. In the limiting case of the higher level having a fixed-point attractor, its fixed states will encode lower level dynamics, which could change quite rapidly. We will see an example of this later on when considering the perceptual categorization of different sequences of chirps subtending birdsongs. This attribute of hierarchically coupled attractors enables the representation of arbitrarily long sequences of sequences and suggests that neuronal representations in the brain will change more slowly at higher levels (Kiebel et al., 2008; see also Botvinick et al., 2007; Hasson, Yang, Vallines, Heeger, & Rubin, 2008). One can turn this argument on its head and use the fact that we are able to recognize sequences of sequences (e.g., Chait, Peoppel, de Cheveigné, & Simon, 2007) as an existence proof for this sort of generative model. In the examples that follow, we will try to show how autonomous dynamics furnish generative models of sensory input, which behave much like real brains, when measured electrophysiologically.

A Synthetic Avian Brain

The toy example used here deals with the generation and recognition of birdsongs (Laje & Mindlin, 2002). We imagine that birdsongs are produced by two time-varying control parameters that control the frequency and amplitude of vibrations emanating from the syrinx of a songbird (see Fig. 17.2). There has been an extensive modeling effort using attractor models at the biomechanical level to understand the generation of birdsong (e.g., Laje, Garnder, & Mindlin, 2002). Here we use the attractors at a higher level to provide time-varying control over the resulting sonograms. We drive the syrinx with two states of a Lorenz attractor, one controlling the frequency (between 2 and 5 KHz) and the other (after rectification) controlling the amplitude or volume. The parameters of the Lorenz attractor were chosen to generate a short sequence of chirps every second or so. To endow the generative model with a hierarchical structure, we placed a second Lorenz attractor, whose dynamics were an order of magnitude slower, over the first. The states of the slower attractor entered as control parameters (known as the Raleigh and Prandtl number) to control the dynamics exhibited by the first. These dynamics could range from a fixed-point attractor, where the states of the first are all zero, through to quasi-periodic and chaotic behavior, when the value of the Prandtl number exceeds an appropriate threshold (about 24) and induces a bifurcation. Because higher states evolve more slowly, they switch the lower attractor on and off, generating distinct songs, where each song comprises a series of distinct chirps (see Fig. 17.3).

Song Recognition

This model generates spontaneous sequences of songs using autonomous dynamics. We generated

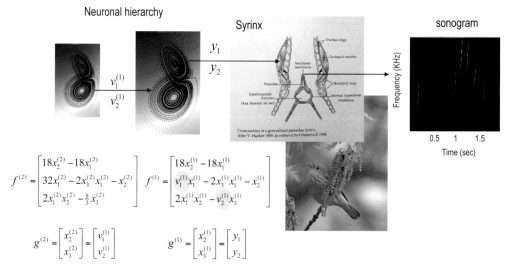

Figure 17.2 Schematic showing the construction of the generative model for birdsongs. This comprises two Lorenz attractors, where the higher attractor delivers two control parameters (gray circles) to a lower level attractor, which, in turn, delivers two control parameters to a synthetic syrinx to produce amplitude and frequency modulated stimuli. This stimulus is represented as a sonogram in the right panel. The equations represent the hierarchical dynamic model in the form of Equation 5.

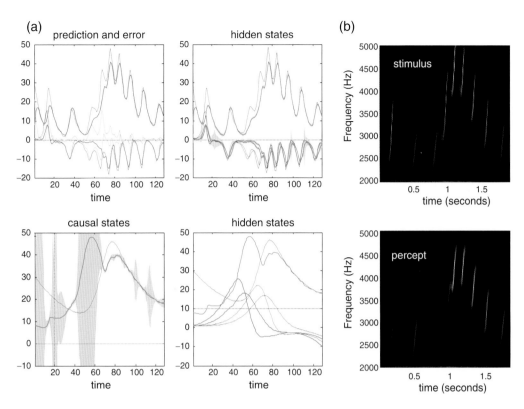

Figure 17.3 Results of a Bayesian inversion or deconvolution of the sonogram shown in Figure 17.2. (*a*) Upper panels show the time courses of hidden and causal states. (*Upper left*) These are the true and predicted states driving the syrinx and are simple mappings from two of the three hidden states of the first-level attractor. The solid lines respond to the conditional mode and the dotted lines to the true values. The discrepancy is the prediction error and is shown as a broken red line. (*Upper right*) The true and estimated hidden states of the first-level attractor. Note that the third hidden state has to be inferred from the sensory data. Confidence intervals on the conditional expectations are shown in gray and demonstrate a high degree of confidence, because a low level of sensory noise was used in these simulations. The panels below show the corresponding causes and hidden states at the second level. Again the conditional expectations are shown as solid lines and the true values as broken lines. Note the inflated conditional confidence interval halfway through the song when the third and fourth chirps are misperceived. (*b*) The stimulus and percept in sonogram format, detailing the expression of different frequencies generated over peristimulus time.

a single song, corresponding roughly to a cycle of the higher attractor and then inverted the ensuing sonogram (summarized as peak amplitude and volume) using the message-passing scheme described in the previous section. The results are shown in Figure 17.3 and demonstrate that, after several hundred milliseconds, the veridical hidden states and supraordinate causes can be recovered. Interestingly, the third chirp is not perceived, in that the first-level prediction error was not sufficient to overcome the dynamical and structural priors entailed by the model.

However, once the subsequent chirp had been predicted correctly the following sequence of chirps was recognized with a high degree of conditional confidence. Note that when the second and third chirps in the sequence are not recognized, first-level prediction error is high and the conditional confidence about the causes at the second level is low (reflected in the wide 90% confidence intervals). Heuristically, this means that the synthetic bird listening to the song did not know which song was being emitted and was unable to predict subsequent chirps.

Structural and Dynamic Priors

This example provides a nice opportunity to illustrate the relative roles of structural and dynamic priors. Structural priors are provided by the top-down inputs that dynamically reshape the manifold of the low-level attractor. However, this attractor itself contains an abundance of dynamical priors that unfold in generalized coordinates. Both provide important constraints on the evolution of sensory states, which facilitate recognition. We can selectively destroy these priors by lesioning the top-down connections to remove structural priors or by cutting the intrinsic connections that mediate dynamic priors. The latter involves cutting the self-connections in Figure 17.1 among the causal and state units. The results of these two simulated lesion experiments are shown in Figure 17.4. The top panel shows the percept as in the previous panel, in terms of the predicted sonogram and prediction error at the first and second level. The subsequent two panels show exactly the same information but without structural (middle) and dynamic (lower) priors. In both cases, the synthetic bird fails to recognize the sequence with a corresponding inflation of prediction error, particularly at the last level. Interestingly, the removal of structural priors has a less marked effect on recognition than removing the dynamical priors. Without dynamical priors there is a failure to segment the sensory stream and although there is a preservation of frequency tracking, the dynamics per se have completely lost their sequential structure. Although it is interesting to compare structural and dynamics priors, the important message here is that both are necessary for veridical perception and that removal of either leads to suboptimal inference. Both of these empirical priors prescribe dynamics that enable the synthetic bird to predict what will be heard next. This leads to the question, What would happen if the song terminated prematurely?

Omission and Violation of Predictions

We repeated the aforementioned simulation but terminated the song after the fifth chirp. The corresponding sonograms and percepts are shown

with their prediction errors in Figure 17.5. The left panels show the stimulus and percept as in Figure 17.4, while the right panels show the stimulus and responses to omission of the last syllables. These results illustrate two important phenomena. First, there is a vigorous expression of prediction error after the song terminates abruptly. This reflects the dynamical nature of the recognition process because, at this point, there is no sensory input to predict. In other words, the prediction error is generated entirely by the predictions afforded by the dynamic model of sensory input. It can be seen that this prediction error (with a percept but no stimulus) is almost as large as the prediction error associated with the third and fourth stimuli that are not perceived (stimulus but no percept). Second, it can be seen that there is a transient percept, when the omitted chirp should have occurred. Its frequency is slightly too low, but its timing is preserved in relation to the expected stimulus train. This is an interesting stimulation from the point of view of ERP studies of omission-related responses. These simulations and related empirical studies (e.g., Nordby, Hammerborg, Roth, & Hugdahl, 1994; Yabe, Tervaniemi, Reinikainen, & Näätänen, 1997) provide clear evidence for the predictive capacity of the brain. In this example, prediction rests upon the internal construction of an attractor manifold that defines a family of trajectories, each corresponding to the realization of a particular song. In the last simulation, we look more closely at perceptual categorization of these songs.

Perceptual Categorization

In the previous simulations, we saw that a song corresponds to a sequence of chirps that are preordained by the shape of an attractor manifold that is controlled by top-down inputs. This means that for every point in the state-space of the higher attractor there is a corresponding manifold or category of song. In other words, recognizing or categorizing a particular song corresponds to finding a fixed location in the higher state-space. This provides a nice metaphor for perceptual categorization; because the neuronal states of the higher attractor represent, implicitly, a category

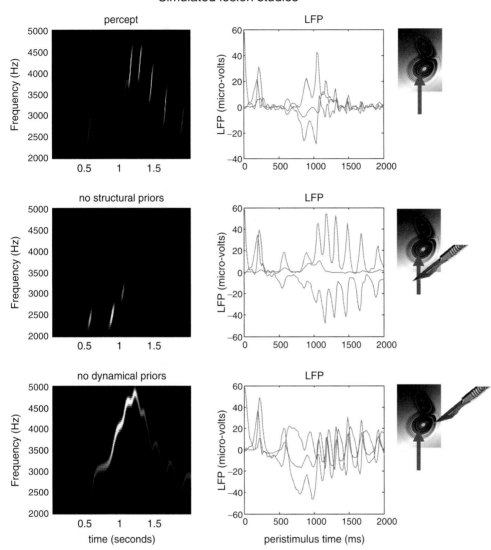

Simulated lesion studies

Figure 17.4 Results of simulated lesion studies using the birdsong model of the previous figures. The left panels show the percept in terms of the predicted sonograms, and the right panels show the corresponding prediction error (at both levels); these are the differences between the incoming sensory information and the prediction and the discrepancy between the conditional expectation of the second-level cause and that predicted by the second-level hidden states. (*Top row*) The recognition dynamics in the intact bird. (*Middle row*) The percept and corresponding prediction errors when the connections between the hidden states at the second level and their corresponding causes are removed. This effectively removes structural priors on the evolution of the attractor manifold prescribing the sensory dynamics at the first level. (*Lower panels*) The effects of retaining the structural priors but removing the dynamical priors by cutting the connections that mediate inversion in generalized coordinates. These results suggest that both structural and dynamical priors are necessary for veridical perception.

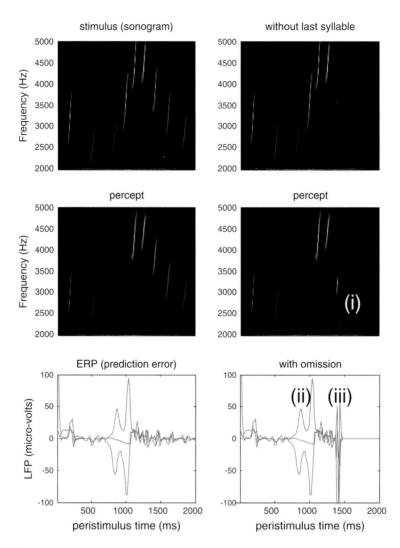

Figure 17.5 Omission-related responses. Here, we have omitted the last few chirps from the stimulus. The left-hand panels show the original sequence and responses evoked. The right-hand panels show the equivalent dynamics on omission of the last chirps. The top panels show the stimulus and the middle panels the corresponding percept in sonogram format. The interesting thing to note here is the occurrence of an anomalous percept after termination of the song on the lower right (i). This corresponds roughly to the chirp that would have been perceived in the absence of omission. The lower panels show the corresponding (precision-weighted) prediction error under the two stimuli at both levels. A comparison of the two reveals a burst of prediction error when a stimulus is missed (ii) and at the point that the stimulus terminates (iii) despite the fact that there is no stimulus present at this time. The darker lines correspond to prediction error at the first level, and the lighter lines correspond to prediction error at the second level.

of song. Inverting the generative model means that, probabilistically, we can map from a sequence of sensory events to a point in some perceptual space, where this mapping corresponds to perceptual recognition or categorization. This can be demonstrated in our synthetic songbird by ignoring the dynamics of the second-level attractor and exposing the bird to a song and letting the states at the second level optimize their location in perceptual space, to best predict the sensory input. To illustrate this, we generated three songs by fixing the Raleigh and Prandtl variables to three distinct values. We then placed uninformative priors on the second-level causes (that were previously driven by the hidden states of the second-level attractor) and inverted the model in the usual way. Figure 17.6a shows the results of this simulation for a single song. This song comprises a series of relatively low-frequency chirps emitted every 250 milliseconds or so. The causes of this song (song C in panel b) are recovered after the second chirp, with relatively tight confidence intervals (the blue and green lines in the lower left panel). We then repeated this exercise for three songs. The results are shown in Figure 17.6b. The songs are portrayed in sonogram format in the top panels and the inferred perceptual causes in the bottom panels. The left panel shows the evolution of these causes for all three songs as a function of peristimulus time and the right shows the corresponding conditional density in the causal or perceptual space of these two states after convergence. It can be seen that for all three songs the 90% confidence interval encompasses the true values (red dots). Furthermore, there is very little overlap between the conditional densities (gray regions), which means that the precision of the perceptual categorization is almost 100%. This is a simple but nice example of perceptual categorization, where sequences of sensory events with extended temporal support can be mapped to locations in perceptual space, through Bayesian deconvolution of the sort entailed by the free-energy principle.

Conclusion

This chapter has suggested that the architecture of cortical systems speaks to hierarchical generative models in the brain. The estimation or inversion of these models corresponds to a generalized deconvolution of sensory inputs to disclose their causes. This deconvolution could be implemented in a neuronally plausible fashion, where neuronal dynamics self-organize when exposed to inputs to suppress free energy. The focus of this paper has been on the nature of the hierarchical models and, in particular, models that show autonomous dynamics. These models may be relevant for the brain because they enable sequences of sequences to be inferred or recognized. We have tried to demonstrate their plausibility, in relation to empirical observations, by interpreting the prediction error, associated with model inversion, with observed electrophysiological responses. These models provide a graceful way to map from complicated spatiotemporal sensory trajectories to points in abstract perceptual spaces. Furthermore, in a hierarchical setting, this mapping may involve trajectories in perceptual spaces of increasingly higher order.

The ideas presented in this chapter have a long history, starting with the notion of neuronal energy (Helmholtz, 1860), covering ideas like efficient coding and analysis by synthesis (Barlow, 1961; Neisser, 1967) to more recent formulations in terms of Bayesian inversion and predictive coding (e.g., Ballard, Hinton, & Sejnowski, 1983; Dayan, Hinton, & Neal, 1995; Kawato, Hayakawa, & Inui, 1993; Mumford, 1992; Rao & Ballard, 1998). This work has tried to provide support for the notion that the brain uses attractors to represent and predict causes in the sensorium (Byrne, Becker, & Burgess, 2007; Deco & Rolls, 2003; Freeman, 1987; Tsodyks, 1999).

Acknowledgments

The Wellcome Trust funded this work. We would like to thank our colleagues for invaluable discussion about these ideas and Marcia Bennett for helping prepare this manuscript.

Software note

All the schemes described in this paper are available in Matlab code as academic freeware

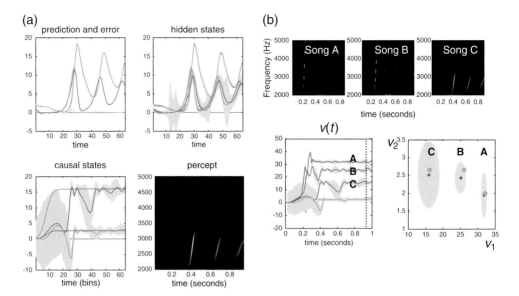

Figure 17.6 (*a*) Schematic demonstration of perceptual categorization. This figure follows the same format as Figure 17.3. However, here there are no hidden states at the second level, and the causes were subject to stationary and uninformative priors. This song was generated by a first-level attractor with fixed control parameters of $v_1^{(1)} = 16$ and $v_2^{(1)} = 8/3$, respectively. It can be seen that, on inversion of this model, these two control variables, corresponding to causes or states at the second level, are recovered with relatively high conditional precision. However, it takes about 50 iterations (about 600 milliseconds) before they stabilize. In other words, the sensory sequence has been mapped correctly to a point in perceptual space after the occurrence of the second chirp. This song corresponds to song C on the right. (*b*) The results of inversion for three songs each produced with three distinct pairs of values for the second-level causes (the Raleigh and Prandtl variables of the first-level attractor). (*Upper panel*) The three songs shown in sonogram format corresponding to a series of relatively high-frequency chirps that fall progressively in both frequency and number as the Raleigh number is decreased. (*Lower left*) These are the second-level causes shown as a function of peristimulus time for the three songs. It can be seen that the causes are identified after about 600 milliseconds with high conditional precision. (*Lower right*) This shows the conditional density on the causes shortly before the end of peristimulus time (dotted line on the left). The blue dots correspond to conditional means or expectations, and the gray areas correspond to the conditional confidence regions. Note that these encompass the true values (red dots) used to generate the songs. These results indicate that there has been a successful categorization, in the sense that there is no ambiguity (from the point of view of the synthetic bird) about which song was heard.

(http://www.fil.ion.ucl.ac.uk/spm). The simulation figures in this paper can be reproduced from a graphical user interface called from the DEM toolbox.

REFERENCES

Angelucci, A., Levitt, J. B., Walton, E. J., Hupe, J. M., Bullier, J., & Lund, J. S. (2002). Circuits for local and global signal integration in primary visual cortex. *Journal of Neuroscience, 22*, 8633–8646.

Ballard, D. H., Hinton, G. E., & Sejnowski, T. J. (1983). Parallel visual computation. *Nature, 306*, 21–26.

Barlow, H. B. (1961). Possible principles underlying the transformation of sensory messages. In W. A. Rosenblith (Ed.), *Sensory communication* (pp. 217–234). Cambridge, MA: MIT Press.

Botvinick, M. M. (2007). Multilevel structure in behaviour and in the brain: A model of Fuster's hierarchy. *Philosophical Transactions of the Royal Society of London B: Biological Sciences*, *362*(1485), 1615–1626.

Breakspear, M., & Stam, C. J. (2005). Dynamics of a neural system with a multiscale architecture. *Philosophical Transactions of the Royal Society of London B: Biological Sciences*, *360*, 1051–1107.

Byrne, P., Becker, S., & Burgess, N. (2007). Remembering the past and imagining the future: A neural model of spatial memory and imagery. *Psychology Review*, *114*(2), 340–375.

Canolty, R. T., Edwards, E., Dalal, S. S., Soltani, M., Nagarajan, S. S., Kirsch, H. E., Berger, M. S., Barbaro, N. M., & Knight, R. T. (2006). High gamma power is phase-locked to theta oscillations in human neocortex. *Science*, *313*, 1626–1628.

Chait, M., Poeppel, D., de Cheveigné, A., & Simon, J. Z. (2007). Processing asymmetry of transitions between order and disorder in human auditory cortex. *Journal of Neuroscience*, *27*(19), 5207–514.

Dayan, P., Hinton, G. E., & Neal, R. M. (1995) The Helmholtz machine. *Neural Computation*, *7*, 889–904.

Deco, G., & Rolls, E. T. (2003). Attention and working memory: A dynamical model of neuronal activity in the prefrontal cortex. *European Journal of Neuroscience*, *18*(8), 2374–2390.

DeFelipe, J., Alonso-Nanclares, L., & Arellano, J. I. (2002). Microstructure of the neocortex: Comparative aspects. *Journal of Neurocytology*, *31*, 299–316.

Efron, B., & Morris, C. (1973) Stein's estimation rule and its competitors an empirical Bayes approach. *Journal of the American Statistical Association*, *68*, 117–130.

Felleman, D. J., & Van Essen, D. C. (1991). Distributed hierarchical processing in the primate cerebral cortex. *Cerebral Cortex*, *1*, 1–47.

Feynman, R. P. (1972). *Statistical mechanics*. Reading, MA: Benjamin.

Freeman, W. J. (1987). Simulation of chaotic EEG patterns with a dynamic model of the olfactory system. *Biological Cybernetics*, *56*(2-3), 139–150.

Friston, K. (2008). Hierarchical models in the brain. *PLoS Computational Biology*, *4*(11), e1000211.

Friston, K. J. (1997). Transients, metastability, and neuronal dynamics. *NeuroImage*, *5*(2), 164–171.

Friston, K. J. (2003). Learning and inference in the brain. *Neural Networks*, *16*, 1325–1352.

Friston, K. J. (2005). A theory of cortical responses. *Philosophical Transactions of the Royal Society of London B: Biological Sciences*, *360*, 815–836.

Friston, K., Kilner, J., & Harrison, L. (2006). A free energy principle for the brain. *Journal of Physiology - Paris*, *100*(1-3), 70–87.

Friston, K. J., et al. (2007). Variational Bayes and the Laplace approximation. *NeuroImage*, *34*, 220–234.

Friston, K. J., et al. (2008). DEM: A variational treatment of dynamic systems. *NeuroImage*, *41*(3), 849–85.

Haken, H., Kelso, J. A. S., Fuchs, A., & Pandya, A. S. (1990). Dynamic pattern-recognition of coordinated biological motion. *Neural Networks*, *3*, 395–401.

Hasson, U., Yang, E., Vallines, I., Heeger, D. J., & Rubin, N. (2008) A hierarchy of temporal receptive windows in human cortex. *Journal of Neuroscience*, *28*, 2539–2550.

Helmholtz, H. (1860/1962). *Handbuch der physiologischen optik.* (Vol. 3., J. P. C. Southall Trans., Ed.) New York: Dover.

Hinton, G. E., & von Camp, D. (1993). Keeping neural networks simple by minimising the description length of weights. In *Proceedings of COLT-93* (pp. 5–13).

Hupe, J. M., James, A. C., Payne, B. R., Lomber, S. G., Girard, P., & Bullier, J. (1998). Cortical feedback improves discrimination between figure and background by V1, V2 and V3 neurons. *Nature*, *394*, 784–787.

Jirsa, V. K., Fuchs, A., & Kelso, J. A. (1998). Connecting cortical and behavioral dynamics: bimanual coordination. *Neural Computation*, *10*, 2019–2045.

Kass, R. E., & Steffey, D. (1989) Approximate Bayesian inference in conditionally independent hierarchical models (parametric empirical Bayes models). *Journal of the American Statistical Association*, *407*, 717–726.

Kawato, M., Hayakawa, H., & Inui, T. (1993). A forward-inverse optics model of reciprocal connections between visual cortical areas. *Network*, *4*, 415–422.

Kiebel, S. J., Daunizeau, J., & Friston, K. J. (2008). A hierarchy of time-scales and the brain. *PLoS Computational Biology*, *4*(11), e1000209.

Kopell, N., Ermentrout, G. B., Whittington, M. A., & Traub, R. D. (2000). Gamma rhythms and beta rhythms have different synchronization properties. *Proceedings of the National Academy of Sciences USA*, *97*, 1867–1872.

Laje, R., Gardner, T. J., & Mindlin, G. B. (2002). Neuromuscular control of vocalizations in birdsong: a model. *Physical Review. E, Statistical, Nonlinear, and Soft Matter Physics*, *65*, 051921.1-8.

Laje, R., & Mindlin, G. B. (2002). Diversity within a birdsong. *Physical Review Letters*, *89*, 288102.

London, M., & Häusser, M. (2005). Dendritic computation. *Annual Review of Neuroscience*, *28*, 503–532.

MacKay, D. J. C. (1995). Free-energy minimisation algorithm for decoding and cryptoanalysis. *Electronics Letters*, *31*, 445–447.

Maunsell, J. H., & van Essen, D. C. (1983). The connections of the middle temporal visual area (MT) and their relationship to a cortical hierarchy in the macaque monkey. *Journal of Neuroscience*, *3*, 2563–2586.

McCrea, D. A., & Rybak, I. A. (2008). Organization of mammalian locomotor rhythm and pattern generation. *Brain Research Reviews*, *57*(1), 134–146.

Mumford, D. (1992). On the computational architecture of the neocortex. II. The role of cortico-cortical loops. *Biological Cybernetics*, *66*, 241–251.

Murphy, P. C., & Sillito, A. M. (1987). Corticofugal feedback influences the generation of length tuning in the visual pathway. *Nature*, *329*, 727–729.

Neal, R. M., & Hinton, G. E. (1998). A view of the EM algorithm that justifies incremental sparse and other variants. In M. I. Jordan (Ed.), *Learning in graphical models* (pp.355–368) Dordrecht Kulver Academic Press.

Neisser, U. (1967). *Cognitive psychology*. New York: Appleton-Century-Crofts.

Nordby, H., Hammerborg, D., Roth, W. T., & Hugdahl, K. (1994). ERPs for infrequent omissions and inclusions of stimulus elements. *Psychophysiology*, *31*(6), 544–552.

Rabinovich, M., Huerta, R., & Laurent, G. (2008). Neuroscience: Transient dynamics for neural processing. *Science*, *321*(5885), 48–50.

Rao, R. P., & Ballard, D. H. (1998). Predictive coding in the visual cortex: A functional interpretation of some extra-classical receptive field effects. *Nature Neuroscience*, *2*, 79–87.

Rockland, K. S., & Pandya, D. N. (1979). Laminar origins and terminations of cortical connections of the occipital lobe in the rhesus monkey. *Brain Research*, *179*, 3–20.

Rosier, A. M., Arckens, L., Orban, G. A., & Vandesande, F. (1993). Laminar distribution of NMDA receptors in cat and monkey visual cortex visualized by [3H]-MK-801 binding. *Journal of Comparative Neurology*, *335*, 369–380.

Sherman, S. M., & Guillery, R. W. (1998). On the actions that one nerve cell can have on another: Distinguishing "drivers" from "modulators." *Proceedings of the National Academy of Sciences USA*, *95*, 7121–7126.

Tsodyks, M. (1999). Attractor neural network models of spatial maps in hippocampus. *Hippocampus*, *9*(4), 481–489.

Yabe, H., Tervaniemi, M., Reinikainen, K., & Näätänen, R. (1997). Temporal window of integration revealed by MMN to sound omission. *NeuroReport*, *8*(8), 1971–1974.

Zeki, S., & Shipp, S. (1988). The functional logic of cortical connections. *Nature*, *335*, 311–331.

CHAPTER 18
Sequence Memory for Prediction, Inference, and Behavior

Jeff Hawkins, Dileep George, and Jamie Niemasik

In this chapter we propose a mechanism that the neocortex may use to store sequences of patterns. Storing and recalling sequences is necessary for making predictions, recognizing time-based patterns, and generating behavior. Since these tasks are major functions of the neocortex, the ability to store and recall time-based sequences is likely a key attribute of many, if not all, cortical areas. Previously, we have proposed that the neocortex can be modeled as a hierarchy of memory regions, each of which learns and recalls sequences. This chapter proposes how each region of neocortex might learn the sequences necessary for this theory. The basis of the proposal is that all the cells in a cortical column share bottom-up receptive field properties, but individual cells in a column learn to represent unique incidences of the bottom-up receptive field property within different sequences. We discuss the proposal, the biological constraints that led to it, and some results modeling it.

PREDICTION AND SEQUENCE MEMORY

Prediction is a ubiquitous function of the brain. During every moment of our waking life, our brains are trying to predict what sights, sounds, and tactile sensations will be experienced next. Previously, we have proposed a theory for how the neocortex learns a model of the world from sensory data, and how it uses this model to make predictions and infer causes (George & Hawkins, 2005; Hawkins & Blakeslee, 2004; Hawkins &

George, 2006). We refer to this theory as hierarchical temporal memory (HTM). HTM models the neocortex as a tree-shaped hierarchy of memory regions, in which each memory region learns common sequences of patterns (Fig. 18.1). Representations of sequences are passed up the hierarchy, forming the elements of sequences in upper regions, and predictions of the next elements in sequences are passed down the hierarchy. By training on time-varying sensory patterns, an HTM builds a spatial and temporal model of the world. HTMs are modeled as a form of Bayesian network, where sequence memory forms the core learning method for each region in the network. When sequence memory is implemented in a probabilistic way, it naturally leads to probabilistic predictions at every level of the hierarchy.

Hierarchical temporal memory is just one example of a class of hierarchical learning models designed to mimic how the neocortex learns, infers, and predicts. Similar models include HMAX (Riesenhuber & Poggio, 1999) and convolutional neural networks (LeCun & Bengio, 1995). Both these models use hierarchical representations and form groups of spatial patterns at each level in the hierarchy. In both cases, no temporal order is maintained within these groups. Thus, the models are most suitable for spatial pattern recognition, as they cannot recognize time-based patterns or make predictions. Another similar model to HTM is the hierarchical hidden Markov model (HHMM) (Fine, Singer, & Tishby, 1998). HHMMs learn sequences at each level of a hierarchy, much

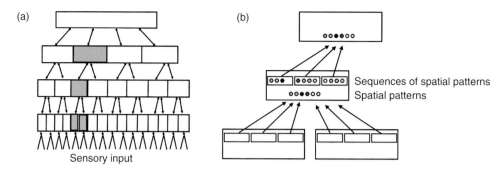

Figure 18.1 (*a*) **A conceptual diagram of a hierarchical temporal memory model (HTM) of neocortex. Models such as this replicate the hierarchical connectivity of neocortical regions and treat the entire system as a Bayesian network.** (*b*) **Four connected regions from** (*a*), **illustrating the feedforward pathway. Circles indicate spatial patterns that form the elements of learned sequences. Small rectangles indicate learned sequences of patterns. Relatively constant representations of sequences are passed up the hierarchy, where they combine to form the individual elements of sequences in parent regions. Not shown is the feedback pathway. Each region uses its sequence memory to predict what elements will likely occur next and passes this prediction down the hierarchy. The unfolding of learned sequences is the foundation of prediction.**

like HTMs, and therefore are able to recognize temporal patterns and make predictions. However, HHMMs are strictly temporal—they do not have the ability to infer spatial patterns.

HTM combines the best of all these models. It is a self-learning model that is inherently temporal, and it can infer and make predictions about spatial and temporal patterns.

HTMs learn by storing sequences of patterns in each memory region. The basic idea is that patterns that frequently occur together in time share a common cause and can be grouped together. Time acts a teacher, indicating which patterns mean the same thing, even though they may be spatially dissimilar. When implemented in a hierarchy, the net result is that fast-changing sensory inputs result in slower changing patterns as you ascend the hierarchy. Relatively stable patterns at the top of the hierarchy can unfold in time to produce faster changing patterns at the bottom of the hierarchy. The theory postulates that recall of sequences leads to prediction, thought, and motor behavior.

In this chapter, we will not fully review HTM or exhaustively contrast it to other hierarchical memory models. Instead we want to focus on a core feature of HTM (and HHMM) that is intimately tied to prediction; specifically, how might sequences be stored in neocortex?

CONSTRAINTS ON SEQUENCE MEMORY

Using a computer and linear computer memory, it is easy to store sequences. Every time you make an audio recording or save a text file, you are storing a sequence of patterns. However, this kind of memory is not sufficient for the kind of learning and recall that brains need to do. Real-world sensory data are never exactly the same, they are noisy, and they do not come with markers indicating when sequences begin and end. The simple approach of storing every pattern that occurs will consume too much memory and be unmanageable.

The following is a set of requirements or "constraints" that a biological sequence memory must meet that are different than linear computer memory.

Probabilistic Prediction

Our sequence memory must make probabilistic predictions of future events from noisy inputs. Data sensed from the world are ambiguous at any time instant. Therefore, what is available to the sequence memory at any instance is a distribution of the likely states of the sequence. Similarly, our predictions must be distributions over possible next states. This is a strong constraint and eliminates many possible memory mechanisms. For example, when we listen to someone speaking, the words we hear are often ambiguous in isolation. From this ambiguous input, we anticipate what words will be said next. We usually cannot predict exactly, but some words are more likely than others. Our memory system must be able to handle ambiguity in its input, and all predictions should be distributions—sometimes over large numbers of possible elements.

Simultaneous Learning and Recall

We cannot make a clear distinction between when our memory system is learning and when it is recalling. It must be able to learn, or extend learned sequences, while simultaneously recalling and predicting what is likely to occur next.

Auto-Associative Recall

Learned sequences are recalled auto-associatively. This is similar to the game of "name that tune." As inputs arrive, the memory has to decide which learned sequences best match the input. An input may match multiple learned sequences or none. Our memory system must be able to recognize sequences even if it is presented with a partial sequence from the middle of a previously learned sequence. In a computer it is possible to implement auto-associative recall using repetitive search algorithms, but brains do not work this way. We desire a memory mechanism that is naturally auto-associative.

Variable-Order Memory

To correctly predict what is likely to happen next, it is often necessary to use knowledge of events that occurred some time in the past. Imagine we have two sequences of letters, "ABCDE" and "YBCDZ." Both sequences contain the same three-element sequence "BCD" but vary in the first and last elements. Our memory system must be able to correctly predict the last element of the sequence based on an input that occurred many time steps earlier, a situation that is sometimes referred to as the "branching problem."

The branching problem forces upon us an important constraint: The internal representation of an afferent pattern must change depending on the temporal context in which it occurs. For example, in the previous example, the representation for the elements "B," "C," and "D" must be somehow different when preceded by "A" than by "Y."

In mathematical terms, the number of previous inputs required to predict the next input is known as Markov order. When only one previous input is necessary, the model is first order. Let X_t represent the input at time t. In a first-order model, X_t+_1 does not depend on any previous input besides the prior input, X_t. If we want to know the distribution over what might occur next, $P(X_t+_1)$, we do not need to know anything that happened in the past (X_{t-1} through X_0); we only need to know the current input, X_t. Specifically:

$$P\left(X_{t+1}|X_t, X_{t-1}, X_{t-2},..., X_0\right) = P\left(X_{t+1}|X_t\right)$$

But in our example with the letter sequences, if we see "ABCD" or "YBCD," we need to go all the way back to the first letter to predict the one that comes next. This requires a fourth-order model:

$$P\left(X_{t+1}|X_t, X_{t-1}, X_{t-2},..., X_0\right)$$
$$= P\left(X_{t+1}|X_t, X_{t-1}, X_{t-2}, X_{t-3}\right)$$

Keeping track of these long dependencies allows us to use the initial letter, "A" or "Y," to predict the final letter, "E" or "Z." However, the amount of memory required to keep track of long dependencies grows exponentially with the order of the model, quickly becoming infeasible to store and to learn. Therefore we desire a variable-order Markov model. Variable-order models learn long sequences (high-order) as necessary, but use short sequences (low-order) for other parts of the data. They allow us to learn complex sequences with manageable amounts of resources.

Biological Constraints

We propose that a sequence memory mechanism that meets these theoretical constraints must exist in all regions of neocortex, in all sensory modalities. Given our belief of the central importance of sequence memory for neocortical function, whatever mechanism the brain uses for sequence memory should be prevalent throughout the neocortex. Therefore, any proposed mechanism should map to one or more prominent features of neocortical anatomy.

SEQUENCE MEMORY IN THE NEOCORTEX

Our theory of biological sequence memory is inspired by the previous work of Rodriguez, Whitson, and Granger (2004), although they used it in a different functional context and with a different biological mapping. We feel it is important to reintroduce this memory technique in the current context of hierarchical neocortical models and give it an expanded biological and mathematical foundation.

The basics of this idea are fairly simple, and they are explained in Figure 18.2a–c. In biological terms, we can think of the cells in a neocortical column as having the same bottom-up receptive field properties. This is a well-known phenomenon believed to occur throughout the neocortex. Within a particular cortical column, there might be dozens of cells within a layer all exhibiting similar or identical feedforward receptive field properties. Although these cells exhibit similar responses to a purely feedforward input, in our model these cells learn to form different responses in the context of natural sequences. Only some of these cells will be active when that feedforward pattern occurs within a learned sequence.

Consider an analogy. Imagine we have a column of cells that respond to the sound made when we say the word "to." Because in English the words "to," "two," and "too" are homonyms, each of these words spoken in isolation will invoke the same response among these co-columnar cells. However, these words are not interchangeable in context. Imagine we hear the sentences "I sat next to," "Can I come too?" and "The number after one is two." In these three phrases, the final words have different meanings, and we perceive them as different. For us to perceive these homonyms as different, our brains must use different neural activations for them.

We propose that through the course of training, individual cells form horizontal connections to previously active cells in nearby columns (Fig. 18.2c). These horizontal connections form

the basis of sequence memory. When a cell is activated by a horizontal connection prior to receiving its feedforward activation, it will inhibit its co-columnar cells, thus guaranteeing a unique representation for the feedforward pattern in the context of a previously learned sequence.

BIOLOGICAL IMPLICATIONS OF SEQUENCE MEMORY MODEL

The proposed model for sequence memory provides a theoretical basis for the columnar organization and horizontal connections observed throughout the neocortex. It also provides a simple mechanism for what we believe is a ubiquitous need for prediction and learning in hierarchical learning models in general.

As a biological model it is speculative and has numerous requirements for it to work. We now will discuss some of these implications before describing how we implemented a software algorithm to mimic the biological theory and tested it within our HTM models.

Sparsification of Response

A prediction of this proposal is that general cell activity in neocortex should become more sparse and selective when receiving input in naturally occurring sequences versus receiving spatial inputs in temporal isolation or random order. A more specific variation of this prediction is that co-columnar cells should exhibit similar responses to simple stimuli, but they should be become more sparse and selective when presented with natural sequences. There are several studies that have observed such behavior. Yen, Baker, and Gray (2007) reported that in cat striate cortex, classical columnar organization (which is usually determined via simple stimuli such as bars and gratings) changes dramatically and becomes sparser when the animal is subjected to complex time-varying natural images. Similar results were shown by Vinje and Gallant (2000) in macaque V1. Here they found that input from outside a cell's classic receptive field increased sparseness. This result was observed when the animal was subjected to a time-varying simulated natural viewing stimulus, and the effect was

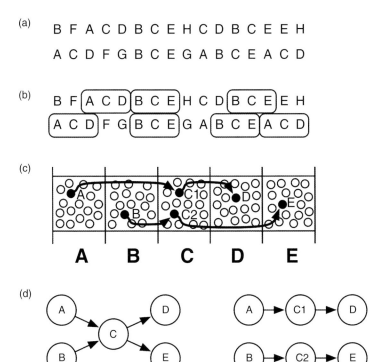

Figure 18.2 (*a*) **Hypothetical sequence of inputs. Letters A through H represent bottom-up input patterns to five columns of cells. Within this sequence of inputs are repeating subsequences intermixed with nonrepeating elements.** (*b*) **Sequence** (*a*) **in which two common subsequences, A-C-D and B-C-E, are highlighted. A second-order Markov model is necessary to differentiate these sequences. In general we require a memory mechanism that can learn and represent sequences of arbitrarily high order.** (*c*) **Proposed manner in which the neocortex represents the sequences highlighted in** (*b*). **The five columns each respond to a different bottom-up input. Shown is one layer of cells, representing neurons that all respond to their column's bottom-up inputs. After training, individual neurons become part of a particular temporal sequence. Filled circles indicate neurons that participate in the two sequences highlighted in** (*b*). **Arrows illustrate lateral excitatory connections. Two neurons, C1 and C2, are used in column C because input C occurs in both sequences. This permits the memory to correctly predict "D" after the input sequence A-C and "E" after the input sequence B-C. The length and Markov order of the memory is limited by the number of cells in a particular layer within a column. Not shown are required inhibitory pathways.** (*d*) **First-order Markov model of transitions learned from** (*a*). **Correct prediction from state C is not possible because the input that preceded C is not captured.** (*e*) **Result of applying the state-splitting algorithm first proposed by Cormack and Horspool (1987) to** (*d*). **Both C1 and C2 respond to a purely bottom-up pattern C, but C1 uniquely responds if A occurs before C, and C2 uniquely responds if B occurs before C. Accurate prediction after input C is possible because C1 will be active if A occurred previously, while C2 will be active if B occurred previously. These states map directly onto the cortical model in** (*c*). **Unlike the biological equivalent, the state-splitting technique has no a priori limit to the length of sequences or the number of sequences in which a bottom-up input can appear.**

somewhat increased under free natural viewing. Machens, Wehr, and Zador (2004) found that rat auditory cortex exhibited increased sparseness when subjected to complex natural sounds. They report that only 11% of the responses to natural sounds could be attributed to the classical receptive field property of the cells, and they suggested the remainder was due to the interactions between frequencies and the time-varying properties of the neural encoding.

These and similar studies have been largely or partially motivated by demonstrating the existence of sparse encoding, which is an efficient method of representation in neural tissue (Olshausen & Field, 1996). Our HTM models similarly employ sparse encoding, but here we suggest that our sequence memory model is one means, and perhaps a primary one, to achieve it.

Inhibitory Requirements

A specific inhibitory effect is required for our proposal to work in neocortical tissue. When a column of cells is activated primarily from a feedforward input, all or a majority of the excitatory cells within a layer of a column should be active together. But if that same feedforward pattern occurs within a learned sequence, we only want one or a few cells to be active. This requires that an excitatory lateral input to one or a few cells inhibit all the other cells in the near proximity. This laterally induced inhibition must be stronger and faster than the feedforward excitation.

Distributed Representations

We assume that the neocortex uses distributed representations in two ways. First, we do not assume that individual cells are sufficient to represent anything. Although our figures show individual cells representing patterns within sequences, this is only a convenience. We assume that in almost all cases multiple cells are simultaneously active, although the pattern of activation will always be sparse.

Representations also are distributed in a second sense. Bayesian networks in general, and HTM models in particular, assume that activations are distributed. Every region of the hierarchy passes a distribution of potentially active sequences to its parent regions. Again, the figure in this chapter does not show this, but our software models are implemented this way. The neocortex works with probabilistic inputs and makes probabilistic predictions.

Efficient Computation

The memory system must use information from previous inputs when making predictions, and both the history of inputs and the forward predictions are distributions over many states. Performing this calculation in a brute-force manner is not biologically realistic in terms of capacity or speed. Our biological model performs the calculation using dynamic programming, a mechanism first described by Bellman (1957). Refer to George (2008) §4.6.2 for a detailed mapping of the biological theory to dynamic programming equations.

Cortical Layers

We believe the sequence model we have described occurs among pools of neurons within the same layer of neocortex, using lateral connections to cells in the same layer of other columns. We do not believe the effect is likely to occur across cortical layers unless evidence exists of strong interlaminar lateral connections.

Previously, we have proposed why the different cell layers observed in neocortex might exist (Hawkins, 2007). It is not our intention to review these proposals here, but a brief overview might be useful. Cellular layers 2–6 all exhibit lateral connections, although there are differences. In our view, these differences reflect the kind of sequences that can be learned, and sequence learning is occurring in some form in layers 2–6.

Hierarchical memory models—and in particular HTM—need to make a distinction between information flowing up the hierarchy and information flowing down the hierarchy. In a crude way, you can think of downward flowing information as expectation and upward flowing information as reality. Bayesian theory tells us that these two streams of information must remain segregated but that they must also be combined to form a local belief at each level of the hierarchy (Pearl, 1988). Because sequence memory is required both in the feedforward path and in the feedback path, we believe that some cell layers are learning feedforward sequences (layers 4 and 3) and other layers are learning feedback sequences (layers 2 and 6). Layer 5 is where they are combined to form a belief. The main point here is that we believe sequence memory is occurring in multiple cell layers and that there are theoretical reasons this should be so.

Sequence Timing

When we learn a melody, part of the memory of the melody is the duration of each note, which varies from note to note. Similarly, when we memorize a poem or a dance step, we remember the duration for each element in the sequence. We can speed up or slow down a recalled sequence, but the absolute duration of the sequence elements are stored and can be recalled.

As described so far, our sequence memory model has no means of storing the duration of sequence elements, and it has no means of changing the rate at which a sequence is recalled. Our sequence memory mechanism therefore needs a neural mechanism that can encode the durations of sequence elements. This neural mechanism should exist in all regions of the neocortex and should be tightly coupled with the sequence memory mechanism proposed in this chapter. Previously (Hawkins & Blakeslee, 2004), we have proposed such a duration mechanism involving layer 5 pyramidal cells, which project to nonspecific thalamic nuclei, which project to neocortical layer 1, which form synapses with apical dendrites of pyramidal cells in layers 2, 3, and 5. It is beyond the scope of this chapter to describe this mechanism further.

When a human learns a melody, there is an upper limit to the duration of individual notes that can be learned of about 1 second. This is why musicians need to count for notes or rests that are longer than 1 second. Assuming that a similar limit exists in other modalities, the sequence memory proposed here can learn arbitrarily long sequences of elements where the duration of each element is between a few tens of milliseconds and about 1 second. In a software implementation, the duration limits need not be fixed but could depend on the parameters of the model and the resources allocated to it.

Memory Capacity

Our proposed biological model tells us something about the capacity of sequence memory. Consider an analogy to music. Imagine we have 12 columns each with 50 cells, where each column represents 1 of the 12 musical tones in Western music. Such a memory can learn melodies and melodic phrases, but there is a limit to number and length of the sequences that can be stored. At one extreme it could learn a single sequence of 600 notes using exactly 50 of each of the 12 tones. If the memory were allocated this way, the system could only recognize the single melody, but it could do so auto-associatively when presented with any portion of the melody, or even a partially garbled portion of the melody. In addition, it would be able to predict the next note or the entire remaining portion of the melody. At another extreme, the memory could learn 100 sequences of six notes each. The point is there are a fixed number of states that can be allocated to a few long sequences or many short sequences or any combination in between.

It might appear that such a memory system is too limited to store all the information we have in our brains. A human can memorize a tremendous amount of temporally associated information, including long speeches, long pieces of music, lengthy journeys, and so on. The answer to this objection is that capacity of hierarchical temporal memory derives primarily from the hierarchy, not the sequence memory in each node (George, 2008). The hierarchy allows learned sequences to be used over and over in different combinations. When memorizing a speech with a hierarchy of sequence memories, the speech is stored as a series of phrases at one level of the hierarchy, the phrases are decomposed into a series of words at the next lower level, and each word is decomposed into a series of phonemes at the next lower level.

THE STATE-SPLITTING ALGORITHM

Over the past 3 years, we have been creating and testing models of hierarchical temporal memory in software. During this time we have tried several different sequence memory techniques, starting with the simplest method of storing all afferent sequences, and progressing to complex methods such as Prediction Suffix Trees (Ron, Singer, & Tishby, 1996; Seldin, Bejerano, & Tishby, 2001). In the end, we have settled on a sequence memory model we call state-splitting, depicted in Figure 18.2d,e. State-splitting was inspired by and maps closely to our proposed biological sequence memory mechanism. Like other techniques, state-splitting generates variable-order Markov models, which can capture complex dependencies within sequences. However, state-splitting is the only sequence memory model we have found that meets all of the aforementioned constraints and maps well to neocortical anatomy. And we have found state-splitting to be simpler to implement than some other methods.

The state-splitting technique was first described by Cormack and Horspool (1987), although they used the algorithm for data compression and in a nonbiological context. We borrow their technique and apply it to prediction and inference in an HTM setting.

Splitting States

State-splitting deviates from our proposed biological sequence memory in one significant way. In the biological model we start with a column of cells that share bottom-up receptive field properties and then assign the cells to unique sequences. By contrast, in the state-splitting model we start with a single state and then split the state as we learn sequences (similar to adding neurons as we need them). State-splitting accomplishes the same goal as the biological model, but there is no limit on the number of assignable elements for each column, and no resources are wasted overrepresenting inputs that only appear in a few sequences.

The state-splitting algorithm begins with one state per input pattern. During learning, it observes the activation of states, and it counts a transition between state i and state j if input j is active immediately after input i is active. The mechanism also works if more than one state is active at a particular point in time. The sequence of activations is tracked in a Markov chain T, a matrix in which $T_{i,j}$ contains the number of transitions from state i to state j. Periodically, we examine T to determine whether some states belong to multiple sequences. Any such state is split to create one or more new copies.

Intuitively, we wish to split a state when we believe it reliably participates in more than one sequence. To test for this, we check whether a state frequently follows a particular state (i.e., it clearly participates in a sequence), and we also check whether it follows other states as well

(i.e., it may appear in other sequences). From Cormack and Horspool (1987) we borrow the two parameters min_cnt1 and min_cnt2. We split state t into two states when there exists a state s for which the two conditions hold:

$$T_{s,t} \geq min\_cnt1$$

$$\sum_{i, i \neq s} T_{i,t} \geq min\_cnt2$$

After the split, we consider the system to be in the new state t' if s is active previously, and otherwise the system is in the original state t. Thus, by construction, the states automatically participate in separate sequences. Through multiple splits, states may participate in many sequences.

We continue learning transitions in the new Markov chain T, which now has an expanded set of states. But even though we still treat the model as first order, it is now implicitly higher order. States that have been split are constructed to activate after a specific predecessor; thus, some states contain higher order information by bundling together inputs from multiple time steps. Figure 18.2d shows the initial first-order model built from the frequent sequences highlighted in Figure 18.2b. The algorithm chooses to split state C into C1 and C2, where C1 originates from A and C2 originates from B. The new model is shown in Figure 18.2e. Although only first-order transitions are maintained, splitting C allows the model to capture the second-order information necessary to recognize the two sequences and form correct predictions.

Identifying Sequences

We have described the algorithm used to build the variable-order memory necessary for modeling sequences and making predictions. HTM requires another component of sequence memory, which identifies individual sequences to communicate with the parent regions in the hierarchy. We believe there are biological equivalents, but they are beyond the scope of this chapter.

Experimental results

We wish to verify that the state-splitting algorithm can be used to model the statistics of real-world sensory data. In this section, we demonstrate the performance of the algorithm on motion-capture data of human subjects.

Motion-capture data are recorded with a camera that measures the position and joint angles of an actor in a special suit. We obtained data from the Carnegie Mellon Graphics Lab Motion Capture Database, available at http://mocap.cs.cmu.edu. Data are recorded from 32 joints at each point in time. We use sequences of these joint angles for training and testing our model.

The data also are sufficient for us to render stick-figure representations of the actors. Figure 18.3a shows three example poses. When the poses do not

appear in a sequence, it is difficult to recognize which action the subject is performing, and it would not be possible to predict next likely poses.

We train on a file of many sequences, with 239 poses in total. Before building the temporal model, we quantize the poses to 66 quantization points. Each input to the state-splitting algorithm is the index of the quantization point with the lowest Euclidean distance to the original input. Using this quantization, we transform each input from a dense vector to a single index. We then learn the Markov chain with these indices and apply the state-splitting algorithm. We pass over the same data five times in total to produce more splits and create a higher order model.

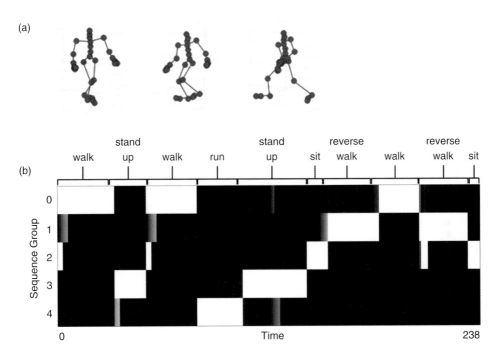

Figure 18.3 (*a*) Three separate motion-capture inputs from a human subject. Each input is a set of angles from 32 joints. When shown a sequence of such poses, humans have no difficulty recognizing activities such as running, walking, and sitting. However, actions are difficult or impossible to recognize from static poses such as these because many poses could be part of several different actions. (*b*) Unsupervised classification of motion-capture sequences. The state-splitting algorithm described in this chapter was shown a sequence of 239 poses in which the subject repeatedly performed four different actions ("walk," "run," "sit," and "stand up"). As an extra test, the "walk" sequences were also played backward as a fifth action ("reverse walk"), guaranteeing that the exact same poses were used but in a different temporal order. The vertical axis represents the five sequences groups, learned without supervision. The horizontal axis shows the time progression of the 239 poses. The labels at the top of the chart indicate what action the subject was performing at that time. The learned sequences closely match the subjects performed actions, demonstrating that the state-splitting method was able to learn the sequences.

To ascertain whether the resultant Markov chain accurately models the data, we apply a sequence-identification algorithm to discover five sequence groups. Figure 18.3b shows the result of playing a long segment of the training data and tracking the activation of the five groups. Although the groups were labeled without supervision, each one clearly corresponds to a particular action. We observe that the group activations switch appropriately when the subject switches actions, with only occasional errors at the intersections. We happily note that the "walk" and "reverse walk" sequences are correctly distinguished, proving that temporal order is being used.

The results in Figure 18.3b demonstrate learning and inference with higher order sequences, using the state-splitting algorithm. It is a straightforward matter to generate predictions from the temporal models within individual nodes in an HTM. Generating predictions using the entire hierarchy together is one of our current areas of research.

Source code for the state-splitting algorithm and the motion-capture example is available from http://www.numenta.com.

Conclusion

The neocortex can be viewed as a memory system that builds a model of the world for inference, prediction, and behavior. We claim that all these goals can be achieved using a hierarchically organized memory system, in which each node in the hierarchy uses probabilistic sequence memory to group patterns together. The hierarchical organization of the neocortex is well documented, and Bayesian theory provides a basis for understanding how hierarchies can infer causes in the face of ambiguity. In this chapter we have proposed a simple yet powerful technique for how regions of neocortex might learn probabilistic sequences. The technique relies on columnar organization of cells that share bottom-up receptive field properties. Through lateral connections, individual cells learn to represent bottom-up patterns within specific sequences. Although simple, the proposed sequence memory technique solves the difficult tasks of learning sequences of arbitrarily

high order from distributed inputs, recognizing time-based patterns, and making distributed predictions.

Acknowledgments

We gratefully thank Bobby Jaros for implementing the state-splitting algorithm and creating the test suite for motion-capture data. We also thank Bruno Olshausen for assisting with references.

References

Bellman, R. (1957). *Dynamic programming*. Princeton, NJ: Princeton University Press.

Cormack, G. V., & Horspool, R. N. S. (1987). Data compression using dynamic Markov modeling. *Computer Journal, 30*, 541–550.

Fine, S., Singer, Y., & Tishby, N. (1998). The hierarchical hidden Markov model: Analysis and applications. *Machine Learning, 32*, 41–62.

George, D. (2008). *How the brain might work: A hierarchical and temporal model for learning and recognition*. Unpublished doctoral dissertation, Stanford University.

George, D., & Hawkins, J. (2005). A hierarchical Bayesian model of invariant pattern recognition in the visual cortex. *Proceedings of the International Joint Conference on Neural Networks, 3*, 1812–1817.

Hawkins, J. (2007). Hierarchical temporal memory: Biological mapping to neocortex and thalamus. Retrieved July 1, 2010, from http://www.numenta.com/for-developers/education/biological-background-htm.php.

Hawkins, J., & Blakeslee, S. (2004). *On intelligence*. New York: Times Books.

Hawkins, J., & George, D. (2006). Hierarchical temporal memory: Concepts, theory, and terminology. Retrieved July 1, 2010, from http://www.numenta.com/Numenta_HTM_Concepts.pdf.

LeCun, Y., & Bengio, Y. (1995). Convolutional networks for images, speech, and time-series. In M. A. Arbib (Ed.), *The handbook of brain theory and neural networks* (pp. 255–258). Cambridge, MA: MIT Press.

Machens, C. K., Wehr M. S., & Zador, A. M. (2004). Linearity of cortical receptive fields measured with natural sounds. *Journal of Neuroscience, 24*, 1089–1100.

Olshausen, B., & Field, D. J. (1996). Emergence of simple-cell receptive field properties by learning a sparse code for natural images. *Nature, 381,* 607–609.

Pearl, J. (1988). *Probabilistic reasoning in intelligent systems: Networks of plausible inference.* San Francisco: Morgan Kaufmann.

Riesenhuber, M., & Poggio, T. (1999). Hierarchical models of object recognition in cortex. *Nature Neuroscience, 2,* 1019–1025.

Rodriguez, A., Whitson, J., & Granger, R. (2004). Derivation and analysis of basic computational operations of thalamocortical circuits. *Journal of Cognitive Neurosciences, 16,* 856–877.

Ron, D., Singer, Y., & Tishby, N. (1996). The power of amnesia: Learning probabilistic automata with variable memory length. *Machine Learning, 25,* 117–149.

Seldin, Y., Bejerano, G., & Tishby, N. (2001). Unsupervised sequence segmentation by a mixture of switching variable memory Markov sources. In *Proceedings of the Eighteenth International Conference on Machine Learning,* 513–520.

Vinje, W., & Gallant, J. (2000). Sparse coding and decorrelation in primary visual cortex during natural vision. *Science, 287,* 1273–1276.

Yen, S-C., Baker, J., & Gray, C. M. (2007). Heterogeneity in the responses of adjacent neurons to natural stimuli in cat striate cortex. *Journal of Neurophysiology, 97,* 1326–1341.

CHAPTER 19
Prediction, Sequences, and the Hippocampus

John Lisman and A. David Redish

There is now strong evidence that the activity in the rodent hippocampus can reflect predictive information about potential future events and places, particularly on the order of several seconds in the future. Moreover, while animals can predict outcomes in simple conditioning tasks without a hippocampus (Corbit & Balleine, 2000), the hippocampus is necessary for predictions that involve novel sequences or temporal gaps (Dusek & Eichenbaum, 1998; O'Keefe & Nadel, 1978; Redish, 1999), particularly when this prediction requires the integration of spatially and temporally separated information (Cohen & Eichenbaum, 1993; Redish, 1999). In this chapter we will review the evidence that hippocampal representations show predictive sequences during behaviors that depend on hippocampal integrity.

In a general sense, any memory could contribute to the ability to form predictions, but the memory of sequences has special utility. Suppose that the sequence ABC has occurred in the past. The subsequent appearance of A can serve as a cue for the recall of this sequence. To the extent that a sequence that has been observed once will tend to recur, the cued recall of BC is a prediction that BC is likely to happen next.

Research on the role of the hippocampus in memory sequences has progressed rapidly over the last decade due to three major developments. First, it has now become standard to monitor a large number of neurons in awake, behaving rats (Buzsáki, 2004; Wilson & McNaughton, 1993). Second, new developments in analytical methods have enabled the study of how neural ensembles represent space on a fast time scale, thereby eliminating the need to average over long, potentially variable time frames (Brown, Frank, Tang, Quirk, & Wilson, 1998; Johnson, Fenton, Kentros, & Redish, 2009; Johnson, Jackson, & Reddish, 2008; Zhang, Ginzburg, McHaughton, & Sejnowski, 1998). Third, it is now clear that the hippocampus cannot be understood solely in terms of a simple rate code. Rather, important additional information is encoded by a temporal code in which cellular firing is organized by oscillations in the theta (7–10 Hz) and gamma (40–100 Hz) range.

We will begin by describing these oscillations and the way they organize information. We will then review experimental evidence that the hippocampus retrieves memory sequences and can utilize this information to guide behavior. We then turn to open questions, such as the mechanism of sequence retrieval, how far in the future the sequences can predict, and whether there is a "constructive" form of prediction about situations that have not previously occurred.

THETA/GAMMA PHASE CODE AND PHASE PRECESSION

The oscillations of the hippocampus are easily observed in the local field potential of the rat. These oscillations depend strongly on behavioral state (Buzsáki, 2006; O'Keefe & Nadel, 1978; Vanderwolf, 1971). During movement, the local field potential is primarily characterized by strong oscillations in the theta frequency range (7–10 Hz). At the same time there is also a faster oscillation in the gamma frequency range (40–100 Hz) (Bragin et al., 1995). These dual oscillations are shown schematically in Figure 19.1. In contrast, during slow-wave sleep and inattentive rest, the local field potential is characterized by a broader frequency distribution and much less prominent theta and gamma. This state (termed large-amplitude irregular activity [LIA]) is punctuated by brief events called sharp waves characterized by 180–220 Hz ripples. Although pauses characterized by inattention (eating, grooming, resting) tend to show LIA, pauses characterized by active attention (e.g., during anxiety, fear, and decision making) show continued theta (Gray & McNaughton, 2000; Johnson & Redish, 2007; O'Keefe & Nadel, 1978; Vanderwolf, 1971). As we will see shortly, certain types of memory processes only occur during periods of theta oscillations.

When one utilizes firing rate as an indicator of cell activity, the activity defines the place field

of the place cell. This field is generally a relatively small fraction of the environment (see center panel in Fig. 19.3G). The place fields of different cells occur in different locations; thus, place cells collectively code for the animal's position within an environment. Two lines of evidence, however, indicate that this description is incomplete. Cells sometimes fire spikes outside their main place fields, for example, at feeder sites (Jackson, Johnson, & Redish, 2006; Jensen & Lisman, 2000; O'Keefe & Nadel, 1978) and at decision points (Johnson & Redish, 2007). As we will see, this additional firing (extra-field firing) may actually reflect information processing ("thinking") about a different location—that of the cell's main place field rather than the animal's current location. The second line of evidence relates to aspects of neural coding that go beyond what can be accounted for by a rate code. As a rat crosses the place field of a cell, the firing shows temporal coding: Spikes fire with a systematic timing (phase) relationship to ongoing theta oscillations. Moreover, this relationship changes

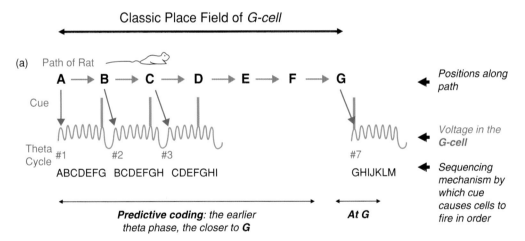

Figure 19.1 Schematic illustrating theta phase precession. The place field of the illustrated cell covers a small part of a path; this part is labeled by successive letters of the alphabet—the firing starts at A and stops when the rat moves past G. Voltage (intracellular) traces show successive theta cycles (1–7), each of which has seven gamma subcycles. Firing occurs near the peak of a gamma cycle and with earlier and earlier theta phase as the rat runs from left to right. This is termed *phase precession*. The precession process can be understood as resulting from a sequencing (chaining) mechanism within each theta cycle in which the cue (current position) triggers sequential readout from different cells representing successive positions (e.g., A–G) along the path. This is termed a *sweep*. The cell illustrated represents the position G. Firing at positions A–F is predictive of the rat being at G.

as the rat moves through the place field, a phenomenon known as "phase precession" (Dragoi & Buzsáki, 2006; Maurer & McNaughton, 2007; O'Keefe & Recce 1993; Skaggs, McNaughton, Wilson, & Barnes, 1996). This phenomenon is shown in Figure 19.2A and illustrated schematically in Figure 19.1. If a rat moves through a place field at average velocity, firing occurs during about 8–12 theta cycles (i.e., a total duration of about 1–2 seconds; Maurer & McNaughton, 2007). Phase precession is most clearly seen on linear tracks as the rat runs through the place field. The cell initially fires during late phases of the theta cycle, but on each successive theta cycle, firing occurs at an earlier and earlier phase. Models of phase precession have suggested that phase precession contains both retrospective and prospective (predictive) components. As we will

review later, it has now been definitively shown that the phase precession has a predictive component.

An issue that determines the information capacity of a phase code is how finely the phase of theta can be divided. Recent experimental work strongly supports the theoretical suggestion that the coding scheme used by the hippocampus is a theta/gamma discrete phase code (Lisman, 2005; Lisman & Idiart, 1995). According to this hypothesis, the gamma oscillations that occur during a theta cycle themselves control firing (i.e., firing can occur at only a restricted phase of a gamma cycle). Thus, there will be approximately 5–14 gamma cycles in each theta cycle (7 Hz/40–100 Hz), and this will result in a corresponding number of discrete times at which firing may occur. Consistent with this

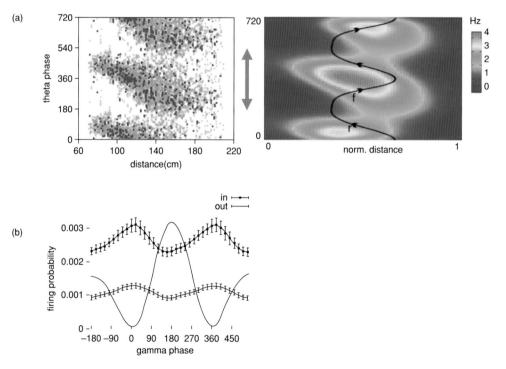

Figure 19.2 **Phase locking of spikes to gamma and theta oscillations.** (*A*) (*Left*) **As a rat moves through a place field (distance), theta phase systematically changes over 360 degrees (red arrow). Green dots, all spikes; blue dots during high gamma power.** (*Right*) **Averaged data from many cells with color code for rate.** (*B*) **During theta phase precession, spiking is gamma locked. Closed circles indicate probability of spiking as a function of gamma phase when rat is in the place field. The gamma waveform in the field potential is plotted as a solid line. (Adapted from Senior, Huxter, Allen, O'Neill, & Csicsvari, 2008.)**

hypothesis, recent work (Fig. 19.2B) has found that the firing of hippocampal pyramidal cells is gamma-modulated while the theta phase precession is occurring (Senior, Huxter, Allen, O'Neill, & Csicsvari, 2008). The cells that fire during a given gamma cycle define an ensemble (i.e., a spatial code for a memory item). Overall, then, about 5–14 items can be coded for during a theta cycle, each in a given gamma subcycle of a theta cycle. This coding scheme provides a framework for understanding the phase precession in the hippocampus (see later discussion), but it may also be related to the capacity limits of working memory networks in cortex (Lisman & Idiart, 1995).

PROSPECTIVE CODING: PREDICTING UPCOMING PLACES

Soon after phase precession was discovered it was suggested that the phenomenon implies a process in which the represented location sweeps across positions in the direction of travel (Skaggs, McNaughton, Wilson, & Barnes, 1996). Two early models specifically proposed that phase precession should be interpreted as a sweep *ahead* of the animal (Jensen & Lisman, 1996; Tsodyks, Skaggs, Sejnowski, & McNaughton, 1996).

An important aspect of this interpretation (Fig. 19.1) is that the spatial resolution of the system is much finer than the size of the place field: the "true place field" (which we designate here by a letter) is taken to be about one-seventh the size of the apparent place field (the entire field where rate is elevated). Thus, we can think of positions A, B, C, D, E, F, G as seven subparts of an apparent place field (with different cells representing each position and firing in different gamma cycles of the theta cycle). As we will explain in the text that follows, the firing of the "G–cell" illustrated in Figure 19.1 at positions A–F is actually a prediction about the distance to the true place field, G.

To further clarify this interpretation, let us first consider what happens during a single theta cycle, a phenomenon we term a "sweep." Suppose that one is recording from a cell representing position G ahead of where the rat is now (position A).

It might at first seem that this cell should not fire until the animal gets to G; however, in the context of a predictive process based on phase coding, firing of the G-cell at position A at late theta phases can be understood as a prediction that the rat is approaching G. The process that causes the G-cell to fire when the animal is at position A can be understood mechanistically as a chaining process that occurs within a theta cycle: If the rat is at position A, the cells representing position A are cued to fire at the beginning of the theta cycle (i.e., in the first gamma cycle). The chaining process then fires the next cells in the spatial sequence (these represent position B and fire in the second gamma cycle). This chaining process continues until the G-cell fires at the end of the theta cycle (in the last gamma cycle within the theta cycle). There is thus a "sweep" of activity from location A to location G during this theta cycle.

A key to understanding the phase precession is that the cue will change over time as the animal runs; this will change the character of sweeps in successive theta cycles. Thus, when the second theta cycle occurs, the rat will have proceeded farther along and so is now at B. Given that B is now the cue, the sweep that occurs in the second theta cycle will be B, C, D, E, F, G, H. It can be seen that whereas in the first theta cycle, the G-cell fired in the last gamma cycle, in the second theta cycle, the G-cell now fires in the next to last gamma cycle, that is, with earlier theta phase. It thus follows that as long as the rat keeps moving, the G-cell will fire with earlier and earlier phase on each successive theta cycle.

EVIDENCE FOR PROSPECTIVE CODING IN HIPPOCAMPUS

In support of this interpretation, several experiments show that many spikes fired by place cells actually represent a position ahead of the animal. First, studies of phase precession in cells with omnidirectional place fields have shown that firing during the late components of theta (early firing in a pass through the place field, i.e., the predictive components) fire as the animal approaches a specific location from any direction. That is, as the animal approaches the position from the left, these spikes are fired to the left

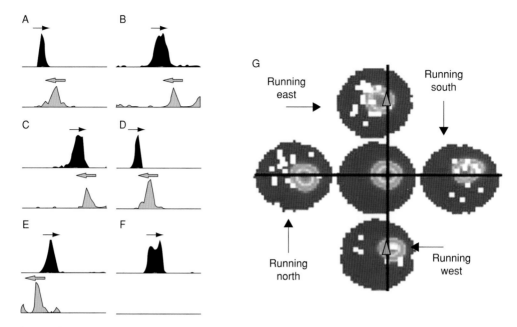

Figure 19.3 Predictive or retrospective aspect of place field firing. (*A–F*) Firing rate as function of position for rats running leftward or rightward on a linear track (as indicated by arrows). A–D are examples of prospective coding (the position being predicted is at the overlap of the arrows and is termed the "true place field"). (*E*) Example of retrospective coding. (Modified from Battaglia, Sutherland, & McNaughton, 2004.) (*G*) Predictive coding in a 2D environment. The size of the environment is indicated in blue and shown five times for different conditions. The central version indicates the concept of the classic place field, the rat explores the environment through motions in all directions, and the firing rat is indicated in a color code (red highest). The place field is centered in the red region. Peripheral plots show firing rate computed for *unidirectional* passage through the region. Predictive coding is illustrated by the fact that when running east, most spikes are to the left of the black line, whereas when running west, they are to the right. The cell can be thought of as predicting arrival to the region marked by the pink triangle. This region would constitute the "true place field." (Modified from Huxter, Senior, Allen, & Csicsvari, 2008.)

of the point; as the animal approaches the position from the right, these spikes are fired to the right of that point. This has been seen (Fig. 19.3) on both the cue-rich 1D linear track (Battaglia, Sutherland, & McNaughton, 2004) and in the standard 2D cylinder foraging task (Huxter, Senior, Allen, & Csicsvari, 2008). These experiments suggest that the information about position implicated by firing of the cell (the "true place field" of the cell) is actually a small central point corresponding to where the rat is during the firing at early phases of the theta cycle (the central portion of the classic omnidirectional place field in 2D, the later portion of the unidirectional place field in 1D).

Second, Johnson and Redish (2007) found that when a rat comes to a difficult choice point on a maze and shows behavioral evidence of searching behavior (the animal alternately looks left and right, a behavior termed *vicarious trial and error* [VTE]; Meunzinger, 1938; Tolman, 1939), neural ensembles within the hippocampus encode future positions ahead of the animal (Fig. 19.4). During these behavioral pauses, the animal appears attentive to its surroundings and the hippocampal local field potential remains in the theta state (Johnson & Redish, 2007; O'Keefe & Nadel, 1978; Vanderwolf, 1971). Decoding represented positions from hippocampal ensembles showed that there are sweeps of firing that

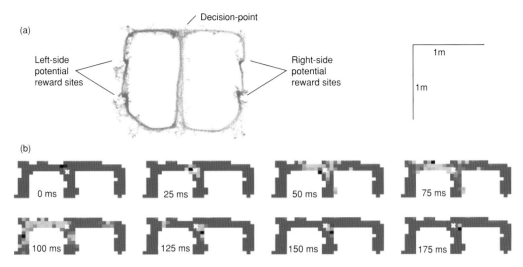

Figure 19.4 Decoded hippocampal neural ensembles at a choice point shows a sweep to the left, progressing from a decision point, around a corner to a goal location through the course of 140 ms. (*A*) **All position samples from a cued-choice task. (*B*) Decoded representations at fine time scales. Color indicates posterior decoded probability. White x indicates location of the animal. (Modified from Johnson & Redish, 2007.)**

represent successive positions along one or the other arms of the maze. These sweeps show directionality away from the choice point (Fig. 19.4). These sweeps can be interpreted analogously to the prospective cued-chaining interpretation of phase precession reviewed in the preceding section. In the cued-chaining interpretation, the observed phase precession is a series of sweeps (ABCDEFG, BCDEFGH, etc.) in which each sweep is a predictive process that differs from the preceding one because of a changing cue. The sweeps observed by Johnson and Redish may be a single instance of one of these chained sequences.

Finally, on tasks with highly repeated paths (such as running back and forth on a linear track, or running around a circular track), place fields expand backwards along the direction of travel, such that on later laps within a day, the place field gains a leader region in front of the place field that was seen on the first laps. This is termed *place field expansion* (Blum & Abbott, 1996; Mehta, Barnes, & McNaughton, 1997). It has now been established that place field expansion does not cause phase precession—place field expansion can be inhibited, while leaving the

basic phase precession intact (Ekstrom, Meltzer, McNaughton, & Barnes, 2001; Shen, Barnes, McNaughton, Skaggs, & Weaver, 1997). The effect of place field expansion is to lengthen the first part of the phase precession, which can be viewed as the learned ability to predict yet further ahead in each theta cycle (Blum & Abbott, 1996; Jensen & Lisman, 2005; Mehta et al., 1997; Redish, 1999; Redish & Touretzky, 1998). This means that as the animal repeatedly observes regular sequences, the sweeps occurring during each theta cycle reach further into the future (ABCDEFGHIJ instead of just ABCDEFG), allowing an earlier prediction of approach to a location.

MANIPULATING THE SPATIAL CUE FOR SEQUENCE RECALL

The interpretation of the phase precession as reflecting a cued sequence-recall process depends on the assumption that the retrieval process is cued on each theta cycle by the current position of the rat (Fig. 19.1). It follows that the phase precession should depend on the velocity of the rat. Suppose, for instance, that the rat ran so fast that by the second theta cycle it was already at G. In this case, proper prediction would imply that firing should occur only on two theta cycles and the entire change in phase (from late to early) should occur in two theta cycles. Consistent with this, a systematic study of the velocity dependence of phase precession indicated that phase precession could be more accurately described by spatial rather than temporal traversal (Geisler, Robbe, Zugaro, Sirota, & Buzsáki, 2007; Maurer & McNaughton, 2007; O'Keefe & Recce, 1993; Skaggs & McNaughton, 1996). At average velocity, the phase advance is equivalent to 0.5–1 gamma period per theta cycle; when the rat runs slower, the phase advance is less and when the rat runs faster, the phase advance is greater.

A further test of the importance of changing cues is to put the rat in a running wheel. If the phase precession is due to internal dynamics, to proprioceptive feedback from running, or even from some general motivational or speed-of-travel signal, phase precession should still occur. However, if phase precession is primarily driven by an updating of current position cues, then phase precession should be abolished. Recordings from the Buzsáki lab (Czurkó, Hirase, Csicsvari, & Buzsáki, 1999; Hirase, Czurkó, Csicsvari, & Buzsáki, 1999) found that under simple conditions, phase precession vanished on the running wheel; instead, individual cells fired at a set phase of theta.

PHASE PRECESSION IN THE NONSPATIAL DOMAIN

The ease with which the spatial location of the rat can be studied can lead to the impression that the rat hippocampus is uniquely processing spatial information rather than being a general-purpose memory device. However, lesion experiments in rats indicate that the hippocampus is also necessary for the memory of nonspatial (odor) sequences (Fortin, Agster, & Eichenbaum, 2002; Manns, Howard, & Eichenbaum, 2007; but see also Dudchenko, Wood, & Eichenbaum, 2000). This helps to bring together the rat literature with the human literature, where the hippocampus clearly has a role in many nonspatial aspects of episodic memory (reviewed in Cohen & Eichenbaum, 1993).

Two recent studies have demonstrated phase precession in the rat in the nonspatial domain. In the first of these studies (Lenck-Santini, Fenton, & Muller, 2008), the rat was removed from a ledge and dropped (see also Lin et al., 2005 for a nonpredictive comparison). Within a certain time, the rat had to jump back on the ledge to avoid a shock. Theta oscillations and phase precession were observed after the rat was picked up (just before being dropped) and again in the short period just before the rat jumped to avoid the shock (Fig. 19.5). This nonspatial phase precession can be interpreted as a prediction of

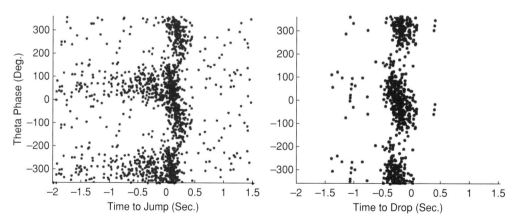

Figure 19.5 Phase precession in a nonspatial domain. (*Left*) Theta firing phase varies with time before the rat jumps to avoid a shock. (*Right*) Theta firing phase varies with time before the rat is dropped. (**From Lenck-Santini, Fenton, & Muller, 2008.**)

being dropped and a prediction of jumping. An alternative interpretation of the first finding, that the rat was predicting *where* it was going to be dropped, was rejected because the same firing occurred irrespective of where in the environment the rat was dropped.

In the second of these studies (Pastalkova, Itskov, Amarasingham, & Buzsáki 2008), a rat had to run on a running wheel for a short period during the delay period of a working memory task. When the rat was allowed to leave the running wheel, it could complete its path to a reward site that alternated between trials. During the brief period on the running wheel, phase precession occurred (compare the previous finding that no phase precession occurs if the rat is simply running indefinitely on the wheel). The phase precession in these experiments can be interpreted as using time as a cue (or equivalently, as traversing a sequence of internally generated states; Levy, 1996; Levy, Sanyal, Rodriguez, Sullivan, & Wu, 2005) and what is being predicted is a future event (i.e., being dropped, jumping, or getting off the wheel). According to this interpretation, on each successive theta cycle, the (internal) temporal cue is advanced (just as the spatial cue is advanced during running on the linear track); thus, the chaining process on each successive theta cycle leads to earlier and earlier theta phase firing of the cells representing the event.

UTILIZATION OF SEQUENCE RETRIEVAL TO GUIDE BEHAVIOR

Evidence is beginning to suggest that the predictions that occur during sweeps are actually used by the animal to guide behavior. Johnson and Redish (2007) found that the direction of the sweep was strongly correlated with the direction of the animal's motion, but was not necessarily correlated with the final decision made. Johnson and Redish also found that these sweeps occurred at decision points and during error correction when animals were performing VTE-like behaviors. These behaviors are known to be hippocampally dependent (Hu & Amsel, 1995), related to hippocampal activity as measured by c–fos (Hu, Xu, & Gonzalez-Lima, 2006), and necessary for

proper decision making (Meunzinger, 1938; Tolman, 1939). The single sweeps observed by Johnson and Redish generally occurred during a single theta cycle and had a velocity ~4–15 times faster than during the actual traversal of these paths. These sweeps are thus exactly what one would predict if the animal had to rapidly recall its experience down the two arms of the maze to make the correct decision about which way to turn.

Additional evidence for a behavioral function of sweeps is provided by the experiments of Lenck-Santini et al. (2008), who examined hippocampal activity in the moments before the rat jumped out of the chamber to avoid a predictable shock. In such internally timed tasks, there is a strong buildup of theta activity before the animal acts (O'Keefe & Nadel, 1978; Terrazas, Gothard, Kung, Barnes, & McNaughton, 1997; Vanderwolf, 1971). If this buildup of theta is disrupted, the animal often does not act. It is during this buildup that the phase precession occurs. Lenck-Santini et al. found that a well-trained rat injected with the cholinergic antagonist scopolamine sometimes failed to jump to avoid the shock. There was a strong correlation between these instances and the failure to see the buildup of theta power before the jump. Interruption of theta (and the concomitant phase precession) may have interfered with the planning of the jump.

POSSIBLE MECHANISMS OF PHASE PRECESSION

There is now substantial evidence that sweeps (and phase precession) can be viewed as a predictive process, but the underlying mechanisms are less certain. Several models have been proposed. One class of models is the dual-oscillator models (Burgess, Barry, & O'Keefe, 2007; Hasselmo, Giocomo, & Zilli, 2007; O'Keefe & Recce, 1993); we refer readers to an excellent critique of such models (Mauer & McNaughton, 2007). Here we focus on cued chaining models.

In such models (Jensen & Lisman, 1996; Maurer & McNaughton, 2007; Tsodyks et al., 1996) asymmetric weights exist between the cells representing subsequent positions along the track (e.g., the synapses of A cells onto B cells; the synapses of B cells onto C cells, etc.).

Thus, if after the asymmetric weights are formed the animal subsequently comes to A, the A cells can retrieve the B-G sequence by a simple excitatory chaining process that utilizes the asymmetric weights. This sequence will occur during a theta cycle, thereby producing a sweep. Importantly, the processes postulated are not linked to the spatial aspects of place cells and so can be generalized to all forms of memory.

The proposition that the asymmetric weights thought to underlie the phase are learned through experience makes a strong prediction: Phase precession should not occur on the first pass through a novel environment. Experimental tests of this prediction have given a somewhat mixed answer. Rosenzweig and colleagues (2000) reported that cells could show phase precession even on the first lap on a novel track, but this study did not attempt to quantify phase precession. In the most systematic study to date, Cheng and Frank (2008) report that phase precession is weak on first exposure to a novel track, but it rapidly becomes stronger with further experience. These results suggest that there are both learning-dependent and learning-independent components of the phase precession. One possibility is that the learning-independent component could be due to intrinsic single-cell biophysics (Harris et al., 2002; Kamondi, Acsady, Wang, & Buzsáki, 1998; Magee, 2001) either in hippocampus (O'Keefe & Recce, 1993) or in entorhinal cortex (Burgess et al., 2007; Hasselmo et al., 2007) and may be related to nonpredictive components (such as would occur in the dual-oscillator model; Maurer & McNaughton, 2007).

One potential resolution to the learning-independent components of phase precession is to hypothesize that there are prewired directionally dependent asymmetric weights within the system (Samsonovich & McNaughton, 1997). However, the connection matrix needed to implement a directionally dependent weight matrix in hippocampal place cells is very complicated due to the remapping properties seen therein (Maurer & McNaughton, 2007; Redish & Touretzky, 1997). Alternatively, because entorhinal cells do not remap between environments (Fyhn, Treves, Moser, & Moser, 2007; Quirk, Muller, Kubie, & Ranck, 1992), a prewired map

could exist in entorhinal cortex (Redish, 1999; Redish & Touretzky, 1997) encoded by the grid cells therein (Hafting, Fyhn, Molden, Moser, & Moser, 2005). The existence of directional information within the entorhinal cortex (Hafting, Fyhn, Bonnevie, Moser, & Moser, 2008), in conjunction with a preexisting map, could allow prediction of future locations without the animal having ever experienced the path between these locations.

A recent review emphasized a second major objection to the cued chaining models (Maurer & McNaughton, 2007): In certain environments, place fields have omnidirectional fields. In these environments, learning processes that drive synaptic learning should produce *symmetric* weights (Muller, Kubie, & Saypoff, 1991; Redish & Touretzky, 1998). Symmetric weights should lead to excitation of both A and C when an animal is at the intermediate location B, contrary to the data showing that phase precession and sweeps produce unidirectional sequences (i.e., the sequence is either ABCD or DCBA depending on which way the rat is moving). One potential resolution to this problem would be to assume that there is a small directional component that causes cells to fire in one direction but not the other. Directionally dependent inhibitory interneurons have been found in hippocampus (Leutgeb, Ragozzino, & Mizmori, 2000), which could selectively inhibit activity behind the animal. Alternatively, visual cues coming from the lateral entorhinal cortex (Hargreaves, Rao, Lee, & Knierim, 2005; Leutgeb et al., 2008), which would depend on which direction the rat is headed, may change the firing rates sufficiently to break the symmetry.

Simple retrieval or construction?

We have reviewed the evidence that the process of sequence recall can be observed in the hippocampus and that several variants can now be studied in detail. As we have argued, simple recall of sequences can be viewed as a form of prediction. To the extent that the world is governed by fixed sequences, cued sequence recall is a prediction of what will happen next. However, recall may not simply be a replay of past sequences. As noted at the beginning of this chapter, tasks that depend on hippocampal integrity tend to be those tasks that require integration of separate components, while simple sequence recall tends to be hippocampally independent. For example, the hippocampus is not involved in the generation of simple expectancies, as used in typical instrumental learning tasks (Corbit & Balleine, 2000), but it is involved in accommodating complex changes in contingencies (as in contingency degradation tasks; Corbit, Ostlund, & Balleine, 2002). This ability to deal with complexity might allow the hippocampus to combine information to produce a prediction of events that never happened. From a cognitive perspective, it seems clear that both simple recall of memories and constructive processes take place. What is much less clear is where these processes take place and the particular role of the hippocampus. Perhaps the hippocampus is best described as a simple memory device: The predictive processes that occur during cued recall act as a relatively faithfully replay of the original events, and these events are then integrated by other brain regions to construct predictions. Alternatively, the hippocampus may itself integrate information to form constructions. A recent study of patients with hippocampal damage (Hassabis, Kumaran, Vann, & Maguire, 2007) suggests that the role of the hippocampus is in the integration of separate components rather than the simple retrieval of memories. At this point, the electrophysiological evidence only provides support for retrieval. Whether the hippocampus can also construct never-experienced predictions is still an open question.

TIMESCALES

An important limitation of the predictive process described thus far is that is it deals with a rather small temporal and spatial scale. The phase precession and sweeps discussed earlier are predictions about locations less than a meter from the current position that the rat will typically come to in several seconds. Human cognitive abilities depend on the ability to predict much further in the future. Whether rats have this ability is controversial (Roberts et al., 2008).

Several mechanisms could potentially provide prediction further in the future. The experiments described in this chapter were all done in the dorsal hippocampus, but cells in the ventral entorhinal cortex and hippocampus have much larger fields (Jung, Wiener, & McNaughton, 1994; Kjelstrup et al., 2008). Sweeps in these more ventral aspects could thus proceed much further in the future than sweeps in dorsal aspects (Maurer & McNaughton, 2007). Another possibility relates to the temporal scale of the hippocampal inputs through chunking (Miller, 1956; Newell, 1990) or the action of a working memory buffer (Jensen & Lisman, 2005). It is possible that the information in each successive gamma cycle (Fig. 19.1) could represent events separated by large times. A final possibility is simply that the information at the end of a sweep could be looped back to provide the cue for another sweep, thereby extending the range of temporal associations.

CONCLUSION

The ability to electrophysiologically monitor ensembles in the hippocampus provides a way of addressing many of the issues raised in this review. It should now be possible to study the timescales of prediction, analyze the mechanisms involved, and determine the degree to which the process can be viewed as simple retrieval as opposed to construction. These questions will not only be important in their own right but also provide a starting point for understanding how other brain regions interact with the hippocampus, for example, by providing cues that stimulate hippocampal prediction or by utilizing the hippocampal output to guide behavior.

ACKNOWLEDGMENTS

We thank Adam Johnson, Ed Richard, and Matthijs van der Meer for helpful comments on an early version of the chapter. ADR was supported by MH080318. JL was supported by R01 NS027337 and P50 MH060450.

REFERENCES

Battaglia, F. P., Sutherland, G. R., & McNaughton, B. L. (2004). Local sensory cues and place cell directionality: Additional evidence of prospective coding in the hippocampus. *Journal of Neuroscience, 24*, 4541–4550.

Blum, K. I., & Abbott, L. F. (1996). A model of spatial map formation in the hippocampus of the rat. *Neural Computation, 8*, 85–93.

Bragin, A., Jando, G., Nadasdy, Z., Hetke, J., Wise, K., & Buzsáki, G. (1995). Gamma (40–100 Hz) oscillation in the hippocampus of the behaving rat. *Journal of Neuroscience, 15*, 47–60.

Brown, E. N., Frank, L. M., Tang, D., Quirk, M. C., & Wilson, M. A. (1998). A statistical paradigm for neural spike train decoding applied to position prediction from ensemble firing patterns of rat hippocampal place cells. *Journal of Neuroscience, 18*, 7411–7425.

Burgess, N., Barry, C., & O'Keefe, J. (2007). An oscillatory interference model of grid cell firing. *Hippocampus, 17*, 801–812.

Buzsáki, G. (2004). Large-scale recording of neuronal ensembles. *Nature Neuroscience, 7*, 446–451.

Buzsáki, G. (2006). *Rhythms of the brain*. New York: Oxford University Press.

Cheng, S., & Frank, L. M. (2008). New experiences enhance coordinated neural activity in the hippocampus. *Neuron, 57*, 303–313.

Cohen, N. J., & Eichenbaum, H. (1993). *Memory, amnesia, and the hippocampal system*. Cambridge, MA: MIT Press.

Corbit, L. H., & Balleine, B. W. (2000). The role of the hippocampus in instrumental conditioning. *Journal of Neuroscience, 20*, 4233–4239.

Corbit, L. H., Ostlund, S. B., & Balleine, B. W. (2002). Sensitivity to instrumental contingency degradation is mediated by the entorhinal cortex and its efferents via the dorsal hippocampus. *Journal of Neuroscience, 22*, 10976–10984.

Czurkó, A., Hirase, H., Csicsvari, J., & Buzsáki, G. (1999). Sustained activation of hippocampal pyramidal cells by "space clamping" in a running wheel. *European Journal of Neuroscience, 11*, 344–352.

Dragoi, G., & Buzsáki, G. (2006). Temporal encoding of place sequences by hippocampal cell assemblies. *Neuron, 50*, 145–157.

Dudchenko, P. A., Wood, E. R., & Eichenbaum, H. (2000). Neurotoxic hippocampal lesions have no effect on odor span and little effect on odor recognition memory but produce significant impairments on spatial span, recognition, and alternation. *Journal of Neuroscience, 20*, 2964–2977.

Dusek, J. A., & Eichenbaum, H. (1998). The hippocampus and transverse patterning guided by olfactory cues. *Behavioral Neuroscience, 112*, 762–771.

Ekstrom, A. D., Meltzer, J., McNaughton, B. L., & Barnes, C. A. (2001). NMDA receptor antagonism blocks experience-dependent expansion of hippocampal "place fields." *Neuron, 31*, 631–638.

Fortin, N. J., Agster, K. L., & Eichenbaum, H. B. (2002). Critical role of the hippocampus in memory for sequences of events. *Nature Neuroscience, 5*, 458–462.

Fyhn, M., Treves, A., Moser, M-B., & Moser, E. I. (2007). Hippocampal remapping and grid realignment in entorhinal cortex. *Nature, 446*, 190–194.

Geisler, C., Robbe, D., Zugaro, M., Sirota, A., & Buzsáki, G. (2007). Hippocampal place cell assemblies are speed-controlled oscillators. *Proceedings of the National Academy of Sciences USA, 104*, 8149–8154.

Gray, J., & McNaughton, N. (2000). *The neuropsychology of anxiety*. Oxford, UK: Oxford University Press.

Hafting, T., Fyhn, M., Bonnevie, T., Moser, M-B., & Moser, E. I. (2008). Hippocampus-independent phase precession in entorhinal grid cells. *Nature, 453*, 1248–1252.

Hafting, T., Fyhn, M., Molden, S., Moser, M-B., & Moser, E. (2005). Microstructure of a spatial map in the entorhinal cortex. *Nature, 436*, 801–806.

Hargreaves, E. L., Rao, G., Lee, I., & Knierim, J. J. (2005). Major dissociation between medial and lateral entorhinal input to dorsal hippocampus. *Science, 308*, 1792–1794.

Harris, K. D., Henze, D. A., Hirase, H., Leinekugel, X., Dragol, G., Czurko, A., & Buzsáki, G. (2002). Spike train dynamics predicts theta-related phase precession in hippocampal pyramidal cells. *Nature, 417*, 738–741.

Hassabis, D., Kumaran, D., Vann, S. D., & Maguire, E. A. (2007). Patients with hippocampal amnesia cannot imagine new experiences. *Proceedings of the National Academy of Sciences USA, 104*, 1726–1731.

Hasselmo, M. E., Giocomo, L. M., & Zilli, E. A. (2007). Grid cell firing may arise from interference of theta frequency membrane potential oscillations in single neurons. *Hippocampus, 17*, 1252–1271.

Hirase, H., Czurkó, A., Csicsvari, J., & Buzsáki, G. (1999). Firing rate and theta-phase coding by hippocampal pyramidal neurons during 'space clamping.' *European Journal of Neuroscience, 11*, 4373–4380.

Hu, D., & Amsel, A. (1995). A simple test of the vicarious trial-and-error hypothesis of hippocampal function. *Proceedings of the National Academy of Sciences USA, 92*, 5506–5509.

Hu, D., Xu, X., & Gonzalez-Lima, F. (2006). Vicarious trial-and-error behavior and hippocampal cytochrome oxidase activity during Y-maze discrimination learning in the rat. *International Journal of Neuroscience, 116*, 265–280.

Huxter, J. R., Senior, T. J., Allen, K., & Csicsvari, J. (2008). Theta phase-specific codes for two-dimensional position, trajectory and heading in the hippocampus. *Nature Neuroscience, 11*, 587–594.

Jackson, J. C., Johnson, A., & Redish, A. D. (2006). Hippocampal sharp waves and reactivation during awake states depend on repeated sequential experience. *Journal of Neuroscience, 26*, 12415–12426.

Jensen, O., & Lisman, J. E. (1996). Hippocampal CA3 region predicts memory sequences: Accounting for the phase precession of place cells. *Learning and Memory, 3*, 279–287.

Jensen, O., & Lisman, J. E. (2000). Position reconstruction from an ensemble of hippocampal place cells: contribution of theta phase encoding. *Journal of Neurophysiology, 83*, 2602–2609.

Jensen, O., & Lisman, J. E. (2005). Hippocampal sequence-encoding driven by a cortical multi-item working memory buffer. *Trends in Neurosciences, 28*, 67–72.

Johnson, A., Fenton, A. A., Kentros, C., & Redish, A. D. (2009). Looking for cognition in the structure in the noise. *Trends in Cognitive Sciences, 13*, 55–64.

Johnson, A., Jackson, J., & Redish, A. D. (2008). Measuring distributed properties of neural representations beyond the decoding of local variables—implications for cognition. In C. Hölscher & M. H. J. Munk (Eds.), *Mechanisms of information processing in the brain: Encoding of information in neural populations and networks* (pp. 95–119). Cambridge, England: Cambridge University Press.

Johnson, A., & Redish, A. D. (2007). Neural ensembles in CA3 transiently encode paths forward of the animal at a decision point. *Journal of Neuroscience, 27*, 12176–12189.

Jung, M. W., Wiener, S. I., & McNaughton, B. L. (1994). Comparison of spatial firing characteristics of the dorsal and ventral hippocampus of the rat. *Journal of Neuroscience, 14*, 7347–7356.

Kamondi, A., Acsády, L., Wang, X.-J., & Buzsáki, G. (1998). Theta oscillations in somata and dendrites of hippocampal pyramidal cells in vivo: Activity-dependent phase-precession of action potentials. *Hippocampus, 8*, 244–261.

Kjelstrup, K. B., Solstad, T., Brun, V. H., Hafting, T., Leutgeb, S., Witter, M. P., Moser, E. I., & Moser, M-B. (2008). Finite scale of spatial representation in the hippocampus. *Science, 321*, 140–143.

Lenck-Santini, P-P., Fenton, A. A., & Muller, R. U. (2008). Discharge properties of hippocampal neurons during performance of a jump avoidance task. *Journal of Neuroscience, 28*, 6773–6786.

Leutgeb, J. K., Henriksen, E. J., Leutgeb, S., Witter, M. P., Moser, M.-B., & Moser, E. I. (2008). Hippocampal rate coding depends on input from the lateral entorhinal cortex. *Society for Neuroscience Abstracts.315*, 961–966.

Leutgeb, S., Ragozzino, K. E., & Mizmori, S. J. (2000). Convergence of head direction and place information in the CA1 region of hippocampus. *Neuroscience, 100*, 11–19.

Levy, W. B. (1996). A sequence predicting CA3 is a flexible associator that learns and uses context to solve hippocampal-like tasks. *Hippocampus, 6*, 579–591.

Levy, W. B., Sanyal, A., Rodriguez, P., Sullivan, D. W., & Wu, X. B. (2005). The formation of neural codes in the hippocampus: Trace conditioning as a prototypical paradigm for studying the random recoding hypothesis. *Biological Cybernetics, 92*, 409–426.

Lin, L., Osan, R., Shoham, S., Jin, W., Zuo, W., & Tsien, J. Z. (2005). Identification of network-level coding units for real-time representation of episodic experiences in the hippocampus. *Proceedings of the National Academy of Sciences USA, 102*, 6125–6130.

Lisman, J. (2005). The theta/gamma discrete phase code occurring during the hippocampal phase precession may be a more general brain coding scheme. *Hippocampus, 15*, 913–922.

Lisman, J., & Idiart, M. A. (1995). Storage of 7 +/-2 short-term memories in oscillatory sub-cycles. *Science, 267*, 1512–1515.

Magee, J. C. (2001). Dendritic mechanisms of phase precession in hippocampal CA1 pyramidal neurons. *Journal of Neurophysiology, 86*, 528–532.

Manns, J. R., Howard, M. W., & Eichenbaum, H. (2007). Gradual changes in hippocampal activity support remembering the order of events. *Neuron*, *56*, 530–540.

Maurer, A. P., & McNaughton, B. L. (2007). Network and intrinsic cellular mechanisms underlying theta phase precession of hippocampal neurons. *Trends in Neurosciences*, *30*, 325–333.

Mehta, M. R., Barnes, C. A., & McNaughton, B. L. (1997). Experience-dependent, asymmetric expansion of hippocampal place fields. *Proceedings of the National Academy of Sciences USA*, *94*, 8918–8921.

Meunzinger, K. F. (1938) Vicarious trial and error at a point of choice. I. A general survey of its relation to learning efficiency. *Journal of Genetic Psychology*, *53*, 75–86.

Miller, G. (1956). The magical number seven, plus or minus two: Some limits on our capacity for processing information. *Psychological Review*, *63*, 81–97.

Muller, R. U., Kubie, J. L., & Saypoff, R. (1991). The hippocampus as a cognitive graph. *Hippocampus*, *1*, 243–246.

Newell, A. (1990). *Unified theories of cognition*. Cambridge, MA: Harvard University Press.

O'Keefe, J., & Nadel, L. (1978). *The hippocampus as a cognitive map*. Oxford, England: Clarendon Press.

O'Keefe, J., & Recce, M. (1993). Phase relationship between hippocampal place units and the EEG theta rhythm. *Hippocampus*, *3*, 317–330.

Pastalkova, E., Itskov, V., Amarasingham, A., & Buzsáki, G. (2008). Internally generated cell assembly sequences in the rat hippocampus. *Science*, *321*, 1322–1327.

Quirk, G. J., Muller, R. U., Kubie, J. L., & Ranck, J. B., Jr. (1992). The positional firing properties of medial entorhinal neurons: Description and comparison with hippocampal place cells. *Journal of Neuroscience*, *12*, 1945–1963.

Redish, A. D. (1999). *Beyond the cognitive map: From place cells to episodic memory*. Cambridge, MA: MIT Press.

Redish, A. D., & Touretzky, D. S. (1997). Cognitive maps beyond the hippocampus. *Hippocampus*, *7*, 15–35.

Redish, A. D., & Touretzky, D. S. (1998). The role of the hippocampus in solving the Morris water maze. *Neural Computation*, *10*, 73–111.

Roberts, W. A., Feeney, M. C., Macpherson, K., Petter, M., McMillan, N., & Musolino, E. (2008). Episodic-like memory in rats: Is it based on when or how long ago? *Science*, *320*, 113–115.

Rosenzweig, E. S., Ekstrom, A. D., Redish, A. D., McNaughton, B. L., & Barnes, C. A. (2000). Phase precession as an experience-independent process: Hippocampal pyramidal cell phase precession in a novel environment and under NMDA-receptor blockade. *Society for Neuroscience Abstracts*, *26*, 982.

Samsonovich, A. V., & McNaughton, B. L. (1997). Path integration and cognitive mapping in a continuous attractor neural network model. *Journal of Neuroscience*, *17*, 5900–5920.

Senior, T. J., Huxter, J. R., Allen, K., O'Neill, J., & Csicsvari, J. (2008). Gamma oscillatory firing reveals distinct populations of pyramidal cells in the CA1 region of the hippocampus. *Journal of Neuroscience*, *28*, 2274–2286.

Shen, J., Barnes, C. A., McNaughton, B. L., Skaggs, W. E., & Weaver, K. L. (1997). The effect of aging on experience-dependent plasticity of hippocampal place cells. *Journal of Neuroscience*, *17*, 6769–6782.

Skaggs, W. E., McNaughton, B. L., Wilson, M. A., & Barnes, C. A. (1996). Theta phase precession in hippocampal neuronal populations and the compression of temporal sequences. *Hippocampus*, *6*, 149–173.

Terrazas, A., Gothard, K. M., Kung, K. C., Barnes, C. A., & McNaughton, B. L. (1997). All aboard! What train-driving rats can tell us about the neural mechanisms of spatial navigation. *Society for Neuroscience Abstracts*, *23*, 506.

Tolman, E. C. (1939). Prediction of vicarious trial and error by means of the schematic sow-bug. *Psychological Review*, *46*, 318–336.

Tsodyks, M. V., Skaggs, W. E., Sejnowski, T. J., & McNaughton, B. L. (1996). Population dynamics and theta rhythm phase precession of hippocampal place cell firing: A spiking neuron model. *Hippocampus*, *6*, 271–280.

Vanderwolf, C. H. (1971). Limbic-diencephalic mechanisms of voluntary movement. *Psychological Review*, *78*, 83–113.

Wilson, M. A., & McNaughton, B. L. (1993). Dynamics of the hippocampal ensemble code for space. *Science*, *261*, 1055–1058.

Zhang, K., Ginzburg, I., McNaughton, B. L., & Sejnowski, T. J. (1998). Interpreting neuronal population activity by reconstruction: Unified framework with application to hippocampal place cells. *Journal of Neurophysiology*, *79*, 1017–1044.

CHAPTER 20
The Neurobiology of Memory-Based Predictions

Howard Eichenbaum and Norbert J. Fortin

There are two general areas of considerable research activity aimed at understanding how we consciously make predictions about future events, one of which seeks to identify the brain structures that underlie imagining the future in humans and the other on the evolution of predicting future events through studies on animals.

In the research on humans, several clinical case studies have noted that patients with severe amnesia due to brain damage are impaired not only in remembering past experiences but also in describing personal future events (Talland, 1965; Tulving, 1985). Consistent with these findings, Yadin and Carruthers (2005) reminded us that the ancient philosophers viewed memory for the past and imagining the future as intimately linked. Considerable recent interest in the link between remembering the past and imagining the future was stimulated by a report that amnesic patients with primary damage to the hippocampus cannot imagine new experiences, and they are particularly deficient in generating a spatial context into which elements of a possible future experience can be bound (Hassabis, Kumaran, Vann, & Maguire, 2007). Complementary evidence from functional imaging studies showed that a largely overlapping brain network, including the hippocampus, is involved in remembering personal past experiences and in imagining future events (Addis, Wong, & Schacter, 2007).

Why are the same brain areas that support laying down memories the same ones used in conceiving the future? The answer, many think, can be found in Bartlett's (1932) early studies on remembering. In contrast to some more modern views of memory as an accurate and detailed record of past events, Bartlett introduced us to the reconstructive nature of recollection, by which we piece together memories of past events from a patchwork of salient details of specific experiences remembered within a framework of our knowledge about how the world works. This characterization of memory for past experiences also bears great similarity with how one might characterize the imagining of future events. Precisely along these lines, Schacter and Addis (2007) proposed the *constructive episodic simulation* hypothesis that explains "memory for the future" in terms of a system that flexibly recombines details from past events (episodic memories) within a plausible scenario (semantic knowledge). They suggested that the hippocampus might play a specific role in recombining stored information into future event simulations, based on evidence that this structure performs a similar sort of relational processing for information contained in past events (Eichenbaum & Cohen, 2001). Building on this framework, Bar (2007) proposed that much of the brain's default activity involves using analogies and associations to make predictions that presensitize brain representations involved in perception and thinking.

The other area of research that has focused on imagining the future concerns whether animals have the capacities to recall the past and predict the future, with implications for how this capacity evolved in humans. Some of the most creative work on this question has explored the capacities of scrub jays to remember particular foods that were cached at a particular time and place, capturing Tulving's (1983) characterization of episodic memory as containing a combination of "what," "where," and "when" prior experiences occurred (Clayton & Dickinson, 1998). This line of research has also recognized a close connection between remembering the past and imagining the future (Clayton, Bussey, & Dickinson, 2003; Suddendorf, 2006). Thus, more recent studies have extended the capacity of scrub jays to cache food in ways that reflect future planning (Raby, Alexis, Dickinson, & Clayton, 2007). Whether these abilities truly contain conscious awareness of past or future experiences has been challenged (Suddendorf & Busby, 2003; Suddendorf & Corballis, 2007). Nevertheless, there are now several examples of situations where different species can remember what happened when and where, and behave intuitively as if thinking ahead even beyond their immediate needs (e.g., Correia, Dickinson, & Clayton, 2007; De Kort, Dickinson, & Clayton, 2005; Mulcahy & Call, 2006; Zentall, 2005).

Regardless of whether the evidence justifies the conclusion that animals recall the past and imagine the future remains an area of controversy. This work has generated considerable effort toward the development of objective criteria for these capacities, rather than limiting the definitions of these abilities to subjective aspects of mental experience that can only be expressed verbally. In particular, Clayton and her colleagues highlighted three specific features of episodic recall and future planning that are shared by animals: *(1)* that the contents of the memory contain what, when, and where information, *(2)* that the what-where-when information is closely integrated into a single representation for which remembering one kind of information automatically retrieves the other features, and *(3)* that recovered information can be deployed flexibly to behave adaptively across many situations, including predictions about future events (Clayton et al., 2003).

Here we will consider how our recent work offers an opportunity to bridge the research in humans and animals. Both lines of study have highlighted a strong connection between remembering the past and imagining the future. The studies on humans have discovered that the hippocampal system is central to both remembering the past and imagining the future and have suggested that the relational processing supported by this system may play the same role in both kinds of cognition. The studies on animals have suggested that what-when-where memories are integrated representations and that these memories can be deployed creatively to solve new problems. Our own research program has been aimed to understand the neural circuitry that supports recalling past experiences (Eichenbaum, 2000, 2004; Eichenbaum, Dudchencko, Wood, Shapiro, & Tanila, 1999; Eichenbaum, Yonelinas, & Ranganath, 2007; Fortin, 2008). However, when viewed in light of these recent findings, our work can also help answer the following questions: *(1)* Do animals have the capacities for recollection and prediction? and *(2)* What are the fundamental information-processing functions of the hippocampus that support both remembering the past and imagining the future? In the text that follows we will first consider these questions with regard to recalling the past, then address predicting the future.

DO ANIMALS HAVE THE CAPACITY TO RECALL THE PAST, AND IS THIS CAPACITY SUPPORTED BY THE HIPPOCAMPUS?

The distinctive nature of episodic recall, or recollection, is perhaps best illustrated by William James' (1890) prescient characterization of recollection (what he called "memory"): "What memory goes with is… a very complex representation, that of the fact to be recalled plus its associates… known in one integral pulse of consciousness… and demanding probably a vastly more intricate brain-process than that on which any simple sensorial image depends." Thus, James' (1890) early writings remarkably captured both the contents of our present-day view of recollection (fact plus associates) and its retrieval dynamics (integral pulse of consciousness), and contrasted recollection with something like familiarity (a "sensorial image"). Though initially rooted in introspection, the study of recollection has also been approached experimentally in recent years, by directly comparing the contributions of recollection and of familiarity to recognition memory (Yonelinas, 2002). In a recognition memory task, subjects can recognize a recently presented stimulus in two ways: They can recollect the specific experience (e.g., "I remember seeing the word 'cat' because it made me think of my childhood cat"), or they may simply have a sense that the particular item is familiar (e.g., "I don't distinctly remember seeing 'cat,' but I'm confident it was on the list"). The two processes are fundamentally distinct in terms of their retrieval dynamics. Recollection involves the ability to recall a specific experience along with its spatial and temporal context and is best characterized by a threshold process, whereas familiarity is based on the strength of a perceptual match of the current memory cue to previously experienced stimuli and is viewed as an incremental process (i.e., there are degrees of familiarity).

In studies on humans, the use of receiver operating characteristic (ROC) analyses of recognition memory performance is one of the most compelling methods to explore the differences in retrieval dynamics between recollection and familiarity. In a typical experiment, subjects initially study a list of words, then distinguish re-presentations of those words as "old" from additional words as "new." The resulting ROC analysis plots "hits," correct identifications of old items, against "false alarms," incorrect identifications of new items as old, across a range of response bias levels typically measured by confidence ratings. The resulting ROC curve typically involves an asymmetric function characterized by an above-zero threshold of recognition at the most conservative criterion (zero false alarm rate) and thereafter a curvilinear performance function (Yonelinas 2001; see Fig. 20.1a). The positive Y-intercept is viewed as an index of recollection, whereas the degree of curvature reflects familiarity as typical of a signal-detection process (Fig. 20.1b,c; Parks & Yonelinas, 2007, but see Wixted, 2007). A body of experiments indicates

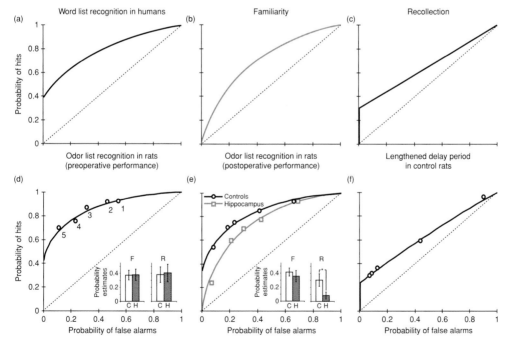

Figure 20.1 ROCs for recognition performance in humans and rats. (*a–c*) Performance of humans in verbal recognition (adapted from Yonelinas, 2001). (*d–f*) Performance of rats in odor recognition (Fortin et al., 2004). (*d*) Normal rats tested with a 30-min delay. Insets: recollection (R) and familiarity (F) estimates. (*e*) Postoperative performance with a 30-min delay. (*f*) Control rats tested with a 75-min memory delay. Diagonal dotted lines represent chance performance across criterion levels. C, control group; H, hippocampal group. Error bars indicate SEM; *, *p* < .05.

that the human hippocampus is differentially involved in recollection and not familiarity (Eichenbaum et al., 2007; but see Squire, Wixted, & Clark, 2007).

Are animals also capable of recollection? Given the controversy about whether animals have these capacities (Suddendorf & Busby, 2003; Suddendorf & Corballis, 2007), it behooves us to provide evidence for the validity of such studies on animals. To answer this question, we adapted the ROC approach used in humans and examined the retrieval dynamics of recognition memory in rats. We used a recognition task that exploits rats' superb memory capacities with odors, and we varied their response biases by manipulation of reward payoffs and response effort (Fortin, Wright, & Eichenbaum, 2004). Similar to the findings on humans, we found that the ROC curve of intact rats was asymmetric (Fig. 20.1d), containing both a recollection component (above-zero Y-intercept) and a strong familiarity (curvilinear) component. Furthermore, following selective hippocampal damage, the recollection component of the ROC function was lost, sparing the familiarity component, that is, the ROC function became fully symmetrical and curvilinear (Fig. 20.1e). Importantly, simply reducing the strength of memory by extending the retention period resulted in a different pattern characterized primarily by loss of the familiarity signal, indicating that hippocampal damage does not just reduce the strength of memories (Fig. 20.1f). These findings indicate that, according to measures of retrieval dynamics defined in studies on humans, rats have the capacity for recollection and normally employ both recollection and familiarity to make recognition judgments. Also, as in humans, the rat hippocampus plays a critical and selective role in this ability to recall the past.

DO ANIMALS USE INTEGRATED WHAT-WHEN-WHERE REPRESENTATIONS TO REMEMBER UNIQUE EVENTS, AND ARE THESE REPRESENTATIONS SUPPORTED BY THE HIPPOCAMPUS?

The previous experiment investigated recollection in terms of its distinct retrieval dynamics, but it did not explore the *content* of what is recalled as an animal remembers past experiences. In an attempt to shed light on whether rats integrate what-when-where information, suggested as defining criteria for recollection by Clayton et al. (2003) and James (1890), we trained rats on a task that required them to remember when and where each of a list of odors (what) had recently been experienced (Ergorul & Eichenbaum, 2004). Rats began each trial by serially sampling each of four odors located along different walls of a square arena (Fig. 20.2a). Then "what-when-where" memory was subsequently tested in a choice between two of the stimuli, randomly selected from the four presented items, in which the animal was rewarded for selecting the earlier presented item. Because each trial involved a novel sequence of odors and locations, and because the animals did not know in advance which two odors would be tested on any particular trial, they had to remember each odor and when and where it was experienced on that unique trial. Normal rats performed well on selecting which odor had appeared in a particular location at a particular time (Fig. 20.2b). Additional measures indicated that performance was not based simply on memory for location, such that animals were less accurate in their initial approach to a stimulus before they could smell the odor than the final choice following sampling of the odor at that location. Also, on probe trials when the odor was left out of the stimulus, choice performance fell to chance, indicating rats relied on the appropriate odor to make the final choice. These observations indicate that rats normally use integrated representations of which odor was presented in each place to make the judgment about when the stimuli were sampled. Furthermore, selective damage to the hippocampus reduced choice performance to chance, and rats with hippocampal damage tended to initially approach the wrong stimulus location (Fig. 20.2c). These findings indicate that normal rats use an integrated representation of what happened where and when. Furthermore, "what-where-when" memory depends on the hippocampus and, in the absence of a hippocampal representation, rats are influenced by other brain systems to repeat the most recently rewarded spatial response.

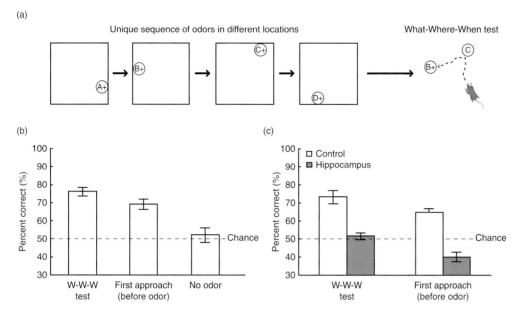

Figure 20.2 What-where-when memory in rats. (*a*) In the sample phase of every trial, rats were presented with four odors in a series (A+ → B+ → C+ → D+), each at a different location on a platform.
Subsequently, what-where-when memory was tested by presenting a choice between two cups from the
list (e.g., B vs. C), and animals were rewarded for selecting the earlier presented item. The experimenter
took note of which cup was approached first (e.g., C), and of which cup the animal selected (e.g., B). +,
reinforced stimulus. (*b*) Presurgical performance of normal rats (mean ± SEM) in what-where-when
tests, first cup approached, and in no-odor probe tests. (*c*) Postsurgical performance of control and hippocampal lesion groups. Dashed line, chance level.

What is the nature of the neural representation in the hippocampus that supports integrated
"what-when-where" memory? To address the
"what" and "where" components of recognition
memory, we recorded the activity patterns of hippocampal principal neurons in rats performing
an odor recognition task in which the stimuli
were presented in any of several locations (Fig.
20.3a; Wood, Dudchencko, & Eichenbaum, 1999).
We observed that during the period when the rats
sampled the odors, some hippocampal cells fired
differentially in association with specific odors
("what"), and other cells were activated when the
rat sampled any odor at a particular location
("where"; Fig. 20.3b). In addition, yet other cells
fired in association with whether the odor
matched or differed from that of the previous
trial, regardless of odor identity or location, indicating additional representation of the recognition status of each odor. Finally, the largest subset

of hippocampal neurons reflected the integration
of these event features by firing differentially in
association with a particular combination of the
odor, the location where it was sampled, and
whether the odor was recognized as the same.
These findings indicate that hippocampal neurons, both individually and as a population, represent the critical memory stimulus along with its
location and its meaningful context. In an additional recent study we also found that, when rats
encode a sequence of odors, hippocampal neurons carry information not only about the odors
and where they were sampled but also a gradually
changing ensemble code that represents the temporal context of each odor sampling event that
predicts subsequent memory accuracy (Manns,
Howard, & Eichenbaum, 2007; see also Fortin,
Agster, & Eichenbaum, 2002). The combined
findings from our recording studies complement
the data from the experiments that examined the

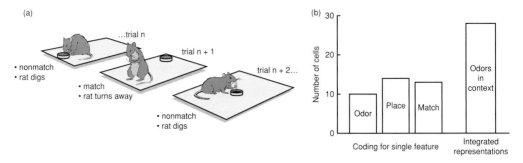

Figure 20.3 Hippocampal coding for *what* and *where* events occurred in an odor recognition task. (*a*) Trial *n* represents a non-match trial where the odor differs from that presented on the previous trial, and the rat digs to find a buried reward. On the next trial (*n+1*), the same scent is repeated, though in a different location. Since rats learned that no reward is available in such match trials, the animal refrains from digging in the cup and turns away. On the subsequent trial (*n + 2*), the odor again differs from the previous trial, and the animal digs for a buried reward. Note that the position of the cup is independent of the match/nonmatch contingency. (*b*) The proportion of individual cells that coded for a single feature (a specific odor, place, or match/nonmatch status) or for an integrated representation of these features (e.g., firing to odor A only when it was presented in the northwest corner).

effects of hippocampal damage, and they show that neuronal ensembles within the hippocampus encode integrated "what-when-where" representations of unique experiences.

CAN RATS PREDICT THE FUTURE, AND DOES THIS ABILITY INVOLVE THE HIPPOCAMPUS?

The aforementioned considerations have focused on whether animals have the capacity for recollection and on the contribution of the hippocampus to this ability. Our observations indicate that animals do have the ability for recollecting past experiences, as tested by objective measures of retrieval dynamics and memory content. Also, our observations indicate that the hippocampus plays a critical role in recollective memory and that it does so through representations of items (what) in their spatial (where) and temporal (when) context. Does the same hippocampal memory processing that underlies recollection also support predicting the future? Our position in addressing this question begins with the premise that imagining the future depends on much of the same neural machinery that is needed to remember the past, and it involves what Schacter

and Addis (2007) called *constructive episodic simulation*. According to this view, the hippocampus participates in creating a "memory for the future" by assisting in the adaptive and flexible recombination of information from past events within a plausible scenario. We extend this notion here, proposing that constructive episodic simulation requires the participation of the hippocampus in the initial learning of multiple episodic and semantic memories that overlap in information content, and the consequent ability to integrate them into a network that links memories by their common elements and thereby represents relations among memories. When called upon to imagine the future, hippocampal processing constitutes a "surfing" of the network, recovering past events and episodes that can be applied in a variety of ways. In particular, such a relational memory network can support the capacity to make inferences that predict relationships among items that have never been experienced together. By this view, relational processing by the hippocampus provides a mechanism by which information from our vast array of episodic and semantic memories can be accessed flexibly to reconstruct a past experience and to imagine the outcomes of events that have not yet occurred. Importantly, the capacity for predicting events that have never occurred is viewed as qualitatively different from predictions about events that have also previously occurred, for example, predicting that a reward will be given for repeating a behavioral response that has previously resulted in reward.

We have explored the acquisition of multiple overlapping memories and their integration into relational networks that support flexible, inferential, predictive judgments on novel problems. One study examined the ability of rats to learn a set of arbitrary associations between pairs of odors, wherein sets of pairs shared a common element (Bunsey & Eichenbaum, 1996; Fig. 20.4a). In this study animals were trained on two sets of overlapping odor-paired associates (A-B and B-C, or X-Y and Y-Z). On each trial, they were presented with the first element of one paired associate (A or X) then presented with a choice between the second elements of both paired associates (B vs. Y); a reward was given for selecting the correctly assigned associate (B given A, or Y given X). Thus, subjects were required to learn the associations A-B and X-Y. Subsequently, subjects were trained on the second set of pairs wherein the former second element became the first element of the new pairings (B-C, or Y-Z). Following success in learning all four associations, we tested whether the representations of the overlapping paired associations had been interleaved into relational memory networks (A-B-C and X-Y-Z). If the relational network exists, and if the animal has the ability to employ these networks to make novel predictions, then they should be able to make the associative inferences A-C and X-Z. Note that rats should be able to make these judgments as predictions, that is, guesses about associations on which they had never been trained. To test this capacity, we presented rats with one of the first elements from the initial pairs (A or X) and then tested them with the second elements from the second pairs (C vs. Z). On these probe trials no rewards were given, and we measured their preference for the inferential choice. Normal rats learned the paired associates and showed strong transitivity in the form of the ability to make the correct predictions in the probe tests (Fig. 20.4b).

Rats with selective hippocampal lesions also learned the odor pairs over several trials but were severely impaired in the probes, showing no evidence of transitivity and prediction.

In another experiment, we extended the number of associations that rats had to integrate into a relational memory network that had an organized structure (Dusek & Eichenbaum, 1997; Fig. 20.5a). To accomplish this, rats learned a hierarchical series of overlapping odor choice judgments (A > B, B > C, C > D, D > E; where ">" means "should be chosen over"), then were probed on the relationship between indirectly related items (e.g., B > D). Thus, in this problem, rats had to learn a series of distinct but overlapping pairings, for example, choose A over B, choose B over C, and so on, then integrate them by their common elements to form a hierarchical relational memory network (A > B > C > D > E). The critical test involved probing whether rats could predict the relationship between two elements that had never been experienced together. Because any probe that involved an end anchoring item (A or E) could be judged based on consistent experience with that item (A was always rewarded, E was never rewarded), the only pure predictive probe was B versus D, wherein these stimuli had never appeared together during training and had been equally associated with reward. Normal rats learned the series and showed robust transitive inference in the ability to predict the correct item on the B > D probe test (Fig. 20.5b). Rats with hippocampal damage also learned each of the initial premises but failed to show transitivity. The combined findings from these studies show that rats with hippocampal damage can learn even complex associations, such as those embodied in the odor paired-associates and conditional discriminations. But, without a hippocampus, they do not interleave the distinct experiences according to their overlapping elements to form a relational network that supports flexible and inferential memory expression to make the correct prediction. Studies on humans have similarly indicated a selective role for the hippocampus in supporting inferences from memory (Heckers, Zalezak, Weiss, Ditman, & Titone, 2004; Preston, Shrager, Dudukovic, & Gabrieli, 2004).

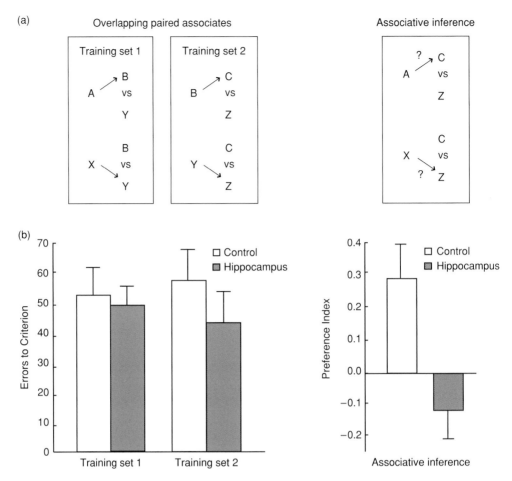

Figure 20.4 Associative inference in rats. (*a*) Rats initially learned two sets of overlapping paired associates (A-B, X-Y, B-C, X-Y, and Y-Z). Subsequently, rats were probed with novel pairings (A vs. C, A vs. Z, or X vs. C, X vs. Z), which can only be solved by associative inference (A-B-C or X-Y-Z). (*b*) Both groups of animals successfully learned the two sets of overlapping paired associates. However, only control animals correctly predicted the association in the novel pairings, by showing a preference for the transitive items. These findings indicate that an intact hippocampus is necessary for interleaving the representations of the overlapping paired associates into a relation memory network, which supports associative inference.

There is also substantial complementary evidence from the analyses of firing patterns of hippocampal neurons that hippocampal neurons encode elements that are common among different experiences—these representations could provide links between distinct memories that allow the formation of relational memory networks (reviewed in Eichenbaum, 2004). For example, in the Wood et al. (1999) study on odor

recognition memory introduced earlier, some neurons fired associated with the same odor across trials where the odor was sampled at different locations and with different meanings (Fig. 20.3b). Other cells fired during a particular phase of the approach toward any stimulus cup across trials that occurred at different places. Others fired differentially as the rat sampled at a particular location, across trials with different

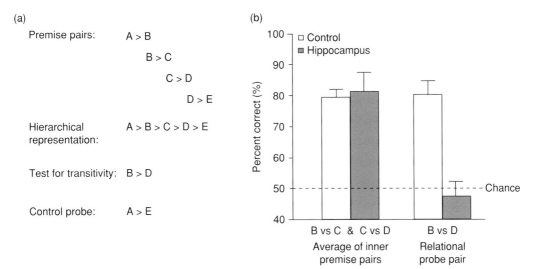

Figure 20.5 Transitive inference in rats. (*a*) Rats learned a series of overlapping premise pairs, presented as odor choice judgments (A > B, B > C, C > D, D > E; where ">" means "should be chosen over"). The series of premise pairs could be integrated by their common elements to form a hierarchical relational memory network (A>B>C>D>E). The critical tests involved probing whether rats could predict the relationship between elements that had never been experienced together: the pure predictive probe B vs. D, and the probe A vs. E, which can be solved using the reward history of the items (A was always rewarded in the premise pairs, whereas E never was). (*b*) Both groups learned the premise pairs (only average of inner premise pairs is shown), but only control rats showed robust transitive inference in the ability to predict the correct item on the relational probe pair (B vs. D).

odors and meanings. Yet other cells fired differentially associated with the recognition status of the odor, across many trials with different odors and at different locations. The observation that hippocampal cells might link experiences by the encoding of common features has also been highlighted in recent studies on monkeys and humans (Hampson, Pons, Stanford, & Deadwyler, 2004; Kreiman, Kock, & Fried, 2000). This combination of findings across species provides compelling evidence that hippocampal networks represent common elements among the distinct episodes that could serve to link memories obtained into a relational network.

HOW DOES THE HIPPOCAMPUS SUPPORT REMEMBERING THE PAST AND IMAGING THE FUTURE?

Bar (2007) has suggested that a frequent off-line (default) function of the declarative memory system is to explore future possibilities through activation and recombination of memories. The findings reviewed here are entirely consistent with this notion, and they offer evidence about the nature of hippocampal representations that can support this function. Data from other studies suggest how the relational representations of the hippocampus emerge in the circuitry of the medial temporal lobe and how the memory and predictive functions of the hippocampus are seamlessly connected (Eichenbaum et al., 2007). The medial temporal lobe is composed of the hippocampus and the immediately surrounding parahippocampal region. Anatomical studies of this region show a segregation of inputs through the parahippocampal region such that representations of distinct items (e.g., people, objects, events) and information about the context in which those items are experienced ("where" and "when") are processed in distinct areas (Burwell & Amaral, 1998; Suzuki & Amaral, 1994). What, when, and where information converge on and are associated within the hippocampus. Subsequently, when an item is presented as a memory cue, the hippocampus may complete the full pattern and mediate a recovery of the contextual representations, as well as representations of associated items in the appropriate areas of the parahippocampal region (Eichenbaum et al., 2007). According to this view, the recovery of context and item associations constitutes the experience of recollection.

Here we speculate that imagining the future is based on similar information processing. Representations of information that is common to multiple memories will likely generate the activation of representations of associated item and contextual information for multiple overlapping memories. Furthermore, this information is likely delivered to brain areas that are the recipients of medial temporal output that perform logical processing, including prefrontal areas, that can then assess the validity of relationships between information that is only indirectly related via the common associates. Consider, for example, the associative inference problem described earlier. Having been trained on A-B and B-C, when an animal is first asked whether there is a relationship between A and C, hippocampal activations will generate the common associate B and send this information to prefrontal areas. The prefrontal system, then, may evaluate these associations and deduce the indirect association between A and C. Notably, within this conception, the hippocampus itself supplies recovered memories in the service of constructing a plausible future; the hippocampus does not itself generate future scenarios but leaves this constructive processing to cortical systems (for another view, see Chapter 19).

We suggest this paradigm for cortical and hippocampal roles in information processing provides a basis for memory-based prediction that can be applied across many more complex problems in predicting the future. Although it is unlikely that animals are capable of the same elaborate mental simulation of the future as humans (Suddendorf & Busby, 2003), we argue that the same medial temporal lobe memory processing that supports this capacity in humans is also present in animals, suggesting that the fundamental features of memory-based prediction extend to animals as well.

References

Addis, D. R., Wong, A. T., & Schacter, D. L. (2007). Remembering the past and imagining the future: Common and distinct neural substrates during event construction and elaboration. *Neuropsychologia*, *45*, 1363–1377.

Babb, S. J., & Crystal, J. D. (2005). Discrimination of what, when, and where: Implications for episodic-like memory in rats. *Learning and Motivation*, *36*, 177–189.

Bar, M. (2007). The proactive brain: Using analogies and associations to generate predictions. *Trends in Cognitive Sciences*, *11*, 280–289.

Bartlett, F. C. (1932). *Remembering: A study in experimental and social psychology*. Cambridge, England: Cambridge University Press.

Bunsey, M., & Eichenbaum, H. (1996). Conservation of hippocampal memory function in rats and humans. *Nature*, *379*, 255–257.

Burwell, R. D., & Amaral, D. (1998). Cortical afferents of the perirhinal, postrhinal, and entorhinal cortices of the rat. *Journal of Comparative Neurology*, *398*, 179–205.

Clayton, N. S., Bussey, T. J., & Dickinson, A. (2003). Can animals recall the past and plan for the future? *Nature Reviews Neuroscience*, *4*, 685–691.

Clayton, N. S., & Dickinson, A. (1998). Episodic-like memory during cache recovery by scrub jays. *Nature*, *395*, 272–274.

Correia, S. P. C., Dickinson, A., & Clayton, N. S. (2007). Western scrub jays anticipate future needs independently of their current motivational state. *Current Biology*, *17*, 856–861.

De Kort, S. R., Dickinson, A., & Clayton, N. S. (2005). Retrospective cognition by food-caching western scrub jays. *Learning and Motivation*, *36*, 159–176.

Dudai, Y., & Carruthers, M. (2005). The Janus face of mnemosyne. *Nature*, *434*, 567.

Dusek, J. A., & Eichenbaum, H. (1997). The hippocampus and memory for orderly stimulus relations. *Proceedings of the National Academy of Sciences USA*, *94*, 7109–7114.

Eichenbaum, H. (2000). A cortical-hippocampal system for declarative memory. *Nature Reviews Neuroscience*, *1*, 1–50.

Eichenbaum, H. (2004). Hippocampus: Cognitive processes and neural representations that underlie declarative memory. *Neuron*, *44*, 109–120.

Eichenbaum, H., & Cohen, N. J. (2001). *From conditioning to conscious recollection: Memory systems of the brain.* Oxford, England: Oxford University Press.

Eichenbaum, H., Dudchencko, P., Wood, E., Shapiro, M., & Tanila, H. (1999). The hippocampus, memory, and place cells: Is it spatial memory or a memory space? *Neuron, 23,* 209–226.

Eichenbaum, H, Fortin, N. J., Ergorul, C., Wright, S. P., & Agster, K. L. (2005). Episodic recollection in animals: "If it walks like a duck and quacks like a duck…" *Learning and Motivation, 36,* 190–207.

Eichenbaum, H., Yonelinas A. R., & Ranganath, C. (2007). The medial temporal lobe and recognition memory. *Annual Review of Neuroscience, 20,* 123–152.

Ergorul, C., & Eichenbaum, H. (2004). The hippocampus and memory for "what," "when," and "where." *Learning and Memory, 11,* 397–405.

Fortin, N. J. (2008). Navigation and episodic-like memory in mammals. In R. Menzel (Ed.) & J. Byrne (Series Ed.), *Learning and memory: A comprehensive reference: Vol. 1. Learning theory and behavior* (pp. 385–418). Oxford, England: Elsevier.

Fortin, N. J., Agster, K. L., & Eichenbaum, H. (2002). Critical role of the hippocampus in memory for sequences of events. *Nature Neuroscience, 5,* 458–462.

Fortin, N. J., Wright, S. P., & Eichenbaum, H. (2004). Recollection-like memory retrieval in rats is dependent on the hippocampus. *Nature, 431,* 188–191.

Hampson, R. E., Pons, T. P., Stanford, T. R., & Deadwyler, S. A. (2004). Categorization in the monkey hippocampus: A possible mechanism for encoding information into memory. *Proceedings of the National Academy of Sciences USA, 101,* 3184–3189.

Hassabis, D., Kumaran, D., Vann, S. D., & Maguire, E. A. (2007). Patients with hippocampal amnesia cannot imagine new experiences. *Proceedings of the National Academy of Sciences, 104,* 1726–1731.

Heckers, S., Zalezak, M., Weiss, A. P., Ditman, T., & Titone, D. (2004). Hippocampal activation during transitive inference in humans. *Hippocampus, 14,* 153–162.

James, W. (1890). *The principles of psychology* (Vols. 1-2). New York: Holt.

Kreiman, K., Kock, C., & Fried, I. (2000). Category specific visual responses of single neurons in the human medial temporal lobe. *Nature Neuroscience, 3,* 946–953.

Manns, J. R., Howard, M., & Eichenbaum, H. (2007). Gradual changes in hippocampal activity support remembering the order of events. *Neuron, 56,* 530–540.

Mulcahy, N. J., & Call, J. (2006). Apes save tools for future use. *Science, 312,* 1038–1040.

Parks, C. M., & Yonelinas, A. P. (2007). Moving beyond pure signal-detection models: Comment on Wixted (2007). *Psychology Review, 114,* 188–202.

Preston, A., Shrager, Y., Dudukovic, N. M., & Gabrieli, J. D. E. (2004). Hippocampal contribution to the novel use of relational information in declarative memory. *Hippocampus, 14,* 148–152.

Raby, C. R., Alexis, D. M., Dickinson, A., & Clayton, N. S. (2007). Planning for the future by western scrub jays. *Nature, 445,* 919–921.

Schacter, D. L., & Addis, D. R. (2007). The cognitive neuroscience of constructive memory: Remembering the past and imagining the future. *Philosophical Transactions of the Royal Society of London B: Biological Sciences, 362,* 773–786.

Schacter, D. L., Addis, D. R., & Buckner, R. L. (2007). Remembering the past to imagine the future: The prospective brain. *Nature Reviews Neurosciences, 8,* 657–661.

Squire, L. R., Wixted, J. T., & Clark, R. E. (2007). Recognition memory and the medial temporal lobe: A new perspective. *Nature Reviews Neuroscience, 8,* 872–883.

Suddendorf, T. (2006). Foresight and evolution of the human mind. *Science, 312,* 1006–1007.

Suddendorf, T., & Busby, J. (2003). Mental time travel in animals? *Trends in Cognitive Sciences, 7,* 391–396.

Suddendorf, T., & Corballis, M. C. (2007). The evolution of foresight: What is mental time travel, and is it unique to humans? *Behavioral and Brain Sciences, 30,* 399–351.

Suzuki, W. A., & Amaral, D. G. (1994). Perirhinal and parahippocampal cortices of the macaque monkey: Cortical afferents. *Journal of Comparitive Neurology, 350,* 497–533.

Talland, G. A. (1965). *Deranged memory: A psychonomic study of the amnesic syndrome.* New York: Academic Press.

Tulving, E. (1983). *Elements of episodic memory* Oxford, England; Clarendon.

Tulving, E. (1985). Memory and consciousness. *Canadian Journal of Psychology, 26,* 1–2.

Wixted, J. T. (2007). Dual-process theory and signal-detection theory of recognition memory. *Psychology Review, 114,* 188–202.

Wood, E., Dudchenko, P. A., & Eichenbaum, H. (1999). The global record of memory in hippo-campal neuronal activity. *Nature, 397,* 613–616.

Yonelinas, A. P. (2001). Components of episodic memory: The contribution of recollection and familiarity. *Philosophical Transactions of the Royal Society of London, 356B,* 1363–1374.

Yonelinas, A. P. (2002). The nature of recollection and familiarity: A review of 30 years of research. *Journal of Memory and Language, 46,* 441–517.

Zentall, T. R. (2005). Animals may not be stuck in time. *Learning and Motivation, 36,* 208–225.

CHAPTER 21
Predicting Not to Predict Too Much: How the Cellular Machinery of Memory Anticipates the Uncertain Future

Yadin Dudai

Human language commonly associates memory with the past. But memories are made mostly for the sake of present and future. Experience-dependent modifications in the individual's behavior draw on the past to permit better adapted responses to ongoing reality as well as to the reality to come. Being able to anticipate even limited types or aspects of events is expected to endow the species with significant advantages. Under certain contextual and temporal conditions, our brain seems to be able to do just that. This requires that the plasticity machinery in the brain operate under the assumption that the future is uncertain and that information stored is likely to require quick and recurrent updating. This assumption should be reflected at multiple levels of organization of the brain, including the synaptic and cellular level.

Defining "future"

For the brain, "future" is anytime between a fraction of a second and a lifetime ahead. Except aging and ultimately the end of life, the further away the future, the less certain it is. The immediate cognitive future is practically inseparable from the present. If 20 milliseconds or so is taken to be an estimate of the duration of cognitive present, or the hypothetical "cognitive beat" (Dudai, 2002), but even simple actions take longer to complete (Baddeley, 2007; Thorpe, Fize, & Marlot, 1996;

Van Tuernnout, Hagoort, & Brown, 1998), then every ongoing behavior incorporates future tense. Ample evidence indeed indicates that the brain anticipates the world on a momentary basis (Anokhin, 1974; e.g., Naya, Yoshida, & Miyashita, 2001; Shima & Tanji, 1998). Furthermore, selectionist ("Darwinian") theories of brain function consider stimulus-driven selection of endogenously generated internal pre-representations, some of which fit better than others to respond to the future event, as instrumental in our adaptive interaction with the world (Heidmann, Heidmann, & Changeux, 1984; Young, 1979). Again, by definition, pre-representations are expected to precede the relevant "teaching" stimulus by a fraction of a second. (See also Bar, 2007 on proposed fast priming of memory representations in facilitating perception and cognition, and Fox, Snyder, Vincent, & Raichle, 2007 for an example of brain imaging data that might be construed to reflect pre-representations.)

In the present discussion, "future" means further away from the present than fractions of a second only. It makes sense to also exclude from the discussion longer time windows that are still short enough to allow attentional control. This is because for all practical purpose, in everyday life, the brain may still consider as present, or at most "present progressive," a brief ongoing potential narrative that unfolds under attentional control. Hence, the time of operation of working memory, that is, seconds to tens of seconds, is left out. Furthermore, there is evidence that neurons can still reach decisions on the state of their recently activated synapses even hours after the offset of a stimulus (Frey & Morris, 1997). Because these cellular processes could be considered as time-locked to direct consequence of the stimulus, none is considered here as involving "future" with regard to that stimulus. All together, although the brain clearly differentiates distinctive poststimulus time slices at the second, minute, and hour range (Coltheart, 1999; Frey & Morris, 1997; Fusi, Drew, & Abbot, 2005; Gilboa, Chen, & Brenner, 2005; Hare, Doherty, Camerer, Schultz, & Rangel, 2008; Hasson, Yang, Vallines, Heger, & Rubin, 2008; Smith, Ghazizadeh, & Shacmeher, 2006; Toib, Lyakhov, & Marom, 1998), this poststimulus time window is here neglected.

The "future" in the context of this discussion is considered to start when memory becomes long-term. Here the assumption is made that short-term memory could still readily adapt to ongoing events, but once the brain decides that the information is important enough to be stored in the long-term, the updating of that information becomes a particularly interesting challenge that involves balancing stability with plasticity. But when does long-term memory start? The answer to this question depends on the discipline. For neurologists, for example, long-term is memory that lasts for more than a few minutes, whereas for cellular and molecular neurobiologists who investigate behaving animals, it is memory that lasts more than a few hours, and practically, over 24 hours (Dudai, 2002). Because the following discussion draws heavily on cellular and molecular data, I have selected the molecular neurobiology view on when memory could be considered as long-term. The question posed in the title of this discussion could hence be rephrased as "How the cellular machinery of *long-term* memory anticipates the uncertain future, where the future lies at least a day head."

It should also be noted that the present discussion addresses "primitives" of memory, that is, basic mechanisms shared by different memory systems. It is likely that in addition to the current rich repertoire of taxonomies of memory systems

(Roediger, Dudai, & Fitzpatrick, 2007; Tulving, 2007; Tulving & Fergus, 2000), one could easily conceive a taxonomy based on the relative role of present or future in the alleged goal of the system. In such a taxonomy, for example, skill and habit will be more present-oriented than episodic memory, whose function is assumed to involve reconstruction of future scenarios and imagination (Addis, Wong, & Schacter, 2007; Atance & O'Neill, 2005; Dudai & Carruthers, 2005; Hassabis, Kumaran, Vann, & Maguire, 2007; Suddendorf & Corballis, 1997; Tulving, 1983). However, the claim made here is that regardless of the weight that evolution had assigned to anticipation of change in the function of the specific memory system, in most memory systems, if not in all of them, there is a built-in capacity to anticipate change.

THE LONG-TERM MEMORY ~f(GROWTH) PARADIGM

A conceptual paradigm that has dominated biological models of learning and memory for over a century now considers learning as a stimulus that triggers a local developmental shift, which involves local growth processes in the brain. Memory is the outcome of these local growth processes. Holt (1931) epitomizes this view: "Growth and learning are one continuous process, to the earlier phases of which we give the one name, and to the later… phases we give the other." He was not, of course, the first to suggest the memory~growth analogy. Attempts to translate this idea into specific biological algorithms and mechanisms preceded even the introduction of concepts like neurons and synapses into the jargon of the brain sciences: "For every act of memory," says Bain (1872), "… there is a specific grouping or coordination of sensations and movements, by virtue of specific growth in the cell junctions." Elaborate experience-dependent growth theories followed (e.g. Hebb, 1949; Kappers, 1917), paving the way to the proposal (Monne, 1949), and then to the discovery (Flexner, Flexner, & Stellar, 1963), that de novo macromolecular synthesis, so characteristic of developmental shifts and growth, is required for long-term memory. The introduction of the concept of memory consolidation (Muller & Pilzecker, 1900) seemed also to fit the idea that memories mature over time, similarly to organs and organisms.

Consolidation refers to the progressive post-acquisition stabilization of the memory trace (Dudai, 2004; McGaugh, 2000). The term is used to denote hypothetical memory stabilization processes at different levels of brain organization. Molecular neurobiologists refer to postencoding stabilization of synaptic or cell-wide information storage, which occurs over hours or days after encoding (cellular consolidation; Dudai & Morris, 2000; Dudai, 2004). Systems and cognitive neuroscientists refer to postencoding reorganization of information in distributed corticohippocampal circuits, which requires weeks, months, possibly even years to complete (systems consolidation; Dudai & Morris, 2000; Dudai, 2004).

The classic consolidation hypothesis connotes two interrelated attributes of long-term memory. One is irreversibility, the other stability (forgetting and lesions notwithstanding). The textbook account of both cellular and systems consolidation was until recently that consolidation occurs just once per item. Furthermore, it was assumed that once consolidation is over, the memory item becomes resistant to a variety of amnesic agents, such as inhibitors of protein synthesis.

USE REINSTATES FRESH PLASTICITY IN OLD MEMORIES

The textbook account of memory consolidation is, however, undergoing significant revisions in recent years. This might not come as a surprise to those who follow the cognitive literature, since the notion that memory items gain stability once consolidated does not sit well with ample evidence from human cognitive psychology, which again and again portrayed recollection as constructive, casting doubts on the stability and veracity of retrieved facts and episodes (Bartlett, 1932; Loftus & Loftus, 1980; Schacter, 1995). Unfortunately, the historical dissociation between the practitioners of cognitive psychology and brain researchers tends to hinder proper cross-fertilization and cross-migration of concepts

(Roediger et al., 2007; Wixted, 2004,). Over the years, animal studies did contribute evidence that items in long-term memory are less stable then previously assumed and that they can regain their sensitivity to amnesic agents upon reactivation in retrieval (Misanin, Miller, & Lewis, 1968; Sara, 2000). But this phenomenon, dubbed "reconsolidation," was somewhat pushed under the rug in view of the dominance of the consolidation dogma. Ultimately, the data made their impact, and in recent years the study of "reconsolidation" became a major focus of interest in both human and animal research (Alberini, 2005; Dudai, 2004; Nader, Schafe, & LeDoux, 2000 ; Nader, 2003).

The current majority view in the field of memory research—as judged by bibliometry, and definitely not without opposition—is that items in memory become transiently sensitive to a variety of amnesic agents immediately after encoding and then again immediately after retrieval. This transient susceptibility to amnesia is taken to imply that encoding and retrieval trigger in the neuronal substrate of the memory a special process and physical state. This postactivation state (Dudai, 2007) is called "consolidation" when it occurs after encoding and "reconsolidation" when it occurs after retrieval. In terms of the cellular and circuit mechanisms involved, reconsolidation is not a faithful replay of consolidation (Alberini, 2005; Bahar, Dorfman, & Dudai, 2004; Debiec & LeDoux, 2004; Dudai, 2004; Lee, Everitt, & Thomas, 2004; von Hertzen & Giese, 2005). Both processes do, however, share dependence on de-novo macromolecular synthesis. It was reported by some (Parsons, Gafford, Baruel, Riedner, & Helmestetter, 2006) but not others (Duvarci, Nader, & Ledoux, 2008) that whereas consolidation requires both protein and mRNA synthesis, reconsolidation requires protein but not mRNA synthesis. The extent to which macromolecular reorganization, whether cell-wide or synapse specific, takes place in reconsolidation vis-à-vis consolidation is hence yet to be determined. The crucial point, however, is not the identity of the detailed cellular and circuit mechanisms, but rather the finding that upon its reactivation, the long-term trace re-enters an unstable state that shares characteristics with postencoding consolidation.

An additional difference between consolidation and reconsolidation is that whereas cellular consolidation is a universal process, that is, detected in every form of learning and every species tested so far, reconsolidation seems to occur only under certain conditions (Dudai, 2004, 2006). To date, several boundary conditions have been identified that constrain reconsolidation, including the dominance of the trace (i.e., its ability to control behavior after retrieval; Eisenberg, Kobilo, Berman, & Dudai, 2003), competition with concomitant memory extinction, and, most pertinent to the context of this discussion, conditions that promote new encoding in or immediately after retrieval (Morris et al., 2006; Pedreira, Perez-Questa, & Maldonado, 2004).

If the reactivated long-term trace regains augmented plasticity, does it mean that the original trace can be completely erased? A close look at the data and discussions in the field distinguishes three versions of the reconsolidation hypothesis (Dudai, 2004). The "strong version" of the reconsolidation hypothesis posits that the regained plasticity applies to all the elements of the original memory and may indeed end up in the erasure of that memory. The "intermediate version" posits that there is a core memory which is stable and unaffected by the reconsolidation, but some stored elements of the original trace can still be modified and even erased. The weak version proposes that the original trace is actually unaffected in the process and that the plasticity refers only to new information that is added to the older memory in the context of retrieval. The latter version does not deviate from the classical consolidation hypothesis, as it simply says that new information consolidates; it is not really "reconsolidation." It is yet unclear which of the other versions fits reality better, the strong or the intermediate. Anyway, even if upon memory reactivation the core representation becomes sensitive to amnesic agents, related memory associations seem to be spared (Debiec, Doyere, Nader, & LeDoux, 2006).

It is important to appreciate that the fact that reconsolidation is usually unveiled by the use of amnesic agents does not imply that in real life, reconsolidation results in the weakening of the trace. Amnesic agents are only a tool to infer function from dysfunction (Dudai, 2002). Reconsolidation might also provide an opportunity for the strengthening of the trace (Frenkel, Maldonado, & Delorenzi, 2005; Sara, 2000; Tronson, Wiseman, Olausson, & Taylor, 2006). This, together with the finding that reconsolidation is promoted by the induction of an encoding state in the retrieval situation (Morris et al., 2006), raises the possibility that the role of reconsolidation is to update memory, that is, to adapt the reactivated memory to the new circumstances of the retrieval context (Dudai, 2004; Sara, 2000). However, whereas the consolidation hypothesis postulates that the original memory is securely consolidated, updating notwithstanding, the reconsolidation hypothesis, even in its intermediate version (see earlier discussion), assumes that at least part of the original trace regains susceptibility to change. Some data (Rodriguez-Ortiz et al., 2008) but not other (Tronel, Milekic, & Alberini, 2005) support a role for reconsolidation in updating of long-term memories. The current discrepancy on the role of reconsolidation in updating in different systems and paradigms might be related to boundary conditions on reconsolidation, which are not yet completely understood (Dudai, 2006).

PLASTIC OPPORTUNITIES IN THE ABSENCE OF EXPLICIT RETRIEVAL

Recent evidence indicates that long-term and remote memory are susceptible to certain amnesic agents even in the absence of explicit memory reactivation. These agents are inhibitors of an atypical isozyme of protein kinase C (PKC), called PKMζ. PKCs are composed of a catalytic subunit and a regulatory subunit, which are attached via a proteineous hinge. The regulatory subunit inhibits the catalytic subunit by a pseudosubstrate domain. In the absence of the regulatory subunit, the enzyme becomes constitutively active, or autonomous. PKMζ is an autonomous form of PKCζ, which is formed in the brain by alternative splicing of PKCζ pre-mRNA. PKMζ can be inhibited by a number of selective inhibitors, particularly the cell-permeable pseudosubstrate inhibitory peptide, ZIP. PKMζ has been reported to be critical in the maintenance of long-term potentiation (LTP) in the hippocampus (Ling et al., 2002). Two sequential steps are required for the persistent increase in PKMζ activity that maintains LTP (Kelly, Crary, & Sacktor, 2007). One is de novo synthesis of PKMζ from PKMζ mRNA in the dendrite. This is regulated by several enzymes, including preexisting PKMζ. The other is formation of a complex with the enzyme phosphoinositide-dependent kinase-1 (PDK1): Though PKMζ is autonomous in the sense that second messengers required to activate PKC are not required, it still must be phosphorylated by PDK1 for optimal catalytic activity. The persistently active PKMζ phosphorylates synaptic substrates, which modify the microstructure of the synapse. This ultimately leads to a substantial increase in the number of functional postsynaptic AMPA-type glutamate receptors, which persistently enhances synaptic transmission (Ling, Benardo, & Sacktor, 2006).

Long-term spatial information in the hippocampus, which is subserved by LTP, was shown to critically depend on persistent activity of PKMζ (Pastlakova et al., 2006). This was demonstrated by the microinfusion of ZIP into the hippocampus of the behaving rat; scrambled ZIP had no effect. Although the hippocampus is well known to play a critical role in some types of memory, it is the neocortex that is considered to serve as the ultimate repository of multiple types of long-term memory in the mammalian brain (Dudai, 2002; Squire & Bayley, 2007). Using similar methods, it has indeed been found that microinfusion of ZIP into the neocortex rapidly erases remote memory associations (3 months old), but not familiarity, in the behaving rat (Shema, Hazvi, Sacktor, & Dudai, 2009; Shema, Sacktor, & Dudai, 2007). The affected brain area can, however, reacquire readily a new memory association. These data suggest that PKMζ permanently maintains long-term memory, and it is thus a target for amnesic agents as long as the memory persists. When the enzymatic activity is blocked for a short while (less than 2 hours, and probably minutes only), the experience-dependent synaptic modifications seem to collapse and the memory disappears with them. One possibility is that the target of PKMζ is a "tag" that dephosphorylates rapidly, and in its absence, though the enzymatic activity recovers from the inhibition, the enzyme cannot locate the proper phosphorylation site anymore.

Two major conclusions emerge from the recent findings concerning the role of PKMζ in maintaining long-term memory. First, inhibitors can cause rapid, irreversible amnesia even in the absence of explicit memory reactivation. Thus, postretrieval "reconsolidation" is not the only window of opportunity in which an item in long-term memory can be modified, at least in a laboratory setting, once postencoding consolidation had been completed. Second, neuronal changes that subserve long-term memory are not indelible modifications of synaptic structure but remain dependent on ongoing enzymatic activity and, thus, are capable of rapid and dynamic alterations by experimental manipulations.

What might the physiological role be of such potential to rapidly erase long-term memory? Three main possibilities come to mind. First, that in situ, the cellular mechanism that requires persistent phosphorylation by PKMζ is regulated in a more graded and discriminative manner than by ZIP inhibition in the artificial laboratory setting, resulting in real life in restricted fast modulation of local synaptic properties and memory rather than in complete memory erasure. Such rapid, local modulation of long-term synaptic plasticity might, for example, be useful in the course of fast incorporation of new experience into existing associative knowledge schemas in the neocortex (Tse et al., 2007), without necessarily activating all the affected associations at the time of change. Second, rapid inhibition of PKMζ in specific synapses may indeed lead to rapid stepwise shift of synapses to a basal level of efficacy or even to a silent state. This might be useful in conditions in which the previous accumulating modifications culminate in catastrophic "freezing" (e.g., a stable local minimum trap) of the computational abilities of the circuit, a situation which might be remedied by "rebooting." And third, as computational models suggest (Amit, 1989; Hopfield, 1982), circuits may saturate, potentially requiring erasure to create space for storing new information.

Selective inhibitors of PKMζ are so far the only agents found to be capable of rapidly erasing long-term and remote memory in the mammalian brain in the absence of explicit memory reactivation. Since the phosphorylation of a target protein can be reversed by protein phosphatases, further research on protein phosphatase inhibitors may identify additional types of memory erasers, including, possibly, long-term memory erasers (Mansuy & Shenolikar, 2006). These agents could cast further light on key elements of the molecular machinery that keep long-term memory going, and on the potential role of erasure in modifying long-term memory in the behaving brain.

On memory metaphors

"Freezing" and "rebooting," as used earlier, are computer-age metaphors. More accurately, they are palimpsest-type metaphors anchored in technological and cultural contexts much older than the computer age. Metaphors are abundant in the science of memory (Dudai, 2002; Roediger, 1980). The problem with them is that although they help us in organizing our thoughts, they are also potentially misleading and promote fixation of conceptual paradigms (Dudai, 2002). Storehouse, a dominant metaphor in memory research, epitomizes the problem. The storehouse metaphor connotes stability, whereas memory is dynamic. The data on reconsolidation, as well as on the ability to rapidly erase long-term memory associations without damaging new learning, only augment the dynamic nature of memory.

The classic time-based classification of memory distinguishes short- from long-term memory. This classification is known as the "dual-trace" hypothesis. It posits a transient, reverberating short-term trace "that carries the information until the growth change is made" (Hebb, 1949), and a long-term, stabilized trace, which is the outcome of the postulated growth change (for other terms used to describe the same or similar ideas, such as primary vs. secondary memory, see Dudai, 2002). Combined with the

consolidation hypothesis, the orthodox version of the dual-trace hypothesis could be construed to depict the memory trace, once consolidated, as being stored as is over time, used, then redeposited until next use (Fig. 21.1A; for an example of a more relaxed version of the dual-trace hypothesis in the context of systems consolidation, see Nadel & Moscovitch, 1997). An alternative conceptual framework was proposed, which portrays memory items in two alternating states: active and inactive (Fig. 21.1B; Lewis, 1979). Active is the state of the trace on and immediately after encoding and retrieval. Occasionally the trace might also become activated independent of encoding and retrieval. Otherwise the trace is inactive. The trace fluctuates between the active-inactive states of cycles. This could be dubbed as "the cyclic model." The data on consolidation and reconsolidation combined indicate that whenever active, the trace enters a special state (postactivation state; Dudai, 2007), in which it is highly plastic and susceptible to interference by amnesic agents. This is different from the classic dual-trace hypothesis, which does not predict augmented plasticity after retrieval, that is, reconsolidation. Whereas the dual-trace model depicts the ontogeny of a memory item as a unidirectional, deterministic function, the reconsolidation hypothesis is in line with the cyclic model. A modified version of the cyclic model takes into account the reports that long-term memory is susceptible to certain amnesic agents even in the absence of explicit reactivation of the trace. This modified cyclic model raises the possibility that the long-term trace can be updated whether active or inactive (Fig. 21.1C).

It is noteworthy that the active-inactive type of model does not nullify the existence of some type of consolidation, that is, it does not preclude an initial maturation phase for each item in memory. As noted earlier, studies that compare consolidation to reconsolidation show that reconsolidation is not a faithful recapitulation of memory, and studies on the role of PKMζ in neural plasticity and memory show that memories are not sensitive to PKMζ inhibitors in the first hours after training. All this implies that the properties of a fresh memory are different from those of an old memory (see also Berman & Dudai, 2001).

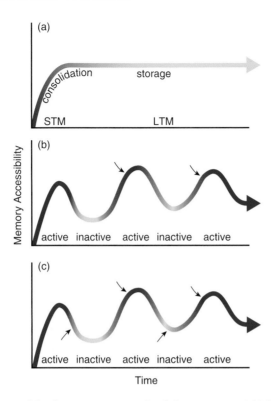

Figure 21.1 Schematic models of memory states and stability over time. (*a*) The dual-trace model classifies memory into a transient, short-term phase (short-term memory, STM) and a stable, long-term trace (long-term memory, LTM). The latter is generated by synaptic and cell-wide growth-like processes in the course of postencoding consolidation. Amnesic agents can disrupt the memory trace during consolidation but lose their effectiveness once consolidation is over. Consolidation according to this model occurs just once per item. This type of model does not refer specifically to the fate of the trace after retrieval, and it assumes, usually implicitly, that when new information is interwoven into old knowledge, the new information undergoes consolidation without altering plasticity in the older, consolidated memory. (*b*) The cyclic model depicts two states of memory, active (black) and inactive (gray), which alternate over time. Activity is time locked to encoding or retrieval. This type of model still predicts an initial consolidation period (on or immediately after encoding of the new memory item) but then allows for consolidation-like processes to occur more than once per item, that is, allows "reconsolidation." Recent data suggest that reconsolidation is not a faithful recapitulation of consolidation. One possibility is that reinstated plasticity in reactivated memory allows some sort of memory reorganization or updating (in the scheme, arrows representing new information merge with the old information only when the memory is in an active state). (*c*) A modified version of the cyclic model that takes into account recent reports that long-term memory is susceptible to certain amnesic agents even in the absence of explicit reactivation of the trace. This model raises the possibility that the long-term trace can be updated whether active or inactive (again, as in *B*, arrows represent new information merging with the existing one to generate an updated representation).

But once long-term memory is established, active-inactive models assume that the memory is still malleable and not stored as an indelible consolidated item. Coming back to metaphors, whereas the combination of the dual-trace model with the consolidation hypothesis connotes the storehouse metaphor, the more recent data on the high plasticity of the long-term trace and the cyclic models that stem from these data favor a Phoenix metaphor: Occasionally, items in memory may get the opportunity to be born anew.

On being just stable enough

In an influential account, Marr (1982) distinguished three levels of description or analysis in information-processing machines: (*a*) the level of the computational theory, that is, what are the goals of the computations and the logic of the strategy to carry them out; (*b*) the levels of representations and algorithms, that is, how can the computations be implemented in terms of "input" and "output" representations and of the algorithms for the transformation of "input" into "output"; and (*c*) the level of hardware implementation, that is, the way the representations and algorithms are implemented in the hardware of the machine, which, in the case of the brain, is the biological material, spanning from molecules to cells, circuits, and brain organs.

Taking the anthropocentric adaptationist approach, which posits that biological systems had evolved to achieve a goal and, furthermore, that we can identify that goal (and see Gould & Lewontin, 1979 for a critique), one could start the analysis of memory systems by defining their goal. Such an approach is likely to culminate in assignment of different goals to different memory systems, since, as noted previously, systems as different as emotional or motor conditioning, skill, priming, semantic or episodic memory had probably evolved under different selection pressures for different purposes. Yet one could still simplify and generalize by proposing a common goal for all memory systems. It is tempting to propose that this universal goal is to optimize adaptive responses to stimuli in the changing milieu of the individual.

The algorithmic and hardware route taken to the aforementioned goal seems to navigate among conflicting pressures. On the one hand, once a proper response is installed, either by the species experience (i.e., innate response programs) or by individual experience or, usually, by their combination, stability is advantageous since it ensures fast response and saves on the energy needed to learn anew. On the other hand, since the milieu changes, plasticity should permit fast changes in the existing response, should the conditions require such changes. On top of it, anticipating future events and trends permits

preparative steps and fast adaptive response. Summation of these requirements probably underlies basic plastic attributes of the memory trace of the type described earlier. Hence, following encoding, initial consolidation converts the trace into a state that is just stable enough that it will last until the next encounter with the proper stimulus, but at same time be amenable to change once the proper stimuli or contexts, or anticipations, change significantly. Under these constraints, a system that opens windows of augmented plasticity only when effective cues concerning the relevant specific situation become available could be beneficial, since it could reduce the risk of unwarranted change, restricting change to when it is needed only. Reconsolidation provides such a cue-locked delineated window of opportunity. The existence of privileged plasticity windows is a type of metaplasticity, that is, the plasticity of neural plasticity (Abraham & Tate, 1997). As other variants of metaplasticity, it reflects a dynamic balance between the need to change, to resist excessive change, and the metabolic price of both (Dudai, 2002).

The question could then be raised why is it that the trace can be rapidly changed or even erased with a PKMζ inhibitor outside the consolidation or reconsolidation windows. The possibility should not be excluded that this reflects inherent mechanistic shortcoming of the system and not adaptivity (e.g., Gould & Lewontin, 1979). In other words, that the susceptible part of the cellular long-term plasticity machinery, which collapses as a consequence of transient interruption of the persistent kinase activity, is not a target for cellular regulation in vivo. However, several hypothetical possibilities that assume physiological regulation of this site were raised earlier. Of these, the one most appealing in my view is the possibility to facilitate fast incorporation of new experience into existing associative knowledge schemas in the neocortex (Tse et al., 2007) in the absence of superfluous activation of indirect association (Debiec et al., 2006).

In conclusion, biological memory systems have evolved the basic capacity to anticipate an uncertain future by combining neuronal plasticity and metaplasticity mechanisms so that they can encode experience in a reasonably robust way on the one hand but update it quickly on the other. It would be of interest to determine whether this capacity is exploited differentially in different memory systems according to the relative weight of the requirement for stability versus anticipation of change in each system. Such differential reliance on plasticity that results in stability and on metaplasticity that permits future destabilization may account also for differences in the veracity of long-term items in different memory systems.

ACKNOWLEDGMENTS

I am grateful to Omri Barak and Joseph E. LeDoux for discussion of memory models. My research is supported by grants from the Israeli Science Foundation (ISF), the US-Israel Binational Science Foundation (BSF), and the Minerva Foundation.

REFERENCES

Abraham, W. C., & Tate, W. P. (1997). Metaplasticity: A new vista across the field of synaptic plasticity. *Progress in Neurobiology, 52*, 303–323.

Addis, D. R., Wong, A. T., & Schacter, D. L. (2007). Remembering the past and imagining the future: Common and distinct neural substrates during event construction and elaboration. *Neuropsychologia, 45*, 1363–1377.

Alberini, C. M. (2005). Mechanisms of memory stabilization: Are consolidation and reconsolidation similar or distinct processes? *Trends in Neuroscience, 28*, 51–56.

Amit, D. J. (1989). *Modeling brain function. The world of attractor model networks.* Cambridge, England: Cambridge University Press.

Anokhin, P. K. (1974). *Biology and neurophysiology of the conditioned reflex and its role in adaptive behavior.* Oxford, England: Pergamon Press.

Atance, C. M., & O'Neill, D. K. (2005). The emergence of episodic future thinking in humans. *Learning and Motivation, 36*, 126–144.

Baddeley, A. (2007). *Working memory, thought, and action.* New York: Oxford University Press.

Bahar, A., Dorfman, N., & Dudai, Y. (2004). Amygdalar circuits required for either consolidation or extinction of taste aversion memory are not required for reconsolidation. *European Journal of Neuroscience, 19*, 1115–1118.

Bain, A. (1872). *Mind and body: The theories of their relation.* London: Henry King.

Bar, M. (2007). The predictive brain: Using analogies and associations to generate predictions. *Trends in Cognitive Sciences, 11*, 280–289.

Berman, D. E., & Dudai, Y. (2001). Memory extinction, learning anew, and learning the new: Dissociations in the molecular machinery of learning in cortex. *Science, 291*, 2417–2419.

Bartlett, E. C. (1932). *Remembering: A study in experimental and social psychology.* London: Cambridge University Press.

Coltheart, V. (Ed.) (1999). *Fleeting memories. Cognition of brief visual stimuli.* Cambridge, MA: MIT Press.

Debiec, J., & LeDoux, J. E. (2004). Disruption of reconsolidation but not consolidation of auditory fear conditioning by noradrenergic blockade in the amygdale. *Neuroscience, 129*, 267–272.

Debiec, J., Doyere, V., Nader, K., & LeDoux, J. E. (2006). Directly reactivated, but not indirectly reactivated, memories undergo reconsolidation in the amygdala. *Proceedings of the National Academy of Sciences USA, 103*, 3428–3433.

Dudai, Y. (2002). *Memory from A to Z. Keywords, concepts, and beyond.* Oxford, England: Oxford University Press.

Dudai, Y. (2004). The neurobiology of consolidation, or, how stable is the engram. *Annual Review of Psychology, 55*, 51–86.

Dudai, Y. (2006). Reconsolidation: The advantage of being refocused. *Current Opinions in Neurobiology, 16*, 174–178.

Dudai, Y. (2007). Post-activation state: A critical rite of passage of memories. In B. Bontempi, A. J. Silva, & Y. Christen (Eds.), *Memories: Molecules and circuits, research and perspectives in neurosciences* (pp. 69–82). Heidelberg, Germany: Springer.

Dudai, Y., & Carruthers, M. (2005). The Janus face of mnemosyne. *Nature, 434*, 567.

Dudai, Y., & Morris, R. G. M. (2000). To consolidate or not to consolidate: What are the questions? In J. J. Bolhuis (Ed.), *Brain, perception, memory: Advances in Cognitive Sciences* (pp. xx–xx), Oxford, England: Oxford University Press.

Duvarci, S., Nader, K., & Ledoux, J. E. (2008). De novo mRNA synthesis is required for both consolidation and reconsolidation of fear memories in the amygdala. *Learning and Memory, 15*, 747–755.

Eisenberg, M., Kobilo, T., Berman, D.E., & Dudai, Y. (2003). Stability of retrieved memory: Inverse correlation with trace dominance. *Science, 301,* 1102–1104.

Flexner, J. B., Flexner, L. B., & Stellar, E. (1963). Memory in mice as affected by intracerebral puromycin. *Science, 141,* 57–59.

Fox, M. D., Snyder, A. Z., Vincent, J. L., & Raichle, M. E. (2007). Intrinsic fluctuations within cortical systems account for intertrial variability in human behavior. *Neuron, 56,* 171–184.

Frenkel, L., Maldonado, H. H., & Delorenzi, A. (2005). Memory strengthening by a real-life episode during reconsolidation: An outcome of water deprivation via brain angiotensin II. *European Journal of Neuroscience, 22,* 1757–1766.

Frey, U., & Morris, R. G. M. (1997). Synaptic tagging and long-term potentiation. *Nature, 385,* 533–536.

Fusi, S., Drew, P. J., & Abbott, L. F. (2005). Cascade models of synaptically stored memories. *Neuron, 45,* 599–611.

Gilboa, G., Chen, R., & Brennner, N. N. (2005). History-dependent multiple-time-scale dynamics in a single-neuron model. *Journal of Neuroscience, 25,* 6479–6489.

Gould, S. J., & Lewontin, R. C. (1979). The spandrels of San Marco and the Panglossian paradigm: A critique of the adaptationist programme. *Proceedings of the Royal Society of London B: Biological Sciences, 203,* 581–598.

Hare, T. A., O'Doherty, J., Camerer, C. F., Schultz, W., & Rangel, A. (2008). Dissociating the role of the orbitofrontal cortex and the striatum in the computation of goal values and predictions errors. *Journal of Neuroscience, 28,* 5623–5630.

Hassabis, D., Kumaran, D., Vann, S. D., & Maguire, E. A. (2007). Patients with hippocampal amnesia cannot imagine new experiences. *Proceedings of the National Academy of Sciences USA, 104,* 1726–1731.

Hasson, U., Yang, E., Vallines, I., Heeger, D. J., & Rubin, N. (2008). A hierarchy of temporal receptive windows in human cortex. *Journal of Neuroscience, 28,* 2539–2550.

Hebb, D. O. (1949). *The organization of behavior: A neuropsychological theory.* New York: Wiley.

Heidmann, A., Heidmann, T. M., & Changeux, J-P. (1984). Stabilization selective de representation neuronals per resonance entre "prerepresentations" spontanees du raseau cerebral et "percepts" evoques par interactions avec le monde exterieur []. *Comptes Rendus de l'Academie des Sciences de Paris Serie III, 299,* 839–843.

Holt, E. B. (1931). *Animal drive and the learning process.* New York: Holt.

Hopfield, J. J. (1982). Neural networks and physical systems with emergent collective computational abilities. *Proceedings of the National Academy of Sciences USA, 79,* 2554–2558.

Kappers, C. U. A. (1917). Further considerations on neurobiotaxis. IX. An attempt to compare the phenomenon of neurobiotaxis with other phenomena of taxis and tropism. The dynamic polarization of the neurone. *Journal of Comparative Neurology, 27,* 261–298.

Kelly, M. T., Crary, J. F., & Sacktor, T. C. (2007). Regulation of protein kinase Mzeta synthesis by multiple kinases in long-term potentiation. *Journal of Neuroscience, 27,* 3439–3444.

Lee, J. L. C., Everitt, B. J., & Thomas, K. L. (2004). Independent cellular processes for hippocampal memory consolidation and reconsolidation. *Science, 304,* 839–843.

Lewis, D. J. (1979). Psychobiology of active and inactive memory. *Psychology Bulletin, 86,* 1054–1083.

Ling, D. S., Benardo, L. S., & Sacktor, T. C. (2006). Protein kinase Mzeta enhances excitatory synaptic transmission by increasing the number of active postsynaptic AMPA receptors. *Hippocampus, 16,* 443–452.

Ling, D. S., Benardo, L. S., Serrano, P. A., Blace, N., Kelly, M. T., Crary, J. F., & Sacktor, T. C. (2002). Protein kinase Mzeta is necessary and sufficient for LTP maintenance. *Nature Neuroscience, 5,* 295–296.

Loftus, E. F., & Loftus, G. R. (1980). On the permanence of stored information in the human brain. *American Psychologist, 35,* 409–420.

Mansuy, I. M., & Shenolikar, S. (2006). Protein serine/threonine phophatases in neuronal plasticity and disorders of learning and memory. *Trends in Neuroscience, 29,* 679–686.

Marr, D. (1982). *Vision.* San Francisco: Freeman.

Martin, S. J., Grimwood, P. D., & Morris, R. G. M. (2000). Synaptic plasticity and memory: An evaluation of the hypothesis. *Annual Review of Neuroscience, 23,* 649–711.

McGaugh, J. L. (2000). A century of consolidation. *Science, 287,* 248–251.

Misanin, J. R., Miller, R. R., & Lewis, D. J. (1968). Retrograde amnesia produced by electroconvulsive shock after reactivation of a consolidated memory trace. *Science, 159,* 554–555.

Monne, L. (1949). Structure and function of neurones in relation to mental activity. *Biological Reviews of the Cambridge Philosophical Society*, *24*, 297–315.

Morris, R. G. M., Inglis, J., Ainge, J. A., Olverman, H. J., Tulloch, J., Dudai, Y., & Kelly, P. A. T. (2006). Memory reconsolidation: Sensitivity of spatial memory to inhibition of protein synthesis in dorsal hippocampus during encoding and retrieval. *Neuron*, *50*, 479–489.

Muller, G. E., & Pilzecker, A. (1900). Experimentelle Beitrgae zur Lehre und Gedachtnis []. *Zeit. Psychol. 1*, 1–300.

Nadel, L., & Moscovitch, M. (1997). Memory consolidation, retrograde amnesia and the hippocampal complex. *Current Opinions in Neurobiology*, *7*, 217–227.

Nader, K. (2003). Memory traces unbound. *Trends in Neuroscience*, *26*, 65–72.

Nader, K., Schafe, G. E., & LeDoux, J. E. (2000). Fear memories require protein synthesis in the amygdala for reconsolidation after retrieval. *Nature*, *406*, 722–726.

Naya, Y., Yoshida, M., & Miyashita, Y. (2001). Backward spreading of memory-retrieval signal in the primate temporal cortex. *Science*, *291*, 661–664.

Parsons, P. R., Gafford, G. M., Baruch, D. E., Riedner, B. A., & Helmestetter, F. J. (2006). Long-term stability of fear memory depends on the synthesis of protein but not mRNA in the amygdala. *European Journal of Neuroscience*, *23*, 1853–1859.

Pastalkova, E., Serrano, P., Pinkhasova, D., Wallace, E., Fenton, A. A., & Sacktor, T. C. (2006). Storage of spatial information by the maintenance mechanism of LTP. *Science*, *313*, 1141–1144.

Pedreira, M. E., Perez-Questa, L. M., & Maldonado, H. (2004). Mismatch between what is expected and what actually occurs triggers memory reconsolidation or extinction. *Learning and Memory*, *11*, 579–585.

Plato. (1961). *The collected dialogues*. (E. Hamilton & H. Cairns, Eds.). Princeton, NJ: Princeton University Press.

Rodriguez-Ortiz, C. J., Garcia_DeLaTorre, P., Benavidez, E., Ballesteros, M. A., & Bermudez-Rattoni, F. (2008). Intrahippocampal anisomycin infusions disrupt previously consolidated spatial memory only when memory is updated. *Neurobiology of Learning and Memory*, *89*, 352–359.

Roediger, H. L., III. (1980). Memory metaphors in cognitive psychology. *Memory and Cognition*, *8*, 231–246.

Roediger, H. L., Dudai, Y., & Fitzpatrick, S. M. (Eds.). (2007). *Science of memory: Concepts*. New York: Oxford University Press.

Sara, S. J. (2000). Retrieval and reconsolidation: Toward a neurobiology of remembering. *Learning and Memory*, *7*, 73–84.

Schacter, D. L. (Ed.). (1995). *Memory distortions*. Cambridge, MA: Harvard University Press.

Shema, R., Hazvi, S., Sacktor, T. C., & Dudai, Y. (2009). Boundary conditions for the maintenance of memory by PKMζ in neocortex. *Learning and Memory*, *16*, 122–128.

Shema, R., Sacktor, T. C., & Dudai, Y. (2007). Rapid erasure of long-term memory associations in cortex by an inhibitor of PKMzeta. *Science*, *317*, 951–953.

Shima, K., & Tanji, J. (1998). Role for cingulate motor area cells in voluntary movement selection based on reward. *Science*, *282*, 1335–1338.

Smith, M. A., Ghazizadeh, A., & Shadmehr, R. (2006). Interacting adaptive processes with different timescales underlie short-term motor learning. *PLoS Biology*, *4*, 1035–1043.

Squire, L. R., & Bayley, P. J. (2007). The neuroscience of remote memory. *Current Opinions in Neurobiology*, *17*, 185–196.

Suddendorf, T., & Corballis, M. C. (1997). Mental time travel and the evolution of the human mind. *Genetic, Social and General. Psychology Monographs*, *123*, 133–167.

Thorpe, S., Fize, D., & Marlot, C. (1996). Speed of processing in the human visual system. *Nature*, *381*, 520–522.

Toib, A., Lyakhov. V., & Marom, S. (1998). Interaction between duration of activity and time course of recovery from slow inactivation in mammalian brain Na+ channels. *Journal of Neuroscience*, *18*, 1893–1903.

Tronel, S., Milekic, M. H., & Alberini, C. M. (2005). Linking new information to a reactivated memory requires consolidation and not reconsolidation mechanisms. *PLoS Biol*, *3*, 1630–1638.

Tronson, N. C., Wiseman, S. L., Olausson, P., & Taylor, J. R. (2006). Biderctional behavioural plasticity of memory reconsolidation depends on amygdalar protein kinase A. *Nature Neuroscience*, *9*, 167–169.

Tse, D., Langston, R. F., Kakeyama, M., Bethus, I., Spooner, P. A., Wood, E. R., Witter, M. P., &

Morris, R. G. M. (2007). Schemas and memory consolidation. *Science, 316,* 76–82.

Tulving, E. (1983). *Elements of episodic memory.* Oxford, England: Oxford University Press.

Tulving, E. (2007). Are there 256 kinds of memory? In J. S. Nairne (Ed.), *The foundations of remembering. Essays in honor of Henry L. Roediger, III* (pp. 39–52). New York: Psychology Press.

Tulving, E., & Fergus, F. I. M. (Eds.). (2000). *The Oxford handbook of memory.* New York: Oxford University Press.

van Turennout, M., Hagoort, P., & Brown, C. M. (1998). Brain activity during speaking: From syntax to phonology in 40 milliseconds. *Science, 280,* 572–574.

von Hertzen, L. S. J., & Giese, K. P. (2005). Memory reconsolidation engages only a subset of immediate-early genes induced during consolidation. *Journal of Neuroscience, 25,* 1935–1942.

Wixted, J. (2004). The psychology and neuroscience of forgetting. *Annual Review of Psychology, 55,* 235–269.

Young, J. Z. (1979). Learning as a process of selection and amplification. *Journal of the Royal Society of Medicine, 72,* 801–814.

CHAPTER 22
The Retina as Embodying Predictions about the Visual World

Michael J. Berry II and Gregory Schwartz

We commonly think of the retina as akin to a camera: It forms a light-sensitive layer in the back of the eye that converts photons into a neural signal and then transmits this neural image in pixel-map form to the central brain. Standard neuroscience textbooks describe some additional features of retinal processing, but they still largely confirm this view. Ganglion cells come in ON and OFF-types with center-surround antagonism, but otherwise they form a pixel map themselves and have light responses that embody little more than a linear filtering operation on the raw visual data. However, the picture that emerges from retinal anatomy and biochemistry is far more elaborate. Not only does the retina have three layers of principal neurons, each capable of carrying out its own image-processing operations on the raw visual data, but within the five major cell types—photoreceptor, horizontal, bipolar, amacrine, and ganglion cells—there are numerous subtypes (Rodiech, 1998).

Photoreceptors include rods, which function at night, and cones, which function during the day, and cones have three types with different visual pigments (in the primate). The bipolar cells are divided broadly into ON- and OFF-types, which have different glutamate receptors, either maintaining or inverting the polarity of the signal transmitted from photoreceptors. Within these two broad types, there are a total of 12 anatomical types (in mouse), which now have been shown to possess unique molecular markers (Wassle, Puller, Muller, & Haverkamp, 2009).

Ganglion cells are commonly divided into at least 15 anatomical types (Masland, 2001), which all seem to form mosaics that tile visual space with their dendrites (in the mammal). The neural activity in each cell type is thought of as forming one "channel" of visual information sent in parallel to the central brain.

Most impressive of all, the amacrine cells are thought to come in 25 or more anatomical types (MacNeil & Masland, 1998). Several of the better-known amacrine cell types have been associated with specific feature selectivities, such as starburst cells (Demb, 2007), polyaxonal cells (Olveczky et al., 2003), and AII amacrine cells (Munch et al., 2009). The anatomical, biochemical, and functional diversity of the amacrine cell population is truly staggering, and the functional role of most of these cells is not yet known.

Against this backdrop of anatomical complexity, it hardly seems plausible that the retina accomplishes scarcely more than a linear filtering operation. And, in fact, there are a number of more complex, nonlinear computations that have been described in the retina, including directionally selective motion responses originally reported in 1963 (Barlow & Hill, 1963), other complex motion responses, such as motion anticipation (Berry et al., 1999), selectivity to object motion (Olveczky et al., 2003), approaching motion (Munch et al., 2009), and motion reversal (Schwartz, Taylor, Fisher, Harris, & Berry, 2007), as well as selectivity to violations of temporally periodic patterns (Bullock, Hofmann,

Nahm, New, & Prechtl, 1990; Schwartz, Harris, Shrom, & Berry, 2007). Another category of complex retinal processing is adaptation. Examples go back to light adaptation (Dowling, 1987) and contrast gain control (Shapley & Enroth-Cugell, 1984), but more recently they include adaptation to contrast and spatial scale (Smirnakis, Berry, Warland, Bailek, & Meister, 1997), wide-field motion (Olveczky, Baccus, & Meister, 2007), and a number of second-order stimulus statistics, including horizontal and vertical stripes (Hosoya, Baccus, & Meister, 2005).

We argue that many of these forms of complex image processing can be described as either explicitly or implicitly embodying a prediction about the visual stimulus. Such a description may form a useful framework for understanding why the retina performs these operations and for generating new experiments to probe retinal function. In fact, this idea has a venerable history, originally describing the spatiotemporal processing of the classical receptive field as an operation that reduces redundancy and produces an efficient neural code (Atick, 1992; Barlow, 1961). However, the many parallel channels of visual information together form a neural code that is highly redundant at the level of the entire ganglion cell population (Puchalla, Schneidman, Harris, & Berry, 2005). As a result of this multiplicity, some ganglion cells fire selectively when retinal predictions come true, while others fire following a violation. Instead, we suggest that the population neural code separates visual information into two broad streams, tagging information as either predictable or surprising. These separate streams are useful, because the behavioral value of the same visual information can differ greatly depending on whether it was predicted or surprising.

To be sure, the retina's predictions are modest compared to those of the entire brain. But because the retina's anatomical complexity is on the same order as other circuits, such as the cortical column, the retina's capabilities may also be similar to those of individual local circuits elsewhere in the brain. Thus, an enumeration of the retina's predictive capabilities and an analysis of their underlying circuit mechanisms may provide essential building blocks for understanding the more sophisticated predictions carried out in the rest of the brain.

PREDICTING MOTION

Motion is one of the most common types of visual pattern encountered by the retina. The retinal image moves either because of the motion of objects in the environment or because of the motion of the observer, including body and eye movements. Recent evidence suggests that the retina has mechanisms to predict both of these types of motion.

As an object moves smoothly along a trajectory, we must constantly make a prediction about its future position. To react appropriately, for example, to hit or catch a ball, we must be able to perform this task with very little delay. Our visual system, however, has an intrinsic delay of at least 30–100 ms (Maunsell, & Gibson, 1992) due in part to the transduction of light into electrical activity in photoreceptors. Researchers have measured our perception of movement by presenting a moving bar along with a second bar briefly flashed in alignment with the first. At the time of the flash, when the two bars are in exact alignment, subjects report seeing the moving bar traveling ahead of the flashed bar (Nijhawan, 1994). Experiments with similar stimuli have shown that the prediction of smooth motion begins in the retina (Berry et al., 1999).

A bar was presented to a patch of retina, and the firing rate of each ganglion cell was measured and plotted as a function of the distance from the center of the bar. Interpolating these measurements from a group of ganglion cells measured simultaneously gave a representation of the spatial distribution of activity called the neural image (Fig. 22.1A). For a bar flashed at a single location, the neural image formed a hump with a peak near the bar center. For a moving bar, however, the neural image was shifted in the direction of motion so that the peak was near the leading edge. An interesting and important property of motion anticipation is that it effectively corrects for the retina's own response delay, enabling the retina to represent the current position of a smoothly moving object, rather than its location several hundred milliseconds in the past.

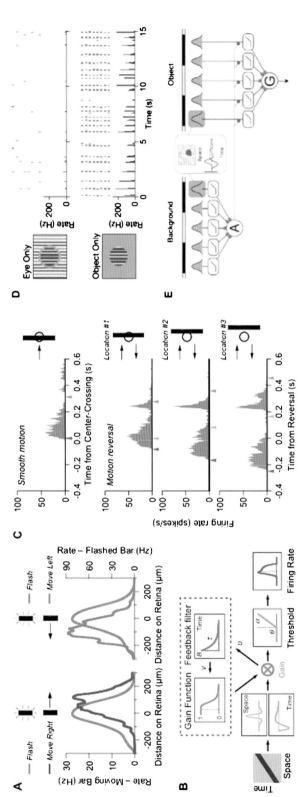

Figure 22.1 Motion prediction. (A) Motion anticipation in the retina (adapted from Berry, Brivanlou, Jordan, & Mesiter, 1999). Neural image of a population of retinal ganglion cells to a flashed bar (red) and bars moving to the right (blue) and to the left (green). (B) A linear-nonlinear (LN) model with gain control can account for motion anticipation. The stimulus (moving bar in this example) is first passed through a linear filter measured from the spatial and temporal properties of the classical receptive field. The filtered signal then undergoes gain control before being rectified to produce the ganglion cell's firing rate. (C) Response to smooth motion and reversals (adapted from Schwartz, Taylor, Fisher, Harris, & Berry, 2007). The firing rate of a single ganglion cell when presented with a smoothly moving bar (*upper*) and a reversing bar at three different reversal locations (*lower three panels*). Time zero for the reversing bar plot corresponds to the time of the reversal. Arrows represent the crossing times of the leading edge of the bar entering the receptive field center (blue), re-crossing the center following reversal (green), and leaving the receptive field surround (magenta). (D) Object motion–sensitive ganglion cells (adapted from Olveczky, Baccus, & Meister, 2003). Spike rasters and firing rate histograms for the same retinal ganglion cell during two different visual motion conditions. In the "eye only" condition, a random stripe pattern over the receptive field center and a different random strip pattern in the background jittered synchronously. In the "object only" condition, the pattern covering the receptive field jittered while the background remained gray. (E) A schematic of the mechanism proposed to underlie object motion sensitivity. The entire visual field is covered by both ON and OFF bipolar cell receptive fields (inset). The excitatory bipolar inputs to the ganglion cell (G) pass through a rectifying nonlinearity. A polyaxonal amacrine (A) also receives excitatory input from the bipolars and provides inhibition onto the bipolar terminals.

A model of ganglion cell responses consisting of a linear receptive field in space and time, a feedback gain control step, and a static nonlinearity (Fig. 22.1B) was able to predict the shift in the neural image for bars of different contrast. The model works as follows: (*1*) due to a ganglion cell's extended receptive field, an approaching object triggers excitation from some distance away; (*2*) due to delays in retinal processing, excitation arrives when the object is roughly centered over the ganglion cell; (*3*) then, contrast gain control shuts off the response, so that peak firing occurs at this time. While this motion anticipation effect in the retina shifts the neural image to the leading edge only over a certain range of speeds, the simple mechanism underlying the effect is likely to be implemented at higher levels of visual processing, perhaps augmenting the range and robustness of the prediction (Berry et al., 1999).

If the retina is constantly predicting the movement of objects along a smooth trajectory, what happens when this prediction is abruptly violated by a change in direction? We know that the visual system rapidly begins a new prediction to account for the change in circumstances. For example, football players learn to anticipate the position of the ball during the smooth trajectory of a forward pass in order to catch it, but when a ball suddenly changes direction after a deflection or bounces irregularly on the turf following a fumble, one must reset this prediction to start anticipating the new trajectory. The retina responds to at least one such violation of a motion prediction, firing a burst of spikes at a fixed time after the reversal of direction of a moving object (Schwartz et al., 2007).

An example of this reversal response in a ganglion cell is shown in Figure 22.1C. The cell fired as the bar moved continuously through its receptive field in one direction (top). When the bar reversed and passed the receptive field in the other direction, the cell fired an additional burst of spikes approximately 250 ms after the reversal (bottom three panels). For reversals at different positions, this burst was locked to the time of reversal (time axis), not the time the bar re-entered the center of the receptive field (green arrows).

The fact that the extra burst of spikes occurred at a fixed time after reversals at multiple positions meant that it occurred as a synchronous burst for a group of ganglion cells with different receptive field positions (see Fig. 22.5A). This synchronous burst represents a unique signal that could be distinguished in the population from the response to a smoothly moving bar using a simple decoding mechanism (Schwartz et al., 2007). Thus, the reversal response could be read out downstream of the retina as a violation of the ongoing smooth motion prediction. While the mechanism of the reversal response remains unknown, it is likely to involve novel processing within the retinal circuit, as the gain control model that explains the motion anticipation effect fails to capture the invariance of response latency at different reversal positions.

Motion anticipation and the synchronous burst following motion reversal represent, respectively, the instantiation of a prediction about moving objects in the visual environment and the response to the violation of that prediction. Along with the motion of external objects, our own bodies and eyes move continuously, causing rapid movements of the retinal image. Does the retina deliver a signal that can disambiguate the motion of objects from self-motion?

When presented with a texture covering the whole visual field that jitters in a random fashion modeled after the statistics of eye movements, a subset of ganglion cells fired very few spikes. The same jittering texture presented in a restricted location in the receptive field of the cells elicited large firing events (Olveczky et al., 2003; Fig. 22.1D). Cells with this response pattern were found in both salamander and rabbit and were called "object motion sensitive" (OMS) based on their ability to fire selectively for motion that is not wide field.

Movement of the observer, either by body or eye movements, causes the entire retinal image to move coherently, while motion of an object causes changes in only one area of the image. If self-motion is the default or "predicted" cause of image change on the retina, then differential motion in only a subset of the visual field (or the incoherent motion of foreground and background) is a violation of that prediction. Thus, OMS cells can be viewed as responding to this violation, but remaining silent during the predicted state of coherent motion across the whole visual field.

Polyaxonal amacrine cells have been identified as a key component of the mechanism of OMS cells (Fig. 22.1E; Baccus, Olveczky, Manu, & Meister, 2008; Olveczky et al., 2003). Signals in these wide-field amacrine cells are caused by motion of the background. When the background and foreground move coherently, excitation in the receptive field center is canceled by inhibition from the amacrine cells and the OMS ganglion cells do not fire. Incoherent motion destroys this alignment of excitatory and inhibitory signals, and the OMS cells are able to respond. The mechanism of object motion sensitivity is essentially a specialized case of the phenomenon of lateral inhibition that is so common across multiple stages of sensory systems.

PERIODIC PATTERNS

The problem of making predictions about the sensory world can be reframed in terms of pattern recognition. To make accurate predictions, our sensory systems must recognize predictable patterns. One example of such a pattern in the visual environment is a periodicity: a pattern of light that repeats at a fixed interval.

Periodic visual patterns abound in the natural world, and many have specific behavioral relevance to animals. The motion of other animals—the crawling of an insect, the swimming of a fish, the flapping wings of a bird, even the gait of a human—is often periodic, and recognizing these patterns is essential in identifying predator and prey. Additionally, the visual system encounters periodic patterns caused by both external factors, like the flicker created on the ground by sunlight filtered through swaying trees or created underwater from waves on the surface (Passaglia, Dodge, Herzong, Jackson, & Barlow, 1997), and by internal factors, like the high-frequency jitter of the retinal image caused by fixational eye movements (Bengi & Thomas, 1972).

It has long been known that the human visual system represents periodic patterns. Numerous studies have demonstrated an electroencephalogram (EEG) signal after a disruption in an auditory periodic pattern called the "mismatch negativity" (Klinke, Fruhstorfer, & Finkenzeller, 1968). Similar signals have also been seen in the visual and somatosensory domains (Rogers, Papanicolaou, Baumann, & Eisenberg, 1992; Sutton, Tueting, Zubin, & John, 1967). Recent work has demonstrated that the retina itself contains remarkably sophisticated capabilities for recognizing periodic patterns.

Following work on the human mismatch negativity, Bullock and colleagues presented periodic sequences of flashes to a number of species of teleost fish, rays, and turtles (Bullock et al., 1990; Bullock, Karamursel, & Hofmann, 1993; Karamursel, & Bullock, 1994). In local field potential recordings from both the optic tectum and the optic nerve, they observed a characteristic response after the end of such flash sequences. The timing of this response depended on the frequency of the preceding flash sequence; it occurred later for flash trains with a long interval between flashes and earlier for flash trains with a shorter interflash interval (Fig. 22.2A). Based on the relationship between preceding stimulus frequency and response latency, they called the phenomenon the "omitted stimulus potential" arguing that the signal was related to the predicted time of the next (omitted) flash in the sequence.

Recordings of spike trains from individual retinal ganglion cells in salamander and mouse revealed a similar phenomenon called the omitted stimulus response (OSR; Schwartz et al., 2007, Fig. 22.2B). Over a range of stimulus frequencies, the timing of the OSR was precisely locked not to the last flash in the sequence but to the omitted flash (Fig. 22.2C). Violations of more complex patterns, like alternating big and small flashes or long and short intervals, also elicited a response in some ganglion cells (Fig. 22.1D,E). The OSR was present for periodicities in both space and time, like an oscillating bar or a drifting grating that suddenly stopped (Fig. 22.2F,G). Subsequent studies showed that the OSR was robust to jitter in the timing of the flashes (imperfect periodicity) yet sensitive enough to detect an offset as small as 1 millisecond in an otherwise perfectly periodic sequence (Schwartz & Berry, 2008). The mechanism of the OSR remains an area of active research.

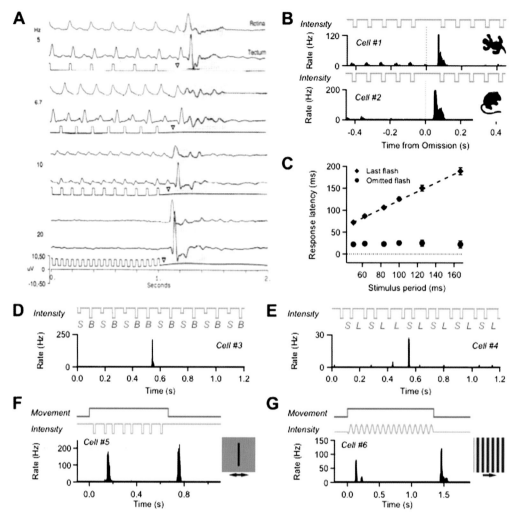

Figure 22.2 Predicting periodic patterns. (*A*) Local field potentials from the optic nerve (labeled "retina") and optic tectum of a teleost fish in response to sequences of bright flashes at different frequencies (adapted from Bullock, Hofmann, Nahm, New, & Prechtl, 1990). Arrows indicate the time the next flash would have occurred had the sequence continued. (*B*) The firing rates of ganglion cells in salamander (*upper*) and mouse (*lower*) following the omission of a single flash in a periodic sequence (adapted from Schwartz, Harris, Shrom, & Berry, 2007). (*C*) The latency of the burst of spikes following the end of a periodic sequence is plotted for sequences at different periods. Points are averages over 76 ganglion cells in salamander (error bars are SEM). Dotted line is slope unity. (*D and E*) Some ganglion cells respond to violation of more complex patterns like alternating big and small flashes (*D*) or long and short intervals between flashes (*E*). (*F and G*) Cells also respond to violations of spatiotemporal patterns like the sudden stop of an oscillating bar (*F*) or a drifting grating (*G*).

ADAPTATION EMBODIES PREDICTION

The OSR represents the violation of an explicit and precise prediction about the visual stimulus, but more broadly any form of adaptation embodies the recognition of the previous pattern of sensory stimuli along with the prediction that this pattern will continue in the future.

Adaptation in a sensory system is a process by which the input-output function of a neural circuit is modified according to a change in the stimulus statistics. The retina adapts to a variety of stimulus parameters, including mean luminance (Shapley & Enroth-Cugell, 1984), temporal contrast and spatial scale (Smirnakis, Berry, Warland, Bailek, & Meister, 1997), wide-field motion (Olveczky et al., 2007), as well as a number of higher order statistics (Hosoya et al., 2005). Once the system reaches its adapted state, it is able to transmit information about the stimulus more efficiently, in some cases approaching a state that optimizes information transfer (Brenner, Bialek, & de Ruyter van Steveninck, 2000). A key assumption in this formulation is that once the system has adapted, the statistics of the sensory stimulus remain fixed long enough for the adaptation to be beneficial; if previous observations had no predictive power about future stimuli, there would be no reason to adapt.

Experiments on the dynamics of temporal contrast adaptation in the retina have made this idea more explicit. A full-field temporally modulated light was presented to the retina with the contrast of the stimulus switching periodically between high and low values. Following the switch to high contrast, retinal ganglion cells immediately increase their firing rate and then slowly decrease their firing to a steady-state level. The high-to-low contrast transition causes a sharp decline in firing and then a slow increase (Fig. 22.3A). These changes in the firing rate of ganglion cells while the contrast remains fixed are evidence that the retina is adapting its processing of visual inputs.

Adaptation can be thought of as a mechanism that matches the limited dynamic range of ganglion cell firing rates to the expected range of light intensities in the visual world. Thus, when the temporal contrast of the stimulus changes, the retina should change its sensitivity in a manner roughly proportional to the contrast. This adaptive rescaling can be seen in the firing rate of ganglion cells (Meister & Berry, 1999) as well as in the excitatory input current to a ganglion cell (Fig. 22.3B, Kim & Rieke, 2001). In these data, a linear-nonlinear model was formulated to relate the visual stimulus to the measured input current. After choosing linear kernel amplitudes to best match the nonlinear function at both values of stimulus contrast (right), the kernel amplitude was seen to scale with the

contrast of the stimulus, while retaining a similar shape (left). Such adaptive rescaling serves to improve or even maximize the transmission of visual information, as has been demonstrated for a similar form of adaptation in the fly visual system (Brenner et al., 2000).

The time scale of adaptation following a transition to higher contrast is systematically faster than for a transition to lower contrast (Fig. 22.3A). This property can be understood from a Bayesian formulation of how any sensor could estimate the current temporal contrast of the world. Such estimation requires multiple samples of the light level. If the prior expectation is that the world has low contrast, then following a switch to high contrast, the sensor will very quickly see extreme values of light intensity that are very unlikely given this prior. Thus, an optimal contrast estimator will quickly increase its estimate of the contrast. However, following a transition to lower contrast, there will be many values of light intensity that are moderate and quite likely, so that it will take a longer amount of time for an optimal estimator to decrease its estimate (DeWeese & Zador, 1998).

Further evidence that retinal adaptation embodies useful predictions about future visual stimuli comes from an experiment similar to the one shown in panel A, but where the authors varied the period at which contrast remains constant (Wark, Fairhall, & Rieke, 2009). For short contrast switching periods, the adaptation was fast; for longer switching periods, it was slower (Fig. 22.3C). In fact, the time constant of retinal adaptation increased monotonically with the time period of constant stimulus statistics. This work demonstrated that the retina not only builds a model of current contrast, it also builds a representation of how frequently contrast changes. In a world where changes are predictably slow, the retina can integrate for a long time to establish an accurate measurement of the stimulus statistics. When changes are rapid, there is little time for the circuit to integrate, so adaptation must take place more quickly.

Recent work has shown that the retina can adapt to many statistical properties of the visual world beyond the mean luminance and contrast. Hosoya et al. (2005) recorded the responses of

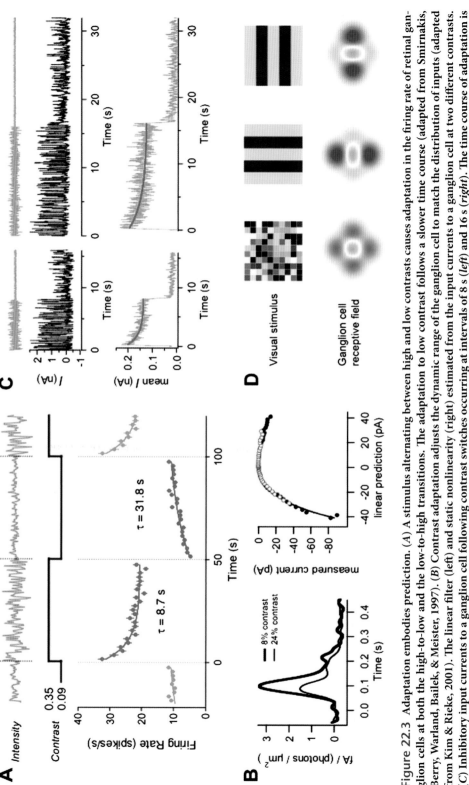

Figure 22.3 Adaptation embodies prediction. (*A*) A stimulus alternating between high and low contrasts causes adaptation in the firing rate of retinal ganglion cells at both the high-to-low and the low-to-high transitions. The adaptation to low contrast follows a slower time course (adapted from Smirnakis, Berry, Warland, Bailek, & Meister, 1997). (*B*) Contrast adaptation adjusts the dynamic range of the ganglion cell to match the distribution of inputs (adapted from Kim & Rieke, 2001). The linear filter (left) and static nonlinearity (right) estimated from the input currents to a ganglion cell at two different contrasts. (*C*) Inhibitory input currents to a ganglion cell following contrast switches occurring at intervals of 8 s (*left*) and 16 s (*right*). The time course of adaptation is proportional to the switching period (adapted from Wark, Fairhall, & Rieke, 2009). (*D*) Schematic of the results of adaptation to different spatial patterns: randomly flickering checkerboard (*left*), horizontal (*center*), or vertical (*right*) stripes. The receptive field surround (blue) becomes elongated along the axis of the stripes, and the center (red) becomes stronger along the orthogonal axis. This makes cells less sensitive to the adapted pattern and more sensitive to the orthogonal orientation (adapted from Hosoya, Baccus, & Meister, 2005).

salamander and rabbit retinal ganglion cells while altering various properties of the stimulus. For each statistical property they changed, the cells displayed a greater sensitivity to the novel stimulus than the adapted stimulus. In one example, the retina was stimulated with randomly flickering horizontal bars. The receptive fields of the ganglion cells became elongated horizontally, making the cells more sensitive to vertical bars (Fig. 22.3D). In another experiment, the researchers presented a full-field stimulus that alternated between strong positive and strong negative correlations. Following adaptation to the positively correlated pattern, ganglion cells exhibited a highly biphasic linear filter that was very sensitive to the negative correlation stimulus. Conversely, following the negatively correlated stimulus, the filter became more monophasic and showed greater sensitivity to the positively correlated stimulus.

As future work uncovers the functions of the many subtypes of interneurons and ganglion cells, we are likely to discover many more phenomena in which the retina adapts to abstract, high-level statistics of the visual scene. Such results will strengthen the interpretation of the retinal circuit as a highly sophisticated pattern detector that constantly makes predictions about its visual environment.

PREDICTION AND THE CLASSICAL RECEPTIVE FIELD

The idea of retinal processing as embodying predictions goes back to seminal work by Barlow (1961). Barlow noticed that natural visual scenes have extensive correlation, such that the light intensity at one location is likely to be similar to the light intensity at adjacent locations in visual space. The center-surround antagonism of the classical receptive field computes differences in light intensity, suppressing the response to regions of uniform light intensity, and thus enhancing edges. As a result, the population of ganglion cells would not send to the brain multiple messages reporting the same light intensity in adjacent spatial locations, but instead would report the "surprising" edges, thus constituting a

more efficient use of costly resources, such as energy-intensive action potentials.

Srinivasan and Laughlin developed a quantitative theory that built upon the idea that retinal processing removes redundant or predictable information from the neural code of the ganglion cells (Srinivasan, Laughlin, & Dubs, 1982). They proposed that the antagonistic surround of the classical receptive field may be viewed as making a prediction about what the light level will be in the receptive field center region (Fig. 22.4A). Such a prediction is possible because of the regularities in natural visual images. Furthermore, the quality of the prediction should depend on the reliability of the data that can be collected in the receptive field surround: At low light level, noise in the estimation of the light intensity will degrade the prediction. As a result of this poorer quality prediction, there should be less subtraction carried out by the surround at low light levels than at high. Srinivasan et al. (1982) put statistics of photon counting together with measurements of the degree of regularity of the light intensity in natural images to produce an estimate of the optimal spatial transfer function of a ganglion cell, and these results agreed qualitatively with how the center-surround balance changes at different light levels (Fig. 22.4B).

Srinivasan et al. went on to apply this idea to the case of temporal processing, assuming a very simple model of temporal correlation in natural vision. This model of the predictive temporal filter was strongly biphasic at high light levels, thereby suppressing the response to constant light intensity, and became more monophasic at low light levels. The suppression of constant stimuli can be interpreted as embodying the very simple prediction that the light intensity at one location will not change in time, as is typically the case in natural vision, if the animal is not moving (Dong & Atick, 1995). Again, the predictive temporal kernel becomes monophasic at low light level because the prediction is of poor quality. This behavior agreed qualitatively with ganglion cells at both high and low light levels; this model also agreed very closely with the temporal kernel of a second-order neuron in the fly visual system (large monopolar cell), which is analogous to retinal bipolar cells (Fig. 22.4C). Van Hateren extended this idea using a more detailed model of natural scene statistics, finding similarly good agreement with the temporal filter of large monopolar cells (van Hateren, 1992). Later, Atick made the proposal that retinal processing reduces redundancy in the ganglion cell representation more quantitative, demonstrating impressive agreement with experiment over seven orders of magnitude in light level with no free parameters that depended on light level (Atick, 1992). Thus, the spatial and temporal processing of classical receptive field can be also thought of as embodying spatial and temporal predictions about the visual stimulus, based primarily on the statistics of natural visual scenes.

While these classic results are compelling and have been highly influential to our view of computation in local neural circuits, they contain significant flaws. If retinal processing is geared toward achieving an efficient neural code, then the redundancy of visual information in the ganglion cell population should be low, but direct measurement reveals that the population actually has quite high redundancy (Puchalla et al., 2005). Models of redundancy reduction explicitly or implicitly assume that the ganglion cells come in one functional type that tile visual space

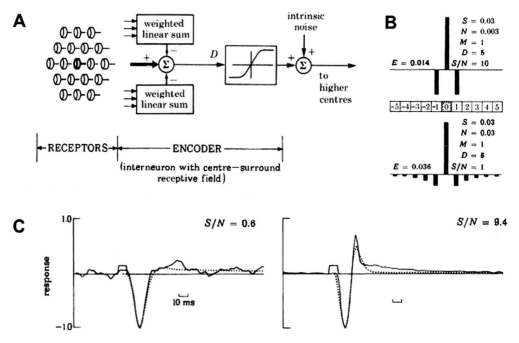

Figure 22.4 Center-surround antagonism in space and time create predictive encoders. (*A*) Schematic of the predictive computation performed by a retinal circuit with a spatial receptive field consisting of center and surround (adapted from Srinivasan, Laughlin, & Dubs, 1982). One "center" receptor (dark lines) provides excitatory input while the "surround" receptors provide inhibition; each receptor input has its own weight. With this organization of inputs, a downstream cell computes the difference between the predicted light intensity (provided by the weighted sum of the surround receptors) and actual value of the center receptor. Intrinsic noise is added after the summation step. (*B*) Receptor weights for the center receptor (position 0) and 10 surround receptors are depicted by bar height and are computed to optimize the predictive computation. When noise is low and thus signal to noise ratio is high (*top*), the optimal predictive encoder has a narrow receptive field. With more noise (*bottom*), the receptive field becomes broad. (*C*) Experimentally measured linear filters from fly large monopolar neurons (solid lines) along with optimal predictive filters (dashed lines). Under conditions of low signal to noise ratio (*left*), the filter is monophasic. At high signal to noise ratio (*right*), it becomes more biphasic.

with minimal overlap, but anatomy and physiology reveal at least 15 cell types (Masland, 2001) with a total coverage of visual space of ~60-fold (Segev, Puchalla, & Berry, 2006). We can reconcile these differences by thinking of redundancy reduction as applying to each cell type individually, but not to the choice of multiple cell types in the entire ganglion cell population. Thus, the question remains: How can we interpret the function of the multiple, redundant visual channels formed by all the types of ganglion cells?

PARALLEL CHANNELS FOR SURPRISING AND PREDICTABLE VISUAL INFORMATION

We have seen that many of the retina's computations can be understood as embodying different kinds of prediction about the visual world. In many of these cases, the ganglion cells selectively fire when there is a violation of the retinal prediction, in accord with the principle of efficient coding. However, an efficient code is one in which neurons only encode the surprising features in their stimulus, not the predictable parts. This might not always be a good idea. In many cases, events in the visual world that the retina has already predicted constitute the most reliable information that the retina can transmit to the brain. In fact, Barlow himself has later emphasized the value of redundancy for robust coding and, perhaps more important, for the potential of later circuits to learn statistically unusual patterns in the stimulus (Barlow, 2001).

For all of these reasons, we do not think that the goal of predictive retinal processing is to achieve an efficient code per se. And, in fact, we observe in many cases that individual ganglion cells fire not just for surprising or novel stimuli but also for predictable stimuli. One example is a ganglion cell that responds to smoothly moving objects with correctly anticipated firing, but then also fires following a motion reversal (Fig. 22.5A). Another example is a cell that fires not just at the start or end of a periodic flash sequence (the surprising events) but also during the sequence (the predictable part) (Fig. 22.5B). So what is an alternative to efficient coding that incorporates these facts and takes into account the many parallel channels of visual information?

We propose that a major goal of retinal processing is to separate visual information into two broad streams: one that represents surprising information, as in an efficient code, but another that represents predictable information. One of the reasons why this might be advantageous is that the behavioral significance of an event in the visual world can be completely different, depending on whether that event was predicted or surprising. For instance, if a small prey object is where the visual system expects it to be, then the animal may want to initiate feeding behavior, but if that same object's location is unexpected, then striking is unlikely to succeed.

A schematic example of this idea of parallel channels of predictable and surprising information is illustrated in Fig. 22.5C. Here, an object suddenly appears, triggering the surprise channel. Then, the object remains in place, triggering activity in the predicted channel. Notice that this channel encodes the same information as before, namely that this same object is still at the same location. Next, the object suddenly begins moving, initially triggering the surprise channel, but then switching over to the predicted channel after enough time has elapsed for correct motion anticipation. Similar events follow motion reversal. Interestingly, when an object stops moving, there is no transient, synchronized response, as for motion reversal (Schwartz et al., 2007). This can be understood if we recall that motion anticipation allows the retina to represent the true, present location of a moving object (Berry et al., 1999). When the object stops moving, it is still at the same location, and consequently there is no surprise about its location. (One might hypothesize, though, that higher level brain circuits that extrapolate a moving object's position will be surprised by a sudden cessation of motion.) Finally, the surprise channel is again active when the object disappears.

PREDICTION AND THE NEURAL CODE

How can the retina represent predictable versus surprising events if ganglion cells respond in both cases? The answer lies in the population code. For the example of motion reversal, the response is transient and tightly synchronized

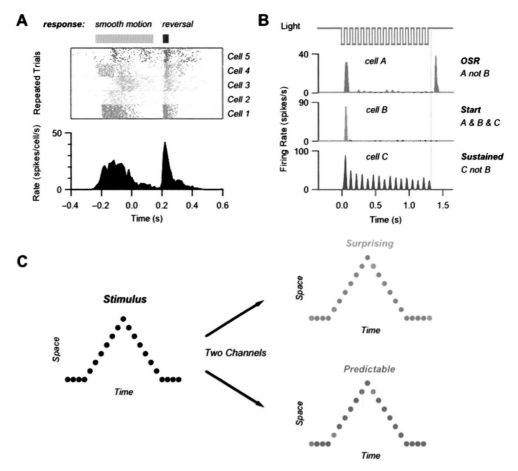

Figure 22.5 Encoding predicted and surprising events. (*A*) (*Upper*) Spike rasters from five simultaneously recorded ganglion cells responding to a reversing bar. (*Lower*) Population firing rate calculated by averaged over trials and cells. Each cell responds both to the smooth motion and the reversal, but the smooth motion responses are prolonged and asynchronous while the reversal responses are transient and synchronous. (*B*) Three ganglion cells responding to a periodic flash sequence (trace above), illustrating different response classes. Firing patterns among different pairs of cells can uniquely identify "start," "sustained," and "omitted flash" sections of the stimulus. (*C*) Space-time representation of an object that appears, begins to move, reverses direction, stops, and disappears. We speculate that retinal processing divides these events into predictable (blue) and surprising (red) channels of visual information encoded by distinct populations of retinal ganglion cells.

over a large group of cells (Fig. 22.5A). Thus, a simple, linear readout circuit that pools over many ganglion cells (50+) could perfectly discriminate motion reversal from smooth motion, even though such discrimination is not possible using individual cells (Schwartz et al., 2007). For the example of periodic temporal sequences, the extreme heterogeneity of individual ganglion cell responses means that the brain can interpret the stimulus as a violation of the expected pattern when "start/end" cells fire *and* "start only" cells are silent (Fig. 22.5B). Similarly, the brain can infer the presence of a predicted flash when a "sustained" cell fires but any kind of "start" cell is silent. Finally, all surprising stimuli need not be lumped together. The unpredictable first flash can be distinguished from the equally unpredictable flash omission by requiring that *both* "start/

end" and "start only" cells fire (which has greater certainty than the firing of a "start only" cell by itself).

One interesting property of the retina code is that in many circumstances, the surprising information is represented by transient, synchronized firing, while the predictable information is represented by sustained firing. Examples include the following: (*1*) smooth motion that elicits sustained firing versus motion reversal or motion initiation that both elicit transient firing; (*2*) the appearance of an object, which initially elicits transient firing in most ganglion cells, which is then followed by sustained firing in a subset of ganglion cells as long as the object remains in place; (*3*) a sudden change in stimulus statistics, like contrast, causes a high transient firing rate and then a slow adaptation to baseline. This pattern should be viewed as a general theme, rather than as a strict rule, as some cases violate this pattern; for instance, the sustained response to a periodic flash sequence is a set of transient bursts. This general theme makes intuitive sense, as predictable sensory events allow continued integration of information and thus benefit by being distributed in time, while surprising sensory events should trigger a rapid update of the central brain's model of the world and thus benefit by being transient and highly synchronized.

These features of combinatorial codes allow us to propose a hypothesis about why the retina has so many parallel channels: namely, that evolution has equipped the retina with circuitry to make predictions about a large set of simple spatiotemporal patterns in the visual world. Each kind of prediction is useful to the animal, so the retina would like to make as many predictions as it possibly can, given constraints of its circuitry, such as limited numbers of long-range processes and a lack of recurrent excitation. Because the retina does not exhibit structural plasticity in the adult, it is effectively limited to predictions about stimulus patterns that are generically valid in all visual environments, such as the prediction that an object moving smoothly at moderate speed will continue at roughly the same speed in the next several hundred milliseconds. Notice that because most retinal predictions are not encoded by strictly dedicated neurons that refrain from firing under any other circumstance, the retina must use multiple cell types and there is significant redundancy among these different cell types. However, as long as the goal of retinal processing is not an efficient code at the population level, this added redundancy is not a problem. Instead, it is the inevitable consequence of attempting to pack many predictive computations into the retina.

PREDICTION IN OTHER NEURAL CIRCUITS?

There is nothing unprecedented about the architectural complexity of the retina. Other local circuits in the brain, such as the cortical column and the hippocampal loop, have multiple layers of principal neurons along with very diverse populations of inhibitory interneurons (Klausberger & Somogyi, 2008; Markram et al., 2004). Consequently, one expects that these local circuits should have similar or greater computational power than the retina. This suggests that other local circuits, such as the cortical column, may also have the capability to predict a large set of patterns in their inputs, as can the retina. For instance, the basic ingredients of motion anticipation—spatially extended pooling of excitatory inputs plus time-delayed negative feedback—are so simple that many cortical circuits are likely to share these properties. If a cortical map then organizes sensory information so that typical sensory sequences activate a "smooth trajectory" on this cortical map, then the same machinery that produces retinal motion anticipation would result in a higher-level form of cortical anticipation.

If many local circuits in a sensory-motor pathway are able to carry out their own predictions, what are the differences in the predictions carried out at different stations, and how can they be linked together in a useful way? One interesting property of neurons that fire selectively to the beginning and end of a predictable spatiotemporal sequence is that their responses can serve to encode the entire sequence as a single "object." Then, if the next local circuit in the pathway can make predictions about these signals, what will emerge is selectivity to a higher-order pattern composed of subpatterns. Thus, the representation of information in the "surprise" channel makes possible a powerful and scalable form of hierarchical pattern detection. In such a mechanism, local circuits higher in the pathway may not need different or more complex pattern recognition mechanisms. Instead, they can achieve increasingly complex pattern detection merely because the class of stimuli represented by their input signals becomes more complex.

MECHANISMS OF PREDICTIVE COMPUTATION

One of the benefits of studying predictive computation in the retina is that this circuit is highly accessible and anatomically ordered, thus allowing detailed dissection of the cellular and synaptic mechanisms underlying predictive computation. So, in this context, what are some of the lessons we have learned from the retina about predictive computations in local circuits? One of the striking observations is that retinal predictions are not carried out using the same kind of algorithms that an engineer might chose. For instance, object motion selectivity does not involve a retinal neuron explicitly calculating the wide-field velocity vector and then "subtracting" this vector from a locally computed vector. Instead, it uses transient selective responses from a wide-field amacrine cell network that briefly veto responses to local motion in ganglion cells. Similarly, motion anticipation does not involve computing the past velocity vector of a moving object and then adding excitation to ganglion cells representing positions ahead of the moving object. Furthermore, this mechanism does not appear "cognitive" in any sense, even though it effectively implements a simple kind of prediction. Thus, the retina tends to use computational "tricks" that are good enough to achieve the desired result over a useful range of stimulus conditions, but which do not perfectly achieve the most general solution.

Another theme that emerges from retinal computation is that inhibition is often the key factor in conferring specific sensitivity. For example, polyaxonal amacrine cells give rise to object motion sensitivity, AII amacrines give rise to approaching motion sensitivity, and starburst amacrine cells confer direction selectivity. These

forms of inhibition serve to "veto" a specific visual pattern, making the ganglion cells selective. Correspondingly, the amacrine cells are the most anatomically and biochemically diverse cell class in the retina.

To be sure, the idea of retinal computation as embodying predictions may not be fruitful for all of the image processing carried out by the retina. However, this idea helps to bring many different, seemingly unrelated examples of complex retinal computation into a single unifying framework. This framework then gives us an appreciation for the computational power of not just the retina but also other local neural circuits, suggests new classes of experiments to more fully elaborate the computational and predictive capabilities of the brain, and helps us understand the detailed cellular mechanisms underlying these fascinating neural computations.

REFERENCES

Atick, J. J. (1992). Could information theory provide an ecological theory of sensory processing? *Network*, *3*, 213–251.

Baccus, S. A., Olveczky, B. P., Manu, M., & Meister, M. (2008). A retinal circuit that computes object motion. *Journal of Neuroscience*, *28*(27), 6807–6817.

Barlow, H. B. (1961). Possible principles underlying the transformations of sensory messages. In W.A. Rosenblith (Ed.). *Sensory communication, contributions* (pp. 217–234. Cambridge, MA: MIT Press.

Barlow, H. (2001). Redundancy reduction revisited. *Network*, *12*(3), 241–253.

Barlow, H. B., & Hill, R. M. (1963). Selective sensitivity to direction of movement in ganglion cells of the rabbit retina. *Science*, *139*, 412–414.

Bengi, H., & Thomas, J. G. (1972). Studies on human ocular tremor. In R. M. Kenedi (Ed.), *Prospectives in biomedical engineering* (pp. 281–292). London: Macmillen.

Berry, M. J., II, Brivanlou, I. H., Jordan, T. A., & Mesiter, M. (1999). Anticipation of moving stimuli by the retina. *Nature*, *398*(6725), 334–338.

Brenner, N., Bialek, W., & de Ruyter van Steveninck, R. (2000). Adaptive rescaling maximizes information transmission. *Neuron*, *26*(3), 695–702.

Bullock, T. H., Hofmann, M. H., Nahm, F. K., New, J. G., & Prechtl, J. C. (1990). Event-related potentials in the retina and optic tectum of fish. *Journal of Neurophysiology, 64*(3), 903–914.

Bullock, T. H., Karamursel, S., & Hofmann, H. M. (1993). Interval-specific event related potentials to omitted stimuli in the electrosensory pathway in elasmobranchs: an elementary form of expectation. *Journal of Comparitive Physiology, 172*(4), 501–510.

Demb, J. B. (2007). Cellular mechanisms for direction selectivity in the retina. *Neuron, 55*(2), 179–186.

DeWeese, M. R., & Zador, A. (1998). Assymetric dynamics in optimal variance adaptation. *Neural Computation, 10*, 1179–1202.

Dong, D. W., & Atick, J. J. (1995). Statistics of natural time-varying images. *Network, 6*, 345–358.

Dowling, J. E. (1987). *The retina: An approachable part of the brain*. Cambridge, MA: Harvard University Press.

Hosoya, T., Baccus, S. A., & Meister, M. (2005). Dynamic predictive coding by the retina. *Nature, 436*(7047), 71–77.

Kim, K. J., & Rieke, F. (2001). Temporal contrast adaptation in the input and output signals of salamander retinal ganglion cells. *Journal of Neuroscience, 21*(1), 287–299.

Karamursel, S., & Bullock, T. H. (1994). Dynamics of event-related potentials to trains of light and dark flashes: Responses to missing and extra stimuli in elasmobranch fish. *Electroencephalography and Clinical Neurophysiology, 90*(6), 461–471.

Klausberger, T., & Somogyi, P. (2008). Neuronal diversity and temporal dynamics: The unity of hippocampal circuit operations. *Science, 321* (5885), 53–57.

Klinke, R., Fruhstorfer, H., & Finkenzeller, P. (1968). Evoked responses as a function of external and stored information. *Electroencephalography and Clinical Neurophysiology, 25*(2), 119–122.

MacNeil, M. A., & Masland, R. H. (1998). Extreme diversity among amacrine cells: Implications for function. *Neuron, 20*(5), 971–982.

Markram, H., Toledo-Rodriguez, M., Wang, Y., Gupta, A., Silberberg, G., & Wu, C. (2004). Interneurons of the neocortical inhibitory system. *Nature Reviews Neuroscience, 5*(10), 793–807.

Masland, R. H. (2001). The fundamental plan of the retina. *Nature Neuroscience, 4*(9), 877–886.

Maunsell, J. H., & Gibson, J. R. (1992). Visual response latencies in striate cortex of the macaque monkey. *Journal of Neurophysiology, 68*(4), 1332–1344.

Meister, M., & Berry, M. J., II. (1999). The neural code of the retina. *Neuron, 22*(3), 435–450.

Munch, T. A., da Silviera, R. A., Siegert, S., Viney, T. J., Awatramani, G. B., & Roska, B. (2009). Approach sensitivity in the retina processed by a multifunctional neural circuit. *Nature Neuroscience, 12*(10), 1308–1316.

Nijhawan, R. (1994). Motion extrapolation in catching. *Nature, 370*(6487), 256–257.

Olveczky, B. P., Baccus, S. A., & Meister, M. (2003). Segregation of object and background motion in the retina. *Nature, 423*(6938), 401–408.

Olveczky, B. P., Baccus, S. A., & Meister, M. (2007). Retinal adaptation to object motion. *Neuron, 56*(4), 689–700.

Passaglia, C., Dodge, F., Herzong, E., Jackson, S., & Barlow, R. (1997). Deciphering a neural code for vision. *Proceedings of the National Academy of Sciences USA, 94*(23), 12649–12654.

Puchalla, J. L., Schneidman, E., Harris, R. A., & Berry, M. J. (2005). Redundancy in the population code of the retina. *Neuron, 46*(3), 493–504.

Rodieck, R. W. (1998). *The first steps in seeing*. Sinauer Associates, Sunderland, MA.

Rogers, R. L., Papanicolaou, A. C., Baumann, S. B., & Eisenberg, H. M. (1992). Late magnetic fields and positive evoked potentials following infrequent and unpredictable omissions of visual stimuli. *Electroencephalography and Clinical Neurophysiology, 83*(2), 146–152.

Schwartz, G., & Berry, M. J., II. (2008). Sophisticated temporal pattern recognition in retinal ganglion cells. *Journal of Neurophysiology, 99*(4), 1787–1798.

Schwartz, G., Harris, R., Shrom, D., & Berry, M. J., II. (2007). Detection and prediction of periodic patterns by the retina. *Nature Neuroscience, 10*(5), 552–554.

Schwartz, G., Taylor, S., Fisher, C., Harris, R., & Berry, M. J., II. (2007). Synchronized firing among retinal ganglion cells signals motion reversal. *Neuron, 55*(6), 958–969.

Segev, R., Puchalla, J., & Berry, M. J., II. (2006). Functional organization of ganglion cells in the salamander retina. *Journal of Neurophysiology, 95*(4), 2277–2292.

Shapley, R. M., & Enroth-Cugell, C. (1984). Visual adaptation and retinal gain controls. *Progress in retinal research*, 1984. 3, 263–346.

Smirnakis, S. M., Berry, M. J., Warland, D. K., Bailek, W., & Meister, M. (1997). Adaptation of retinal processing to image contrast and spatial scale. *Nature, 386*(6620), 69–73.

Srinivasan, M. V., Laughlin, S. B., & Dubs, A. (1982). Predictive coding: a fresh view of inhibition in the retina. *Proceedings of the Royal Society of London B: Biological Sciences, 216*(1205), 427–459.

Sutton, S., Tueting, P., Zubin, J., & John, E. R. (1967). Information delivery and the sensory evoked potential. *Science, 155*(768), 1436–1439.

van Hateren, J. H. (1992). Real and optimal neural images in early vision. *Nature, 360*(6399), 68–70.

Wark, B., Fairhall, A., & Rieke, F. (2009). Timescales of inference in visual adaptation. *Neuron, 61*(5), 750–761.

Wassle, H., Puller, C., Muller, F., & Haverkamp, S. (2009) Cone contacts, mosaics, and territories of bipolar cells in the mouse retina. *Journal of Neuroscience, 29*(1), 106–117.

CHAPTER 23
Making Predictions: A Developmental Perspective

Cristina M. Atance and Laura K. Hanson

Adults think frequently about the future. These thoughts may range from what we will eat for tonight's dinner, what we will pack for an upcoming vacation, or where we will be in our careers several years from now. Bar (2007) argues that such mental projections into the future are an important tool for making predictions. Indeed, it would seem impossible to make an event-based prediction without some capacity to envision how the event will unfold. For example, predicting what we will eat for tonight's dinner is contingent upon envisioning what our day will be like. If we anticipate a long work day filled with teaching and meetings, then our dinner prediction may include leftovers or take-out food, rather than homemade lasagna. Bar (2007) argues that even when our brains are "at rest" (i.e., not engaged in any goal-directed activity) they are continually generating predictions. Making such predictions is adaptive (Suddendorf & Corballis, 1997) because it helps us to prepare for an uncertain future.

Given the ubiquity with which adults think about the future, and the role that such thought might play in generating predictions, an important issue is when the capacity for future thought and predictions emerges in development. In addition, what information do children draw upon to begin to construct notions of the future, and how does this process change with age? To what extent does children's thought about the future rely on their memory for the past? What factors—both cognitive and social—might contribute to children's capacity for future thinking

and making predictions? Do different future-oriented processes require qualitatively different types of predictions?

We address each of these questions in this chapter. In doing so, we argue that the capacity for future-oriented thinking, in the form of expectations, emerges in infancy. We then review findings that show that, by the early preschool years, children begin to construct scripts, which can then be drawn upon to make predictions about the future. However, we argue that preschoolers' conception of the future, and the predictions that they make, extend beyond such scripts. Indeed, as children progress through the preschool years they increasingly take into account the uncertainty and novelty that the future holds. As a result, their conception of the future becomes more flexible, useful, and adaptive.

EXPECTATIONS IN EARLY DEVELOPMENT: THE BASIS FOR MAKING PREDICTIONS?

Developmental research has focused more extensively on children's memories for the past than on their thoughts, or predictions, about the future. Nonetheless, there is research that supports the idea that, from birth, infants' behavior can be described as future oriented. In this section we borrow and extend upon a useful framework developed by Haith (1997) to chart the development of expectations. According to Haith, the simplest form of expectation entails recognizing that what has happened in the past will happen again. To test whether infants recognize this important fact, Haith developed the "Visual Expectation Paradigm," in which infants are presented with a series of pictures that appear and disappear in predictable locations, at predictable times. By 6 weeks of age, babies make anticipatory looks to the location where the picture will next appear, suggesting that they have formed an expectation (Haith, Hazan, & Goodman, 1988). By 2 to 3 months, infants' primitive abilities to form expectations are evidenced by their reduced reaction times to pictures that appear in predictable, versus unpredictable, locations (Haith et al., 1988). These findings support the notion that by early infancy, humans recognize regularities in their environments and use this knowledge to prepare for the future (Haith, 1997).

Although such future-oriented expectations may not qualify as *predictions* per se, they are arguably an important step in the "prediction-making" process. That is, our earliest predictions about the future must rest on the ability to recognize environmental regularities. Nonetheless, as Haith (1997) points out, such early expectations are limited; the next step is to move beyond recognizing repeating patterns and to form expectations based on extrapolations of current trends. For example, adults create scientific models that may use the past as a guide, but they ultimately make predictions about future situations that have no precedent (Haith, 1997). Although infants are clearly incapable of such feats, they do show some ability to make generalizations based on past events.

Baillargeon (2004) reviews findings showing that infants as young as 2.5 months of age look longer at sequences of events in which objects are being covered, placed in containers, or occluded in ways that violate expected outcomes (e.g., the physically impossible event of a tall object being fully occluded by a shorter object). In these studies, increased looking time to an "unexpected" event, as compared to an "expected" event, is taken as evidence that infants have formed an expectation and are surprised when it is violated. In addition to showing that infants form expectations that future events will respect the laws of the physical world (as in the Baillargeon studies),

Téglás, Girotto, Gonzalez, and Bonatti (2007) reported that 12-month-olds expect that, in a future event, the most likely outcome will occur. For example, infants watched a movie in which three red balls and one blue ball bounced inside a container with an open tube at its base (similar to a lottery game draw). The container was then occluded and either the one blue ball, or one of the red balls, exited from it. Infants looked longer at the outcome in which the one blue ball exited. Based on these results, Téglás et al. argued that infants form rational expectations about novel future events based on the possibility of that event occurring, and they do not need to experience outcome frequencies to respond to probabilities and to form expectations.

While infants' expectations in the first year of life may form the building blocks of predictions, Haith (1997) argues that they are nevertheless limited. Most notably, infants' expectations are largely based on information that is perceptually available or, as Haith notes, "…physical actions in a world of objects" (p. 33). Moreover, the infants in the studies just reported seem to be *reacting* to an event in the world—a process that is arguably less sophisticated than *generating* a prediction about the world. However, there exists research on infants' motor planning that suggests that they can anticipate (and possibly even predict) outcomes that are not based on information that is directly perceivable.

For example, McCarty, Clifton, and Collard (1999) presented 9-, 14-, and 19-month-olds with a food-filled spoon, mounted horizontally on two vertical handles. The handle of the spoon was sometimes oriented to the infant's right, and sometimes to the infant's left. Bringing food to the mouth efficiently and without spilling is best achieved by reaching for the handle using a "radial" grip (i.e., an overhand grip in which the thumb is oriented toward the bowl of the spoon). Because most infants in their study were right-hand dominant, of particular interest was how they reached for the spoon when its handle was oriented to the *left* of their midline (or, what the authors referred to as "difficult" trials). Only the 19-month-olds reliably reached for the spoon with their left hands, successfully bringing food to their mouths using the radial grip. In contrast, the 9-month-olds tended to reach with their right hands, thus placing the handle end rather than the bowl end of the spoon in their mouths. Although 14-month-olds often reached with the incorrect hand, they tended to notice the difficulty of placing the spoon in their mouths and so changed their grips prior to completing the action. Arguably, the actions of the 19-month-olds, and possibly the 14-month-olds, reflect "implicit" predictions about how an event will unfold. Specifically, these infants seemed to recognize that grabbing the spoon in an incorrect orientation would not lead to the desirable outcome of actually consuming the food in it. In contrast, the 9-month-olds were unable to predict how the consequences of their actions would affect subsequent outcomes.

It is also during the second year of life that children begin to form expectations based on the experience of others (Haith, 1997). Indeed, many events in our lives are without precedent but can be extrapolated from the events experienced by those around us. If expectations, and eventually predictions, could only be made on the basis of our own past experiences, then we would be incapable of planning for college, buying a first home, or retirement. Luckily, predictions about the future can be made on the basis of analogy—using knowledge about the experiences of others to predict the future (though, interestingly, we may not realize how useful this source of information may be; Gilbert, Killingsworth, Eyre, & Wilson, 2009). There is evidence that this process is also available to very young children.

A well-known example is Bandura's (1965) work, which demonstrates that preschoolers are more likely to imitate modeled behavior when the model has been reinforced, thus showing that they are able to predict future consequences based on the experience of others. More recent research has also shown that infants can tailor their future behavior based on emotional information that they have gleaned from observing the interactions of others (e.g., Repacholi & Meltzoff, 2007; Repacholi, Meltzoff, & Olsen, 2008). For example, Repacholi and Meltzoff devised an "emotion-imitation" procedure in which 18-month-olds watched an adult

(the "emoter") react either with a neutral expression or an angered expression to another adult's action on a particular object. Infants were then given the opportunity to interact with the object while the emoter faced the infant with a pleasant facial expression. Interestingly, infants regulated their actions on the object as a function of the emoter's previous emotional display; if the emoter had reacted negatively to the other adult's action on the object, then the infants tended to avoid imitating this particular action. This finding suggests that infants had formed an expectation of how the emoter would react and tailored their behavior accordingly. Thus, implicit in their thinking may have been the prediction "if 'emoter' got angry with her, 'emoter' might get angry with me."

Finally, very young children are able to form expectations about the world based on their ability to detect the relation between a symbol (e.g., a picture/scale model of a room) and a referent (e.g., the room itself); or what DeLoache (1995; 2000) refers to as "representational insight." For example, DeLoache (2000) showed children various models and pictures that depicted where an object was hidden in a room, and then asked them to retrieve the object in the actual room. By 2.5 years of age, children were able to correctly predict the object's location, as demonstrated by their successful retrieval of it. More recently, Suddendorf (2003) showed that children as young as 2 years of age can use a picture to predict an object's location when the conditions are such that perseverative responding is prevented.

Our discussion of infants' capacity to form expectations is by no means exhaustive but serves to illustrate several important points: *(1)* a future orientation, in the form of expectations, develops shortly after birth; *(2)* infants' expectations gradually become less rooted in the physical world; *(3)* infants and young children form expectations based on their own past experiences, those of others, and on symbols. Although we do not believe that infants' future orientation is akin to adults' capacity to engage in "mental time travel" (e.g., Suddendorf & Corballis, 2007; Tulving, 1985), "prospection" (Buckner & Carroll, 2007), or "simulation" (Schacter, Addis, & Buckner, 2008), it is possible that it forms the building blocks of these abilities.

Using scripts to make predictions

Scripts are spatiotemporally organized sequences that specify the actions, actors, and props most likely to occur during an event (Hudson, Fivush, & Kuebli, 1992; Nelson & Gruendel, 1981). For example, in a restaurant script the typical sequence of events involves sitting down, looking at the menu, ordering food, eating, and paying (Hudson et al., 1992). Children as young as 3 years of age can recount scripts of everyday events. In a "baking cookies" script, a 3-year-old might say, "Well, you bake and eat them" (Nelson & Gruendel, 1981, p. 135). As children age, they include more detail in their scripts, as illustrated by the following "baking cookies" example provided by a 4.5-year-old: "My mommy puts chocolate chips inside the cookies. Then ya put 'em in the oven…Then we take them out, put them on the table, and eat them" (Nelson & Gruendel, 1981, p. 135).

As is clear from the previous examples, children's scripts are temporally organized; that is, they report events in their correct temporal sequence (Hudson et al., 1992). Moreover, after a single experience with an event, children can recount specific, detailed information about this event and can begin to draw on this experience to predict future events (Hudson et al., 1992). For example, after having experienced the event of baking cookies, the next time children bake cookies they can predict that once the cookie dough has been mixed, the dough can be placed in the oven.

Although scripts are a useful source of information for making predictions, they are limited. Because they are necessarily constructed based on our past experiences, we argue that they do not fully incorporate the uncertainty and multiple possibilities that characterize the future. As such, they may result in predictions that are constrained by past experiences and thus lack flexibility. In the following section we review evidence that suggests that throughout the preschool years children's predictions increasingly take into account the uncertainty that is inherent in the future, thus becoming more flexible in their structure.

Beyond scripts: recognizing that the future is uncertain

Atance and O'Neill (2005) devised a task in which 3-year-olds were asked about going on a trip. This particular event was chosen because it is one for which there are many possible outcomes. For instance, in thinking about a trip, one could anticipate such situations as getting hungry, thirsty, or cold. Because the likelihood of each of these situations occurring is unknown, Atance and O'Neill reasoned that, in adults at least, talk about a trip should entail some uncertainty and speculation, and hence less reliance on a script. Of interest was whether this would also characterize young children's talk. Thus, after children were asked to pretend that they would be going on a trip, they were presented with eight items (e.g., juice, food, Band-Aids) that could potentially address a state (e.g., thirst, hunger, or getting hurt) that may arise during their trip. Children were then asked to select three of these items and were afterwards asked to provide explanations for why they had chosen them. Children's responses were coded based on whether they contained a reference to the future, such as "will" "gonna," and "could," and a reference to uncertainty, such as "might" or "if." Across two experiments, 37%–50% of children's explanations referenced future situations (e.g., "when I get hungry") that could arise during their trip. Over half of these explanations also contained an uncertainty marker (e.g., "I might get hurt"), reflecting a nascent understanding that the future is more than a simple recapitulation of the past but is, by nature, uncertain.

The fact that children become increasingly less reliant on scripts when making predictions about the future is nicely demonstrated by Hudson, Shapiro, and Sosa (1995). These authors compared preschool (3-, 4-, and 5-year-old) children's ability to formulate scripts and plans for the familiar events of going to the beach and going grocery shopping. In the "script" condition, children were asked, for example, to "tell me *what happens* when you go to the beach." In contrast, in the "plan" condition, children were asked to "tell me *a plan* for going to the beach." Interestingly, the number of actions children mentioned in the script condition did not increase with age, while the number of actions mentioned in the plan condition did. By age 5, children in the plan condition discussed more preparatory activities in their descriptions (e.g., "You have to bring a beach umbrella so the sun stays out of your face") than children in the script condition, indicating an awareness that planning for an event entails more than simply recounting what typically happens. When presented with potential mishaps, children of all ages were able to provide adequate *remedy* plans. For example, in response to the potential mishap of forgetting your lunch, one child suggested the following remedy plan: "You can get a popsicle from the beach or something" (Hudson et al., 1995, p. 996). However, it was only by age 5 that children were able to provide adequate *prevention* plans to address this mishap (e.g., "Put a cooler out by the front steps," Hudson et al., 1995, p. 996). These data suggest that as children progress through the preschool years, they develop an increased capacity to consider multiple future possibilities, recognize and cope with uncertainty, and make flexible, adaptive predictions about the future.

It is worth noting, however, that Hudson et al. (1995) asked children about familiar events—and thus ones for which children had some level of personal experience. An important question is whether children can make predictions about events that are relatively novel to them. To address this issue, Atance and Meltzoff (2005, Experiment 1) gave children a task that was specifically designed to minimize their reliance on scripts. Three-, 4-, and 5-year-olds were presented with stories and pictorial scenes that depicted novel events, such as walking beside a waterfall, walking through a desert, and hiking up a mountain. Children were then asked to pretend that they would visit these locations and were asked to select one of three items to bring with them. One of these items (e.g., raincoat) was considered to be the correct choice because it could be used to address a future physiological

state (e.g., getting wet), while the other two distracter items (e.g., money, blanket) could not.

Three-, 4-, and 5-year-olds chose the correct item on 74%, 91%, and 97% of the scenarios, respectively. Although this was a significant age-related increase, all age groups chose the correct item more often than would be expected by chance. Children's ability to provide explanations that referenced future states (e.g., "I might get thirsty") also increased with age, with 4- and 5-year-olds doing so significantly more often than 3-year-olds. These results suggest that by 4 years of age, children are able to predict needs that might arise during relatively novel future events. However, it is important to acknowledge that, even in this task, children likely used their script-based knowledge to help guide their choices for the future. That is, although most children had probably not wandered in front of a waterfall, they could nevertheless draw upon their knowledge of going outside on a rainy day to alert them of their need for a raincoat.

One final study that supports the claim that children's predictions about the future become more flexible and less "script bound" with age was conducted by Quon and Atance (2010). This study compared 3-, 4-, and 5-year-olds' ability to remember past events ("past" condition), talk about how events typically unfold ("semantic" or "script" condition), and pre-experience events ("future" condition). The design of the study was between-subjects so that children's responses to one type of question would not influence their responses to another. Children were asked about everyday events such as "breakfast," "going grocery shopping," and "bedtime." In the past condition, children were asked, for example, "What did you eat for breakfast this morning?" in the semantic condition, "What do you eat for breakfast?" and, in the future condition, "What are you going to eat for breakfast tomorrow?" In addition to asking parents to rate the accuracy of their children's responses, Quon and Atance coded responses for what they termed "script indicators" (verbs in the present tense, e.g., "eat" and "go," and words denoting how the event typically unfolds, e.g., "usually" and "always"). They did so to specifically address the hypothesis that younger children would include more of these indicators in their talk about the future than older children, suggesting that younger children are more reliant on scripts when pre-experiencing a future event. Results were consistent with this hypothesis; 5-year-olds used marginally fewer script indicators in their future talk than did 3-year-olds (the 4-year-olds did not differ from either the 3- or 5-year-olds).

The research reviewed in this section suggests that younger children tend to draw more heavily on scripts to make predictions about the future than do older children. Although doing so may initially be highly adaptive because it allows children to begin to make sense of the future, there are likely to be contexts in which such reliance on scripts is detrimental. In the next section, we discuss evidence supporting this claim. In addition, we discuss other contexts that lead children to experience difficulties in making accurate predictions about the future.

FAILURES TO MAKE ACCURATE PREDICTIONS

Recall that Atance and Meltzoff (2005) assessed whether children could anticipate a future physiological state (e.g., getting wet) and then select an item (e.g., raincoat) that could be used to address this state. Although 3-year-olds were proficient at choosing the correct item, they did not tend to explain their choices by making reference to a future state. In contrast, older children's explanations were predominantly future oriented. These findings led Atance and Meltzoff to hypothesize that 3-year-olds may have selected the correct items by making a semantic/thematic association between the scene depicted in the photograph and the correct item. For example, in the "desert" scenario (depicting sand and sun), children may simply have chosen "sunglasses" (the correct choice in this case) because sunglasses are frequently associated with a sunny desert. This process is different from *mentally projecting* oneself into the future to predict a specific need. Thus, in a second experiment, each scenario also included an item that was "associated" with the scene, but that did not address a future state of the self. For example, in the desert scenario, children were asked to choose between sunglasses (correct choice), soap

(distracter item), and a seashell ("semantic associate"). Atance and Meltzoff hypothesized that presenting children with an item that is associated with a scenario, but that does not address a future state of the self, would negatively impact the performance of the 3-year-olds. In other words, if these younger children predominantly rely on scripts to make predictions about the future, then falling prey to the semantic associate is expected.

Results were consistent with this prediction. Whereas in Experiment 1, all three age groups chose the correct item for each scenario at a higher than chance level, for a number of scenarios in Experiment 2, the 3- and 4-year-olds chose the semantic associate as often as the correct item. The performance of the 5-year-olds, in contrast, was not affected by the introduction of the semantic associates. This finding suggests that during the early preschool years children's decisions about a future event are influenced by their knowledge of the thematic structure of an event, rather than by their *predictions* of how they may feel during that event.

Other contexts in which young children experience difficulty making predictions about the future are ones in which they must anticipate a future state that differs from a current one. Both Suddendorf and Corballis (2007) and Tulving (2005) argue that the essence of mental time travel into the future is acting in the present to address a future state that is not currently being experienced (e.g., securing food for the future when one is currently satiated). Although there is debate about whether this criterion should be a defining feature of mental time travel into the future (or "foresight") (Atance & Meltzoff, 2007; Bar, 2007; Raby & Clayton, 2009), it is certainly an adaptive feature of human cognition, and one that does not appear to develop until at least the fifth year of life.

Suddendorf and Busby (2005) designed the following paradigm to test this capacity: First, children spent several minutes in an "empty room." In the experimental condition, this room contained a puzzle board with no pieces, whereas in the control condition no item was present. Children were then led to an "active room," which contained the puzzle pieces and several distracter items (crayons, a coin, and a paint-brush). Following a 5-minute period in the active room, children were asked to choose one item to bring with them to the empty room. The 4- and 5-year-olds in the experimental condition were more likely to select the target item (i.e., puzzle pieces) than children in the control condition. In contrast, 50% of 3-year-olds in both conditions chose the puzzle pieces. This suggests that only the older children were acting in the present to address a future state of the self (e.g., boredom, or the need to play with something) that they were not currently experiencing.

Atance and Meltzoff (2006) also designed a paradigm that measured the extent to which children could anticipate a future state that differed from their current one. Three-, 4-, and 5-year-olds were assigned to one of four conditions. In two of these conditions, children's current state of thirst was manipulated by giving them pretzels to eat, while in the other two conditions, it was not (i.e., no pretzels were given). Subsequently, one group of children who were given pretzels were asked whether they would like to have water or pretzels for *right now*, while the other group was asked whether they would like to have water or pretzels for *tomorrow*. The groups of children who were not given pretzels were also asked to choose between water and pretzels for *right now* or *tomorrow*. Despite children's overwhelming desire for pretzels in the baseline (no pretzels given) conditions (83% in both), children in both intervention conditions (pretzels given) predominantly chose water, whether choosing for *right now* (75%) or for *tomorrow* (92%).

The fact that most children in the intervention condition who were asked about *tomorrow* chose water suggests that they had difficulty overriding their current desire to predict that pretzels would likely be desirable again the next day. Interestingly, there were no age differences detected. Although this could be due to a lack of sensitivity of the particular measure used, it is important to note that adults show a similar bias in their reasoning, as evidenced by their overreliance on current states when making decisions about the future (e.g., Gilbert, Gill, & Wilson, 2002; Nisbett & Kanouse, 1969; Read & van Leeuwen, 1998).

THE RELATION BETWEEN PREDICTIONS AND EPISODIC MEMORY

Implicit in our discussion thus far is the notion that children's memory/understanding of the past plays an important role in their capacity to make predictions about the future. In fact, the strong hypothesis is that without any knowledge of the past, children could not make predictions about the future. In this chapter, we have mainly focused on the role of scripts in children's predictions about the future. Because scripts are constructed based on general knowledge about the world, one could characterize them as reflecting semantic memory. However, it is also important to consider the role that episodic memory may play in the prediction-making process. In fact, several well-known neuropsychological case studies suggest that having relatively intact semantic knowledge is not sufficient to allow an individual to mentally project into his or her personal future (e.g., Klein, Loftus, & Kihlstrom, 2002; Tulving, 2005). In addition, recent studies using functional magnetic resonance imaging (fMRI) show substantial overlap in the brain regions activated when individuals recount a specific past experience and pre-experience a specific future one (e.g., Addis, Wong, & Schacter, 2007; Okuda et al., 2003; Szpunar, Watson, & McDermott, 2007).

The developmental data with respect to this overlap are less conclusive, however. Interestingly, in an early chapter about the origins of future orientation in young children, Benson (1994) describes language data that support various alternative claims: *(a)* that the past is understood before the future (e.g., children learn the term "yesterday" before the term "tomorrow"); *(b)* that the future is understood before the past (e.g., children's spontaneous expressions pertain mainly to the present, then to the present and future, and then to the present, future, and past); and *(c)* that both the past and the future are understood simultaneously. This last view is most consistent with studies by Busby and Suddendorf (2005) and Suddendorf (2010). In the former, 3- to 5-year-olds were asked to recount an event that occurred yesterday and one that would occur tomorrow (parents were asked to rate the accuracy of children's responses). In Experiment 1, 3- and 4-year-olds' accuracy on both questions was positively correlated, with no difference in difficulty between each. In Experiment 2, which also included 5-year-olds, there was no significant correlation between performance on past and future questions, and the two questions were not found to differ in their level of difficulty. More recently, Suddendorf reported a significant correlation both between 3- and 4-year-olds' capacity to report an event that occurred yesterday and one that would occur tomorrow and the quantity of events that were generated in response to both of these time frames.

Finally, Quon and Atance (2010) found that preschoolers were no more accurate in recounting a specific event from their pasts (e.g., the last time they went to the park) than they were in pre-experiencing a specific event in their futures (e.g., the next time they would go to the park). Thus, as a whole, these findings do not provide strong support for the claim that children develop the capacity to think about specific past events before specific future events. They are most consistent with the claim that re-experiencing the past and pre-experiencing the future draw on similar cognitive mechanisms but, even here, additional developmental research is needed to cement this conclusion.

WHAT FACTORS CONTRIBUTE TO CHILDREN'S FORMULATION OF PREDICTIONS?

We have mainly focused on how children's scripts put them on the path to developing an understanding of the future and formulating predictions. However, there are a number of other factors that likely contribute to these processes. One such factor may be conversations with parents. Because time is not a physical entity to be discovered in the world, learning about it must rely on its social construction from language (Nelson, 1996). Indeed, a number of studies have shown that social interaction is critical to the emergence of autobiographical memory (e.g., Farrant & Reese, 2000; Fivush, 1991; Nelson, 1993).

It is possible that children come to understand the future (and make predictions) via a similar mechanism. Hudson (2006) examined how the content and themes in mothers' talk about future events impact their children's future talk. Mothers were asked to talk to their 2.5- and 4-year-old children about familiar and novel future events. Hudson found that the more elaborative (e.g., referring to new information about the event being discussed) and advanced (e.g., using hypothetical or temporal terms, as in "tomorrow, we might go to the beach") language the mothers used to talk about the future events, the more their children were able to contribute to conversations about the future. In addition, the extent to which mothers incorporated temporal language into their talk about future events contributed to their children's understanding of temporal language and temporal concepts. Finally, by making reference to the past and to general knowledge during the conversation (e.g., "What did you do the last time you went to the playground?"), mothers provided cues that helped increase children's contributions and predictions (Hudson, 2006). Interestingly, the type of event being discussed (i.e., familiar vs. novel) did not affect children's participation in making predictions about the future. When talking about novel events, mothers simply made more hypothetical references and predictions to compensate for their children's lack of prior knowledge. These results suggest that children's capacity to make predictions is facilitated by their social interactions and conversations with the people in their world.

The process of making predictions is partly motivated by our need to prepare ourselves for the future and to gain (some) control over how the future will unfold. However, young children have only limited input about what happens in their lives, because many of their daily activities are determined by others. Thus, children may not always be motivated to make predictions because these may have no bearing on how the future events in their lives unfold. Nonetheless, Quon and Atance (2010) hypothesized that young children have more control over certain events in their lives and that, in turn, their predictions about these events will be more accurate than those about events over which they exert little control.

This hypothesis was tested by having parents rate the amount of control (or "input") that their children had over eight different events (e.g., breakfast, eating at a restaurant, supper, going grocery shopping). Based on these parental reports, events were categorized as either "high" or "low" control. When asked about the next time that they would engage in each of these events (e.g., "What are you going to eat for breakfast tomorrow?"), children's predictions were more accurate for the high-control, as compared to the low-control, events. Thus, it seems that children's ability to make predictions might develop in part in response to having control over events in their lives, which in turn allows them to make choices and anticipate future instances of these events.

Inhibitory control may also influence children's capacity to make accurate predictions. Indeed, Bar (2009) argues that "... inhibition can play a powerful role in helping the selective activation of only the most relevant representations as predictions...A lack of inhibition might cause overly broad associative activations and therefore unhelpful, non-specific, predictions" (p. 1240). This may also be true from a developmental perspective. For example, the 3- and 4-year-olds in Atance and Meltzoff's (2005) study who were unable to resist choosing the semantic associates in Experiment 2 may have had difficulty inhibiting the thematic link between the object and the scene in question. This interpretation is consistent with the finding that children's executive functioning skills (including inhibitory control) show marked development during the preschool years (e.g., Carlson & Moses, 2001).

However, the extent to which inhibitory control influences children's ability to make predictions may also depend on the particular task requirements. For example, when children must override a current state to consider a future one (a criterion of Atance and Meltzoff's, 2006, study), inhibitory control may be especially important. But, as noted earlier, it is not clear whether all forms of future thinking need meet this specific criterion. For example, a 3-year-old who has difficulty talking about/predicting what will happen tomorrow may not be limited in her inhibitory control skills but, rather, as Quon and Atance (2010) argue, may lack control over how this event will unfold and may therefore be less apt to make a prediction about it.

Finally, children's developing theory of mind (ToM) skills may also influence their ability to make predictions. Theory of mind is described as the ability to understand and attribute mental states to self and others (Premack & Woodruff, 1978). A number of researchers have argued that the ability to mentally project oneself into the future, an essential aspect of making predictions, is related to ToM and, specifically, to the understanding that others can have different perspectives from one's own (Atance & O'Neill, 2005; Moore, Barresi, & Thompson, 1998; Suddendorf & Corballis, 1997). When projecting oneself into the future to make a prediction, an individual must adopt the perspective of a *future* self, rather than that of *another person*. Similar to theory of mind, future-oriented thinking involves a shift from the immediate, current perspective to an alternative perspective (Buckner & Carroll, 2007). As such, future thinking likely relies at least partially on ToM ability. Consistent with this claim is the finding that there is an overlap in the brain structures underlying these two forms of perspective taking (Buckner & Carroll, 2007). In addition, both future-thinking and ToM skills emerge during the preschool years (e.g., Atance & Jackson, 2009; Wellman & Liu, 2004), although these skills have not been tested on the same group of children to determine whether they are indeed correlated.

Because both inhibitory control and ToM may play an important role in making predictions, it follows that individuals who are impaired in these skills will also be impaired in making predictions. This hypothesis can be explored in children with autism, since these children show deficits in both their ToM and inhibitory control skills (Baron-Cohen, Leslie, & Frith, 1985; Hill, 2004). Jackson and Atance (2008) investigated how children with autism performed on two types of tasks that required making predictions about simple event sequences. In the first type of prediction task that the authors labeled "self-based," children were required to reason about a sequence of events that explicitly involved the self. For example, children were shown an "ant" costume that consisted of an ant "body" (a t-shirt with straw "legs" affixed to the front) and an ant "head" (a hat with two long straw "antennae" attached to the top). Children were then told to pretend that they were going to put on the ant costume and were asked which piece they should put on first. The correct response, "ant body," required children to predict that this part of the costume would not fit over the ant head (because of its long antennae) and thus needed to be put on first. In the second type of prediction task that the authors labeled "mechanical-based," children were required to reason about a sequence of events that involved a purely physical transformation. For example, children were shown an inclined ramp with a large tube at the top and a small tube attached below it. They were then shown two balls—a large one and a small one—and asked which ball they should place into the top tube (i.e., the large one) to knock over a domino that was positioned at the exit of the small tube. The correct response (i.e., the small ball) required children to predict that the large ball would get stuck in the small tube, and thus fail to knock over the domino.

Children with autism scored significantly lower on the self-based tasks than on the mechanical-based tasks, suggesting that they were better able to make predictions about an outcome that involved a physical transformation than one that involved a transformation of the self (typically developing children were also tested in this study and showed no difference in performance on the two types of tasks). Because the tasks were relatively well matched in terms of inhibitory control requirements (i.e., in the ant costume task, children had to inhibit their preference for the more interesting "ant head," and in the ramp task, they had to inhibit their preference to put the large ball into the large tube), Jackson and Atance (2008) argued that performance differences were likely a function of the children with autism's ToM deficits, resulting in a difficulty with projecting into the future to pre-experience an event involving the self.

THE IMPORTANCE OF PREDICTIONS IN CHILDREN'S FUTURE ORIENTATION

It is likely that the capacity to make predictions is crucial to several aspects of children's future orientation, including delay of gratification, prospective memory, and planning. In a classic delay-of-gratification paradigm (e.g., Mischel, Shoda, & Rodriguez, 1989), children are shown a pair of rewards that differ in value (e.g., one vs. two marshmallows) and are then asked to indicate which reward they prefer. Not surprisingly, nearly all children choose the reward of greater value (i.e., two marshmallows). It is then explained to children that they can have the less desirable reward immediately, or that they can wait to obtain the larger reward. This wait period typically lasts between 5 and 15 minutes while children are left alone with the rewards visible to them. The ability to delay gratification in this and similar contexts increases with age (e.g., Mischel et al., 1989; Moore et al., 1998; Thompson, Barresi, & Moore, 1997). The delay of gratification task is described as measuring children's "future-oriented self-control" (Mischel et al., 1989), but it can also be conceptualized as assessing children's ability to make predictions about their future feelings. That is, children who can delay gratification are presumably able to predict that receiving the larger reward later will make them happier than receiving the smaller reward immediately.

Prospective memory is defined as remembering to perform an action at some point in the future (Kerns, 2000). Although described as a form of memory, it is very much a future-oriented process. That is, to remember to perform a required task, one must make a prediction about the future event in question. For example, if a person needs to remember to call a friend before leaving the house, then leaving a portable phone by the front door is a good strategy to trigger memory for this intention. Importantly, this particular strategy may rely on predicting that one will exit by the front door, see the phone, and make the necessary call. Children's prospective memory increases between the ages of 3 and 5 (Atance & Jackson, 2009; Guajardo & Best, 2000) and continues to develop throughout early childhood (Kvavilashvili, Messer, & Ebdon, 2001). As we hypothesized to be the case with delay of gratification, it is possible that children's developing prospective memory skills are partly influenced by their ability to both envision future events and predict how they will unfold.

Planning ability is generally described as involving the representation of, and preparation for, a future goal. Predictions likely form an integral part of the planning process. However, the types of predictions that are made may depend on the particular planning task at hand. For example, in the commonly used Tower of Hanoi task (Klahr & Robinson, 1981), individuals must make a prediction about the outcome of a series of moves that unfold in a particular spatiotemporal sequence. Although the goal (i.e., matching the experimenter's structure) is perceptually available, predicting the sequence of moves necessary to achieve it is a challenging task for young children. Indeed, most 3- and 4-year-olds do not often progress beyond two-disk problems that require two moves to solve (Atance & Jackson, 2009; Carlson, Moses, & Claxton, 2004).

The predictions that children must make in the Tower of Hanoi task differ substantially from those required in other tasks that rely on some level of planning or predicting. For example, if we consider Atance and Meltzoff's (2005) "anticipation of physiological states" task and Busby and Suddendorf's (2005) "tomorrow" task, children can draw in part on memories of the past to formulate their plans/predictions about the future. It is unlikely that this mechanism is available to children for solving the Tower of Hanoi, since this task is a completely novel problem. Moreover, the predictions that must be made in this task do not require mentally projecting the self into the future but, as mentioned, imagining a particular spatiotemporal sequence. These differences imply that the capacity to make predictions in these contexts may not be related.

Support for this argument was provided by Atance and Jackson (2009). Although these authors found that Atance and Meltzoff's (2005) and Busby and Suddendorf's (2005) tasks (categorized as reflecting "mental time travel") were correlated with one another, once the effects of

age and language had been controlled for neither task was correlated with children's performance on the Tower of Hanoi. Atance and Jackson also assessed children's delay of gratification and prospective memory abilities and found that these too were uncorrelated with the mental time travel tasks (again, once the effects of age and language were controlled for). These findings suggest that although all of these types of tasks might rely on the ability to make predictions and contemplate the future, the nature of these predictions is different. These differences include the extent to which children need to draw on past experiences, and the extent to which the self is mentally projected into a future situation.

Conclusions and future directions

In this chapter, we have argued that children's capacity to make predictions undergoes significant developments during the first 5 years of life. The groundwork for making predictions may begin as early as the first few months of life, during which infants develop future-oriented expectations about previously experienced event sequences. By the early preschool years children have become adept at constructing scripts that contain information about how events typically unfold, which can then be used to predict how these same events will unfold the next time. However, with age, children's predictions become more flexible and also begin to incorporate the uncertainty that is inherent in the future—processes that we believe reflect less reliance on script-based knowledge. Identifying the particular factors that allow for this shift is an important question for future research. It will also be important to distinguish between the different forms that predictions about the future may take, and how these may draw on different cognitive capacities. For example, preliminary findings with children with autism suggest that predictions about the "psychological" world rely on different mechanisms than predictions about the "physical" world. Finally, the extent to which various future-oriented behaviors, including delaying gratification and planning, rely on the capacity to make predictions (and, again, the particular form that these predictions may take) is also an important direction for future research.

REFERENCES

Addis, D. R., Wong, A. T., & Schacter, D. L. (2007). Remembering the past and imagining the future: Common and distinct neural substrates during event construction and elaboration. *Neuropsychologia, 45,* 1363–1377.

Atance, C. M., & Jackson, L. K. (2009). The development and coherence of future-oriented behaviors during the preschool years. *Journal of Experimental Child Psychology, 102,* 379–391.

Atance, C. M., & Meltzoff, A. N. (2005). My future self: Young children's ability to anticipate and explain future states. *Cognitive Development, 20,* 341–361.

Atance, C. M., & Meltzoff, A. N. (2006). Preschoolers' current desires warp their choices for the future. *Psychological Science, 17,* 583–587.

Atance, C. M., & Meltzoff, A. N. (2007). How developmental science contributes to theories of future thinking. *Behavioral and Brain Sciences, 30,* 314–315.

Atance, C. M., & O'Neill, D. K. (2005). Preschoolers' talk about future situations. *First Language, 25,* 5–18.

Baillargeon, R. (2004). Infants' physical world. *Current Directions in Psychological Science, 13,* 89–94.

Bandura, A. (1965). Influence of models' reinforcement contingencies on the acquisition of imitative responses. *Journal of Personality and Social Psychology, 1,* 589–595.

Bar, M. (2007). The proactive brain: Using analogies and associations to generate predictions. *Trends in Cognitive Sciences, 11,* 280–289.

Bar, M. (2009). The proactive brain: Memory for predictions. *Philosophical Transactions of the Royal Society of London, 364,* 1235–1243.

Baron-Cohen, S., Leslie, A. M., & Frith, U. (1985). Does the autistic child have a "theory of mind"? *Cognition, 21,* 37–46.

Benson, J. B. (1994). The origins of future orientation in the everyday lives of 9- to 36-month-old infants. In M. M. Haith, J. B. Benson, R. J. Roberts, Jr., & B. F. Pennington (Eds.), *The development of future-oriented processes* (pp. 375–407). Chicago: University of Chicago Press.

Buckner, R. L. & Carroll, D. C. (2007). Self-projection and the brain. *Trends in Cognitive Sciences, 11,* 49–57.

Busby, J., & Suddendorf, T. (2005). Recalling yesterday and predicting tomorrow. *Cognitive Development, 20,* 362–372.

Carlson, S. M., & Moses, L .J. (2001). Individual differences in inhibitory control and children's theory of mind. *Child Development, 72,* 1032–1053.

Carlson, S. M., Moses, L. J., & Claxton, L. J. (2004). Individual differences in executive functioning and theory of mind: An investigation of inhibitory control and planning ability. *Journal of Experimental Child Psychology, 87,* 299–319.

DeLoache, J. S. (1995). Early understanding and use of symbols: The model model. *Current Directions in Psychological Science, 4,* 109–113.

DeLoache, J. S. (2000). Dual representation and young children's use of scale models. *Child Development, 71,* 329–338.

Farrant, K., & Reese, E. (2000). Maternal style and children's participation in reminiscing: Stepping stones in children's autobiographical memory. *Journal of Cognition and Development, 1,* 193–225.

Fivush, R. (1991). The social construction of personal narratives. *Merrill-Palmer Quarterly, 37,* 59–81.

Gilbert, D. T., Gill, M. J., & Wilson, T. D. (2002). The future is now: Temporal correction in affective forecasting. *Organizational Behavior and Human Decision Processes, 88,* 690–700.

Gilbert, D. T., Killingsworth, M. A., Eyre, R. N., & Wilson, T. D. (2009). The surprising power of neighborly advice. *Science, 323,* 1617–1619.

Guajardo, N. R., & Best, D. L. (2000). Do preschoolers remember what to do? Incentive and external cues in prospective memory. *Cognitive Development, 15,* 75–97.

Haith, M. M. (1997). The development of future thinking as essential for the emergence of skill in planning. In S. L. Friedman & E. K. Scholnick (Eds.), *The developmental psychology of planning: Why, how, and when do we plan?* (pp. 25–42). Mahwah, NJ: Erlbaum.

Haith, M. M., Hazan, C., & Goodman, G. S. (1988). Expectation and anticipation of dynamic visual events by 3.5-month-old babies. *Child Development, 59,* 467–479.

Hill, E. L. (2004). Executive dysfunction in autism. *Trends in Cognitive Sciences, 8,* 26–32.

Hudson, J. A. (2006). The development of future time concepts through mother-child conversations. *Merrill-Palmer Quarterly, 52,* 70–95.

Hudson, J. A., Fivush, R., & Kuebli, J. (1992). Scripts and episodes: The development of event memory. *Applied Cognitive Psychology, 6,* 483–505.

Hudson, J. A., Shapiro, L. R., & Sosa, B. B. (1995). Planning in the real world: Preschool children's scripts and plans for familiar events. *Child Development, 66,* 984–998.

Jackson, L. K., & Atance, C. M. (2008). Future thinking in children with autism spectrum disorders: A pilot study. *Journal on Developmental Disabilities, 14,* 40–45.

Kerns, K. A. (2000). The CyberCruiser: An investigation of development of prospective memory in children. *Journal of the International Neuropsychological Society, 6,* 62–70.

Klahr, D., & Robinson, M. (1981). Formal assessment of problem-solving and planning processes in preschool children. *Cognitive Psychology, 13,* 113–148.

Klein, S. B., Loftus, J., & Kihlstrom, J. F. (2002). Memory and temporal experience: The effects of episodic memory loss on an amnesic patient's ability to remember the past and imagine the future. *Social Cognition, 20,* 353–379.

Kvavilashvili, L., Messer, D. J., & Ebdon, P. (2001). Prospective memory in children: The effects of age and task interruption. *Developmental Psychology, 37,* 418–430.

McCarty, M. E., Clifton, R. K., & Collard, R. R. (1999). Problem solving in infancy: The emergence of an action plan. *Developmental Psychology, 35,* 1091–1101.

Mischel, W., Shoda, Y., & Rodriguez, M. L. (1989). Delay of gratification in children. *Science, 244,* 933–938.

Moore, C., Barresi, J., & Thompson, C. (1998). The cognitive basis of future-oriented prosocial behaviour. *Social Development, 7,* 198–218.

Nelson, K. (1993). The psychological and social origins of autobiographic memory. *Psychological Science, 4,* 1–8.

Nelson, K. (1996). *Language in cognitive development: The emergence of the mediated mind.* New York: Cambridge University Press.

Nelson, K., & Gruendel, J. (1981). Generalized event representations: Basic building blocks of cognitive development. In M. E. Lamb & A. L. Brown (Eds.), *Advances in developmental psychology.* (Vol. 1, pp. 21–46). Hillsdale, NJ: Erlbaum.

Nisbett, R. E., & Kanouse, D. E. (1969). Obesity, food deprivation, and supermarket shopping behavior. *Journal of Personality and Social Psychology, 12,* 289–294.

Okuda, J., Fujii, T., Ohtake, H., Tsukiura, T., Tanji, K., Suzuki, K., et al. (2003). Thinking of the future and past: The roles of the frontal pole and the medial temporal lobes. *Neuroimage, 19,* 1369–1380.

Premack, D., & Woodruff, G. (1978). Does the chimpanzee have a theory of mind? *Behavioral and Brain Sciences, 1,* 515–526.

Quon, E., & Atance, C. M. (2010). A comparison of preschoolers' memory, knowledge, and anticipation of events. *Journal of Cognition and Development, 11,* 37–60.

Raby, C. R., & Clayton, N. S. (2009). Prospective cognition in animals. *Behavioural Processes, 80,* 314–324.

Read, D., & van Leeuwen, B. (1998). Predicting hunger: The effects of appetite and delay on choice. *Organizational Behavior and Human Decision Processes, 76,* 189–205.

Repacholi, B. M., & Meltzoff, A. N. (2007). Emotional eavesdropping: Infants selectively respond to indirect emotional signals. *Child Development, 78,* 503–521.

Repacholi, B. M., Meltzoff, A. N., & Olsen, B. (2008). Infants' understanding of the link between visual perception and emotion: "If she can't see me doing it, she won't get angry" *Developmental Psychology, 44,* 561–574.

Schacter, D. L., Addis, D. R., & Buckner, R. L. (2008). Episodic simulation of future events: Concepts, data, and application. *Annals of the New York Academy of Sciences, Special Issue: The Year in Cognitive Neuroscience, 1124,* 39–60.

Suddendorf, T. (2003). Early representational insight: Twenty-four-month-olds can use a photo to find an object in the world. *Child Development, 74,* 896–904.

Suddendorf, T. (2010). Linking yesterday and tomorrow: Preschooler's ability to report temporally displaced events. *British Journal of Developmental Psychology, 28,* 491–498.

Suddendorf, T., & Busby, J. (2005). Making decisions with the future in mind: Developmental and comparative identification of mental time travel. *Learning and Motivation, 36,* 110–125.

Suddendorf, T., & Corballis, M. C. (1997). Mental time travel and the evolution of the human mind. *Genetic, Social, and General Psychology Monographs, 123,* 133–167.

Suddendorf, T., & Corballis, M. C. (2007). The evolution of foresight: What is mental time travel, and is it unique to humans? *Behavioral and Brain Sciences, 30*, 299–313.

Szpunar, K. K., Watson, J. M., & McDermott, K. B. (2007). Neural substrates of envisioning the future. *Proceedings of the National Academy of Sciences, 104*, 642–647.

Téglás, E., Girotto, V., Gonzalez, M., & Bonatti, L. (2007). Intuitions of probabilities shape expectations about the future at 12 months and beyond. *Proceedings of the National Academy of Sciences, 104*, 19156–19159.

Thompson, C., Barresi, J., & Moore, C. (1997). The development of future-oriented prudence and altruism in preschoolers. *Cognitive Development, 12*, 199–212.

Tulving, E. (1972). Episodic and semantic memory. In E. Tulving (Ed.), *Organization of memory* (pp. 381–403). New York: Academic Press.

Tulving, E. (1985). Memory and consciousness. *Canadian Psychology, 26*, 1–12.

Tulving, E. (2005). Episodic memory and autonoesis: Uniquely human? In H. S. Terrace, & J. Metcalfe (Eds.), *The missing link in cognition: Origins of self-reflective consciousness* (pp. 3–56). New York: Oxford University Press.

Wellman, H. M., & Liu, D. (2004). Scaling theory-of-mind tasks. *Child Development, 75*, 523–541.

CHAPTER 24
Prospective Decision Making in Animals: A Potential Role for Intertemporal Choice in the Study of Prospective Cognition

Lucy G. Cheke, James M. Thom, and Nicola S. Clayton

Animals regularly engage in future-oriented behaviors, from nest-building to hibernation. Clearly these behaviors are functionally prospective, but the extent to which they are controlled by cognitive processes remains an open question. Migrating birds, for example, travel long distances to avoid cold winters, without ever having experienced a winter, warmer climates, or the dangers of travel. These birds are unable to *know* what it is they are avoiding and why this course of action benefits them. Indeed, when two bird populations with different migratory paths are cross-bred, the resulting offspring migrate in a direction halfway between that of their parents (Berthold, Heilbig, Mohr, & Querner, 1992), suggesting that direction of migration is genetically determined. From this example we can see that not all prospective behaviour can be considered to involve awareness of the future, but may instead be an automatic responses to natural (e.g., seasonal changes in day length or hormones), or learned, cues.

Much of the recent literature has focused on identifying behaviors that demonstrate what Suddendorf and Corballis (2007) term a "declarative" future concept: an awareness of a future time, or as we shall herein refer to it, prospective cognition. This endeavor has encountered two main difficulties. The first problem is ruling out behaviors that have no need for *any* prospective

cognition (e.g., migration), and the second is determining what *type* of prospective cognition underlies a given behavior. Predominantly, this means differentiating between behaviors resulting from a representation of a generalized rule-based future and those that arise from a detailed, contextualized representation of a specific future event.

EPISODIC VERSUS SEMANTIC PROSPECTIVE COGNITION

Anyone who has watched a cat lie in wait outside a mouse-hole can have no doubt that this creature has some kind of anticipation of events yet to come. However, it has proven difficult to unambiguously demonstrate *awareness* of a future time, ruling out alternative explanations (e.g. Mulcahy & Call, 2006; Raby, Alexis, Dickinson, & Clayton, 2007).

Most animal prospection research has looked for one particular form of prospective cognition: the ability to imagine oneself in a future scenario, termed "episodic future thinking" (Atance & O'Neill, 2001) or "episodic prospection," which constitutes the prospective element of "mental time travel" (Suddendorf & Corballis, 1997). Mental time travel (MTT) describes the ability to "transport at will into the personal past, as well as into the future" (Tulving, 1993 p. 67)— to re-experience or pre-experience episodes in personal time. There is now considerable evidence supporting a common mechanism underlying these processes. Episodic recollection of the past and episodic future thinking engage common mental processes (Schacter, Addis, & Buckner, 2007), involve the same neural substrates (Addis, Wong, & Schacter, 2007), are impaired in the same patients (Hassabis, Kumaran, Vann, & Maguire, 2007b; Tulving, 1985), develop simultaneously in children (Suddendorf & Busby, 2003, 2005), and decline at the same time in the elderly (Addis, Wong, & Schacter, 2008). However, episodic prospection is not the only form that prospective cognition can take.

Tulving (1972, 1985) contrasts "episodic" memory for specific life events and "semantic" memory for timeless facts, capturing this distinction by showing that episodically retrieved events are "remembered" while semantically retrieved events are "known." Raby and Clayton (2009) differentiate between two analogous types of prospective cognition, "semantic" and "episodic" prospection. They describe semantic prospection as the ability to represent a generalized future based on one's previous experience of the world, and of regularly occurring events. Such a distinction is supported by several lines of evidence. Episodic amnesic patients who can describe likely events in the public domain, or in generalized scenarios such as visiting a restaurant, are unable to envisage episodes in their personal future and report a feeling of blankness when asked to do so (Atance & O'Neill, 2001; Klein, Loftus, & Kihlstrom, 2002; Tulving, 2005). Furthermore, it seems that thinking about the self in the future may involve different brain regions and develop later in infancy than contemplating episodes in someone else's future. Brain regions activated during both episodic recall and imagination of oneself in a future scenario are significantly less active while imagining a familiar individual in that scenario (Szpunar, Watson, & McDermott, 2007), while young children appear to develop the ability to plan for the future needs of another child at a younger age than the ability to plan for their own future needs (Russell, Alexis, & Clayton, 2010).

This idea of a plurality of prospective mechanisms has great appeal, and the argument for a framework in which episodic simulation is complemented by non-episodic processes appears to be strong. However, the concept of a "semantic cognitive system," responsible for both decontextualized knowledge of the world, as well as the use of this information to form future-oriented plans, seems to be poorly defined. Certainly the evidence for a dissociation between episodic and semantic memory is convincing, and the use of semantic knowledge in executing prospective behavior is very plausible. However, while episodic simulation appears to engage certain component processes of episodic memory, there are only sparse links between semantic memory mechanisms and non-episodic planning. As Raby and Clayton note, there is no necessary dissociation between the content of episodic and semantic memories, so we shall hesitate in labeling any prospective system as "semantic" simply because it utilizes overlapping stores with semantic memory. To err on the side of caution, therefore, we shall refer to these components as "episodic" and "non-episodic" prospective cognition hereafter.

It is one thing to acknowledge a distinction between the different types of prospective cognition, but another to distinguish between these type of cognition and identify which of them is involved in the control of any given behavior.

What constitutes episodic prospection?

As yet there is only one coherent theory for the identification of episodic prospection in animals. Suddendorf and Corballis (1997, 2007) argue that for an animal to act flexibly to secure future needs requires the ability to conceive of itself as having needs other than those currently being experienced. Furthermore, to act for these future needs, the individual must be capable of representing the future in a way that evokes a drive state related to it. Thus, the animal must be able to trigger in itself a drive state based on future needs rather than current ones, essentially envisaging itself in a future affective scenario, or "pre-experiencing" an internal state.

Suddendorf and Corballis (1997) argue that while animals are capable of predicting likely future events based on past regularities, they cannot conceptualize specific future occurrences. Like Köhler (1927), they suggest that nonhuman anticipations of the future "do not go beyond the context of the present" (p. 15) and argue that animals cannot disassociate themselves from their present mental state to consider future events from the perspective of their future selves. This is the "Bischof-Köhler hypothesis": Nonhuman animals cannot anticipate future needs or drive states and are therefore bound to a present, defined by their current motivational state. Much research has been aimed at falsifying this hypothesis.

Naqshbandi and Roberts (2006) presented squirrel monkeys with a choice between one or four thirst-inducing pieces of date. This was followed by training that choice of the larger quantity would lead to a period of water deprivation six times longer than that following choice of the smaller quantity. At test, the monkeys' choice of the larger quantity dropped from 70% to 25% after the first trial. The authors suggest that since the monkeys were not thirsty at the time of the choice, this preference reversal indicates anticipation of future thirst. A comparison study conducted with rats showed no reversal of preference; subjects continued to choose the larger quantity of thirst-inducing food, despite the future discomfort this caused. To control for the possibility that the larger quantity of dates had become associated with greater thirst felt immediately after their consumption, a second experiment was conducted in which the water deprivation was equal for both choices. The monkey then chose the larger amount of dates on 75% of trials. Although it has been argued that the gradual learning of this behavior implies associative processes (Shettleworth, 2007b; Suddendorf & Corballis, 2007), it is not clear to us that speed of learning can be used as evidence for *type* of learning; associative learning can occur within a single trial or take hundreds of trials to appear. By standard operant learning criteria, the action and reinforcer in this study (food choice and return of water) were not sufficiently temporally contiguous to allow associative learning, nor were conditions met for the "long delay" associative learning demonstrated by Lett (1975). However, the results of this study must nonetheless be treated with caution since they present the behaviour of only two subjects.

Another challenge to the Bischof-Köhler hypothesis comes from work with the western scrub–jay (*Aphelocoma californica*). Correia, Dickinson, and Clayton (2007) fed scrub-jays to satiety on a particular food and then gave them the opportunity to eat and cache that food as well as an alternative food type. Later, subjects were fed to satiety on the other food type before being allowed to retrieve their caches. This design ensures that the jays experienced a qualitatively different motivational state when caching from that experienced at the time of recovery. On the first trial, birds predominantly cached the food that they had not been sated on before caching. However, on the second and third trials, a significantly higher proportion of the birds' caches were of the food that they had been sated on before caching but would *not* be sated on before recovery. What makes this study convincing is that there is no discernible difference between the caching and recovery episodes other than the bird's internal state and the temporal order of events. To differentiate between the two, the bird must be aware that its current and future motivational states will differ and understand that an action in the present can have consequences for this future state. Furthermore, the use of specific satiety made it possible to ensure that the subjects' motivational states at these two times were different, and therefore any action taken in the morning that was of benefit in the afternoon cannot have been due to a current drive state.

In a critique of these studies, Suddendorf and Corballis (2008) suggest that Correia and colleagues' birds may have learned not to cache items that are of little value at recovery—a rule such as "fine to eat but not good to cache." This type of learning has been demonstrated in scrub-jays that cease caching an item that has been regularly degraded at recovery (Clayton, Dally, Gilbert, & Dickinson, 2005). However, since Correia and colleagues' birds were pre-fed *both* foods at some point during the day, an incentive learning account (e.g., Balleine & Dickinson, 1998; Dickinson & Balleine, 1994) would predict decreased caching of *both* foods since a food's incentive value is insensitive to *when* it had a low value (Clayton et al., 2008). At the very least, then, the difference in the proportions of the two food types cached must reflect some cognitive representation of a different situation in which the value of these food types will be different. This debate illustrates the difficulty in interpreting what nature of future concept is necessary for particular behaviors.

It has recently been argued (Cheke & Clayton, 2010) that falsification of the Bischof-Köhler hypothesis, while providing undisputable evidence for prospective cognition in animals, would not be sufficient to identify what *type* of prospective cognition was involved. Cheke and Clayton suggest that the ability to learn that a "food item or tool will gain a value later that it does not current possess" (p. 13) does not necessitate pre-experience of a future valuation, but rather a concept of change over time, something that could be encompassed within non-episodic prospective cognition. Osvath and Osvath (2008) argue that, intuitively, pre-experiencing future drive states while in the opposite state is hard to do and may therefore be an inappropriate mechanism for the control of prospective behavior in such contexts. Indeed, human adults struggle to accurately predict their own future motivational states; for example, we tend to order a high-calorie snack for our (sated) future selves when presently hungry (Read & van Leeuwen, 1998) and buy more in the supermarket if food-deprived while shopping (Nisbett & Kanouse, 1969). Furthermore, children fail to meet their own future needs until at least five years of age, suggesting that this ability develops significantly later than episodic cognition (Atance & Meltzoff, 2006).

Raby and Clayton (2009) argue that much prospective cognition in humans is aimed at the fulfillment of a *current* motivational state; "cold weather might prompt you to book a holiday in the sun with a considerable amount of planning, forward thinking and mental time travel involved" (p. 7), so it is unhelpful to set a criterion for animal prospective cognition that specifically excludes such behaviors. They cite Noser and Byrne's (2007) finding that chacma baboons will travel to areas whose resources are likely to be quickly diminished early in the day,

bypassing more plentiful food sources which they return to later. While almost certainly driven by current hunger, this behavior may indicate understanding that one food source will degrade before the other, and the ability to forgo the immediately available food to utilize this information.

How do we differentiate between types of prospective representation?

Osvath and Osvath (2008) argue that to be able to differentiate between an understanding of change in value over time and a pre-experience of a future event, one must emphasize the unique characteristics of that future event. Like Mulcahy and Call (2006), their experiment exploited a tool transportation paradigm. This study replicated that study's finding that apes will choose a functional tool for use in accessing a reward temporally and physically distant from the act of choosing. However, this study included important manipulations. The second experiment required subjects to choose between functional and nonfunctional tools as well as a valued food reward. Their success in this condition suggests that they overcame their present drive state to achieve a future goal. Interestingly, subjects preferred having one tool and one grape over two tools, suggesting that the tool had not acquired strong reinforcing properties itself. In a final experiment, the apes chose a novel functional tool over novel nonfunctional but visually similar tools. The authors argue that this condition emphasizes the peculiarities of the future event, such that the choice of the functional tool in the absence of the apparatus necessitates not only an understanding that tools that are not useful now will be useful later but to envisage *how* the tool might be used later. The authors therefore argue that subjects mentally pre-experience their future encounter with the apparatus to rehearse the potential functionality of the novel tools.

Osvath and Osvath (2008) argue that requiring subjects to resist an immediately accessible reward in favor of a larger future reward is a more appropriate paradigm to investigate future planning because pre-experiencing a drive state while also experiencing a *competing* drive state is easier than when experiencing the *opposite* state. The authors argue that it is important to "ensure that the self-control setting offers competition between different desires…the immediate reward must be qualitatively distinct from the future one; otherwise the outcome of the choice would only be an expression of inhibitory strength and not of the ability to distinguish the future oriented drive from the present oriented one" (p. 3). As we discuss in more detail later, choices between immediate and delayed rewards may be dominated by impulsivity, but exertion of self-control must be motivated by *some* representation of the delayed reward this will allow. Furthermore, it is potentially unhelpful to model "future-orientated drives" as a single process in competition with a unitary "present-orientated" one; as we have hinted at earlier, there may be multiple types of future representation, all of which may influence future-oriented decision making. The focus of this chapter will be to illustrate how modeling prospective cognition as an interaction between many processes may allow researchers to investigate subtleties and quantifiable patterns in prospective behavior rather than concerning themselves chiefly with dichotomous categorization.

In humans, there is a large, well-documented body of research on the ways in which people make choices about present and future outcomes, termed "intertemporal choice" (ITC). That people are able to choose a large delayed reward over a small immediate one is not what interests theorists in this area, but rather the situations in which they *do not* do so; in particular, the way in which people discount future rewards relative to their temporal distance, that is, how far they are away in time.

TEMPORAL DISCOUNTING IN HUMANS

The term "temporal discounting" describes the devaluation of an outcome because receipt of that outcome will not occur now, but at some point in the future. For example, when asked, "Would you prefer $54 today or $55 in 117 days?" (Kirby & Marakovic, 1996), most people would opt for the smaller, but immediately available sum.

The notion that outcome value is discounted with delay is inherited from the field of economics. The idea is that individuals treat delayed

outcomes as less valuable than immediate ones to maximize their utility in an unpredictable world where delay may reduce the probability of an outcome actually occurring. This idea is termed the Discounted Utility Theory. The behavior this theory postulates is typically modeled by an exponential function (Fig. 24.1), with a constant rate of discounting over all delays. However, actual devaluation of delayed reward is not consistent across all delays. For example, Ainslie and Haendel (1983) found that most people prefer $50 immediately to $100 in 6 months, but would opt for $100 in a year over $50 in 6 months, despite the difference in delay and magnitude between the two options being identical. Consequently human temporal discounting is better modeled by hyperbolic (e.g., Rachlin, Raineri, & Cross, 1991; Raineri & Rachlin, 1993) or quasi-hyperbolic (e.g., Laibson, 1997; McClure, Laibson, Loewenstein, & Cohen, 2004a) functions rather than an exponential one. The advantage of using a hyperbolic (or quasi-hypebolic) function is that such equations are able to describe the decrease in discounting rate with delay to choice outcome, such that the

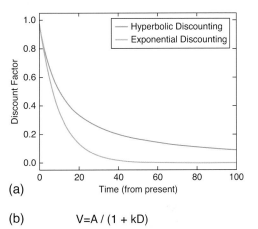

(a)

(b) $V = A / (1 + kD)$

Figure 24.1 (*a*) **Comparison of the discount factors of hyperbolic and exponential discounting. In both cases, k = 1.** (*b*) **Hyperbolic discounting equation; V is the value of the delayed reward, A is the monetary amount, and D is the delay. k is the hyperbolic discounting constant, which varies between individuals. Higher values of k correspond to steeper discounting.**

choice between two rewards is less affected by the difference in delay between them the more *both* are delayed.

Here an important distinction must be made between between competing views of the explanatory power of these models. The more conservative view is that these functions model behavior, without making any presumptions concerning psychological processes. Following this account, hyperbolic and quasi-hyperbolic hypotheses are indistinguishable as they both predict (or rather, have been designed to explain) the same behavior. Alternatively, we can propose a *real* representation of outcome value, which is discounted with respect to time according to one process, or the interaction of several processes (generating hyperbolic or quasi-hyperbolic patterns respectively). We will adopt the former position because the necessary use of experiential paradigms in animal research (see below) intertwines subjective valuation with those processes governing knowledge of the ITC itself. In other words, it is difficult using such paradigms to disambiguate whether a future reward is devalued, or whether it is outside of comprehension altogether. For this reason, and because it is unclear that performance modelled in restrictive instrumental paradigms generalises to the broader concept of ITC we refer to, we will not distinguish further between hyperbolic and quasi-hyperbolic models.

MENTAL TIME TRAVEL AND INTERTEMPORAL CHOICE

We suggest that ITC may provide an invaluable paradigm with which to investigate the contribution of episodic cognition to decision -making. Furthermore, knowledge of those situations that most encourage the formation and use of different types of prospective representations and most influence the interaction between prospection and behavior may yield insights into the underlying mechanisms involved in MTT as well as non-episodic prospection. Tulving describes three core features of episodic cognition: subjective perception of time, self-referential processing, and autonoetic consciousness (Tulving, 2002). All three of these aspects appear to influence

ITCs in humans. Here we shall briefly discuss each of them in turn.

Subjective Time

It has been suggested that the hyperbolic pattern of temporal discounting in humans may in part result from a present bias in the perception of time - that we perceive time delays as longer the closer they occur to the present.

During a temporal discounting task, Zauberman and colleagues (2009) asked subjects "how long" they considered a given duration to be, thus assessing its subjective temporal distance. The researchers found that the discounting function over *subjective* time was less hyperbolic than that over *real* time. Thus, the hyperbolic function seen in temporal discounting may arise partially from the way time is mentally represented by subjects. Further, the flexibility of time perception—mediated by attention paid to it— hints at the involvement of mental representations of the subjective experience of the passage of time in ITCs, even when those delays are not being directly experienced. For example, representing delays in terms of dates rather than a number of days elicits less discounting of future rewards in hypothetical choices (Read, Frederick, Orsel, & Rahman, 2005).

The MTT hypothesis suggests an individual is able to "time travel" in a similar way into the past and future (Suddendorf & Corballis, 1997). This symmetry is also apparent in discounting of hypothetical reinforcers. Yi, Gatchalian, and Bickel (2006; see also Bickel, Yi, Kowal, & Gatchalian, 2008) found that discounting of both past and future rewards was approximately hyperbolic and occurred at similar rates. There was also similar evidence for past/future symmetry of the magnitude effect; very small rewards were devalued more than very large sums, with respect to time.

Self-Referential Processing

[Peter] remembers his own states, whilst he only conceives Paul's. Remembrance is like direct feeling; its object is suffused with a warmth and intimacy to which no object of mere conception ever attains. (James, 1890, p. 148)

The "warmth and intimacy" to which James refers encapsulates the uniquely personal nature of episodic memories—one's mind projects oneself into one's own past. Tulving (1985) argues that such self-projection requires self-referential processes, a view mirrored by Suddendorf and Corballis's claims that self-awareness is a prerequisite for mental time travel (1997). As has been reviewed earlier in this chapter, there is some evidence that prospection of personal events seem to be mediated episodically while the future events in others' lives or the public domain may not be (e.g., Atance & O'Neill, 2001; Russell et al., 2010; Szpunar et al., 2007; Tulving, 2005).

This difference in prospection concerning oneself or another individual is reflected in intertemporal decision making. For example, Pronin, Olivola, and Kennedy (2008) found that subjects were far less likely to choose to a large delayed reward over a small immediate one when choosing for themselves than for another person.

The specific self-referential processing to which Tulving refers is metacognition, that is, a conscious awareness of one's own thoughts and feelings (Suddendorf & Corballis, 1997, 2007). This awareness also plays a role in ITC. Metcalfe and Mischel (1999) describe a range of short-term self-regulatory strategies that are dependent upon the subject's awareness of the influence of his or her own affect and impulsivity (for example, choosing to hide a piece of food that must be resisted). Strotz (1956) and Laibson (1997) also describe the use of long-term commitment mechanisms to make far-sighted plans, such as limiting one's future choices, in the knowledge of one's inevitable reversal of preference to immediate consumption.

Autonoesis

> We seldom confuse the feeling that we are remembering a past event with the feeling that we are looking at the world, that we are imagining what is on the other side of the mountain, or that we are dreaming. (Tulving, 2002, p. 2)

The episodically remembered event is not only experienced rather than merely conceived of, but it is done so in the explicit awareness of what this experience is. Tulving's term "autonoesis" refers to the conscious awareness that what is being experienced during remembering is a re-experience of a life episode rather than direct perception or imagination. The phenomenological characteristic of "re-experience" and the associated "self-knowing" consciousness is considered to be a central defining feature of episodic memory in humans, and it is supported by evidence that vivid remembering of events coincides with the activation of the sensory cortices, suggesting that we really do resense the sights and sounds of our remembered experiences (Wheeler, Petersen, & Buckner, 2000).

The extent to which future scenarios are "experienced" in temporal discounting can be manipulated by attentional priming. Pronin and colleagues' study (2008) found that encouraging a representational strategy to reduce the emotional salience of monetary reinforcers elicited reduced temporal discounting, leading to decision-making for the self that was similar to that for other subjects, suggesting that the amount one "experiences" a future scenario affects the intertemporal decision made. Metcalfe and Mischel (1999) review cognitive strategies aimed at reducing impulsivity in ITC and suggest that the most effective method may be to elicit task-irrelevant affective motivation (such as concentrating on the hedonic properties of pretzels while trying to resist a marshmallow). These affective responses may provide a means of drawing excitation away from the task-relevant affective responses that may lead to impulsive action. These affective responses are stimulus driven; thus, for elicitation to occur in the absence of such stimuli, the subject must internally create the sensation of stimulus perception, essentially pre-experiencing the stimulus.

A ROLE FOR MENTAL TIME TRAVEL IN TEMPORAL DISCOUNTING?

To summarize, attentional mediation of the subjective perception of time, and the extent to which a future outcome is represented as an "experience" influences ITCs. Furthermore, differences in delay discounting for self and others, as well as the use of certain self-control strategies and commitment mechanisms, provide evidence for metacognitive self-referential processing in human ITCs. We therefore argue that such choices exhibit qualities that are symptomatic of the contribution of episodic prospective cognition. Indeed, Boyer (2008) argues that encouraging prospective behavior by countering discounting of delayed outcomes is the adaptive function of episodic future-thinking. This account gains some support from the apparent attenuation of temporal discounting of hypothetical rewards to be received at some real life event in the subject's future (Peters & Büchel, 2010). As such, we believe that ITC provides a good paradigm for investigating the contribution of MTT to behavior.

With this in mind, the next section will be dedicated to an exploration of the processes that may be involved in temporal discounting in humans. Paradigms for assessing ITC can be very broadly divided into three types: long-term hypothetical, experiential, and delayed gratification.

Discounting of Hypothetical Rewards

The majority of temporal discounting research in humans is conducted using large variations in reward and delay amount. Choices involving rewards over any delays longer than the overall task length are necessarily assessed by presenting the magnitude and delay options linguistically. These choice tasks typically involve a series of small soon rewards (SSRs), and larger, later rewards (LLRs) (e.g., Green, Myerson, Lichtman, Rosen & Fry, 1996; Green, Myerson, & Ostaszewski, 1999). The immediate rewards are typically presented in both ascending and descending order, so as to find the point at which, in both ascending and descending titrations, subjects demonstrate a reversal in preference. This is labeled the *indifference point*—the SSR that is equal in subjective value to a given LLR (Fig. 24.2). The indifference points for different delays and LLRs may be plotted graphically, allowing patterns of discounting to be quantified by measuring the area under a discounting curve (Myerson, Green, & Warusawitharana, 2001) or by providing a model of good fit.

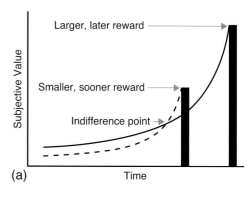

(a)   Time

(b) $k = ((LDR/SIR)-1)/Delay$

Figure 24.2 (*a*) **A hyperbolic discounting function graph; preference switches to the smaller outcome as its time of presentation draws near. (*b*) Mazur's (1987) hyperbolic equation, solved for k at the indifference point between the LDR and SIR at the stated delay.**

It has been reliably found (e.g., Green & Myerson, 2004; Green et al., 1997; Kirby, 1997; Kirby & Marakovic, 1996; Kirby, Petry, & Bickel, 1999; Thaler, 1981) that small delayed outcomes (e.g., $25–$35) are discounted more quickly than larger rewards (e.g., $75–$85). Investigation of this "magnitude effect" is made feasible by the use of hypothetical rewards (Green et al., 1996). This practice has drawn some criticism, but within-subject studies have found no systematic difference in discounting of hypothetical and real rewards (Johnson & Bickel, 2002; Lagorio & Madden, 2005).

Experiential Discounting

Intertemporal decisions in experiential tasks require the subject to learn the magnitudes and delays by experiencing them (e.g., Allen, Moeller, Rhoades, & Cherek, 1998; Cherek & Lane, 1999; Lane, Cherek, Pietras, & Tcheremissine, 2003b; Lane, Cherek, Rhoades, Pietra, & Tcheremissine, 2003c; Pietras, Cherek, Lane, Tcheremissine, & Steinberg, 2003; Reynolds & Schiffbauer, 2004). Subjects experience delays by waiting for the reward to arrive, at which time it may be consumed if it is a primary reinforcer, such as food, or simply gained possession of (thought to be pseudo-consummatory) in the case of monetary reinforcers. The outcome delays and magnitudes used in these tasks are constrained by task length and financial considerations, so the sums of money involved are typically much smaller (e.g., 5–15 cents) than those in hypothetical choices, and the delays are limited to seconds and minutes. Also, waiting for the outcome means the delay takes on an extra dimension as an "opportunity cost." Despite these differences, experiential discounting is well-modeled by a hyperbolic function (Reynolds & Schiffbauer, 2004), and it correlates moderately with performance on a hypothetical discounting task (Lane, Cherek, Pietra, & Tcheremissine, 2003a).

Delayed Gratification

In the delay of gratification procedure, the participant must resist a small reward throughout a delay until a large reward becomes available. Research has shown that individual differences in performance on delay of gratification tasks in 4-year-old children are predictive of cognitive and social competence in later life (Mischel, Shoda, & Rodriguez, 1989).

There are two common paradigms for the study of delayed gratification. In the Mischel procedure (Mischel, 1974), the participant is presented with a consumable treat and informed (or trained) that after waiting for a given delay he or she will receive a double quantity of this treat, while acting to end the delay will mean the receipt of only a single item. This paradigm is used to examine levels of self-control ("willpower"), generally in animals and preschool children. However, this actually tests two skills: the ability to make the initial choice between an immediate or delayed reward, and the ability to maintain that decision throughout the delay. These two parts have been shown to be relatively independent in young children (Toner, Holstein, & Hetherington, 1977).

In the accumulation procedure (Toner & Smith, 1977), rewards accumulate gradually throughout the waiting period such that the subject is not confronted with a dichotomous choice between a single immediate or delayed reward. Here an inability to wait the full delay, but wait for a proportion of it, does not result in a complete absence of reward.

THEORIES OF INTERTEMPORAL CHOICE

Thus we see that ITCs can be assessed using highly varied hypothetical rewards and delays, or small experienced rewards and delays, and by means of a single choice or sustained self-control. Berns, Laibson, and Loewenstein (2007) argue that ITCs are mediated by complex interactions between three aspects: self-control, reinforcer anticipation, and representation. For the purposes of our argument here we shall concentrate on self-control and representation. There are a number of theories of how these two elements may affect human temporal discounting.

Some argue that the pattern of temporal discounting in humans results from the interactions between two variables rather than a single process (Laibson, 1997). One example of a quasi-hyperbolic discounting model proposes two sets of processes: "β processes," concerned with immediate rewards, and "δ processes," which mediate decisions involving delayed outcomes. McClure and colleagues (2004a) used functional magnetic resonance imaging (fMRI) to show that parts of the limbic system associated with the midbrain dopamine system are preferentially activated during decisions between an immediate and a delayed reward while lateral prefrontal cortical (PFC) areas and the posterior parietal cortex (PPC) were engaged uniformly during ITCs regardless of the delay involved. The authors argue that limbic system regions, and parts of the PFC and PPC, mediate the β and δ processes, respectively. This position is supported by the strong correlation between the relative activation of these areas and the decision eventually made.

Given the involvement of the limbic system in emotional processing, this region's role in evaluating immediate rewards (rather than "sooner" rewards generally) is consistent with the idea that levels of emotional impulsivity affect ITCs. The contrast between stimulus-driven emotional impulsivity and a more flexible, cognitive system for evaluating and comparing delayed rewards is encapsulated in Metcalfe and Mischel's (1999) "hot/cool" framework for mediating decisions about delaying gratification (Table 24.1). The hot system is presented as a collection of

Table 24.1 Characteristics of the Hot and Cool Systems

Hot System	Cool System
Emotional	Cognitive
"Go"	"Know"
Simple	Complex
Reflexive	Reflective
Fast	Slow
Develops early	Develops late
Accentuated by stress	Attenuated by stress
Stimulus control	Self-control

Source: Reconstructed from Metcalfe & Mischel, 1999.

stimulus-driven "spots" that directly elicit behavior-driving motivational and emotional states. The cool system consists of an array of interconnected nodes, representing individual features of an outcome and its context. This second system appears to share many structural similarities with the popular concept of a semantic tree: Stimulus-driven activity at a few given nodes causes local reverberation around the system, resulting in a disparate representation of an entity in terms of its constituent components. The authors focus upon decisions requiring willpower, where the two systems as wholes should be in conflict. They also note that the cool system's flexibility means it need not necessarily conflict with the hot system in every circumstance.

In delayed gratification tasks, detection of the small reward activates a "hot spot," eliciting a strong desire to take and consume it. However, the subject's knowledge of the task, processed by the cool system, drives the subject to inhibit impulsive responding in favor of waiting for the larger reward. The behavioral outcome emerges as the outputs of one system dominate those of another. Traditional learning theory assumes that sensory exposure to a delayed outcome should increase representational salience, enabling delay of gratification. The contrary finding that exposure encourages impulsive action (Metcalfe & Mischel, 1999) is consistent with priming of the stimulus-driven hot system. The authors also review the role of the cool system in allowing the subject to manipulate incoming perceptual information to facilitate

cognitive strategies that enhance the outputs of cool relative to hot processes. They emphasize the role of metacognitive reflection on the disadvantageous influence of impulsive behavior in implementing these strategies.

Trope and Liberman (2003) propose that the nature of future outcome representations, termed "construals," varies systematically with the temporal distance of the represented event from the present. In this theory, events in the distant future are represented by a few "high-level" construals encapsulating their perceived essence in an ultimate and decontextualized form. By contrast, "low-level" construals dominate representations of the near future and are responsible for constructing an event's incidental, contextual details. For example, a meal to be eaten in the near future might be represented mostly in terms of its taste, while a distantly future meal might be represented with greater reference to its healthiness. The authors argue that the subjective value of a future goal is determined by the combined value of the different construals representing that goal, and as such that time-dependent changes in the level at which an outcome is construed will cause temporal changes in preference. Specifically, if the high-level construals of a reward have a lower subjective value than the lower-level construals (i.e., the essence is less valued than the details), then delayed rewards will be discounted; while low-value low-level construals and high-value high-level construals would cause the value of a reward to increase with delay. Similarly, if the delay were represented as contextual rather than fundamental, it would be construed at a low level. If this were so, the hyperbolic pattern would result, in part, from a reduction in low-level construal with time, causing the delay to wield a systematically decreasing influence over outcome preference. It may also be possible to explain the magnitude effect using differences in outcome construal. Thaler (1981) suggests that small sums are mentally represented as current accounts for immediate everyday expenses (life's details), and large sums as saving accounts for use in the distant future (for life-defining events such as a marriage).

Trope and Liberman (2003) suggest that there are few functional differences between the two accounts just reviewed. Indeed, they may be complementary; different patterns of construal may signify a distinction between subcomponents of the cool system. Certainly it is likely that prospective construals are cognitive rather than affective entities, particularly given their role in long-term prediction and evaluation. It is also not implausible that affective stimuli might be construed within a cognitive network, as well as eliciting behavior more directly via hot spots. We speculate that the functional foci of the two theories are also complementary, examining different aspects of Berns and colleagues' integrative framework of willpower, anticipation, and representation (2007). Long-term evaluations and predictions are mediated by cognitive outcome representations, the natures of which are determined by delay from the present. Interactions between these cognitive representations dominate intertemporal decisions where the sooner reward is not immediate, nor are the rewards involved available for immediate perception. However, presence of such a reward activates hot spots, leading to conflict between stimulus-driven impulsivity and the subject's long-term cognitive goals.

While these discussions may seem irrelevant to the literature on prospective cognition in animals, we hold that many parallels may be drawn between ideas of episodic and non-episodic representations and Construal Level Theory, and we suggest that the two may be compatible, even complementary. Trope and Liberman's (2003) heuristics dictating the relative dominance of low- and high-level construals could be considered to reflect fluctuations in the application of episodic and non-episodic representations. This view draws on similarities between an episodically constructed scene and an event represented by low-level construals. Most definitions of MTT emphasize the contextual details contained in such representations. Indeed, it seems that the construction of detailed contextualized "scenes," as compared to isolated objects, is impaired in patients with episodic amnesia (Hassabis, Kumaran, & Maguire, 2007a). We propose, then, that episodic processes generate scenes from the personal past and future by uniting the plethora

of details associated with such events, and that these are construed at a low level.

Within the framework of this overarching Just-So story, then, intertemporal decisions are mediated by interactions between stimulus-driven affective drives and the cumulative output of multiple cognitive outcome representations. In situations requiring willpower, the resultant behavior is determined by competition between broad affective (hot) and cognitive (cool) systems (Metcalfe & Mischel, 1999). However, willpower is just one key factor, alongside outcome representation (Berns et al., 2007). When certain affective stimuli are unavailable, the hot system's outputs are diminished and competition between these two systems gains less influence over behavior. Interactions between qualitatively different outcome representations will then acquire control over behavior according to the strength of, as well as the subjective value ascribed to, those representations. The relative strengths of different representational types may be governed by a plethora of heuristics, notably those sensitive to delay (Trope & Liberman, 2003).

We argue that these cool nodes encompass prospective cognition as whole, including both episodic and non-episodic representations. The relational mnemonic processes of episodic cognition may be furthermore required to unite disparate nodes into a coherent representation of a future event. It is these processes that give the cool system its "spatiotemporal" properties (Metcalfe & Mischel, 1999). The contribution of episodic cognition to outcome representation may reduce over delay, giving way to non-episodic representation (equating to "low-level" and "high-level" construals, respectively). This process can be manipulated by the application of attentional strategies to emphasize either the contextual features of a greatly delayed outcome (for example, actively imagining what the extra money could be spent on) or the more semantic features of a less delayed outcome (such as effects of inflation on value).

If the various characteristics of human intertemporal decision making *do* signify the involvement of episodic cognition, similar characteristics in nonhuman ITCs may indicate the involvement of episodic processes here, too. The benefit of this line of investigation is that it allows the analysis not only of the potential presence or absence of such mechanisms, but how they contribute to decisions that involve many processes, including impulsivity and non-episodic prospective cognition. In particular, one is able to investigate how these mechanisms might be consciously harnessed by an individual to manipulate his or her own decision making, both in overcoming immediate impulsivity and reducing the impact of future impulsivity or preference reversal.

RESEARCH INTO INTERTEMPORAL CHOICE IN NONHUMAN ANIMALS

There has been a substantial amount of research into intertemporal decision making in nonhuman animals. The broad conclusion of this body of research is that most animal species wait only a few seconds for delayed benefits (e.g., Ainslie, 1974; Mazur, 1987; Ramseyer, Pelé, Dufour, Chauvin, & Thierry, 2006; Stevens, Hallina, & Hauser, 2005b; Tobin, Logue, Chelonis, Ackermann, & May, 1996). This apparent discontinuity between humans' ability to wait years for a large reward and nonhuman animals inability to wait even a few minutes has been used to suggest that patience is a uniquely human trait (McClure, York, & Montague, 2004b; Roberts, 2002; Tobin & Logue, 1994). However, there are significant methodological differences between human and animal research, which may account for much of the seemingly impulsive behavior of nonhuman subjects.

METHODOLOGICAL DIFFERENCES

Human discounting studies involving long delays all use linguistic instructions (Green et al., 1996; Kirby, 1997). By contrast, discounting paradigms for nonlinguistic subjects are necessarily experiential—subjects must learn about reward sizes and delays by experiencing them (e.g., Green, Fischer, Perlow, & Sherman, 1981; Mazur, 2000; Richards, Mitchell, de Wit, & Seiden, 1997). These differences could plausibly contribute to the large

disparity in human and nonhuman discounting performance. Firstly, knowledge of delay and outcome magnitudes in experiential tasks is bounded, that is, the subject cannot be sure of his or her decision's result, as one's predictions are only based upon previous trials. This uncertainty is likely to be compounded by noise, which affects all perceptual inputs from past experience, but would not exert such an influence over more linguistic representations. Any uncertainty about the reliability of the reward's arrival could lead to faster discounting of delayed rewards. This uncertainty need not be restricted to the task scenario itself but can result from a subject's past history, as has been demonstrated in human subjects (Ostaszewski, Green, & Myerson, 1998). Thus, it is possible that even if the details of the task were sufficiently appreciated by the animal subject, lack of predictability and stability in the subject's general life may lead to fast discounting of delayed rewards.

Differences in the motivational qualities of primary and secondary rewards may also contribute to disparities in outcome discounting between humans and animals. Having no utility of its own, money is valuable only by virtue of its economic equivalence to directly rewarding goods; it can also be exchanged for an almost infinite variety of these goods, meaning that its value is largely independent of the influence of any given drive state. There is evidence that delay has a different effect on valuation of monetary and primary rewards. Odum and Rainaud (2003) found slower discounting of hypothetical sums of money than imaginary food and alcohol rewards of equivalent financial value by typical adults. Rosati and colleagues (2007) found that human participants were more than three times more willing to wait for small amounts of money than for small amounts of food (for a similar finding with a more typical format of hypothetical questions see Estle, Green, Myerson & Holt, 2007). Furthermore, while 40% of subjects would wait for money *every time*, not one subject waited every time for food. As such, human research using money cannot be considered directly comparable to animal research using food, which may simply encourage increased impulsivity, or may tap different mechanisms altogether. Indeed, Rosati and colleagues found that human adults were *less* willing to wait for a larger delayed food reward than were chimpanzees, suggesting that when it comes to primary rewards, humans are not uniquely patient. It is also conceivable that the high discount rate for food seen in animals results partially from the relatively small quantities of food used, when compared with the sums of money involved in human hypothetical tasks.

The unique qualities of money mean that it maintains its utility even in vast quantities; as such amounts may still be consumed quickly with little or no effect on satiety. In particular, the ceiling on food consumption imposed by satiety provides a plausible explanation for the notable lack of effect of outcome magnitude on discount rates—the magnitude range of consumable primary reinforcers may be too small to reveal any such effect. A more ecologically valid alternative may be to embrace those species that hoard food, thereby maintaining external energy reserves not constrained by gut volume, as internal reserves are.

Of most concern, however, is the possibility that non-human subjects are not aware that a delayed reward is on offer. As stated above, animal studies are necessarily experiential, but if arrival of the delayed outcome is temporally beyond limits of a given subject's awareness (or 'temporal horizon'), then the instrumental contingency between the choice action and reward will be degraded. In this situation, the behavior resulting in presentation of the delayed outcome will be perceived as unrewarded, and that behavior will be extinguished. This would be indistinguishable from impulsive choice, though clearly psychologically very different. To overcome this problem we recommend using ecologically-valid paradigms, with causal aspects of the ITC being relevant to the natural behavior of the subject species to ensure maximal attentional engagement and understanding. We further suggest the study of innately prospective action such as food-storing, where impulsive preference and limited temporal horizons posit opposite predictions (with the caveat that a complete absence of delay discounting cannot be attributed to prospective thought until lack of awareness of the temporal aspects of the ITC has been ruled out as a confound).

COMPARABILITY OF DELAYED GRATIFICATION WITH SINGLE-CHOICE PROCEDURES

Most animal ITC research has used the delayed gratification paradigm. However, this procedure is qualitatively different from the hypothetical or experiential procedures used with adult humans, and it may elicit different results. Reynolds, de Wit, and Richards (2002) found similar k-values for rats in delay discounting and delayed gratification tasks, and so argue that the processes measured by these procedures are the same, or at least are the same in rats (Rachlin, 2000). However, apart from the danger inherent in interpreting null results, Reynolds and colleagues procedure involved a choice between an immediate or delayed reward. As McClure and colleagues (2004a) demonstrated, in humans different brain areas may be involved in decisions concerning immediate rewards and delayed rewards. We have speculated that decisions involving immediate reinforcers activate hot spots that compete with cognitive systems for control of behavior. As such, ITCs between delayed rewards would reduce the role of self-control, allowing behavior to be predominantly driven by the interaction between cognitive systems. An example of this difference can be seen in Rachlin and Green's (1972) work with pigeons. The authors demonstrated that pigeons offered a choice between a small immediate reward and a larger reward delayed by 4 seconds invariably prefer the small, immediate reward. However, when choosing between a delay followed by this choice and a delay followed by restriction to the large delayed reward only, the pigeons' choice depended on the length of the delay. When the delay was small, the pigeons chose the alternative leading to a choice (and then chose the small, immediate reward). When the delay was large, the pigeons chose the alternative leading to restriction to the large delayed reward only. Thus, the pigeons were more able to choose the larger, more delayed reward the more *both* rewards were delayed from the present.

There may also be an effect of *type* of delayed gratification task used. For example, Metcalfe and Mischel (1999) highlight the importance of reward visibility on the inability to inhibit impulsive action; however, much animal research is conducted using the accumulation procedure, which encourages attentional focus on the accumulating reward. It also reduces the opportunity to use commitment mechanisms because the animal cannot make a single choice and then entirely remove itself from the situation to wait out the delay without temptation. The Mischel procedure may also be problematic in this respect if the action to end the delay becomes sufficiently associated with the reward that it continually leads to the activation of reward hot spots.

One way in which this kind of stimulus-driven impulsivity can be reduced is self-distraction. Young children will increase their own success on delay of gratification tasks by engaging in distracting play or thought (Miller & Karniol, 1976; Mischel, Ebbesen, & Zeiss, 1972; Toner & Smith, 1977). There is some evidence that animals are able to do the same. For example, pigeons in a Mischel task, which would wait for a delayed reward on only 4% of trials, increased their success rate to 78% when provided with a distracter activity (Grosch & Neuringer, 1981). Chimpanzees in an accumulation delay of gratification task were shown to obtain significantly more pieces of candy when toys were available than when they were not (Evans & Beran, 2007b). Furthermore, they spent significantly more time manipulating the toys when the candies were within reach (and therefore had to be resisted) than when they were not. The proportion of time spent manipulating the toys was positively correlated with the number of candies obtained. Overall, the chimpanzees were able to wait up to 18 minutes, with an average waiting time of 7.5 minutes.

Providing a means of self-distraction allows the animal to act to reduce its own impulsivity, but changes in task design may be a better strategy for the researcher. In Pelé and colleagues' recent work with long-tailed macaques (2009), it was found that while subjects were able to wait a maximum of 1 minute in a standard accumulation delay of gratification task, they could wait up to 10 minutes for a larger reward in a social exchange task, which involved inhibiting consumption of the smaller reward so as to be able to exchange it for the larger reward after a delay. This result is comparable to results obtained with chimpanzees that indicate that they are able to postpone the return of the small reward by up to 8 minutes (Dufour, Pele, Sterck, & Thierry 2007). Both the chimpanzee and macaque studies demonstrated that the longer the delay, the *earlier* subjects gave up, suggesting that they made a decision with an awareness of the options, rather than being simply unable to continue waiting. An important finding of the macaque paper, however, was that if the subjects were given the option of *immediately* returning the smaller reward in order to commit themselves to the delay, not only were they willing to do so, but their delay tolerance more than doubled, in some individuals surpassing 40 minutes (Pelé et al., 2009). Thus, unlike Reynolds and colleagues' (2002) results with rats, macaques seem to benefit from the opportunity to commit themselves to a choice, suggesting that it is the consumption inhibition that limits them in alternative paradigms rather than an inability to represent the future reward.

INTERTEMPORAL CHOICE AS A PARADIGM FOR THE INVESTIGATION OF MENTAL TIME TRAVEL IN ANIMALS

We have reviewed a number of perspectives on ITC. Broadly, we posit that intertemporal decisions between immediate and delayed rewards involve competition between affective and cognitive processes, but that when neither reward is immediate, the competition exists primarily between different types of outcome representation, or levels of construal.

Thus, we argue that when faced with an ITC between two nonimmediate rewards, the behavioral outcome of this decision depends on the relative strength of various prospective representations. The relative contribution of episodic representations diminishes with the temporal distance of the event being represented, to be replaced by representations of the decontextualized "essence" of the event. In line with this view, the contribution of both episodic and non-episodic prospective cognition to the intertemporal decisions of nonhuman animals can be investigated by assessing preference across different non-immediate time delays. In humans, the relative strength or value of these representations can be manipulated by attentional priming of either the essential (superordinate) or contextual (subordinate) features of the delay or the outcomes. If similar manipulations were to produce analogous effects in animal subjects, then this might suggest that comparable processes feed into non-human ITC. These manipulations may reveal the involvement of prospective representations in decisions, even if the behavioral outcome of these decisions implies otherwise. It is after all not unlikely that in situations where impulsivity dominates, cognitive representations may be present, but outcompeted.

Suddendorf and Corballis suggest that one possessing mental time travel must have a representation of the future that is capable of evoking a drive state different from that currently being experienced. To make a decision for a current motivational state that relies on actively sabotaging future behavior (i.e., commitment strategies), one must also be able to conceive of oneself as having a future drive state that is different from that currently being experienced. Thus, while much research into ITC in animals has, arguably, employed paradigms that weight the response bias toward impulsivity, nonhuman animals may, to greater or lesser extents, be able to overcome this impulsivity with cognitive strategies and commitment mechanisms involving prospective representations. What is in question, one would hope, is not whether they are successful in overcoming impulsivity, but what these representations are and how animals are able to use them. That macaques were willing to hand back a small treat to commit themselves to long delays until receipt of a large treat, and the fact that pigeons preferred to limit their own future choices, suggests tentatively that these species may be able to represent their own future impulsivity and act in the present to ameliorate its negative impact. This is a potentially fruitful area for the investigation of the Bischof-Köhler hypothesis.

In summary, we believe that research into prospective cognition in animals should not be focused on a dichotomous presence/absence debate over a unitary mechanism. We suggest that ITC offers a fruitful framework within which to investigate prospective cognition in a more multivariate manner; to explore what different representations may be involved and what external and internal influences affect the relative strength of these contributions. However, until now the methods used to explore intertemporal decision making in animals have encouraged impulsive responding, which may mask the contribution of other prospective processes. We suggest that the use of two nonimmediate rewards, delayed by different amounts and invisible to the subject, will allow the influence of cognitive processes to be explored.

REFERENCES

Addis, D. R., Wong, A. T., & Schacter, D. L. (2007). Remembering the past and imagining the future: Common and distinct neural substrates during event construction and elaboration. *Neuropsychologia*, 45, 1363–1377.

Addis, D. R., Wong, A. T., & Schacter, D. L. (2008). Age-related changes in the episodic simulation of future events. *Psychological Science*, 19, 33–41.

Ainslie, G., & Haendel, V. (1983). The motives of will In E. Gottheil, K. Druley, T. Skolda, & H. Waxman (Eds.), *Etiologic aspects of alcohol and drug abuse* (pp. 119–140),. Springfield, IL: Charles C. Thomas.

Ainslie, G. W. (1974). Impulse control in pigeons. *Journal of the Experimental Analysis of Behaviour*, 21, 485–489.

Allen, T. J., Moeller, F. G., Rhoades, H. M., & Cherek, D. R. (1998). Impulsivity and history of drug dependence. *Drug and Alcohol Dependency*, 50, 137–145.

Atance, C. M., & Meltzoff, A. N. (2006). Preschoolers' current desires warp their choices for the future. *Psychological Science*, 17, 583–587.

Atance, C. M., & O'Neill, D. K. (2001). Episodic future thinking. *Trends in Cognitive Sciences*, 5, 533–539.

Balleine, B., & Dickinson, A. (1998). The role of incentive learning in instrumental outcome revaluation by sensory-specific satiety. *Animal Learning and Behavior*, 26, 46–59.

Berns, G. S., Laibson, D., & Loewenstein, G. (2007). Intertemporal choice—toward an integrative framework. *Trends in Cognitive Sciences, 11,* 482–488.

Berthold, P., Heilbig, A. J., Mohr, G., & Querner, U. (1992). Rapid microevolution of migratory behaviour in a wild bird species. *Nature, 360,* 668–670.

Bickel, W. K., Yi, R., Kowal, B. P., & Gatchalian, K. M. (2008). Cigarette smokers discount past and future rewards symmetrically and more than controls: Is discounting a measure of impulsivity? *Drug Alcohol Depend, 96,* 256–262.

Boyer, P. (2008). Evolutionary economics of mental time travel? Trends in Cognitive Sciences, 12, 219-224.

Cheke, L. G., & Clayton, N. S. (2010). Mental time travel in animals. *WIREs Cognitive Science, 1,* 1–16.

Cherek, D. R., & Lane, S. D. (1999). Laboratory and psychometric measurements of impulsivity among violent and nonviolent female parolees. *Biological Psychiatry, 46,* 273–280.

Clayton, N. S., Correia, S. P. C., Raby, C. R., Alexis, D. M., Emery, N. J., & Dickinson, A. (2008). Response to Suddendorf & Corballis (2008) in defence of animal foresight. *Animal Behaviour, 76,* 9–11.

Clayton, N. S., Dally, J., Gilbert, J., & Dickinson, A. (2005). Food caching by western scrub-jays (*Aphelocoma californica*) is sensitive to the conditions at recovery. *Journal of Experimental Psychology: Animal Behavioural Processes, 31,* 115–124.

Correia, S. P., Dickinson, A., & Clayton, N. S. (2007). Western scrub-jays anticipate future needs independently of their current motivational state. *Current Biology, 17,* 856–861.

Dickinson, A., & Balleine, B. (1994). Motivational control of goaldirected action. *Animal Learning and Behavior, 22,* 1–18.

Dufour, V., Pele, M., Sterck, E. H., & Thierry, B. (2007). Chimpanzee (Pan troglodytes) anticipation of food return: Coping with waiting time in an exchange task. *Journal of Comparative Psychology, 121,* 145–155.

Estle, S. J., Green, L., Myerson, J. & Holt, D. D. (2007). Discounting of Monetary and Directly Consumable Rewards. *Psychological Science, 18,* 58-63.

Evans, T. A., & Beran, M. J. (2007b). Chimpanzees use self-distraction to cope with impulsivity. *Biology Letters, 22,* 599–602.

Green, L., Fisher, E. B., Perlow, S., & Sherman, L. (1981). Preference reversal and self-control: Choice as a function of reward amount and delay. *Behaviour Analysis Letters, 1,* 43–51.

Green, L., & Myerson, J. (2004). A discounting framework for choice with delayed and probabilistic rewards. *Psychology Bulletin, 130,* 769–792.

Green, L., Myerson, J., Lichtman, D., Rosen, S., & Fry, A. (1996). Temporal discounting in choice between delayed rewards: The role of age and income. *Psychology and Aging, 11,* 79–84.

Green, L., Myerson, J., & McFadden, E. (1997). Rate of temporal discounting decreases with amount of reward. *Memory and Cognition, 25,* 715–723.

Green, L., Myerson, J., & Ostaszewski, P. (1999). Discounting of delayed rewards across the life span: Age differences in individual discounting functions. *Behavioural Processes, 46,* 89–96.

Grosch, J., & Neuringer, A. (1981). Self-control in pigeons under the Mischel paradigm. *Journal of the Experimental Analysis of Behavior, 35,* 3–21.

Hassabis, D., Kumaran, D., & Maguire, E. A. (2007a). Using imagination to understand the neural basis of episodic memory. *Journal of Neuroscience, 27,* 14365–14374.

Hassabis, D., Kumaran, D., Vann, S. D., & Maguire, E. A. (2007b). Patients with hippocampal amnesia cannot imagine new experiences. *Proceedings of the National Academy of Sciences USA, 104,* 1726–1731.

James, W. (1890). *The principles of psychology.* New York: Dover.

Johnson, M. W., & Bickel, W. K. (2002). Within-subject comparison of real and hypothetical money rewards in delay discounting. *Journal of the Experimental Analysis of Behavior, 77,* 129–146.

Kirby, K. N. (1997). Bidding on the future: Evidence against normative discounting of delayed rewards. *Journal of Experimental Psychology, 126,* 54–70.

Kirby, K. N., & Marakovic, N. E. (1996). Delay-discounting probabilistic rewards: Rates decrease as amounts increase. *Psychonomic Bulletin and Review, 3,* 100–104.

Kirby, K. N., Petry, N. M., & Bickel, W. K. (1999). Heroin addicts have higher discount rates for delayed rewards than non-drug-using controls. *Journal of Experimental Psychology: General, 128,* 78–87.

Klein, S. B., Loftus, J., & J. F. Kihlstrom. (2002). Memory and temporal experience: The effects of episodic memory loss on an amnesic's patient ability to remember the past and imagine the future. *Social Cognition, 20,* 353–379.

Kohler, W. (1927). *The mentality of apes*. London: Routledge and Kegan Paul.

Lagorio, C. H., & Madden, G. J. (2005). Delay discounting of real and hypothetical rewards III: Steady-state assessments, forced-choice trials, and all real rewards. *Behavioural Processes*, 69, 173–187.

Laibson, D. (1997). Golden eggs and hyperbolic discounting. *Quarterly Journal of Economics*, 112, 443–477.

Lane, S. D., Cherek, D. R., Pietras, C. J., & Tcheremissine, O. V. (2003a). Measurement of delay discounting using trial-by-trial consequences. *Behavioural Processes*, 64, 287–303.

Lane, S. D., Cherek, D. R., Pietras, C. J., & Tcheremissine, O. V. (2003b). Measurement of delay discounting using trial-by-trial consequences. *Behavioural Processes*, 64, 287–303.

Lane, S. D., Cherek, D. R., Rhoades, H. M., Pietras, C. J., & Tcheremissine, O. V. (2003c). Relationships among laboratory and psychometric measures of impulsivity: Implications in substance abuse and dependence. *Addictive Disorders and Their Treatment*, 2, 33–40.

Lett, B. T. (1975). Long delay learning in the T-maze. *Learning and Motivation*, 6, 80–90.

Mazur, J. E. (1987). An adjusting procedure for studying delayed reinforcement. In M. L. Commons, J. E. Mazur, J. A. Nevin, & H. Rachlin (Eds.), *The effect of delay and of intervening events on reinforcement value* (Vol. 5, pp. 55–73). Hillsdale, NJ: Erlbaum.

Mazur, J. E. (2000). Tradeoffs among delay, rate, and amount of reinforcement. *Behavioural Processes*, 49, 1–10.

McClure, S. M., Laibson, D. I., Loewenstein, G., & Cohen, J. D. (2004a). Separate neural systems value immediate and delayed monetary rewards. *Science*, 306, 503–507.

McClure, S. M., York, M. K., & Montague, P. R. (2004b). The neural substrates of reward processing in humans: The modern role of fMRI. *Neuroscientist*, 10, 260–268.

Metcalfe, J., & Mischel, W. (1999). A hot/cool-system analysis of delay of gratification: Dynamics of willpower. *Psychological Review*, 106, 3–19.

Miller, D. T., & Karniol, R. (1976). Coping strategies and attentional mechanisms in self-imposed and externally imposed delay situations. *Journal of Personality and Social Psychology*, 34, 310–316.

Mischel, W. (1974). Processes in delay of gratification In L. Berkowitz (Ed.), *Advances in experimental social psychology* (Vol. 7, pp. xx–xx). New York: Academic Press.

Mischel, W., Ebbesen, E. B., & Zeiss, A. R. (1972). Cognitive and attentional mechanisms in delay of gratification. *Journal of Personality and Social Psychology*, 21, 204–218.

Mischel, W., Shoda, Y., & Rodriguez, M. I. (1989). Delay of gratification in children. *Science*, 244, 933–938.

Mulcahy, N. J., & Call, J. (2006). Apes save tools for future use. *Science* 312, 1038–1040.

Myerson, J., Green, L., & Warusawitharana, M. (2001). Area under the curve as a measure of discounting. *Journal of the Experimental Analysis of Behavior*, 76, 235–243.

Naqshbandi, M., & Roberts, W. A. (2006). Anticipation of future events in squirrel monkeys (Saimiri sciureus) and rats (Rattus norvegicus): Tests of the Bischof-Kohler hypothesis. *Journal of Comparitive Psychology*, 120, 345–357.

Nisbett, R. E., & Kanouse, D. E. (1969). Obesity, food deprivation, and supermarket shopping behavior. *Journal of Personality and Social Psychology*, 12, 289–294.

Noser, R., & Byrne, R. W. (2007). Travel routes and planning of visits to out-of-sight resources in wild chacma baboons, *Papio ursinus*. *Animal Behaviour*, 73, 257–266.

Odum, A. L., & Rainaud, C. P. (2003). Discounting of delayed hypothetical money, alcohol, and food. *Behavioural Processes*, 64, 305–313.

Ostaszewski, P., Green, L., & Myerson, J. (1998). Effects of inflation on the subjective value of delayed and probabilistic rewards. *Psychonomic Bulletin and Review*, 5, 324–333.

Osvath, M., & Osvath, H. (2008). Chimpanzee (Pan troglodytes) and orangutan (Pongo abelii) forethought: Self-control and pre-experience in the face of future tool use. *Animal Cognition*, 11, 661–674.

Pelé, M., Dufour, V., Micheletta, J., & Thierry, B. (2010). Long-tailed macaques display unexpected waiting abilities in exchange tasks. *Animal Cognition*, 13, 263–271.

Pietras, C. J., Cherek, D. R., Lane, S. D., Tcheremissine, O. V., & Steinberg, J. L. (2003). Effects of methylphenidate on impulsive choice in adult humans. *Psychopharmacology (Berlin)*, 170, 390–398.

Peters, J. & Büchel, C. (2010). Episodic Future Thinking Reduces Reward Delay Discounting through an Enhancement of Prefrontal-Mediotemporal Interactions. Neuron, 66, 138-148.

Pronin, E., Olivola, C. Y., & Kennedy, K. A. (2008). Doing unto future selves as you would do unto others: Psychological distance and decision making. *Personality and Social Psychology Bulletin*, 34, 224–236.

Raby, C. R., Alexis, D. M., Dickinson, A., & Clayton, N. S. (2007). Planning for the future by western scrub-jays. *Nature*, 445, 919–921.

Raby, C. R., & Clayton, N. S. (2009). Prospective cognition in animals. *Behavioural Processes*, 80, 314–324.

Rachlin, H. (2000). *The science of self-control.* Cambridge, MA: Harvard University Press.

Rachlin, H., & Green, L. (1972). Commitment, choice and self-control. *Journal of the Experimental Analysis of Behavior*, 17, 15–22.

Rachlin, H., Raineri, A., & Cross, D. (1991). Subjective probability and delay. *Journal of the Experimental Analysis of Behavior*, 55, 233–244.

Raineri, A., & Rachlin, H. (1993). The effect of temporal constraints on the value of money and other commodities. *Journal of Behavioral Decision Making*, 6, 77–94.

Ramseyer, A., Pelé, M., Dufour, V., Chauvin, C., & Thierry, B. (2006). Accepting loss: The temporal limits of reciprocity in brown capuchin monkeys. *Proceedings of the Royal Society of London B: Biological Sciences*, 273, 179–184.

Read, D., Frederick, S., Orsel, B., & Rahman, J. (2005). Four score and seven years from now: The date/delay effect in temporal discounting. *Management Science*, 51, 1326–1335.

Read, D., & van Leeuwen, B. (1998). Predicting hunger: The effects of appetite and delay on choice. *Organizational Behavior and Human Decision Processes*, 76, 189–205.

Reynolds, B., de Wit, H., & Richards, J. B. (2002). Delay of gratification and delay discounting in rats. *Behavioural Processes*, 59, 157–168.

Reynolds, B., & Schiffbauer, R. (2004). Measuring state changes in human delay discounting: An experiential discounting task. *Behavioural Processes*, 67, 343–356.

Richards, J. B., Mitchell, S. H., de Wit, H., & Seiden, L. S. (1997). Determination of discount functions in rats with an adjusting-amount procedure. *Journal of the Experimental Analysis of Behavior*, 67, 353–366.

Roberts, W. A. (2002). Are animals stuck in time? *Psychology Bulletin*, 128, 473–489.

Rosati, A. G., Stevens, J. R., Hare, B., & Hauser, M. D. (2007). The evolutionary origins of human patience: Temporal preferences in chimpanzees, bonobos, and human adults. *Current Biology*, 17, 1663–1668.

Russell, J., Alexis, D. M., & Clayton, N. S. (2010). Episodic future thinking in 3- to 5-year-old children: The ability to think of what will be needed from a different point of view. *Cognition*, 114 56–71.

Schacter, D. L., Addis, D. R., & Buckner, R. L. (2007). Remembering the past to imagine the future: the prospective brain. *Nature Reviews Neuroscience*, 8, 657–661.

Shettleworth, S. J. (2007b). Studying mental states is not a research program for comparative cognition. *Behavioral and Brain Sciences*, 30, 332–333.

Stevens, J. R., Hallinan, E. V., & Hauser, M. D. (2005b). The ecology and evolution of patience in two New World monkeys. *Biology Letters*, 1, 223–226.

Strotz, R. H. (1956). Myopia and Inconsistency in dynamic utility maximisation. *Review of Economic Studies*, 23, 165–180.

Suddendorf, T., & Busby, J. (2003). Mental time travel in animals? *Trends in Cognitive Sciences*, 7, 391–396.

Suddendorf, T., & Busby, J. (2005). Making decisions with the future in mind: Developmental and comparative identification of mental time travel. *Learning and Motivation*, 36, 110–125.

Suddendorf, T., & Corballis, M. C. (1997). Mental time travel and the evolution of the human mind. *Genetic, Social and General Psychology Monographs*, 123, 133–167.

Suddendorf, T., & Corballis, M. C. (2007). The evolution of foresight: What is mental time travel, and is it unique to humans? *Behavior and Brain Sciences*, 30, 299–351.

Suddendorf, T., & Corballis, M. C. (2008). New evidence for animal foresight? *Animal Behaviour*, 75, e1–e3.

Szpunar, K. K., Watson, J. M., & McDermott, K. B. (2007). Neural substrates of envisioning the future. *Proceedings of the National Academy of Sciences USA*, 104, 642–647.

Thaler, R. (1981). Some empirical evidence on dynamic inconsistency. *Economics Letters*, 8, 201–207.

Tobin, H., & Logue, A. W. (1994). Self-control across species (Columba livia, Homo sapiens, and Rattus norvegicus). *Journal of Comparative Psychology*, 108, 126–133.

Tobin, H., Logue, W., Chelonis, J. J., Ackermann, K. T., & May, J. G. (1996). Self-control in the monkey

Macaca fascicularis. Animal Learning and Behavior, 24, 168–174.

Toner, I. J., Holstein, R. B., & Hetherington, E. M. (1977). Reflection-impulsivity and self-control in preschool children. *Child Development, 48,* 239–245.

Toner, I. J., & Smith, R. A. (1977). Age and overt verbalization in delay-maintenance behavior in children. *Journal of Experimental Child Psychology, 24,* 123–128.

Trope, Y., & Liberman, N. (2003). Temporal construal. *Psychology Review, 110,* 403–421.

Tulving, E. (1972). Episodic and semantic memory. In T. E & D. W (Eds.), *Organisation of memory* (pp. 381–403). New York: Academic Press.

Tulving, E. (1985). Memory and consciousness. *Canadian Psychology, 26,* 1–12.

Tulving, E. (1993). What is episodic memory? *Current Directions in Psychological Science, 2,* 67–70.

Tulving, E. (2002). Episodic memory: From mind to brain. *Annual Review of Psychology, 53,* 1–25.

Tulving, E. (2005). Episodic memory and autonoesis: Uniquely human? In H. Terrace & J. Metcalfe (Eds.), *The missing link in cognition: Evolution of self-knowing consciousness* (pp. 3–56). New York: Oxford University Press.

Wheeler, M. E., Petersen, S. E., & Buckner, R. L. (2000). Memory's echo: Vivid remembering reactivates sensory-specific cortex. *Proceedings of the National Academy of Sciences USA, 97,* 11125–11129.

Yi, R., Gatchalian, K. M., & Bickel, W. K. (2006). Discounting of past outcomes. *Experimental and Clinical Psychopharmacology, 14,* 311–317.

Zauberman, G., Kim, B. K., Malkoc, S. A., & Bettman, J. R. (2009). Discounting time and time discounting: Subjective time perception and intertemporal preferences. *Journal of Marketing Research, 46,* 543–556.

CHAPTER 25
Mental Time Travel and the Shaping of the Human Mind

Thomas Suddendorf, Donna Rose Addis, and Michael C. Corballis

Clive Wearing is an English musician. As an acknowledged expert on early music, he had built up a musical career with the BBC when he was infected at the age of 46 with the herpes simplex virus. The virus effectively destroyed his hippocampus and left him profoundly amnesic. The nature of his amnesia illustrates the distinction between semantic memory, which is memory for enduring facts about the world, and episodic memory, which is a personal record of the past (Tulving, 1983). Wearing's semantic memory is largely intact, as is his procedural memory. He retains a normal vocabulary, recognizes his wife and family, and can still play the piano and conduct a choir. His episodic memory, though, is profoundly impaired. He has sufficient short-term memory to be able to converse, but he quickly forgets about topics he spoke about or experienced just moments earlier. He is continually under the impression that he has just woken up or just recovered from being dead. His conscious experience is entirely of the present and is well captured in the book *Forever Today*, written by his wife Deborah (Wearing, 2005).

Neuropsychological evidence reveals that deficits in episodic and semantic memory are doubly dissociated, implying distinct mechanisms. As with Clive Wearing, most cases of amnesia, especially those resulting from damage to the hippocampus, are characterized by severe deficits in episodic memory, while semantic memory remains largely intact (Aggleton & Brown, 1999; Scoville & Milner, 1957; Tulving,

Schacter, McLachlan, & Moscovitch, 1988; VarghaKhadem et al., 1997). Indeed, the very term "memory" is usually taken to mean episodic memory, as when William James wrote, "Memory requires more than the mere dating of an event in the past. It must be dated in my past" (James, 1890, p. 650). Yet in a degenerative condition known as semantic dementia, semantic memory is grossly impaired, yet episodic memory remains surprisingly unaffected (Hodges & Graham, 2001).

Retrieval of episodic memories involves the conscious reliving of past events, a sort of mental journey into the past (Tulving, 1983). In recent years, evidence has accumulated that the episodic-memory system is also involved in mental travel into the future, suggesting a general concept of mental time travel (Suddendorf & Corballis, 1997, 2007). Conceiving of future events, of course, involves a process of active construction of events that have not yet occurred, but the more general process of mental time travel highlights the evidence that episodic memory, too, is better conceived as a conscious act of construction, rather than a faithful re-enactment of the past. Indeed, if the only function of episodic memory was to record the past, it might be expected to function in a reproductive manner, like a video recorder (Suddendorf & Corballis, 1997). However, the slew of errors and distortions that episodic memory is vulnerable to shows us this is not the case (Schacter, 1999; Schacter & Addis, 2007). The primary role of episodic memory, then, may be to provide information from the past for the simulation of the future. Indeed, natural selection can only work on what memory can offer for present and future fitness rather than on the accuracy of the past record per se (Suddendorf & Busby, 2005; Suddendorf & Corballis, 1997).

In spite of the dissociation between semantic and episodic memory, there must be some links between them. The encoding of episodic memories must to some extent depend on semantic memories that are already in place (Tulving, 2002); a remembered visit to a restaurant, for example, must depend in part on one's knowledge of what a restaurant is and what happens there. Indeed, descriptions of episodic memories and future simulations comprise both episodic and semantic details that are woven together into a narrative of the experience (e.g., Addis, Wong, & Schacter, 2008; Levine. Svoboda, Hay, & Winocur, 2002). Individual episodes, having drawn on semantic elements, are then related to the self in subjectively sensed time. This allows the experience of an event to be stored separately from the semantic system and to be retrieved in what Tulving called "episodic retrieval mode" (Tulving, 2002). Just as they are during encoding, retrieved episodic memories are interwoven with elements of semantic memory. The episodic details of an event are not retrieved in isolation of the context that semantic information can provide (Levine et al., 2002). This would apply, we suggest, not only to the reconstruction of past events but also to the construction of future ones, and even to storytelling—the construction of fictional episodes that permeate folklore, literature, stage drama, film, and television (Hassabis, Kumaran, Vann, & Maguire, 2007b; Suddendorf & Corballis, 2007).

In this chapter, we review neuroscientific evidence for the continuity of mental time travel into the past and future, and we consider what, if anything, might be uniquely human about mental time travel. We go on to suggest that human language may have evolved primarily for the communication of episodes, whether from the past or the imagined future, or indeed in the form of fiction. We conclude with some speculation as to when and why mental time travel evolved in hominin evolution.

NEUROPSYCHOLOGICAL AND NEUROIMAGING EVIDENCE

The title of Deborah Wearing's book, *Forever Today*, also captures the fact that Clive Wearing is as unable to imagine future events as he is incapable of remembering past ones. It is becoming clear that this is true of other profoundly amnesic patients as well (Hassabis et al., 2007b; Klein, Loftus, & Kihlstrom, 2002; Rosenbaum et al., 2005; Tulving, 1985). In one study, for example, patients with bilateral hippocampal damage and intact premorbid semantic memory were given cue words and short descriptions of scenarios and asked to generate new experiences from them. Their scores for the detail and coherence of the imagined scenarios fell well below those of a control group (Hassabis et al., 2007b). Interestingly, this study suggests that the hippocampus may play a critical role, not only in terms of retrieving details from episodic memory to be utilized for an imagined scenario but also for the integration of such details into a coherent event. Moreover, it seems such processes are not unique to imagining future events per se, but they apply more generally to the construction of any fictitious scenario (Hassabis et al., 2007b; Rosenbaum et al., 2005).

Consistent with neuropsychological data, functional brain imaging also reveals a strong overlap in brain activity between backward and forward mental time travel. In one study, positron emission tomography (PET) revealed activity in the frontal poles and medial temporal lobes, including hippocampal and parahippocampal regions, to tasks involving both remembered past and imagined future episodes (Okuda et al., 2003). Although most areas showed equivalent activation to both past and future tasks, areas in the anteromedial pole showed greater activation to future than to past tasks, and greater activation to both tasks the more distant the episode in time. A more recent study showed that hippocampal activity, too, was greatly increased for future events that were more distant from the present (Addis & Schacter, 2008). These effects may reflect the degree of construction required, with higher levels of construction for more distant events.

Based on this and on other work using functional magnetic resonance imaging (fMRI) (Addis, Wong, & Schacter, 2007; Szpunar, Watson, & McDermott, 2007), Schacter and colleagues identify a "core network" that is used not just for remembering the past, but that functions adaptively and is even more actively recruited when integrating information from past experiences to construct mental simulations about possible future events (Schacter et al., 2007). The prominent components of this network include regions of the medial prefrontal cortex, the lateral and medial parietal cortex (including precuneus and retrosplenial cortex), and the lateral and medial temporal lobes, including notably the hippocampus. Activity is intercorrelated across these regions and with activity in the hippocampal formation. While some recent studies challenge this finding, reporting more activity for past than future events (Botzung, Denkova, & Manning, 2008; D'Argembeau, Xue, Lu, Van der Linden, & Bechara, 2008; Hassabis, Kumaran, & Maguire, 2007a), it is important to note that in these studies future events are not being imagined during the scan. Rather, they are constructed outside of the scanner and then recalled during the scan. Memories of imagined events are typically less detailed than memories of real experiences and thus recruit fewer hippocampal resources during retrieval. This further supports the core network being more actively recruited when one must use episodic memory to construct and imagine a new event online.

Moreover, these findings challenge the traditional view that the role of the hippocampus is to hold episodic memories for a limited period of time until they are consolidated in other neocortical areas (Squire, 1992; Squire, Starck, & Clark, 2004). The alternative view, more consistent with these and other recent results, is that the hippocampus is always necessary for the retrieval of detailed episodic experiences, including remote ones (Moscovitch et al., 2005). By this account, the extent of hippocampal involvement likely depends on the vividness of the internal representation, whether of past episodes or imagined future ones (Hassabis et al., 2007b). Confirming this, Addis and Schacter (2008) also found more detailed representations to be associated with increased posterior hippocampal activity. This probably reflects the retrieval of information, necessary when remembering as well as imagining events. In contrast, future event detail was associated with greater activity in the anterior hippocampus, possibly reflecting the recombination of details into a coherent event.

The reported phenomenological richness of imagined events (D'Argembeau & Van der Linden, 2004), as well as the number of imagined events reported (Spreng & Levine, 2006), decreases with temporal distance into both past and future. There are further parallels in the development of mental time travel into past and future across the life span, both in terms of initial emergence (Busby & Suddendorf, 2005) and eventual decline (Addis et al., 2008). The neural and cognitive evidence linking episodic memory to imagining the future is increasingly recognized (e.g., Hassabis & Maguire, 2009; Schacter & Addis, 2009).

UNIQUELY HUMAN?

In a detailed account of the nature of episodic memory, Tulving (1983) proposed that it was uniquely human. It was later proposed more generally that mental time travel was unique to our species and that the main adaptive advantage must lie with foresight (Suddendorf & Corballis, 1997, 2007). This does not mean that nonhuman animals do not behave in a manner oriented to the future. The futures of animals and their offspring often depend on instinctive behaviors, such as food-caching, migrations, and nest-building, as well as on learned behaviors and semantic memory (Suddendorf & Corballis, 2007). Semantic knowledge can be important for prospection, but it must be distinguished from episodic future thinking. For example, knowledge of where Paris is located, what language is spoken there, and how to get there will clearly enhance the prospects of making a trip to that city. Episodic memories of experiences in Paris, though, allow conscious construction of imagined future events there, including perhaps friends that one might meet there, places one might revisit, specific restaurants and perhaps specific dishes, and so forth. More generally, episodic memory provides a vocabulary from which to construct possible scenarios and to compare them off-line to optimize future behavior. This ability to act with specific, individually anticipated future events in mind may account for why human behavior is so immensely flexible and, as we shall argue further next, why humans have evolved open-ended communication systems.

The claim that only humans are capable of episodic memory and episodic foresight has posed a challenge to animal researchers. One of the difficulties has been to demonstrate memory that is truly episodic, and not merely semantic or procedural. For example, does the dog that returns to where a bone is buried remember actually burying it, or does it simply know where it is buried? One suggestion is that episodic memory in nonhuman animals might be defined in terms of *what* happened, *where* it happened, and *when* it happened—the so-called www criteria. It has been proposed that scrub jays meet these criteria, because of experimental evidence that they can select the locations of food they have previously cached not only according to the type of food that is stored there but also according to how long it has been stored, implying that they remember when it was stored. For example, they will recover recently cached worms in preference to nuts, since fresh worms are more palatable, but if the worms have been cached for too long they will retrieve nuts, because the worms will have decayed and become unpalatable (Clayton & Dickinson, 1998). Further, if another jay observes them caching food, they will later recache it, presumably to prevent the observer from stealing the food. They will only do this, however, if they have themselves stolen food in the past (Emery & Clayton, 2001). Clayton and colleagues (Clayton, Bussey, & Dickinson, 2003) concluded that scrub jays can not only remember the what, where, and when of past events but can also anticipate the future by taking steps to avoid future theft.

A recent study suggests that meadow voles, too, have a similar capacity (Ferkin, Combs, del Barco-Trillo, Pierce, & Franklin, 2008). Male voles were first allowed to explore two chambers, one containing a pregnant female 24 hours prepartum, and the other containing a female that was neither lactating nor pregnant. Twenty-four hours later, they were again given access to the chambers, now empty and clean, and spent more time exploring the chamber that had contained the previously pregnant female than the one that had housed the other female. This suggests that they had remembered the pregnant female and her location and had understood that she would now be in postpartum estrus, a state of heightened sexual receptivity. In another condition they first explored a chamber containing a female in postpartum estrus and another containing a female that was neither lactating nor pregnant, and was not in estrus. Twenty-four hours later they were again allowed to explore the now-empty cages, and they showed no preference for the chamber that had housed the female in estrus. This suggests that they realized the female would no longer be in a state of heightened receptivity.

Several other recent experiments have documented that various species of mammals and birds may pass the www criteria (for reviews, see Dere, Huston, & Silva, 2005; Suddendorf & Corballis, 2007; Zentall, 2006). If this entails that these species can travel mentally in time, then we are in need of a fundamental reconsideration of animal welfare and ethics (Lea, 2001; Suddendorf & Corballis, 2007). The extent to which animals live in the present has a major impact on their capacity for suffering—if they can mentally revisit a past traumatic event or anticipate future pain, as humans do, then considerations for their welfare would need to take this into account when attempting to minimize their suffering (see Mendl & Paul, 2008, for a detailed discussion).

It remains possible, though, that these ingenious studies do not prove that the animals actually remember or anticipate episodes. For example, associative memory might be sufficient to link an object with a location, and a time tag or "use by" date might then be attached to the representation of the object to update information about it (Suddendorf & Corballis, 2007). Moreover, "how long ago" can be empirically distinguished from "when," so the ability of scrub jays to recover food depending on how long ago it was cached need not actually imply that they remember when it was cached. As evidence for this, a recent study suggests that rats can learn to retrieve food in a radial maze on the basis of how long ago it was stored, but not on when it was stored, suggesting that "episodic-like memory in rats is qualitatively different from episodic memory in humans" (Roberts et al., 2008).

More generally, the www criteria may not be sufficient to demonstrate true episodic memory. Most of us know where we were born, when we were born, and indeed what was born, but this is semantic memory, not episodic memory (Suddendorf & Busby, 2003). Conversely, one can imagine past and future events and be factually wrong about what, where, and when details (in fact, we are often mistaken). This double dissociation, then, strongly suggests that we should not equate mental time travel with www memory.

Nonhuman animals and very young children may be limited in their foresight in a number of different ways (Suddendorf & Corballis, 2007). One variant on the claim to human uniqueness is the so-called Bischof-Köhler hypothesis, which states that only humans can flexibly anticipate their own future mental states of need and act in the present to secure them (Bischof-Köhler, 1985; Bischof, 1978; Suddendorf & Corballis, 1997). Again, an experiment with scrub jays has been claimed as a counterexample. The birds were prefed with one type of food for 3 hours and then allowed to cache the prefed and an alternative food. They were subsequently prefed with the alternative food before being allowed to recover what they had cached. On the second and third trials, the birds cached more of the food on which they were satiated, on the apparent understanding that they would be hungry for this food at later recovery, thus challenging the Bischof-Köhler hypothesis (Correia, Dickinson, & Clayton, 2007). Closer analysis of the data, however, suggests that this interpretation is misleading. Although the birds cached a greater proportion of food for which they would later be hungry, the absolute number of items stored did not change in any meaningful way. The six birds in the critical condition cached an average of 0.7 items of the prefed food on the first trial, and 1.2 items and 0.8 items on the second and third trials, respectively. Thus, they did not increasingly

store the food that was more desirable in the future (Suddendorf & Corballis, 2008).

The most promising challenge to the Bischof-Köhler hypothesis so far comes from great apes. In one study, orangutans and bonobos learned to use a tool to extract grapes from an apparatus in a test room. They were later given a choice of tools, some appropriate and other inappropriate for extracting grapes, and significantly chose appropriate ones for later access to the test room (Mulcahy & Call, 2006). In a similar experiment, two chimpanzees and an orangutan were shown, on a single trial, how to use a plastic hose as a straw to obtain juice from an apparatus, and on subsequent trials, prior to access to the test room an hour later, chose this tool in preference to others. In one critical condition, the animals were offered grapes, their favorite food, along with the other tools, and chose the hose more often than the grapes, suggesting that obtaining a large amount of fruit juice in the future may have been valued more than a small instant grape reward (Osvath & Osvath, 2008). In both studies, the experimenters took pains to rule out alternative explanations, such as simple association between tool and later reward, but there continue to be some methodological concerns (see Suddendorf, 2006; Suddendorf, Corballis, & Collier-Baker, 2009, for critical analyses).

So far, examples of putative mental time travel in nonhuman species appear limited to situations with a strong instinctive component. They do suggest ways in which animals might adapt their behavior to maximize future reward, but so far they have little of the flexibility and generality of mental time travel in humans. Humans can simulate virtually any event and evaluate it in terms of likelihood and desirability. It has been argued that this human faculty may by likened to a theatre production in that we employ mental analogs to a stage, a playwright, actors, a set, a director, an executive producer, and a broadcaster (Suddendorf & Corballis, 2007). These sophisticated mental roles may be employed to simulate future events, just as readily as to imagine the minds of others (theory of mind) and entirely fictional stories (Buckner & Carroll, 2007; Hassabis et al., 2007b; Suddendorf & Corballis, 1997). Animals may be restricted in their capacity to travel mentally in time by limits in any of these domains. For example, just as a playwright is responsible for creating new stories, mental simulations of novel future events requires open-ended generativity—our ability to combine and recombine a limited set of items into virtually unlimited ways (something not evident in any of the animal studies). Our memories for episodes are made up of combinations of people, actions, objects, and places, along with qualities such as time of day, season, emotional states, and the like. Imagined future events are similarly constructed, and we may in fact compose different scenarios depending on various contingencies, such as the weather, or who is likely to show up. Indeed, it may be the generative component that most clearly distinguishes mental time travel in humans from future-directed capacities in other species. This generativity is also characteristic of other human faculties such as navigation, number, theory of mind, and language (Corballis, 2003). Language is often regarded as the most distinct of human faculties (e.g., Hauser Chomsky, & Fitch, 2002), and much of what humans talk about (or broadcast) are the mental simulations of past events and future possibilities (Szagun, 1978).

Language

Testing for episodic memory in humans is normally reliant on language, which is why it is difficult to devise ways of testing for it in nonhuman animals. This raises the possibility that the evolution of language itself is intimately connected with the evolution of mental time travel. Language is exquisitely designed to express "who did what to whom, what is true of what, where, when and why," as Pinker (2003) put it—a combination of w's that goes well beyond the www criteria—and these are precisely the qualities needed to recount episodic memories. The same applies to the expression of future events—who will do what to whom, or what will happen to what, where, when and why, and what are we going to do about it. When considering the future, the conditional may also be important— if it rains, then X will happen; if it doesn't, we may enjoy Y. To a large extent, then, the stuff of

mental time travel is also the stuff of language (Corballis & Suddendorf, 2007).

Language allows personal episodes and plans to be shared, enhancing the ability to plan and construct viable futures. To do so, though, requires ways of representing the elements of episodes: people, objects, actions, qualities, times of occurrence, and so forth. Language may well have begun as pantomime, with the use of bodily gestures to mimic events (Donald, 1991), with gestures becoming conventionalized, and thus more arbitrary and less representational, in the interests of greater economy and efficiency. According to this scenario, vocal gestures gradually replaced manual ones as the dominant mode (Corballis, 2003; Rizzolatti & Sinigalglia, 2007), although most people still gesture manually as they speak.

The recounting of mental time travel places a considerable and perhaps uniquely human burden on communication, since there must be ways of referring to different points in time—past, present, and future—and to locations other than that of the present. Different cultures have solved these problems in different ways. Many languages use tense as a way of modifying verbs to indicate the time of an episode, and to make other temporal distinctions, such as that between continuous action and completed action. Some languages, such as Chinese, have no tenses but indicate time through other means, such as adverbs or aspect markers (Lin, 2005). The language spoken by the Pirahã, a tribe of some 200 people in Brazil, has only a very primitive way of talking about relative time, in the form of two tense-like morphemes that seem to indicate simply whether an event is in the present or not, and Pirahã are said to live largely in the present (Everett, 2005).

Reference to space may have a basis in hippocampal function; as noted earlier, current theories suggest that the hippocampus provides the mechanism for retrieval of memories based on spatial cues. It has also been suggested that in humans the hippocampus may encompass temporal coding, perhaps through analogy with space; thus, most prepositions referring to time are borrowed from those referring to space. In English, for example, words such as *at*, *about*, *around, between, among, along, across, opposite, against, from, to,* and *through,* are fundamentally spatial, but they are also employed to refer to time, although a few, such as *since* or *until,* apply only to the time dimension (O'Keefe, 1996). It has been suggested that the hippocampus may have undergone modification in human evolution, such that the right hippocampus is responsible for retrieval of spatial information, and the left for temporal (episodic or autobiographical) information (Burgess, Maguire, & O'Keefe, 2002). It remains unclear whether the left-hippocampal specialization is a consequence of left-hemispheric specialization for language or of the incorporation of time into human consciousness of past and future, but either way it reinforces the link between language and mental time travel.

The most striking parallel between language and mental time travel has to do with generativity. We generate episodes from basic vocabularies of events, just as we generate sentences to describe them. It is the properties of generativity and recursiveness that perhaps most clearly single out language as a uniquely human capacity (Hauser et al., 2002). The rules governing the generation of sentences about episodes must depend partly on the way in which the episodes themselves are constructed, but added rules are required by the constraints of the communication medium itself. Speech, for example, requires that the account of an event that is structured in space-time be linearized, or reduced to a temporal sequence of events. Sign languages allow more freedom to incorporate spatial as well as temporal structure, but they still require conventions. For example, in American Sign Language, the time at which an event occurred is indicated spatially, with the continuum of past to future running from behind the body to the front of the body.

Of course, language is not wholly dependent on mental time travel. We can talk freely about semantic knowledge without reference to events in time, as typically required by the education industry—and indeed this very chapter. But it is mental time travel that forced communication to incorporate the time dimension, and to deal with reference to elements of the world, and

combinations of those elements, that are not immediately available to the senses. It is these factors, we suggest, that were in large part responsible for the development of grammars. Given the variety of ways in which grammars are constructed, such as the different ways in which time is marked in different languages, we suspect that grammar is not so much a product of some innately determined universal grammar (Chomsky, 1988; O'Keefe, 1996) as it is a product of culture and human ingenuity, constrained by brain structure (Christiansen & Chater, 2008). Through language, then, we see not just language itself, but the structure of human thought, and how it is composed of basic elements including "events, states, things, substances, places, and goals" (Pinker, 2007)—and times. And the generativity of language reflects the generativity of the underlying thought processes themselves.

Evolutionary considerations

Instinct, learning, and memory are adaptations that enhance the fitness of animals and shape their futures. Episodic memory is a form of memory, possibly unique to humans, that further allows the fine tuning of behavior, based on specific episodes in the past. It allows us to imagine future episodes, make specific plans, and compare different scenarios. Language, we suspect, coevolved with mental time travel to allow the sharing of episodic information, sometimes to the point that we confuse events that have actually happened in our lives with those told to us by others, or even with those gleaned from fictional accounts.

Mental time travel and grammatical language probably evolved during the Pleistocene (Corballis, 2003; Suddendorf & Corballis, 1997, 2007). Survival pressures brought about by changes in climate and the replacement of a forested environment by the more exposed savannah necessitated greater social cohesion, more detailed future planning, and more effective communication. Brain size increased dramatically in the genus *Homo* during the Pleistocene, reaching a peak with the large-brained Neanderthals and precursors to modern humans perhaps 500,000 years ago. It has been suggested that the emergence of the genus

Homo was also accompanied by a prolongation of the period of development from infancy to adulthood, and that an extra stage, known as childhood, was inserted into the sequence of developmental stages (Locke & Bogin, 2006). Childhood lasts from age 2½ to about age 7, roughly the period during which both mental time travel and grammatical language develop.

There can be little doubt that flexible foresight became a key human survival strategy (Suddendorf, 2006) and that humans have taken the quest for securing future survival to a new level. Consider, for example, Norway's construction of a "doomsday" seed bank designed to withstand global catastrophes to protect all known varieties of the world's crop. Yet, in spite of our strong reliance on foresight, humans are notoriously fallible with our predictions. For example, we display systematic errors in predicting the affective consequences of future action. Gilbert and Wilson (2007) recently reviewed these biases and concluded that several characteristics of mental simulation are the main contributors to these pervasive errors. Simulations tend to be unrepresentative, since they are often based on the most recent or most salient aspects of episodic memory, rather than on the most representative sampling. They often tend to reflect the gist of an event but fail to represent many details, and they often fail to take into account different future contexts in which events occur. The systematic biases in misapprehending how we will feel when a future event becomes the here and now is an essential problem for anyone in pursuit of happiness, and Gilbert (2006) offers the following simple solution to the dilemma: Ask someone else who is or has been where we project ourselves as going. Their advice, on average, will be a far better guide to what it will be like than one's own biased simulations. This resonates with our proposal that one adaptive function of language may be to allow us to improve our mental time travel by drawing on the descriptions others can offer of what the future may hold. Undoubtedly, language allows us to learn from other individuals' experiences as no other animal can.

Whether this also leads to greater happiness remains debatable. Unlike perhaps psychologists,

evolution does not care for our happiness, and errors in affective forecasting are only errors if they negatively affect survival and reproduction. As with reconstruction of past events, it is not accuracy per se but the fitness consequences of foresight that matter. Systematic biases and errors may thus in fact serve adaptive purposes. For example, humans generally tend to expect more positive events than is rational to expect, and this optimism bias has specific neural correlates (Sharot, Ricardi, Raio, & Phelps, 2007). Though we may often be wrong with our optimism, this positive mental stance may have profound selective advantages over a more realistic (and possibly bleak) perspective. Foresight, fallible and biased as it often may be, must have made a net positive contribution to fitness. Indeed, it is arguably our most formidable weapon. The price we might have had to pay for this includes unique psychological stresses and disorders (e.g., Brune, 2006, makes the case for obsessive-compulsive disorder).

In this chapter, we proposed that human language evolved in the first instance for the sharing of mental time travel. After reviewing the growing neuroscientific evidence linking episodic memory and episodic foresight, we discussed data from nonhuman animals. On current evidence, mental time travel, like language, appears to reflect something uniquely human. This is not to say, however, that language and mental time travel are drawing on the same neurocognitive machinery. Language and mental time travel are clearly dissociable in modern humans. The total collapse of our faculty for mental time travel leaves a linguistically sophisticated person such as Clive Wearing trapped in the present and unable to conduct his life without the extensive support of others who can look ahead.

Acknowledgments

The writing of this manuscript was supported in part by an Australian Research Council Discovery Grant (DP0770113) to T. S.

References

Addis, D. R., & Schacter, D. L. (2008). Effects of detail and temporal distance of past and future events on the engagement of a common neural network. *Hippocampus, 18*, 227–237.

Addis, D. R., Wong, A. T., & Schacter, D. L. (2007). Remembering the past and imagining the future: Common and distinct neural substrates during event construction and elaboration. *Neuropsychologia, 45*, 1363–1377.

Addis, D. R., Wong, A. T., & Schacter, D. L. (2008). Age-related changes in the episodic simulation of future events. *Psychological Science, 19*, 33–41.

Aggleton, J. P., & Brown, M. W. (1999), Episodic memory, amnesia and the hippocampal-anterior thalamic axis. *Behavioral and Brain Sciences, 22*, 425–489.

Bischof-Köhler, D. (1985). Zur Phylogenese menschlicher Motivation [On the phylogeny of human motivation]. In L. H. Eckensberger & E. D. Lantermann (Eds.), *Emotion und Reflexivität* (pp. 3–47). Vienna, Austria: Urban & Schwarzenberg.

Bischof, N. (1978). On the phylogeny of human morality. In G. S. Stent (Ed.), *Morality as biological phenomenon* (p. 53–74). Berlin: Dahlem Konferenzen.

Botzung, A., Denkova, E., & Manning, L. (2008). Experiencing past and future personal events: Functional neuroimaging evidence on the neural bases of mental time travel. *Brain and Cognition, 66*, 202–212.

Brune, M. (2006). The evolutionary psychology of obsessive-compulsive disorder—the role of cognitive meta-representation. *Perspectives in Biology and Medicine, 49*, 317–329.

Buckner, R. L., & Carroll, D. C. (2007). Self-projection and the brain. *Trends in Cognitive Sciences, 11*, 49–57.

Burgess, N., Maguire, E. A., & O'Keefe, J. (2002). The human hippocampus and spatial and episodic memory. *Neuron, 35*, 625–641.

Busby, J., & Suddendorf, T. (2005). Recalling yesterday and predicting tomorrow. *Cognitive Development, 20*, 362–372.

Chomsky, N. (1988). *Language and problems of knowledge: The Managua lectures.* Cambridge, MA: MIT Press.

Christiansen, M., & Chater, N. (2008). Language as shaped by the brain. *Behavioral and Brain Sciences, 31*, 489–509.

Clayton, N. S., Bussey, T. J., & Dickinson, A. (2003). Can animals recall the past and plan for the future? *Nature Reviews Neuroscience, 4*, 685–691.

Clayton, N. S., & Dickinson, A. (1998). Episodic-like memory during cache recovery by scrub jays. *Nature, 395*, 272–278.

Corballis, M. C. (2003). *From hand to mouth: The origins of language.* Princeton, NJ: Princeton University Press.

Corballis, M. C., & Suddendorf, T. (2007). Memory, time and language. In C. Pasternak (Ed.), *What makes us human?* (pp. 17–36). Oxford, England: Oneworld.

Correia, S. P. C., Dickinson, A., & Clayton, N. S. (2007). Western scrub-jays anticipate future needs independently of their current motivational state. *Current Biology, 17*, 856–861.

D'Argembeau, A., & Van der Linden, M. (2004). Phenomenal characteristics associated with projecting oneself back into the past and forward into the future: Influence of valence and temporal distance. *Consciousness and Cognition, 13*, 844–858.

D'Argembeau, A., Xue, G., Lu, Z. L., Van der Linden, M., & Bechara, A. (2008). Neural correlates of envisioning emotional events in the near and far future. *NeuroImage, 40*, 398–407.

Dere, E., Huston, J. P., & Silva, M. A. S. (2005). Episodic-like memory in mice: Simultaneous assessment of object, place and temporal order memory. *Brain Research Protocols, 16*, 10–19.

Donald, M. (1991). *Origins of the human mind: Three stages in the evolution of culture and cognition.* Cambridge, MA: Harvard University Press.

Emery, N. J., & Clayton, N. S. (2001). Effects of experience and social context on prospective caching strategies by scrub jays. *Nature, 414*, 443–446.

Everett, D. L. (2005). Cultural constraints on grammar and cognition in Piraha—Another look at the design features of human language. *Current Anthropology, 46*, 621–646.

Ferkin, M. H., Combs, A., del Barco-Trillo, J., Pierce, A. A., & Franklin, S. (2008). Meadow voles, Microtus pennsylvanicus, have the capacity to recall the "what," "where," and "when" of a single past event. *Animal Cognition, 11*, 147–159.

Gilbert, D. T. (2006). *Stumbling on happiness.* New York: A.A. Knopf.

Gilbert, D. T., & Wilson, T. D. (2007). Prospection: Experiencing the future. *Science, 317*, 1351–1354.

Hassabis, D., Kumaran, D., & Maguire, E. A. (2007a). Using imagination to understand the neural basis of episodic memory. *Journal of Neuroscience, 27*, 14365–14374.

Hassabis, D., Kumaran, D., Vann, S. D., & Maguire, E. A. (2007b). Patients with hippocampal amnesia cannot imagine new experiences. *Proceedings of the National Academy of Sciences USA, 104*, 1726–1731.

Hassabis, D., & Maguire, E. A. (2009). The construction system of the brain. *Philosophical Transactions of the Royal Society of London B: Biological Sciences, 364*, 1263–1271.

Hauser, M. D., Chomsky, N., & Fitch, W. T. (2002). The faculty of language: What is it, who has it, and how did it evolve? *Science, 298*, 1569–1579.

Hodges, J. R., & Graham, K. S. (2001). Episodic memory: Insights from semantic dementia. *Philosophical Transactions of the Royal Society of London B: Biological Sciences, 356*, 1423–1434.

James, W. (1890). *The principles of psychology*. London: Macmillan.

Klein, S. B., Loftus, J., & Kihlstrom, J. F. (2002). Memory and temporal experience: The effects of episodic memory loss on an amnesic patient's ability to remember the past and imagine the future. *Social Cognition, 20*, 353–379.

Lea, S. E. G. (2001). Anticipation and memory as criteria for special welfare consideration. *Animal Welfare, 10*, S195–208.

Levine, B., Svoboda, E., Hay, J. F., & Winocur, G. (2002). Aging and autobiographical memory: Dissociating episodic from semantic retrieval. *Psychology and Aging, 17*, 677–689.

Lin, J. W. (2005). Time in a language without tense: The case of Chinese. *Journal of Semantics, 23*, 1–53.

Locke, J. L., & Bogin, B. (2006). Language and life history: A new perspective on the development and evolution of human language. *Behavioral and Brain Sciences, 29*, 259–280.

Mendl, M., & Paul, E. S. (2008). Do animals live in the present? Current evidence and implications for welfare. *Applied Animal Behaviour Science, 113*, 357–382.

Moscovitch, M., Rosenbaum, R. S., Giboa, A., Addis, D. R., Westmacott, R., Grady, C., McAndrews, B., Levine, B., Black, S., Wincour, G., & Nadel, L. (2005). Functional neuroanatomy of remote episodic, semantic and spatial memory: A unified account based on multiple trace theory. *Journal of Anatomy, 207*, 35.

Mulcahy, N. J., & Call, J. (2006). Apes save tools for future use. *Science, 312*, 1038–1040.

O'Keefe, J. (1996). The spatial prepositions in English, vector grammar, and the cognitive map theory. In P. Bloom (Ed.), *Language and Space* (pp. 277–316). Cambridge, MA: MIT Press.

Okuda, J., Fujii, T., Ohtake, H., Tsukiura, T., Tanji, K., Suzuki, K., Kawashima, R., Fukuda, H., Itoh, M., & Yamadori, A. (2003). Thinking of the future and past: The roles of the frontal pole and the medial temporal lobes. *Neuroimage, 19*, 1369–1380.

Osvath, M., & Osvath, H. (2008). Chimpanzee *(Pan troglodytes)* and orangutan *(Pongo abelii)* forethought: self-control and pre-experience in the face of future tool use. *Animal Cognition, 12*, 661–674.

Pinker, S. (2003). Language as an adaptation to the cognitive niche. In M. H. Christiansen & S. Kirby (Eds.), *Language evolution* (pp. 16–37). Oxford, England: Oxford University Press.

Pinker, S. (2007). *The stuff of thought*. New York: Viking.

Rizzolatti, G., & Sinigalglia, C. (2007). *Mirrors in the brain*. Oxford, England: Oxford University Press.

Roberts, W. A., Feeney, M. C., MacPherson, K., Petter, M., McMillan, N., & Musolino, E. (2008). Episodic-like memory in rats: Is it based on when or how long ago? *Science, 320*, 113–115.

Rosenbaum, R. S., Kohler, S., Schacter, D. L., Moscovitch, M., Westmacott, R., Black, S. E., Gao, F. Q., & Tulving, E. (2005). The case of KC: Contributions of a memory-impaired person to memory theory. *Neuropsychologia, 43*, 989–1021.

Schacter, D. L. (1999). The seven sins of memory— insights from psychology and cognitive neuroscience. *American Psychologist, 54*, 182–203.

Schacter, D. L., & Addis, D. R. (2007). The ghosts of past and future. *Nature, 445*, 27–27.

Schacter, D. L., & Addis, D. R. (2009). On the nature of medial temporal lobe contributions to the constructive simulation of future events. *Philosophical Transactions of the Royal Society of London B: Biological Sciences, 364*, 1245–1253.

Scoville, W. B., & Milner, B. (1957). Loss of recent memory after bilateral hippocampal lesion. *Journal of Neurology, Neurosurgery and Psychiatry, 20*, 11–21.

Sharot, T., Riccardi, A. M., Raio, C. M., & Phelps, E. A. (2007). Neural mechanisms mediating optimism bias. *Nature, 450*, 102–106.

Spreng, R. N., & Levine, B. (2006). The temporal distribution of past and future autobiographical events across the lifespan. *Memory and Cognition, 34,* 1644–1651.

Squire, L. R. (1992). Memory and the hippocampus: A synthesis from findings with rats, monkeys and humans. *Psychological Review, 99,* 195–231.

Squire, L. R., Starck, C. E., & Clark, R. E. (2004). The medial temporal lobe. *Annual Review of Neuroscience, 27,* 279–306.

Suddendorf, T. (2006). Foresight and evolution of the human mind. *Science, 312,* 1006–1007.

Suddendorf, T., & Busby, J. (2003). Mental time travel in animals? *Trends in Cognitive Sciences, 7,* 391–396.

Suddendorf, T., & Busby, J. (2005). Making decisions with the future in mind: Developmental and comparative identification of mental time travel. *Learning and Motivation, 36,* 110–125.

Suddendorf, T., & Corballis, M. C. (1997). Mental time travel and the evolution of the human mind. *Genetic Social and General Psychology Monographs, 123,* 133–167.

Suddendorf, T., & Corballis, M. C. (2007). The evolution of foresight: What is mental time travel and is it unique to humans? *Behavioral and Brain Sciences, 30,* 299–313.

Suddendorf, T., & Corballis, M. C. (2008). New evidence for animal foresight? *Animal Behaviour, 75,* e1–e3.

Suddendorf, T., Corballis, M. C., & Collier-Baker, E. (2009). How great is great ape foresight? *Animal Cognition, 12,* 751–754.

Szagun, G. (1978). On the frequency of use of tenses in English and German children's spontaneous speech. *Child Development, 49,* 898–901.

Szpunar, K. K., Watson, J. M., & McDermott, K. B. (2007). Neural substrates of envisioning the future. *Proceedings of the National Academy of Sciences USA, 104,* 642–647.

Tulving, E. (1983). *Elements of episodic memory.* Oxford, England: Clarendon Press.

Tulving, E. (1985). Memory and consciousness. *Canadian Psychology, 26,* 1–12.

Tulving, E. (2002). Episodic memory: From mind to brain. *Annual Review of Psychology, 53,* 1–25.

Tulving, E., Schacter, D. L., McLachlan, D. R., & Moscovitch, M. (1988). Priming of semantic autobiographical knowledge - a case-study of retrograde-amnesia. *Brain and Cognition, 8,* 3–20.

VarghaKhadem, F., Gadian, D. G., Watkins, K. E., Connelly, A., VanPaesschen, W., & Mishkin, M. (1997). Differential effects of early hippocampal pathology on episodic and semantic memory. *Science, 277,* 376–380.

Wearing, D. (2005). *Forever today.* New York: Doubleday.

Zentall, T. R. (2006). Mental time travel in animals: A challenging question. *Behavioural Processes, 72,* 173–183.

AUTHOR INDEX

SUBJECT INDEX

Note: Page references followed by "*f*" and "*t*" denote figures and tables, respectively.